Antebellum American Culture

Antebellum American Culture

An Interpretive Anthology

David Brion Davis
Yale University

D. C. HEATH AND COMPANY
Lexington, Massachusetts □ Toronto

To Toni, With Love

Preface

One of the prime benefits students gain from studying history is the amazing realization that people and societies change, that life a short time ago was very different, and that if people had made different choices in the past we would lead very different lives today. Nothing can deepen this realization better than primary source documents: Only documents really confront the student with the strange and fascinating "pastness of the past." Unfortunately such documents never entirely "speak for themselves." The student needs explanatory context and meaningful identification, which must at least begin with who, when, where, why, what—and since as a historian I am concerned with underlying reasons, I have attempted in this book to add another and somewhat antiquated "W": wherefore. I hope that this *interpretive anthology* will provoke new questions and suggest new ways of making the past more immediately and concretely accessible.

It is no easy task to enter into the minds and feelings of people long dead, such as the antebellum Americans. Their language and style of thought are foreign, and their emotions and sensitivities seem in some ways constricted and hemmed-in. It is difficult for us to imagine their largely rural and parochial world, almost wholly dependent on horses and water-power, water-transport, and wood-burning stoves and fireplaces for heat in subzero winters. In many respects the physical environment of even middle-class Americans of the antebellum period—a highly privileged group in the world of that time—would shock us.

Except for lightning, they were unfamiliar with electricity; they knew nothing of automobiles, airplanes, plastics, supermarkets, radios, television, paved highways, antibiotics, or modern plumbing. In most ways their environment was closer to that of the ancient Greeks or medieval Europeans than to our own. Furthermore, whether church-goers or not, they believed with few exceptions in a patriarchal God, in an afterlife, and in a literal heaven and hell where the virtuous would be rewarded and sinners punished. They were also confident that the future would bring continuing progress—progress in morals, technology, standard of living, and social justice. Consequently, they paid reverence to humanity as a whole, including past and future generations, and thought more often and more hopefully of the twentieth century than we have done for the twenty-first.

Unfortunately, the material "progress" of the late twentieth century is swiftly eradicating the landscape and last physical reminders of the preautomotive past. We are faced with an increasing need, expressed on different levels of authenticity, for establishing meaningful links with a vanishing world. Thankfully, we are also faced with a growing wealth of documentary material in American history that is rapidly being enriched by new discoveries and new techniques of analysis. We have begun to recognize the inadequacy of the conventional textbook structuring of American history, such as an "age" keyed to a political figure like Andrew Jackson; or a "spirit" or "ferment" that gives rise to reform or creative expression. These categories do little to illuminate the lives of people who seem at once to have been freer and less free than ourselves, who confronted the "head" of problems to which we have seen the "tail"—and whose choices and motives help explain how we got to where we are.

A case can be made, therefore, for an interpretive anthology, one that starts from scratch or at least takes a fresh look at available documents. There should be nothing sacred about the traditional use of documents to supplement or amplify a text, chapter by chapter, unit by unit. While this anthology can be used to supplement a text, it should also suggest innovative ways of reading, using, and understanding historical sources—ways that bridge the conventional topical and compartmental categories of American history.

Because this anthology is intended for student use, I have sometimes modernized spelling, punctuation, and capitalization in the interest of readability. In general, I have changed inconsistently capitalized words to lower case except when the capitalization of such words as Nature, State, Providence, Divine, and Union was probably meant to convey some special meaning. I have Americanized most British spellings and have changed "&c." to "etc." On occasion, I have eliminated unnecessary commas when they seemed to pose an obstacle to clear comprehension. Unusual or archaic words are defined within brackets or explained in footnotes.

The preparation of this anthology was greatly aided by two classes of Yale undergraduates who struggled through blurred reproductions of minute nineteenth-century print, and whose class papers and discussions furthered my own thinking and confirmed my enthusiasm for the project. My wife Toni, to whom the book is dedicated, repeatedly saved my own prose from unnecessary complexities and obscurities. I am much indebted to Lois Rule, who typed most of the manuscript. Both the editorial staff and the management of D. C. Heath have shown continuing commitment to the book. Above all, I am grateful to Steven Mintz, of the History Department at Oberlin College, who in many respects is a coeditor of this anthology. The basic themes and organization grew out of our discussions of antebellum culture, and he supplied the tens of thousands of pages from which I made the final selections. As an assistant, colleague, and friend he contributed immeasurably to this book.

DAVID BRION DAVIS
Orange, Connecticut

Contents

UNIT TWO

Struggles Over Access to Wealth and Power 99

1

"The Anxious Spirit of Gain" 105

2

Access to Land 129

3

The Changing Uses of Law

4

"Improvements": Transportation and Corporations

5

The Politics of Opportunity

5

The Quest for New Social Harmonies   441

6

Transcending Human History: Americans as "Pioneers of the World"   453

Introduction: Organization and Themes

I have tried to derive my organizational themes from the actual concerns, perceptions, and explanations of antebellum Americans. For example, one of the underlying themes of this book is the uneasy and self-conscious concern with union and disunion, with the procedures and processes likely to ensure a harmony of interests and a voluntary cohesion of social groups ranging from the family to the nation at large. Because antebellum Americans thought of themselves as citizens of a *new* nation founded on rational principles and dependent on the consent of the governed, they could not take unity for granted. They could not presuppose a spontaneous and unthinking loyalty to family, clan, king, church, or regional traditions. Although most nineteenth-century Americans still regarded the Bible as a divinely revealed guide to life, they knew that honest people could disagree on Biblical interpretation. There was thus a sense of urgency in defining creeds, principles, and what we would call ideologies which could evoke assent from as many Americans as possible. This appeal for self-conscious affirmation could take the form of religious or political conversion. It also focused attention on the dangers of inauthentic forms of unity that might disguise deeper divisions and polarities. For example, northern reformers accused the national political parties of conveying merely an appearance of unity that disguised a growing hegemony, at the North's expense, of the southern slaveholding aristocracy.

A second broad theme is the dedication to *improvement*—material, moral, religious, and intellectual. Proud of the achievements of their fathers and confident of their superiority to every other nation on earth, antebellum Americans were also convinced that every institution and aspect of life could be improved. In this faith they were inspired by the example and promise of the Revolution, by the impressive spectacle of physical and territorial growth —the conquest and settlement of a vast wilderness, and by the early triumphs of science and technology. Even the more religious minds tended to conclude that piety could be extended by increased productivity, that happiness and holiness could be measured by various statistical gains. Yet at times the sheer boundlessness of America's growth aroused spasms of doubt. Again and again we hear voices expressing understandable alarm over the "anxious spirit of gain," the wild scramble for land and speculative fortune that seemed to be leading toward a competitive jungle of selfishness, fraud, and conspiracy against the public good. The remedies proposed for these evils included an amplification and reinvigoration of law, and above all, an intensified diffusion of education, religion, and other forms of "moral influence."

Faith in irresistible progress was also qualified by a growing consciousness that various groups of outsiders, notably Indians and blacks, were excluded from both the opportunities and culture that gave rise to the "anxious spirit of gain." Here the remedy of moral influence, leading to the goal of acculturation and assimilation, directly collided with an alternative remedy of expatriation and physical removal. The plight of such outsiders in a supposedly "open society" ties in with our first theme regarding the basis of social and national cohesion. Were the unity and promise of American life to be based on white supremacy?

The third major theme, America's world mission, was at once an extension of faith in improvement and an expression of nationalistic unity that for a time appeared to dissolve, or at least coat over, internal divisions, conflicts, and polarities. The ideal of America as a redeemer nation, "the last, best hope of earth," was rooted in Christian visions of universal freedom from sin, war, and tyranny—the so-called millennium or thousand years of peace and brotherhood that would supposedly culminate human history. What gave this ancient dream more immediate promise was the success of the American colonists in throwing off European tyranny and the subsequent triumphs, as Americans perceived them, in extending an orderly and prosperous civilization over the eastern third of the continent. From religion and politics to town-building and engineering, antebellum culture was pervaded by a heightened belief in human *ability*. It seemed that any goal could be achieved, from the individual renunciation of alcohol or slaveholding to the moral regeneration of the world, by an act of wholehearted assent, an act of sheer will. Enthusiasm for fulfilling America's high mission was a unifying force, especially when this mission seemed to be threatened by Old World enemies or rivals. But the traditional polarization between New World and Old also raised the specter of betrayal—of American tories or subversive agents who in some way served the reactionary or revolutionary causes of a corrupt Europe. Hence the very sacredness of America's mission, which could not be openly challenged by any group, invited accusations that opponents of various kinds were either secretly or unwittingly in league with America's enemies. Ironically, a united commitment to national mission ultimately aggravated the questions of cohesion and group identity posed by the first general theme of union and disunion.

As the selections in this book will show, these abstract themes overlap and interlock in a variety of historical contexts and concrete situations. This anthology is organized in four broad Units, each containing between thirty-three and forty-one selections. Each Unit is divided into five or six topical Parts. For example, in Unit Three, "The Plight of Outsiders in an 'Open Society,'" Part 4 contains ten selections on the topic, "The Nonfreedom of 'Free Blacks.'" Although I have tried to preserve some sense of chronological progression *within* each Unit, my primary aim is to illuminate meaningful connections and interrelationships through a carefully selected sequence of topics. It is this thematic sequence, coupled with extensive analytic and explanatory headnotes, that makes this book an interpretive anthology. The Unit introductions and headnotes also provide a chronological framework. However, students who are unfamiliar with the broad outline of antebellum American history will find it useful to refer to the Chronological Chart, 1820–1860, pages 469–472, and to a textbook, such as Bernard Bailyn et al., *The Great Republic.*

In Unit One, we begin with "Socialization and the Problem of Influence," or, in other words, with the institutions and techniques that were supposed to make individuals responsible members of a democratic society. For nineteenth-century Americans such shaping of character logically preceded all other questions. The Founding Fathers had repeatedly stressed that the success of the American experiment in self-government would depend on the virtue and public spirit of the entire citizenry. Succeeding generations hailed the family as the key institution for developing a capacity for self-government. They also promoted public schools as indispensable auxiliaries to the family in ensuring social stability and moral improvement. The topics covered in Unit One include "family government," childrearing, education, the role of women, problems of discipline and delinquency, self-culture and self-improvement, the feminist movement, and divorce.

In Unit Two, "Struggles Over Access to Wealth and Power," we move outward from the family and schoolroom to what antebellum Americans considered the more "masculine" sphere—competitive enterprise and politics. Here we are less concerned with the conventional chronology of economic and political history than with two pervasive themes of American culture: the raising of individual expectations, which feed a speculative spirit of gain; and the fear of being "had"—of being unfairly excluded from equal access to America's vast resources. The merging of such fears and aspirations led to successive struggles over the ground rules governing the access to wealth and power. In developing these broad themes, Unit Two moves from "the anxious spirit of gain" to land speculation, town-building, and the California gold rush; from the demand for western land to the extension of law on the frontier; from the protest of eastern labor to the adaptation of law to the needs of free enterprise; and from the financing of internal improvements to the ideology of political parties and expressions of sectional rivalry.

The fear of being excluded and victimized by the unchecked power of a hostile majority was by no means unrealistic. The fate of the powerless is illustrated in Unit Three, "The Plight of Outsiders in an 'Open Society.'" Although the nation was dedicated to religious freedom, there were limits of tolerance that were tested whenever religious groups challenged certain vital cultural norms. The definition of cultural norms leads us from religious dissent to the great controversies over the fate of the American Indians. We then pursue the questions of assimilation, cultural identity, and exclusion in selections devoted to Hispanic and Chinese-Americans, ghetto-dwellers, free blacks, black slaves, and the polarized South.

In Unit Four we turn from the sharp disparities and polarities of American life to "Ideals of Progress, Perfection, and Mission." For in the last analysis, it was the commitment to such ideals that gave a distinctive stamp to ante-bellum consciousness, persuading Americans of different geographic sections and ethnic backgrounds that the conflicts documented in previous Units amounted to more than struggles for material self-interest. In the nineteenth century, visions of a better life drew their inspiration from the progress of science and technology, which still seemed to confirm the belief in a natural order designed by its Creator for the instruction and improvement of humanity. Religious revivalism, the second broad topic in Unit Four, also nourished faith in a higher social and historical purpose. After examining the quest for technological and moral perfection, we then move on through various reform movements to grandiose dreams of America's mission of emancipating the world from the sins and bondage of the past. Unit Four concludes with documents that transfer such millenarian symbolism to the sectional crisis precipitating the Civil War. The conflict over Negro slavery links back to the concluding selections of Units Two and Three, which examine this ultimate American contradiction from other perspectives. The theme of the nation as a "house divided" also echoes the appeals in Unit One for familial discipline, harmony, and solidarity.

As indicated above, the selections deal with aspects of political, economic, legal, and social life that illuminate central patterns of antebellum American culture. By "culture" I mean something more than the so-called high culture of elite intellectual and artistic activity; and something less than a generalized and anthropological "way of life." The selections focus on the ways in which "history" was experienced and symbolized—the ways in which people perceived, structured, explained, and argued over what was happening, who was doing what to whom, what to fear and what to fight for.

There remains the question of representativeness—of *whose* culture? First of all, I have not conceived antebellum American culture as a static or monolithic entity, but rather as a *process* involving dissent, contradiction, adaptation, and appropriation. In the selections that follow we hear the voices of blacks, Indians, a Chicano, a Chinese-American, radicals, conservatives, and moderates. Over twelve percent of the selections were written by women; over eighteen percent by Southerners. Some of the "elitist" sources cast invaluable light on how non-elites lived and were treated. Yet in the interest of representativeness it would be absurd as well as impossible to establish quotas reflecting the actual constituency of the antebellum population. The "average" antebellum American—a white, Protestant farmer—is not represented in this anthology. The typical farmer, artisan, or housewife had little opportunity to record his or her reflections on life or to relate immediate daily cares to a larger frame of meaning. Our authors include people who had worked as farmers, artisans, housewives, millgirls, and slaves, but almost by definition they were exceptional men and women who sought by the written word to exert some kind of public influence.

In a sense, this anthology is a study of Americans trying to exert public influence: It is heavily weighted toward the Northeast, and especially New England, precisely because that region tended to monopolize the printed word as it implemented a prolonged campaign of cultural imperialism. One of the central events of the antebellum era—an event that was to have a profound impact on the post-Civil War decades—was the success of northeastern elites in defining, preempting, and disseminating their own versions of "American culture." Although they failed to politicize this culture in the form of a national party, a relatively few writers, preachers, and reformers succeeded in standardizing a set of middle-class norms and fashions that applied to education, taste, sex roles, sensibility, and the very meaning of moral "respectability." One must remember that there were virtually no authoritative media to compete with the tens of millions of copies of standardized and didactic schoolbooks like McGuffey's Eclectic Readers. These schoolbooks prepared a mass audience for such phenomenal and long-term bestsellers as *Uncle Tom's Cabin* and *Little Women*—books that shaped the moral standards of countless American youth. Northeastern models also had a multiplier effect, since they were assimilated and adapted to local conditions by regional "tastemakers" in Illinois, California, and even the Deep South.

The "official" middle-class culture by no means won acceptance from all Americans. However, it was increasingly able to define nonaccepters as aliens, outsiders, and degenerates. In addition, it established the criteria of permissible dissent, thereby narrowing the range of cultural options. If this cultural hegemony was always incomplete and always resisted, its strength lay in fusing class interest with what seemed to be an impartial, uplifting, and commonsense view of moral progress. As we shall see, even radical reformers and dissident free blacks were susceptible, in varying degrees, to the norms of the official moralistic culture. If I have given disproportionate space to such New Englanders as the famous Beecher family, it is because they created the standards and symbols of Americanism which later generations of immigrants and rebels would ultimately confront.

Unit One

Socialization and the Problem of Influence

Introduction

The American Revolution accentuated the self-assertive confidence of individual Americans. It sanctioned subsequent challenges to every form of traditional privilege. Increasingly, wielders of authority felt the need to explain and justify appeals for obedience, whether from children in homes or from restive citizens who questioned the justice of certain laws. The early decades of the nineteenth century witnessed a marked decline of deference to authority of all kinds—to the supposedly upper classes and higher social orders, to local magistrates, to the clergy, and to family patriarchs. As American communities became more democratic, social rules depended for their effectiveness on at least a belief in their having won popular consent. The belief that such consent had been given depended in turn on the persuasive power of various kinds of influence. Though "influence" had once suggested occult, magic, or invisible forces that determined behavior (as in astrology), in politics the term became associated, especially in the eighteenth century, with the more worldly favors and patronage that linked self-interest to a particular faction or party. By the early nineteenth century, it was moral and psychological influence that Americans increasingly saw as the key to both social order and social power.

1

The most enduring form of influence is socialization. As applied to children, socialization pertains to the training and discipline required to suppress many immediate desires and to generate a sensitivity to the needs, feelings, opinions, and conventions of a given social group. Socialization, by internalizing norms of duty and responsibility, prepares the child for work, fellowship, and citizenship. In earlier times, this process had been thought of mainly in religious terms—as the breaking of a child's sinful will and the instilling through terror of a respect for divinely instituted authority. While such attitudes persisted well into the nineteenth century, they were increasingly modified by changing social conditions and the widespread view that children, instead of being inherently vicious, were highly malleable like fresh clay. This theory of malleability, which appeared in both religious and secular forms, evoked both optimism and alarm. Given proper moral influence, the republic could be assured of continuing security, order, and progress. But because of the absence of authoritarian institutions, there were no ultimate protections against the effects of corrupting environments or the failure of socialization.

This Unit addresses the problem of creating a harmonious social order based on individual consent. In the early nineteenth century, Americans of quite different persuasions could agree that it was within the family matrix that social rules are originally defined and assimilated, and that family interactions therefore build the foundation for all larger, external conceptions of authority, legitimacy, consent, duty, and discipline. The prevailing system of values, rooted in the Judeo-Christian tradition, prescribed the monogamous, patriarchal family as the eternal and unchanging norm for all peoples, a secure anchorage in otherwise stormy seas of political and social change. Yet the family alone could not bear the full burden of socialization. By the antebellum period, families had increasingly lost the reinforcement of an established church, a stable and homogeneous community, a system of apprenticeship, and other traditional social controls. Hence the theme of socialization and influence leads us to various substitutes such as the Society for the Reformation of Juvenile Delinquents, the public school movement, and a vast new literature devoted to self-culture and self-improvement. As we shall see, the attempt to exert influence by the printed word focused particular attention on the role of women as mothers, educators, and moral saviors of the republic. Ironically, the glorification of female influence ultimately encouraged feminist redefinitions of duty and familial consent as radical alternatives to the supposedly corrupting authority of the patriarchal home.

In Part 1, we begin with "The Art and Responsibilities of Family Government." From the time of Plato and Aristotle, political theorists had insisted that the government of families is closely related to the government of nations. Since the authority of a father had traditionally been likened to that of a king, the relation between family government and democratic government remained problematic. On the one hand, for conservatives the supposedly unchangeable structure of legitimate family government might make democracy "safe" by ensuring a respect for order, justice, and communal purpose. These virtues could not really be guaranteed by laws and constitutions, which were always subject to revision. But America's great political experiment might be secured if families succeeded in internalizing "checks and balances" within the moral character of future generations. As we see in the initial selections, this was the high responsibility assigned to the family by writers who pictured the institution as a bulwark against anarchy and thus as a substitute for the bayonets, religious establishments, and oligarchic rule of most of the world outside America.

On the other hand, it was impossible to insulate the American family from the leveling influence of democratic ideals. Heman Humphrey, in the first selection of Part 1, complains that "our children hear so much about liberty and equality, and are so often told how glorious it is to be 'born free and equal,'" that they are submitting with increasing reluctance to parental authority. Moreover, even conservatives like Humphrey tended to admit that in governing children persuasion and moral influence were more effective than trying to break disobedient wills. Women, according to a growing number of writers of both sexes, had special gifts for coaxing "cheerful obedience" and for peacefully resolving family conflicts. Women were also said to be the only group in America uncontaminated by the competitive struggle for wealth and power. Therefore, if families were to serve as the nation's primary source of moral values and as a counterforce to acquisitive self-interest, their mission would largely depend on the regenerative powers of American women.

All parts of the nation were concerned with the problems of family government in a democratic society. But Northeasterners tended to monopolize the literature on childrearing, the new responsibilities of women, and the need for alternative methods of socialization and moral influence to remedy the deficiencies of family government. This was partly because the Northeast, and especially New England, had well-established traditions of public schooling, journalism, and publishing. The growth of large cities and the arrival in the Northeast of hundreds of thousands of immigrants heightened the region's awareness of ethnic and religious diversity, to say nothing of widening extremes of poverty and wealth. These dramatic social transformations aggravated alarm over the effectiveness of family discipline.

The Northeast also led a national trend toward a more heavily female population. By 1860 it was the only region in which females had begun to outnumber males. Furthermore, in the Northeast more middle-class women were postponing marriage or not marrying at all; more girls and women were attending school and working as wage earners; and native-born women were having fewer children and ceasing childbearing at an earlier age. These demographic changes were closely related to the expansion of a market economy and to the destruction of domestic industries that had once employed the women and older children of families. For the middle class, at least, children of eight or ten years of age were no longer an economic asset; instead of working at family industries or being bound out as servants or apprentices, they were becoming consumers of education designed to improve their happiness and productivity as adults. Rising income and the availability of manufactured goods also provided middle-class women with greater leisure and with higher expectations of self-fulfillment. Along with Protestant clergymen, New England women, in particular, became innovators as teachers, publicists, novelists, and organizers. If other sections of the country were less articulate about questions of self-culture, moral improvement, and finding alternatives to the "absorbing passion for gain," they nevertheless contained important groups and classes who eagerly read northeastern books, journals, and sermons. Later on, in Unit Three, we will sample some of the southern writing on socialization and discipline as it pertained to the distinctive institution of Negro slavery.

The theme of Part 2 is "The Discipline and Self-Discipline of the Young." Since the very survival of a republican form of government supposedly depended on parental effectiveness in producing good citizens, it followed that society as a whole had a compelling interest in rectifying parental failures. In Part 2 we move outward from the middle-class family to the discovery, as early as the 1820s, that gangs of juveniles in America's larger cities roamed the streets and lived beyond the reach of moral influence. For example, male and female missionaries in their campaign to distribute Bibles and religious tracts throughout New York City found not only noxious garrets and tenements filled with destitute and diseased adults, but children who appeared to have no knowledge of right and wrong. In the words of the women who later ran the New Mission House at Five Points, the worst slum area, New York City swarmed with vagrants who had gone through "infancy and childhood without a mother's care or a father's protection: born in sin, nurtured in crime; . . . the young heart crushed before its tiny call for affection has met one answering response." The failure or even absence of family government supposedly explained the alarming increase of beggary, theft, prostitution, and drunkenness, even among children. And for reformers this failure dramatized the need for creating substitute families in the form of asylums, houses of refuge, and schools.

Such institutions were seen essentially as extensions of family government. Whether administered by the state or by benevolent societies, the houses of refuge and even penitentiaries were designed for moral rehabilitation, a form of socialization. Like idealized families, they aimed at subduing aggression, evoking guilt, developing self-control and respect for order, all for the "good" of their inmates. They presumed to act in the name of benevolence and to employ such devices as solitary confinement in the interest of love. As a result of these preconceptions, reformers tended to exaggerate the voluntary consent of the people they strove to help, and thus remained blind to the coercions of power when used for moral ends. For example, the Reverend Thomas L. Harris, in the selection entitled "The Problem of Unwilling Submission," fervently calls for a house of refuge to which all juveniles found engaged in beggary or theft "should be removed"; yet he also pictures the same home being open to all children who voluntarily want "to secure its advantages."

This typical desire to disguise punishment by identifying it as a means for self-improvement and social progress helps to explain why American penitentiaries could be internationally hailed as humanitarian innovations that would ultimately eradicate crime. The blurring of familial and penal functions also helps us understand the startling fact that prison reformers exhorted American parents to adopt the methods of constant surveillance, vigilance, and regimented order that had supposedly proven effective in penitentiaries. The same techniques of management, including the enlistment of sibling, or peer-group pressure, were prescribed for families, schools, colleges, and factories.

Part 3 deals with "The Schoolroom as an Extended Family." The movement for state-wide systems of public schools encouraged the most unprecedented arguments for public paternalism. In the eyes of Horace Mann, the celebrated champion of public schools, every state "is morally bound to enact a code of laws legalizing and enforcing infanticide, or a code of laws establishing free schools." Mann's alternatives are revealing, even if intended only as a shocking rhetorical device to dramatize both the absolute right of every child to proper sustenance and education and the belief that denying such rights "would be equivalent to a sentence of death." The logical conclusion of this reasoning was that life itself had negative value unless open to the improvements and perfections of modern civilization. It should be stressed that Mann was a naive idealist committed to vindicating the claims on society of newborn children. He appealed to the state as the only force that could open "imprisoned minds and hearts." His vision, like that of many reformers, focused on the deprivation of victims, not on the possible abuses of self-righteous power. He remained blind to the dangers of an all-or-nothing definition of educational rights.

Actually, Mann barely touched on the right of every newborn infant to "sustenance and shelter and care," which constituted a claim to "a portion of pre-existent property." He could demand that the government "step in and fill the parent's place," but could imagine no program that would bolster parental competence and self-respect. Prodded on by reformers like Mann, Massachusetts built the nation's first state-wide system of graded schools and educational bureaucracy, complemented by special institutional care for the physically handicapped and delinquent. But these expressions of state paternalism did little to counteract the effects of economic inequality or to challenge the dominant liberal values of voluntarism and self-improvement.

In higher education, there was also a growing tension between paternalistic guidance and the ideal of self-reliance, between the received culture of the past and the utilitarian needs of the present. In the selection entitled "What Is a Young Man Fitted For, When He Takes His Degree?", a Yale College committee not only admits the need for some accommodation to the "spirits and wants of the age" and to "the business character of the nation," but affirms that ultimately "the scholar must form himself, by his own exertions." The same 1830 report takes it for granted that college students should be subjected to rote learning, mechanical recitations, and constant personal surveillance, but also presumes that such dependence and tutelage are suitable only for a brief apprenticeship stage culminating in a liberal education that gives "a commanding influence in society, and a widely extended sphere of usefulness."

In Part 4, we turn to "Advice on Self-Culture and Sexual Identity." The authors of such "advice literature" aimed at a youthful audience no longer subjected to strict parental, institutional, or communal controls. Even as late as 1870, only two percent of the seventeen-year-olds graduated from high school and barely one percent of persons aged eighteen to twenty-four were attending institutions of higher education. Yet in the antebellum period, an increasing number of young people were migrating to the cities or to the West. Probably the majority of such mobile youth were untouched by the literature, public lectures, and institutions devoted to self-improvement. But in an age when villages mushroomed into cities, when immense tracts of wilderness gave way to farmland, when new classes of men rose from obscurity to power as merchants, brokers, speculators, and manufacturers, anything seemed possible. William Ellery Channing captured one of the central ideas of the age when he wrote, "it matters little what or where we are now." Improvement—whether individual or national, spiritual or material—was not merely an ideal but, for men like Channing and Ralph Waldo Emerson, a universal duty. Though in most other respects Channing and Emerson had little in common with religious revivalists like Charles Grandison Finney, they shared a common faith of communicating to the American public the liberating effects of an act of will. As Channing put it, "we can stay or change the current of thought," meaning not only the correction of thought but the correction of actions flowing from thought.

It is cheering to think that every human being contains latent powers for shaping his or her own destiny, and that farmers, mechanics, and factory girls can be inspired to improve themselves by their own exertions. Yet there was a certain paradox in depending on self-professed experts to prescribe the techniques for becoming self-reliant. By the 1840s a market society had already begun to commercialize the popular yearning for liberation and self-fulfillment. If from one point of view Americans had become more emancipated from the prescriptions of family tradition and local custom, from another point of view they were becoming hardly less dependent on the latest fashions, mostly accessible at a price, concerning everything from the choice of a spouse to the ways to get rich. The content of such how-to-do-it literature, which we sample in Part 4, tells us little about how spouses were actually chosen or fortunes made. But the immense market for such literature does suggest a widespread uncertainty over how decisions should be made. The uncertainty also suggests a growing belief in the insufficiency of family and communal guidance.

The dispensers of advice were still largely preoccupied with the nation's morality. Their claims of authority and impartiality usually rested on some clerical or religious background. This clerical influence probably accounts for the repeated emphasis on self-denial in a literature ostensibly devoted to self-improvement. Faced with America's unparalleled opportunities, a young man should beware, according to Channing, "lest your motives sink as your condition improves." Various lectures on "how to get rich" warned against the kind of bold ventures and speculations that were in fact producing new fortunes, and recommended instead a kind of caution and frugality implying at least temporary contentment with one's lot.

Similarly, tracts on "female culture" advised the American woman to find strength in submission, to "be plastic herself if she would mold others." But in the selections entitled "The 'Restless, Anxious Longing' of American Women," this cult of home and motherhood becomes subtly transformed into a covert attack on the violence, exploitation, and insensitivity of a male-dominated society. The marriageable woman, we learn, not only has the duty to spurn any suitor who smells of tobacco or alcohol, but knows "that though it may be expedient for her to marry, it is her privilege to be single." Catharine Beecher, who exercised that privilege in her own life, proceeds to map out a campaign that would enable an army of underemployed women to educate "the vast multitude of neglected American children all over our land." Hence women's liberation and fulfillment, in teaching and social service, become at once an answer to family failure and a moral antidote to the self-seeking and callousness of the masculine world of "business."

The selections in Part 5, "Feminist Alternatives," take up and extend Catharine Beecher's indictment of "the evils suffered by American women." Beginning with the concrete grievances of New England mill girls, the protest expands to a more general complaint against men treating women, in Sarah Grimké's words, as "pretty toys" or "mere instruments of pleasure." Though the feminist movement developed out of the antislavery movement and originally focused on public discrimination against female reformers, it soon challenged the patriarchal family as a kind of analogue to Negro slavery. Like enslavement, traditional marriage was charged with stripping a woman of her basic rights and separate human identity, subjecting her to the nearly absolute will of a husband-master. Thus radical feminism leads us back to the theme of family government and to the effects of egalitarian ideals on the process of socialization.

Heman Humphrey, in the first selection of Part 1, pleads for the *appearance*, at least, of parental unity in dealing with children. Otherwise, and here Humphrey paraphrases St. Mark in the New Testament, "your house being 'divided against itself cannot stand.'" In contrast, radical feminists concluded that "marriage does not differ, in any of its essential features, from chattel slavery." For them, the mere appearance of unity could not conceal the stifling of women's capacity for moral and intellectual improvement or disguise the underlying violence of "myriads of discordant and disordered households." Ernestine Rose, in the concluding section of this Unit, calls for an end to hypocrisy by legalizing easy divorce.

Divorce failed to become a central issue for most feminists of this period, but the very charge that "marriage is the *slavery of woman*" drew its resonance from a larger national debate over the emancipation of Negro slaves, the limits of federal authority, and the legitimacy of southern threats of disunion. Conversely, the sectional struggle acquired more vivid meaning from the rhetoric of domestic discord. It was no accident that Abraham Lincoln, in the most daring and provocative speech of his career (a selection from which appears near the end of this volume), declared that " 'A house divided against itself cannot stand.' " Unlike Humphrey, Lincoln was attacking the hypocrisy of pretending that the government could "endure, permanently half *slave* and half *free*." Unlike Rose, he denied the right and desirability of secession: "I do not expect the Union to be *dissolved*—I do not expect the house to *fall*—but I *do* expect it will cease to be divided." Either slavery or freedom would prevail: "It will become *all* one thing, or *all* the other."

The parallel between national and family government cannot be pressed too far. But what linked the two in a uniquely American way was an outlook of uncertainty and hope concerning the consensual basis of unity. As the following selections suggest, Americans increasingly looked to moral influence as the means of ensuring order and unity with consent. When moral influence failed—whether in dealing with delinquent children or, in northern eyes, with a delinquent and rebellious South—the goal of moral improvement was used to justify the coercions of physical power.

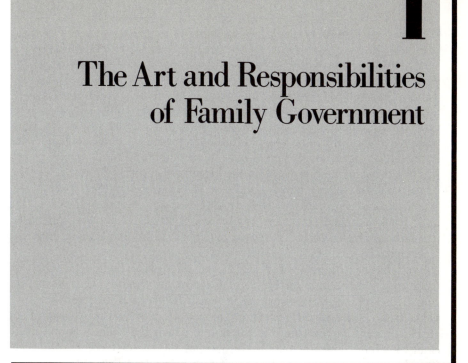

1

The Art and Responsibilities
of Family Government

A. Family Government and National Government

• *Heman Humphrey (1840)*

From the Old Testament prophets and ancient Greek philosophers to Sigmund Freud, social theorists have emphasized the primal (and often unconscious) connections between family authority and tribal or national government. Confronted by the political and social upheavals of the 1830s (the so-called Age of Jackson, for which Jackson was only one symbol), conservatives like Heman Humphrey could draw on this tradition and portray the patriarchal family as history's stabilizing remnant and hope. Yet in making this argument, Humphrey concedes much to the genial, democratic pressures which had aggravated the problems of parenthood. And ironically, from one point of view, Humphrey's arguments for family autonomy can be interpreted as a "radical" defiance of the encroachments of the state. Humphrey (1779–1861) was a native New Englander who worked as a school teacher and farmhand before entering Yale College at the age of twenty-five. A pioneering temperance preacher, he later became president of Amherst College, two years after its founding, and remained in that influential position for twenty-two years.

Heman Humphrey (1840)

Every family is a little state, or empire within itself, bound together by the most endearing attractions, and governed by its patriarchal head, with whose prerogative no power on earth has a right to interfere. Nations may change their forms of government at pleasure, and may enjoy a high degree of prosperity under different constitutions; and perhaps the time will never come, when any *one* form will be adapted to the circumstances of all mankind. But in the family organization there is but one model, for all times and all places. It is just the same now, as it was in the beginning, and it is impossible to alter it, without marring its beauty, and directly contravening the wisdom and benevolence of the Creator. It is at once the simplest, the safest and the most efficient organization that can be conceived of. Like everything else, it may be perverted to bad purposes; but it is a divine model, and must not be altered.

Every father is the constituted head and ruler of his household. God has made him the supreme earthly legislator over his children, accountable, of course, to Himself, for the manner in which he executes his trust; but amenable to no other power, except in the most extreme cases of neglect, or abuse. The will of the parent is the law to which the child is bound in all cases to submit, unless it plainly contravenes the law of God. Children are brought into existence and placed in families, not to follow their own wayward inclinations, but to look up to their parents for guidance; not to teach, but to be taught; not to govern but to be governed.

. . .

And as no power on earth may forcibly take the reins out of a parent's hands, neither may he abandon his post, or refuse to act as the viceregent of God in his own house. When a father finds himself surrounded by a rising family, it is too late for him to decide whether or not he will assume the responsibility of supporting and educating his children. That question is already settled. . . . These are duties which every head of a family *must* perform. If he neglect them, it is at his peril. . . . He is not indeed precluded from availing himself of the assistance of others, by sending his children abroad for a part of their education, when he thinks it will be for their advantage; but let him not forget that he is accountable to God for the judicious exercise of this discretion. The authority which he cannot exercise over his children when they are away from home, he must delegate to those who receive them under their care; and in no case may he place them where they will be left to themselves, and exposed without counsel or restraint, to bad influences.

. . .

Although, as I have already remarked, the state has no right to interfere with the domestic arrangements of families, except in extreme cases, it is

SOURCE: Heman Humphrey, *Domestic Education* (Amherst, Mass.: J. S. and C. Adams, 1840), pp. 16, 18–19, 21–24, 26, 32–33.

nevertheless true, that in order to become good citizens in after life, children must be accustomed to cheerful subordination in the family, from their earliest recollection. I know that those who grow up without restraint by the fire-side, and whose youth is consequently as wild as the winds, *can* be governed afterwards by absolute power. The bayonet of the Czar and the scimitar of the Sultan can tame them and keep them in subjection. But it may well be doubted whether anything like a free constitutional government can ever be maintained over a people, who have not been taught the fifth commandment in their childhood.[1] I do not believe it can. . . . It has been said a thousand times, that the practicability of maintaining a highly republican form of government has been *tried* and is *settled* in the United States, however it may have failed everywhere else. I wish it were so: but I am afraid the question is settled, so far *only* as we have gone. What the future may disclose, who can certainly tell? It is yet a grand desideratum, whether we have religion and virtue and intelligence enough to sustain our blessed institutions. The danger is, that our liberties will degenerate into licentiousness, and that the growing laxity of family government in this country will hasten on the fearful crisis. There is, if I am not deceived, a reaction in our unparalleled political freedom, upon our domestic relations. It is more difficult than it was, half, or even a quarter of a century ago, for parents to "command their household after them." Our children hear so much about liberty and equality, and are so often told how glorious it is to be "born free and equal," that it is hard work to make them understand for what good reason their liberties are abridged in the family; and I have no doubt this accounts, in multitudes of instances, for the reluctance with which they submit to parental authority. The boy wants to be "his own man," long before his wisdom teeth are cut; and the danger lies in conceding the point to him under the notion that our fathers were quite too rigid and that a more indulgent domestic policy, corresponding with the "spirit of the age," is better. This may be the way to make *rulers* enough for a hundred republics; but not to make a single good *subject*. I repeat, therefore, that if it is important to secure a prompt obedience to the wholesome laws of the state, then is family government indispensably necessary, and the father who takes no care to control his own sons, is not himself a patriot, if he is a good citizen.

Moreover, without family government there will be very little *self-government* in any community. If you do not restrain the waywardness of your child, in its early developments, and thus assist him to get the mastery of it while yet the conquest is comparatively easy, it will be in vain for you to expect him ever to gain that self-control which is so essential to his happiness and safety. Nothing is better settled by the experience of all ages, than that the will grows stubborn—that evil passions become impetuous by indulgence; and that indulged they will be, by the child, if they are not held in check by parental authority. In this view, a greater misfortune can hardly befall a

---

[1] The fifth commandment is to honor one's father and mother.

young person, than to be left to himself. The consequence is, that before reason and conscience can assert their supremacy, bad habits are formed, and his depraved inclinations have time to ripen into such maturity, that to bring them into subjection is infinitely more difficult than if the work had been commenced in the nursery.

. . .

It is thought by some, that the government of children must be very easy, if not even a delightful task. I do not recollect, however, that I ever heard this sentiment expressed by a parent who had been placed in circumstances to make the trial, and who had succeeded in any tolerable degree. As a general rule, persons know how to manage families much better before they have them, than afterwards. Those who are most astonished at the failure of their friends in this important matter, and see no difficulty at all in holding the reins, have no children to govern. The bachelor who boards in his brother's family, or goes to spend a few weeks with a married sister, understands the thing perfectly, and can discourse most eloquently upon family government, by the hour together. He has it all at his fingers ends, from A to Z, and knows exactly what to do from sunrise till bed-time. Oh how he wishes he could have the management of these lawless little urchins for a month. He would stop their crying and romping, or he would quit the premises. How parents can have so little tact, and be so indulgent, is entirely beyond his comprehension. But it is often exceedingly amusing to see how the tables are turned when he comes to have a family of his own. Poor man! the children spoil his beautiful theories a great deal faster than he ever made them. What the matter is, he cannot tell; but it is infinitely more difficult to govern children than it used to be.

. . .

If parents are not of one heart and one mind, in regard to this matter, it will be found extremely difficult, if not impossible, to rule their household well. And how many families suffer from this want of *unity!* The father and mother, instead of "seeing eye to eye," and directing all their efforts to one point, differ essentially, both in theory and practice. As they do not think alike, they move in opposite directions. One parent, perhaps, is too stern, and the other too lax and indulgent. Or if one has correct views of parental authority, and the manner in which it should be exercised, the other looks at the whole subject in a very erroneous point of light. What one regards as a serious fault, the other overlooks as an excusable foible. Where one thinks the rod is called for, the other is entirely opposed to it. Where one is actuated by principle and good judgment, in the painful administration of necessary discipline, the other is swayed by a morbid tenderness, which would screen the little culprit, perhaps to his undoing. . . . What can the father do if the mother takes the part of the child? Or what can the mother do, if the father comes in and takes the darling boy out of her hands? Discuss these matters between yourselves as much as you please; but never let your children know or suspect, that you are not perfectly agreed. . . . Think alike, if possible. At all events, strengthen each other's hands, and never *seem* to differ. Let your children see, that in the administration of government, you are one—that you have one heart and one aim—and that nothing is to be hoped for, from any appeal that can be made to either. Take the opposite course; let the jarring of interfering and conflicting action be felt, and your house being "divided against itself cannot stand."

B. The Mission of American Women

• *Catharine Beecher* (1842)

Beginning, like Humphrey, with the theme of parental authority and the need for subordination, Catharine Beecher moves on to consider the status of American women. For a comparative perspective, she quotes extensively from the second volume of Alexis de Tocqueville's now-classic *Democracy in America*, which had been published in 1840, only a year before the first edition of her own book. Although Tocqueville seems to be arguing against sexual equality, Beecher seizes upon the passages that accord American women a "superior moral influence." Disavowing any feminist demand for equal rights, Beecher then proceeds to equate women's mission with the mission of America itself; in the hands of America's wives, mothers, and sisters she places the fate of democratic institutions. The argument illustrates Beecher's brilliance in revolutionizing what had traditionally been thought of as a submissive feminine role.

A member of America's most famous evangelical family (her father Lyman and five of her brothers were ministers), Catharine Beecher (1800–1878) became skilled at covert rebellion as she struggled to reconcile her own feminine identity with the Beecher sense of family mission. After her fiancé was killed in a shipwreck, Catharine turned away from marriage but became the nation's first expert on "domestic science." Her *Treatise on Domestic Economy*, reprinted nearly every year from 1841 to 1856, was essentially a how-to-do-it manual on the practical details of household management. Its impact has been likened to that of Dr. Benjamin Spock's *Baby and Child Care* in the decades after World War II. As a teacher, lecturer, fundraiser, and organizer, Catharine Beecher was also notable for promoting the cause of higher education for women and for popularizing the idea that teaching was a profession for which women were uniquely suited.

Catharine Beecher (1842)

Society could never go forward, harmoniously, nor could any craft or profession be successfully pursued, unless . . . superior and subordinate relations be instituted and sustained.

But who shall take the higher, and who the subordinate, stations in social and civil life? This matter, in the case of parents and children, is decided by the Creator. He has given children to the control of parents, as their superiors, and to them they remain subordinate, to a certain age, or so long as they are members of their household. And parents can delegate such a portion of their authority to teachers and employers, as the interests of their children require.

In most other cases, in a truly democratic state, each individual is allowed to choose for himself, who shall take the position of his superior. No woman is forced to obey any husband but the one she chooses for herself; nor is she obliged to take a husband, if she prefers to remain single. So every domestic, and every artisan or laborer, after passing from parental control, can choose the employer to whom he is to accord obedience, or, if he prefers to relinquish certain advantages, he can remain without taking a subordinate place to any employer.

• • •

The tendencies of democratic institutions, in reference to the rights and interests of the female sex, have been fully developed in the United States; and it is in this aspect, that the subject is one of peculiar interest to American women. In this country, it is established, both by opinion and by practice, that woman has an equal interest in all social and civil concerns; and that no domestic, civil, or political institution is right, which sacrifices her interest to promote that of the other sex. But in order to secure her the more firmly in all these privileges, it is decided, that, in the domestic relation, she take a subordinate station, and that, in civil and political concerns, her interests be intrusted to the other sex, without her taking any part in voting, or in making and administering laws. The result of this order of things has been fairly tested, and is thus portrayed by M. de Tocqueville, a writer, who, for intelligence, fidelity, and ability, ranks second to none.

"There are people in Europe [Tocqueville writes], who, confounding together the different characteristics of the sexes, would make of man and woman, beings not only equal, but alike. They would give to both the same functions, impose on both the same duties, and grant to both the same rights. They would mix them in all things,—their business, their occupations, their pleasures. It may readily be conceived, that, by *thus* attempting to make one sex equal to the other, both are degraded; and, from so preposterous a

---

SOURCE: Catharine Beecher, A *Treatise on Domestic Economy* (Boston: T. H. Webb, 1842), pp. 26–34, 36–38.

medley of the works of Nature, nothing could ever result, but weak men and disorderly women.

"It is not thus that the Americans understand the species of democratic equality, which may be established between the sexes. They admit, that, as Nature has appointed such wide differences between the physical and moral constitutions of man and woman, her manifest design was, to give a distinct employment to their various faculties; and they hold, that improvement does not consist in making beings so dissimilar do pretty nearly the same things, but in getting each of them to fulfil their respective tasks, in the best possible manner. The Americans have applied to the sexes the great principle of political economy, which governs the manufactories of our age, by carefully dividing the duties of man from those of woman, in order that the great work of society may be the better carried on.

"In no country has such constant care been taken, as in America, to trace two clearly distinct lines of action for the two sexes, and to make them keep pace one with the other, but in two pathways which are always different. American women never manage the outward concerns of the family, or conduct a business, or take a part in political life; nor are they, on the other hand, ever compelled to perform the rough labor of the fields, or to make any of those laborious exertions, which demand the exertion of physical strength. No families are so poor, as to form an exception to this rule.[1]

• • •

"Nor have the Americans ever supposed, that one consequence of democratic principles is the subversion of marital power, or the confusion of the natural authorities in families. They hold, that every association must have a head, in order to accomplish its object; and that the natural head of the conjugal association is man. They do not, therefore, deny him the right of directing his partner; and they maintain, that in the smaller association of husband and wife, as well as in the great social community, the object of democracy is, to regulate and legalize the powers which are necessary, not to subvert all power.

• • •

"Although the travellers, who have visited North America differ on a great number of points, they agree in remarking, that morals are far more strict, there, than elsewhere. . . . In America, all books, novels not excepted, suppose women to be chaste; and no one thinks of relating affairs of gallantry.

"It has often been remarked that, in Europe, a certain degree of contempt lurks, even in the flattery which men lavish upon women. Although a European frequently affects to be the slave of woman, it may be seen, that he never sincerely thinks her his equal. In the United States, men seldom compliment women, but they daily show how much they esteem them. They

---

[1] Tocqueville was referring to white families, since elsewhere he commented extensively on the "exception" of Negro slavery.

constantly display an entire confidence in the understanding of a wife, and a profound respect for her freedom. They have decided that her mind is just as fitted as that of a man to discover the plain truth, and her heart as firm to embrace it, and they have never sought to place her virtue, any more than his, under the shelter of prejudice, ignorance, and fear.

"It would seem, that in Europe, where man so easily submits to the despotic sway of woman, they are nevertheless curtailed of some of the greatest qualities of the human species, and considered as seductive, but imperfect beings, and (what may well provoke astonishment) women ultimately look upon themselves in the same light, and almost consider it as a privilege that they are entitled to show themselves futile, feeble, and timid. The women of America claim no such privileges.

"It is true, that the Americans rarely lavish upon women those eager attentions which are commonly paid them in Europe. But their conduct to women always implies, that they suppose them to be virtuous and refined; and such is the respect entertained for the moral freedom of the sex, that, in the presence of a woman, the most guarded language is used, lest her ear should be offended by an expression. In America, a young unmarried woman may, alone, and without fear, undertake a long journey.

"As for myself, I do not hesitate to avow that, although the women of the United States are confined within the narrow circle of domestic life, and their situation is, in some respects, one of extreme dependence, I have nowhere seen women occupying a loftier position; and if I were asked, now I am drawing to the close of this work, in which I have spoken of so many important things done by the Americans, to what the singular prosperity and growing strength of that people ought mainly to be attributed, I should reply,—*to the superiority of their women.*"

This testimony of a foreigner, who has had abundant opportunities of making a comparison, is sanctioned by the assent of all candid and intelligent men, who have enjoyed similar opportunities.

It appears, then, that it is in America, alone, that women are raised to an equality with the other sex; and that, both in theory and practice, their interests are regarded as of equal value. They are made subordinate in station, only where a regard to their best interests demands it, while, as if in compensation for this, by custom and courtesy, they are always treated as superiors. Universally, in this country, through every class of society, precedence is given to woman, in all the comforts, conveniences, and courtesies, of life.

In civil and political affairs, American women take no interest or concern, except so far as they sympathize with their family and personal friends; but in all cases, in which they do feel a concern, their opinions and feelings have a consideration, equal, or even superior, to that of the other sex.

In matters pertaining to the education of their children, in the selection and support of a clergyman, in all benevolent enterprises, and in all questions relating to morals or manners, they have a superior influence. In such concerns, it would be impossible to carry a point, contrary to their judgement and feelings; while an enterprise sustained by them, will seldom fail of success.

If those who are bewailing themselves over the fancied wrongs and injuries of women in this nation, could only see things as they are, they would know, that, whatever remnants of a barbarous or aristocratic age may remain in our civil institutions, in reference to the interests of women, it is only because they are ignorant of them, or do not use their influence to have them rectified; for it is very certain that there is nothing reasonable, which American women would unite in asking, that would not readily be bestowed.

The preceding remarks, then, illustrate the position, that the democratic institutions of this country are in reality no other than the principles of Christianity carried into operation, and that they tend to place woman in her true position in society, as having equal rights with the other sex; and that, in fact, they have secured to American women a lofty and fortunate position, which, as yet, has been attained by the women of no other nation.

· · ·

To us is committed the grand, the responsible privilege, of exhibiting to the world the beneficent influences of Christianity, when carried into every social, civil, and political institution; and, though we have, as yet, made such imperfect advances, already the light is streaming into the dark prison-house of despotic lands, while startled kings and sages, philosophers and statesmen, are watching us with that interest, which a career so illustrious, and so involving their own destiny, is calculated to excite. They are studying our institutions, scrutinizing our experience, and watching for our mistakes, that they may learn whether "a social revolution, so irresistible, be advantageous or prejudicial to mankind."

· · ·

But the part to be enacted by American women, in this great moral enterprise, is the point to which special attention should here be directed.

The success of democratic institutions, as is conceded by all, depends upon the intellectual and moral character of the mass of the people. If they are intelligent and virtuous, democracy is a blessing; but if they are ignorant and wicked, it is only a curse, and is much more dreadful than any other form of civil government, as a thousand tyrants are more to be dreaded than one. It is equally conceded, that the formation of the moral and intellectual character of the young is committed mainly to the female hand. The mother forms the character of the future man; the sister bends the fibres that are hereafter to be the forest tree; the wife sways the heart, whose energies may turn for good or for evil the destinies of a nation. Let the women of a country be made virtuous and intelligent, and the men will certainly be the same. The proper education of a man decides the welfare of an individual; but educate a woman, and the interests of a whole family are secured.

If this be so, as none will deny, then to American women, more than to any others on earth, is committed the exalted privilege of extending over the world those blessed influences, which are to renovate degraded man, and "clothe all climes with beauty."

No American woman, then, has any occasion for feeling that hers is an humble or insignificant lot. The value of what an individual accomplishes is to be estimated by the importance of the enterprise achieved, and not by the particular position of the laborer. The drops of heaven which freshen the earth, are each of equal value, whether they fall in the lowland meadow, or the princely parterre.[1] The builders of a temple are of equal importance, whether they labor on the foundations, or toil upon the dome.

Thus, also, with those labors which are to be made effectual in the regeneration of the earth. And it is by forming a habit of regarding the apparently insignificant efforts of each isolated laborer, in a comprehensive manner, as indispensable portions of a grand result, that the minds of all, however humble their sphere of service, can be invigorated and cheered. The woman, who is rearing a family of children; the woman, who labors in the school-room; the woman, who, in her retired chamber, earns with her needle the mite, which contributes to the intellectual and moral elevation of her country; even the humble domestic, whose example and influence may be molding and forming young minds, while her faithful services sustain a prosperous domestic state;—each and all may be animated by the consciousness, that they are agents in accomplishing the greatest work that ever was committed to human responsibility. It is the building of a glorious temple, whose base shall be coextensive with the bounds of the earth, whose summit shall pierce the skies, whose splendor shall beam on all lands; and those who hew the lowliest stone, as much as those who carve the highest capital, will be equally honored when its top-stone shall be laid, with new rejoicings of the morning stars, and shoutings of the sons of God.

C. The Feminine Regeneration of Everyday Life

• *Mrs. A. J. Graves* (1843)

Little is known about Mrs. A. J. Graves, but she was one of many writers who echoed or played variations on Catharine Beecher's themes. Rejecting the excesses of feminism while sympathizing with the movement's spirit, Mrs. Graves sees women as an uplifting and unifying force within households fragmented by the economy's division of labor and by the "absorbing passion for gain, and the pressing demands of business." Her critique of male arrogance and complacency is as sharp as that of any feminist. She provides us with a rare glimpse of an emerging modern condition: husbands and wives whose daily concerns are so specialized and so far removed from each other that little common ground remains for communication. In the end, Mrs. Graves supports the increasingly popular image of home as a haven and refuge in a heartless world. She finds hope in the image of a newly enlightened domestic woman, the last custodian of culture and civilization.

---

[1] A parterre is an ornamental flowerbed.

Mrs. A. J. Graves (1843)

The great principles of liberty and equal rights, which are about to overthrow the long-existing institutions of despotism, and are stirring the hearts of men of every station, in every clime, have penetrated even into the quiet havens of domestic life. While men are fiercely contending for their prerogatives upon the world's arena, without seeming yet to have settled what should be their relative position in regard to each other, women have come forward to claim immunities which ancient usage has long denied them. "The Rights of Woman" are almost as warmly and wildly contested as "The Rights of Man"; and there is a revolution going on in the female mind at the present day, out of which glorious results may arise; though in this, as in all other revolutions, ultraism and fanaticism may retard the development of good by their excesses, and their disregard of the dictates of sound wisdom and sober discretion. We lament the erratic course of many of our female reformers, believing that they have inflicted deep injury where they intended good, by drawing woman away from her true and allotted sphere—domestic life.

. . .

To woman it belongs . . . to elevate the intellectual character of her household, to kindle the fires of mental activity in childhood, and to keep these steadily burning with advancing years . . . The men of our country, as things are constituted among us, find but little time for the cultivation of science and general literature—studies so eminently calculated to refine the mind and purify the taste, and which furnish so exhaustless a fund of elevated enjoyment to the heart. And this is the case even with those who have acquired a fondness for intellectual pursuits in early life. The absorbing passion for gain, and the pressing demands of business, engross their whole attention. Thus the merchant becomes a merchant, and nothing more; and the mind of the lawyer is little else than a library of cases and precedents, of legal records and commentaries. The physician loses sight of the scientific studies to which his profession so naturally directs him, contents himself with the same beaten track, and becomes a mere practitioner or operator. And the mechanic and agriculturist too often settle down into mere manual laborers, by suffering practical details wholly to occupy their minds as well as their bodies. The only relief to this absorbing devotion to "material interests" is found in the excitement of party politics.

These two engross the whole moral, intellectual, and physical man; and, to be convinced of this, we need not follow the American to his place of business or to political meetings—we have only to listen to his fireside conversation. It might be supposed that the few waking hours he spends at home in the bosom of his family, he would delight to employ upon such subjects as would interest and improve his wife and children, and that he

SOURCE: Mrs. A. J. Graves, *Woman in America: Being an Examination into the Moral and Intellectual Condition of American Female Society* (New York: Harper and Brothers, 1843), pp. xiii–xiv, 62–67.

would avail himself of these opportunities to refresh his wearied mind with new matters of thought. But in place of this, what is the perpetual theme of his conversation? Business and politics, six per cent, bank discounts, stock-jobbing, insolvencies, assets, liabilities—cases at court, legal opinions and decisions—neuralgia, gastric irritation, fevers, etc.—Clay, Webster, the Bank bill, and other political topics of the day: these are the subjects incessantly talked about by the male members of the family when at home, and which the females, of course, are neither expected to take any special interest in nor to understand. Or perhaps the wife may take her turn in relating the history of the daily vexations she experiences in her household arrangements, while the husband's eye is gazing on vacancy, or his mind is occupied by his business cares. Woman should be made to take an intelligent interest in her husband's affairs, and may be benefited by a knowledge of the value of money, its best mode of investment; or by being instructed in the laws of physiology and of hygiene; but she can receive neither pleasure nor profit from hearing the cabalistic terms familiar only to the initiated in the mysteries of financiering, or the occult words and phrases which the professional man employs to communicate his knowledge or the results of his observations. The husband should doubtless sympathize with the wife in her domestic trials; but he cannot, nor ought he to, become interested in every trivial vexation she may meet with. There should, then, be some common ground on which both may meet with equal pleasure and advantage to themselves and to their offspring; and what is there so appropriate to this end as *intellectual pursuits?*

What a certain writer has said of sons, may also be said, with equal truth, of many husbands: "they seem to consider their homes as mere places of boarding and lodging"; and, we may add, forget that it is the dwelling-place of their wives and children. So long as they provide for the physical wants of their families, they think their duty is fulfilled; as though shelter, food, and clothing could satisfy the necessities of immortal minds. They are liberal, perhaps, even to profusion, in surrounding their families with all that can minister to physical comfort, and the indulgence of vanity and pride, but they neglect to excite or to satisfy the more exalted desire for intellectual adorning and spiritual improvement. It is here our men are wanting; and female influence must supply the defect. A mother should sedulously cultivate the intellectual tastes of her children, and surround them with objects calculated to stimulate and gratify their ambition for knowledge. Her own mind should not only be richly stored with the wisdom of the past, but she should keep herself familiar with the current literature of the day, with the progress of science, and the new and useful truths it is constantly bringing to light. Out of all this fullness of knowledge she should communicate freely to her children, and labor by her conversation gently to draw her husband away from his contracted sphere of thought, to enter with her upon a more extended field of observation and reflection. She should entice him to forget his business and his politics, and to devote the few hours he spends at home to those higher pleasures of the mind, which will not only yield a delightful refreshment at the time, but enable him to return with renewed vigor to the routine of his daily labors.

2

The Discipline and Self-Discipline of the Young

A. Instilling a Capacity for Self-Government

- *Samuel Goodrich* (1838)
- *Lydia M. Child* (1831)

By the 1820s Americans expressed a growing interest in the techniques for managing and influencing children. This concern, while dependent intellectually on the theories of John Locke and subsequent eighteenth-century philosophers, was related to more general trends accentuating the importance and value of the individual child. The waning of belief in original sin contributed to a sense of parental responsibility, for if the children were born essentially "good" yet malleable, their fate would depend on whether parents created a good or bad environment. We do not have sufficient evidence to rank one cause above another, but there can be no doubt that by the early nineteenth-century children were benefiting from improved standards of diet, hygiene, and safety. The proof is a marked decline in infant and child mortality, particularly from accidents and other easily preventable causes. Between 1810 and 1825, there was also a pronounced decline of fertility within marriage. This abrupt shift, beginning in New England, led for the first time to average families of under six children. Parents could now invest more emotional commitment as well as material

21

resources in each child. And it was upon American mothers, who gained in life expectancy with fewer childbirths and improved obstetrical care, that the hopes and burdens of child-rearing chiefly fell.

Here the assumptions of environmentalism are concisely summarized by Samuel Goodrich (1793–1860), whose books for children, written under the pen name "Peter Parley," sold several million copies. The son of a Connecticut minister, Goodrich was a largely self-educated literary entrepreneur whose gift-book "annuals" included some of Nathaniel Hawthorne's first stories.

Lydia M. Child (1802–1880), one of the nation's first self-supporting women-of-letters, presents a remarkably modern and "child-centered" argument for parental sensitivity and self-restraint. But note that Child's purpose is to make the parental restraint of children as "invisible" as possible. The daughter of a prosperous Massachusetts baker and the wife of an erratic lawyer-reformer, Child herself remained childless. After teaching school, she won acclaim in 1824 for a romantic novel about love between an Indian brave and a white maiden. Her popularity later suffered when, as an ardent abolitionist, she attacked northern laws prohibiting racial intermarriage. Child had a long and varied career as a reformer, editor, and prolific writer.

Samuel Goodrich (1838)

It is obvious that the faculties of man, commencing at birth, proceed in their development through several stages, before they reach maturity. These are usually denominated infancy, childhood, and youth. We may consider these as embracing the first seventeen years of life, and remark that during this period the foundation of the physical, mental, and moral character is usually laid. This fact arises from the susceptibility of our nature during this portion of our existence. We are then like plaster, prepared by the molder, soft and impressible, taking forms and images from every thing we may chance to touch. But as this plaster soon grows hard, and retains ever after the traces made upon it, so the impressions made upon youth become indurated in manhood. The imitative and reflective tendencies of childhood and youth, operating on their plastic nature, also render this a decisive period of life in the formation of character. Children mark the peculiarities of those around, and incline to copy them. They are also as mirrors, catching reflections on every hand, and often retaining traces of the images casually thrown upon them, for the remainder of life.

I am aware that there is a great difference in the character of children as to their ductility. Some are facile in their dispositions; others are more obstinate and unyielding. But these diversities do not affect the substantial

SOURCE: Samuel Goodrich, *Fireside Education* (New York: Perkins and Marvin, 1838), pp. 62–63.

truth of the remark, that the general outline of every man's character is formed by education, and that too within the first seventeen years of his life. It is within this period that the basis of his physical constitution is laid, the frame-work of the understanding formed, the leading features of the moral character decided. And however much these may all seem to depend upon nature, they depend much more upon influences which are brought to bear upon them at this plastic period of life.

Lydia M. Child (1831)

The good old fashioned maxim that "example is better than precept," is the best thing to begin with. The great difficulty in education is that we give *rules* instead of inspiring *sentiments*. The simple fact that your child never saw you angry, that your voice is always gentle, and the expression of your face always kind, is worth a thousand times more than all the rules you can give him about not beating his dog, pinching his brother, etc. It is in vain to load the understanding with rules, if the affections are not pure. In the first place, it is not possible to make rules enough to apply to all manner of cases; and if it were possible, a child would soon forget them. But if you inspire him with right *feelings*, they will govern his *actions*. All our thoughts and actions come from our affections; if we love what is good, we shall think and do what is good. Children are not so much influenced by what we say and do in particular reference to them, as by the general effect of our characters and conversation. They are in a great degree creatures of imitation. If they see a mother fond of finery, they become fond of finery; if they see her selfish, it makes them selfish; if they see her extremely anxious for the attention of wealthy people, they learn to think wealth is the only good.

Those whose early influence is what it should be, will find their children easy to manage, as they grow older.

An infant's wants should be attended to without waiting for him to cry. At first, a babe cries merely from a sensation of suffering—because food, warmth, or other comforts necessary to his young existence, are withheld; but when he finds crying is the only means of attracting attention, he soon gets in the habit of crying for everything. To avoid this, his wants should be attended to, whether he demand it or not. Food, sleep, and necessary comforts should be supplied to him at such times as the experience of his mother may dictate. If he has been sitting on the floor, playing quietly by himself a good while, take him up and amuse him, if you can spare time, without waiting for weariness to render him fretful. Who can blame a child for fretting and screaming, if experience has taught him that he cannot get his wants attended to in any other manner?

SOURCE: Lydia M. Child, *The Mother's Book* (Boston: Carter and Hendee, 1831), pp. 22–23, 24–26.

When a little child has been playing, and perhaps quarrelling, out of doors, and comes in with his face all of a blaze, sobbing and crying, it is an excellent plan to take him by the hand and say, "What is the matter, my dear boy? Tell me what is the matter. But, how dirty your face is! Let me wash your face nicely, and wipe it dry, and then you shall sit in my lap and tell me all about it." If he is washed gently, the sensation will be pleasant and refreshing, and by the time the operation is finished, his attention will be drawn off from his vexations; his temper will be cooled, as well as his face. Then seat him in your lap, encourage him to tell you all about his troubles, comb his hair gently in the mean time, and in a few minutes the vexation of his little spirit will be entirely soothed. This secret of calling off the attention by little kind offices is very valuable to those who have the care of invalids, or young children.

. . .

By such expedients as I have mentioned, ill-humor and discontent are driven away by the influence of kindness and cheerfulness; "evil is overcome with good." Whipping and scolding could not have produced quiet so soon; and if they could, the child's temper would have been injured in the process.

I have said that example and silent influence were better than direct rules and commands. Nevertheless, there are cases where rules must be made; and children must be taught to obey implicitly. For instance, a child must be expressly forbidden to play with fire, to climb upon the tables, etc. But whenever it is possible, restraint should be invisible.

B. Neutralizing Sibling Rivalry

• *Catharine Sedgwick* (1841)
• *Jacob Abbott* (1841)

Sibling conflict, from the time of Cain and Abel, has presented a continuing challenge to parental ideals of discipline. The selection from Catharine Sedgwick's novel *Home*, taken from a chapter entitled "A Glimpse at Family Government," concerns the response of various family members to sibling conflict that has led to a sudden act of violence. Jacob Abbott, in *The Rollo Code of Morals*, is more directly concerned with prescribing rules for resolving petty disputes between brothers and sisters.

Like Catharine Beecher, Catharine Sedgwick (1789–1867) was the daughter of an imposing and conservative father—though Theodore Sedgwick, a member of the Continental Congress, a Federalist Senator, Congressman, and justice of the Massachusetts supreme court, was far more aristocratic than Lyman Beecher. Although Catharine Sedgwick also shared Catharine Beecher's teenage experience of losing a mother, caring for younger siblings, and adjusting to a new stepmother, the death of her father, when she was still in her early twenties, opened the way for her rejection of his Calvinist creed. Sedgwick's conversion to the Unitarianism of William

Ellery Channing coincided with her emergence in the 1820s as the nation's leading woman novelist. In view of the selection below, it is perhaps significant that Sedgwick took an active part in prison reform. Remaining single herself, she published a novel in 1857 entitled *Married or Single?*, which was designed to "lessen the stigma placed on the term, old maid."

Jacob Abbott (1803–1879), a Congregational minister and, for a time, professor of mathematics and science at Amherst College, moved into educational reform and school administration before becoming a prolific and internationally known writer. Of the 180 volumes Abbott wrote, the most famous were the juvenile *Rollo* series, which were read by children in all parts of the country well into the twentieth century. As an educator Abbott was dedicated to the goal of instilling self-control as an alternative to an authoritarian regimen. The priggish tone of this selection should not distract attention from his emphasis on self-reliance and on developing what today would be termed "interpersonal skills." For Abbott, the family, a microcosm of the larger social world, was a democratic testing ground where children had to learn how to resolve conflicting claims and counterclaims.

The selection from Sedgwick's novel concerns a model middle-class family, the Barclays. Before we come on the scene, four-year-old Haddy has punched a hole in the precious kite of ten-year-old Wallace, and has then playfully poked the kitten's head through the hole. Wally, in a flash of anger, has just thrown the kitten into a tub of scalding water. The question now posed is how the family will deal with this shocking loss of control. Note that decisive parental influence is exerted only at the beginning of the story.

Catharine Sedgwick (1841)

The children were all sobbing. Wallace stood pale and trembling. His eye turned to his father, then to his mother, then was riveted on the floor. The children saw the frown on their father's face, more dreaded by them than ever was flogging, or dark closet with all its hobgoblins.

"I guess you did not mean to, did you, Wally?" said little Haddy, whose tender heart was so touched by the utter misery depicted on her brother's face, that her pity for him overcame her sense of her own and pussy's wrongs. Wallace sighed deeply, but spoke no word of apology or justification. The children looked at Wallace, at their father, and their mother, and still the portentous silence was unbroken. The dinnerbell rung. "Go to your own room, Wallace," said his father. "You have forfeited your right to a place among us. Creatures who are the slaves of their passions are, like beasts of prey, fit only for solitude."

SOURCE: Catharine Sedgwick, *Home* (Boston: James Munroe and Co., 1841), pp. 22–26.

"How long must Wallace stay up stairs?" asked Haddy, affectionately holding back her brother who was hastening away.

"Till he feels assured," replied Mr. Barclay, fixing his eye sternly on Wallace, "that he can control his hasty temper; at least so far as not to be guilty of violence towards such a dear good little girl as you are, and murderous cruelty to an innocent animal;—till, sir, you can give me some proof that you dread the sin and danger of yielding to your passions so much that you can govern them. The boy is hopeless," he added in a low voice to his wife, as Wallace left the room.

"My dear husband! hopeless at ten years old, and with such a good, affectionate heart as his? We must have patience."

A happy combination for children is there in an uncompromising father and an all-hoping mother. The family sat down to table. The parents were silent, serious, unhappy. The children caught the infection, and scarcely a word was said above a whisper. There was a favorite dish on the table, followed by a nice pudding. They were eaten, not enjoyed. The children realized that it was not the good things they had to eat, but the kind looks, the innocent laugh, and cheerful voice, that made the pleasure of the social meal.

"My dear children," said their father, as he took his hat to leave them, "we have lost all our comfort to-day, have not we?"

"Yes, sir,—yes, sir," they answered in a breath.

"Then learn one lesson from your poor brother. Learn to dread doing wrong. If you commit sin, you must suffer, and all that love you must suffer with you; for every sin is a violation of the laws of your Heavenly Father, and he will not suffer it to go unpunished."

. . .

The days passed on. Wallace went to school as usual, and returned to his solitude, without speaking or being spoken to. His meals were sent to his room, and whatever the family ate, he ate. For the Barclays took care not to make rewards and punishments out of eating and drinking, and thus associate the duties and pleasures of a moral being with a mere animal gratification. "But ah!" he thought, as he walked up and down his apartment,[1] while eating his pie or pudding, "how different it tastes from what it does at table!" and though he did not put it precisely in that form, he felt what it was that "sanctified the food." The children began to venture to say to their father, whose justice they dared not question, "How long Wally has stayed up stairs!" and Charles, each day, eagerly told how well Wallace behaved at school.

. . .

Two weeks had passed when Mr. Barclay heard Wallace's door open, and heard him say, "Can I speak with you one minute before dinner, sir."

"Certainly, my son." His father entered and closed the door.

---

[1] "Apartment" means merely, his room.

"Father," said Wallace, with a tremulous voice but an open, cheerful face, "I feel as if I had a right now to ask you to forgive me, and take me back into the family."

Mr. Barclay felt so too, and kissing him, he said, "I have only been waiting for you, Wallace; and, from the time you have taken to consider your be-setting sin, I trust you have gained strength to resist it."

"It is not consideration only, sir, that I depend on; for you told me I must wait till I could give you *proof*; so I had to wait till something happened to try me. I could not possibly tell else, for I always do resolve, when I get over my passion, that I never will get angry again. Luckily for me,—for I began to be horribly tired of staying alone,—Tom Allen snatched off my new cap and threw it in the gutter. I had a book in my hand, and I raised it to send at him; but I thought just in time, and I was so glad I had governed my passion, that I did not care about my cap, or Tom, or any thing else. 'But one swallow doesn't make a summer,' as Aunt Betsey says; so I waited till I should get angry again. It seemed as if I never should; there were provoking things happened, but somehow or other they did not provoke me,—why do you smile, father?"

"I smile with pleasure, my dear boy, to find that one fortnight's resolute watchfulness has enabled you so to curb your temper that you are not easily provoked."

"But stay, father, you have not yet heard all; yesterday, just as I was putting up my arithmetic which I had written almost to the end without a single blot, Tom Allen came along and gave my inkstand a jostle, and over it went on my open book; I thought he did it purposely,—I think so still, but I don't feel so sure. I did not reflect then,—I doubled my fist to strike him."

"O, Wallace!"

"But I did not, father, I did not,—I thought just in time. There was a horrid choking feeling in my throat, and angry words seemed crowding out; but I did not even say, 'Blame you.' [1] I had to bite my lips, though, so that the blood ran."

"God bless you, my son."

"And the best of it all was, father, that Tom Allen, who never before seemed to care how much harm he did you, or how much he hurt your feelings, was really sorry; and this morning he brought me a new blank book nicely ruled, and offered to help me copy my sums into it; so I hope I did *him* some good as well as myself, by governing my temper."

$$\cdot \quad \cdot \quad \cdot$$

Others may think with Aunt Betsey, that Wallace's punishment was out of proportion to his offence; but it must be remembered, that it was not the penalty for a single offence, but for a habit of irascibility that could not be cured without serious and repeated efforts. Mr. Barclay held whipping, and all such summary modes of punishment, on a par with such nostrums in

---

[1] "Blame you" was a nineteenth-century euphemism for "damn you."

medicine as peppermint and lavender, which suspend the manifestation of the disease, without conducing to its cure. He believed the only effectual and lasting government,—the only one that touches the springs of action, and in all circumstances controls them, is *self*-government. It was this he labored to teach his children. The process was slow but sure. It required judgment, and gentleness, and, above all, patience on the part of the parents; but every inch of ground gained was kept.

Jacob Abbot (1841)

Every child ought to be desirous of gaining an influence over his brothers and sisters, and especially over those who are younger than himself; and he should endeavor to exert this influence, when it is gained, in going good. It is a high and noble aim, to attempt to gain an influence over mind. A child makes a great effort, when he is small, to learn to drive a nail with a hammer, or to cut with an axe. And it is quite an accomplishment for him when he has acquired it; though, after all, it is only the art of managing inert wood and iron. To learn to ride a horse, or to drive a yoke of oxen while his father holds the plough, is a higher attainment still,—for the nature of a living animal is higher than that of wood and iron. But to gain an ascendency over human minds is a higher object still. It requires greater skill, and it is a nobler kind of power. And yet children may possess it. We often find a sister, who, by kind and winning manners, a conciliatory and forgiving spirit, inflexible justice, and steadiness of moral principle, has acquired a strong influence over her brothers and sisters; and, sometimes, too, a boy, who has, by the same means, acquired a like ascendency, and can lead and guide those around him pretty much as he will. All children ought to aim at acquiring this power; all might possess it,—for such an influence, when it is in its greatest perfection, is mutual: each one exerts it over the others. George will do what James wishes, and James, in his turn, will comply with the wishes of George.

When this influence is once obtained, it ought to be used as a means of doing good. Every child can do a great deal to induce his brothers and sisters to do right, or, if he will pervert his influence, he can excite or encourage them to do wrong. A younger brother is easily induced to do what he sees one doing who is older than himself, and whom he has been accustomed to look upon as his leader and guide. How careful, then, ought every one to be, that his example and influence should be on the right side! How great is the guilt of leading a young and confiding brother or sister into sin!

· · ·

Disputes arise among brothers and sisters, about property and rights, as well as about words. There is a little more excuse for this than for the other.

SOURCE: Jacob Abbott, *The Rollo Code of Morals: or The Rules of Duty for Children* (Boston: Crocker and Brewster, 1841), pp. 91–94.

And, in fact, it is sometimes right to insist upon our rights, rather than yield to the demands of the unreasonable. By constantly yielding to them, we may make them more and more unreasonable. When such cases occur, we must maintain our own cause mildly, though firmly, and by actions rather than words. To stand disputing, scolding, and recriminating, is a very poor way of regaining lost rights, or securing any valuable object whatever.

Cases of little importance ought not to be referred to parents for decision. A boy who had been out at play, came in towards evening, and went into the parlor, and placed a chair near the fire, intending to sit down and read. While he was gone out for a book, his sister came in and took his chair, not knowing that her brother had placed it there. When he saw her, he came up roughly, and took hold of his sister's arm, saying, "Get out of my chair." His sister would not move. She said that it was not his chair; she had found it empty, and had a good right to sit in it. After some more harsh words, the boy went out to complain to his mother.

Now, he ought to have considered that the mere hearing and deciding of the question would put his mother to a far greater degree of inconvenience and trouble, than it would occasion him to get another chair. Even if he was right, and was fairly entitled to the chair, he ought to give up his title, for he could not recover it without doing his mother more injury than he would have suffered himself by losing it. Thus the whole question was not worth the trouble it would take to consider it. The amount at issue was not worth the trial. There may, indeed, possibly be some cases of such open and unqualified oppression, that, though the amount be small, it is best to complain, rather than allow so bad a spirit to be successful; but these cases are rare. In nearly all the instances of disputes among children, both parties think they are right. One or both are biased and blinded, but they think they are right. Neither of them intends to do the other wilful injustice; and therefore it is better to yield one's claims rather than put parents to an inconvenience and trouble more than the claim is worth.

C. The Problem of Unwilling Submission

- *Society for the Reformation of Juvenile Delinquents* (1829)
- *Prison Discipline Society* (1829)
- *Thomas L. Harris* (1850)

Even by the 1820s, missionaries and reformers, many from rural backgrounds, were discovering children in the slums of New York and Boston who lived in a different universe from the rosy-cheeked Rollos and Barclays. For the urban poor, the question was not which chair to sit in but how to eat and survive.

Fired by religious optimism, reformers of the 1820s and 1830s spoke confidently of rescuing and reclaiming all juvenile delinquents. We have heard Lydia M. Child advising mothers to avoid conflict by anticipating the wants of infants; as a substitute parent, the Society for the Reformation of Juvenile Delinquents now seeks to prevent crime by removing youth from the sources of temptation and corruption. Like dutiful parents, the reformers profess to act out of love and compassion. But as the Boston Prison Discipline Society complains, frequent escapes from the house of reformation dramatize the problem of "unwilling submission." Remember that Wallace Barclay, while punished by solitary confinement, achieved self-mastery only after his *willing submission* to the principle that his father knew what was best for him. That, of course, was the adult ideal as embodied in popular fiction. In practice, the Prison Discipline Society appealed to the policy of "unceasing vigilance," as recently perfected in Auburn, Sing Sing, and other penitentiaries. Ironically, while penal reformers looked upon prisons and asylums as extensions of family government, they increasingly urged families to adopt institutional techniques of control.

When we jump forward to 1850, we see that the sanguine expectations of the 1820s were far from being fulfilled. Thomas L. Harris (1823–1906) was an English-born Universalist mystic and spiritualist. His sermon, affirming that only institutionalized love could save eight thousand of New York City's children from a life of crime, led to the founding of the New York Juvenile Asylum. As noted in the introduction to Unit One, Harris is ambiguous on the question of willing versus unwilling submission. He later experimented with socialistic communities in New York State and California.

Society for the Reformation of Juvenile Delinquents (1829)

It must be satisfactory to those with whom this charity originated, and to those by whose exertions it has been and is supported, to find that it is not only approved at home, but that it has attracted the attention of those in other countries, whose minds are bent on the amelioration of the condition of mankind. If it were possible that any feelings but those of pure benevolence could mix with the consideration of this subject, we might feel a pride in the reflection, that our young country which has so lately assumed the rank of an independent nation, was the first to adopt with any efficacy, the penitentiary system of prison discipline, and the first to attempt to prevent the commission of crimes, by seeking out the youthful and unprotected, who were in the way of temptation, and by religious and moral instruction, by

---

SOURCE: *Fourth Annual Report*, Society for the Reformation of Juvenile Delinquents in the City of New-York (New York: Mahlon Day, 1829), pp. 6–10.

imparting to them useful knowledge, and by giving them industrious and orderly habits, rescuing them from vice, and rendering them valuable members of society.

. . .

Previously to the establishment of the House of Refuge, there were more than five hundred young persons annually committed, in the city of New-York, either as criminals or vagrants; now the officers of justice do not find half that number . . . so that the effects of the institution are not only felt by those who are committed to its care, but the community at large feels its benign influence in the diminution of crime. Its operation, in this respect, is not only in the present time, but future generations will be rendered more pure and virtuous, by the reformation of the depraved youths of the present race,[1] who, if they were left to their ordinary course, would have been matured in vice. . . . Very generally, the children who are committed to this asylum are orphans, or if not, they are so neglected, or misled by their parents, as to be in a worse condition than if they had none—deserted and in poverty, often in absolute want, and without a roof under which they can claim shelter; not only without religious or moral instruction, but in many instances taught to be vicious by precept as well as by example, these unfortunate children are found offending against the laws. Frequently the younger persons who are received in the House of Refuge are so totally devoid of moral instruction, that they evince an entire want of a knowledge of right and wrong. It has happened that when one has been questioned as to his former course of life, and asked how he obtained means of subsistence, he has answered, by begging and stealing, with apparently, as little consciousness that he was making a disgraceful confession, as if he had said that he had found a support from some honest employment. Under such circumstances, what could be more unjust than to visit the young delinquent with the same kind or degree of punishment, which would be due to a deliberate offender of mature years?

To confine these youthful criminals in our loathsome and crowded prisons [not meaning penitentiaries], where no, or scarcely any, distinction can be made between the young and old, or between the more and less vicious, where little can be learned but the ways of the wicked, and from whence they must be sent to encounter new wants, new temptations, and to commit new crimes, is to pursue a course, as little reconcilable with justice as humanity; yet, till the House of Refuge was established there was no alternative.

. . .

In almost every case . . . the discipline of the institution works a reformation. The moral faculties are awakened, the thoughts of the young offender are turned, often with regret, upon his past life, and he is led to resolve on

---

[1] "Race" refers here to "present generation," who constitute the "roots" (an original meaning of "race") of future generations.

a better course. In many instances, the child not only thinks of his future condition in this world, but his mind is filled with a concern for his eternal, as well as his temporal welfare; a conviction is produced that our happiness in this life, as well as in that which is to come, depends on a due application of our moral and physical faculties. The transition of a being from a life of want, ignorance, idleness, corruption and hopelessness, to the enjoyments in the Refuge of comfort, to the relief which is afforded to the mind, by constant and useful employment, to the knowledge of good and evil, to the hope of obtaining an honest living, and to the consolations of religion, must be to him as a new birth.

Prison Discipline Society (1829)

In the house of reformation at South Boston, before the boys were subject to unceasing vigilance, there were frequent escapes, which indicated a habit of discontent, and unwilling submission; there was besides but little industry, in the shop or school-room; few cases of reformation; and generally a state of things affording little satisfaction to the directors or friends of the institution. . . . In the prisons at Sing Sing and Auburn [in New York State], whenever an overseer leaves his place, even for a few minutes, he calls another to take it, so that the supervision may be uninterrupted. To all this vigilance, and the benefits of it, there is a striking contrast in some of the penitentiaries, and in the county prisons generally. . . . So long as it is supposed that any class of prisons can be properly managed without unceasing vigilance, so long they will remain nurseries of vice. This brings into view a principle of very extensive application to families, schools, academies, colleges, factories, mechanics' shops; i. e. the importance of unceasing vigilance. If therefore, this society [the Prison Discipline Society] does in any degree magnify the importance of unceasing vigilance in government, it will be useful in this respect.

. . .

This Society shows the importance of family government.—Among the causes of crime, the neglect of family government stands next to intemperance: it is, in fact, not unfrequently the cause of intemperance. Youth, when unrestrained and neglected by their parents, find their way to the tavern and the grog-shop; and others, whose parents have attempted unsuccessfully to govern them, have not become abandoned to vice, till they forsook their father's house. It is the confession of many convicts from the prisons at Auburn and Wethersfield [Connecticut], that the course of vice, which brought them to the prison, commenced in disobedience to their parents, or in their parents' neglect.

SOURCE: *Fourth Annual Report*, Prison Discipline Society (Boston: T. R. Marvin, 1829), pp. 297–98.

Thomas L. Harris (1850)

A spectacle is presented in our midst which might rather seem the dream of an insane fancy, than the reality of a Christian age. The recent report of the Chief of Police [of New York City] discloses the fact that THREE THOUSAND CHILDREN, from eight years and upwards, in the lower wards of our city, gain subsistence solely by theft, beggary, or unnamable vice. If we add to this estimate those under eight years who are growing up under the same influences, brothers and sisters of these, and if we extend our survey to include the entire city, we shall arrive at the conclusion that eight thousand children are involved in this extremity of evil. And thus our infant population is decimated, not by a conscription, not by a famine, not by a pestilence, but by a destroying curse that eats from body to soul and involves the whole nature in its ruin.

It is hard to speak of this in calm language or in cool blood. Little children, one in ten in the lower wards, sent out to pilfer, to importune, to sink into utter depths of personal degradation, spending their days in vice among each other and in war against mankind, returning at nightfall to yield up their wages of fraud and shame to unnatural owners or more unnatural parents, and then devoting the night to low revelry, sinking soul and body in one common hell! From these nurseries of crime come the bold and unscrupulous enemies of society, who furnish votes to the demagogue, torches to the incendiary, and weapons to the assassin: from these come those pale and miserable unfortunates [prostitutes] whose life is a continual destruction of purity and virtue: from these come those corrupters of the young, parasites and panderers, who remorselessly destroy the children of opulence and station, plundering them though ministering to vice. . . . This devouring vortex is fed continually by the unfortunate, the intemperate, the exhausted poor, who, losing all self-respect with the loss of property, or virtue, or standing, or health, hide themselves in miserable dens, where their children grow up deformed and embruted, and from whence they issue to their evil trades.

• • •

The question before us is simply this: What is to be done; how is this evil to be destroyed; how are these children to be rescued; how are the increasing multitudes who press on in the future to be preserved from the doom which has overtaken so many in the present and the past? Sympathies, unless they flow to practical action, are uselessly excited. . . .

I would answer this question by saying, that what these children need is kindness, education, renumerative labor. If they had breathed an atmosphere of love; if their faculties of mind and heart had been properly cultivated—if labor had been provided for all of them who were willing to do, this terrible

SOURCE: Thomas L. Harris, *Juvenile Depravity and Crime in Our City* (New York: Charles B. Norton, 1850), pp. 10–13.

evil would never have arisen to its height. We must then, as a community, —proceed to organize a *Home for Children.* It should seek to accomplish three results: *Reformation, Education, Remunerative Employment.* Its doors should be open for all children wishing through compliance with its rules to secure its advantages. All children found engaged in beggary or theft should be removed to its shelter.

3

The Schoolroom as an Extended Family

A. The Demand for Public Schools

- *Philadelphia Working Men's Committee* (*1830*)
- *Philadelphia* National Gazette (*1830*)

Until the second quarter of the nineteenth century, the education of Americans was informal, unsystematic, and dependent on parental initiative and ability to pay. Some "free" schools expected parents to pay a small fee, and most tax-supported schools were intended only for the children of paupers. Though many artisans had long sent their children to what were known in New York City as "common pay schools," the Working Men's movement of the late 1820s expressed a growing fear that unequal educational opportunities were contributing to a hardening of class distinctions and to the permanent debasement of all people who worked with their hands. Beginning in Philadelphia and New York City, the movement spread rapidly to smaller towns throughout the country. The Working Men's agitation for free tax-supported schools was short-lived but produced a number of remarkable reports and manifestos. Here, a Philadelphia Working Men's committee points realistically to the barriers that deterred or prevented poor families from sending their children to school. One proposed solution is schools that combine literary and scientific instruction with training in manual skills. The report anticipates angry resistance from affluent taxpayers, and it was quick in coming. The editorial in the *National Gazette* is a sample.

Philadelphia Working Men's Committee (1830)

An opinion is entertained by many good and wise persons, and supported to a considerable extent, by actual experiment, that proper schools for supplying a judicious infant [small child] training, would effectually prevent much of that vicious depravity of character which penal codes and punishments are vainly intended to counteract. Such schools would, at least, relieve, in a great measure, many indigent parents, from the care of children, which in many cases occupies as much of their time as would be necessary to earn the children a subsistence. They would also afford many youth an opportunity of participating in the benefits of the public schools, who otherwise must, of necessity, be detained from them.

. . .

The original element of despotism is a monopoly of talent, which consigns the multitude to comparative ignorance, and secures the balance of knowledge on the side of the rich and the rulers. If then the healthy existence of a free government be, as the committee believe, rooted in the will of the American people, it follows as a necessary consequence, of a government based upon that will, that this monopoly should be broken up, and that the means of equal knowledge (the only security for equal liberty) should be rendered, by legal provision, the common property of all classes.

. . .

When the committees contemplate their own condition, and that of the great mass of their fellow laborers; when they look around on the glaring inequality of society, they are constrained to believe, that until the means of equal instruction shall be equally secured to all, liberty is but an unmeaning word, and equality an empty shadow, whose substance to be realized must first be planted by an equal education and proper training in the minds, in the habits, in the manners, and in the feelings of the community.

. . .

[A] radical defect in the best system of common schools yet established, will be found in its not being adapted to meet the wants and necessities of

---

SOURCE: Report of Working Men's Committee, Philadelphia, from *Working Man's Advocate* (New York: March 6, 1830), pp. 1–2. Reprinted in John R. Commons, *et al.*, eds., *A Documentary History of American Industrial Society*, Vol. V (Cleveland: Arthur H. Clark Co., 1910–1911; New York: Russell and Russell, 1958), pp. 98–100, 102–103, 106–107.

those who stand most in need of it. Very many of the poorest parents are totally unable to clothe and maintain their children while at school, and are compelled to employ their time, while yet very young, in aiding to procure a subsistence. In the city of New York, a much more efficient system of education exists than in this city, and common schools have been in successful operation for the last ten or twelve years; yet there are at the present time upwards of 24,000 children between the ages of 5 and 15 years, who attend no schools whatever, and this apparently criminal neglect of attending the schools is traced, chiefly, to the circumstance just mentioned. It is evidently therefore, of no avail, how free the schools may be, while those children who stand most in need of them, are, through the necessity of their parents, either retained from them altogether, or withdrawn at an improper age, to assist in procuring a subsistence. . . .

The committees, therefore, believe, that one school, at least, should be established in each county, in which some principle should be adopted, calculated to obviate the defects that have been alluded to, and by which the children of all who desire it, may be enabled to procure, at their own expense [that is, by manual labor while at school] a liberal and scientific education. They are of the opinion that a principle fully calculated to secure this object, will be found in a union of agricultural and mechanical with literary and scientific instruction.

. . .

When we behold the hundreds, perhaps thousands of youth, who, between the ages of 14 and 21 are daily and nightly seduced around or into the innumerable dens of vice, licensed and unlicensed, that throng our suburbs, we are constrained to believe that in many if not in most cases, the unconquerable habit that destroys the morals, ruins the constitution, sacrifices the character, and at last murders both soul and body of its victim, is first acquired during the thoughtless period of juvenile existence. This plan of education,[1] however, by its almost entire occupation of the time of the pupils, either in labor, study, or recreations; by the superior facilities it affords for engrossing their entire attention, and by its capability of embracing the whole juvenile population, furnishes, we believe, the only rational hope of ultimately averting the ruin which is threatened by this extensive vice.

The committee are aware that any plan of common and more particularly of equal education that may be offered to the public, is likely to meet with more than an ordinary share of opposition. It is to be expected that political demagogism, professional monopoly, and monied influence, will conspire as hitherto . . . against every thing that has promised to be an equal benefit to the whole population. Nevertheless, the appearance, that something will

---

1 "This plan of education . . ." refers to the plan of combining formal schooling with manual labor in agriculture and the "mechanic arts," a plan that originated at Hofwyl, Switzerland and aroused much enthusiasm and experimentation in the United States.

now be done for the intellectual as well as every thing for the physical improvement of the state are certainly very promising. The public mind is awake and favorably excited, while the press also is somewhat active on this subject.

Philadelphia *National Gazette* (1830)

. . . [T]he scheme of Universal Equal Education at the expense of the state, is virtually "Agrarianism." [1] It would be a compulsory application of the means of the richer, for the direct use of the poorer classes; and so far an arbitrary division of property among them. The declared object is, to procure the opportunity of instruction for the child or children of every citizen; to elevate the standard of the education of the working classes, or equalize the standard for all classes; which would, doubtless, be to lower or narrow that which the rich may now compass. But the most sensible and reflecting possessors of property sufficient to enable them to educate their children in the most liberal and efficacious way, and upon the broadest scale, would prefer to share their means for any other purpose, or in any other mode, than such as would injuriously affect or circumscribe the proficiency of their offspring. A public meeting of "the Mechanics and other Working Men of the City and County of New York," was held in the city, on the 17th inst. [the present month], and among the principles for which they have "resolved" to contend, we find the following: "In Education—The adoption of a general system of instruction, at the expense of the state, which shall afford to children, however rich or poor, equal means to obtain useful learning. To effect this, it is believed that a system of direct taxation will not be necessary, as the surplus revenue of the state and United States governments will, in a very few years, afford ample means—but even if it were necessary to resort to direct taxation to accomplish this all-important object, and the amount paid by the wealthy should be far greater than that paid by our less eligibly situated fellow-citizens, an equivalent to them would be found in the increased ability and usefulness of the educated citizen to serve and to promote the best interests of the state; in the increased permanency of our institutions—and in the superior protection of liberty, person and property."

Thus, a direct tax for "the equal means of obtaining useful learning" is not deemed improbable, and it is admitted that the amount which would be paid by the wealthy would be "far greater" than that paid by their "less eligibly situated fellow citizens." Here, we contend, would be the action, if not the name, of the Agrarian system. Authority—that is, the state—is to

---

source: Philadelphia *National Gazette*, editorial, August 19, 1830, p. 2. Reprinted in Commons, *et al.*, *Documentary History*, Vol. V, pp. 110–12, *op. cit.*

[1] "Agrarianism" meant the equal division of landed property; for many conservatives it was equivalent to communism.

force the more eligibly situated citizens to contribute a part (which might be very considerable) of their means, for the accommodation of the rest; and this is equivalent to the idea of an actual, compulsory partition of their substance. The more thriving members of the "mechanical and other working classes" would themselves feel the evil of the direct taxation; they would find that they had toiled for the benefit of other families than their own. One of the chief excitements to industry, among those classes, is the hope of earning the means of educating their children respectably or liberally: that incentive would be removed, and the scheme of state and equal education be thus a premium for comparative idleness, to be taken out of the pockets of the laborious and conscientious. . . .

B. The "Parental" State

• *Horace Mann* (1846)

The conservative taxpayer ideology articulated in 1830 by the Philadelphia *National Gazette* remained the most imposing obstacle to educational reformers. Here, it is the target of Horace Mann's opposing ideology in support of tax-supported free education for all.

Mann's cause was triumphant, first in Massachusetts, last in the South. Liberals have rightly regarded him as a heroic figure who pointed the way to the ideals of the modern democratic state. He argues that private property, far from being an absolute right, is held in trusteeship for future generations and for the general public good. He imparts the vision of "parental government" (Massachusetts, not the federal government) reaching out through a network of benign schools and asylums to the young, the poor, and the disadvantaged. He sees nothing coercive or authoritarian about the state promoting industry to prevent poverty, or diffusing knowledge and virtue to prevent vice and crime. Yet the question can be raised whether reformers like Mann were not imposing their own version of "the culture of virtuous principles" on society, and thereby changing the very meaning of political power. One may note that Mann was bitterly opposed to liquor, tobacco, profanity, and ballet dancing, and that his image of virtue, to be inculcated in public schools, would later be resisted by many immigrant groups. Note also that Mann capitalizes State, Heaven, Giver, Providence, and Nature, and compares the state's furnishing of education to "Heaven's bounties of light and air." In effect, he tends to make the secular state an agency of Providence, counteracting the effects of what his Calvinist forebears had thought of as original sin.

Horace Mann (1796–1859) had struggled as a child with the terrors provoked by Calvinist sermons. A convert to Unitarianism, he attended Brown University, was admitted to the Massachusetts bar, and rose to political eminence in the Massachusetts legislature. In 1837, after helping to secure passage for an innovative education bill, he surprised his associates by abandoning his successful law practice and becoming the first secretary of the new state board of education. In this administrative position he gathered exhaustive information, publicized the shortcomings of existing schools, and fought successfully for a longer school year, standardized texts, and higher standards and pay for teachers. The following selection is taken from one of Mann's twelve classic *Annual Reports*.

Horace Mann (1846)

. . . In the district-school-meeting, in the town-meeting, in legislative halls, everywhere, the advocates for a more generous education could carry their respective audiences with them in behalf of increased privileges for our children, were it not instinctively foreseen that increased privileges must be followed by increased taxation. Against this obstacle, argument falls dead. The rich man who has no children declares that the exaction of a contribution from him to educate the children of his neighbor is an invasion of his rights of property. The man who has reared and educated a family of children denounces it as a double tax when he is called upon to assist in educating the children of others also; or, if he has reared his own children without educating them, he thinks it peculiarly oppressive to be obliged to do for others what he refrained from doing even for himself. Another, having children, but disdaining to educate them with the common mass, withdraws them from the public school, puts them under what he calls "selecter influences," and then thinks it a grievance to be obliged to support a school which he [regards with contempt]. . . .

It seems not irrelevant, therefore . . . to inquire into the nature of a man's right to the property he possesses; and to satisfy ourselves respecting the question, whether any man has such an indefeasible title to his estates, or such an absolute ownership of them, as renders it unjust in the government to assess upon him his share of the expenses of educating the children of the community up to such a point as the nature of the institutions under which he lives, and the well-being of society, require.

I believe in the existence of a great, immortal, immutable principle of natural law, or natural ethics,—a principle antecedent to all human institutions, and incapable of being abrogated by any ordinance of man,—a principle of divine origin, which proves the *absolute right* to an education of every human being that comes into the world; and which, of course, proves the correlative duty of every government to see that the means of that education are provided for all.

SOURCE: Horace Mann, *Tenth Annual Report of the Secretary of the Board of Education* (1846), in *The Life and Works of Horace Mann* (Boston: Lee and Shepard, 1891), Vol. IV, pp. 114–17, 128–29, 131–34.

In regard to the application of this principle of natural law,—that is, in regard to the extent of the education to be provided for all at the public expense,—some differences of opinion may fairly exist under different political organizations; but, under our republican government, it seems clear that the minimum of this education can never be less than such as is sufficient to qualify each citizen for the civil and social duties he will be called to discharge.

. . .

To any one who looks beyond the mere surface of things, it is obvious that the primary and natural elements or ingredients of all property consist in the riches of the soil, in the treasures of the sea, in the light and warmth of the sun, in the fertilizing clouds and streams and dews, in the winds, and in the chemical and vegetative agencies of Nature. In the majority of cases, all that we call *property*, all that makes up the valuation or inventory of a nation's capital, was prepared at the creation, and was laid up of old in the capacious storehouses of Nature. For every unit that a man earns by his own toil or skill, he receives hundreds and thousands, without cost and without recompense, from the all-bountiful Giver. A proud mortal, standing in the midst of his luxuriant wheat-fields or cotton-plantations, may arrogantly call them his own; yet what barren wastes would they be, did not Heaven send down upon them its dews and its rains, its warmth and its light, and sustain, for their growth and ripening, the grateful vicissitude of the seasons!

. . .

The claim of a child, then, to a portion of pre-existent property, begins with the first breath he draws. The new-born infant must have sustenance and shelter and care. If the natural parents are removed, or parental ability fails; in a word, if parents either cannot or will not supply the infant's wants, —then society at large—the government having assumed to itself the ultimate control of all property—is bound to step in and fill the parent's place. To deny this to any child would be equivalent to a sentence of death, a capital execution of the innocent,—at which every soul shudders. It would be a more cruel form of infanticide than any which is practised in China or in Africa.

. . .

In obedience to the laws of God and to the laws of all civilized communities, society is bound to protect the natural life of children; and this natural life cannot be protected without the appropriation and use of a portion of the property which society possesses. We prohibit infanticide under penalty of death. We practise a refinement in this particular. The life of an infant is inviolable, even before he is born; and he who feloniously takes it, even before birth, is as subject to the extreme penalty of the law as though he had struck down manhood in its vigor, or taken away a mother by violence from the sanctuary of home where she blesses her offspring. But why preserve the natural life of a child, why preserve unborn embryos of life, if we do not intend to watch over and to protect them, and to expand their subsequent existence into usefulness and happiness? As individuals, or as an organized community, we have no natural right, we can derive no authority or countenance from reason, we can cite no attribute or purpose of the divine nature, for giving birth to any human being, and then inflicting upon that being the curse of ignorance, of poverty, and of vice, with all their attendant calamities. We are brought, then, to this startling but inevitable alternative, —the natural life of an infant should be extinguished as soon as it is born, or the means should be provided to save that life from being a curse to its possessor; and, therefore, every State is morally bound to enact a code of laws legalizing and enforcing infanticide, or a code of laws establishing free schools.

The three following propositions, then, describe the broad and ever-during [enduring] foundation on which the common-school system of Massachusetts reposes:—

The successive generations of men, taken collectively, constitute one great commonwealth.

The property of this commonwealth is pledged for the education of all its youth, up to such a point as will save them from poverty and vice, and prepare them for the adequate performance of their social and civil duties.

The successive holders of this property are trustees, bound to the faithful execution of their trust by the most sacred obligations; and embezzlement and pillage from children and descendants have not less of criminality, and have more of meanness, than the same offences when perpetrated against contemporaries.

. . .

Massachusetts is *parental* in her government. More and more, as year after year rolls by, she seeks to substitute prevention for remedy, and rewards for penalties. She strives to make industry the antidote to poverty, and to counterwork the progress of vice and crime by the diffusion of knowledge and the culture of virtuous principles. She seeks not only to mitigate those great physical and mental calamities of which mankind are the sad inheritors, but also to avert those infinitely greater moral calamities which form the disastrous heritage of depraved passions. Hence it has long been her policy to endow or to aid asylums for the cure of disease. She succors and maintains all the poor within her borders, whatever may have been the land of their nativity. She founds and supports hospitals for restoring reason to the insane; and, even for those violators of the law whom she is obliged to sequestrate from society, she provides daily instruction and the ministrations of the gospel at the public charge. To those who, in the order of Nature and Providence, have been bereft of the noble faculties of hearing and of speech, she teaches a new language, and opens their imprisoned minds and hearts to conversation with men and to communion with God; and it hardly transcends the literal truth to say that she gives sight to the blind. . . . The public highway is not more open and free for every man in the community than is the public schoolhouse for every child; and each parent feels that a free education is as secure a part of the birthright of his offspring as Heaven's bounties of light and air. The State not only commands that the means of education shall be provided for all, but she denounces [proclaims] penalties against all individuals, and all towns and cities, however populous or powerful they may be, that shall presume to stand between her bounty and its recipients. In her righteous code, the interception of knowledge is a crime. . . .

C. The Dilemmas of Democratic Discipline

• *Horace Mann (1844)*
• *Joseph Hale (1845)*

School taxes were not the only source of controversy surrounding Horace Mann. More orthodox Protestants violently objected to Mann's drive to secularize the schools by allowing teachers to only read from the Bible, without delivering sectarian commentary. Another battle erupted in 1844 when a committee of the Association of Masters of Boston Public Schools publicly attacked Mann's *Seventh Annual Report*, which they interpreted as a personal censure of their traditional methods of disciplining intractable students. Mann responded with a blistering *Reply*, from which the selection below is taken. His appeal to "moral means" of influence and his mockery of the doctrine of "unconditional surrender" recall the themes we have encountered in the writings of Graves, Child, and Sedgwick. The issue, as seen both by Mann and by Joseph Hale, who here gives a *Rejoinder* to Mann's *Reply*, was whether some coercion was inevitable in any system of authority and subordination.

On the surface, the differences between Mann and Hale seem to be mere quibbles. Mann admits that teachers must "resort to physical coercion" (meaning, presumably, the whip) after all moral means have failed. Hale is no less for love and virtue and resents any insinuation that traditionalists try to whip civilization into their pupils (by the 1840s no Northerner, no matter how conservative, would relish the inevitable comparison with slavedrivers in the South). But beneath Hale's religious vocabulary, which was losing conviction even then and which is alien to most modern readers, important issues are being raised, issues that are still relevant today. For example, is there not an element of hypocrisy in pretending that "moral means" of control, including verbal reproof, are wholly virtuous and innocent? Is there not a danger that welfare states and institutions will so perfectly systematize selfishness, in Hale's words, "as to conceal its own machinery" and make evil appear good and self-interest appear benevolent? Hale insists on calling evil and punishment by their true names. Yet for all his belief in divine authority and innate sin, Hale acknowledges that, in reality, teachers depend on the way pupils and their parents *interpret* punishment. This ultimate reliance on public opinion is a dramatic illustration of the dilemmas of authority and discipline in a democratic society.

Horace Mann (1844)

At different times, in my Reports, Lectures, and other writings, I have dwelt, at some length, on the subject of "School Discipline"; and have been led to consider, more particularly, *one* of its instrumentalities, namely *corporal punishment*. This has been forced upon me; for the perusal of sixteen hundred reports of the school committees, together with other authentic and unquestionable evidence, has left no room to doubt, that the rod has been, not very unfrequently, abused, in our schools; and, in the hands of inexperience and passion and ignorance, has been the coarse substitute for wisdom and affection and knowledge. But I am no ultraist on this point. I have never taken a one-sided view of this subject. I have reproved disobedience and insubordination, on the part of the pupil, as earnestly as I have ever reprehended severity on the part of the teacher; and I have always defended the resort to physical coercion after moral means had been tried and failed.

. . .

Let us now examine this section of the "Remarks," and see from which end of the scale its motive-powers, and its implements for "School Discipline," have been selected.

. . .

Authority, Force, Fear, Pain! These motives, taken from the nethermost part of the nethermost end of the scale of influences [i.e., hell], are to be inscribed on the lintels and door-posts of our schoolhouses, and embroidered on the phylacteries of the teachers' garments. These are the motives, by which the children of Boston,—and if this doctrine prevails, the children of the State also,—are to be so trained. . . . Throughout this whole section, *conscience* is no where referred to, as one of the motive-powers in the conduct of children. The *idea* seems not to have entered into the mind of the writer, that any such agency could be employed in establishing the earliest, as well as the latest relations, between teacher and pupil. That powerful class of motives which consists of affection for parents, love for brothers and sisters, whether older or younger than themselves, justice and the social sentiment towards schoolmates, respect for elders, the pleasures of acquiring knowledge, the duty of doing as we would be done by, the connection between present conduct, and success, estimation, eminence, in future life, the presence of an unseen eye,—not a syllable of all these is set forth with any earnestness, or insisted upon, as the true source and spring of human actions.

. . .

Was it not, and is it not, one of the grand objects in the institution and support of Common Schools, to bring those children who are cursed by a vicious parentage, who were not only "conceived and brought forth," but

SOURCE: Horace Mann, *Reply to the Remarks of Thirty-one Boston Schoolmasters* (Boston: J. N. Bradley & Co., 1844), pp. 119, 126, 130–31, 136–37.

have been nurtured in "sin"; who have never known the voice of love and kindness; who have daily fallen beneath the iron blows of those parental hands that should have been outstretched for their protection;—was it not, and is it not, I say, one of the grand objects of our schools to bring this class of children under humanizing and refining influences; to show them that there is something besides wrath and stripes and suffering, in God's world? . . . Or is the teacher,—the man whom the beneficent laws of the State, and the unequalled bounty of the city, have sent out after these lambs who have been driven from the sheepfold of Christ,—is he to say, because they are not *already* under "higher and more refined motives," he has no "resource" but to redouble the stripes, and send deeper the pain, until their froward and passionate minds shall acknowledge the abstract loveliness of the doctrine of "unconditional surrender?"

Joseph Hale (1845)

Admitting, then, and earnestly urging, that all possible moral incentives and persuasives should be used without stint or measure, in bringing both old and young to a sense of duty,—advice, expostulation, entreaty, affection, conscience, religion,—let me avow openly that I meant, and still mean, to espouse the naked doctrine, that physical coercion is, in certain cases, necessary, natural, and proper; and, therefore, equally honorable, when used in its true relation, with any other agency, to both giver and receiver; and to scout [discredit] the sickly and ridiculous notion, that all use of pain and compulsion is disgraceful and degrading, derogating from the dignity of our nature, and indicating low purposes and debasing tendencies.

"Corporal punishment, considered in itself, is an evil," it is said [by Mann]. So are reproof and censure in any form, and a thousand other agencies. But things are to be regarded, not as good or evil in themselves, but in their relations. "All evils natural, are moral goods." To speak of things, then, apart from their use, is really to say nothing whatever about them. Such forms of words answer very well to syllogize one into absurdity, but they can never lead to the truth.

Sympathy, I have said, is the predominant feature of the age. I believe it. I believe that its ascendency is abnormal. I believe that there is much pseudo-philanthropy abroad. . . . This loftiest human theory is fast swelling itself to the point of explosion. Those who think this the foundation principle of our nature, and the limits of our highest destiny, will of course regard its growing supremacy as the progress of the race towards perfection; and will seem to catch the coming swell of that universal consonance, when all the discordant elements of humanity shall be resolved into perfect harmony, by

SOURCE: Joseph Hale, *Rejoinder to the "Reply" of the Hon. Horace Mann* (Boston: C. C. Little and J. Brown, 1845), pp. 52–54, 56–60.

the fullest recognition of the high, and denial of the low. Perfection belongs not to the finite, but to the Infinite.

We may, indeed, extend selfishness over so wide a field, as to seem to annihilate it by its very magnificence; may sink the individual in the community, or association, or corporation; merge self-love into philanthropy; convert *I* into *We*; and blend the race, en masse, into one grand brotherhood of mutual love and worship, which would seem to put paradise to the blush, and to make an immortality on earth, far preferable to the worship of God in heaven. Thus, selfishness having become so perfectly systematized as to conceal its own machinery, man would *love* all, because he *is* all, and all is his. . . . It is this vain desire to spiritualize and deify the natural man, that leads us to mistake a faith in the human, for a faith in the divine.

Relying thus upon education merely, for all results, and starting from the broad principle, suggested by natural pride, though denied by revelation, that the human will is in harmony with the Divine will, we slide imperceptibly into the belief, that even the moral evil which we witness in the world, and therefore cannot deny, is an accident to be avoided, and not an innate growth to be plucked up by the roots and cast away; that only perfect example is necessary to make perfect character; that temptation, and struggle, and conflict may be dispensed with. We thus become prepared for the doctrine, that the impulses of love alone will lead us into all duty. This is the natural doctrine of the human heart; the very instinct of that elemental selfishness, which forms the basis and nucleus of all finite and individual existence.

• • •

[T]his same selfishness continues to control the affections and govern all the actions of the individual, modified only by his relations to those about him, as far and as fast as he understands them. He naturally loves every thing as it affects himself. Why should he not? He gradually learns that his relation to others is a necessary relation, and he discovers the value and true use of it. But in the exercise of this social nature, he is still himself the centre of all his associations, and must ever be, throughout the whole progress of his merely human development. Yet his highest destiny is, to renounce himself and submit to God, as the only proper object of all worship.

• • •

Sympathy, or mutual love, is right, understood as imperfection, but wrong, considered as perfection, and made the basis of what professes to be a complete philosophy, whose prevalence promises to revolutionize the action of the human heart, and to harmonize a nature whose very elements are discordant. Admitting it, then, as the promise of something higher, we are bound to deny our faith in it as a final result, since, attempting to rise by its own merits, and rejecting the idea of its own baseness, inferiority, and consequent subjection, it cuts man off from his last and highest destiny,—the perfect love and worship of God,—by excusing him from his first and lowest duty, implicit obedience and submission to His authority and ordinances.

If I am said to dwell upon what are called religious doctrines, I answer that the subject itself, when viewed in its widest relations, inclines that way. Any person, in treating a subject, must give it that range which it has in his own mind. If then all authority is of God, and must be obeyed, it becomes indispensable, in order to settle the question whether compulsion may ever be absolutely necessary or not, that we decide whether there is in the nature of man an innate element of evil, prompting him to rebellion. If there is, then compulsion results from resistance; if not, then the impulses are all that is necessary to secure duty; temptation is at an end; virtue is a negation; vice a nonentity; repentance a work of supererogation. In the former case, force may be necessary, because there are conflicting elements in the character; in the latter, force is inappropriate, because the character is the result of circumstances, depending not upon choice but upon opportunity. Every teacher, therefore, must regard what to him are the highest relations of his pupils.

Again, then, I say, that believing in virtue and vice, in positive good and positive evil, in cheerful obedience and wilful disobedience, in humility and pride, I would teach obedience as duty in every relation. I would reveal, rather than conceal, its obligations. I would plainly set forth its tendency and claims, and enforce it as early as possible. But I would aim at the spirit, rather than at the letter, of obedience. I would rather produce a consciousness of wrong and a wish to do better, even though ill-feeling might prevent the most prompt compliance, than compel the overt act while the heart should remain in a state of rebellion. I would by no means encourage too sensitive a regard to external compliances. The teacher's chief aim, excepting only those cases in which the disobedience of the subject may operate upon others by way of example, is to awaken the proper feelings in the child. For this reason, it is clearly a matter of great moment, that children, as well as teachers, should have sound views in regard to the nature, tendencies, and purposes of punishment. No pupil ought to regard his teacher as committing an outrage upon him by inflicting needed pain, or as entering the lists with him for a trial of strength; he should look upon a punishment as an act of kindness, done for his good. The teacher should, in every case, satisfy himself that the punishment he is about to inflict will be likely to benefit the child, and will be understood and received by him aright. He cannot, of course, always know this, but he is to be persuaded of it in his own mind.

The feelings with which punishments are viewed by the pupil being, then, an important consideration, it follows that the prevalence of false notions in regard to their utility and propriety must greatly increase the difficulty of using them, as well as the anxiety that results from their use. Indeed, such is the sensitiveness on this subject, that a teacher having inflicted punishment feels almost obliged to enter into an argument to prove that he has done right; lest he sacrifice the affection of his pupils, and encounter the charge of brutality from those, whose confidence and sympathy are indispensable to him. If a child is induced to regard physical punishment not merely as painful, but as disgraceful, as an indignity offered to his very nature, as a misapplication of means showing want of skill in the teacher, he will be apt to consider himself as being more sinned against than sinning. Thus, setting himself up to judge the actions of the teacher, he, of course, is not likely to be profited by the infliction.

. . .

A teacher should not be made to feel that he is constrained in his intercourse with his pupils. The guidance and control of them should be left as much as possible to him. His interest in and love for them, and their confidence and respect for him, should be carefully guarded, and every avenue to distrust and disaffection should be effectually closed. The parent should regard the teacher as his own representative, and should encourage him in the exercise of the utmost frankness and faithfulness. Indeed, the teacher must be, to a great extent, the intellectual and moral parent of his pupil. Supposing, then, the worst case, that a parent is obliged to entrust his child in the care of one in whom his own confidence is weak, he had better make up for the deficiency of the teacher by his own efforts, than diminish the pupil's respect and love for that teacher. The teacher and parent are so related, that either, by thwarting the other, is undermining his own authority.

. . .

Parents should remember that their confidence and support are the strong arm of the teacher's influence. Without these he is crippled and discouraged, and the more [he has such confidence and support], the more fond and faithful he is.

The false notions that prevail to some extent in the community in regard to government, are very unfavorable to docility and obedience. Children should not hear the authority of their parents and teachers called in question. They should not be allowed to speak disrespectfully of their own or of each other's parents and teachers, and he who through the press, or in any other way, encourages this, whatever he may intend, is a disorganizer; is weakening and dissolving the primal bond of civil society, and sapping the foundations of social order.

D. A Struggle for Mastery

• *Edward Eggleston* (1871)

Both Horace Mann and Joseph Hale seem remote from the actual conditions of rural schoolrooms, especially in the West and South. Edward Eggleston (1837–1902), descended from a Virginia family, was born and raised in rural Indiana and was thoroughly familiar with the backwoods school in the antebellum period. His novel, *The Hoosier Schoolmaster*, expressed the postwar enthusiasm for folklore and local dialect, and was immensely popular in both Europe and America. It presents aspects of antebellum culture which were seldom written about until after the Civil War.

In earlier chapters, we meet the "schoolmaster," young and bookish Ralph Hartsook, who applies for a teaching job at "Flat Crick." Old Jack Means, a trustee who runs the school, says that no other teachers have applied because the boys "driv off the last two, and licked the one afore them like blazes." "You see," Old Means goes on, while he shaves shingles and his sons split wood, "it takes grit to apply for this school. The last master had a black eye for a month." It turns out that the head bully is Bud Means, Jack's brawny and muscular eldest son. From the outset, Bud and Bill Means begin testing Ralph Hartsook, first by taking him on a coon hunt. When Bud threatens him in the schoolroom, Ralph admits he could not win a fight but sternly lays down the law: "You'll do the fighting and I'll do the teaching." During various showdowns, Ralph tries to win over the most respected and influential pupils, and establishes a reputation for shrewd maneuvers. Here, in the crucial "struggle for mastery," the class has determined to shut Ralph out of the schoolhouse and thus make him the laughingstock of the community. Though Ralph wins this battle, he meets a new crisis (not included here) when he is wrongly suspected of courting Bud's girlfriend, and Bud threatens to "thrash" him if he doesn't leave town. In the end, when the confusion over girls is straightened out, Ralph and Bud become good friends, and the teacher marries Hannah, the "bound girl" servant of the Means family. As his pupil, Hannah had earlier "spelled Ralph down" in a spelling bee.

Edward Eggleston (1871)

Nothing but the bulldog in the slender, resolute young master had kept down the rising storm. A teacher who has lost moral support at home, can not long govern a school. Ralph had effectually lost his popularity in the district, and the worst of it was that he could not divine from just what quarter the ill wind came. . . .

He had expected a petition for a holiday on Christmas day. Such holidays are deducted from the teacher's time, and it is customary for the boys to "turn out" the teacher who refuses to grant them, by barring him out of the school-house on Christmas and New Year's morning. Ralph had intended to grant a holiday if it should be asked, but it was not asked. Hank Banta was the ringleader in the disaffection, and he had managed to draw the surly Bud, who was present this morning, into it. It is but fair to say that Bud was in favor of making a request before resorting to extreme measures, but he was overruled. He gave it as his solemn opinion that the master was mighty peart, and they would be beat anyhow some way, but he would

SOURCE: Edward Eggleston, *The Hoosier Schoolmaster: A Story of Backwoods Life in Indiana* (New York: Grosett & Dunlap, 1899; originally published 1871), pp. 105–10.

lick the master fer two cents ef he warn't so slim that he'd feel like he was fighting a baby.

•   •   •

But Bud, discouraged as he was with the fear of Ralph's "cute," went like a martyr to the stake and took his place with the rest in the school-house at nine o'clock at night. It may have been Ralph's intention to preoccupy the school-house, for at ten o'clock Hank Banta was set shaking from head to foot at seeing a face that looked like the master's at the window. He waked up Bud and told him about it.

"Well, what are you a-tremblin' about, you coward?" growled Bud. "He won't shoot you; but he'll beat you at this game, I'll bet a hoss, and me, too, and make us both as 'shamed of ourselves as dogs with tin-kittles to their tails. You don't know the master, though he did duck you. But he'll larn you a good lesson this time, and me too, like as not." And Bud soon snored again, but Hank shook with fear every time he looked at the blackness outside the windows. He was sure he heard foot-falls. He would have given anything to have been at home.

When morning came, the pupils began to gather early. A few boys who were likely to prove of service in the coming siege were admitted through the window, and then everything was made fast, and a "snack" was eaten.

"How do you 'low he'll get in?" said Hank, trying to hide his fear.

"How do I 'low?" said Bud. "I don't 'low nothin' about it. You might as well ax me where I 'low the nex' shootin' star is a-goin' to drap. Mr. Hartsook's mighty onsartin. But he'll git in, though, and tan your hide fer you, you see ef he don't. *Ef* he don't blow up the school-house with gunpowder!" This last was thrown in by way of alleviating the fears of the cowardly Hank, for whom Bud had a great contempt.

•   •   •

"I don't believe he'll come," said Hank, with a cold shiver. "It's past school-time."

"Yes, he will come, too," said Bud. "And he 'lows to come in here mighty quick. I don't know how. But he'll be a-standin' at that air desk when it's nine o'clock. I'll bet a thousand dollars on that. *Ef* he don't take it into his head to blow us up!" Hank was now white.

Some of the parents came along, accidentally of course, and stopped to see the fun, sure that Bud would thrash the master if he tried to break in. . . .

"There's the master," cried Betsey Short, who stood out in the road shivering and giggling alternately. For Ralph at that moment emerged from the sugar-camp[1] by the school-house, carrying a board.

"Ho! ho!" laughed Hank, "he thinks he'll smoke us out. I guess he'll find us ready." The boys had let the fire burn down, and there was now nothing but hot hickory coals on the hearth. . . .

Ralph's voice was now heard, demanding that the door be opened.

---

[1] A grove of sugar maples and a boiling house.

"Let's open her," said Hank, turning livid with fear at the firm, confident tone of the master.

Bud straightened himself up. "Hank, you're a coward. I've got a mind to kick you. You got me into this blamed mess, and now you want to crawfish. You jest tech one of these 'ere fastenin's, and I'll lay you out flat of your back afore you can say Jack Robinson."

The teacher was climbing to the roof with the board in hand.

"That air won't win," laughed Pete Jones outside. He saw that there was no smoke. Even Bud began to hope that Ralph would fail for once. The master was now on the ridge-pole of the school-house. He took a paper from his pocket, and deliberately poured the contents down the chimney.

Mr. Pete Jones shouted "Gunpowder!" and set off down the road to be out of the way of the explosion. . . .

But Ralph emptied the paper, and laid the board over the chimney. What a row there was inside! The benches that were braced against the door were thrown down, and Hank Banta rushed out, rubbing his eyes, coughing frantically, and sure that he had been blown up. All the rest followed, Bud bringing up the rear sulkily, but coughing and sneezing for dear life. Such a smell of sulphur as came from that school-house!

Betsey had to lean against the fence to giggle.

As soon as all were out, Ralph threw the board off the chimney, leaped to the ground, entered the school-house, and opened the windows. The school soon followed him, and all was still.

"Would he thrash?" This was the important question in Hank Banta's mind. And the rest looked for a battle with Bud.

"It is just nine o'clock," said Ralph, consulting his watch, "and I'm glad to see you all here promptly. I should have given you a holiday if you had asked me like gentlemen yesterday. On the whole, I think I shall give you a holiday, anyhow. The school is dismissed."

And Hank felt foolish.

And Bud secretly resolved to thrash Hank or the master, he didn't care which.

And Mirandy looked the love she could not utter.

And Betsey giggled.

E. Schools and Mills for Girls

• *Lucy Larcom* (1889)

> Again we turn to postwar reminiscence, though here not in the form of fiction. Lucy Larcom (1824–1893) first recalls her informal, coeducational schooling in a "dame school" in Beverly, Massachusetts. The maternal "Aunt Hannah" manages to combine some teaching with cooking, spinning, housework, and babysitting. Given the prejudices of the time, it is surpris-

ing that the "class" includes a black child who seems, however, to have been kept in a state of permanent humiliation. Note the evidence of changing sex roles, especially the growing expectation that girls should "cultivate and *make use* of their individual powers." Note also the suggestion that a large family is not necessarily an economic benefit.

At the age of eleven, after the death of her father, Lucy Larcom goes to work in the Lowell textile mills. Initially she enjoys the sense of independence and peer-group companionship, but increasingly feels frustrated by the shutting off of educational opportunity. Fortunately, she later made her mark as a contributor to the *Operative's Magazine* and *Lowell Offering*. After moving to Illinois, she taught school and became an accomplished poet and writer.

Lucy Larcom (1889)

Aunt Hannah used her kitchen or her sittingroom for a schoolroom, as best suited her convenience. We were delighted observers of her culinary operations and other employments. If a baby's head nodded, a little bed was made for it on a soft "comforter" in the corner, where it had its nap out undisturbed. But this did not often happen; there were so many interesting things going on that we seldom became sleepy.

Aunt Hannah was very kind and motherly, but she kept us in fear of her ferule,[1] which indicated to us the possibility of smarting palms. This ferule was shaped much like the stick with which she stirred her hasty pudding for dinner,—I thought it was the same,—and I found myself caught in a whirl-wind of family laughter by reporting at home that "Aunt Hannah punished the scholars with the pudding-stick."

There was one colored boy in school, who did not sit on a bench, like the rest, but on a block of wood that looked like a backlog turned endwise. Aunt Hannah often called him a "blockhead," and I supposed it was because he sat on that block. Sometimes, in his absence, a boy was made to sit in his place for punishment, for being a "blockhead" too, as I imagined. I hoped I should never be put there. Stupid little girls received a different treatment, —an occasional rap on the head with the teacher's thimble; accompanied with a half-whispered, impatient ejaculation, which sounded very much like "Numskull!" I think this was a rare occurrence, however, for she was a good-natured, much-enduring woman.

One of our greatest school pleasures was to watch Aunt Hannah spinning on her flax-wheel, wetting her thumb and forefinger at her lips to twist the

SOURCE: Lucy Larcom, *A New England Girlhood* (Boston: Houghton Mifflin and Co., 1889), pp. 42–45, 120–21, 152–57.

[1] A flat stick used for punishment by striking a child's hand; originally, a stalk of giant fennel.

thread, keeping time, meanwhile, to some quaint old tune with her foot upon the treadle.

. . .

I began to go to school when I was about two years old, as other children about us did. The mothers of those large families had to resort to some means of keeping their little ones out of mischief, while they attended to their domestic duties. Not much more than that sort of temporary guardianship was expected of the good dame who had us in charge.

But I learned my letters in a few days, standing at Aunt Hannah's knee while she pointed them out in the spelling-book with a pin, skipping over the "a b abs" into words of one and two syllables, thence taking a flying leap into the New Testament, in which there is concurrent family testimony that I was reading at the age of two years and a half. Certain it is that a few passages in the Bible, whenever I read them now, do not fail to bring before me a vision of Aunt Hannah's somewhat sternly smiling lips, with her spectacles just above them, far down on her nose, encouraging me to pronounce the hard words.

. . .

The Voice in the Book seemed so tender! Somebody was speaking who had a heart, and who knew that even a little child's heart was sometimes troubled. And it was a Voice that called us somewhere; to the Father's house, with its many mansions, so sunshiny and so large.

. . .

Everybody about us worked, and we expected to take hold of our part while young. I think we were rather eager to begin, for we believed that work would make men and women of us.

I, however, was not naturally an industrious child, but quite the reverse. When my father sent us down to weed his vegetable-garden at the foot of the lane, I, the youngest of his weeders, liked to go with the rest, but not for the sake of the work or the pay. I generally gave it up before I had weeded half a bed. It made me so warm! and my back did ache so! I stole off into the shade of the great apple-trees, and let the west wind fan my hot cheeks, and looked up into the boughs, and listened to the many, many birds that seemed chattering to each other in a language of their own. What was it they were saying? and why could not I understand it? Perhaps I should, sometime. I had read of people who did, in fairy tales.

. . .

My father had always strongly emphasized his wish that all his children, girls as well as boys, should have some independent means of self-support by the labor of their hands; that every one should, as was the general custom, "learn a trade." Tailor's work—the finishing of men's outside garments—was the "trade" learned most frequently by women in those days, and one or more of my older sisters worked at it; I think it must have been at home, for I somehow or somewhere got the idea, while I was a small child, that the chief end of woman was to make clothing for mankind.

. . .

It was not in my mother's nature closely to calculate costs, and in this way there came to be a continually increasing leak in the family purse. The older members of the family did everything they could, but it was not enough. I heard it said one day, in a distressed tone, "The children will have to leave school and go into the mill."

There were many pros and cons between my mother and sisters before this was positively decided. The mill-agent did not want to take us two little girls, but consented on condition we should be sure to attend school the full number of months prescribed each year. I, the younger one, was then between eleven and twelve years old.

I listened to all that was said about it, very much fearing that I should not be permitted to do the coveted work. For the feeling had already frequently come to me, that I was the one too many in the overcrowded family nest. Once, before we left our old home, I had heard a neighbor condoling with my mother because there were so many of us, and her emphatic reply had been a great relief to my mind:—

"There is n't one more than I want. I could not spare a single one of my children."

But her difficulties were increasing, and I thought it would be a pleasure to feel that I was not a trouble or burden or expense to anybody. So I went to my first day's work in the mill with a light heart. The novelty of it made it seem easy, and it really was not hard, just to change the bobbins on the spinning-frames every three quarters of an hour or so, with half a dozen other little girls who were doing the same thing. When I came back at night, the family began to pity me for my long, tiresome day's work, but I laughed and said,—

"Why, it is nothing but fun. It is just like play."

And for a little while it was only a new amusement; I liked it better than going to school and "making believe" I was learning when I was not. And there was a great deal of play mixed with it. We were not occupied more than half the time. The intervals were spent frolicking around among the spinning-frames, teasing and talking to the older girls, or entertaining ourselves with games and stories in a corner, or exploring, with the overseer's permission, the mysteries of the carding-room, the dressing-room, and the weaving-room.

I never cared much for machinery. The buzzing and hissing and whizzing of pulleys and rollers and spindles and flyers around me often grew tiresome. I could not see into their complications, or feel interested in them. But in a room below us we were sometimes allowed to peer in through a sort of blind door at the great water-wheel that carried the works of the whole mill. It was so huge that we could only watch a few of its spokes at a time, and part of its dripping rim, moving with a slow, measured strength through the darkness that shut it in. It impressed me with something of the awe which comes to us in thinking of the great Power which keeps the mechanism of the universe in motion. . . .

There were compensations for being shut in to daily toil so early. The mill itself had its lessons for us. But it was not, and could not be, the right sort of life for a child, and we were happy in the knowledge that, at the longest, our employment was only to be temporary.

When I took my next three months at the grammar school, everything there was changed, and I too was changed. The teachers were kind, and thorough in their instruction; and my mind seemed to have been ploughed up during that year of work, so that knowledge took root in it easily. It was a great delight to me to study, and at the end of the three months the master told me that I was prepared for the high school.

But alas! I could not go. The little money I could earn—one dollar a week, besides the price of my board—was needed in the family, and I must return to the mill. It was a severe disappointment to me, though I did not say so at home. I did not at all accept the conclusion of a neighbor whom I heard talking about it with my mother. His daughter was going to the high school, and my mother was telling him how sorry she was that I could not.

"Oh," he said, in a soothing tone, "my girl hasn't got any such head-piece as yours has. Your girl doesn't need to go."

Of course I knew that whatever sort of a "head-piece" I had, I did need and want just that very opportunity to study. I think the resolution was then formed, inwardly, that I *would* go to school again, some time, whatever happened. I went back to my work, but now without enthusiasm. I had looked through an open door that I was not willing to see shut upon me.

* * *

In the older times it was seldom said to little girls, as it always has been said to boys, that they ought to have some definite plan, while they were children, what to be and do when they were grown up. There was usually but one path open before them, to become good wives and housekeepers. And the ambition of most girls was to follow their mothers' footsteps in this direction; a natural and laudable ambition. But girls, as well as boys, must often have been conscious of their own peculiar capabilities,—must have desired to cultivate and *make* use of their individual powers. When I was growing up, they had already begun to be encouraged to do so. We were often told that it was our duty to develop any talent we might possess, or at least to learn how to do some one thing which the world needed, or which would make it a pleasanter world.

F. Lessons on "A House Divided"

• *William H. McGuffey* (1857)

At school or at home, a key instrument of socialization was the juvenile anthology or "reader." In the 1830s, innovations in printing technology greatly increased the cheapness and accessibility of the printed word; the standardization of texts meant that millions of schoolchildren were being exposed to the same examples and lessons. The most famous and successful nineteenth-century readers were those written by William H. McGuffey (1800–1873), which are reported to have sold a staggering 122,000,000 copies. Born in Pennsylvania and reared in frontier Ohio, McGuffey became a professor of languages and college president before moving to the University of Virginia, where he taught moral philosophy. He was also trained as a Presbyterian minister. If the lesson below seems ludicrously sentimental and moralistic, one must realize that several generations of children were steeped in this sort of reading. What was its effect and function? Note that the selection is meant to be read aloud to help get rid of the kind of dialects and mispronunciations later celebrated by writers like Eggleston and Twain. The subject of alcoholism is a way of getting at wider themes of moral influence, violence, and family division, which we have encountered before in other contexts.

William H. McGuffey (1857)

The Intemperate Husband

REMARK.—Take care not to let the voice grow weaker and weaker, as you approach the end of the sentence.

ARTICULATE correctly. Do not say *full-es* for full-*est*; *suf-rin* for suf-fer-ing; *sur-es* for sur-*est*; *un-feel-in* for un-feel-ing; *fren's* for friends; *beau-ti-fl'y* for beau-ti-ful-ly; *ga-zin* for gaz-ing; *vi-er-lits* for vi-o-lets; *ag-er-ni-zing* for ag-o-niz-ing; *fea-ters* nor *fea-tshurs* for feat-ures.

1. THERE was one modification of her husband's persecutions, which the fullest measure of Jane Harwood's piety could not enable her to bear unmoved. This was unkindness to her feeble and suffering boy. It was at first commenced as the surest mode of distressing her. It opened a direct avenue to her heart.

2. What began in perverseness, seemed to end in hatred, as evil habits sometimes create perverted principles. The wasted invalid shrunk from his father's glance and footstep, as from the approach of a foe. More than once had he taken him from the little bed which maternal care had provided for him, and forced him to go forth in the cold of the winter storm.

3. "I mean to harden him," said he. "All the neighbors know that you make such a fool of him, that he will never be able to get [earn] a living. For my part, I wish I had never been called to the trial of supporting a useless boy, who pretends to be sick only that he may be coaxed by a silly mother."

4. On such occasions, it was in vain that the mother attempted to protect her child. She could neither shelter him in her bosom, nor control the

---

SOURCE: William H. McGuffey, *New Fifth Eclectic Reader* (Cincinnati: Van Antwerp, Bragg and Co., 1866; originally printed 1857), pp. 155–60. The story is by Lydia Sigourney, "the Sweet Singer of Hartford."

frantic violence of the father. Harshness, and the agitation of fear, deepened a disease which might else have yielded. The timid boy, in terror of his natural protector, withered away like a blighted flower. It was of no avail that friends remonstrated with the unfeeling parent, or that hoary-headed men warned him solemnly of his sins. *Intemperance* had destroyed his respect for man, and his fear of God.

• • •

8. The mother knew that the hectic fever had been long increasing, and saw there was such an unearthly brightness in his eye, that she feared his intellect wandered. She seated herself on his low bed, and bent over him to soothe and compose him. He lay silent for some time.

9. "Do you think my father will come?" Dreading the agonizing agitation which, in his paroxysms of coughing and pain, he evinced at the sound of his father's well-known footstep, she answered "I think not, love. You had better try to sleep."

10. "Mother, I wish he would come. I do not feel afraid now. Perhaps he would let me lay my cheek to his once more, as he used to do when I was a babe in my grandmother's arms. I should be glad to say goodby to him before I go to my Savior."

• • •

2. The father entered carelessly. She pointed to the pallid, immovable brow. "See, he suffers no longer." He drew near, and looked on the dead with surprise and sadness. A few natural tears forced their way, and fell on the face of the first-born, who was once his pride. The memories of that moment were bitter. He spoke tenderly to the emaciated mother; and she, who a short time before was raised above the sway of grief, wept like an infant, as those few affectionate tones touched the sealed fountains of other years.

• • •

7. [The father] returned from the funeral in much mental distress. His sins were brought to remembrance, and reflection was misery. For many nights, sleep was disturbed by visions of his neglected boy. Sometimes he imagined that he heard him coughing from his low bed, and felt constrained to go to him, in a strange disposition of kindness, but his limbs were unable to obey the dictates of his will.

8. Conscience haunted him with terrors, and many prayers from pious hearts arose, that he might now be led to repentance. The venerable man who had read the Bible at the burial of his boy, counseled and entreated him, with the earnestness of a father, to yield to the warning voice, and to "break off his sins by righteousness, and his iniquities by turning unto the Lord."

9. There was a change in his habits and conversation, and his friends trusted it would be permanent. She, who, above all others, was interested in the result, spared no exertion to win him back to the way of truth, and soothe his heart into peace with itself, and obedience to his Maker.

10. Yet was she doomed to witness the full force of grief, and of remorse for intemperance, only to see them utterly overthrown at last. The reviving virtue, with whose indications she had solaced herself, and even given thanks that her beloved son had not died in vain, was transient as the morning dew.

11. Habits of industry, which had begun to spring up, proved themselves to be without root. The dead, and his cruelty to the dead, were alike forgotten. . . .

12. The friends who had alternately reproved and encouraged him, were soon convinced their efforts had been of no avail. Intemperance, "like the strong man armed," took possession of a soul that lifted no cry to God, and girded on no weapon to resist the destroyer.

EXERCISES.—What effect was produced upon the father by the death of his child? What were his friends disposed to hope? How did intemperance take possession of him? Why was he unsuccessful, do you suppose, in his resistance to intemperate habits?

G. "What Is a Young Man Fitted For, When He Takes His Degree?"

• *Reports on the Course of Instruction in Yale College* (1830)

Though it may seem a large jump from McGuffey's schoolbooks to the curriculum at Yale, American colleges in the antebellum period were still glorified boarding schools and considered part of an extended family. For example, these *Reports* of 1830 take for granted the "parental character of college government," which functions as "a substitute for the regulations of a family." The emphasis on internal policing and surveillance echoes the concerns of the Prison Discipline Society (Part 2 above).

But the Yale committee (Jeremiah Day was president of Yale) is also dedicated to building the "foundations" of a superior education—not simply cultivating moral sentiment, but training the mind to know *how* to learn. The committee's justifications for liberal education are strikingly similar to those used in recent times, at least until the 1950s. And the arguments are directed against challenges that have persisted to the present day —that a liberal education is not relevant to "the spirits and wants of the age"; that it fails to equip students for any vocation or profession. The immediate issue, the required study of the "dead languages," Latin and Greek, had raised the whole question of "the object and plan of education in the college." The committee is sensitive to democratic and utilitarian pressures, and shows particular concern over winning the support of rising groups of merchants, manufacturers, and commercial farmers. Committed to the preservation and transmission of the Old World's classical culture—as the highest form of socialization—they are also determined to keep up with the hustle and bustle of America's physical expansion. Against the divisions and fragmentations of American life, they uphold the classical ideals of roundedness, wholeness, and balance. But ultimately, they acknowledge that it is up to the student himself to fuse the models and wisdom of the past with the needs of the future: "The scholar must form himself, by his own exertions." This phrase forms a bridge to our next section on "Self-Culture."

Reports on the Course of Instruction in Yale College (1830)

We are decidedly of the opinion, that our present plan of education admits of improvement. We are aware that the system is imperfect: and we cherish the hope, that some of its defects may ere long be remedied. We believe that changes may, from time to time, be made with advantage, to meet the varying demands of the community, to accommodate the course of instruction to the rapid advance of the country, in population, refinement, and opulence. We have no doubt that important improvements may be suggested by attentive observation of the literary institutions in Europe; and by the earnest spirit of inquiry which is now so prevalent, on the subject of education.

The guardians of the college appear to have ever acted upon the principle, that it ought not to be stationary, but continually advancing. Some alteration has accordingly been proposed, almost every year, from its first establishment. It is with no small surprise, therefore, we occasionally hear the suggestion, that our system is unalterable; that colleges were originally planned in the days of monkish ignorance; and that, "by being immovably moored to the same station, they serve only to measure the rapid current of improvement which is passing by them."

How opposite to all this, is the real state of facts, in this and the other seminaries in the United States. Nothing is more common, than to hear those who revisit the college, after a few years absence, express their surprise at the changes which have been made since they were graduated. Not only the course of studies, and the modes of instruction, have been greatly varied; but whole sciences have, for the first time, been introduced; chemistry, mineralogy, geology, political economy, etc. By raising the qualifications for admission, the standard of attainment has been elevated. . . . Improvements, we trust, will continue to be made, as rapidly as they can be, without hazarding the loss of what has been already attained.

• • •

What then is the appropriate object of a college? It is not necessary here to determine what it is which, in every case, entitles an institution to the *name* of a college. But if we have not greatly misapprehended the design of

SOURCE: [Jeremiah Day and James Kingsley], *Reports on the Course of Instruction in Yale College; by a Committee of the Corporation and Academical Faculty* (New Haven: Hezekiah Howe, 1830), pp. 5–16, 26–27, 29–30.

the patrons and guardians of this college, its object is to LAY THE FOUNDATION of a SUPERIOR EDUCATION: and this is to be done, at a period of life when a substitute must be provided for *parental superintendence.* The ground work of a thorough education, must be broad, and deep, and solid. For a partial or superficial education, the support may be of looser materials, and more hastily laid.

The two great points to be gained in intellectual culture, are the *discipline* and the *furniture* of the mind; expanding its powers, and storing it with knowledge. The former of these is, perhaps, the more important of the two. A commanding object, therefore, in a collegiate course, should be to call into daily and vigorous exercise the faculties of the student. Those branches of study should be prescribed, and those modes of instruction adopted, which are best calculated to teach the art of fixing the attention, directing the train of thought, analyzing a subject proposed for investigation; following, with accurate discrimination, the course of argument; balancing nicely the evidence presented to the judgment; awakening, elevating, and controlling the imagination; arranging, with skill, the treasures which memory gathers; rousing and guiding the powers of genius. All this is not to be effected by a light and hasty course of study; by reading a few books, hearing a few lectures, and spending some months at a literary institution. The habits of thinking are to be formed by long continued and close application. . . . In the course of instruction in this college, it has been an object to maintain such a proportion between the different branches of literature and science, as to form in the student a proper *balance* of character. From the pure mathematics, he learns the art of demonstrative reasoning. In attending to the physical sciences, he becomes familiar with facts, with the process of induction, and the varieties of probable evidence. In ancient literature, he finds some of the most finished models of taste. By English reading, he learns the powers of the language in which he is to speak and write. By logic and mental philosophy, he is taught the art of thinking; by rhetoric and oratory, the art of speaking. By frequent exercise on written composition, he acquires copiousness and accuracy of expression. By extemporaneous discussion, he becomes prompt, and fluent, and animated. . . .

No one feature in a system of intellectual education is of greater moment than such an arrangement of duties and motives as will most effectually throw the student upon the *resources of his own mind.* Without this, the whole apparatus of libraries, and instruments, and specimens, and lectures, and teachers, will be insufficient to secure distinguished excellence. The scholar must form himself, by his own exertions. The advantages furnished by a residence at a college, can do little more than stimulate and aid his personal efforts. The *inventive* powers are especially to be called into vigorous exercise. However abundant may be the acquisitions of the student, if he has no talent at forming new combinations of thought, he will be dull and inefficient. The sublimest efforts of genius consist in the creations of the imagination, the discoveries of the intellect, the conquests by which the dominions of science are extended. But the culture of the inventive faculties is not the *only* object of a liberal education. The most gifted understanding cannot greatly enlarge the amount of science to which the wisdom of ages has contributed. If it were possible for a youth to have his faculties in the highest state of cultivation, without any of the knowledge which is derived from others, he would be but poorly fitted for the business of life. To the discipline of the mind, therefore, is to be added instruction. . . .

A most important feature in the colleges of this country is, that the students are generally of an age which requires, that a substitute be provided for *parental superintendence*. When removed from under the roof of their parents, and exposed to the untried scenes of temptation, it is necessary that some faithful and affectionate guardian take them by the hand, and guide their steps. This consideration determines the *kind* of government which ought to be maintained in our colleges. As it is a substitute for the regulations of a family, it should approach as near to the character of parental control, as the circumstances of the case will admit. It should be founded on mutual affection and confidence. It should aim to effect its purpose, principally by kind and persuasive influence; not wholly or chiefly by restraint and terror. Still, punishment may sometimes be necessary. There may be perverse members of a college, as well as of a family. There may be those whom nothing but the arm of law can reach.

The parental character of college government requires that the students should be so collected together, as to constitute one family; that the intercourse between them and their instructors may be frequent and familiar. . . .

In giving the course of instruction, it is intended that a due proportion be observed between *lectures*, and the exercises which are familiarly termed *recitations*; that is, examinations in a text-book. The great advantage of lectures is, that while they call forth the highest efforts of the lecturer, and accelerate his advance to professional eminence; they give that light and spirit to the subject, which awaken the interest and ardor of the student. They may place before him the principles of science, in the attractive dress of living eloquence. Where instruments are to be explained, experiments performed, or specimens exhibited, they are the appropriate mode of communication. But we are far from believing, that *all* the purposes of instruction can be best answered by lectures alone. They do not always bring upon the student a pressing and definite responsibility. He may repose upon his seat, and yield a passive hearing to the lecturer, without ever calling into exercise the active powers of his own mind. This defect we endeavor to remedy, in part, by frequent examinations on the subjects of the lectures. Still it is important, that the student should have opportunities of retiring by himself, and giving a more commanding direction to his thoughts, than when listening to oral instruction. To secure his steady and earnest efforts, is the great object of the daily examinations or recitations. In these exercises, a text-book is commonly the guide. A particular portion of this is assigned for each meeting. In this way only, can the responsibility be made sufficiently definite. If it be distributed among several books upon the same subject, the diversity of statement in these, will furnish the student with an apology for want of exactness in his answers. Besides, we know of no method which will more effectually bewilder and confound the learner, on his first entrance upon a new science, than to refer him to half a dozen different authors, to be read at the same time. He will be in danger of learning nothing effectually. When he comes to be engaged in the study of his *profession*, he may find his way through the maze, and firmly establish his own opinions, by taking days or weeks for the examination of each separate point. Text-books are, therefore, not as necessary in this advanced stage of education, as in the course at college, where the time allotted to each branch is rarely more than sufficient for the learner to become familiar with its elementary principles. These [principles] with a few exceptions, are not new and controverted points, but such as have been long settled; and they are exhibited to the best advantage, in the consistent and peculiar manner of some eminent writer. . . .

If we mistake not, some portion of the popularity of . . . oral instruction is to be set to the account of the student's satisfaction, in escaping from the demand for mental exertion. It is to secure the unceasing and strenuous exercise of the intellectual powers, that the responsibility of the student is made so constant and particular. For this purpose, our semi-annual *examinations* have been established. These, with the examination of the seniors in July, occupy from twelve to fourteen days in a year. Each class is divided into two portions, which are examined in separate rooms at the same time, seven or eight hours a day. A committee is present on the occasion, consisting of gentlemen of education and distinction from different parts of the state. The degree of correctness with which each student answers the questions put to him in the several branches, is noted on the spot, and entered in a record, permanently kept by the faculty. But to the instructors, the daily examinations in the recitation rooms are a more unerring test of scholarship than these public trials. The latter answer the purpose of satisfying the inquiries of strangers.

· · ·

In the internal police of the institution, as the students are gathered into one family, it is deemed an essential provision, that some of the officers should constitute a portion of this family; being always present with them, not only at their meals, and during the business of the day; but in the hours allotted to rest. The arrangement is such, that in our college buildings, there is no room occupied by students, which is not near to the chamber of one of the officers. . . .

The tutor of a division has an opportunity, which is enjoyed by no other officer of the college, of becoming intimately acquainted with the characters of his pupils. It is highly important that this knowledge should be at the command of the faculty. By distributing our family among different individuals, minute information is acquired, which may be communicated to the Board, whenever it is called for. . . .

The collegiate course of study, of which we have now given a summary view, we hope may be carefully distinguished from several *other* objects and plans, with which it has been too often confounded. It is far from embracing *every thing* which the student will ever have occasion to learn. The object is not to *finish* his education; but to lay the foundation, and to advance as far in rearing the superstructure, as the short period of his residence here will admit. If he acquires here a thorough knowledge of the principles of science, he may then, in a great measure, educate himself. He has, at least, been taught *how* to learn. With the aid of books, and means of observation, he may be constantly advancing in knowledge. Wherever he goes, into whatever company he falls, he has those general views, on every topic of interest, which will enable him to understand, to digest, and to form a correct opinion, on the statements and discussions which he hears. . . .

The course of instruction which is given to the undergraduates in the college, is not designed to include *professional* studies. Our object is not to teach that which is peculiar to any one of the professions; but to lay the foundation which is common to them all. There are separate schools for medicine, law, and theology, connected with the college, as well as in various parts of the country; which are open for the reception of all who are prepared to enter upon the appropriate studies of their several professions. With these, the academic course is not intended to interfere.

But why, it may be asked, should a student waste his time upon studies which have no immediate connection with his future profession? Will chemistry enable him to plead at the bar, or conic sections qualify him for preaching, or astronomy aid him in the practice of physic [medicine]? Why should not his attention be confined to the subject which is to occupy the labors of his life? In answer to this, it may be observed, that there is no science which does not contribute its aid to professional skill. "Every thing throws light upon every thing." The great object of a collegiate education, preparatory to the study of a profession, is to give that expansion and balance of the mental powers, those liberal and comprehensive views, and those fine proportions of character, which are not to be found in him whose ideas are always confined to one particular channel. When a man has entered upon the practice of his profession, the energies of his mind must be given, principally, to its appropriate duties. But if his thoughts never range on other subjects, if he never looks abroad on the ample domains of literature and science, there will be a narrowness in his habits of thinking, a peculiarity of character, which will be sure to mark him as a man of limited views and attainments. Should he be distinguished in his profession, his ignorance on other subjects, and the defects of his education, will be more exposed to public observation. On the other hand, he who is not only eminent in professional life, but has also a mind richly stored with general knowledge, has an elevation and dignity of character, which gives him a commanding influence in society, and a widely extended sphere of usefulness. His situation enables him to diffuse the light of science among all classes of the community.

Is a man to have no other object, than to obtain a *living* by professional pursuits? Has he not duties to perform to his family, to his fellow citizens, to his country; duties which require various and extensive intellectual furniture?

. . .

As our course of instruction is not intended to complete an education in theological, medical, or legal science; neither does it include all the minute details of *mercantile, mechanical,* or *agricultural* concerns. These can never be effectually learned, except in the very circumstances in which they are to be practiced. The young merchant must be trained in the counting room, the mechanic, in the workshop, the farmer, in the field. But we have, on our premises, no experimental farm or retail shop; no cotton or iron manufactory; no hatter's, or silver-smith's, or coach-maker's establishment. For what purpose, then, it will be asked, are young men who are destined to these occupations, ever sent to a college? They should not be sent, as we think, with an expectation of *finishing* their education at the college; but with a view of laying a thorough foundation in the principles of science preparatory to the study of the practical arts. As every thing cannot be learned in four years, either theory or practice must be, in a measure at least, postponed to a future opportunity. But if the scientific theory of the arts is *ever* to be acquired, it is unquestionably first in order of time. The corner stone must be laid, before the superstructure is erected. . . .

The question may be asked, What is a young man fitted for, when he takes his degree? Does he come forth from the college qualified for business? We answer, no,—if he stops here. His education is begun, but not completed. Is the college to be reproached for not accomplishing that which it has never undertaken to perform?

. . .

Another serious difficulty with which we have to contend, is the impression made on the minds of a portion of our students, from one quarter and another, that the study of any thing for which they have not an instinctive relish, or which requires vigorous and continued effort, or which is not immediately connected with their intended professional pursuits, is of no practical utility. They of course remain ignorant of that which they think not worth the learning. We are concerned to find, that not only students, but their parents also, seem frequently more solicitous for the *name* of an education, than the substance.

. . .

Young men intended for active employments ought not to be excluded from the colleges, merely on the ground that the course of study is not specially adapted to their pursuits. This principle would exclude those also who are intended for the professions. In either case, the object of the undergraduate course, is not to finish a preparation for business; but to impart that various and general knowledge, which will improve, and elevate, and adorn any occupation. Can merchants, manufacturers, and agriculturists, derive no benefit from high intellectual culture? They are the very classes which, from their situation and business, have the best opportunities for reducing the principles of science to their practical applications. The large estates which the tide of prosperity in our country is so rapidly accumulating, will fall mostly into their hands. Is it not desirable that they should be men of superior education, of large and liberal views, of those solid and elegant attainments, which will raise them to a higher distinction, than the mere possession of property; which will not allow them to hoard their treasures, or waste them in senseless extravagance; which will enable them to adorn society by their learning, to move in the more intelligent circles with dignity, and to make such an application of their wealth, as will be most honorable to themselves, and most beneficial to their country?

The active, enterprising character of our population, renders it highly important, that this bustle and energy should be directed by sound intelligence, the result of deep thought and early discipline. The greater the impulse to action, the greater is the need of wise and skillful guidance. . . . Light and moderate learning is but poorly fitted to direct the energies of a nation, so widely extended, so intelligent, so powerful in resources, so rapidly advancing in population, strength, and opulence. Where a free government gives full liberty to the human intellect to expand and operate, education should be proportionably liberal and ample. When even our mountains, and rivers, and lakes, are upon a scale which seems to denote, that we are destined to be a great and mighty nation, shall our literature be feeble, and scanty, and superficial?

4

Advice on Self-Culture
and Sexual Identity

A. Self-Culture

- *William Ellery Channing* (1838)
- *Manual of Self-Education* (1842)
- *Henry Ward Beecher* (1846)

William Ellery Channing (1780–1842) stood at the fountainhead of American religious liberalism. After graduating from Harvard, Channing first served as a tutor for a Virginia planter family and then, in 1803, became pastor of the Federal Street Church in Boston. Though noncombative and retiring by nature, he became embroiled by 1815 in the great "Unitarian controversy" which bitterly divided New England Congregationalism between the traditionalists, who believed in inherent human depravity (original sin), and the liberals, who stressed a universal capacity for moral improvement. As Channing puts it here, the liberals believed in our ability "to see in ourselves germs and promises of a growth to which no bounds can be set. . . ."

Channing soon emerged as the leading spokesman for American Unitarianism, and his vision of a latent divinity in human nature exerted a profound influence on reformers like Horace Mann and on writers like Ralph Waldo Emerson. But unlike Emerson and the group known as Transcendentalists, Channing by no means rejected belief in the miracles record-ed in the New Testament or in the supernatural basis of Christianity. Occu-pying a half-way house between Calvinism and romantic reform, he still identified self-culture with the suppression of sensual appetites. Like so many reformers, whether orthodox or liberal in theology, he also saw abstention from alcohol as a key symbol of self-control and self-improvement. Here, he is particularly concerned with curbing the luxurious excesses of the rich and with elevating the standards of working-class behavior. Fearing both an amoral plutocracy and a riotous mobocracy, he presents self-culture as the only means of moving toward common ethical norms—norms that will bind the people, without coercion, in a common pursuit of self-restraint and virtue.

By the time of Channing's death in 1842, the nation was already flooded with cheap tracts, books, and periodicals offering advice on everything from etiquette and courtship to "how to get rich." These popularizers of self-culture often drew on the arguments and themes of men like Channing—for example, the first issue of *Manual of Self-Education: A Magazine for the Young* begins with a long quotation from Channing (without naming him). But the popularizers were also attuned to market demand and were telling the public what it wanted to hear. By the 1840s, a growing number of Americans were eager for advice on all aspects of "self-improvement," from health and physical fitness to the cultivation of their minds.

In dispensing advice, no figure had achieved greater prominence by the 1850s than Henry Ward Beecher (1813–1887). Though Henry was the son of Lyman Beecher and the younger brother of Catharine Beecher and Harriet Beecher Stowe, his own ascent to fame was slow and owed more to personal magnetism than to family or to originality of mind. Serving eight years as a preacher in Indianapolis before moving to Plymouth Church in Brooklyn in 1847, Beecher perfected an informal, homespun, yet florid style perfectly synchronized to the tastes and concerns of the urban middle class. In many ways Beecher's immensely popular *Seven Lectures to Young Men* anticipates the tone and appeal of the "advice columns" in twentieth-cen-tury newspapers. Upholding traditional values, such as the need for patience, contentment, and solid foundations, Beecher also shows his familiarity with dreams of glittering success. Addressing a weekly congregation of over two thousand members and acquiring a voice of respected authority on public issues, Beecher savored his own success. But after the Civil War his repu-tation became clouded when Elizabeth Tilton, a feminist and Sunday school teacher at Plymouth Church, confessed to her husband that she had had sexual relations with Beecher. The resulting scandal and sensational trial (Theodore Tilton finally brought suit against Beecher, his former friend and associate) dramatized the growing anxiety over marriage and women's subordination—questions to which we shall soon turn.

William Ellery Channing (1838)

Self-culture is something possible; it is not a dream; it has foundations in our nature. Without this conviction, the speaker will but declaim, and the hearer listen, without profit. There are two powers of the human soul which make self-culture possible—the self-searching and the self-forming power. We have first the faculty of turning the mind on itself; of recalling its past, and watching its present operations; of learning its various capacities and susceptibilities, what it can do and bear, what it can enjoy and suffer; and of thus learning in general what our nature is, and what it was made for. It is worthy of observation, that we are able to discern, not only what we already are, but what we may become, to see in ourselves germs and promises of a growth to which no bounds can be set, to dart beyond what we have actually gained, to the idea of perfection as the end of our being. It is by this self-comprehending power that we are distinguished from the brutes, which give no signs of looking into themeslves. . . .

But self-culture is possible, not only because we can enter into and search ourselves; we have a still nobler power, that of acting on, determining, and forming ourselves. This is a fearful as well as glorious endowment, for it is the ground of human responsibility. We have the power not only of tracing our powers, but of guiding and impelling them; not only of watching our passions, but of controlling them; not only of seeing our faculties grow, but of applying to them means and influences to aid their growth. We can stay or change the current of thought; we can concentrate the intellect on objects which we wish to comprehend; we can fix our eyes on perfection, and make almost everything speed us towards it. This is, indeed, a noble prerogative of our nature. Possessing this, it matters little what or where we are now; for we can conquer a better lot, and even be happier for starting from the lowest point. Of all the discoveries which men need to make, the most important, at the present moment, is that of the self-forming power treasured up in themselves. . . . Improve, then, your lot. Multiply comforts, and still more, get wealth, if you can, by honorable means, and if it does not cost too much. A true cultivation of the mind is fitted to forward you in your worldly concerns, and you ought to use it for this end. Only, beware, lest this end master you; lest your motives sink as your condition improves; lest you fall victims to the miserable passion of vying with those around you in show, luxury, and expense. Cherish a true respect for yourselves. Feel that your nature is worth more than everything which is foreign to you. He who has not caught a glimpse of his own rational and spiritual being, of something within himself superior to the world and allied to the Divinity, wants the true spring of that

SOURCE: William Ellery Channing, *Self-Culture* (London: John Chapman, 1844), pp. 8–9, 24–25.

purpose of self-culture, on which I have insisted as the first of all the means of improvement.

I proceed to another important means of self-culture, and this is, the control of the animal appetites. To raise the moral and intellectual nature, we must put down the animal. Sensuality is the abyss in which very many souls are plunged and lost. Among the most prosperous classes, what a vast amount of intellectual life is drowned in luxurious excesses! . . . Whoever would cultivate the soul, must restrain the appetites. . . . Above all, let me urge on those who would bring out and elevate their higher nature, to abstain from the use of spirituous liquors. This bad habit is distinguished from all others by the ravages it makes on the reason, the intellect; and this effect is produced to a mournful extent, even when drunkenness is escaped. Not a few men, called temperate, and who have thought themeslves such, have learned, on abstaining from the use of ardent spirits, that for years their minds had been clouded, impaired by moderate drinking, without their suspecting the injury. Multitudes in this city [Boston] are bereft of half their intellectual energy, by a degree of indulgence which passes for innocent. Of all the foes of the working class, this is the deadliest. Nothing has done more to keep down this class, to destroy their self-respect, to rob them of their just influence in the community, to render profitless the means of improvement within their reach, than the use of ardent spirits as a drink.

Manual of Self-Education (1842)

It is the design of this publication, humble as are its merits, to aid actively in promoting the education and moral advancement of American youth. Appealing directly to them as a class, it is intended to be, as far as it is in the power of its contributors to make it, a guide and an assistant in the formation of character, the acquisition of knowledge, and the culture and discipline of the mind. The inherent qualities that constitute character are to a human being of all other things the most important. How necessary, then, that the principles of mental and moral development should be made familiar before the habits get fixed, and the attention absorbed in material interests!

We shall endeavor to show, as a primary object of our labors, that the destiny of each individual is, to a large extent, in his own possession; and shall strive to awaken in our readers, and to stimulate into methodical action, the power they have over themselves.

• • •

But what shall be said of those unfortunate sons of penury and toil, who, bereft of the means of education in its more extended import, are yet ambitious of intellectual distinction? To such we would come as the messenger

source: *Manual of Self-Education: A Magazine for the Young*, Vol. I (New York: August, 1842), pp. 1–4, 66–67.

of glad tidings. Full well do we appreciate their difficulties and embarrassments, and it shall be the studied object of our efforts to be of service to this class of persons. And we believe there is no class to whom advice and proper instruction is of more value.

It will be one of our objects to take up in proper order the several sciences and other branches of knowledge, and discuss their relative merits, the peculiar advantages of their pursuit, the best method of investigation, and the most suitable text books for study. . . .

Few subjects are of more interest in the family circle than the choice of a profession or occupation for life for its younger members. This, instead of being decided alone by the arbitrary behests of the parent, or the momentary caprice of the son, should be determined by the application of well-established principles, derived from a thorough knowledge of character and of the circumstances of the several parties. We entertain a hope that we shall be able, by occasional discussions of this subject, to be of much service to our readers. We do not consider it so much involved in obscurity, as that no true light can be shed upon it. On the contrary, we see no reason why a young man cannot at an early age be enabled from his own reflections to select such a course for his future employment, as shall tend most happily to his earthly welfare and moral advancement.

The importance of adequate physical development can hardly be too much insisted on. One of the first observations of intelligent foreigners is said to be relative to the attenuated forms and delicate appearance of our young people. We propose presenting a regular series of articles upon the subject of physical culture. In these we shall strive to encourage bodily sports of a healthy and animating description. These, together with the arts of swimming and riding on horseback, will be fully explained and illustrated by wood cut engravings. In connexion with this subject, we shall lay before our readers a general system of instructions, exhibiting the more obvious laws of health and disease so necessary to be understood by every individual.

The arts of address, of conversation, and of social intercourse generally, will be dwelt upon, and illustrated and explained by all the lights that can be borrowed from the suggestions of experience and the maxims of philosophy.

Young Men's Associations for Mutual Improvement have of late years become, in their capacity for usefulness, among the most important institutions in our country. We believe that they are yet susceptible of much improvement, and shall appropriate a department of our journal to this purpose. We are in possession of much valuable matter relative to the working of Mechanics' Institutes in Europe, and have had no little experience in the modes of operation of these and other Lyceum Institutions here, which we entertain a hope can be made available to the satisfaction and improvement of our readers.

To each of the different classes of young persons to whom our labors are addressed, we propose appropriating a department to subjects exclusively applicable to their own situation and views in life. Thus, "The Young

Lady," "The Young Merchant," "The Young Mechanic," "The Young Student," will each receive their portion in due season.

* * *

How to get Rich.—Almost every merchant has been rich, or at least prosperous, at some point of his life; and if he is poor now, he can see very well how he might have avoided the disaster which overthrew his hopes. He will probably see that his misfortunes arose from neglecting some of the following rules:—Be industrious. Every body knows that industry is a fundamental virtue in the man of business. But it is not every sort of industry which tends to wealth. Many men work hard to do a great deal of business, and after all make less money than they would if they did less. Industry should be expended in seeing to all the details of business—in careful finishing up of each separate undertaking, and in the maintenance of such a system as will keep every thing under control.

Be economical. This rule also is familiar to every body. Economy is a virtue to be practiced every hour in a great city. It is to be practiced in pence as much as in pounds. A shilling a day saved, amounts to an estate in the course of a life. Economy is especially important in the outset of life, until the foundations of an estate are laid. Many men are poor all their days, because when their necessary expenses were small, they did not seize the opportunity to save a small capital, which would have changed their fortunes for the whole of their lives. . . .

Do not be in a hurry to get rich. Gradual gains are the only natural gains, and they who are in haste to be rich, break over sound rules, fall into temptations and distress of various sorts, and generally fail of their object. There is no use in getting rich suddenly. The man who keeps his business under his control, and saves something from year to year, is always rich. At any rate, he possesses the highest enjoyment which riches are able to afford.

Henry Ward Beecher (1846)

The scheming speculations of the last ten years have produced an aversion among the young to the slow accumulations of ordinary industry, and fired them with a conviction that shrewdness, cunning, and bold ventures, are a more manly way to wealth. There is a swarm of men, bred in the heats of adventurous times, whose thoughts scorn pence and farthings, and who humble themselves to speak of dollars;—*hundreds* and *thousands* are their words. They are men of *great* operations. Forty thousand dollars is a moderate profit of a single speculation. They mean to own the bank; and to look down, before they die, upon Astor and Girard.[1] The young farmer becomes

---

SOURCE: Henry Ward Beecher, *Lectures to Young Men* (Boston: J. P. Jewett and Co., 1846), pp. 26–28.

[1] John Jacob Astor and Stephen Girard were considered the wealthiest Americans of the time.

almost ashamed to meet his schoolmate, whose stores line whole streets, whose stocks are in every bank and company, and whose increasing money is already well nigh inestimable. . . .

Every few years, commerce has its earthquakes, and the tall and toppling warehouses which haste ran up, are first shaken down. The hearts of men fail them for fear; and the suddenly rich, made more suddenly poor, fill the land with their loud laments. But nothing strange has happened. When the whole story of commercial disasters is told, it is only found out that they, who slowly amassed the gains of useful industry, built upon a rock; and they, who flung together the imaginary millions of commercial speculations, built upon the sand. . . .

Parents, equally wild, foster the delusion. Shall the promising lad be apprenticed to his uncle, the blacksmith? The sisters think the blacksmith so very smutty; the mother shrinks from the ungentility of his swarthy labor; the father, weighing the matter prudentially deeper, finds that a *whole life* had been spent in earning the uncle's property. These sagacious parents, wishing the tree to bear its fruit before it has ever blossomed, regard the long delay of industrious trades as a fatal objection to them. The son, then, must be a rich merchant, or a popular lawyer, or a broker; and these, only as the openings to speculation.

B. The "Restless, Anxious Longing" of American Women

- *Young Lady's Own Book* (1833)
- *William Alcott* (1850)
- *Sarah C. Edgarton* (1843)
- *Catharine Beecher* (1846)

For self-improvement, young males were told to be temperate, frugal, and industrious; a separate body of literature advised young females to be neat, orderly, and submissive. Particularly in the 1820s and 1830s, this literature was almost obsessively traditional, proclaiming—as in the first selection here —that woman is "the weaker vessel," "conscious of inferiority," apparently created only to serve men. But as we have seen in earlier selections by Catharine Beecher and Mrs. A. J. Graves (Part 1, B and C), the celebration of woman's special "sphere" of domesticity provided a basis for asserting female hegemony over manners and morals.

William Alcott (1798–1859) was a crusading school reformer, doctor, pioneer in health and physical education, and prolific author—his *Juvenile Rambler* was one of the nation's first magazines designed for children; for a time he edited Samuel Goodrich's *Parley's Magazine*; and his *Young Man's Guide*, published in 1833, went through twenty-one editions in the next twenty-five years. His *Letters to a Sister* not only set high standards for selecting a mate but suggested that young men should expect a thorough screening for moral blemishes, a screening that presumably would not end on the day of marriage.

Sarah Edgarton (1819–1848), also a writer of juvenile literature, seems on first sight to be echoing the themes of the *Young Lady's Own Book*, especially in rejecting "the absurd doctrine of physical independence." Yet Edgarton goes on to talk of self-reliance and of woman's "birthright of an independent existence." Though she died at twenty-nine, two years after marrying a minister, Edgarton also enjoyed a successful career as a poet, editor, and writer.

We have already seen that Catharine Beecher, while paying allegiance to the values of domesticity, was in reality a "career woman" who had considerable impact on popular American culture. This selection from Catharine Beecher's *Evils Suffered by American Women and American Children* can be read as a transitional link between the literature of domesticity and feminism. Stopping short of any avowal of women's rights, Catharine Beecher still gives vent to women's grievances—to their exploitation in factories and in the needle trades; to the frustrations of women of talent and education whose abilities go unused in a society that professes to value ability above all else; and to women's "restless, anxious longing for they know not what. . . ." As a supposedly impartial investigator, exposing conditions in the Lowell textile mills by appealing to "facts" without expressing the "impressions" of her own mind, Beecher's rhetoric is strikingly similar to that of the so-called progressive reformers of the early twentieth century. With almost subversive wit, she turns the sexual stereotypes of her time against the male-dominated society. If women are the gentler sex, superior to men in moral sensitivity, they should not be laboring in factories but should be in schools teaching America's children. Beecher's grandiose scheme may seem visionary, but in the next decades women would increasingly replace men as teachers in elementary schools. Apart from her faith in "a well-devised plan" for saving America's children and providing employment for America's women, be sure to note Beecher's remarks on domestic servants, her concern over an emerging "principle of caste," and her sense of female solidarity or sisterhood, apart from class.

Young Lady's Own Book (1833)

Domestic comfort is the chief source of her influence, and the greatest debt society owes her; for happiness is almost an element of virtue, and nothing conduces more to improve the character of men than domestic peace. A woman may make a man's home delightful, and may thus increase his motives for virtuous exertion. She may refine and tranquillize his mind,—may turn away his anger or allay his grief. Her smile may be the happy influence to gladden his heart, and to disperse the cloud that gathers on his brow. And

SOURCE: *Young Lady's Own Book* (Philadelphia: Key, Mielke, and Biddle, 1833), pp. 13–15, 20.

she will be loved in proportion as she makes those around her happy,—as she studies their tastes, and sympathizes in their feelings. In social relations, adaptation is therefore the true secret of her influence.

Where want of congeniality impairs domestic comfort, the fault is generally chargeable on the female side; for it is for woman, not for man, to make the sacrifice, especially in indifferent matters. She must, in a certain degree, be plastic herself if she would mold others. . . .

Domestic life is a woman's sphere, and it is there that she is most usefully as well as most appropriately employed. But society, too, feels her influence, and owes to her, in great measure, its balance and its tone. She may be here a corrective of what is wrong, a moderator of what is unruly, a restraint on what is indecorous. Her presence may be a pledge against impropriety and excess, a check on vice, and a protection to virtue.

• • •

Nothing is so likely to conciliate the affections of the other sex as a feeling that woman looks to them for support and guidance. In proportion as men are themselves superior, they are accessible to this appeal. On the contrary, they never feel interested in one, who seems disposed rather to offer, than to ask assistance. There is, indeed, something unfeminine in independence. It is contrary to nature, and therefore it offends. We do not like to see a woman affecting tremors, but still less do we like to see her acting the amazon. A really sensible woman feels her dependence. She does what she can, but she is conscious of inferiority, and therefore grateful for support. She knows she is the weaker vessel, and that it is as such that she should receive honor; and, in this view, her weakness is an attraction, not a blemish.

William Alcott (1850)

. . . [N]o young man that is duly enlightened by the Gospel of Christ, and by the public sentiment, so as to see that the use of tobacco is not only offensive to a large portion of female society, but absolutely incompatible with the golden rule, which requires us to do to others as we would wish them in similar circumstances to do to us, and yet persists in his foolish, not to say wicked habit, is fit for the friendship or even for the intimate society of a young woman. . . .

If his teeth, and breath, and perspiration do not reveal the secret, his clothes will. They retain the odor of this virulent narcotic with a most wonderful tenacity, and for a long time. But I hardly need say this to a young woman of New England.

The use of alcohol, in such moderate quantities as are retained in small beer [weak beer], and weak wines and cider, it may not be quite so easy to detect in the habits of a young man. And yet there are methods, of which

SOURCE: William Alcott, *Letters to a Sister* (Buffalo: G. H. Derby and Co., 1850), pp. 183–85, 187.

you may lawfully avail yourself, which enable you to *guess*. Nor need you be very scrupulous about instituting an inquiry on the subject, when there is strong circumstantial or hearsay evidence in the case. He who is likely to be offended by such a course, is as unworthy of your hand as he is unfit for your friendship.

.   .   .

Straws, we are told, show which way the wind blows. Or in other words, little things afford an index to the character. A young man who wears his shoes negligently, will be so much the more apt to be negligent about business, other things being equal. I say other things being equal—because such a remark is indispensable. This, *other things being equal*, includes more than most people are aware.

I will even go a step further, and say that a young man who manages not only his dress, but his ordinary business in a slipshod way, will be apt to manage the matter of friendship in a slipshod manner. Beware, therefore, in your selection, of one who may be slipshod for life!

Sarah C. Edgarton (1843)

I think a woman greatly misjudges her own happiness in making it depend so entirely upon the charms of her fortune, and the gratification of her affections. She is too much inclined to the belief that she is a dependent creature. I would not inculcate the absurd doctrine of physical independence; nor ground my arguments on the supposition that woman can render herself indifferent to exterior circumstances. But the same good Being who has given to the minutest insect some instrument of self preservation, sent not into the world the most beautiful creation of his hands to be the sport of circumstances, and the victim of feeling. . . .

It seems to be a prevalent idea that there is something wrong either in the education or in the position of woman. Her rights are discussed, her sphere disputed, and her very privileges seem to be subjects of doubt and inquiry. One claims for her a place in the halls of legislation, in the pulpit, the lecture-room, and at the polls. He would see her clad, like Joan of Arc, in the panoply of war, with helm on her head and shield at her heart. Another not less devoted to her happiness would make her, like the Lares,[1] a household divinity, presiding at the hearthstone—the mother of children, the tender nurse, the frugal housewife, and nothing more.

I think these contending advocates for the sex are both at fault in making exterior condition the source of female influence and happiness. If woman's mind and heart are right it is not of essential importance whether her opera-

SOURCE: Sarah C. Edgarton, "Female Culture," *Mother's Assistant*, Vol. III (1843), pp. 94–95.

[1] In ancient Rome, the benevolent gods of the household.

tions are in private, and upon her household, or whether they take a more open and blustering sphere of duty. The most she wants is not a character, a power and independence which erects "liberty poles," and shouts "freedom" from the forum; but the calm, still, holy consciousness of mental and moral power, the elevation and strength which is born of knowledge, of thought, and of self-reliance.

The education which will fit a woman to be the companion of man, in intellect, as well as in feeling, will subtract in the minutest degree, from those qualities which render her lovely in domestic life. Indeed, can any woman be so valuable to a husband, as one who is capable of sharing the confidence of his mind as well as his heart? She is but half wedded who cannot enter into the intellectual sympathies of her companion.

And then, again, woman is not necessarily born for marriage. She has the birthright of an independent existence; and to this birthright she owes reverence as a holy gift. Her motto should be "equal to either fortune"—and at all times let her remember, that though it may be expedient for her to marry, it is her privilege to be single.

Catharine Beecher (1846)

Ladies and Friends,

The immediate object which has called us together, is an enterprise now in progress, the design of which is *to educate destitute American children, by the agency of American women.* It is an effort which has engaged the exertions of a large number of ladies of various sects, and of all sections in our country, and one which, though commencing in a humble way and on a small scale, we believe is eventually to exert a most extensive and saving influence through the nation. . . .

Few are aware of the deplorable destitution of our country in regard to the education of the rising generation, or of the long train of wrongs and sufferings endured by multitudes of young children from this neglect.

The last twelve years I have resided chiefly at the West, and my attention has been directed to the various interests of education. In five of the largest western states I have spent from several weeks to several months—I have traveled extensively and have corresponded or conversed with well-informed gentlemen and ladies on this subject in most of the western states. And I now have materials for presenting the real situation of vast multitudes of American children, which would "cause the ear that heareth it to tingle." But I dare not do it. It would be so revolting—so disgraceful—so heart-rending—so incredible—that in the first place, I should not be believed; and

source: Catharine Beecher, *The Evils Suffered by American Women and American Children: The Causes and the Remedy* (New York: Harper and Brothers, 1846), pp. 3, 5–12.

in the next place, such an outcry of odium and indignation would be aroused as would impede efforts to remedy the evil. The only thing I can safely do is to present some statistics, which cannot be disputed, because they are obtained from *official documents,* submitted by civil officers to our national or state legislatures. Look then at the census, and by its data we shall find that *now* there are nearly *a million* adults who cannot read and write, and more than *two million* children utterly illiterate, and entirely without schools. Look at individual states, and we shall find Ohio and Kentucky, the two best supplied of our western states, demanding *five thousand* teachers each, to supply them in the same ratio as Massachusetts is supplied. *Ten thousand* teachers are now needed in Ohio and Kentucky alone, to furnish schools for more than two hundred thousand children, who otherwise must grow up in utter ignorance.

· · ·

Thus it is that two millions of American children are left without any teachers at all, while, of those who go to school, a large portion of the youngest and tenderest are turned over to coarse, hard, unfeeling men, too lazy or too stupid to follow the appropriate duties of their sex.

And thus it has come to pass, that while every intelligent man in the Union is reading and saying every day of his life that unless our children are trained to intelligence and virtue, the nation is ruined; yet there is nothing else for which so little interest is felt, or so little done. Look now at that great body of intelligent and benevolent persons, who are interesting themselves for patriotic and religious enterprises. We see them sustaining great organizations, and supporting men to devote their whole time to promote enterprises which draw thousands and hundreds of thousands [of dollars] for their support. There is one organization to send missionaries to the heathen and to educate heathen children; another to furnish the Bible; another to distribute tracts; another to educate young men to become ministers; another to send out home missionaries. . . . But our two millions of *little children,* who are growing up in heathenish darkness, enchained in ignorance, and in many cases, where the cold law provides for them, enduring distress of body and mind [from male teachers] greater than is inflicted on criminals, where is the benevolent association for their relief? Where is there a periodical supported by the charitable, to tell the tale of their wrongs? . . .

I wish now to point out certain causes which have exerted a depressing influence upon our sex in this land; for we shall find that the very same effort, which aims to benefit the children of our country, will tend almost equally to benefit our own sex. The first cause that bears heavily on our sex is the fact that in our country, the principle of *caste,* which is one of the strongest and most inveterate in our nature, is strongly arrayed against *healthful and productive labor.*

To understand the power of this principle, see what sacrifices men and women make, and what toils they endure, to save themselves from whatever sinks them in station and estimation. And this is a principle which is equally powerful in high and low, rich and poor. To observe how it bears against healthful and productive labor, let any woman, who esteems herself in the higher grades of society, put the case as her own, and imagine that her son, or brother, is about to marry a young lady, whose character and education are every way lovely and unexceptionable, but who, it appears, is a *seamstress*, or a *nurse*, or a *domestic*, and how few are there, who will not be conscious of the opposing principle of *caste*. But suppose the young lady to be one who has been earning her livelihood by writing poetry and love stories, or who has lived all her days in utter idleness, and how suddenly the feelings are changed! Now, all the comfort and happiness of society depend upon having that work properly performed, which is done by nurses, seamstresses, chamber-maids, and cooks; and so long as this kind of work is held to be degrading, and those who perform it are allowed to grow up ignorant and vulgar, and then are held down by the prejudices of caste, every woman will use the greatest efforts, and undergo the greatest privations, to escape from the degraded and discreditable position. And this state of society is now, by the natural course of things, bringing a just retribution on the classes who cherish it. Domestics are forsaking the kitchen, and thronging to the work-shop and manufactory, and *mainly* under the influence of the principle of *caste*; while the family state suffers keenly from the loss. Meantime the daughters of wealth have their intellectual faculties and their sensibilities developed, while all the household labor, which would equally develop their physical powers, and save from ill-health, is turned off to hired domestics, or a slaving mother. The only remedy for this evil is, securing a proper education for all classes, and making productive labor honorable, by having all classes engage in it.

The next cause which bears severely on the welfare of our sex, is the *excess of female population* in the older states from the disproportionate emigration of the other sex. By the census we find in only three of the small older states, *twenty thousand* more women than men, and a similar disproportion is found in other states. . . .

Meantime, capitalists at the East avail themselves of this excess of female hands. Large establishments are set up in eastern cities to manufacture cloth-ing. Work of all kinds is got from poor women, at prices that will not keep soul and body together; and then the articles thus made are sold for prices that give monstrous profits to the capitalist, who thus grows rich on the hard labors of our sex. Tales there are to be told of the sufferings of American women in our eastern cities, so shocking that they would scarcely be credited, and yet they are true beyond all dispute.

The following extracts, from some statistics recently obtained in New-York city, verify what has been stated.

"There are now in this city, according to close estimates, *ten thousand* women who live by the earnings of the needle. On an average, these women, by working twelve or fourteen hours-a-day, can earn only *twelve and a half cents*, with which they are to pay for rent, fuel, clothes, and food." Here follow the prices paid for various articles of women's work at the clothing stores, and then the following:—"A great multitude of women are employed in making men's and boys' caps. We are told by an old lady, who lives by this work, that when she begins at sunrise and works till midnight, she earns *fourteen cents a-day!* That is, *eighty-four cents* a-week, for incessant toil every waking hour, and this her sole income for every want! A large majority of these women are American born; some have been rich, many have enjoyed the ease of competence; some are young girls without homes; some are widows; some the wives of drunken husbands. The manner in which these women live; the squalidness, unhealthy location and nature of their habitations; their total want of recreation, or of intellectual or moral improvement; their forlorn situation in all respects, *may* be imagined, but we assure the public, that it would require an extremely active imagination to conceive the reality.

. . .

Let us now turn to another class of our countrywomen—the *female operatives* in our shops and mills. Unfortunately, this subject cannot be freely discussed without danger of collision with the vast pecuniary and party interests connected with it. I therefore shall simply *state facts*, without expressing the impressions of my own mind.

Last year, I spent several days in Lowell [Massachusetts], for the sole purpose of investigating this subject. I conversed with agents, overseers, clergymen, physicians, editors, ladies resident in the place, and a large number of the operatives themselves. All seemed disposed to present the most favorable side of the picture; and nothing unfavorable was said except as drawn forth by my questions. . . .

Let me now present the facts I learned by observation or inquiry on the spot. I was there in mid-winter, and every morning I was wakened at *five*, by the bells calling to labor. The time allowed for dressing and breakfast was so short, as many told me, that both were performed hurriedly, and then the work at the mills was begun by lamp-light, and prosecuted without remission till twelve, and chiefly in a standing position. Then half an hour only allowed for dinner, from which the time for going and returning was deducted. Then back to the mills, to work till seven o'clock, the last part of the time by lamp-light. Then returning, washing, dressing, and supper occupied another hour. Thus ten hours only remained for recreation and sleep. Now eight hours' sleep is required for laborers, and none in our country are employed in labor more hours than the female operatives in mills. Deduct eight hours for sleep and only *two hours* remain for shopping, mending, making, recreation, social intercourse, and *breathing the pure air*. For it must be remembered that all the hours of labor are spent in rooms where lamps, together with from forty to eighty persons, are exhausting the healthful principle of the air, where the temperature, both summer and winter, on account of the work, must be kept at 70°, and in some rooms at 80°, and where the air is loaded with particles of cotton thrown from thousands of cards, spindles, and looms.

. . .

In regard to *intellectual advantages,* such as night schools, lectures, reading, and composition, all time devoted to these must be taken from the hours required for recreation or needful repose. . . .

I asked one of the young operatives if they could not take turns in reading aloud while sewing. She replied that they were all either too tired, or they wished a little time to talk, and so they never succeeded when they attempted it. As to the periodical, the *Lowell Offering,* I found that out of six thousand women, many of them school-teachers, but about *twenty* were contributors to its pages, while the best pieces were written by the two lady editors, neither of whom are operatives, though both had been so at former periods. All written by actual operatives is probably done in hours which should have been given to sleep.

• • •

Now, without expressing any opinion as to the influence, on health and morals, of taking women away from domestic habits and pursuits, to labor with men in shops and mills, I simply ask if it would not be *better* to put the thousands of men who are keeping school for young children into the mills, and employ the women to train the children?

Wherever education is most prosperous, there woman is employed more than man. In Massachusetts, where education is highest, five out of seven of the teachers are women; while in Kentucky, where education is so much lower, five out of six of the teachers are men.

Another cause of depression to our sex is found in the fact that there is no profession for women of education and high position, which, like law, medicine, and theology, opens the way to competence, influence, and honor, and presents motives for exertion. Woman ought never to be led to married life except under the promptings of pure affection. To marry for an establishment, for a position, or for something to do, is a deplorable wrong. But how many women, for want of a high and honorable profession to engage their time, are led to this melancholy course. This is not so because Providence has not provided an ample place for such a profession for woman, but because custom or prejudice, or a low estimate of its honorable character, prevents her from entering it. The educating of children, that is the true and noble profession of a woman—that is what is worthy the noblest powers and affections of the noblest minds.

Another cause which deeply affects the best interests of our sex is the contempt, or utter neglect and indifference, which has befallen this only noble profession open to woman. There is no employment, however disagreeable or however wicked, which custom and fashion cannot render elegant, interesting, and enthusiastically sought. A striking proof of this is seen in the military profession. This is the profession of *killing our fellow-creatures,* and is attended with everything low, brutal, unchristian, and disgusting; and yet what halos of glory have been hung around it, and how the young, and generous, and enthusiastic have been drawn into it! If one-half the poetry, fiction, oratory, and taste thus misemployed had been used to embellish and elevate the employment of training the mind of childhood, in what an altered position should we find this noblest of all professions!

As it is, the employment of teaching children is regarded as the most wearying drudgery, and few resort to it except from necessity; and one very reasonable cause of this aversion is the utter neglect of any arrangements for *preparing* teachers for this arduous and difficult profession. The mind of a young child is like a curious instrument, capable of exquisite harmony when touched by a skillful hand, but sending forth only annoying harshness when unskillfully addressed. To a teacher is committed a collection of these delicate contrivances; and, without experience, without instruction, it is required not only that each one should be tuned aright, but that all be combined in excellent harmony: as if a young girl were sent into a splendid orchestra, all ignorant and unskillful, and required to draw melody from each instrument, and then to combine the whole in faultless harmony. And in each case there are, here and there, individual minds, who, without instruction, are gifted by nature with aptness and skill in managing the music either of matter or of mind; but that does not lessen the folly, in either case, of expecting the whole profession, either of music or of teaching, to be pursued without preparatory training.

.   .   .

There is another class of evils, endured by a large class of well-educated, unmarried women of the more wealthy classes, little understood or appreciated, but yet real and severe. It is the suffering that results from the *inactivity of cultivated intellect and feeling.*

.   .   .

Now every woman whose intellect and affections are properly developed is furnished for just such an illustrious work as this [teaching]. And when such large capacities and affections are pent up and confined to the trifling pursuits that ordinarily engage our best educated young women between school life and marriage, suffering, and often keen suffering, is the inevitable result. There is a restless, anxious longing for they know not what; while exciting amusements are vainly sought to fill the aching void. A teacher, like myself, who for years has been training multitudes of such minds, and learning their private history and secret griefs, knows, as no others can, the great amount of suffering among some of the loveliest and best of the youthful portion of our sex from this cause. True, every young lady *might*, the moment she leaves the school-room, commence the exalted labor of molding young minds for eternity, who again would transmit her handiwork from spirit to spirit, till thousands and thousands receive honor and glory from her hands. But the customs and prejudices of society forbid; and instead of this, a little working of muslin and worsted, a little light reading, a little calling and shopping, and a great deal of the high stimulus of fashionable amusement, are all the aliment her starving spirit finds. And alas! Christian parents find no way to remedy this evil! . . .

It is the high character of my countrywomen, and the great power and influence they thus command, which has been my chief encouragement in laboring in this cause. In the aristocratic countries of Europe, the wrongs of the neglected and oppressed are so inwrought in the framework of society, that it is an almost hopeless task to attempt to rectify them. All that can be done is to try to *alleviate, at least a little*. But to us opens a fairer prospect. Every one of the evils here portrayed, it is in the power of American women fully to remedy and remove. Nothing is wanting but a knowledge of the evils, and a well-devised plan for uniting the energies of our countrywomen in the effort, and the thing will be speedily and gloriously achieved.

It is the immediate object of this enterprise now presented, to engage American women to exert the great power and influence put into their hands, to remedy the evils which now oppress their countrywomen, and thus, at the same time, and by the same method, to secure a proper education to the vast multitude of neglected American children all over our land.

The plan is, to begin on a small scale, and to take women already qualified intellectually to teach, and possessed of missionary zeal and benevolence, and, after some further training, to send them to the most ignorant portions of our land, to raise up schools, to instruct in morals and piety, and to teach the domestic arts and virtues. The commencement of this enterprise, until we gain confidence by experiment and experience, will be as the opening of a very small sluice. But so great is the number of educated and unemployed women at the East, and so great the necessity for teachers at the West, that as soon as the stream begins to move, it will grow wider and deeper and stronger, till it becomes as the river of life, carrying health and verdure to every part of our land. . . .

This will prove the true remedy for all those *wrongs of women* which her mistaken champions are seeking to cure by drawing her into professions and pursuits which belong to the other sex. When all the mothers, teachers, nurses, and domestics are taken from our sex, which the best interests of society demand, and when all these employments are deemed *respectable*, and are filled by *well-educated* women, there will be no supernumeraries found to put into shops and mills, or to draw into the arena of public and political life.

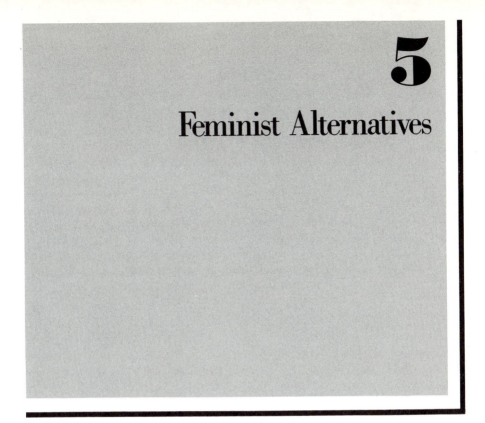

5

Feminist Alternatives

A. Militant Mill-Girls

• *Harriet Robinson* (1898)

We have seen how debates over the nature of family government and the socialization of children led to changing conceptions of female influence. While the *Young Lady's Own Book* claimed in 1833 that woman's "domestic comfort is the chief source of her influence," by the 1840s Catharine Beecher not only demanded that women be given a critical public role as teachers but pointed to the reality of exploited female labor in factories and sweatshops. Of course, most American women had always worked—at preserving and preparing food, for example, and at spinning yarn, weaving cloth, and making clothes, candles, and other household necessities (in the South, slave women did heavy field work). From the 1820s on, however, there was a marked decline in household production, except on the frontier or as "out work" for merchants who furnished the materials and marketed the product. As the selection below makes clear, the changing nature of women's work could seem liberating—in contrast to women's slavish subordination in many households, a factory at least offered female companionship and independent earnings, however small. Harriet Robinson notes that desperate wives sometimes fled to factories as a refuge from punitive husbands. But while Robinson's view of the Lowell mills is generally more favorable than that of Catharine Beecher, she also underscores women's economic dependence and marginal economic role. When read together with the selection by Lucy Larcom (Part 3, E), we glimpse a system where female wage-earners contributed the necessary margin for family subsistence, for male upward mobility or male education.

Harriet Hanson Robinson (1825–1911) was born in Boston, the daughter of a carpenter who died when she was six. At age ten she began working as a bobbin doffer[1] in a Lowell textile mill, and she was only eleven when she participated in the strike of 1836 described below. Such strikes against wage-cutting were the first manifestation of collective protest by women. Harriet Hanson—she did not marry William S. Robinson, an antislavery journalist, until 1848—was one of the few links between such labor militancy and the later feminist movement. Taking full advantage of the schools and libraries provided by paternalistic mill-owners, she became a contributor to the *Lowell Offering* and then a coworker with her husband in the antislavery cause. After the Civil War, Mrs. Robinson was a feminist leader, working closely with Susan B. Anthony in the National Woman Suffrage Association. The selection here should be read as the reminiscence of an elderly veteran of the women's rights cause.

Harriet Robinson (1898)

The laws relating to women were such, that a husband could claim his wife wherever he found her, and also the children she was trying to shield from his influence; and I have seen more than one poor woman skulk behind her loom or her frame when visitors were approaching the end of the aisle where she worked. Some of these [women] were known under assumed names, to prevent their husbands from trusteeing their wages.[2] It was a very common thing for a male person of a certain kind to do this, thus depriving his wife of all her wages, perhaps, month after month.

· · ·

The law took no cognizance of woman as a money-spender. She was a ward, an appendage, a relict [remnant]. Thus it happened, that if a woman did not choose to marry, or, when left a widow, to re-marry, she had no

---

SOURCE: Harriet Robinson, *Loom and Spindle, or Life Among the Early Mill Girls* (Boston: T. Y. Crowell, 1898), pp. 66–69, 76–77, 83–85.

[1] A doffer removes full bobbins from a textile machine.
[2] That is, garnishing their wages, as a creditor might do to a debtor. Legally, a husband had claim to his wife's earnings and property.

choice but to enter one of the few employments open to her, or to become a burden on the charity of some relative.

In almost every New England home could be found one or more of these women, sometimes welcome, more often unwelcome, and leading joyless, and in many instances unsatisfactory, lives. The cotton-factory was a great opening to these lonely and dependent women. From a condition approaching pauperism they were at once placed above want; they could earn money, and spend it as they pleased.

. . .

Some of the mill-girls helped maintain widowed mothers, or drunken, incompetent, or invalid fathers. Many of them educated the younger children of the family, and young men were sent to college with the money furnished by the untiring industry of their women relatives.

Indeed, the most prevailing incentive to our labor was to secure the means of education for some *male* member of the family. To make a *gentleman* of a brother or a son, to give him a college education, was the dominant thought in the minds of a great many of these provident mill-girls. I have known more than one to give every cent of her wages, month after month, to her brother, that he might get the education necessary to enter some profession.

. . .

ONE of the first strikes of cotton-factory operatives that ever took place in this country was in Lowell, in October, 1836. When it was announced that the wages were to be cut down, great indignation was felt, and it was decided to strike, *en masse*. This was done. The mills were shut down, and the girls went in procession from their several corporations to the "grove" on Chapel Hill, and listened to "incendiary" speeches from early labor reformers.

One of the girls stood on a pump, and gave vent to the feelings of her companions in a neat speech, declaring that it was their duty to resist all attempts at cutting down the wages. This was the first time a woman had spoken in public in Lowell, and the event caused surprise and consternation among her audience.

. . .

My own recollection of this first strike (or "turn out" as it was called) is very vivid. I worked in a lower room, where I had heard the proposed strike fully, if not vehemently, discussed: I had been an ardent listener to what was said against this attempt at "oppression" on the part of the corporation, and naturally I took sides with the strikers. When the day came on which the girls were to turn out, those in the upper rooms started first, and so many of them left that our mill was at once shut down. Then, when the girls in my room stood irresolute, uncertain what to do, asking each other, "Would you?" or "Shall we turn out?" and not one of them having the courage to lead off, I, who began to think they would not go out, after all their talk, became impatient, and started on ahead, saying, with childish bravado, "I don't care what you do, *I* am going to turn out, whether any one else does or not"; and I marched out, and was followed by the others.

As I looked back at the long line that followed me, I was more proud than I have ever been since at any success I may have achieved, and more proud than I shall ever be again until my own beloved state gives to its women citizens the right of suffrage.

B. The Discovery of Female Enslavement

- *Sarah Grimké* (1838)
- *Wendell Phillips* (1840)
- *"Declaration of Sentiments"* (1848)
- *The* Lowell Courier's *Response* (1848)

The following selections are not intended to present a rounded picture of the early feminist movement, but rather to illustrate the relationship between feminist protest and the wider themes of domestic order, sexual roles, and the search for noncoercive bonds of unity. In other words, we are concerned with the effect on the traditional limits of sexual identity and domestic relations of expanding boundaries of possibility—in Channing's words, the faith that "we can fix our eyes on perfection, and make almost everything speed us towards it."

By the 1830s, women were actively involved in labor reform and made up an indispensable core of the rank-and-file supporters of temperance and antislavery. While there had long been isolated advocates of women's rights, the immediate source of feminist agitation was resentment over attempts by male reformers to impose traditional sexual restrictions on the public activities of female abolitionists.

Sarah Grimké (1792–1873) was one of the first abolitionists to test the boundaries of sexual propriety and to launch a counterattack against the entire ideology that limited women's moral influence to a segregated "sphere." She was the very model of a "self-formed" woman. Along with her younger sister Angelina, she cast off her heritage as the daughter of a wealthy, slaveholding South Carolina family; she abandoned Episcopalianism for Quakerism, and then rebelled against the discipline of orthodox Quakerism. As a convert to militant abolitionism, she captivated audiences of New England women and then defied the taboo against lecturing to mixed crowds of both sexes. It was the resulting furor, especially from the clergy, that provoked her public defense of sexual equality. On the surface, Grimké seems to share many of Catharine Beecher's complaints—a contempt for "fashionable" women, a scorn for the idea that woman's highest calling is serving a husband, and an outrage over inequalities in wages and education. But whereas Beecher feared drawing women "into the arena of public and political life," Grimké saw sexual segregation as a counterpart to racial "spheres" in the South—that is, as a justification for the supremacy of one group and the enslavement of another.

By 1840, when American abolitionists traveled to London for the first World's Anti-Slavery Convention, the American antislavery movement had become deeply divided over the issue of women's rights. The conservatives who insisted on confining women to a separate sphere of activity had withdrawn from the American Anti-Slavery Society, giving control to the radical followers of William Lloyd Garrison. At London, a controversy immediately exploded over the seating of delegates to the convention—or more specifically, over whether women would be barred from *access* to a public forum and public influence even when they carried credentials naming them as official representatives of American antislavery organizations. The debate opened when Wendell Phillips (1811–1884), a wealthy Boston Brahmin, a spellbinding orator, and a Garrisonian, moved that a committee be appointed to prepare a correct list of all members of the convention including all persons bearing credentials from any antislavery body. Here, in an excerpt from the resulting debate, Phillips answers the charge that seating women would offend British public opinion. A Glasgow minister then contends that separate sexual spheres have been ordained by the Word of God —an argument that carried enormous weight in America as well as Britain.

Female abolitionists were permanently embittered by the decision to exclude them from open participation in an international convention, a convention supposedly dedicated to the high moral cause of universal emancipation. Increasingly, they saw parallels between their own powerlessness and the legal status of slaves. Lucretia Mott (1793–1880) and Elizabeth Cady Stanton (1815–1902), two of the women who had felt humiliated at the London convention, continued to ponder the grievances of women. In 1848 they organized at Seneca Falls, New York the first convention in history devoted to women's rights. In drafting a "Declaration of Sentiments" modeled on the Declaration of Independence, Stanton included the right of suffrage. One of her few supporters on this point was the former slave and prominent black abolitionist, Frederick Douglass. The Declaration was signed by sixty-eight women and thirty-two men. The excerpt from the *Lowell Courier* is a sample of the kind of condescending ridicule heaped on the early feminists.

Sarah Grimké (1838)

During the early part of my life, my lot was cast among the butterflies of the *fashionable* world; and of this class of women, I am constrained to say, both from experience and observation, that their education is miserably deficient; that they are taught to regard marriage as the one thing needful, the only

SOURCE: Sarah Grimké, *Letters on the Equality of the Sexes and the Condition of Women* (Boston: Issac Knapp, 1838), pp. 46–48, 50–51.

avenue to distinction; hence to attract the notice and win the attentions of men, by their external charms, is the chief business of fashionable girls. They seldom think that men will be allured by intellectual acquirements, because they find, that where any mental superiority exists, a woman is generally shunned and regarded as stepping out of her "appropriate sphere," which, in their view, is to dress, to dance, to set out to the best possible advantage her person, to read the novels which inundate the press, and which do more to destroy her character as a rational creature, than any thing else. Fashionable women regard themselves, and are regarded by men, as pretty toys or as mere instruments of pleasure. . . .

There is another and much more numerous class in this country, who are withdrawn by education or circumstances from the circle of fashionable amusements, but who are brought up with the dangerous and absurd idea, that *marriage* is a kind of preferment; and that to be able to keep their husband's house, and render his situation comfortable, is the end of her being. Much that she does and says and thinks is done in reference to this situation; and to be married is too often held up to the view of girls as the *sine qua non* of human happiness and human existence. For this purpose more than for any other, I verily believe the majority of girls are trained.

• • •

There is another way in which the general opinion, that women are inferior to men, is manifested, that bears with tremendous effect on the laboring class, and indeed on almost all who are obliged to earn a subsistence, whether it be by mental or physical exertion—I allude to the disproportionate value set on the time and labor of men and of women. A man who is engaged in teaching, can always, I believe, command a higher price for tuition than a woman—even when he teaches the same branches, and is not in any respect superior to the woman. This I know is the case in boarding and other schools with which I have been acquainted, and it is so in every occupation in which the sexes engage indiscriminately. As for example, in tailoring, a man has twice, or three times as much for making a waistcoat or pantaloons as a woman, although the work done by each may be equally good. In those employments which are peculiar to women, their time is estimated at only half the value of that of men. A woman who goes out to wash, works as hard in proportion as a wood sawyer, or a coal heaver, but she is not generally able to make more than half as much by a day's work.

Wendell Phillips (1840)

[Wendell Phillips, of Massachusetts]: I would merely ask whether any man can suppose that the delegates from Massachusetts or Pennsylvania can take upon their shoulders the responsibility of withdrawing that list of delegates

SOURCE: Elizabeth Cady Stanton, *et al., History of Woman Suffrage,* Vol. I (Rochester, N.Y.: Fowler and Wells, 1889), pp. 58–59.

from your table, which their constituents told them to place there, and whom they sanctioned as their fit representatives, because this Convention tells us that it is not ready to meet the ridicule of the morning papers, and to stand up against the customs of England. In America we listen to no such arguments. If we had done so we had never been here as abolitionists. It is the custom there not to admit colored men into respectable society, and we have been told again and again that we are outraging the decencies of humanity when we permit colored men to sit by our side. When we have submitted to brick-bats, and the tar tub and feathers in America, rather than yield to the custom prevalent there of not admitting colored brethren into our friendship, shall we yield to parallel custom or prejudice against women in Old England? We can not yield this question if we would; for it is a matter of conscience. But we would not yield it on the ground of expediency. In doing so we should feel that we were striking off the right arm of our enterprise. We could not go back to America to ask for any aid from the women of Massachusetts if we had deserted them, when they chose to send out their own sisters as their representatives here. We could not go back to Massachusetts and assert the unchangeableness of spirit on the question. We have argued it over and over again, and decided it time after time, in every society in the land, in favor of the women. We have not changed by crossing the water. We stand here the advocates of the same principle that we contend for in America. We think it right for women to sit by our side there, and we think it right for them to do the same here.

• • •

The Rev. A. Harvey, of Glasgow: It was stated by a brother from America, that with him it is a matter of conscience, and it is a question of conscience with me too. I have certain views in relation to the teaching of the Word of God, and of the particular sphere in which woman is to act. I must say, whether I am right in my interpretations of the Word of God or not, that my own decided convictions are, if I were to give a vote in favor of females, sitting and deliberating in such an assembly as this, that I should be acting in opposition to the plain teaching of the Word of God. I may be wrong, but I have a conscience on the subject, and I am sure there are a number present of the same mind.

"Declaration of Sentiments" (1848)

The history of mankind is a history of repeated injuries and usurpations on the part of man toward woman, having in direct object the establishment of an absolute tyranny over her. To prove this, let facts be submitted to a candid world.

He has never permitted her to exercise her inalienable right to the elective franchise.

SOURCE: Stanton, *et al.*, *History of Woman Suffrage*, Vol. I, pp. 70–71.

He has compelled her to submit to laws, in the formation of which she had no voice.

He has withheld from her rights which are given to the most ignorant and degraded men—both natives and foreigners.

Having deprived her of this first right of a citizen, the elective franchise, thereby leaving her without representation in the halls of legislation, he has oppressed her on all sides.

He has made her, if married, in the eye of the law, civilly dead.

He has taken from her all right in property, even to the wages she earns.

He has made her, morally, an irresponsible being, as she can commit many crimes with impunity, provided they be done in the presence of her husband. In the covenant of marriage, she is compelled to promise obedience to her husband, he becoming, to all intents and purposes, her master—the law giving him power to deprive her of her liberty, and to administer chastisement.

He has so framed the laws of divorce, as to what shall be the proper causes, and in case of separation, to whom the guardianship of the children shall be given, as to be wholly regardless of the happiness of women—the law, in all cases, going upon a false supposition of the supremacy of man, and giving all power into his hands.

After depriving her of all rights as a married woman, if single, and the owner of property, he has taxed her to support a government which recognizes her only when her property can be made profitable to it.

He has monopolized nearly all the profitable employments, and from those she is permitted to follow, she receives but a scanty remuneration. He closes against her all the avenues to wealth and distinction which he considers most honorable to himself. As a teacher of theology, medicine, or law, she is not known.

He has denied her the facilities for obtaining a thorough education, all colleges being closed against her.

He allows her in church, as well as state, but a subordinate position, claiming apostolic authority for her exclusion from the ministry, and, with some exceptions, from any public participation in the affairs of the church.

He has created a false public sentiment by giving to the world a different code of morals for men and women, by which moral delinquencies which exclude women from society, are not only tolerated, but deemed of little account in man.

He has usurped the prerogative of Jehovah himself, claiming it as his right to assign for her a sphere of action, when that belongs to her conscience and to her God.

He has endeavored, in every way that he could, to destroy her confidence in her own powers, to lessen her self-respect, and to make her willing to lead a dependent and abject life.

Now, in view of this entire disfranchisement of one-half the people of this country, their social and religious degradation—in view of the unjust laws above mentioned, and because women do feel themselves aggrieved, oppressed, and fraudulently deprived of their most sacred rights, we insist that they have immediate admission to all the rights and privileges which belong to them as citizens of the United States.

The *Lowell Courier's* Response (1848)

"Progress," is the grand bubble which is now blown up to balloon bulk by the windy philosophers of the age. The women folks have just held a convention up in New York State, and passed a sort of "bill of rights," affirming it their right to vote, to become teachers, legislators, lawyers, divines, and to do all and sundries the "lords" may, and of right now do. They should have resolved at the same time, that it was obligatory also upon the "lords" aforesaid, to wash dishes, scour up, be put to the tub, handle the broom, darn stockings, patch breeches, scold the servants, dress in the latest fashion, wear trinkets, look beautiful, and be as fascinating as those blessed morsels of humanity whom God gave to preserve that rough animal man, in something like a reasonable civilization. "Progress!" Progress, forever!

C. "Discordant and Disordered Households"

• *The Lily (1849 and 1855)*

Amelia Jenks Bloomer (1818–1894) attended the Seneca Falls convention but did not sign the "Declaration of Sentiments." Her magazine, *The Lily*, initially focused on temperance, education, and unjust marriage laws, but then became devoted to "the Emancipation of Woman from Intemperance, Injustice, Prejudice and Bigotry." Its columns, letters, and reprintings from other papers show how the feminist challenge led to a reexamination of the realities of marriage, home, and family—supposedly the very source of social cohesion and responsible self-government (as we have seen in the first selections of Unit One). Note that by 1855 the editor (Mrs. Bloomer had by then sold the periodical) feels free to publish a letter proclaiming that "marriage is the *slavery of woman*," but admits to censoring remarks on "free love."

SOURCE: From the *Lowell* [Mass.] *Courier*. Reprinted in Stanton, *et al.*, *History of Woman Suffrage*, Vol. I (appendix), p. 804.

The Lily (1849)

I am anxious to say a few words about *Home*. The song tells us "there is no place like" it. And the song is right. But how few homes there are in the world! Or how many "homes which are no homes!" It is enough to make one sick to look at it. Not one home in ten is deserving of the name. And what wonder! Look at it.

A young man meets a pretty face in the ballroom, falls in love with it, courts it, "marries it," goes to housekeeping with it—and boasts of having a home to go to, and a wife. The chances are nine to ten he has neither. His pretty face soon gets to be an old story—or becomes faded or freckled, or fretted—and as that face was all he wanted, all he "paid attention to," all he sat up with, all he bargained for, all he swore to "love, honor, and pro-tect,"—he gets sick of his trade; knows a dozen faces which he likes better; gives up staying at home evenings; consoles himself with cigars, oysters, whiskey punch and politics; and looks upon his "home" as a very indifferent boarding house. A family of children grow up about him; but neither he nor his "face" knows anything about training them; so they come up helter-skelter—made toys of when babies, dolls when boys and girls, drudges when young men and women—and so passing year after year, and not one quiet, happy, hearty, homely hour is known throughout the whole household.

.   .   .

There are many other kinds of ill-assorted "marriages," and they all result in unhappy "homes." What else could be expected?—Young folks get their ideas of the holiest relation in life from the novel. Or when this is not the case, they, in most instances, have no idea at all of it, but are governed in their choice and conduct by their feelings, their passions, or their imagined interests. Thus the marriage union is prostituted throughout the civilized world, and the terrible retribution is seen in myriads of discordant and dis-ordered households.

The Lily (1855)

There is no more important question than this of marriage, and the time has now come to give it a thorough examination. In order to arrive at the truth on any subject, it is necessary that all the various and conflicting views in relation to it be presented and examined, and the advocates of the different theories be allowed the most perfect freedom in presenting the views they may entertain.

SOURCE: "Home Sweet Home," from the Lynn *Pioneer*. Reprinted in *The Lily*, Vol. I (Seneca Falls, N.Y., February 1, 1849).

SOURCE: Letter on "the marriage institution." Printed in *The Lily*, Vol. VII (July 15, 1855).

In speaking of marriage, we, of course, speak of it as it *is*, and not of a system that *might* be, called marriage. My first point, then, is (and which no advocate of Woman's Rights can dispute) that marriage *as it is*, is such an outrage upon justice and purity, so degrading to woman, so destructive to all humanity's highest interests, that a system worthy to be embraced and cherished must be so entirely different from it, as to deserve a different name.

Marriage is the *slavery of woman*. Marriage does not differ, in any of its essential features, from chattel slavery. The slave's earnings belong to the master, the earnings of the wife belong to the husband. The right of another to claim one's earnings, constitutes one a slave. In this respect, the essential feature of slavery, the wife and the chattel slave stand on a level. They may wear fine clothes, and "fare sumptuously every day," but in both cases the clothes they wear and the food they eat is the property of the master, and may be changed or withheld at his pleasure. If woman is endowed with one right more sacred than another, it is the right to her own children; but the wife nor the slave mother have no such right. In either case the legal owner of the child, as well as the mother, may separate them at will. Either the master or the husband, in his conduct, may be manly and pure; but it is, in either case, simply because she is too good [for him] to exercise the power placed in his hands. If there is any difference between chattel slavery and the popular system of marriage, that difference is incidental and not essential.

FRANCIS BARRY.

Berlin Heights, Ohio, June, '55.

We have taken the liberty to omit a portion of this communication—not because we have any fears of "Error, when truth is left free to combat it," but because a discussion about "Free Love" would, in our view, be of no benefit to our readers.

D. A House Divided: Divorce

• *Ernestine Potowsky Rose* (*1860*)

Feminists divided over the question of divorce. At the Tenth National Women's Rights Convention, Wendell Phillips moved to table resolutions for easier divorce on the grounds that disputes over marriage were unrelated to the goals of the women's rights movement and could only damage the cause. This position was unsuccessfully challenged by Ernestine Potowsky Rose (1810–1892). Born in Russian Poland, the daughter of a rabbi, Ernestine Potowsky had rebelled at an early age against the subordination of Jewish women. In England, she had become associated with a group of radical reformers, one of whom she married. After emigrating to America in 1836, she and her husband had led the fight in New York State for a law granting married women the right to own property. A socialist and free-thinker (rejecting all institutional religion), Mrs. Rose became known as

"Queen of the Platform" as she toured many states lecturing on antislavery, temperance, and women's rights. From the mid-1850s to the great struggles for woman suffrage after the Civil War, she was a close friend and asssociate of Susan B. Anthony. Though in the following selection Mrs. Rose seems to represent the antithesis of Heman Humphrey (Part 1, A) and to fulfill his worst fears of a "house divided," she sees herself as an upholder of "true marriages" which will be strengthened by removing the barrier of "indissolubility."

In actuality, by the 1860s several states had adopted divorce laws that were even more permissive than the one Rose proposed. In Connecticut, for example, divorce could be granted for any "misconduct" that "permanently destroys the happiness of the petitioner and defeats the purposes of the marriage relation." Ironically, by the 1880s a new group of reformers, inspired by religious ideals similar to those of Heman Humphrey, succeeded in repealing such liberal legislation and in making divorce more difficult. It is conceivable that this reaction owed something to the insistence on unity engendered by the Civil War and to the frank acceptance of coercion as a means for keeping "houses," whether families or nations, together.

Ernestine Potowsky Rose (1860)

ERNESTINE L. ROSE said:—Mrs. President—The question of a divorce law seems to me one of the greatest importance to all parties, but I presume that the very advocacy of divorce will be called "Free Love." For my part (and I wish distinctly to define my position), I do not know what others understand by that term; to me, in its truest significance, love must be free, or it ceases to be love. In its low and degrading sense, it is not love at all, and I have as little to do with its name as its reality.

· · ·

Mr. [Horace] Greeley tells us, that, marriage being a Divine institution, nothing but death should ever separate the parties; but when he was asked, "Would you have a being who, innocent and inexperienced, in the youth and ardor of affection, in the fond hope that the sentiment was reciprocated, united herself to one she loved and cherished, and then found (no matter from what cause) that his profession was false, his heart hollow, his acts cruel, that she was degraded by his vice, despised for his crimes, cursed by his very presence, and treated with every conceivable ignominy—would you have her drag out a miserable existence as his wife?" "No, no," says he; "in

SOURCE: Speech of Ernestine Potowsky Rose at Tenth National Woman Rights Convention, New York, May 10–11, 1860. Printed in Stanton, *et al.*, *History of Woman Suffrage*, Vol. I, pp. 729–31.

that case, they ought to separate." Separate? But what becomes of the union divinely instituted, which death only should part? (Applause.)

. . .

But what is marriage? A human institution, called out by the needs of social, affectional human nature, for human purposes, its objects are, first, the happiness of the parties immediately concerned, and, secondly, the welfare of society. Define it as you please, these are only its objects; and therefore if, from well-ascertained facts, it is demonstrated that the real objects are frustrated, that instead of union and happiness, there are only discord and misery to themselves, and vice and crime to society, I ask, in the name of individual happiness and social morality and well-being, why such a marriage should be binding for life?—why one human being should be chained for life to the dead body of another? "But they may separate and still remain married." What a perversion of the very term! Is that the union which "death only should part"? . . .

I therefore ask for a divorce law. Divorce is now granted for some crimes; I ask it for others also. It is granted for a state's prison offense. I ask that personal cruelty to a wife, whom he swore to "love, cherish, and protect," may be made a heinous crime—a perjury and a state's prison offense, for which divorce shall be granted. Willful desertion for one year should be a sufficient cause for divorce, for the willful deserter forfeits the sacred title of husband or wife. Habitual intemperance, or any other vice which makes the husband or wife intolerable and abhorrent to the other, ought to be sufficient cause for divorce. I ask for a law of divorce, so as to secure the real objects and blessing of married life, to prevent the crimes and immoralities now practiced, to prevent "Free Love," in its most hideous form, such as is now carried on but too often under the very name of marriage, where hypocrisy is added to the crime of legalized prostitution. "Free Love," in its degraded sense, asks for no divorce law. It acknowledges no marriage, and therefore requires no divorce. I believe in true marriages, and therefore I ask for a law to free men and women from false ones. (Applause.)

But it is said that if divorce were easily granted, "men and women would marry to-day and unmarry to-morrow." Those who say that, only prove that they have no confidence in themselves, and therefore can have no confidence in others. But the assertion is false; it is a libel on human nature. It is the indissoluble chain that corrodes the flesh. Remove the indissolubility, and there would be less separation than now, for it would place the parties on their good behavior, the same as during courtship.

Unit Two

Struggles Over Access to Wealth and Power

Introduction

In Unit One we began with the family and schoolroom as agencies for internalizing a form of self-government intended to provide the foundation, in the absence of authoritarian institutions, for noncoercive order, stability, and community. We concluded with debates over the limits of women's sphere and influence, and with a radical challenge to the patriarchal family as a remnant of the undemocratic and hierarchical societies of the Old World. The feminist demand for equal rights and privileges ties in with the central theme of Unit Two: the struggle over the ground rules—political, economic, and constitutional—governing the *access* of individuals and groups to wealth and power.

By the 1820s, there was sudden and widespread concern over the definition or redefinition of such rules. The death of hallowed figures like John Adams and Thomas Jefferson (who both died on July 4, 1826, exactly fifty years after the adoption of the Declaration of Independence) symbolized the passing of a heroic generation of Founding Fathers who, at least in nostalgic retrospect, had succeeded in balancing individual liberty with republican simplicity, order, and self-restraint. While Americans of the 1820s reaffirmed their loyalty to republican institutions, congratulated themselves on their growing prosperity, and rededicated themselves to the high mission of leading the world toward liberty, they also voiced a multitude of fears: fears that public virtue was giving way to the selfish pursuit of wealth; that communities which had once been well-ordered and like-minded were dissolving into competitive factions, sects, and classes; that the interests of the honest, hard-working majority were being subverted by fraud, conspiracy, secret societies, or alliances between powerful bankers, merchants, and politicians. The effectiveness of rules, whether in a game or in society at large, depends on mutual trust that the rules will be observed and that they conform to fundamental standards of equity and justice. At bottom, what characterized the 1820s and 1830s was a mood of uncertainty that severely strained the fragile networks of American trust.

This uncertainty was largely a response to the great unleashing of expansive energies in the period from 1815 to the mid-1830s—a period following the Napoleonic wars and the War of 1812 when both America and Western Europe plunged through dizzying stages of economic growth punctuated by sudden shocks of financial crisis. In America, the financial panic of 1819 ended a period of wild land speculation fueled by the reckless expansion of credit. The subsequent depression aroused widespread hostility, particularly among farmers and artisans, toward banking corporations and other groups that had used political influence to gain economic privilege. This demand for equality of opportunity was only intensified by economic recovery which was accompanied in the 1820s by the fastest rate of urbanization of any decade in the nineteenth century. Adding to the sense of revolutionary change was the incredibly rapid settlement of regions from New York State to the Ohio and Mississippi valleys; the beginning of the "transportation revolution" with its destructive impact on local markets and household industries; and an increase in regional specialization, most dramatically marked by the extension of cotton cultivation in the Old Southwest and the rise of textile manufacturing in New England. Though most Americans professed to believe in maximizing growth and opportunity while ensuring the orderly creation of new communities, they grew more watchful and suspicious as rival leaders, interests, towns, states, and regions maneuvered to win a larger share of the rewards generated by national expansion. What some men interpreted as making the most of opportunity, others interpreted as sharp practice, fraud, or conspiracy. In a world where anything seemed possible and nothing certain, it became difficult to apply traditional standards of a fair price, of contractual rights, of liability for one's dependents—standards that presumed that "morality" was not a category to be isolated from "economics" or "the law."

Since our approach to such questions is thematic, the selections in Unit Two cut across the conventional boundaries of social, economic, legal, and political history. Disputes over rules governing access to wealth and power imply a prior drive, quest, or aspiration. Hence, Part 1 concerns "the anxious spirit of gain," a phrase used by a Whig essayist in 1845 to describe the American people's obsession with work, ambition, and getting ahead. The questions raised by this phrase involve more than the traditional European contempt for American "materialism" or a snobbish disdain for money-getting on the part of people who have already gotten their money, although both these elements may be detected in certain selections. What is the meaning for humanity, the selections seem to ask, when the onrush of history removes most previous barriers to thought, effort, and aspiration? One may begin with the enormous release of individual energy, the almost frantic willingness to try new routes for fear, as Alexis de Tocqueville puts it, "of missing the shortest cut to happiness." This risk-taking drive and acceptance of impermanence leads us on to such classic exhibits of American go-getting as building-lot speculation in early Chicago and gold prospecting in California. Concern over the disintegration of all conceptions of stability, predictability, and community is mixed with almost admiring wonder at American audacity. The spectacle of striking it rich becomes so commonplace, prices and expectations become so absurd, that a new kind of community seems to arise from the very sharing of absurdity and unpredictable luck. Yet the selections on California by Walter Colton and Bayard Taylor also suggest that this mood of "practical equality" and trust is limited to those who share at least theoretical access to the gambling casino of life. There are Indians and Mexicans who stand outside, as well as other outsiders we shall come to in Unit Three.

Land was the great and seemingly inexhaustible source of American wealth and power. After the Revolution, the creation of a viable nation depended essentially on the cession of the western land claims of the original states to the federal government, and on shaping an acceptable and workable national policy for "extinguishing" Indian claims; for surveying, dividing, and classifying the public domain; and for encouraging orderly settlement. Such a policy was framed and implemented in the early national period (1783– 1820). In Part 2 we move on to several representative responses, beginning with the demand for free homesteads as both a natural right and a prerequisite for economic independence. Originally, this "agrarian" demand for equal access to the public domain came not from Western farmers but from radical artisans and other urban "working men" who regarded the sale of public property as an encouragement to monopoly and special privilege. In subsequent selections, we trace the growing tension between the appeal to political pressure—"Vote Yourself a Farm"—and the traditional Anglo-American assumption that society can remain free only so long as law protects private property from the tyranny of demagogues who play on the ignorance and cupidity of the majority. "Law," in this conservative sense, did not mean statutes enacted by legislators who might be susceptible to momentary public passion or corruption, but the esoteric and somewhat mysterious body of English rules and precedents known as the common law.

The common law, further defined in Part 3, was hailed by conservatives like Supreme Court Justice Joseph Story as the great stabilizing and boundary-making institution so desperately needed in a land of constant flux and uncertainty. Like the family as portrayed in Unit One, the common law was supposedly a source of unchanging norms and principles that would make democracy safe, restricting the powers of reckless legislators, ensuring the rights of property and of unpopular minorities, protecting the interests of posterity against the short-sighted needs of what Jefferson called "the living generation." But also like the family, the common law could not be insulated from the pragmatic and egalitarian influences of American society. The law was interpreted or "expounded" not by demigods but by judges who represented particular class and regional interests within "the living generation." Hence, in Part 3 we consider the attacks on "judge-made law" and on the "artificial barriers" imposed by common law, and then turn to some of the crucial transformations of common-law principles, especially with respect to "waste," contract, and legal liability.

The main thrust of such transformations was toward laissez-faire—toward freeing entrepreneurs from the legal risks and restrictions associated with traditional concepts of fair exchange and communal responsibility. Increasingly, judges and legislators assumed that the public good would be furthered by economic growth, and that economic growth would be encouraged by giving maximum liberty to the "will" of buyers and sellers, employers and employees. But economic growth also required certain kinds of direct government aid, particularly in constructing improved modes of transportation and in making it easier for more individuals to share the privileges and benefits gained from limited liability corporations. Part 4 concerns government involvement in such "improvements," beginning with the landmark *Charles River Bridge* case, which gave judicial blessing to a proliferation of competing corporations. After some discussion of the financing of canals and railroads, Part 4 concludes with the appeal by William Leggett, a radical Jacksonian, for general laws of incorporation that would enable every man to become an entrepreneur.

Having surveyed the broad setting within which rules and principles were redefined, we move in Part 5 to political ideology—to three samples of style and rhetoric that characterized a new politics of opportunity. We are not concerned here with the history of parties, elections, voting behavior, or sectional conflict. It is sufficient to note that the local economic, social, and cultural conflicts of the 1820s aroused a widespread popular interest in politics. As increasing numbers of Americans sought political outlets for their everyday grievances and aspirations, politicians responded by offering rival programs designed to maximize the popular vote. By the late 1820s various state factions coalesced in support of Andrew Jackson's candidacy for President, creating a national Democratic party which remained the majority party of the nation for thirty years. But as with any popular American sport, the health of the so-called Second Party System depended on competition between relatively equal opponents. Otherwise, it would have been difficult to maintain partisan loyalty, to keep political emotions at a high pitch, or to convince the public that political choices made a crucial difference in everyone's life. Though it took some time for anti-Democrats from the local and state levels to move from the National Republican and Antimasonic parties toward a more effective national identity as Whigs, by 1840 they were able to defeat the Democrats in a presidential election. Thereafter, for nearly fourteen years, Whigs matched Democrats as a national and nearly equal power. Leaders of both parties sought to exploit or manufacture conflicts, dramatizing party differences while also tuning their programs to shifting public demands. As mass parties, both the Whigs and the Democrats claimed to serve the people's true interests. Each party also claimed to be the true embodiment of America's Revolutionary heritage, defending freedom, equality, and self-government from various antirepublican perils.

The purpose of Part 5 is to compare the ways in which Antimasons, Democrats, and Whigs sought to mobilize a broad constituency by attacking a privileged and self-serving "power," an exclusive clique or party which aimed at denying the people equal access to the rewards of national growth. The truth of such charges is not our concern, though it can be said that all three parties could muster enough facts to make a plausible case. For cultural analysis, the main points are the distinctive pattern given to presentations of "them" and "us," and the appeal to an overriding fear of being deceived by false professions of patriotism and public spirit, and thereby excluded from benefits quietly reserved for those with special privileges (or "connections," as Americans tended to translate the word). It was precisely because America had repudiated special privilege in the formal sense of aristocratic ranks and orders that politics became a game—of the most serious kind—in which every party claimed to represent the true interests of the *excluded* people. Since no incumbent party could possibly avoid the realities of patronage and special connections, the game consisted of proving that the incumbents were insincere and were in fact partial to their friends.

This game of democratic one-upmanship, even when cynically played, probably helped to prevent an entrenchment and perpetuation of power, at least in regions not dominated by a single party. The two-party system also diluted radicalism and extremism, including that of northern reformers and southern disunionists. The real catch was that democratic rhetoric and procedures were never intended to include *all* the people. As we shall see in Unit Three, a large segment of the American population had no chance of competing for equal access to wealth and power. In the North, such outcasts were often disenfranchised and disregarded. In the South, as black slaves, they made up the basic labor force and hence were not disregarded.

Part 6, on the fear of sectional exclusion, touches on some of the consequences of this fact. As John C. Calhoun makes clear, in the concluding selection, the North's increasing gains in strategic superiority "might be endured without the hazard of destruction to the South" if it were not for the question of slavery and race. Although the two sections had weathered periodic confrontations over slavery, beginning with the Constitutional Convention, the striking fact was the repeated success of compromise and the compelling weight in both North and South of moderate opinion. Despite

Calhoun's deathbed warnings to the South, compromise prevailed again in 1850, the year with which we conclude Unit Two. Yet however wrongheaded he may have been in other respects, Calhoun was surely right on three counts: that black slavery was a question of "vital importance" to the South, involving the very basis of the region's "social organization"; that "every portion of the North," not simply abolitionists, held "views and feelings more or less hostile" to slavery; and that such a moral and cultural discrepancy, when combined with the North's accelerating gains in wealth and power, meant ultimate destruction of the South's social organization; that is, unless the North could be persuaded or coerced into restoring the former "equilibrium" between the two sections and guaranteeing an absolute parity in political power. Calhoun's last futile warning and demand represent the most ominous expression of both the fear of exclusion and the yearning for some permanent "settlement" or contract that could not be eroded by America's limitless aspirations and anxious spirit of gain.

A. The Discontents of Limitless Aspiration

- *Alexis de Tocqueville (1840)*
- *J. N. Bellows (1843)*
- *Henry W. Bellows (1845)*

As a young man, the French nobleman Alexis de Tocqueville (1805–1859) was fascinated by democracy but ambivalent toward what he regarded as its irresistible progress in world history. A trip to America in 1831, ostensibly to study the new penitentiary system, gave him the opportunity to blend hypothesis with personal observation and ultimately to present a comprehensive analysis of democracy, which he saw as a universal historical force, now manifested in its first concrete and self-containing setting. In this selection, on American "restlessness" in the midst of prosperity, Tocqueville's approach is essentially that of a social psychologist. The American environment, including laws and customs, has not only promoted economic growth and material abundance but has swept away all limits to individual dreams and expectations. No condition of life (except slavery) is prescribed by fate, birth, or law. But precisely because there are no checks on aspiration, no one is satisfied with his present condition. Perpetual hope mixes with perpetual anxiety. In their daily experience, Americans encounter the harsh reality of a new barrier, universal competition, which prevents them from attaining the perfect equality and happiness they desire. Tocqueville's ingenious theory suggests that the fear of failure, in a land so obsessed with success, would be extraordinarily poignant. While concerned with explaining Americans' restlessness, he also suggests why Americans would be acutely sensitive to the rules governing their access to wealth and power.

The writings of Tocqueville and other European travelers were often interpreted by Americans as a critique of pursuing material wealth at the cost of an impoverished culture. In *Hunt's Merchants' Magazine* a writer from New Hampshire, J. N. Bellows, presents a typical defense of America's priorities while agreeing essentially that Americans are a restless, "serious," and striving people. Bellows' use of specific detail reminds us that Tocqueville's generalizations are abstract and oversimplified. Bellows' reference to canals and to the clearing of land also points to some of the links between individual opportunity and public policy.

The third selection was written by Henry W. Bellows (1814–1882), minister of the First Unitarian Church in New York City, a prominent editor, clubman, founder of Antioch College, and president of the United States Sanitary Commission during the Civil War. In this essay, Henry Bellows returns to the apparent paradox of "excessive anxiety" in the midst of unparalleled prosperity and opportunity. Unlike J. N. Bellows, he does not associate the culture America lacks with theatres, festivals, and "light amusements," nor does he believe that material progress is a stage of growth which must precede the "graces of humanity." Expanding on Tocqueville's argument, Henry Bellows finds American life at once enriched and impoverished by the same force: "the concentration of the [human] faculties upon an object, which in its very nature is unattainable—the perpetual improvement of the outward condition." Americans are at once free to pursue happiness as they see fit and enslaved by a single-minded and insatiable pursuit of success. No profession escapes the compulsions of competitive work. The spirit of enterprise is so all-consuming that ". . . we labor for bread, and labor for pride, and *labor* for pleasure." When all the pleasures and values of life are identified with individual self-betterment, there can be no criteria or standards of judgment independent of the "anxious spirit of gain."

Alexis de Tocqueville (1840)

In certain remote corners of the Old World you may still sometimes stumble upon a small district which seems to have been forgotten amid the general tumult, and to have remained stationary while everything around it was in motion. The inhabitants are for the most part extremely ignorant and poor;

SOURCE: Alexis de Tocqueville, *Democracy in America*, Vol. II (Boston: C. C. Little & J. Brown, 1841), Second Book, ch. 13.

they take no part in the business of the country, and they are frequently oppressed by the government; yet their countenances are generally placid, and their spirits light.

In America I saw the freest and most enlightened men, placed in the happiest circumstances which the world affords; it seemed to me as if a cloud habitually hung upon their brow, and I thought them serious and almost sad even in their pleasures.

The chief reason of this contrast is that the former do not think of the ills they endure—the latter are for ever brooding over advantages they do not possess. It is strange to see with what feverish ardor the Americans pursue their own welfare; and to watch the vague dread that constantly torments them lest they should not have chosen the shortest path which may lead to it.

A native of the United States clings to this world's goods as if he were certain never to die; and he is so hasty in grasping at all within his reach, that one would suppose he was constantly afraid of not living long enough to enjoy them. He clutches everything, he holds nothing fast, but soon loosens his grasp to pursue fresh gratifications.

In the United States a man builds a house to spend his latter years in it, and he sells it before the roof is on; he plants a garden, and lets it [rents] just as the trees are coming into bearing; he brings a field into tillage, and leaves other men to gather the crops; he embraces a profession, and gives it up; he settles in a place, which he soon afterward leaves, to carry his changeable longings elsewhere. If his private affairs leave him any leisure, he instantly plunges into the vortex of politics; and if at the end of a year of unremitting labor he finds he has a few days' vacation, his eager curiosity whirls him over the vast extent of the United States, and he will travel fifteen hundred miles in a few days, to shake off his happiness. Death at length overtakes him, but it is before he is weary of his bootless chase of that complete felicity which is for ever on the wing.

At first sight there is something surprising in this strange unrest of so many happy men, restless in the midst of abundance. The spectacle itself is however as old as the world; the novelty is to see a whole people furnish an exemplification of it.

. . . He who has set his heart exclusively upon the pursuit of worldly welfare is always in a hurry, for he has but a limited time at his disposal to reach it, to grasp it, and to enjoy. The recollection of the brevity of life is a constant spur to him. Besides the good things which he possesses, he every instant fancies a thousand others which death will prevent him from trying if he does not try them soon. This thought fills him with anxiety, fear, and regret, and keeps his mind in ceaseless trepidation, which leads him perpetually to change his plans and his abode.

If in addition to the taste for physical well-being a social condition be superadded, in which the laws and customs make no condition permanent, here is a great additional stimulant to this restlessness of temper. Men will then be seen continually to change their track, for fear of missing the shortest cut to happiness.

It may readily be conceived, that if men, passionately bent upon physical gratifications, desire eagerly, they are also easily discouraged: as their ultimate object is to enjoy, the means to reach that object must be prompt and easy, or the trouble of acquiring the gratification would be greater than the gratification itself. Their prevailing frame of mind then is at once ardent and relaxed, violent and enervated. Death is often less dreaded than perseverance in continuous efforts to one end.

The equality of conditions leads by a still straighter road to several of the effects which I have here described. When all the privileges of birth and fortune are abolished, when all professions are accessible to all, and a man's own energies may place him at the top of any one of them, an easy and unbounded career seems open to his ambition, and he will readily persuade himself that he is born to no vulgar destinies. But this is an erroneous notion, which is corrected by daily experience. The same equality which allows every citizen to conceive these lofty hopes, renders all the citizens less able to realize them; it circumscribes their powers on every side, while it gives freer scope to their desires. Not only are they themselves powerless, but they are met at every step by immense obstacles, which they did not at first perceive. They have swept away the privileges of some of their fellow-creatures which stood in their way; but they have opened the door to universal competition: the barrier has changed its shape rather than its position. When men are nearly alike, and all follow the same track, it is very difficult for any one individual to walk quick and cleave a way through the dense throng which surrounds and presses him. This constant strife between the propensities springing from the equality of conditions and the means it supplies to satisfy them, harasses and wearies the mind.

It is possible to conceive men arrived at a degree of freedom which should completely content them; they would then enjoy their independence without anxiety and without impatience. But men will never establish any equality with which they can be contented. Whatever efforts a people may make, they will never succeed in reducing all the conditions of society to a perfect level; and even if they unhappily attained that absolute and complete depression, the inequality of minds would still remain, which, coming directly from the hand of God, will for ever escape the laws of man. However democratic then the social state and the political constitution of a people may be, it is certain that every member of the community will always find out several points about him which command his own position; and we may foresee that his looks will be doggedly fixed in that direction. When inequality of conditions is the common law of society, the most marked inequalities do not strike the eye; when everything is nearly on the same level, the slightest are marked enough to hurt it. Hence the desire of equality always becomes more insatiable in proportion as equality is more complete.

Among democratic nations men easily attain a certain equality of conditions; they can never attain the equality they desire. It perpetually retires from before them, yet without hiding itself from their sight, and in retiring draws them on. At every moment they think they are about to grasp it; it escapes at every moment from their hold. They are near enough to see its charms, but too far off to enjoy them; and before they have fully tasted its delights, they die. . . .

In democratic ages enjoyments are more intense than in the ages of aristocracy, and especially the number of those who partake in them is larger. But, on the other hand, it must be admitted that man's hopes and his desires are often blasted, the soul is more stricken and perturbed, and care itself more keen.

J. N. Bellows (1843)

Gentlemen travelers and bookmakers, by way of reproach, call us the *trading-nation*, a people devoted to gain; they lament our want of chivalry, our neglect of light amusements; they wonder we do not better support our theatres and other places of public resort, and say we are too sombre and gloomy by half for our national health. . . .

But a few years ago, the country we inhabit was a wilderness. Hardly was the land cleared on the coast, and dotted with towns and villages; hardly had New York, and Boston, and Philadelphia assumed the name and character of cities, before the great west became an object of interest to our own people, and to the immigrant from foreign lands. The story of the resources of this continent reached the ears of the starved and oppressed European; a gleam of hope lighted up his care-worn features, as he heard of a free life on a fertile soil, by the banks of wide, navigable rivers, skirted by woods that abounded with game, where food, fuel, and peace, could be had for the asking. We had enough to do to welcome our new friends, as every one knows. The wants of a population, increasing in the west by magical numbers, made demands upon the comparatively old portions of the country to supply them. The great [Erie] canal, connecting the lakes with the Hudson, was one of these wants. The genius of a [DeWitt] Clinton devised and planned it, and it is the pattern improvement of this time. The magnitude, completion, and success of it, has given hope and confidence to every subsequent effort of the kind; and it has been of as great benefit in its consequences upon internal improvements, as it has as a highway for the wealth of the western valleys. . . .

As soon as we had breathing-time, we turned our attention to manufactures; that is, as soon as the young men could be spared, and the capital could be spared or made. Then, in places where water-power was abundant, towns and villages sprang into being, and employed not only the labors of the young

SOURCE: J. N. Bellows, "An Explanation of American Characteristics," *Hunt's Merchants' Magazine*, Vol. VIII (New York, 1843), pp. 164–68.

men, but the young women, to such an extent, that cooks and chambermaids became scarce; and, at this time, the majority of those who are technically called servants, in the houses of the opulent, are foreigners, the natives being employed, for the most part, on the farms and in the factories.

. . .

We are a serious people, and if we are not, we ought to be. Let our calumniators recollect that every freeman in this country is a part of the government; that he has to decide great questions daily. No matter what his occupation, or learning, or social standing, his vote weighs in the scale of measures; and he knows it. His leisure is employed in reading or talking upon public concerns, the doings of congress, questions of wide or sectional interest; the weight of his responsibility is upon him—would to God that every man felt it fourfold what he does!—and he considers it excitement enough for him to attend to it. . . .

Is it strange that a people who govern themselves should be averse to those fetes and merriments, which despotisms always encourage to keep out of mind and sight the oppressions they practice? The only way, in years past, that the people of Europe have been kept quiet, has been by arousing their national pride, and employing their feelings in animosities with rival powers. A state of peace is more to be dreaded by any European power, than the most bloody and destructive war; because it gives the people leisure to see the chains that bind them, and they will begin to reason about their condition.

Foreigners mistake our sobriety for sadness, our thoughtfulness for gloom, our thrift for niggardliness, our love of independence for love of money.

. . .

Go to the western immigrant, who consults convenience and expedition in building his log hut, and is glad of any house that will shelter his little family, and say to him, "there, friend, your house is out of all proportion; and where are your fences and your flower-garden? Why don't you paint your gateway, and make gravel walks about your domicil, and set out shrubbery, etc., etc.?" The man will laugh in your face, and perhaps answer you thus: "I have a very warm house; here is a hole in the roof to let out the smoke, and a hole in the door to let in the pigs; it works very well, as you may see." This matter of the pigs might be dispensed with, to be sure, but you would find out that the man is chiefly bent on living first; he feels that he has great fundamental things to attend to before he can accommodate himself to your tastes.

This is our position as a country. We have the land to clear, canals to dig, rail-tracks to lay, water-works to finish; trade, agriculture, and common school education, are the great interests of our people. You may talk to them, write about them, ridicule them, do what you please to divert them from their common-sense track, and you will talk, and write, and ridicule in vain. We cannot do everything to-day. Give us time; and do not expect from our infancy, what only can be found in the manhood of a nation.

Henry W. Bellows (1845)

All strangers who come among us remark the excessive anxiety written in the American countenance. The widespread comfort, the facilities for livelihood, the spontaneous and cheap lands, the high price of labor, are equally observed, and render it difficult to account for these lines of painful thoughtfulness. It is not poverty, nor tyranny, nor overcompetition which produces this anxiety; that is clear. It is the concentration of the faculties upon an object, which in its very nature is unattainable—the perpetual improvement of the outward condition. There are no bounds among us to the restless desire to be better off; and this is the ambition of all classes of society. We are not prepared to allow that wealth is more valued in America than elsewhere, but in other countries the successful pursuit of it is necessarily confined to a few, while here it is open to all. No man in America is contented to be poor, or expects to continue so. There are here no established limits within which the hopes of any class of society must be confined, as in other countries. There is consequently no condition of hopes realized, in other words, of contentment. In other lands, if children can maintain the station and enjoy the means, however moderate, of their father, they are happy. Not so with us. This is not the spirit of our institutions. Nor will it long be otherwise in other countries. That equality, that breaking down of artificial barriers which has produced this universal ambition and restless activity in America, is destined to prevail throughout the earth. But because we are in advance of the world in the great political principle, and are now experiencing some of its first effects, let us not mistake these for the desirable fruits of freedom. Commerce is to become the universal pursuit of men. It is to be the first result of freedom, of popular institutions everywhere. Indeed, every land not steeped in tyranny is now feeling this impulse. But while trade is destined to free and employ the masses, it is also destined to destroy for the time much of the beauty and happiness of every land. This has been the result in our own country. We are free. It is a glorious thing that we have no serfs, with the large and unfortunate exception of our slaves—no artificial distinctions—no acknowledged superiority of blood—no station which merit may not fill—no rounds in the social ladder to which the humblest may not aspire. But the excitement, the commercial activity, the restlessness, to which this state of things has given birth, is far from being a desirable or a natural condition. It is natural to the circumstances, but not natural to the human soul. It is good and hopeful to the interests of the race, but destructive to the happiness, and dangerous to the virtue of the generation exposed to it.

Those unaccustomed, by reading or travel, to other states of society, are probably not aware how very peculiar our manner of life here is. The labo-

SOURCE: [Henry W. Bellows] "The Influence of the Trading Spirit Upon the Social and Moral Life of America," *The American Review: A Whig Journal of Politics, Literature, Art, and Science,* Vol. I (January, 1845), pp. 94–98.

riousness of Americans is beyond all comparison, should we except the starving operatives of English factories. . . . There is no necessity for the custom;
but there is a necessity, weakly constituted as men are, that every individual
should conform greatly to the prevailing habits of his fellows, and the expectations of the community in and with which he deals. It is thus that those
who deeply feel the essentially demoralizing and wretched influences of this
system are yet doomed to be victims of it. Nay, we are all, no matter what
our occupations, more or less, and all greatly, sufferers from the excessive
stimulus under which every thing is done. We are all worn out with thought
that does not develop our thinking faculties in a right direction, and with
feeling expended upon poor and low objects. There is no profession that
does not feel it. The lawyer must confine himself to his office, without
vacation, to adjust a business which never sleeps or relaxes. The physician
must labor day and night to repair bodies, never well from over-exertion,
over-excitement, and over-indulgence. The minister must stimulate himself
to supply the cravings of diseased moral appetites, and to arouse the attention
of men deafened by the noise, and dizzy with the whirl in which they constantly live.

We call our country a *happy* country; happy, indeed, in being the home
of noble political institutions, the abode of freedom; but very far from being
happy in possessing a cheerful, light-hearted, and joyous people. Our agricultural regions even are infected with the same anxious spirit of gain. If ever
the curse of labor was upon the race, it is upon us; nor is it simply now "by
the sweat of thy brow thou shalt earn thy bread." Labor for a livelihood is
dignified. But we labor for bread, and labor for pride, and *labor* for pleasure.
A man's life with us *does* consist of the abundance of the things which he
possesseth. To get, and to have the reputation of possessing, is the ruling
passion. To it are bent all the energies of nine-tenths of our population.
Is it that our people are so much more miserly and earth-born than any
other? No, not by any constitutional baseness; but circumstances have
necessarily given this direction to the American mind. In the hard soil of our
common mother, New England—the poverty of our ancestors—their early
thrift and industry—the want of other distinctions than those of property—
the frown of the Puritans upon all pleasures; these circumstances combined,
directed our energies from the first into the single channel of trade. And in
that they have run till they have gained a tremendous head, and threaten to
convert our whole people into mere money-changers and producers. Honor
belongs to our fathers, who in times of great necessity met the demand for a
most painful industry with such manly and unflinching hearts. But what
was their hard necessity we are perpetuating as our willing servitude! what
they bore as evil we seek as good.

•   •   •

It is said that we are not a happy people. And it is true; for we most
unwisely neglect all those free fountains of happiness which Providence has
opened for all its children. Blessed beyond any people with the means of
living, supplied to an unparalleled extent with the comforts and luxuries of

life, our American homes are sombre and cheerless abodes. There is even in the air of comfort which their well-furnished apartments wear something uncomfortable. They are the habitations of those who do not live at home. They are wanting in a social and cheerful aspect. They seem fitted more to be admired than to be enjoyed. The best part of the house is for the occasional use of strangers, and not to be occupied by those who might, day by day, enjoy it, which is but one proof among many that we love to appear comfortable rather than to be so. Thus miserable pride hangs like a millstone about our hospitality. . . . We are ashamed of any thing but affluence, and when we cannot make an appearance, or furnish entertainments as showy as the richest, we will do nothing. Thus does pride close our doors. Hospitality becomes an event of importance. It is not our daily life, one of our chiefest enjoyments, but a debt, a ceremony, a penance. And not only pride, but anxiety of mind, interferes with sociality. Bent upon one aim, the merchant grudges his thoughts. He cannot expend his energies in social enjoyment. Nay, it is not enjoyment to him; society has nothing of the excitement of business. The excessive pursuit of gain begets a secrecy of thought, a contradiction of ideas, a barrenness of interest, which renders its votary any thing but social or companionable. Conversation incessantly takes an anxious and uninteresting turn; and the fireside becomes only a narrower exchange, and the parlor a more private news-room.

It is rare, on the contrary, to find a *virtuous* American past middle life, who does not regard amusements of all sorts either as childish or immoral; who possesses any acquaintance with or taste for the arts, except it be a natural and rude taste for music; or who reads any thing except newspapers, and only the political or commercial columns of those. It is the want of tastes for other things than business which gives an anxious and unhappy turn to our minds. It cannot be many years before the madness of devoting the whole day to the toils of the countinghouse will be acknowledged; before the claim of body and mind to relaxation and cheerful, exhilarating amusement will be seen. We consider the common suspicion which is felt of amusements among thoughtful people to be one of the most serious evils to which our community is exposed. It outlaws a natural taste, and violates and ruins the consciences of the young, by stamping as sinful what they have not the force to refrain from. It makes our places of amusement low, divides the thoughtful and the careless, the grave and the gay, the old and the young, in their pleasures. Children are without the protection of their parents in their enjoyments. And thus, too, is originated one of the greatest curses of our social state—the great want of intimacy and confidence between children and their parents, especially between fathers and sons.

· · ·

Overt sins are more rare here than elsewhere. As far as morality is restrictive in its nature, it has accomplished a great work in America. The vices or sins which are reducible to statute, or known by name, are generally restrained. We have a large class of persons of extraordinary propriety and faultlessness of life. Our view of morals has a tendency to increase this class.

Our pursuits are favorable to it. The love of gain is one of the most sober of all desires. The seriousness of a miser surpasses the gravity of a devotee. Did not every commercial city draw a large body of strangers to it, and attract many reckless and vicious persons, it would wear a very solemn aspect. The pleasure-seeking, the gay, the disorderly, are never the trading population. Large commercial cities tend to great orderliness and decency of manners and morals. But they also tend to very low and barren views of moral excellence. And the American spirit of our own day illustrates this. Our moral sense operates only in one direction. Our virtues are the virtues of merchants, and not of men. We run all to honesty, and mercantile honesty. We do not cultivate the graces of humanity. We have more conscience than heart, and more propriety than either. The fear of evil consequences is more influential than the love of goodness. There is nothing hearty, gushing, eloquent, in the national virtue. You do not see goodness leaking out from the full vessel at every motion it feels. Our goodness is formal, deliberate, premeditated. The upright man is not benevolent, and the just man is not generous. The good man is not cheerful. The religious man is not agreeable. In other words, our morals are partial, and therefore barren. It is not generally understood how great scrupulousness of character may be united with great selfishness, and how, along with a substantial virtue, there may exist the most melancholy deficiencies. This seems to be very common with us, and to be the natural result of our engrossing pursuits. Every one minds his own business, to the extreme peril of his own soul. The apostolic precept, Mind not thine own things, but also the things of another, is in danger of great neglect.[1] Our social condition makes us wary, suspicious, slow to commit ourselves too far in interest for others. The shyness of the tradesman communicates itself to the manners of the visitor; we learn to live within ourselves; we grow unsocial, unfraternal in feeling; and the sensibility, the affection, the cordiality, the forth-putting graces of a warm and virtuous heart, die of disuse. For our part, we are ready to say, let us have more faults and more virtues; more weaknesses and more grace; less punctilio, and more affluence of heart. Let us be less dignified and more cordial; less sanctimonious and more unselfish; less thriving and more cheerful; less toilsome and more social.

We want, as a people, a rounder character. Our humanity is pinched; our tastes are not generous. The domestic and social virtues languish. . . . Children grow up unknown to their parents. The mature despise their own youth, and have no sympathy with the romance, the buoyancy, the gayety of their children. Enterprise is our only enthusiasm. We grow to be ashamed of our best affections. We are afraid to acknowledge that we derive enjoyment from trifles, and make apologies for being amused with any thing. Thus is the beautiful field of life burnt over, and all its spontaneous flowers and fruitage destroyed; a few towering trunks alone redeeming the landscape.

---

[1] An apostolic precept is a command by one of Christ's apostles.

B. Speculation and Community

- *Timothy Flint* (1826)
- *D. W. Mitchell* (1862)
- *Harriet Martineau* (1837)
- *Walter Colton* (1850)
- *Bayard Taylor* (1850)

For conservatives, the rapid settlement of the West was at once a stimulus to the "anxious spirit of gain" and a threat to the ideal of a stable, ordered, and homogeneous community. For example, Timothy Dwight, the Calvinist president of Yale and the stern guardian of Connecticut as a "land of steady habits," complained in his widely read *Travels* (1821) that pioneers were too idle, passionate, and shiftless to live in "regular society": "They are impatient of the restraints of law, religion and morality; grumble about the taxes, by which Rulers, Ministers, and School-masters are supported; and complain incessantly . . . of the extortions of mechanics, farmers, merchants, and physicians, to whom they are always indebted."

It is precisely this prejudice against backwoodsmen that Timothy Flint (1780–1840) here seeks to counteract. Though Flint was himself a New Englander, a Harvard graduate, and an agent of the Missionary Society of Connecticut, he soon developed a warm sympathy for the people and folkways of the Mississippi Valley. Influenced by European writers who romanticized the shaggy American wilderness, Flint's popular fiction and histories established him as one of the first literary interpreters of the West. He won fame in Europe as well as in the East for his account of Indian wars and his celebration of Daniel Boone. Ironically, in his effort to replace Dwight's image of Westerners as lazy misfits, Flint emphasizes not only wholesome ambition but a worship of "improvement" which leads to extravagant speculation. According to Flint, Westerners are so obsessed with growth and with acquiring access to the latest fashions in education and "culture" that they are exposed to every possible fraud and swindle. Halfamused by these excesses, Flint finally anchors his faith in the sheer abundance of land and physical resources which makes it "difficult for the imagination to assign limits to the future growth and prosperity of the country."

The tension between speculation and ordered community takes on added meaning in the next selection when we skip ahead some thirty years (to the 1850s), glimpsing the West as it appeared to a British visitor, D. W. Mitchell. Though Mitchell is a biased witness, he provides important details on the mechanisms of speculation and especially on the role of government in making land, once the basis of communal stability and generational continuity, as easily transferable as any other form of property. Mitchell also recalls some of the themes of Unit One when he describes the plight of American women, struggling to preserve a home and "family nest" in the face of male restlessness and "temptations to change for the sake of rising in the world more rapidly."

The third selection is written by a more famous British traveler, Harriet Martineau (1802–1876), a religious liberal and a promoter of laissez-faire economics. In the few years before she departed on a lengthy tour of America, in 1834, Martineau had won astonishing authority and influence from a series of fictional tales popularizing the doctrines of Thomas Malthus, David Ricardo, and James Mill. If not an original thinker, Martineau had a keen eye (unfortunately, she was deaf) for the human details of economic behavior. In frontier Chicago, which was just then emerging as a boom town, she encountered a "rage for speculation" ignited by a proposed canal connecting the Great Lakes with the Mississippi waterways. The genuine and spectacular growth of Chicago came somewhat later, with the arrival of the railroad, but Martineau describes a volatile interest in building lots which was at once a characteristic of American urban growth and an illustration of how advance knowledge of projected transportation routes could affect the escalating value of land. Note that, contrary to the common view of Americans as somber and cheerless, Martineau finds "much gaiety" in the midst of business. Perhaps many Americans discovered a certain sense of community and fraternity in the very excitement and unpredictability of striking it rich.

The entire world agreed that such excitement and unpredictability reached its climax in the California gold rush, beginning in 1848, which became, at least in imagination, almost a caricature of the American Dream. The author of our fourth selection, Walter Colton (1797–1851), had the distinction of first publicizing the discovery of gold in the Sacramento Valley and hence of contributing to the sudden influx of prospectors and immigrants from all corners of the globe. Born in Vermont, the son of a humble weaver, Colton managed to rise in the Congregational and missionary establishment until, on the eve of the Mexican War, he became chaplain on the flagship of the American Pacific Squadron, which in 1846 seized Monterey, the capital of Mexican California.

It is a mark of the pervasiveness and influence of New England culture that a man who shared a common education and tradition with Heman Humphrey, Catharine and Henry Ward Beecher, Samuel Goodrich, Jacob Abbott, Timothy Flint, and a multitude of other reformers, educators, journalists, writers, and organizers should have been appointed and then elected by popular vote as the first Anglo-American "alcalde," or chief judge, of the California capital. In accordance with his heritage and ideology, Colton established the first Anglo-American newspaper and schoolhouse in California. But while the following selection from Colton's journal registers a slight echo of Timothy Dwight's fear of social disintegration, in the sense that the gold mines "have upset all social and domestic arrangements in Monterey," Colton is clearly caught up in the contagious enthusiasm and makes no attempt to disguise his longing to shoulder a pickax (at fifty-one, three years before his death) and join the cosmopolitan throng. According to Colton, the gold fields offered sudden access to wealth for nearly everyone, but the reader should not lose sight of the thirty "wild Indians" who were actually the bound slaves to a Mexican ranchero, and who received no share of the $76,844 of the gold they uncovered for seven prospectors in seven weeks and three days.

One of the most informative accounts of gold-smitten California was written by Bayard Taylor (1825–1878), the author of the fifth selection on "Speculation and Community." Taylor's own career offers a dramatic illustration of the deceptiveness of success and failure in a nation that has usually been blind to the dynamics and significance of failure. Of Pennsylvania Quaker background, Taylor was a literary prodigy who at age nineteen escaped a dreary apprenticeship as a printer and was sent off to Europe with commissions to write for the American press. His dazzling success as a journalist and travel writer led to his assignment, by the New York *Tribune*, to cover the California gold rush of 1849. During the 1850s he traveled widely through the Mideast, Asia, and Africa, and wrote many volumes—travel accounts, poetry, ballads, translations. Before he was forty, Taylor was probably the most widely traveled and cosmopolitan of American writers; he continued to receive honors and acclaim. Yet his works were soon dismissed as second-rate, and he has long been forgotten. In a sense, his fate is similar to the young men and women who sought immortality in the gold fields of California, the very gold fields he tried to immortalize in his prose.

Here, we begin with Taylor's arrival by ship in San Francisco—a bustling, polyglot boom town where all traditional prices and values are topsy-turvy. When he speaks of common wages of $15 to $20 a day, one must remember that in the East a laborer's wages (male) were about $1.00 a day, $1.50 for an artisan. The startling theme—especially for Easterners who had had no experience with such drastic inflation—is that community, order, and trust seem to flower in the midst of such chaos. In a climate of affluence and hope, debtors pay their creditors, no one dares to haggle over prices in a store, and strangers of diverse class and background cooperate in self-government. The pervasiveness of opportunity—the lowered thresholds of *access* to wealth, create a mood of "practical equality" and trust. Yet one must make allowance for even Taylor's intolerance of outsiders (the theme of Unit Three). When the prospectors from Mexico ("Sonorians") are expelled, Taylor rejoices.

Timothy Flint (1826)

The people in the Atlantic states have not yet recovered from the horror inspired by the term "backwoodsman." This prejudice is particularly strong in New England, and is more or less felt from Maine to Georgia. When I first visited this country,[1] I had my full share, and my family by far too much for their comfort. In approaching the country, I heard a thousand stories of gougings, and robberies, and shooting down with the rifle. . . . The gentlemen of the towns, even here, speak often with a certain contempt and horror of the backwoodsmen. I have read, and not without feelings of pain, the bitter representations of the learned and virtuous Dr. [Timothy] Dwight, in speaking of them. He represents these vast regions, as a grand reservoir for the scum of the Atlantic states. He characterizes in the mass the emigrants from New England, as discontented coblers, too proud, too much in debt, too unprincipled, too much puffed up with self-conceit, too strongly impressed that their fancied talents could not find scope in their own country, to stay there. It is true there are worthless people here, and the most so, it must be confessed, are from New England. It is true there are gamblers, and gougers, and outlaws; but there are fewer of them, than from the nature of things, and the character of the age and the world, we ought to expect. But it is unworthy of the excellent man in question so to designate this people in the mass. The backwoodsman of the west, as I have seen him, is generally an amiable and virtuous man. His general motive for coming here is to be a freeholder, to have plenty of rich land, and to be able to settle his children about him. It is a most virtuous motive.

• • •

The people here are not yet a reading people. Few good books are brought into the country. The few literary men that are here, seeing nothing to excite or reward their pursuits, seeing other objects exclusively occupy all minds, soon catch the prevailing feeling. The people are too busy, too much occupied in making farms and speculations, to think of literature.

America inherits, I believe, from England a taste for puffing.[2] She has improved upon her model. In your quarter, as well as here, the people are idolaters to the "golden calves." Some favorite man, fashion, or opinion, sweep every thing before them. This region is the paradise of puffers. One puffs up, and another down. As you draw near the influence of the "lord of the ascendant," you will find opinions graduated to his *dicta*. The last stranger that arrives from Kentucky, or the Atlantic country, is but poorly

---

SOURCE: Timothy Flint, *Recollections of the Last Ten Years* (Boston: Cummings, Hilliard, and Co., 1826). Reprinted and edited by C. Hartley Grattan (New York: Alfred A. Knopf, Inc., 1932), pp. 170–71, 179–83.

[1] The Mississippi Valley.
[2] Exaggerated praise or advertising.

introduced to his new residence, if he have not one of these great men to puff a breeze in the sail of his skiff, as he puts himself afloat.

I have been amused in reading puffing advertisements in the newspapers. A little subscription school, in which half the pupils are abecedarians, is a college. One is a Lancastrian school, or a school of "instruction mutuelle." There is the Pestalozzi establishment, with its appropriate emblazoning. There is the agricultural school, the missionary school, the grammar box, the new way to make a wit of a dunce in six lessons, and all the mechanical ways of inoculating children with learning, that they may not endure the pain of getting it in the old and natural way. I would not have you smile exclusively at the people of the West. This ridiculous species of swindling is making as much progress in your country as here. The misfortune is, that these vile pretensions finally induce the people to believe, that there is a "royal road" to learning. The old and beaten track, marked out by the only sure guide, experience, is forsaken. The parents are flattered, deceived, and swindled. Puffing pretenders take the place of the modest man of science, who scorns to compete with him in these vile arts. The children have their brains distended with the "east wind," and grow up at once empty and conceited.

. . . A respectable man wishes to establish himself in a school in those regions. He consults a friend, who knows the meridian of the country. The advice is, call your school by some new and imposing name. Let it be understood, that you have a new way of instructing children, by which they can learn twice as much, in half the time, as by the old ways. Throw off all modesty. Move the water, and get in while it is moving. In short, depend upon the *gullibility* of the people. A school, modelled on this advice, was instituted at St. Louis, while I was there, with a very imposing name. The masters,—professors, I should say,—proposed to teach most of the languages, and all the sciences. Hebrew they would communicate in twelve lessons; Latin and Greek, with a proportionate promptness. . . .

Town-making introduces another species of puffing. Art and ingenuity have been exhausted in devising new ways of alluring purchasers, to take lots and build in the new town. There are the fine rivers, the healthy hills, the mineral springs, the clear running water, the eligible mill-seats, the valuable forests, the quarries of building-stone, the fine steam-boat navigation, the vast country adjacent, the central position, the connecting point between the great towns, the admirable soil, and last of all the cheerful and undoubting predictions of what the town must one day be. I have read more than an hundred advertisements of this sort. Then the legislature must be tampered with, in order to make the town either the metropolis, or at least the seat of justice. . . .

A coarse caricature of this abomination of town-making, appeared in the St. Louis papers. The name was "Ne plus ultra."[1] The streets were laid out

---

[1] The highest point or acme.

a mile in width; the squares were to be sections, each containing six hundred and forty acres. The mall was a vast standing forest. In the centre of this modern Babylon, roads were to cross each other in a meridional line at right angles, one from the south pole to Symmes's hole in the north, and another from Pekin to Jerusalem.

.In truth, while travelling on the prairies of the Illinois and Missouri, and observing such immense tracts of rich soil, of the blackness of ink, and of exhaustless fertility,—remarking the beautiful simplicity of the limits of farms, introduced by our government, in causing the land to be all surveyed in exact squares, and thus destroying here the barbarous prescription, which has in the settled countries laid out the lands in ugly farms, and bounded them by zigzag lines,—contemplating the hedge of verdure that will bound the squares of these smooth and fertile plains,—remarking the beauty of the orchards and improvements, that must ensue,—being convinced that the climate will grow salubrious with its population and improvement,—seeing the guardian genius, Liberty, hovering over the country,—measuring the progress of the future, only by the analogy of the past,—it will be difficult for the imagination to assign limits to the future growth and prosperity of the country. Perhaps on one of these boundless plains, and contiguous to some one of these noble rivers, in view of these hoary bluffs, and where all these means of the subsistence and multiplication of the species are concentered in such ample abundance, will arise the actual "Ne plus ultra."

D. W. Mitchell (1862)

There is a constant struggle going on between the instinctive tendency of the German and Anglo-Saxon races to form a home, in the English social sense of the word, on the one hand; and the counteracting influences of the political condition of the country, the rapid development of business and population, the temptations to change for the sake of rising in the world more rapidly, on the other. The women, the mothers of families especially, very many of them, lead, from these causes, a life of incessant worry and disappointment; again and again they arrange the family nest in some new spot, and when they are able to sit down with some satisfaction are suddenly obliged to abandon the comfortable home. The husband thinks he sees somewhere a fine opening; the family pack up and away they go, perhaps into the midst of the most unsettled population in Christendom—that of the West.

Speculation in real estate has for many years been the ruling idea and occupation of the Western mind. Clerks, laborers, farmers, storekeepers, merely followed their callings for a living, while they were speculating for their fortunes. . . .

source: D. W. Mitchell, *Ten Years in the United States* (London: Smith, Elder and Co., 1862), pp. 322–23, 325–28.

[A]ll classes and people of all kinds became agitated and unsettled, and had their acquisitiveness perpetually excited by land speculations in some shape or other—new railways, roads, proposed villages and towns, gold mines, water-powers, coal mines—some opportunity or other of getting rich all at once by a lucky hit.

. . .

By convenient laws, land was made as easily transferable and convertible as any other species of property. It might and did pass through a dozen hands within sixty days, rising in price at each transfer; in the meantime producing [only] buffaloes and Red Indians. Millions of acres were bought and sold without buyer or seller knowing where they were, or whether they were anywhere; the buyer only knowing that he hoped to sell his title to them at a handsome profit.

. . .

To extend and facilitate these land transactions, these speculations in the Progress of the Country, the system of selling land on time was adopted. The installments of the purchase-money were made payable within various periods (frequently ten years) at low interest, in the first instance. Thus, A., after much thinking, and watching, and saving, or borrowing, secured a corner lot in his favorite city (that was to be), or his half-section in some future garden of the Union (often actually indicated in the deed of sale by the latitude and longitude); this he sold at a profit to B., on a few years' credit (secured, of course, by mortgage); B. did the same to C.; and so on.

It happened that, while this system was going on, the United States government rewarded the services of those who had borne arms in the wars of the country, by giving them land warrants for 80, or 160, or 320 acres, according to services—in all amounting to many millions of acres. So in 1856 the railroad and canal companies and the holders of these land warrants were everywhere selling, selling, selling, in large or small parcels of land, until everybody in the West had a share of God's earth, quietly increasing in value at the rate of perhaps a hundred, or at least twenty per cent. per annum—it was hoped.

Harriet Martineau (1837)

I never saw a busier place than Chicago was at the time of our arrival. The streets were crowded with land speculators, hurrying from one sale to another. A negro, dressed up in scarlet, bearing a scarlet flag, and riding a white horse with housings of scarlet, announced the times of sale. At every street-corner where he stopped, the crowd flocked round him; and it seemed as if some prevalent mania infected the whole people. The rage for speculation might fairly be so regarded. As the gentlemen of our party walked

---

SOURCE: Harriet Martineau, *Society in America* (London, 1837), pp. 350–52.

the streets, store-keepers hailed them from their doors, with offers of farms, and all manner of land-lots, advising them to speculate before the price of land rose higher. A young lawyer, of my acquaintance there, had realized five hundred dollars per day, the five preceding days, by merely making out titles to land. Another friend had realized, in two years, ten times as much money as he had before fixed upon as a competence for life. Of course, this rapid money-making is a merely temporary evil. A bursting of the bubble must come soon. The absurdity of the speculation is so striking, that the wonder is that the fever should have attained such a height as I witnessed. The immediate occasion of the bustle which prevailed, the week we were at Chicago, was the sale of lots, to the value of two millions of dollars, along the course of a projected canal; and of another set, immediately behind these. Persons not intending to game, and not infected with mania, would endeavor to form some reasonable conjecture as to the ultimate value of the lots, by calculating the cost of the canal, the risks from accident, from the possible competition from other places, etc., and, finally, the possible profits, under the most favorable circumstances, within so many years' purchase. Such a calculation would serve as some sort of guide as to the amount of purchase-money to be risked. Whereas, wild land on the banks of a canal, not yet even marked out, was selling at Chicago for more than rich land, well improved, in the finest part of the valley of the Mohawk [in New York State], on the banks of a canal which is already the medium of an almost inestimable amount of traffic. If sharpers and gamblers were to be the sufferers by the impending crash at Chicago, no one would feel much concerned; but they, unfortunately, are the people who encourage the delusion, in order to profit by it. Many a high-spirited, but inexperienced, young man; many a simple settler, will be ruined for the advantage of knaves.

Others, besides lawyers and speculators by trade, make a fortune in such extraordinary times. A poor man at Chicago had a pre-emption right to some land, for which he paid in the morning one hundred and fifty dollars. In the afternoon, he sold it to a friend of mine for five thousand dollars. A poor Frenchman, married to a squaw, had a suit pending, when I was there, which he was likely to gain, for the right of purchasing some land by the lake for one hundred dollars, which would immediately become worth one million dollars.

There was much gaiety going on at Chicago, as well as business.

Walter Colton (1850)

Tuesday, June 20. [1848] My messenger sent to the mines, has returned with specimens of the gold; he dismounted in a sea of upturned faces. As he drew

source: Walter Colton, *Three Years in California* (New York: A. S. Barnes and Co., 1850; reprint, Stanford University Press, 1949), pp. 246–49, 252–53.

forth the yellow lumps from his pockets, and passed them around among the eager crowd, the doubts, which had lingered till now, fled. . . . All were off for the mines, some on horses, some on carts, and some on crutches, and one went in a litter. An American woman, who had recently established a boarding-house here, pulled up stakes, and was off before her lodgers had even time to pay their bills. Debtors ran, of course. I have only a community of women left, and a gang of prisoners, with here and there a soldier, who will give his captain the slip at the first chance. I don't blame the fellow a whit; seven dollars a month, while others are making two or three hundred a day! that is too much for human nature to stand.

• • •

TUESDAY, JULY 18. Another bag of gold from the mines, and another spasm in the community. It was brought down by a sailor from Yuba river, and contains a hundred and thirty-six ounces. It is the most beautiful gold that has appeared in the market; it looks like the yellow scales of the dolphin, passing through his rainbow hues at death. My carpenters, at work on the school-house, on seeing it, threw down their saws and planes, shouldered their picks, and are off for the Yuba. Three seamen ran from the Warren, forfeiting their four years' pay; and a whole platoon of soldiers from the fort left only their colors behind. One old woman declared she would never again break an egg or kill a chicken, without examining yolk and gizzard.

• • •

THURSDAY, AUG. 16. Four citizens of Monterey are just in from the gold mines on Feather River, where they worked in company with three others. They employed about thirty wild Indians, who are attached to the rancho owned by one of the party. They worked precisely seven weeks and three days, and have divided seventy-six thousand eight hundred and forty-four dollars,—nearly eleven thousand dollars to each. Make a dot there, and let me introduce a man, well known to me, who has worked on the Yuba river sixty-four days, and brought back, as the result of his individual labor, five thousand three hundred and fifty-six dollars. . . . Make another dot there, and let me introduce a woman, of Sonoranian birth,[1] who has worked in the dry diggings forty-six days, and brought back two thousand one hundred and twenty-five dollars. Is not this enough to make a man throw down his leger and shoulder a pick? . . .

TUESDAY, AUG. 28. The gold mines have upset all social and domestic arrangements in Monterey; the master has become his own servant, and the servant his own lord. The millionaire is obliged to groom his own horse, and roll his wheelbarrow; and the hidalgo—in whose veins flows the blood of all the Cortes—to clean his own boots! Here is lady L——, who has lived here seventeen years, the pride and ornament of the place, with a broomstick in her jewelled hand!

---

[1] From Sonora, a Mexican province.

Bayard Taylor (1850)

As yet, we were only in the suburbs of the town. Crossing the shoulder of the hill, the view extended around the curve of the bay, and hundreds of tents and houses appeared, scattered all over the heights, and along the shore for more than a mile. A furious wind was blowing down through a gap in the hills, filling the streets with clouds of dust. On every side stood buildings of all kinds, begun or half-finished, and the greater part of them mere canvas sheds, open in front, and covered with all kinds of signs, in all languages. Great quantities of goods were piled up in the open air, for want of a place to store them. The streets were full of people, hurrying to and fro, and of as diverse and bizarre a character as the houses: Yankees of every possible variety, native Californians in *sarapes* and sombreros, Chilians, Sonorians, Kanakas from Hawaii, Chinese with long tails, Malays armed with their everlasting creeses, and others in whose embrowned and bearded visages it was impossible to recognize any especial nationality.

· · ·

Many of the passengers began speculation at the moment of landing. The most ingenious and successful operation was made by a gentleman of New York, who took out fifteen hundred copies of The Tribune and other papers, which he disposed of in two hours, at one dollar a-piece! Hearing of this I bethought me of about a dozen papers which I had used to fill up crevices in packing my valise. There was a newspaper merchant at the corner of the City Hotel, and to him I proposed the sale of them, asking him to name a price. "I shall want to make a good profit on the retail price," said he, "and can't give more than ten dollars for the lot." I was satisfied with the wholesale price, which was a gain of just four thousand per cent!

I set out for a walk before dark and climbed a hill back of the town, passing a number of tents pitched in the hollows. The scattered houses spread out below me and the crowded shipping in the harbor, backed by a lofty line of mountains, made an imposing picture. The restless, feverish tide of life in that little spot, and the thought that what I then saw and was yet to see will hereafter fill one of the most marvellous pages of all history, rendered it singularly impressive. . . .

I was forced to believe many things, which in my communications to The Tribune I was almost afraid to write, with any hope of their obtaining credence. It may be interesting to give here a few instances of the enormous and unnatural value put upon property at the time of my arrival. The Parker House rented for $110,000 yearly, at least $60,000 of which was paid by gamblers, who held nearly all the second story. Adjoining it on the right was a canvas-tent fifteen by twenty-five feet, called "Eldorado," and occupied

SOURCE: Bayard Taylor, *Eldorado; or, Adventures in the Path of Empire* (New York: G. P. Putnam's Sons, 1865; 1st ed., 1850), pp. 55–61, 99–103.

likewise by gamblers, which brought $40,000. On the opposite corner of the plaza, a building called the "Miner's Bank," used by Wright & Co., brokers, about half the size of a fire-engine house in New York, was held at a rent of $75,000. A mercantile house paid $40,000 rent for a one-story building of twenty feet front; the United States Hotel, $36,000; the Post-Office, $7,000, and so on to the end of the chapter. A friend of mine, who wished to find a place for a law-office, was shown a cellar in the earth, about twelve feet square and six deep, which he could have at $250 a month. . . .

The prices paid for labor were in proportion to everything else. The car-man of Mellus, Howard & Co. had a salary of $6,000 a year, and many others made from $15 to $20 daily. Servants were paid from $100 to $200 a month, but the wages of the rougher kinds of labor had fallen to about $8 [a day]. Yet, notwithstanding the number of gold-seekers who were returning en-feebled and disheartened from the mines, it was difficult to obtain as many workmen as the forced growth of the city demanded. . . .

A curious result of the extraordinary abundance of gold and the facility with which fortunes were acquired, struck me at the first glance. All business was transacted on so extensive a scale that the ordinary habits of solicitation and compliance on the one hand and stubborn cheapening on the other, seemed to be entirely forgotten. You enter a shop to buy something; the owner eyes you with perfect indifference, waiting for you to state your want; if you object to the price, you are at liberty to leave, for you need not expect to get it cheaper; he evidently cares little whether you buy it or not. One who has been some time in the country will lay down the money, without wasting words. . . .

This disregard for all the petty arts of money-making was really a refresh-ing feature of society. Another equally agreeable trait was the punctuality with which debts were paid and the general confidence which men were obliged to place, perforce, in each other's honesty. Perhaps this latter fact was owing, in part, to the impossibility of protecting wealth, and consequent dependence on an honorable regard for the rights of others. . . .

. . . Business was over about the usual hour, and then the harvest-time of the gamblers commenced. Every "hell" in the place, and I did not pretend to number them, was crowded, and immense sums were staked at the monte and faro tables. A boy of fifteen, in one place, won about $500, which he coolly pocketed and carried off. One of the gang we brought in the Panama won $1,500 in the course of the evening, and another lost $2,400. . . .

Walking through the town the next day, I was quite amazed to find a dozen persons busily employed in the street before the United States Hotel, digging up the earth with knives and crumbling it in their hands. They were actually gold-hunters, who obtained in this way about $5 a day. After blowing the fine dirt carefully in their hands, a few specks of gold were left, which they placed in a piece of white paper. . . . The presence of gold in the streets was probably occasioned by the leakings from the miners' bags and the sweepings of stores; though it may also be, to a slight extent, native in the earth, particles having been found in the clay thrown up from a deep well.

. . .

The history of law and society in California, from the period of the golden discoveries, would furnish many instructive lessons to the philosopher and the statesman. The first consequence of the unprecedented rush of emigration from all parts of the world into a country almost unknown, and but half reclaimed from its original barbarism was to render all law virtually null, and bring the established authorities to depend entirely on the humor of the population for the observance of their orders. The countries which were nearest the golden coast—Mexico, Peru, Chili, China and the Sandwich Islands—sent forth their thousands of ignorant adventurers, who speedily outnumbered the American population. Another fact, which none the less threatened serious consequences, was the readiness with which the worthless and depraved class of our own country came to the Pacific Coast. From the beginning, a state of things little short of anarchy might have been reasonably awaited.

Instead of this, a disposition to maintain order and secure the rights of all, was shown throughout the mining districts. In the absence of all law or available protection, the people met and adopted rules for their mutual security—rules adapted to their situation, where they had neither guards nor prisons, and where the slightest license given to crime or trespass of any kind must inevitably have led to terrible disorders. Small thefts were punished by banishment from the placers, while for those of large amount or for more serious crimes, there was the single alternative of hanging. . . .

In all the large digging districts, which had been worked for some time, there were established regulations, which were faithfully observed. Alcaldes were elected, who decided on all disputes of right or complaints of trespass, and who had power to summon juries for criminal trials. When a new placer or gulch was discovered, the first thing done was to elect officers and extend the area of order. The result was, that in a district five hundred miles long, and inhabited by 100,000 people, who had neither government, regular laws, rules, military or civil protection, nor even locks or bolts, and a great part of whom possessed wealth enough to tempt the vicious and depraved, there was as much security to life and property as in any part of the Union, and as small a proportion of crime. The capacity of a people for self-government was never so triumphantly illustrated. Never, perhaps, was there a community formed of more unpropitious elements; yet from all this seeming chaos grew a harmony beyond what the most sanguine apostle of Progress could have expected.

The rights of the diggers were no less definitely marked and strictly observed. Among the hundreds I saw on the Mokelumne and among the gulches, I did not see a single dispute nor hear a word of complaint. A company of men might mark out a race of any length and turn the current of the river to get at the bed, possessing the exclusive right to that part of it, so long as their undertaking lasted. A man might dig a hole in the dry ravines, and so long as he left a shovel, pick or crowbar to show that he still intended working it, he was safe from trespass. . . .

The treatment of the Sonorians by the American diggers was one of the exciting subjects of the summer. These people came into the country in armed bands, to the number of ten thousand in all, and took possession of the best points on the Tuolumne, Stanislaus and Mokelumne Rivers. At the Sonorian camp on the Stanislaus there were, during the summer, several thousands of them, and the amount of ground they dug up and turned over is almost incredible. For a long time they were suffered to work peaceably, but the opposition finally became so strong that they were ordered to leave. They made no resistance, but quietly backed out and took refuge in other diggings. In one or two places, I was told, the Americans, finding there was no chance of having a fight, coolly invited them back again! At the time of my visit, however, they were leaving the country in large numbers, and there were probably not more than five thousand in all scattered along the various rivers. Several parties of them, in revenge for the treatment they experienced, committed outrages on their way home, stripping small parties of the emigrants by the Gila route of all they possessed. It is not likely that the country will be troubled with them in future.

Abundance of gold does not always beget, as moralists tell us, a grasping and avaricious spirit. The principles of hospitality were as faithfully observed in the rude tents of the diggers as they could be by the thrifty farmers of the North and West. The cosmopolitan cast of society in California, resulting from the commingling of so many races and the primitive mode of life, gave a character of good-fellowship to all its members; and in no part of the world have I ever seen help more freely given to the needy, or more ready coöperation in any humane proposition. Personally, I can safely say that I never met with such unvarying kindness from comparative strangers.

2

Access to Land

A. The Demand for Land as a Natural Right

- *Memorial to Congress*, Mechanics' Free Press (1828)
- *Thomas Skidmore* (1829)
- *True Workingman* (1846)

By winning independence from Britain and by obtaining, through cession, the western land claims of the original seaboard states, the federal government acquired a "public domain" of over one-quarter billion acres. This national resource, theoretically open to settlement, was as large as the combined areas of modern France, West Germany, Belgium, Holland, and Portugal. The Louisiana Purchase of 1803 added over one-half billion acres (at a purchase price of less than four cents an acre) to this unprecedented sweep of public land. By the census of 1810, the government possessed (disregarding the prior "occupancy" by Indians, a subject we shall deal with in Unit Three) enough public land to provide 104 acres to every man, woman, and child—and in 1810 one-half the American whites were under the age of sixteen, and black slaves comprised nearly one-fifth of the total population. By 1848, as a result of treaties with Spain, Britain, and Mexico, more than a half-billion additional acres had poured into this seemingly limitless cornucopia of public property.

Of course, much of this territory, especially in the arid West, was unsuitable for agriculture, especially for small family farms. Many Americans had no wish to become farmers; millions of others had neither the means nor skills to travel to the transappalachian West and establish themselves in the risky and increasingly commercialized business of agriculture. In a literal sense, it is thus highly misleading to divide acres of public land by population. On the other hand, any understanding of antebellum American culture must take account of two salient facts. First, the public domain, however it might be reserved or apportioned by law, was *public* property. It had been conquered or paid for by collective means, and its ultimate use was thus crucial for the definition and evolution of democratic institutions. Other nations, such as Czarist Russia, opened hundreds of millions of acres of land to new settlement, displacing or exterminating native populations. But only in America was the process of settlement intermeshed with the ideals of popular sovereignty, self-government, and self-betterment. Second, in 1820 approximately 79 percent of the labor force was gainfully employed in agriculture; even by 1850, after decades of immigration and urban growth, the proportion had fallen to only 55 percent. Since the process of "modernization" has long been associated with urbanization and with the uprooting and migration of peasant populations, social scientists have tended to regard a proportionate decline of farmers as an inevitable and beneficial trend. In the late twentieth century, however, this assumption is at least open to question. In view of the disastrous urban crises in many countries, there is a need to reassess the possible benefits of the long dominance of rural life on American culture (it was not until 1920 that the census showed a slight majority of Americans living in places of over 2,500 population). And if the benefits of *continuous* urbanization can no longer be taken for granted, there is also a need to reassess the forgotten alternatives proposed for the use of public lands.

Nineteenth-century Americans perceived the apportionment of land as central to the meaning and success of their democratic experiment. Without trying to summarize the history of public land policy, it can be said that the government moved cautiously toward a policy of encouraging rapid settlement by selling land in smaller minimum parcels (in some regions, forty acres by 1832); by giving grants to veterans and to states (especially to finance canals and other internal improvements that would attract settlement); and by recognizing the "preemption" claims of actual settlers, or squatters, who were eventually allowed to purchase land at the minimum price ($1.25 per acre) in advance of public auction. Despite this seeming responsiveness to public demand, every federal measure seemed to benefit the land companies and speculators who monopolized many of the most promising tracts, often by purchasing the claims of veterans or squatters who happened to acquire potentially valuable land. Such land could then be used as security for bank loans that enabled speculators to acquire still larger tracts. Given the volatile market and expansive economy, the land companies and speculators were eager to promote settlement and to sell their holdings as soon as possible. Hence, market forces prevented any permanent accumulation of vast feudal estates but also rewarded, at public expense, the speculators who were lucky, politically influential, or foresightful. The force of the market, as opposed to relatively minor changes in government policy, is demonstrated by the fact that during the first three decades of the nineteenth century public land sales totaled only 26 million acres, mostly concentrated in the boom years following the War of 1812. In the 1830s, this figure nearly tripled, with a sale of 20 million acres in the speculative mania of 1836. During the partly-depression decade of the 1840s, total land sales fell to less than 18 million acres. As a postscript, one may note that in 1865 the government awarded more than 41 million acres in land grants to private railroads.

The selection from the Philadelphia *Mechanics' Free Press* in 1828 is an expression of the agrarian ideology which drew on Paine and Jefferson and which won the support of radical artisans in the late 1820s and 1830s. The movement to organize a Working Men's party begain in Philadelphia in 1828 and then spread to other cities and towns. Among various other reforms, such as a maximum ten-hour day and free public schools, the Working Men's movement demanded that the people be given free access to the public lands. This demand, as articulated here in a memorial to Congress, rested on three arguments that formed the core of preindustrial radicalism: first, that the natural rights enumerated in the Declaration of Independence can never be secure unless the people have an opportunity for economic independence—that is, an escape from becoming dependent as wage earners or farm tenants; second, that a democratic government, representing all the people, must dispense its favors equally and avoid any policies that create special privilege or monopoly; third, that the goal of national growth and prosperity is best served by encouraging individual enterprise through the rapid settlement and cultivation of the public domain.

In the next selection, Thomas Skidmore (1800?–1832) carries agrarian radicalism to its most extreme conclusions. Born in rural Connecticut, Skidmore drifted up and down the Atlantic seaboard working as a teacher, machinist, and inventor. In 1829 he suddenly acquired prominence as a founder and key leader of the New York Working Men's party, and nearly won election to the New York Assembly. Though Skidmore briefly dominated the New York Working Men's movement, his views were too radical for some of his more pragmatic, middle-class colleagues, and he was, in effect, pushed out of the party. He died from cholera during the epidemic of 1832.

Skidmore's book, *The Rights of Man to Property!*, is significant in two respects. First, it is probably the most revolutionary American work of its time, and therefore helps to define the boundary between the permissible and conceivable levels of dissent, as both were defined by the surrounding culture. Second, for all his radicalism, Skidmore simply extends certain well-known pronouncements of Jefferson, such as the following: (1785) "The earth is given as a common stock for man to labor and live on. If for the encouragement of industry we allow it to be appropriated, we must take care that other employment be provided to those excluded. . . . If we do not, the fundamental right to labor the earth returns to the unemployed"; (1789) ". . . I suppose it be self evident, '*the earth belongs in usufruct* [the right of enjoying all advantages derivable from] *to the living*'; that the dead have neither powers nor rights over it. The portion occupied by any individual ceases to be his when himself ceases to be, and reverts to the society." From such propositions, Skidmore concludes, "I AM; THERE-FORE IS PROPERTY MINE." And on good Jeffersonian grounds, he reasons that any government that refuses to protect fundamental rights deserves to be overthrown. (It should be emphasized that Jefferson did not favor the immediate confiscation and equal division of property!)

While Skidmore was ostracized and soon forgotten, his basic doctrines were diluted and modified, and they won growing acceptance in the northern agitation for free homesteads. The third selection, from the *True Work-ingman* (1846) is still more radical than the Republican party's demands of the 1850s, which led ultimately to the Homestead Act of 1862 (offering 160 acres of the public domain to any citizen who agreed to live on or culti-vate the land for five years). On the radical side of the ledger, the 1846 program stresses the joint ownership of all public lands; it defends the theory (later associated with Marxism) that labor is the source of all eco-nomic value; and it calls for strict limits on the amount of land any one citizen may monopolize or inherit. On the conservative side of the ledger, it envisions no expropriation or revolutionary overthrow of existing institu-tions. Indeed, it looks to land reform as a means of ending all antagonism between labor and capital. And whereas Skidmore looks to the unlimited and possibly tyrannical power of a vague majority, the *True Workingman* attempts to mobilize a workable majority around the catchy slogan of George Henry Evans's National Reformers—later used by the Republicans—"Vote Yourself a Farm."

Memorial to Congress, *Mechanics' Free Press* (1828)

To the Honorable the Senate and the House of Representatives of the United States, in Congress assembled.

The undersigned citizens of the United States, respectfully suggest to Congress the propriety of placing all the public lands, without the delay of sales, within the reach of the people at large, by the right of a title of occupancy only.

Their reasonings on the case, to be brief, are as follows:

SOURCE: *Mechanics' Free Press*, October 25, 1828. Reprinted in John R. Commons, *et al.*, *Documentary History of American Industrial Society*, Vol. V (Cleveland: Arthur H. Clark Co., 1910), pp. 43–45.

1st. That until the public lands shall have been actually put under cultivation, it is clear they will be entirely useless.

2dly. That they are fully satisfied that the present state of affairs, must lead to the wealth of a few, and thus place within their reach the means of controlling all the lands of our country.

3dly. That as all men must occupy a portion of the earth, they have, naturally, a birth-right in the soil: And that while this right shall be subject to the control of others, they may be deprived of life, liberty, and the pursuit of happiness.

4thly. That hence, it is perceived by them, that a true spirit of independence can not be enjoyed, by the great body of the people, nor the exercise of freedom secured to them, so long as the use of the soil is withheld.

. . .

6thly. That the mere sale of these lands can give little ability to the people in sustaining national expenditures. As the relief thus to be derived, could only arise from resources at that time extant, it is clear that this would be but the shifting of existing resources, however insufficient, from the people to the government. But by the widely extensive improvements of an agricultural nature, which the general cultivation of these lands would induce, the people would against the hour of emergency, by large additions to the ordinary revenue, have absolutely created the means of meeting all the prospective expenditures of the most generous administration of the general government.

And, finally, that they deprecate every species of monopoly and exclusive privileges, and more especially all those which produce unnatural exclusions with relation to the public lands. But that it is further respectfully suggested to the Representatives of the people, that should any of the purchasers of these lands for the purpose of speculation, conceive that they are to be injured by the operation of the proposed measure, for which, however, there can be but a remote apprehension entertained, your Memoralists recommend that the purchase money, with interest if necessary, be refunded to them: and that those lands be thus suffered to revert again to the government for the use of the people.

That it is the opinion of your Petitioners that, (the people themselves being, *de facto*, the government) were the public lands thus perpetually held only to their use, it would be, perhaps, the only effectual prevention of future monopoly and the best safeguard of the American Republic.

Thomas Skidmore (1829)

If a man were to ask me, to what I would compare the unequal distribution of property which prevails in the world, and has ever prevailed, I would say,

SOURCE: Thomas Skidmore, *The Rights of Man to Property!* (New York: 1829; New York: Burt Franklin and Co., Inc., 1966), pp. 355–58.

that it reminds me of a large party of gentlemen, who should have a common right to dine at one and the same public table; a part of whom should arrive first, sit down and eat what they chose; and then, because the remaining part came later to dinner, should undertake to monopolize the whole; and deprive them of the opportunity of satisfying their hunger, but upon terms such as those who had feasted, should be pleased to prescribe.

Such, now, is the actual condition of the whole human race. Those who have gone before us, have been the first to sit down to the table, and to enjoy themselves, without interruption, from those who came afterwards; and not content with this enjoyment, they have disposed of the whole dinner, in such a manner, that nine-tenths of the beings that now people this globe, have not wherewith to dine, but upon terms such as these first monopolisers, or those to whom they pretend they have conferred their own power as successors, shall choose to dictate. It is as if after dining till they were satisfied, a general scramble ensued, for what remained on the table; and those who succeeded in filling their pockets and other receptacles, with provisions, should have something to give to their children; but those who should have the misfortune to get none, or having got it, should lose it again, through fraud, calamity, or force, should have none for theirs, to the latest generation.

Such is the exact resemblance of the present order of things. Ye proud and rich possessors of the earth, look at this, and see if it be not so; and being so, and seeing that it is in your power to consent to a more *honorable* method of obtaining title to possession; say, if ye will not do so? I do not ask you because it is in your power to confer any favor by giving such consent; for, this community, and every other, whenever they shall understand their rights, will have power enough in their own hands to do what they shall think fit, without seeking for any acquisition from you; but because it will be more agreeable to your own true happiness, to give such consent freely; than, with the ill, but unavailing grace of reluctance. Three hundred thousand freemen, in this state, hold votes in their hands, which no power that you can command can take out; and of these freemen, more than two hundred and fifty thousand are men whom a preceding generation, together with yourselves and their own ignorance of their rights have conspired to place in situations such that they have no property in the state of which they are citizens; although their title to such property is as good as that of any man that breathes.

The first possession of this state, by the ancestors of its present inhabitants, was acquired by means partaking of the nature of fraud, cunning, purchase and conquest, the latter predominating; acting upon ignorance, and want of the power of resistance.

. . .

But it is not necessary now to say more, in objection to titles obtained by possession, by conquest, or by any other imaginary species of acquisition. It has been shown already throughout these pages, I trust to the satisfaction of the reader, that *title* to property exists for all; and for all alike; not because others have been; nor because they have *not* been; not because they had a certain being for a parent, rather than another being; not because they appear later, or earlier, on the stage of life, than others; not because of purchase, of conquest, of preoccupancy, or what not; but BECAUSE THEY ARE: BECAUSE THEY EXIST. I AM; THEREFORE IS PROPERTY MINE; as much so as any man's, and that without asking any man's permission; without paying any man price; without knowing or caring farther than as my equal right extends, whether any other human being exists, or not. Such is the language of nature; such is the language of right; and such are the principles which will justify any people in pulling down any government, which denies, even to a *single* individual of the human race, his possession, his real tangible possession, of this unalienable right of nature; or its unquestionable equivalent. How much more so, then, is it the duty of any such people, to destroy their own government, when *more than nine-tenths*, it may be, are deprived of rights which the Creator gave them, when he gave them existence?

True Workingman (1846)

Are you an American citizen? Then you are a joint-owner of the public lands. Why not take enough of your property to provide yourself a home? Why not vote yourself a farm?

Remember Poor Richard's saying: "Now I have a sheep and a cow, every one bids me 'good morrow.'" If a man have a house and a home of his own, though it be a thousand miles off, he is well received in other people's houses; while the homeless wretch is turned away. The bare right to a farm, though you should never go near it, would save you from many an insult. Therefore, vote yourself a farm.

Are you a party follower? Then you have long enough employed your vote to benefit scheming office-seekers; use it for once to benefit yourself—vote yourself a farm.

Are you tired of slavery—of drudging for others—of poverty and its attendant miseries? Then, vote yourself a farm.

Are you endowed with reason? Then you must know that your right to life hereby includes the right to a place to live in—the right to a home. Assert this right, so long denied mankind by feudal robbers and their attorneys. Vote yourself a farm. . . .

Would you disarm this aristocracy of its chief weapon, the fearful power of banishment from God's earth? Then join with your neighbors to form a true American party, having for its guidance the principles of the American revolution, and whose chief measures shall be—1. To limit the quantity of land that any one man may henceforth monopolize or inherit; and 2. To make the public lands free to actual settlers only, each having the right to

SOURCE: *True Workingman*, January 24, 1846. Reprinted in Commons *et al., Documentary History*, Vol. VII, pp. 305–7.

sell his improvements to any man not possessed of other land. These great measures once carried, wealth would become a changed social element; it would then consist of the accumulated products of human labor, instead of a hoggish monopoly of the products of God's labor; and the antagonism of capital and labor would forever cease.

B. The Right of Access Versus the Rights of Landlords

• *James Fenimore Cooper* (*1845*)
• *Debates on a Homestead Bill* (*1852*)

The demand for free access to unsettled land increasingly clashed with a concern for secure property rights and a continuity of social order. James Fenimore Cooper (1789–1851), the most famous and successful American writer of the antebellum period, was a Jacksonian Democrat. Cooper nevertheless believed fervently in the virtues of a natural aristocracy and the need for an orderly transition from the wilderness stage of Indian occupancy, which he romanticized in his "Leatherstocking Tales," to a civilized stage of responsible landholders dedicated to public virtue and cautious progress. The privileged son of a New York State land magnate, Cooper harbored a bitter prejudice against Yankee entrepreneurs, speculators, demogagues, and self-made men. Associating democracy with benevolent paternalism, he pitted himself against "the anxious spirit of gain," whether personified in landless squatters or in sharp-dealing businessmen.

Even in the 1820s and 1830s, many of Cooper's novels dealt with what John P. McWilliams terms "the awkward transition between the State of Nature and the State of Civilization," a transition marked by struggle over the first legal and moral boundaries in a "neutral ground" of change and uncertain possibility.[1] But in the 1840s Cooper wrote a little-read trilogy, *The Littlepage Manuscripts*, which gave this theme a much sharper ideological edge. Already embittered by conflicts with the villagers of Cooperstown, New York (a settlement named for his father), Cooper was deeply alarmed by the agrarian radicalism encouraged by the Anti-Rent Wars in the Hudson Valley. Beginning in 1839, tenant farmers violently resisted the efforts of great landlords like the Rensselaers to collect longstanding debts and to enforce semifeudal obligations. By 1845 the Anti-Rent Wars had reached a point that induced the governor to declare a state of insurrection and call out the militia. The landlords, whose unusual privileges were based on colonial land patents, faced a public outcry which soon resulted in a more democratic system of land tenure. Cooper, while continuing to think of himself as a democrat, viewed the political agitation as a form of demagoguery aimed at seizing property for the politically influential at the expense of a minority who had lost public favor. For Cooper, once one accepted

---

[1] *Political Justice in a Republic: James Fenimore Cooper's America* (Berkeley: University of California Press, 1972), p. 10.

the slogan of George Henry Evans's National Reformers, "Vote Yourself a Farm,"[1] there was no security to any property whatever; a slight majority of voters, mobilized by militants on any issue, could overturn any law and gain special privileges for a new elite under the banner of "overthrowing aristocracy."

Cooper's response was to write three bitter novels depicting the social history of land ownership and community building in the Hudson Valley. If the books changed few minds and have little literary merit, they nevertheless succeed in illuminating the complexity of issues involved in antebellum struggles over access to wealth and power—largely because Cooper, even at his worst, was a skilled literary craftsman who managed through the device of fiction to achieve enough *distance* from events to present two or more points of view as a coherent, interrelated whole. He was too gifted a writer to settle for simplistic propaganda or to overlook the ambiguities of human interaction.

Our selection is taken from *The Chainbearer*, the second work in the trilogy. Though set in the 1780s, when the Littlepage family is just beginning to assert their rights to Hudson River Valley land invaded by squatters and speculators, the issues and principles are essentially those of the Anti-Rent Wars of the 1840s (the subject of Cooper's third *Littlepage* volume, *The Redskins* [1846]). An understanding of the selection requires some background. We begin with a dialogue between Mordaunt Littlepage, a young veteran of the Battle of Yorktown and the son of an illustrious patriot who owns extensive tracts of wilderness in Upstate New York, and Susquesus (also called "Sureflint"), an Indian brave who has long been an ally of the Littlepage family. Mordaunt, acting as attorney for his father, is being guided by Susquesus to family lands he has never seen, lands neglected during the Revolution and now being stripped of timber by Yankee squatters and town developers. The voice of Susquesus allows Cooper to express, in innocent and primitive form, the questions that were then being posed by radical agrarians. Cooper thus has a setup for didactic lectures by Littlepage on the foundations of civilization. This could be dismissed as insufferable propaganda if it were not for two qualifications. First, Cooper is committed to racial equality, allowing only for different racial "gifts" according to stages of civilization; second, as a writer who romanticized Indian life he is ambivalent about the moral "progress" of civilization, particularly the appropriation of land by individuals. As in all his novels, the legitimacy of the white man's title depends on Indian consent and sanction.

In the second part of the selection from *The Chainbearer*, we turn to the villain, "Thousandacres" (whose real name is Aaron Timberman), a Yankee squatter whose family has set up a sawmill on the Littlepage estate. Thou-

---

[1] A slogan repeated in our last selection, from the *True Workingman*, which appeared early in 1846 and which we can now interpret within the context of the Anti-Rent War campaign.

sandacres has captured both Mordaunt Littlepage and Andries Coejemans, or "the Chainbearer," an aged but hardy woodsman and surveyor of Dutch descent. Coejemans, who had fought at Yorktown with Mordaunt Littlepage, is for Cooper the symbolic link between wilderness virtues—freedom, competence, and self-reliance—and the lawful boundaries of social order. He is called "the Chainbearer" because he carries the surveyor's chain to establish precise property rights and to mark off plots of land for sale or lease. Like the Indian, he is a man of the woods, a man of free spirit; yet his chain helps establish, according to Cooper's ideology, the only freedom possible within the constraints of civilization. Still, symbolically, he is a man chained, an illiterate, dialect-ridden Dutchman employed by the Littlepages (Mordaunt is a Princeton graduate) to discover what it is that they own. In this confrontation between Thousandacres and his captives, it is Chainbearer who symbolizes and defends law and order against all the agrarian arguments which Thousandacres mouths and which Cooper takes pains to link, even in footnotes, to the radical press of the 1840s. In the end, not included in this selection, Thousandacres' family shoot and kill Chainbearer. Again, it is a sign of Cooper's ambivalence that his own arguments are voiced in almost ludicrous dialect[1] by an aged family servant whose life is perfunctorily sacrificed in accordance with the rules of an equally ludicrous and romantic plot. Whatever his overt message, Cooper seemed to sense that the future belonged to lawless entrepreneurs ("timbermen") who could claim thousands of acres, not to elderly Dutch woodsmen who had become chainbearers, or to educated "little pages" (the name "Mordaunt," meaning "biting, sarcastic," hardly suggests triumphant victory).

The second selection is a sample of Congressional debate on the question of opening the public domain to free homesteads. Before the Civil War, homestead bills had no chance of overcoming southern resistance, based on the fear that the public domain, if monopolized by small family farms, would be excluded from slaveholder settlement. Hence, the Congressional debates of the 1850s mark the final stage, in our period, of the controversy over access to land as a "birthright" and "God-given" resource. But by no means all opponents of free homesteads were southern slaveholders. Josiah Sutherland (1804–1887), who here presents the negative case, was a Democrat and an attorney from the Hudson Valley country that had just emerged from the Anti-Rent Wars. Henry Hastings Sibley (1811–1891), who defends free homesteads, was the son of New Englanders who migrated to the wilderness of the Michigan Territory. After a career as a fur trader in the Far West, Sibley helped to organize the Minnesota Territory and, in 1849, was elected as delegate to Congress. A Democrat, Sibley became Minnesota's first governor after the territory was admitted as a state.

---

[1] Cooper's rendering of Dutch dialect makes difficult reading; I have taken the liberty of changing some of the spelling in the interest of comprehensibility.

James Fenimore Cooper (1845)

[Mordaunt Littlepage] "Oh! How long is it since I saw the patent [a tract of wilderness land owned by Mordaunt's father]. I never saw it, Sureflint; this is my first visit."

[Susquesus] "Dat queer! How you own land, when nebber see him?"

"Among the pale-faces we have such laws that property passes from parent to child; and I inherit mine in this neighborhood from my grandfather, Herman Mordaunt."

"What dat mean, 'herit? How man haf land, when he don't keep him?"

"We do keep it, if not by actually remaining on the spot, by means of our laws and our titles. The pale-faces regulate all these things on paper, Sureflint."

"T'ink dat good? Why not let man take land where he want him, when he want him? Plenty land. Got more land dan got people. 'Nough for ebberybody."

"That fact makes our laws just; if there were not land enough for everybody, these restrictions and divisions might seem to be, and in fact be, unjust. Now, any man can have a farm, who will pay a very moderate price for it. The state sells, and landlords sell; and those who don't choose to buy of one, can buy of the other."

"Dat true 'nough; but don't see need of dat paper. When he want to stay on land, let him stay; when he want to go somewhere, let 'noder man come. What good pay for betterment?"

"So as to have betterments. These are what we call the rights of property, without which no man could aim at being anything more than clad and fed. Who would hunt, if anybody that came along had a right to pick up and skin his game?"

"See dat well 'nough—nebber do; no, nebber. Don't see why land go like skin, when skin go wid warrior and hunter, and land stay where he be."

"That is because the riches of you redmen are confined to movable property, and to your wigwams, so long as you choose to live in them. Thus far, you respect the rights of property as well as the pale-faces; but you must see a great difference between your people and mine!—between the redman and the white man?"

"Be sure, differ; one strong, t'oder weak; one rich, t'oder poor; one great, t'oder little; one drive 'way, t'oder haf to go; one gets all, t'oder keep nuttin'; one march large army, t'oder go Indian file, fifty warrior, p'raps—dat reason t'ing so."

"And why can the pale-faces march in large armies, with cannon, and horses, and bayonets, and the redman not do the same?"

"Cause he no got 'em; no got warrior—no got gun—no got baggonet—no got nuttin'."

SOURCE: James Fenimore Cooper, *The Chainbearer* (New York: G. P. Putnam's Sons, n.d.; first published 1845), pp. 111–15, 318, 320–26, 329.

"You have given the effect for the cause, Sureflint, or the consequences of the reason for the reason itself. I hope I make you understand me. Listen, and I will explain. You have lived much with the white men, Susquesus, and can believe what I say. There are good, and there are bad, among all people. Color makes no difference in this respect. Still, all people are not alike. The white man is stronger than the redman, and has taken away his country, because he knows most."

. . .

[Mordaunt Littlepage] "No, Susquesus; the redskin is as brave as the pale-face; as willing to defend his rights, and as able-bodied; but he does not know as much. He had no gunpowder until the white man gave it to him— no rifle, no hoe, no knife, no tomahawk, but such as he made himself from stones. Now, all the knowledge, and all the arts of life that the white man enjoys and turns to his profit, come from the rights of property. No man would build a wigwam to make rifles in, if he thought he could not keep it as long as he wished, sell it when he pleased, and leave it to his son when he went to the land of spirits. It is by encouraging man's love of himself, in this manner, that he is got to do so much. Thus it is, too, that the father gives to the son what he has learned, as well as what he has built or bought; and so, in time, nations get to be powerful, as they get to be what we call civilized. Without these rights of property, no people could be civilized; for no people would do their utmost, unless each man were permitted to be master of what he can acquire, subject to the great and common laws that are necessary to regulate such matters."

. . .

"A man must work for himself to do his most; and he cannot work for himself unless he enjoys the fruits of his labor. Thus it is, that he must have a right of property in land, either bought or hired, in order to make him cause that land to produce all that nature intended it should produce. On this necessity is founded the right of property; the gain being civilization; the loss ignorance, and poverty, and weakness. It is for this reason, then, that we buy and sell land, as well as clothes, and arms, and beads."

"T'ink, understand. Great Spirit, den, say must have farm?"

"The Great Spirit has said we must have wants and wishes, that can be met, or gratified, only by having farms. To have farms we must have owners; and owners cannot exist unless their rights in their lands are protected. As soon as these are gone, the whole building would tumble down about our ears, Susquesus."

"Well s'pose him so. We see, some time. Young chief [Littlepage] know where he is?"

"Not exactly; but I suppose we are drawing near to the lands of Ravens-nest."

"Well, queer 'nough, too! Own land, but don't know him. See—marked tree—dat sign your land begin."

"Thank you, Sureflint—a parent would not know his own child, when he saw him for the first time. If I am owner here, you will remember that this is my first visit to the spot."

· · ·

Thousandacres had not altogether neglected forms, though so much set against the spirit of the law. We found a sort of court collected before the door of his dwelling, with himself in the centre. . . .

When in the room, Chainbearer [Andries Coejemans] and I seated ourselves near the door, while Thousandacres had a chair on the turf without, surrounded by his sons, all of whom were standing.

· · ·

The silence which occurred after we took our seats must have lasted several minutes. For myself, I saw I was only a secondary person in this interview; old Andries having completely supplanted me in importance, not only in acts, but in the estimation of the squatters. To him they were accustomed [familiar], and accustomed, moreover, to regard as a sort of hostile power; his very pursuit [occupation] being opposed to the great moving principle of their every-day lives. The man who measured land, and he who took it to himself without measurement, were exactly antagonist forces, in morals as well as in physics; and might be supposed not to regard each other with the most friendly eyes. Thus it was that the Chainbearer actually became an object of greater interest to these squatters, than the son of one of the owners of the soil, and the attorney in fact of both.

· · ·

"Chainbearer," commenced Thousandacres, after the pause already mentioned had lasted several minutes, and speaking with a dignity that could only have proceeded from the intensity of his feelings; "Chainbearer, you've been an inimy to me and mine sin' the day we first met. You're an inimy by your cruel callin'; yet you've the boldness to thrust yourself into my very hands!"

"I'm an enemy to all knaves, T'ousantacres, ant I don't care who knows it," answered old Andries, sternly; "t'at ist my trate, ast well ast carryin' chain; ant I wish it to pe known far and near. Ast for pein' your enemy by callin', I may say as much for yourself; since there coult pe no surveyin', or carryin' of chain, til all t'e people help t'emselves to lant, as you haf done your whole life, wit'out as much as sayin' to t'e owners 'By your leaf.'"

· · ·

[Thousandacres] "In talkin' this matter over, young man, I purpose to begin at the beginnin' of things," he said; "for I allow, if you grant any value to titles, and king's grants, and sich sort of things, that my rights here be no great matter. But, beginnin' at the beginnin', the case is very different. You'll admit, I s'pose, that the Lord created the heavens and the 'arth, and that he created man to be master over the last."

· · ·

[Chainbearer] "Well, admittin' all you say, squatter, how does t'at make your right here better t'an t'at of any ot'er man?" demanded Andries, disdainfully.

"Why, reason tells us where a man's rights begin, you'll see, Chainbearer. Here is the 'arth, as I told you, given to man, to be used for his wants. When you and I are born, some parts of the world is in use, and some parts isn't. We want land, when we are old enough to turn our hands to labor, and I make my pitch out here in the woods, say where no man has pitched afore me. Now, in my judgment that makes the best of titles, the Lord's title."

"Well, t'en, you've got your title from t'e Lort," answered Chainbearer, "and you've got your land. I s'pose you'll not take all t'e 'art' t'at is not yet peopled, and I shoult like to know how you wilt run your lines petween you and your next neighpor. Atmittin' you're here in t'e woods, how much of t'e land woult you take for your own religious uses, and how much woult you leaf for t'e next comer?"

"Each man would take as much as was necessary for his wants, Chainbearer, and hold as much as he possessed."

· · ·

"Don't be onreasonable—don't be onreasonable in your questions, Chainbearer; and I'll answer every one on 'em, and in a way to satisfy you, or any judgmatical man. How long do I want the lumber? As long as I've use for it. How long do I want to keep the boys busy? Till they're tired of the place, and want to change works. When a man's aweary of his pitch, let him give it up for another, selling his betterments [improvements], of course, to the best chap he can light on."

"Oh! you't sell your petterments, woult you! What! sell t'e Lort's title, olt T'ousantacres? Part wit' Heaven's gift for t'e value of poor miseraple silver and golt?"

"You don't comprehend Aaron," put in Prudence [Thousandacre's wife], who saw that Chainbearer was likely to get the best of the argument, and who was always ready to come to the rescue of any of her tribe, whether it might be necessary with words, or tooth and nail, or the rifle. "You don't, by no manner of means, comprehend Aaron, Chainbearer. His idee is, that the Lord has made the 'arth for his critturs; that any one that wants land has a right to take as much as he wants, and to use it as long as he likes; and when he has done, to part with his betterments for sich price as may be agreed on."

"I stick to that," joined in the squatter, with a loud hem, like a man who was sensible of relief; "that's my idee, and I'm determined to live and die by it."

"You've lifed py it, I know very well, T'ousantacres; and, now you're old, it's quite likely you'll die by it. As for comprehentin', you don't comprehent yourself. I'll just ask you, in the first place, how much land do you holt on t'is very spot? You're here squattet so completely and finally as to haf built a mill. Now tell me how much land you holt, t'at when I come to squat alongsite of you, our fences may not lap on one anot'er. I ask a simple question, and I hope for a plain ant straight answer. Show me t'e boundaries of your domain, ant how much of t'e world you claim, and how much you ton't claim."

"I've pretty much answered that question already, Chainbearer. My creed is, that a man has a right to hold all he wants, and to want all he holds."

"God help t'e men, t'en, t'at haf to carry chain between you and your neighpors, T'ousantacres; a man's wants totay, may differ from his wants to-morrow, and to-morrow from t'e next tay, and so on to t'e end of time! On your doctrine, not'in' would pe settlet, and all woult be at sixes and sevens."

. . .

[Thousandacres] "Take him away, boys, take him back to the store-house," said the old squatter, rising and moving a little on one side to permit Andries to pass, as if afraid to trust himself too near; "he was born the sarvent of the rich, and will die their sarvent. Chains be good enough for him, and I wish him no greater harm than to carry chains the rest of his days."

"Oh! you're a true son of liberty!" called out the Chainbearer, as he quietly returned to his prison; "a true son of liberty, accordin' to your own conceit! You want eferyt'ing in your own way, and eferyt'ing in your own pocket."

Debates on a Homestead Bill (1852)

[The Honorable Josiah Sutherland, New York] What is this bill, then, Mr. Chairman? What ought it to be called? What ought to be its title? It is in fact a bill to grant to every man or widow in the United States, who is the head of a family, and has no land, and is not worth $500, one hundred and sixty acres of the public domain, on certain conditions, for his or her benefit, and thus more nearly equalize the distribution of property. It should be so entitled—it should be so called. . . .

. . . Who ask for it? Who demand it? Certain associations, called "Industrial Congresses"—offsprings of the German school of socialism, and of the American school of "higher law" transcendentalism—partly political, partly agrarian. Upon what ground do they ask for it? Upon what ground do they demand it? They ask for it, as a gift, as a charity, to better their condition, and to enable them to live without working, at least for others; and, while they ask for it as a gift, as a charity, they at the same time demand it as a matter of right, for which, even if granted, they will owe no thanks to the Government; for they place their right to it upon the natural rights of man, and not upon the Constitution and laws of their country, or the charity of Congress. They ask and demand it upon grounds and theories of the natural rights of man, as I understand them, utterly inconsistent with that great principle, the recognition and security of individual property, which lies at the foundation of all civilized government not only, but of all civilized society; for upon the security of property hangs industry, the mother of all

SOURCE: *Congressional Globe*, Appendix, April 22, and April 24, 1852. Reprinted in Commons, *et al.*, *Documentary History*, Vol. VIII, pp. 68–70, 74–75.

arts, of all science, of all wealth; the mother and supporter of all law, order, governments; of the virtues and charities of individuals, and of the wealth and power of nations, and without which, the whole earth would be but one moral and physical waste. . . .

What is the difficulty with manufactures now? Why does even the manufacturer of iron ask for further protection? Is it a want of a market for his iron? Protect iron to any extent, and we will not be able, in years, to manufacture all the country will want. No; it is the cost of manufacturing it here that calls for the protection. And why the cost here? It is not the cost of the raw material—of the ore, or of the coal. It is, then, the cost of the labor —the high price of labor here. . . .

I am not advocating now, either protection and low wages, or free trade and high wages; but my point is, that this homestead bill will take labor from the manufacturing states to the land states—from the manufactories of the East to the farms of the West—and thereby increase the cost of labor and the cost of manufacturing.

. . . I think this bill is an attack on the rights of property, for I can see no difference in principle, in taking the property of A B and giving it to C D, because he has none; and taking the property of all the people of the United States, and giving it to those only who have no land. I look upon this bill as agrarian, and if it should become a law, as the first only of measures brought forward to more nearly equalize the distribution of property. . . .

• • •

[The Honorable Henry Hastings Sibley, Minnesota Territory] . . . I know the character of the pioneer, and of the men who even now are on their way to the West, and I speak understandingly when I say, that it is such homes as this bill, if adopted, will create, which will ever remain the nurseries of that love of freedom, by which alone our present happy form of government can be perpetuated. . . .

The Government has watched its public domain with a jealous eye, and there are now enactments upon your statute-books, aimed at the trespasser upon it, which should be expunged as a disgrace to the country and to the nineteenth century. Especially is he pursued with unrelenting severity, who has dared to break the silence of the primeval forest by the blows of the American axe. The hardy lumberman, who has penetrated the remotest wilds of the Northwest, to drag from their recesses, the materials for building up towns and cities in the great valley of the Mississippi, has been particularly marked out as a victim. After enduring all the privations, and subjecting himself to the perils incident to his vocation—when he has toiled for months to add, by his honest labor, to the comfort of his fellow-men, and to the aggregate wealth of the nation—he finds himself suddenly in the clutches of the law, for trespassing on the public domain. . . .

The Changing Uses of Law

A. Two Versions of Law for the Frontier

- *David Crockett* (*1834*)
- *Joseph Story* (*1821*)

It would be difficult to find two contemporaries with more contrasting careers and temperaments than those of David Crockett (1786–1836) and Joseph Story (1779–1845). The son of a tavern-keeper in frontier Tennessee, Crocket ran away from home, successfully avoided schooling, failed at farming, and finally won some renown as a hunter and Indian fighter. After drifting to a wilderness settlement in Tennessee, described below, he was informally chosen as a judge, later elected as a colonel in the local militia, and sent to the state legislature. Unfortunately, most of our knowledge depends on the mythic "Davy Crockett" pictured in his autobiographical writings, which were probably ghostwritten, and which were part of a Whig campaign to build up a Western "man of nature" as a rival to Andrew Jackson. In popular image, at least, Crockett was a shrewd, fearless, swaggering fighter whose intuitive good sense was uncontaminated by book learning. He jubilantly divided his time between lumber speculation, swapping tall tales over a bottle of whiskey, capturing enough votes to be elected to Congress, and killing 105 bears in a single season. Whatever the exaggeration, Crockett did serve three terms in Congress. After being defeated by the Jacksonians in Tennessee, he moved southwestward to join the Texan war for independence and died at the Alamo.

Joseph Story's early life was dominated by security, fixity of purpose, and incredible self-discipline. Born in Marblehead, Massachusetts, the son of a wealthy physician, Story soon developed a compulsive will to study. After graduating second in his class at Harvard (William Ellery Channing was first), he plunged into years of concentrated, self-taught legal study, consuming esoteric treatises and reports as avidly as Davy Crockett shot bear. By age thirty-two, Story had established an immensely profitable legal practice, had instituted important law reform as a Massachusetts legislator, had been elected to Congress, and had been appointed an associate justice of the United States Supreme Court. In middle life, Story established record feats of productivity. As a Supreme Court justice he wrote hundreds of opinions, some landmarks in learning and subsequent influence, and rode "circuit" hearing cases through New England. He taught law at the newly-founded Harvard Law School and helped shape the formative stage of American legal education. Most extraordinary was that Story found time to churn out a long shelf of volumes, including his internationally acclaimed *Commentaries,* dealing with an immense sweep of technical legal subjects. With Davy Crockett, he seemed to share only a common hostility toward President Andrew Jackson, who called Story "the most dangerous man in America."

Yet in a wider sense Crockett too, though he brags of never having "read a page in a law book in all my life," is concerned in the selection below with adapting law to peculiar American conditions. Like Story and other judges of his time, Crockett assumes that law is an objective standard, independent of personal taste or self-interest, based ultimately on "principles of common justice and honesty between man and man." For all of his faith in "natural born sense" as the source of true law, Crockett's cavalier attitude toward formal legal procedures can be read as an ultimate *appeal* to legal procedures as a means of vindicating the natural justice of communities outside the reach of established institutions. For example, he takes pride in the fact that the Tennessee legislature confirmed most of the appointments of his informal, frontier "corporation." Even Story could not have exulted more from the thought that "my judgments were never appealed from, and if they had been, they would have stuck like wax. . . ."

Story's 1821 *Address* to the lawyers of Suffolk County (Boston) is a classic account of the painful emergence and progress of a specifically American law, indebted to English precedent but hammered out by American needs and circumstances, slowly overcoming local interest, ignorance, and jealousy. In the following excerpt, Story turns romantic and conventional assumptions upside down. In Kentucky, then celebrated by romanticists as the abode of Daniel Boone and of frontier individualism, Story finds a confusion of land titles that gives rise to a "metaphysical" legal system built on "artificial" principles. In other words, permissiveness leads to chaos and complexity. In the absence of clear and authoritative rules governing the acquisition and transfer of land, law becomes hopelessly difficult, parochial, and untranslatable into the legal language of other jurisdictions. In 1821, many reformers and American nationalists associated such words as "metaphysical" and "artificial" with the system of common law, based on the ancient precedents of English courts. In contrast, Story refers to the "simplicity and certainty" of the *structure* derived from English common law. But he then goes on to associate this simplicity and certainty with the rational order and mathematical precision of federal land policy—the legislative policy of rectangular surveys and subdivisions in advance of settlement. Ironically, Story finds chaos and complexity precisely where Crockett finds spontaneous and natural order—in a disregard for the precedents and learning of the past. Yet both Story and Crockett envision national progress as a "regularizing" process, subjecting local decisions on rights and obligations to the procedures of a larger unity.

David Crockett (1834)

It was just only a little distance in the purchase [in what was to become Giles County, Tennessee], and no order had been established there; but I thought I could get along without order as well as anybody else. And so I moved and settled myself down on the head of Shoal Creek. We remained here some two or three years, without any law at all; and so many bad characters began to flock in upon us, that we found it necessary to set up a sort of temporary government of our own. I don't mean that we made any president, and called him the "government," but we met and made what we called a corporation; and I reckon we called *it* wrong, for it wasn't a bank, and hadn't any deposits; and now they call the bank a corporation. But be this as it may, we lived in the backwoods, and didn't profess to know much, and no doubt used many wrong words. But we met, and appointed magistrates and constables to keep order. We didn't fix any laws for them, though; for we supposed they would know law enough, whoever they might be; and so we left it to themselves to fix the laws.

I was appointed one of the magistrates; and when a man owed a debt, and wouldn't pay it, I and my constable ordered our warrant, and then he would take the man, and bring him before me for trial. I would give judgment against him, and then an order for an execution would easily scare the debt out of him. If any one was charged with marking his neighbor's hogs, or with stealing anything,—which happened pretty often in those days,—I

source: David Crockett, *The Autobiography of David Crockett* (New York: A. L. Burt, 1902), pp. 98–101.

would have him taken, and if there were tolerable grounds for the charge, I would have him well whipp'd and cleared. We kept this up till our legislature added us to the white settlements in Giles county, and appointed magistrates by law, to organize matters in the parts where I lived. They appointed nearly every man a magistrate who had belonged to our corporation. I was then, of course, made a squire, according to law; though now the honor rested more heavily on me than before. For, at first, whenever I told my constable, says I—"Catch that fellow and bring him up for trial,"—away he went, and the fellow must come, dead or alive; for we considered this a good warrant, though it was only in verbal writing [*sic*]. But after I was appointed by the assembly, they told me my warrants must be in real writing, and signed; and that I must keep a book, and write my proceedings in it. This was a hard business on me, for I could just barely write my own name; but to do this, and write the warrants too, was at least a huckleberry over my persimmon. I had a pretty well informed constable, however, and he aided me very much in this business. Indeed, I had so much confidence in him that I told him, when we should happen to be out anywhere, and see that a warrant was necessary, and would have a good effect, he needn't take the trouble to come all the way to me to get one, but he could just fill out one; and then on the trial I could correct the whole business if he had committed any error. In this way I got on pretty well, till by care and attention I improved my handwriting in such a manner as to be able to prepare my warrants, and keep my record book without much difficulty. My judgments were never appealed from, and if they had been, they would have stuck like wax, as I gave my decisions on the principles of common justice and honesty between man and man, and relied on natural born sense, and not on law learning to guide me; for I had never read a page in a law book in all my life.

Joseph Story (1821)

As to the structure of land titles, there is a considerable diversity in the states, and in several of them a great departure from the simplicity and certainty of those derived under the common law. I am not aware that in any part of New England any serious difficulties are to be found on this subject, all titles having had their origin in separate grants derived directly from the government or confirmed by it, and having the usual formalities and certainty of grants of the crown at common law, or of grants by private legislative acts. The only questions, which have been much litigated, are those of boundary, which may and do ordinarily arise under grants between private persons, and of these there have been few of any considerable magnitude. Far different has been the course of proceeding in some other parts of the Union. . . .

SOURCE: Joseph Story, *An Address Delivered Before the Members of the Suffolk Bar* [1821] (Boston: Freeman & Bolles, 1829), pp. 18–21.

The system of land titles in Kentucky is indeed one of the most abstruse branches of local jurisprudence, built up on artificial principles, singularly acute and metaphysical, and quite as curious and intricate, as some of the higher doctrines of contingent remainders and executory devises. It affords an illustrious example of human infirmity and human ingenuity. . . .

The vice of the original system consisted in enabling any persons to appropriate the lands of the state by entries and descriptions of their own, without any previous survey under public authority, and without any such boundaries as were precise, permanent, and unquestionable; and the issuing of grants upon such entries without any inquiry as to the true nature, description, and survey of the lands, and without any attempt to prevent duplicate grants of the same property. If we consider, that Kentucky was at this time a wilderness traversed principally by hunters; that many places must have been but very imperfectly known even to them, and must have received different appellations from occasional and disconnected visitants; if we consider, that the lands were rich, and the spirit of speculation was pushed to a most extravagant extent, and that the spirit of fraud, as is but too common, followed close upon the heels of speculation; if we consider the infinite diversity, which under such circumstances must unavoidably exist in the descriptions of the appropriated tracts of land, arising from ignorance, or carelessness, or innocent mistake, or fraud, or personal rashness;—we ought not to be surprised at the fact, that the best part of Kentucky is oppressed by conflicting titles, and that in many instances there are three layers of them lapping on or covering each other. . . .

The land law of Kentucky, while it stands alone in its subtle and refined distinctions, has attained a symmetry, which at this moment enables it to be studied almost with scientific precision. But ages will probably elapse before the litigations founded on it will be closed; and so little assistance can be gained from the lights of the common law for its comprehension, that to the lawyers of other states, it will forever remain an unknown code with a peculiar dialect, to be explored and studied like the jurisprudence of some foreign nation.

In order to avoid such serious evils, the government of the United States, with a wisdom and foresight which entitle it to the highest praise, has in the system of land laws, which regulate the sales of its own territorial demesnes, given great certainty, simplicity, and uniformity, to the titles derived under it. With a few unimportant exceptions, all lands are surveyed before they are offered for sale. They are surveyed in ranges, and are divided into townships each six miles square, and these are subdivided into thirty-six sections, each one mile square, containing six hundred and forty acres. All the dividing lines run to the cardinal points [the four chief directions of the compass], and of course intersect each other at right angles, except where fractional sections are formed by navigable rivers, or by an Indian boundary line. The subdividing lines of quarter sections are not actually surveyed, but the corners, boundaries, and contents of these, are designated and ascertained by fixed rules prescribed by law; and regular maps of all the surveys are lodged in the proper departments of the government. In this manner, with some few exceptions, the public lands in Alabama, Mississippi, Louisiana, Ohio, Indiana, and Illinois, have been sold; and the system applies universally to all our remaining territorial possessions. The common law doctrines have, in respect to these titles, taken deep root, and flourished; and the waters, which divide the states on the opposite banks of the Ohio [between Kentucky and Ohio], do not form a more permanent boundary of their respective territorial possessions, than the different origin of their land titles does in the character of their local jurisprudence.

B. The Common Law in America

- *Joseph Story* (1829)
- *Henry Dwight Sedgwick* (1824)

In the first selection below, Joseph Story attempts to define the meaning of Anglo-American common law. Yet Story would have been the first to agree that no single definition is adequate, since common law is flexible, indefinite, expansive, and "unwritten" in the sense of being based on judicial custom and precedent, not enacted by lawmakers or systematized in a legal code. What appealed to Story, James Kent, and other American jurists was the thought that English common law provided a body of principles and standards legitimized by centuries of practical experience in reconciling conflicting rights, duties, and interests—"the gathered wisdom of a thousand years." In a nation so diverse as America, intricately divided by state and federal jurisdictions, the common law held promise as a great cohesive agent, an authoritative source of clarity and uniformity. Even more important, for jurists like Story, was the urgent need for upholding against the growing "influence" of public opinion the ideal of government by law and not by men. In the absence of other traditional institutions, the common law remained the only bulwark against sudden gusts of popular enthusiasm or reckless legislation guided by immediate self-interest and blind to long-term social consequences.

By 1829, Story's views were unmistakably conservative. His two-hour inaugural lecture as Dane Professor at Harvard, from which our brief excerpt is taken, was delivered six months after Andrew Jackson's inauguration as President. It was intended to rally every lawyer "as a public sentinel, to watch the approach of danger, and to sound the alarm when oppression is at hand." Story was most concerned with the oppression of the rich and privileged. On the other hand, he firmly believed that any legislative undermining of property rights would also erode the legal protections of the weak, the poor, and the unpopular. Having begun his career as a Jeffersonian Republican, surrounded by reactionary Federalists, Story retained a commitment to science, progress, and republican principles. Though all too aware of the growing attacks on "judge-made law" as aristocratic and essentially un-American, his response is to emphasize the practicality and progressive nature of common law in contrast to statutes, which he sees as abstract, difficult to interpret, and fraught with unintended injustice. If common law requires a *gradual* accommodation to new needs and interests, Story insists on its compatibility with unlimited social progress.

One of the critics Story had in mind was Henry Dwight Sedgwick (1785–1831), the son of a famous Connecticut jurist and statesman and the member of a prominent New England family (he was the brother of Catharine Sedgwick, who appears in Unit One, Part 2, B). Believing that a new age should not be saddled with the fears and prejudices of the past and should be open-minded toward innovation, Sedgwick had broken ranks from the judicial establishment by writing, in 1824, a highly favorable review essay of a blistering attack on the common law. The author of the attack, William Sampson, could hardly have been less congenial to Story's New England Unitarian culture. An Irish radical who had studied law in England, Sampson was also a Catholic and a political exile who did not look with favor on the supposed sanctity of English institutions. He savagely ridiculed the barbarity and superstition surrounding the common law, and urged that America choose the unencumbered path of legislative statute and systematic codification. Sedgwick had the gall to praise Sampson's work in the pages of *The North American Review*, seen by people like Story as the defining voice of American culture. Moreover, Sedgwick used his review as an excuse for advancing his own arguments, more moderate in tone than Sampson's, favoring statute law and codification.

Although Sedgwick's essay appeared nearly five years before Story's *Discourse*, I have reversed the chronological order because Sedgwick's critique requires some understanding of the common law as revered by men like Story. The differences between the two go far beyond an academic debate. They involve the basic standards of fairness and justice that American courts will apply to conflicts over access to wealth and power. Sedgwick is addressing broad questions of ideology and motive, especially the obsolescence of fears of innovation engendered by the French Revolution and hence the dangers, in an era of rapid change and new social needs, of excessive veneration of tradition. In one sense, the differences between Story and Sedgwick are a matter of degree. Sedgwick calls only for removing the "artificial barriers" imposed by common law; Story, who agrees that much of the English common law is inapplicable to America, looks forward to its continuous improvement. Within a few years, however, there would be far more uncompromising attacks on the power of the judiciary and on judge-made law as arbitrary, self-serving, and undemocratic. The defenders of common law won a long and at times uphill battle only by reconciling themselves to legislative authority and adapting common law to the rapidly changing needs of commerce and industry.

Joseph Story (1829)

By the *common* law is sometimes understood that collection of principles, which constitutes the basis of the administration of justice in England, in contradistinction to the maxims of the Roman code, which has universally received the appellation of the *civil* law. The latter has been adopted . . . into the juridical polity of all continental Europe, as a fundamental rule. The former is emphatically the custom of the realm of England, and has no authority beyond her own territory, and the colonies, which she has planted in various parts of the world. It is no small proof of its excellence, however, that where it has once taken root, it has never been superseded; and that its direct progress, or silent sway, has never failed to obliterate the attachment to other codes, whenever the accidents of conquest or cession have brought it within the reach of popular opinion. But there is another sense (which is the most usual sense), in which it is called the *common* law, to distinguish it from the *statute* law, or the positive enactments of the legislature. In this sense the common law is . . . the unwritten law, which cannot now be traced back to any positive text [enactment], but is composed of customs, and usages, and maxims, deriving their authority from immemorial practice, and the recognitions of courts of justice. . . . Much, indeed, of this unwritten law may now be found in books, in elementary treatises, and in judicial decisions. But it does not derive its force from these circumstances. On the contrary, even judicial decisions are deemed but the formal promulgation of rules antecedently existing, and obtain all their value from their supposed conformity to those rules.

When our ancestors emigrated to America, they brought this common law with them, as their birthright and inheritance; and they put into operation so much of it as was applicable to their situation. It became the basis of the jurisprudence of all the English colonies; and, except so far as it has been abrogated or modified by our local legislation, it remains to this very hour the guide, the instructer, the protector, and the ornament of every state within this republic, whose territory lies within our boundaries by the treaty of peace of 1783.[1] May it ever continue to flourish here; for it is the law of liberty, and the watchful and inflexible guardian of private property and public rights.

It is of this common law, in its largest extent, that the Law Institution in this university [Harvard] proposes to expound the doctrines and diversities; and thus to furnish the means of a better juridical education to those who are destined for the profession, as well as to those who, as scholars and gentlemen, desire to learn its general principles.

• • •

SOURCE: Joseph Story, *Discourse Pronounced Upon the Inauguration of the Author, as Dane Professor of Law in Harvard University* (Cambridge, Mass.: E. W. Metcalf and Co., 1829), pp. 5–9.

[1] Story is specifically excluding Louisiana which was under the French civil code.

Whoever will take the trouble to reflect upon the vast variety of subjects, with which it [the common law] is conversant, and the almost infinite diversity of human transactions, to which it applies; whoever will consider how much astuteness and ingenuity are required to unravel or guard against the contrivances of fraud, and the indiscretions of folly, the caprices of the wise and the errors of the rash, the mistakes of pride, the confidence of ignorance, and the sallies of enterprise, will be at no loss to understand, that there will be ample employment for the highest faculties. If he will but add to the account, that law is a science, which must be gradually formed by the successive efforts of many minds in many ages; that its rudiments sink deep into remote antiquity, and branch wider and wider with every new generation; that it seeks to measure the future by approximations to certainty derived solely from the experience of the past; that it must for ever be in a state of progress, or change, to adapt itself to the exigencies and changes of society; that even when the old foundations remain firm, the shifting channels of business must often leave their wonted beds deserted, and require new and broader substructions to accommodate and support new interests. If, I say, he will but add these things to the account, it will soon become matter of surprise, that even the mightiest efforts of genius can keep pace with such incessant demands; and that the powers of reasoning, tasked and subtilized as they must be, to an immeasurable extent, should not be absolutely overwhelmed in the attempt to administer justice.

Henry Dwight Sedgwick (1824)

This extreme artificialness, and technicality of the English common law, both as to its principles and its practice, distinguishes that system very broadly from every other. This distinction is remotely analogous to that which exists between the syllogistic mode of reasoning, and the ordinary style of argument in which a plain man would press his conclusions. . . . Since those periods [of our English ancestors] the condition of the people has undergone a change almost radical, but the laws have not experienced a correspondent revolution. Lands in this country and in England are nearly as much the subject of traffic, as the public stocks, and yet the *theory* of the law of real estate is almost as feudal as it was in those times, when resort was had for national defense, not to the monied sources of the country, but to the lands which were held on the condition of performing military service. Society has grown and spread in every direction; wealth has increased to an immense degree, and its nature changed by the disproportionate increase of personal property; occupations and interests are in a thousand ways extended and diversified; but all this has been done silently and gradually; there has been no revolu-

SOURCE: Henry Dwight Sedgwick, [review of] "An Anniversary Discourse delivered before the Historical Society . . . showing the Origin, Progress, Antiquities, Curiosities, and Nature of the Common Law. By William Sampson," *North American Review*, Vol. XIX (October, 1824), pp. 417–21.

tionary period, no crisis, no epoch when the community, finding itself thrown into new circumstances, was obliged to cast about for new rules or principles to guide it in the emergency.

The lawyers and judges of the common law were not in advance of the age; they did not perceive the alteration that had begun and was going on in the structure of society; on the contrary, they strove to apply old rules, with which only they were acquainted, to new relations and new things. In addition to this, and cooperating with it, was that love of quaintness, refined reasoning, and fanciful analogy, which characterises the early stages of civilization. It was necessarily the combined effects of these circumstances, and of others not here enumerated, to give to the law in the progress of time an air of mystery, inasmuch as its reasons and principles were not to be found in the existing state of things, and its practice was unintelligible, having reference to institutions which had passed away. . . .

The foundation of the English common law is *authority*, that is, the *dicta*, or *sayings*, and the decisions of the judges, handed down from the earliest time to the present, each successive decision being, or being supposed to be, founded on some preceding adjudication, or at least but a new application of a principle already established. This is the theory of the common law, and the practical deviations from it have been rare and slight. The maxim is *stare decisis* [the decision stands]; and no argument *ab inconvenienti* [from what has not been agreed upon], that is, showing the mischievous nature of a principle, is permitted to be urged against a positive decision. Whatever has once been clearly settled, by a competent tribunal, is not again to be drawn into question before a judicial forum, and, if wrong, it can only be corrected by the omnipotence of legislative authority.

There are specious and weighty reasons for this principle. We are told, and truly, that, with regard to a great number of legal questions, they are not subjects of ethics, that there is no right or wrong in the case, but what is made by the law; that it is more important that the rule should be known than that it should be right, for otherwise there would be no guide to conduct, or security in property; that there is no safeguard against judicial tyranny and corruption but in the immutability of the law; and, in short, that innovations are dangerous, and it is most safe and wise to suffer things to remain, as they have been settled by the wisdom and toil of the ancient sages of the law. . . .

In every other branch of human inquiry and intellectual effort, it has been found, and is now for the most part admitted, that the veneration for authority has been one of the principal barriers to human improvement. Rash innovation has indeed been productive of enormous evil; but in its own nature it is conspicuous, and excites attention, and having every habit and tendency of society to oppose, and nothing to favor it but its own merit, it is quickly discarded if found pernicious. This is so true, that many important discoveries and improvements have often sunk under the shock of opposing prejudices, and have again been revived with the happiest effect in after times, and under circumstances more propitious. Disregarded millions have pined and perished under the chains of habit, prejudice, and authority, while there have been comparatively few victims of enticing novelty; but as the fate of these latter has been more marked, it has alone been pointed out as the beacon to alarm. New opinions are often visionary, and introduce confusion, but what have these done compared with the tyranny of the Aristotelian system? The French revolution, the most tremendous innovation which ever convulsed the established order of things, was indeed a moral Vesuvius, but already its fires are extinct, and its desolating lava has mingled with and fertilized the soil. What is that compared with the unvarying despotism, and the changeless castes of the East, where every effort of the intellect, and every impulse of the heart, is repressed not less by the tyranny of custom, and ancient and venerated usage, than by the sword of power.

This excessive veneration for authority binds one age in the chains of another; it tends to preclude improvement. The very idea of improvement is to discover and put in use something better than what has hitherto been known, whereas, the principle upon which the law is administered is to repress all innovation, and to ascertain and declare precisely what our ancestors would have declared in a similar case. This is reversing the proper and natural order of things. The world, as it grows older, in the ordinary course grows wiser, and ought to put away as childish, some things which are fast passing from the ancient and venerable, to the absurd and ridiculous.

. . .

. . . We should be among the last to undervalue institutions [such as the trial by jury] which, whatever might be their origin, and whatever theoretical objections may be urged against them, have been . . . happily applied, and have been matured and perfected by time. But in regard to the English common law, the misfortune is, that time and the advancement of society have not uniformly been permitted to produce the beneficent effect, which they would have done, but for the intervention of artificial barriers.

C. Modifications

- *Van Ness v. Pacard* (1829)
- *Gulian Verplanck* (1835)
- *Farwell v. Boston and Worcester Railroad* (1842)
- *John Ramsey McCulloch* (1826)

As a Supreme Court justice, Joseph Story played an important role in limiting and modifying the force of common law. For example, his opinion in *Van Ness v. Pacard*, the first selection below, concerns the inapplicability to America of the English law of "waste." In England, where courts had tried to protect land from any fundamental alterations by tenants, a tenant was held responsible for cutting timber or erecting buildings and had no right to remove physical "improvements" at the end of a rental term. In *Van Ness,* Story formally acknowledges the general trend of American judicial opinion which had defended the right of tenants to clear land of timber and to remove various fixtures such as barns, fences, and even houses.

The law of contracts formed an even more central part of the inherited rules governing access to wealth. Traditional English law presupposed a relatively static economy in which exchanged goods had an objective value independent of supply and demand. To protect sellers and buyers from fraud or unfairness, the law upheld the principle of giving and receiving *equivalents.* The notion of a just price or customary price, enforceable by law in at least certain kinds of transactions, persisted in colonial America and was only gradually undermined by expanding markets, commercial speculation, and abrupt fluctuations in prices. In response to the demands of merchants and speculators who wanted to reduce the legal risk of practices supposedly promoting national growth, courts moved away from the idea of contract as an objectively fair exchange.

By the 1820s, legal theorists were beginning to conclude, in the words of Morton J. Horwitz, that "the role of contract law was not to assure the equity of agreements but simply to enforce only those willed transactions that parties to a contract believed to be to their mutual advantage."[1] In short, since price was presumably set by mutual agreement, reflecting forces of supply and demand, the law was to deal only with questions like fraud or breach of contract for which there was positive evidence. Thus Gulian Verplanck (1786–1870), who wrote the most systematic redefinition of contract law, stresses in the selection below only the evidence concerning the *will* of contracting parties apart from any ideal of objective value. Verplanck, a New Yorker of Dutch descent, was an innovative lawyer, a Congressman, and a literary figure. Verplanck's redefinition of contract in terms of will and the necessity of individual risk was soon extended and elaborated by Joseph Story and other jurists.

This substitution of market values (such as the beneficial nature of risk) for traditional standards of equity had a profound impact on labor law, particularly the concept of employer liability. Railroads, which used dangerous new technology and which were America's first large-scale business enterprise, became the first and critical testing ground. The question at issue in the landmark case of *Farwell* v. *Boston and Worcester Railroad* was whether a railroad company was "answerable" to an engineer employee who lost his right hand when his train derailed as a result of the carelessness of another employee who tended switches. In a decision that shaped the law of employer liability for decades to come, Chief Justice Lemuel Shaw, of Massachusetts, rules here that the railroad was not bound by customary

---

[1] *The Transformation of American Law, 1780–1860* (Cambridge, Mass.: Harvard University Press, 1977), p. 181.

law regarding the injury to a servant through the negligence of a fellow servant. Much as Verplanck decided that risk was an inevitable part of selling and buying, so Shaw assumes that a job-hunter carefully weighs the risks of a job against the wages proposed, demanding higher wages for more hazardous tasks. Henceforth American courts would increasingly invoke the concept of contract, understood as formalizing an economic bargain, to free entrepreneurs from various traditional perils of liability.

Our final selection concerns a parallel question of regulating unequal bargaining power. Even in the 1820s, defenders of laissez-faire economics launched a campaign against state usury laws which severely punished creditors who charged more than a maximum legal rate of interest. This laissez-faire cause received ideological support from John Ramsey McCulloch (1789–1864), a Scottish disciple of Adam Smith and David Ricardo, whose authoritative works on money and banking were widely reprinted in the United States. In the selection here, McCulloch assumes that the public good will be served by economic growth which can only be maximized by a self-regulating free market. He therefore opposes all the traditional restrictions imposed on making profit from capital. To dwell on the injustice of unequal bargaining between creditors and debtors would, in McCulloch's view, distract attention from the larger picture. During the antebellum period, legislators stopped short of repealing usury laws, but a dramatic easing of penalties made it impossible to enforce maximum rates of interest.

Van Ness v. Pacard (1829)

The common law of England is not to be taken in all respects to be that of America. . . .

The country was a wilderness, and the universal policy was to procure its cultivation and improvement. The owner of the soil as well as the public had every motive to encourage the tenant to devote himself to agriculture and to favor any erection which should aid this result; yet, in the comparative poverty of the country, what tenant could afford to erect fixtures of much expense or value, if he was to lose his whole interest therein by the very act of erection? His cabin or log hut, however necessary for any improvement of the soil, would cease to be his the moment it was finished. It might, therefore, deserve consideration whether, in case the doctrine [of waste] were not previously adopted in a state by some authoritative practice or adjudication; it ought to be assumed by this court as a part of the jurisprudence of such state, upon the mere footing of its existence in the common law. At

---

SOURCE: *Van Ness v. Pacard*, 27 U. S. (2 Pet.) 143.

present it is unnecessary to say more than that we give no opinion on this question. The case which has been argued at the bar may well be disposed of without any discussion of it.

Gulian Verplanck (1835)

The question is, simply, what is the exact measure of that justice which we may claim as a matter of strict right from others—of that justice, which he who violates is not simply hard or avaricious, but absolutely dishonest?

With these objects steadily in view, let us now endeavor to ascertain what are precisely the circumstances which constitute fairness or unfairness in buying and selling. The clue to the accurate solution of this question is, I think, not to be found, where the old lawyers and moralists alone sought it, in metaphysical definitions or logical distinctions. We should rather seek it in some of the plainer truths of political economy.

. . .

A man of large capital in passing through some hamlet in a newly settled country, is impressed with the conviction that from local advantages this now neglected spot is destined to become the centre of commerce to a large and wealthy district. Relying upon this judgment, he determines to buy the property. As land, it is worth almost nothing, and there may be no other bidders for it. But the sagacious proprietor [of the land] has the same views or opinions with him who wishes to buy. The reasoning of each man, as to the greater or less profits which he might derive from a certain sum of money, compared with the profits of the lands; their ideas of the future value of the property itself; all this is private, and personal to each. Neither thinks of communicating such views to the other. In the comparison of mutual offers, the property may be finally disposed of at a price which, to all others than the parties, may seem wild and absurd. Yet each has received, not, to be sure, an equivalent, but, what he himself judges to be, to him, worth more than what he parts with. In such bargains between intelligent and sagacious men, the experience of our own country has a thousand times shown, that it commonly turns out that both were right. If either be a loser, he can only say, that he erred in his calculations.

. . .

Cotton is today sold at ten cents the pound: in a few weeks it rises to fifty; and in another month is to be had at its first cost. The market price, thus irregular as it is, may again be greatly varied by the individual judgments and means of buyers and sellers. There is, then, it is evident, nothing like a permanent value of one commodity, or kind of property, as compared with another.

Still greater is the difference which may be made as to things not subject

SOURCE: Gulian Verplanck, *An Essay on the Doctrine of Contract* (New York: G. and C. Carvill, 1825), pp. 106, 109–10, 114–15, 119–20, 125–27.

to the common estimation of the market, by the speculation, the tastes, wants, or caprices of purchasers.

Can there then be any such thing in the literal sense of the words, as adequacy of price, equality or inequality of compensation? In other words, from the very nature of the thing, price depends solely upon the agreement of the parties, being created by it alone. Mere inequality of price, or rather what appears so in the judgment of a third person, cannot, without reference to something else, be any objection to the validity of a sale, or of an agreement to sell.

· · ·

My knowledge of my own interests, and my personal necessities, my sagacity, natural or acquired, in forming judgments of the state of the market; in brief, all that has been above summed up as constituting the facts and reasoning of a bargain, peculiar to each *individual*, can never be expected by the other party to be communicated; and in most instances it would be impracticable or silly to do so. All know what a wide difference exists among men in these points, and whatever advantage may result from that inequality, is silently conceded in the very fact of making a bargain. It is a superiority on one side—an inferiority on the other, perhaps very great, but they are allowed. This must be so; the business of life could not go on were it otherwise.

Not so with regard to the *common* facts, which immediately and materially affect price in the estimate of the generality of those who buy and sell. It is true, that strict equality of knowledge, as to these points, is just as difficult as with regard to other matters. But the contract is entered into on the supposition, that whatever superiority of knowledge one may have over the other, *no advantage will be taken of it*. This forms the fundamental consideration of the contract.

· · ·

From these views we may deduce a broader rule as to concealment or reservation, which may be laid down as that of strict natural justice. It may be thus expressed.

Whenever any advantage is taken in a purchase, or sale, from the suppression of any fact, (not of an opinion or inference,) *necessarily and materially affecting the common estimate which fixes the present market value of the thing sold; and in regard whereto, the sale alone conclusively proves, that it was presumed by the losing party, that no advantage would be taken; such advantage is gained by* FRAUD.

· · ·

On the other hand, it may be confidently and decisively stated, that,

There is nothing dishonest, or unfair, either in using superior sagacity as to probabilities, or in applying greater skill and better knowledge, as to those facts which do not necessarily enter into the common calculations of those who fix the current price, and concerning which no confidence, express or implied, is reposed.

Farwell v. Boston and Worcester Railroad (1842)

The claim, therefore, is placed, and must be maintained, if maintained at all, on the ground of contract. As there is no express contract between the parties, applicable to this point, it is placed on the footing of an implied contract of indemnity, arising out of the relation of master and servant. It would be an implied promise, arising from the duty of the master to be responsible to each person employed by him, in the conduct of every branch of business, where two or more persons are employed, to pay for all damage occasioned by the negligence of every other person employed in the same service. . . .

The general rule, resulting from considerations as well of justice as of policy, is, that he who engages in the employment of another for the performance of specified duties and services, for compensation, takes upon himself the natural and ordinary risks and perils incident to the performance of such services, and in legal presumption, the compensation is adjusted accordingly. And we are not aware of any principle which should except the perils arising from the carelessness and negligence of those who are in the same employment. These are perils which the servant is as likely to know, and against which he can as effectually guard, as the master. They are perils incident to the service, and which can be as distinctly foreseen and provided for in the rate of compensation as any others. To say that the master shall be responsible because the damage is caused by his agents, is assuming the very point which remains to be proved.

• • •

In applying these principles to the present case, it appears that the plaintiff was employed by the defendants as an engineer, at the rate of wages usually paid in that employment, being a higher rate than the plaintiff had before received as a machinist. It was a voluntary undertaking on his part, with a full knowledge of the risks incident to the employment. . . .

John Ramsey McCulloch (1826)

Before the nature and functions of capital were properly understood, it was believed it could not be increased otherwise than by injuriously abstracting a portion of the national revenue, and that any advantage it might give to the proprietor, must have been obtained at the public expense. It did not occur to our ancestors, that an individual who, by his economy, has accumulated stock, has really added to the wealth of the state, without diminishing

SOURCE: *Farwell v. Boston and Worcester Railroad*, 45 Mass. (4 Met.) 56–59.

SOURCE: John Ramsey McCulloch, *Interest Made Equity* (New York: G. and C. Carvill, 1826), pp. 13–15, 30.

that of others; nor were they aware that this stock, when afterwards expended, as is almost always the case, in the support of productive industry, would afford the means of producing an increased income. But, reckoning as they did, the savings of individuals as so much withdrawn from the public income, it was natural enough that they should endeavor to limit the advantage to be derived from their employment. . . .

But, whatever may have been the causes of the efforts so generally made to regulate and limit the rate of interest, it is certain that, far from succeeding in their object, they have had a precisely opposite effect. Should a borrower find it for his interest to offer 6, 7, or 8 *per cent* for a loan—and, unless it were for his advantage, nothing could possibly induce him to make such an offer—what right has the legislator to interfere, and to prohibit the lender from receiving, and the borrower from paying, more than 4 or 5 *per cent*? Such an interference is not only uncalled for and unnecessary, but it is, in the highest degree, prejudicial. Restrictive laws, instead of reducing, have uniformly contributed to raise the rate of interest. . . .

Thus a capitalist might be inclined to lend a sum at 6 or 7 *per cent*; but, as the law declares that any individual who shall stipulate for more than 5 *per cent* shall, if detected, forfeit *three times the principal*, it is clear, provided there was no method of defeating this statute, that there must be an end of all borrowing, except when the market rate of interest was below the statutory rate. When ever it was above that rate, no person would be able to obtain a single farthing by way of loan. There could, then, be no transference of capital. It would continue locked up in the same hands; and the national prosperity and welfare would, in consequence, suffer severely. Luckily, however, the mutual interest and ingenuity of borrowers and lenders have always proved an overmatch for the enactments of the law. These have done nothing but fetter the transference of stock, and force the borrowers to pay a higher rate of interest for it. What might have been borrowed at 6 *per cent*, had there been no hazard from anti-usurious statutes, is, on account of that hazard, raised to perhaps 8 or 10 *per cent*; and, what is still worse, a contempt for the institutions of society, and a habit of carrying on business in a secret and underhand manner, is generated.

• • •

We trust, however, that we have said enough to show the inexpediency and the pernicious tendency of all such regulations. If a landlord is to be allowed to take the highest rent he can get offered for his land—a farmer the highest price for his raw produce—a manufacturer for his goods—why should a capitalist be restricted and fettered in the employment of his stock? Every principle of natural justice, and of sound political expediency, is outraged by such a distincton.

"Improvements": Transportation and Corporations

A. The Charles River Bridge

- *Isaac Parker* (1829)
- *Roger Taney* (1837)
- *Joseph Story* (1837)

Unit Two began with the individual quest for material improvement, "the anxious spirit of gain" that motivated squatters, speculators, traders, and goldseekers. We then moved on to the redefinition of legal principles intended to provide minimal social cohesion, predictability, and trust as well as a basis for adjudicating the inevitable conflicts of a society rich in virginal resources and dedicated to exploitive opportunity.

The crucial links between the concrete aspirations of individuals and the stratospheric boundaries of law were forged in a middle ground where the decisions of courts and state legislatures overlapped. These testing links involved the profits and wider economic advantages expected from governmental franchises for the public benefit—particularly, charters for improved modes of transportation and corporate forms of enterprise. Only in recent decades have historians begun to appreciate the extent to which "free enterprise" originally relied on legislative and judicial decision. First, the advocates of laissez faire found it necessary to discredit and dismantle an intricate web of protective and restrictive law; they then had to find ways of distinguishing "obsolete" governmental interference from such possibly beneficial measures as land grants, subsidies, tariffs, and acts of incorporation. The *Charles River Bridge* case encapsulated these ambiguous currents at mid-passage.

What made the case far-reaching was the fact that it precisely coincided with the beginnings of a "transportation revolution" which required not only massive public support but painful reassessments of policy. Commercial enterprise had always involved risk, but state franchises had always conveyed a certain degree of security. For example, in the late eighteenth and early nineteenth centuries legislatures had assumed that monopolistic privileges were necessary to attract sufficient investment capital for building or managing bridges, toll roads, and ferries. Customary law also assumed that such privileged proprietors, or grantees, would accept public duties and responsibilities. But by the 1820s, with unprecedented urban growth and expanding markets, there were irresistible pressures to bypass or improve upon the inadequate facilities sanctioned by state charters. In 1827, when the spectacular success of the Erie Canal was just beginning to fire a national fever for "internal improvements," the Massachusetts legislature granted a charter for a new bridge (the Warren Bridge), connecting Boston with Charlestown. While it is clear that the existing Charles River Bridge could not accommodate the growing traffic over the Charles River, it is also clear that the competing Warren Bridge, built within a few minutes' walk of the older bridge, diverted sufficient traffic to bring disastrous losses in revenue to the Charles River Bridge proprietors, who immediately brought suit. It should be added that the Warren Bridge charter called for free passage and state ownership within a maximum of six years, after construction and maintenance costs had been met.

The legal case involved a multitude of technical issues pertaining to prescriptive rights, implied powers, and constitutional law. Here, it is sufficient to know that from 1650 Harvard College had owned the rights to a ferry which had been replaced in 1785 by the Charles River Bridge, whose charter guaranteed Harvard a fixed and supposedly perpetual annuity. In 1829, the Supreme Judicial Court of Massachusetts was evenly divided on the question of whether the Warren Bridge charter had impaired the state's contractual obligations to the proprietors (including Harvard College) of the Charles River Bridge. But what is most striking in the opinion delivered by Chief Justice Isaac Parker, who ultimately favored the claims of the Charles River Bridge proprietors and who is represented in our first selection, is his eager acceptance of the doctrine that progress necessitates risk and failure. Parker (1768–1830), a Federalist and a founder of Harvard Law School, not only repudiates the common-law doctrine that long use creates an exclusive right but embraces the ideology of laissez-faire competition and defends the conclusion that any state promotion of public improvement will inevitably mean that some individuals and communities lose while others win.

By the time the case was finally settled by the United States Supreme Court, in 1837, there were two overriding issues concerning the role of government in the economy. First, since it was admitted that state franchises benefited some groups at the expense of others, it was necessary to justify this partiality in terms other than vested rights or public accountability. Roger Taney (1777–1864), President Jackson's former attorney general and secretary of the treasury, only recently confirmed as Chief Justice of the Supreme Court, deals with this problem by outdoing, in our second selection, even Isaac Parker's tributes to progress, enterprise, and the need for incentive. Ultimately, Taney suggests, the entire public will benefit from the state's promotion of private enterprise.

The second issue was how a state government could meet the demand for improvements without infringing upon existing contractual privileges and understandings and thereby undermining the confidence of investors and propertyholders. As a good Jacksonian, Taney insists on a narrow construction of the rights granted by state charter. But by divesting public grants of any implied privileges, he also equates them with private contracts, implying no public responsibility. In delivering the opinion of the Supreme Court in favor of the Warren Bridge, he at once expands the discretionary power of legislatures and gives judicial blessing to a proliferation of private corporations unbound by customary duties and services to the public.

Joseph Story, in one of his most famous and learned dissents, appeals nostalgically to a lost world of English fairs, markets, and ferries in which exclusive grants were accompanied by public burdens. If Story seemed old-fashioned to his contemporaries in his concern for local history and circumstance and in his reliance on ancient common-law authorities, his arguments in our third selection suggests how far American law had moved from the notion of a corporation as a quasi-public institution. And he is no doubt right in his assertion that the proprietors of the Charles River Bridge would never have accepted a charter which imposed public obligations while reserving to the legislature the specific right to construct competing bridges. In the future, corporations would assume greater risks and fewer duties.

Isaac Parker (1829)

[Chief Justice Isaac Parker] It is the right and the duty of all governments, especially those over new countries, to facilitate the intercourse of business between its subjects by opening new roads and constructing new avenues as the population, and the consequent demands for such improvements, shall increase. In doing this it will often happen, that estates upon old roads are diminished in value; the seat of business may be transferred from one town or village to another; inns and stores, erected with a view to the travel or

SOURCE: *Charles River Bridge* v. *Warren Bridge*, 24 Mass. (7 Pick.) 344, 514.

business as it exists, may become deserted and of little value; but the proprietors would have no claim upon the government for redress, for it is necessarily one of the contingencies on which property is acquired and held, that it is liable to be impaired by future events of this kind.

The whole history and policy of this country from its first settlement, furnish instances of changes and improvements, the effect of which has been to transfer the adscititious [derived from without] value of real estate in one town, resulting from its favorable position for trade, to another, which, by alteration of roads, erection of bridges, or more recent interior settlements, has taken its place as a thoroughfare, or as a place of transit or deposit for articles of merchandise. Losses of this kind never have been, and probably never will be compensated; nor can compensation be reasonably expected by the sufferers, any more than by the dealers in any branch of trade or in any mechanical employment, who find their profits and emoluments diminished and sometimes destroyed by the change of fashion, or by new inventions for carrying on the same branch of business in a cheaper and more acceptable manner. Such losses are the effect of the general system of legislation upon subjects of this nature, adopted in the early part of our history, and constantly practised through all the changes of government; so that property is in fact held upon a tenure which admits of its deterioration in value from causes of this kind.

And I confess I do not see why the same principles do not apply to property in ferries and bridges to a considerable, if not to the whole extent. . . .

Roger Taney (1837)

[Chief Justice Roger Taney] The court are fully sensible that it is their duty, in exercising the high powers conferred on them by the Constitution of the United States, to deal with these great and extensive interests with the utmost caution; guarding, as far as they have the power to do so, the rights of property, and at the same time carefully abstaining from any encroachment on the rights reserved to the states.

• • •

But we are not now left to determine, for the first time, the rules by which public grants are to be construed in this country. The subject has already been considered in this court, and the rule of construction, above stated, fully established [the rule that the rights of grantees are limited by the explicit grant, and that any ambiguity in the contract must be construed in favor of the public]. . . .

But the object and end of all government is to promote the happiness and prosperity of the community by which it is established, and it can never be

---

SOURCE: *Charles River Bridge v. Warren Bridge*, 36 U. S. (11 Pet.) 535, 546–48, 551–52.

assumed that the government intended to diminish its power of accomplishing the end for which it was created. And in a country like ours, free, active and enterprising, continually advancing in numbers and wealth; new channels of communication are daily found necessary, both for travel and trade, and are essential to the comfort, convenience, and prosperity of the people. A state ought never to be presumed to surrender this power, because, like the taxing power, the whole community have an interest in preserving it undiminished. And when a corporation alleges that a state has surrendered for seventy years its power of improvement and public accommodation, in a great and important line of travel, along which a vast number of its citizens must daily pass, the community have a right to insist, in the language of this court above quoted, "that its abandonment ought not to be presumed, in a case in which the deliberate purpose of the state to abandon it does not appear." The continued existence of a government would be of no great value, if by implications and presumptions, it was disarmed of the powers necessary to accomplish the ends of its creation, and the functions it was designed to perform, transferred to the hands of privileged corporations. . . .

No one will question that the interests of the great body of the people of the state, would, in this instance, be affected by the surrender of this great line of travel to a single corporation, with the right to exact toll, and exclude competition for seventy years. While the rights of private property are sacredly guarded, we must not forget that the community also have rights, and that the happiness and well being of every citizen depends on their faithful preservation.

. . .

Indeed, the practice and usage of almost every state in the Union, old enough to have commenced the work of internal improvement, is opposed to the doctrine contended for on the part of the plaintiffs in error. Turnpike roads have been made in succession, on the same line of travel; the latter ones interfering materially with the profits of the first. These corporations have, in some instances, been utterly ruined by the introduction of newer and better modes of transportation and traveling. In some cases railroads have rendered the turnpike roads on the same line of travel so entirely useless, that the franchise of the turnpike corporation is not worth preserving. Yet in none of these cases have the corporations supposed that their privileges were invaded, or any contract violated on the part of the state. . . .

And what would be the fruits of this doctrine of implied contracts on the part of the states, and of property in a line of travel by a corporation, if it should now be sanctioned by this court? To what results would it lead us? If it is to be found in the charter to this bridge, the same process of reasoning must discover it in the various acts which have been passed within the last forty years, for turnpike companies. And what is to be the extent of the privileges of exclusion on the different sides of the road? The counsel who have so ably argued this case, have not attempted to define it by any certain boundaries. How far must the new improvement be distant from the old one? How near may you approach without invading its rights in the privileged line? If this court should establish the principles now contended for, what is to become of the numerous railroads established on the same line of travel with turnpike companies; and which have rendered the franchises of the turnpike corporations of no value? Let it once be understood that such charters carry with them these implied contracts, and give this unknown and undefined property in a line of traveling, and you will soon find the old turnpike corporations awakening from their sleep, and calling upon this court to put down the improvements which have taken their place. The millions of property which have been invested in railroads and canals, upon lines of travel which had been before occupied by turnpike corporations, will be put in jeopardy. We shall be thrown back to the improvements of the last century, and obliged to stand still until the claims of the old turnpike corporations shall be satisfied, and they shall consent to permit these states to avail themselves of the lights of modern science, and to partake of the benefits of those improvements which are now adding to the wealth and prosperity, and the convenience and comfort, of every other part of the civilized world. Nor is this all. This court will find itself compelled to fix, by some arbitrary rule, the width of this new kind of property in a line of travel; for if such a right of property exists, we have no lights to guide us in marking out its extent, unless, indeed, we resort to the old feudal grants, and to the exclusive rights of ferries, by prescription, between towns; and are prepared to decide that when a turnpike road from one town to another had been made, no railroad or canal, between these two points, could afterwards be established. The court are not prepared to sanction principles which must lead to such results.

Joseph Story (1837)

[Justice Joseph Story, dissenting] . . . I maintain that, upon the principles of common reason and legal interpretation, the present grant carries with it a necessary implication that the legislature shall do no act to destroy or essentially to impair the franchise; that (as one of the learned judges of the state court expressed it) there is an implied agreement that the state will not grant another bridge between Boston and Charlestown, so near as to draw away the custom from the old one; and (as another learned judge expressed it) that there is an implied agreement of the state to grant the undisturbed use of the bridge and its tolls, so far as respects any acts of its own, or of any persons acting under its authority. In other words, the state, impliedly, contracts not to resume its grant, or to do any act to the prejudice or destruction of its grant. I maintain that there is no authority or principle established in relation to the construction of crown grants, or legislative grants, which

SOURCE: *Charles River Bridge v. Warren Bridge*, 36 U. S. (11 Pet.) 646–47.

does not concede and justify this doctrine. Where the thing is given, the incidents, without which it cannot be enjoyed, are also given. . . . I maintain that a different doctrine is utterly repugnant to all the principles of the common law, applicable to all franchises of a like nature, and that we must overturn some of the best securities of the rights of property, before it can be established. I maintain that the common law is the birthright of every citizen of Massachusetts, and that he holds the title deeds of his property, corporeal, and incorporeal, under it. I maintain that under the principles of the common law, there exists no more right in the legislature of Massachusetts to erect the Warren Bridge, to the ruin of the franchise of the Charles River Bridge, than exists to transfer the latter to the former, or to authorize the former to demolish the latter. If the legislature does not mean in its grant to give any exclusive rights, let it say so, expressly, directly, and in terms admitting of no misconstruction. The grantees will then take at their peril, and must abide the results of their overweening confidence, indiscretion, and zeal.

My judgment is formed upon the terms of the grant, its nature and objects, its design and duties; and, in its interpretation, I seek for no new principles, but I apply such as are as old as the very rudiments of the common law.

B. Canals and Railroads

- *Ohio Board of Canal Commissioners* (1824)
- *Ohio Board of Canal Commissioners* (1825)
- *Nathan Hale* (1837)

The first selection, taken from an official report submitted in 1824 by the Ohio Board of Canal Commissioners, conveys some of the enthusiasm generated by the success of the Erie Canal even before it had finally been extended to Buffalo. What impressed observers the most was the dramatic lowering of transport costs and hence the dramatic extension of markets. It should be explained that before the canal connected Rochester with New York City, Upstate millers found it difficult to sell flour, and thus the local price of wheat was low. With the canal, the price of wheat doubled, bringing an agricultural and commercial boom to favored sections of Upstate New York.

In the second selection, the same Ohio board considers the option of state construction of canals as opposed to a reliance on chartered companies. Expressing a "Jacksonian" fear of concentrated power (Jackson had not yet been elected President and was not yet known for any hostility to corporations), the Commissioners tend to associate chartered companies with monarchical government. The issues raised resemble those in the later *Charles River Bridge* case, but the assumption that a charter might be irrevocable and beyond the reach of the legislature derives from the Supreme

Court's decision in the *Dartmouth College* case (1819), which ruled that even a quasi-public charter granted by a legislature enjoyed constitutional protection from later infringements by the legislature. In practice, Ohio and most other states chose to borrow the necessary funds for public financing of canals.

By contrast, most of the later construction of railroads was done by private companies, though with generous public support. In the next selection, Nathan Hale (1784–1863) describes the intense regional rivalry that led, even in the 1830s, the first decade of railroad expansion, to a competitive scramble for the key transportation routes of the future. When Hale discusses railroad promotion in relation to regional growth and prosperity, he speaks with the authority of experience. A nephew of the Nathan Hale hanged by the British as a spy, he had given up a law practice in order to purchase and edit a Boston newspaper. Hale was one of the founders of the influential *North American Review* and the *Christian Examiner*. As a journalist and state legislator, he helped publicize various Federalist and Whig causes. In the 1830s, he became one of the nation's leading promoters of railroads and served from 1831 to 1859 as president of the Boston and Worcester Railroad.

Ohio Board of Canal Commissioners (1824)

Though the construction of the great [Erie] canal of New York is a work so grand and imposing, its advantages to the public are not less apparent. The benefits of which have already resulted from that work, although it is not yet completed, are so great as to stagger belief, if they were not capable of proof amounting almost to mathematical demonstration.

That every saving in the expense of transporting the surplus productions of a country to market, is just so much added to the value at home, is a proposition too evident to require proof, and too plain to need illustration. We accordingly find that any article designed for distant market, increases in price, where it is produced, in exact proportion to the diminution in the expense of conveying it to its place of destination, unless affected by accidental circumstances. Taking this rule as a criterion, it is ascertained by information derived from authentic sources, that on the productions of the country exported from the single county of Monroe, situated on the Genesee river in New York, and the property received in return, more than 275,000 dollars was saved during the last season; in other words, so much money was put into the pockets of those who raised that produce for market and those who received such articles as they needed in return. This benefit has resulted

---

SOURCE: [Ohio] Board of Canal Commissioners, *Second Annual Report, Civil Engineer* (January 19, 1828), pp. 75–79.

soley from the Erie canal, and the sum thus saved to a small section of country, would more than pay the interest for one year on all moneys expended in the construction of all the canal lines in that state, which were then completed. This fact alone, speaks volumes in favor of canal navigation, and ought to carry conviction to the mind of every reflecting man.

. . .

Wheat, of which there were near 500,000 bushels floured at the mills in and near Rochester on the Genesee river, during one year ending in November last, was worth no more than 50 cents per bushel, before its price was affected by canal navigation. During the past season it has commanded in Rochester, from 94 to 105 cents per bushel, owing entirely to the canal navigation, between that place and the Hudson river.

Ohio Board of Canal Commissioners (1825)

An important question may present itself for the consideration of the [Ohio] General Assembly, as connected with the proposed improvements; whether the contemplated canals should be made under the authority, and at the expense of the state, or charters should be granted to private companies for that purpose? The commissioners are of opinion, that the work should be undertaken by the state; chartered companies, possessing exclusive privileges, have always been popular in monarchical governments, because their powers and advantages were so much carved out of the sovereign power for the benefit of subjects—so much in fact gained from the monarchy. The judicial tribunals, influenced doubtless by the popular feeling upon this subject soon found means to secure them to the grantees—gave them a character of *immortality*; changed granted privileges, from the sovereign, into a contract between equals, and placed them beyond the reach of his power, under the protection of that ingenious fiction. Our jurisprudence which borrows its principles and reasonings from England, has very gravely adopted this doctrine of immortality in corporations; naturalized and established it as law in our free governments, and stretched over its dogmas, the ægis of the Constitution, so that in effect, whatever is granted to a private company by the legislature is holden to be intangible and irrevocable. A grant made under erroneous impressions, and which in its operation is found detrimental to, or even destructive of the public welfare, whether it involves the exercise of sovereign powers or not is, according to established principles of law, altogether irrevocable. The present generation may in this way not only bind themselves, but their posterity forever; and government, instead of being at all times administered for the benefit of the people and in accordance with their will; may be parcelled out into monopolies, swallowing up their interests

SOURCE: [Ohio] Board of Canal Commissioners, *Third Annual Report, Civil Engineer* (August 16, 1828), pp. 138–40.

and counteracting their wishes. How long a free people will sanction such principles, or how consonant they are to the fundamental maxims of our social fabric, it is not our purpose to inquire; the existence of them, we remark, as evincing the risk and danger of granting to private companies any control over matters of public and general interest. Nothing can be more interesting to the whole community, than great navigable highways through the state, from the Lake [Erie] to the Ohio river, on the routes proposed; it does not consist with the dignity, the interest or the convenience of the state, that a private company of citizens or foreigners (as may happen), should have the management and control of them; the evils of such management cannot be fully foreseen, and therefore cannot be provided against; for experience is the only safe guide in legislation and of the operation of such grants we have no experience. Besides, such works should be constructed with a view to the greatest possible accommodation of our citizens; as a public concern, the public convenience is the paramount object; a private company will look only to the best means of increasing their profits, the public convenience will be regarded only as it is subservient to their emolument. We think therefore, that it would be extremely hazardous and unwise, to entrust private companies with making those canals, which can be made by the state.

Nathan Hale (1837)

The commercial advantages of the city of New York secure to her a decided preëminence over the other ports of the Union. Her unrivalled inland navigation,—her steamboats stretching their regular and rapid voyages to Albany, to Hartford, to Providence, and even to Charleston,—her lines of packets, to Liverpool, to London, to Havre, and to many other ports,—her canals, extending the line of navigation to Lake Champlain and Lower Canada, to Lakes Ontario and Erie, and to the whole western country,—and her unlimited resources in the wealth and enterprise of her citizens, seemed destined to give her, at no remote period, a monopoly of the great foreign trade of the country. The towns of a secondary class, Philadelphia, Baltimore, Boston, and Charleston, were approaching daily the condition of provincial towns, dependent for all the principal operations of commerce on the port of New York. A great part of the domestic trade of Massachusetts had by degrees formed a direct connexion with that city. Canals were dug leading in that direction, from the counties of Hampden, and Hampshire, and even from Worcester, the very centre of the state. Boston, the metropolis formerly of New England, had almost ceased to be the commercial metropolis of her own state. The other cities of the Union were suffering under a similar

SOURCE: Nathan Hale, [Review of] "Chemins de Fer Américains, by Guillaume-Tell Poussin," *North American Review*, Vol. XLIV (April, 1837), pp. 438–39.

influence. The whole trade of the country seemed destined to be restricted to those channels, which were adapted to either steam or canal navigation.

In this state of things, rail-roads were introduced on public routes in England, and became known in this country. It was evident from the first proofs of their efficacy, as a method of traveling, that they were capable of producing a great change in the face of things; that the currents of traffic and of personal intercourse, instead of passing only through channels where water could be made to flow, might be led across mountains, and through every region enlivened by human industry; and that the prosperity of cities, instead of depending on the accident of being placed on a navigable stream, which can float its commerce to a vast interior, would hereafter depend upon the foresight and energy of their inhabitants, in forming for themselves the channels of intercourse, and in supplying them with the fruits of their industry.

These considerations serve to account for the earnestness of the early friends of rail-roads, in endeavoring to impress on the public mind a conviction of their utility and importance; and for the eagerness of the public, in undertaking these improvements, as soon as they become convinced of their utility. Under these circumstances it is not surprising, that in many instances the zeal of those who undertake these works, should far outstrip their ability to carry them into execution; or that among the many judicious projects, which promise successful results, there should be also many, which are likely to disappoint the expectations of their projectors, and still more which are impracticable and visionary.

C. Financing Internal Improvements

- *Charles Francis Adams* (*1840*)
- *American Railroad Journal* (*1851*)

By the mid-1830s, the expected rewards from improved transportation had hypnotized state legislators and attracted massive inflows of investment capital, especially from Britain. The great boom in land sales and in slave-grown cotton induced legislators, especially in the West and South, to extend enormous amounts of public credit to banks, turnpikes, canals, and railroads. Often there were no immediate sources of revenue to justify such mounting public debts. The public debts usually took the form of state bonds purchased by eastern or British investors. The bubble burst in 1837. The reasons were complex but related to a crisis in the international flow of credit. British investors recalled their loans. American banks suspended payment of gold and silver, while most paper currency quickly depreciated in value. Several states defaulted on the interest owed to bondholders. Bankruptcies multiplied. Europeans expressed moral outrage over a supposed breach of trust, and tended to blame America's fiscal irresponsibility on the democratic form of government. For Americans who responded to these charges, the debate involved national honor and the very legitimacy of America's high expectations of material and moral progress.

In 1840, Charles Francis Adams (1807–1886) was ideally equipped to answer European complaints. If his tone seems a bit pompous for a thirty-three year old, it is because he still lived in the imposing shadow of his grandfather, President John Adams, and of his father, President John Quincy Adams. In 1840 his father, after a life of public service, was still a leading figure in Congress; though seventy-three, John Quincy Adams seemed indestructable and would in fact remain in Congress another eight years. Hence, Charles Francis Adams speaks with the care of a son who has been bred for the presidency (though he never became President, one can reasonably argue that his later achievements as America's minister to England during the Civil War were as significant as anything accomplished by his father and grandfather as one-term Presidents).

Charles Francis Adams shared his family's nationalism and their fear of any American subservience to Europe. Having spent his early childhood in Russia, where his father was America's minister, and having then attended boarding school in England, Adams could look upon Europe as familiar ground. Here he is unintimidated by the indignation of the "capitalists of Europe," who had sought to exploit America with "usurious contracts" that imposed excessive rates of interest. In an only half-veiled threat, Adams even suggests possible grounds for debt repudiation. But precisely because he deplores a situation which economically has prolonged America's status as a colonial and debtor nation, Adams insists on the need for national economic unity and coordination. In his view, local jealousy, ignorance, and regional competition have allowed European capitalists to charge unreasonable rates of interest, thus inflating the total public debt and increasing the public cost of internal improvements. Adams has no doubt that such improvements will ultimately prove productive, and that much of the debt can be repaid. His plea for consolidation and planning is in the interest of reducing waste, duplicated effort, and dangerous dependence on Europe.

Though a few figures like Adams called for centralism and a "general plan," the construction of railroads proceeded with even less planning and public accountability than had the construction of canals. In the next selection, an anonymous writer in the *American Railroad Journal* underscores the public benefits derived from railroads but wholly endorses the building and management of railroads by private enterprise, which he shrewdly pictures as "entrusting to people the management of their own affairs," as opposed to "the care of a corrupt legislature." He refrains from adding that if legislatures were corrupt, they were all the more vulnerable to manipulation by railroad promoters seeking charters, land grants, and other favors. The writer does express concern over the spirit of reckless rivalry that leads to a wasteful construction of competing lines on the same route (the question of the proper distance between competing lines is closely related to the

Charles River Bridge case). But after making this bow to the public interest, the writer goes on to describe the actual methods of railroad finance. His picture of life on Wall Street as a "constant contest" in which the strongest emerge as victors can be taken as a preview, in 1851, of the later era of railroad wars and "robber barons."

Charles Francis Adams (1840)

In consequence of the applications for loans, that are perpetually making by the states to the capitalists of Europe, and particularly of London, an obvious necessity arises for the information essential to estimate properly the ability of the respective applicants to fulfill the engagements they are disposed to make. Hitherto, it would certainly seem as if a suitable degree of attention had not been paid to the duty of collecting this, and as if money had been advanced at hap-hazard, with more reference to the tempting nature of the terms offered, than to the resources of the parties offering them. It is high time that this mode of proceeding should be changed; for it will inevitably lead to disappointment upon one side, and irritation upon both. The more usurious a contract is, the more oppressive it will be felt by the borrower; and, if ultimately there should be found an unwillingness to comply with its conditions, amounting in fact to inability, the greater will be the disposition to seek in the severity of those conditions an excuse for non-performance. . . .

Nineteen states out of the twenty-six, and one territory, have authorized the contracting of a debt, which in the aggregate may now be estimated as equal to two hundred millions of dollars. A very large part of this is actually due to foreigners, and consequently subjects the country to a heavy annual drain of money in the form of interest, which must, in most cases, be remitted to Europe at the hazard and expense of the borrowers. It is, therefore, highly incumbent upon every citizen of the United States, if he does not now know, directly to set about understanding, what he has got to represent [show for] the debt thus created, and how far his industry and his capital have been assisted or hazarded by the mode in which the money raised has been spent.

• • •

Of the large amount that has been borrowed within a few years by the states, considerably more than half has been expended in works of internal improvement, such as canals, railways, turnpike roads, etc.; the rest has been made the basis of banking institutions. . . .

SOURCE: Charles Francis Adams, [Review of] "Observations on the Financial Position and Credit of Such of the States of the North American Union as Have Contracted Public Debts, by Alexander Trotter," *North American Review*, Vol. LI (October, 1840), pp. 317–21.

. . . The competition, from being between great sections of country, the West, the East, the South, and the North, as it was in Congress, has been between the several states, and in some cases has degenerated into a contest between the different counties in the same state. In addition to this, there has been no system adopted to make the works executed conduce to the common benefit. The utter want of general plan has led to a hurtful emulation, by which each state strives to secure to itself whatever it may gain from its neighbor, and this at a constant expense of new undertakings to divert trade from one point and to another, which, if carried on, must in the end absorb all the profits attending even the most judiciously executed ones. There can be little hope of permanent profit in any one quarter, where success becomes the signal for new efforts in others to diminish if not to destroy it. Moreover, the extraordinary expense at which all this is carried on by the states would have covered a great many fat jobs given to favorites of the national government, even if we are to suppose that such things do not also sometimes happen with the states themselves. Most of the money which has been raised to pay for these state undertakings, has been borrowed upon terms much less advantageous than it would have been, had the United States been the applicant. The wealthy capitalists of Europe, who would have been glad to advance to the national government the whole sum which has been actually procured, at a very low rate of profit, on account of the general confidence in the security of the loan, have been induced to do the same thing to the separate states only by extraordinary appeals to their avarice, and by the offer to them of terms, which, in many cases, if they had been made in private among individuals at home, would have been reckoned to be highly usurious.

On the whole, therefore, if we strike the balance between centralism and consolidation on the one side, and state pride on the other, we shall perhaps discover that the latter, however good in itself, is apt, when carried to an extreme, to prove, like all other pride, equally expensive and inconvenient.

American Railroad Journal (1851)

Our capacity for production is unlimited, but much of our most fertile lands are worthless, simply because there exists no means of sending their productions to a market. In very many parts of this country corn may be raised at a profit at 20 cents a bushel, while the same article is worth 70 cents in New York. If it could be forwarded for 10 cents per bushel, the producer would make 40 cents additional profit. The reduced cost of transportation (the price remaining the same) measures the increased profits of the seller. But it often happens in many parts of the country, that all surplus beyond the wants of the consumer is *worthless*. A railroad, therefore, gives a value to

SOURCE: "Western Securities," *American Railroad Journal* (January 25, 1851), pp. 56–57.

articles that had no commercial value before, and in this respect, creates wealth where none for practical purposes existed.

It is in this view, that we must estimate the importance of railroads to the West, and the value of their securities. The producing portion of the country is far removed from the consumers. All the surplus products of the West require to be exported, and the capacity to produce is only measured by the means for transportation. The fact, too, that our present agriculture engrosses almost the entire attention of our western people, compels them to *import* all that their own farms and industry do not directly supply. Facilities for transportation, therefore, are what give the ability to purchase. Exports and imports bear the same ratio to each other, because the amount that a farmer can purchase is limited by the amount he can sell. Western railroads, therefore, produce in this way a double result, and create an *import*, while their original and primary object was to facilitate the export trade.

. . .

We go for free railroading, and think that there is less danger in entrusting to people the management of their own affairs, than to commit them to the care of a corrupt legislature. But if we are going to have rival roads, let us build these rivals where they can be made the means of a positive good to some, as well as harm to others. Let the rival occupy if possible a *different* route, where it can be the means of a *local* and *public* good, as well as of private pique or spleen. . . .

Rival lines gave the death blow to English railroads. Millions upon millions were thrown away in the same manner in Massachusetts. We do not like to witness the commencement of such schemes in New York. We have not money enough to throw it away upon them. Such as are based upon ill will or upon speculation are always dangerous, not only in results, but in the influence they exert upon the community, in fostering the same spirit that gave birth to the first. A scheme that has not a legitimate object should never be trusted. Its getters up are looking after their own ends, and the public will find that when these ends are accomplished, that they will be left to shift for themselves. . . .

It may not be inappropriate to state here the usual manner in which securities are negociated. We have already spoken of sales at auction. These are considered safe to be tried only under peculiar circumstances. If one man is seen running through the streets, no person would think of following him. But let ten start together, and every person in sight will join in the chase. If these ten halloo, the rest will halloo in sympathy; and if the leaders act in concert, they will soon acquire such an influence over the feelings of those following, as to have them almost entirely under their control, and ready for any dare-devil exploit that may have been planned. Persons are in this way easily brought into a state, when they "go it blind," indifferent, unconscious even, of any blows or contusions they may receive. So with selling railroad securities at auction. The great mass of operators will of course unite to break down the sale; and will do so, unless it is strongly supported. A few strong names must be selected to lead off, to puff and blow, and manufacture a public sentiment in favor of the what to be sold; to form the nucleus, and start off in the race, and the number and spirit of those that will follow, will bear an exact proportion to the apparent zeal and confident assertion of the leaders. After the public sentiment is brought up to the proper point, the managers must attend the sale, start and sustain the bids at a proper point, and take for the sellers what cannot be disposed of *bona fide*. All this process, as may be well supposed, costs something; so much, that sales made in this manner are only resorted to where a very large amount is to be disposed of. Securities sold at auction often bring more than those sold at private sale, but the expense is great, and the risk still greater. If the parties fail to make a good *hit*, the security loses *caste*, and must then be disposed of as a second-hand article.

When securities are disposed of at *private* sale, the broker or operator to whom they are committed, makes up a *party* of his friends, among whom they are divided, each taking 5, 10, or $20,000; for, notwithstanding we have some pretty capacious maws in Wall Street, it can boast of but few individuals who severally could comfortably digest a mass of bonds of $500,000, without having the functions of his business stomach somewhat deranged. . . . As soon, therefore, as the seller, with the greatest secrecy and confidence, imparts his scheme to the money lender or broker, he communicates with an electric despatch the same to some twenty or thirty others. The whole party must know and discuss the matter, as much as the principal who stands between them and the seller. If the seller, for the purpose of trying the market, and finding out what he can expect to sell for, goes to other operators, he strikes the wires which carry his secrets around another circuit, composed of an equal number of names. In this manner, a person may not have been a day in Wall Street before every important man on 'change [the exchange] will understand his whole scheme as well as the seller does himself. He has thus shown his whole hand, without knowing a card held on the other side. . . .

No person wishes to invest his money in a security that is not popular with *all* parties—that will not always sell without requiring any efforts on his part to give it credit. The frowns of a half-dozen leading operators are often sufficient to damn a good security, which would at once have gone into public favor under the smiles of the same persons. So long, therefore, as purchasers have a plenty of room for choice, they prefer securities that are well known to those which must be pushed and crowded into favor by efforts of their own. Another evil which results from the exposure of a scheme in the manner stated is the fact, that unless securities are "placed" soon after they come into the market, the inference is, that there is some intrinsic defect in them which has prevented a sale. The securities in this way become *shop-worn*, and must be sold as second-hand goods. . . .

When a person comes here for money, he must bear in mind that $400,000 or $500,000 is no small sum. . . . He must remember that money is power, and that the holder can dictate to a great extent his own terms, and above all, he must bear in mind, that he is liable to encounter the opposition of parties he never heard or dreamed of before, and that he will come in contact with those who, for life have made man a study, who, at a glance almost, detect his weak points, and lay their plans accordingly. Life in Wall Street is a constant contest, and he who would sustain himself in it must prove himself superior to those he meets in their own way.

D. Corporations and the Public Interest

- *American Jurist and Law Magazine* (*1830*)
- *William Leggett* (*1834*)

During the antebellum period, there was much debate and confusion over the future significance of corporations. While the corporate form had a long history, as indicated by the anonymous writer in the *American Jurist and Law Magazine*, the modern business corporation was still a novelty in 1830, and it was necessary to explain even to a legal-minded audience its peculiar characteristics: a legal "person" possessing no political or moral capacities but endowed, in theory, with perpetual life. Like many thoughtful Americans of his time, this writer is concerned about the unaccountability of corporations and the need to subject their activities to more public control.

But legislative control was still associated with monopoly and special privilege, especially since corporations could not be formed in most states without special legislative acts, which required considerable political influence. Ironically, then, the Jacksonian movement against aristocracy and special privilege also aimed at widening popular access to the *advantages* of corporate organization. Instead of demanding more political regulation of corporations, radical Jacksonians like William Leggett called for general laws of incorporation that would enable every man to become an entrepreneur. Leggett (1801–1839) was a New York journalist who, in 1829, became part owner and assistant editor of the *Evening Post*, one of the country's most influential Democratic papers. In the years 1834–1835, when the chief editor, William Cullen Bryant, was abroad, Leggett became the ideological spokesman for the extreme anti-bank, anti-monopoly wing of the Democratic party. While most states soon adopted laissez-faire policies, including general incorporation acts which opened the way for the freewheeling irresponsibility of late-nineteenth century companies, Leggett must be understood within a context of small artisan and shopkeeper establishments. In 1834, when he wrote the following editorial, no one was thinking of great trusts, mergers, or railroad lines intended to destroy or blackmail other lines. Indeed, before the 1870s corporations were extremely rare in American industry, despite the impression conveyed by the writer of the first selection. With the exception of the New England textile companies, even the larger manufacturing establishments were typically partnerships or family businesses. Leggett's dream of a kind of participatory capitalism—of preventing concentrated power by opening joint-stock partnerships to all the people—had much in common with the dream of small family-farm homesteads on the public domain. Leggett's overriding fear of special privilege at the public's expense also provides a bridge to the next section, "The Politics of Opportunity."

American Jurist and Law Magazine (1830)

In this country, a corporation is a community of men, possessing, in conformity to constitutional or legislative provision, certain property, income, or rights, and subject to certain burdens, distinct from other men.

The objects in the creation of corporations, were to perpetuate succession, without submitting to the embarrassing forms of administration and guardianship, on the decease of incorporators, and to enable numerous bodies of men, acting under a charter, as municipal, pecuniary, or other associations, to negotiate as an individual.

Our elementary books ascribe the invention of corporations to the Romans, soon after the building of the city. . . . [S]omething like corporate provisions was found indispensably necessary on the first formation of civil society on a more extensive scale than patriarchal governments. The motive of their formation, was to enable communities to sustain their common burdens, and participate their common privileges in a simple, convenient, and equal manner. . . .

In England, trading and stock-holding corporations are not of ancient origin. It was not till recently, that they became numerous there. In our republics, they are still more numerous, and it is difficult to set bounds to the general desire to increase them. This desire naturally grows from the genius of our institutions; for our governments, political and municipal, are founded on corporate principles. In Massachusetts alone, the chartered capital of banks and insurance offices, amounts to about $30,000,000. And the various manufacturing companies have charters to hold a still greater amount. In addition to these, are the various turnpikes, bridges, canals,—and many other corporations, created for the mere purpose of holding and managing wharves, public houses, and other estates. These already embrace a large portion of the property of the state, and some of them are of such an accumulating character, that unless restrained by legislative enactment, judicial construction, or the good sense and discretion of the stockholders, they will absorb the greatest part of the substance of the commonwealth.

SOURCE: "Corporations," *American Jurist and Law Magazine* (October, 1830), pp. 298–301, 307.

The extent of the wealth and power of corporations among us demands that plain and clear laws should be declared for their regulation and restraint. . . .

Such is the language of the English common law, and if it be here in force, it follows, that if A, B, and C, and their associates, are by a legislative act, by a single section created a corporation, without declaring or limiting their operations, they have the power to organize, to perpetuate their existence, by receiving new members, who shall have all the rights of the original corporators, and be considered associates (for they can have no successors), to trade, buy, hold, manage, and sell, any and all estates to an indefinite extent, to make and enforce contracts, all of which they do as an individual, in their corporate name. In fine, they have collectively all the rights and powers of individuals, excepting those of a political and moral character. With the want of political and moral powers, they are of course exempted from corresponding responsibilities.

The quaint language of Lord Coke, and other venerable ancient luminaries of the law, describing corporations as having no souls or consciences, as mere capacities to sue and be sued, has been productive of much mischief, and led to many judicial decisions, which the enlightened reason of this age cannot but deplore. From such doctrines, the managers of corporations have sometimes been led to forget that *they* had souls and moral responsibility; and in the performance of what they deemed their duty, in the corporate name, they have done such things as, on their individual responsibility, they would never have ventured to do.

* * *

It might still, however, be wise for legislatures to reserve more direct control over corporations of future creation than they are accustomed to do in most of the states. The enjoyment of a corporate franchise is not of common right. It is the grant of the whole people of certain powers to a few individuals, to enable them to effect some specific benefit, or promote the general good. When the corporation fails to produce the expected benefit, and far more when its charter is perverted to injurious purposes, the whole people ought to have the power to control the operations, and even to revoke the charter.

William Leggett (1834)

It is not against the objects effected by incorporated companies that we contend; but simply against the false principle, politically and politico-economically, of special grants and privileges. Instead of renewing the charters of insurance companies, or any other companies, about to expire, or

SOURCE: Theodore Sedgwick, Jr., ed., *A Collection of the Political Writings of William Leggett* (New York: Taylor and Dodd, 1840), pp. 142–43.

granting charters to new applicants, we would recommend the passing of one general law of joint stock partnerships, allowing any number of persons to associate for any object . . . permitting them to sue and be sued under their partnership name, to be secure from liability beyond the amount of capital invested, to conduct their business according to their own good pleasure, and, in short, to possess all the powers defined by the revised statutes as belonging to corporations. . . .

The only difference would be that those privileges would no longer be special, but would belong to the whole community, any number of which might associate together, form a new company for the same objects, give due notification to the public, and enter into free competition with pre-existing companies or partnerships; precisely as one man, or set of associated men, may now enter into mercantile business by the side of other merchants, import the same kinds of goods, dispose of them on the same terms, and compete with them in all the branches of their business.

There has been a great deal said about our ultraism and utopianism; and this is the extent of it. By a general law of joint-stock partnerships all the good effects of private incorporations would be secured, and all the evil ones avoided. The humblest citizens might associate together, and wield, through the agency of skillful and intelligent directors, chosen by themselves, a vast aggregate capital, composed of the little separate sums which they could afford to invest in such an enterprise, in competition with the capitals of the purse-proud men who now almost monopolize certain branches of business.

The Politics of Opportunity

A. Antimasonic Revivalism

• *Moses Thatcher* (1830)

The rise of democratic politics depended on popular parties that could turn out voters. To maximize votes, politicians had to find means of arousing the apathetic on more than immediate local issues. The basic political style that emerged in antebellum America, in the South and West as well as in the North, centered on the portrayal of some self-serving, privileged interest which had secretly consolidated power and had begun to shut off equal access to the rewards of national growth. Of course, any successful crusade to "turn the rascals out" needed to be responsive to public moods and to the genuine frustrations, grievances, and aspirations of a large segment of the electorate. But to a striking degree, politicians sought to legitimize any new coalition of interests by picturing their opponents as heirs of the British and Tories—as an un-American elite whose systematic encroachments demanded, on the model of the Declaration of Independence, a proclamation of grievances, a listing (in Jefferson's famous words) of an "assemblage of horrors," "a long train of abuses and usurpations."

While there had been earlier local experiments with this style, antimasonry was the first widespread popular movement to attack special privilege and

183

insist on an unequivocal commitment to equal access to power. Combining the ideology of the American Revolution with the fervor and rhetoric of religious revivalism, the Antimasons taught unforgettable lessons to the most seasoned politicians—in 1830 they captured approximately one-half the popular vote in New York State and also held, in Philadelphia, America's first national political convention. The Antimasons recruited new voters throughout New England and the Middle Atlantic states, and in several regions they remained for a time the major anti-Jacksonian party.

The reasons for this sudden popular outburst can only be briefly outlined here. From the late eighteenth century to the 1820s, the secret order of Freemasons had grown at an astonishing rate. In many parts of the Northeast, its lodges included an impressive proportion of the young male population, particularly men who were upward-mobile, politically active, and increasingly affluent. Membership was especially appealing to ambitious men (including some free blacks who organized separate lodges) who were excluded from the most prestigious centers of local power and whose business travel or change of residence gave extraordinary value to "fraternal" connections that would be honored in distant communities. Freemasonry, in short, can be viewed as a means of adapting to the highly competitive, individualistic, and unpredictable conditions of a society in the first throes of modernization. Membership was a substitute for "ethnicity," in the sense that Freemasonry provided many of the benefits, including in-group charity, solidarity, and social services later associated with ethnic organizations. In other ways, Freemasonry functioned as a substitute church, not only in its rituals, discipline, and hierarchy but in giving members a sense of brotherhood and mutual trust as well as business and political connections. The more that Freemasonry succeeded in providing a sense of privileged identity and special advantages, the more it aroused the suspicion and jealousy of outsiders.

What triggered an organized antimasonic crusade was the kidnapping and probable murder in 1826 of William Morgan, an apostate Freemason who was about to publish an exposé revealing many of the secrets of the order. After Morgan disappeared in Upstate New York, it appeared that the Freemasons were powerful enough to silence newspapers and obstruct the course of justice. By 1830, moral outrage had spread throughout the Northeast and was being translated into political action, often to the advantage of skillful politicians eager to challenge various groups of incumbents. Since antimasonry depended on sustaining a high level of public indignation on a single issue, it soon proved inadequate as the basis for a permanent national party—especially since large numbers of Freemasons either withdrew from the fraternity or were driven underground. More important, however, was the perfection of an anti-elitist rhetoric which soon became a staple of American political culture.

Moses Thatcher (1795–1878), who presents a relatively moderate sample of this rhetoric in the selection below, was a New England minister, an ardent opponent of alcohol and tobacco, and one of the founders of the New-England Anti-Slavery Society. Note that in calling for a national convention he pictures "the people" rallying against an exclusive and autonomous "power" which is no longer subject to the legal, political, and religious rules of the larger society. Thatcher quotes, from an Upstate New York convention, a typical list of grievances modeled on the Declaration of Independence.

Moses Thatcher (1830)

The common cause of our common country, demands the utmost vigilance of an intelligent community. In order that this vigilance may be maintained, it is necessary that corresponding exertions be used to scatter light upon every subject which has an important political bearing. Light being diffused upon such subjects, and the attention of the people being directed to those things which are either salutary or prejudicial to the public good; it argues either a want of moral principle, or a criminal degree of apathy, not to feel interested; and those who feel deeply interested, must *act*. . . .

On this ground, we consider it not only the *right*, but the *obligation*, of citizens of this Commonwealth, in concert with others of our sister states, to assemble for the express purpose of investigating the nature, tendency, and political bearing of Free Masonry.

We are aware that this subject is one of great interest, and, in its own nature, exceedingly delicate; inasmuch as it relates to the opinions and practice of many, who, for talents, learning and integrity, are ranked among the first men in our country. We are, likewise, by no means insensible, that a thorough investigation of this subject must bring us in unpleasant collision with men whom we highly regard for their moral worth, and with many to whom we are bound by the strongest ties of social and relative friendship. We would, therefore, have it distinctly understood, that we have neither collision nor controversy with Masons as *men*, but only with men as *Masons*.

While, however, we are willing to concede to Masons, as *men*, all that is just, honorable, virtuous and praiseworthy, on their part; we are *not* willing to admit, that *all* the talents, and *all* the learning, and *all* the moral worth of our common country are the perquisite of the masonic fraternity. We are not willing to admit that they "are *the* people," and that "wisdom will die with them." However highly we may respect Masons as *men*; we cannot concede, that [Masonic] aprons, sashes, jewels, mitres, secret rites and obligations, or princely titles, can *justly* secure to them prerogatives of honor, profit and trust; or that they are more deserving of public confidence, than any

---

SOURCE: Moses Thatcher, "Address," from *An Abstract of the Proceedings of the Anti-Masonic Convention of Massachusetts* (Boston: John Marsh, 1830), pp. 9–11, 18–19.

other class of citizens. We cannot stand afar off, and "exceedingly fear and quake," because of the "awful mystery," which, for a century past, has hung over this institution. . . .

THE MASONIC FRATERNITY HAVE ERECTED FOR THEMSELVES A DISTINCT, AND INDEPENDENT GOVERNMENT, WITHIN THE JURISDICTION OF THE UNITED STATES. It cannot be denied, that *any* community, arrogating to itself the right of punishing offenders, not recognized by the laws of the land; and, especially, holding in its own power the lives of its members; must, so far, be considered as claiming independence, and refusing, in these respects, to hold itself amenable to any higher authority. But, that the masonic fraternity have done this, and still persist in their claim to independence, has been made to appear by the most satisfactory evidence. The testimony of their own members has abundantly shown, that they have instituted a code of laws, not subject to the supervision of any civil power; and this code is *sanguinary*. The code of laws in this institution, consists in the several "oaths or obligations" of its several degrees, to every one of which a penalty is annexed; and that penalty is *death*. Every Free Mason, in every degree by which he may advance, is made to swear, that he will for ever conceal the secret rites and principles of the institution; his acting himself "under no less *penalty*," than to die a most horrid and barbarous death, if he should ever knowingly or wilfully violate any essential part of his obligation.

•   •   •

We cannot, however, sum up what we have already suggested, and what we might still desire to lay before the citizens of this Commonwealth, in more appropriate language, than that of the Le Roy [New York] Convention, in their Anti Masonic Declaration of Independence.

"That it (the Masonic Institution) is opposed to the genius and design of this government, the spirit and precepts of our holy religion, and the welfare of society generally, will appear from the following considerations:

"It exercises jurisdiction over the persons and lives of citizens of the republic.

"It arrogates to itself the right of punishing its members for offences unknown to the laws of this or any other nation.

"It requires the concealment of crime, and protects the guilty from punishment.

"It encourages the commission of crime, by affording to the guilty facilities of escape.

"It affords opportunities for the corrupt and designing to form plans against government, and the lives and characters of individuals.

"It assumes titles and dignities incompatible with a republican form of government, and enjoins an obedience to them derogatory to republican principles.

"It destroys all principles of equality, by bestowing favors on its own members, to the exclusion of others equally meritorious and deserving.

"It creates odious aristocracies by its obligations to support the interests of its members, in preference to others of equal qualifications.

"It blasphemes the name, and attempts a personification of the Great Jehovah.

"It prostitutes the Sacred Scriptures to unholy purposes, to subserve its own secular and trifling concerns.

"It weakens the sanctions of morality and religion, by the multiplication of profane oaths, and an immoral familiarity with religious forms and ceremonies.

"It destroys a veneration for religion and religious ordinances, by the profane use of religious forms.

"It substitutes the self-righteousness and ceremonies of Masonry for the vital religion and ordinances of the Gospel.

"It promotes habits of idleness and intemperance, by its members neglecting their business to attend its meetings and drink its libations.

"It accumulates funds at the expense of indigent persons, and to the distress of their families, too often to be dissipated in rioting and pleasure, and its senseless ceremonies and exhibitions.

"It contracts the sympathies of the human heart for all the unfortunate, by confining its charities to its own members; and promotes the interests of a few at the expense of the many.

"An institution thus fraught with so many and great evils, is dangerous to our government and the safety of our citizens, and is unfit to exist among a free people: We, therefore, believing it a duty we owe to God, our country, and to posterity, resolve to expose its mystery, wickedness and tendency, to public view—and we exhort all citizens, who have a love of country and a veneration for its laws, a spirit of our holy religion, and a regard for the welfare of mankind, to aid us in the cause which we have espoused."

B. Democratic Ideology

• *Andrew Jackson* (1837)

Andrew Jackson (1767–1845) won national fame as the military hero who crushed Indian resistance in the Old Southwest, who defeated a supposedly invincible British army at the Battle of New Orleans, and who temporarily seized Spanish Florida, preparing the way for its annexation to the United States (for Jackson's Indian policy, see Unit Three, Part 2, B). Jackson was in his late fifties when he began to emerge as a national political leader, intent first on exposing the "deep intrigue" of presidential rivals like William Crawford and Henry Clay, then on denouncing the "corrupt bargain" which in 1825 had allegedly put the "monarchical" John Quincy Adams in the White House. Even men who distrusted or hated Jackson—including Jefferson, Adams, Webster, Clay, Calhoun, and Lincoln—agreed that he was the dominant figure of his age. Yet even after he had been elected President in 1828, Jackson had taken few clear stands on the pressing issues of the time.

It was Jackson's charisma and personal style that originally defined the Democratic party, polarizing state and local factions as if he were a national magnetic force. Few Americans could remain neutral about "Old Hickory." By the mid-1830s, however, Jackson had spelled out a political philosophy based on the premise that government intervention in the economy inevitably creates special privilege for some groups at the expense of others. In the interest of maximizing liberty and equality, Jacksonian Democrats opposed a national bank, protective tariffs, federal aid for internal improvements, the distribution of federal revenues to the states, and other measures that might lead to concentrations of power.

On March 4, 1837, the day when Jackson completed his second term as President and was succeeded by his own handpicked protégé, Martin Van Buren, "Old Hickory" reviewed the history of his administrations and summed up the leading principles of the Democratic party. The central theme of Jackson's address to his "fellow citizens" is ingeniously simple. It concerns America's proud heritage, present greatness, and future mission, all of which are threatened from within by "intriguers and politicians" reinforced by the "money power." There is no more eloquent and comprehensive statement of the Democratic version of the politics of opportunity.

Andrew Jackson (1837)

We have now lived almost fifty years under the Constitution framed by the sages and patriots of the Revolution. The conflicts in which the nations of Europe were engaged during a great part of this period, the spirit in which they waged war against each other, and our intimate commercial connections with every part of the civilized world rendered it a time of much difficulty for the government of the United States. . . . But we have passed triumphantly through all these difficulties. Our Constitution is no longer a doubtful experiment, and at the end of nearly half a century we find that it has preserved unimpaired the liberties of the people, secured the rights of property, and that our country has improved and is flourishing beyond any former example in the history of nations.

. . .

In the legislation of Congress also, and in every measure of the general government, justice to every portion of the United States should be faithfully observed. No free government can stand without virtue in the people and a lofty spirit of patriotism, and if the sordid feelings of mere selfishness shall usurp the place which ought to be filled by public spirit, the legislation

SOURCE: James D. Richardson, ed., *A Compilation of the Messages and Papers of the Presidents, 1789–1897* (New York: Bureau of National Literature, 1969), Vol. IV, pp. 1512, 1517–27.

of Congress will soon be converted into a scramble for personal and sectional advantages. Under our free institutions the citizens of every quarter of our country are capable of attaining a high degree of prosperity and happiness without seeking to profit themselves at the expense of others; and every such attempt must in the end fail to succeed, for the people in every part of the United States are too enlightened not to understand their own rights and interests and to detect and defeat every effort to gain undue advantages over them; and when such designs are discovered it naturally provokes resentments which can not always be easily allayed. Justice—full and ample justice—to every portion of the United States should be the ruling principle of every freeman, and should guide the deliberations of every public body, whether it be state or national.

It is well known that there have always been those amongst us who wish to enlarge the powers of the general government, and experience would seem to indicate that there is a tendency on the part of this government to overstep the boundaries marked out for it by the Constitution. Its legitimate authority is abundantly sufficient for all the purposes for which it was created, and its powers being expressly enumerated, there can be no justification for claiming anything beyond them. Every attempt to exercise power beyond these limits should be promptly and firmly opposed, for one evil example will lead to other measures still more mischievous; and if the principle of constructive powers or supposed advantages or temporary circumstances shall ever be permitted to justify the assumption of a power not given by the Constitution, the general government will before long absorb all the powers of legislation, and you will have in effect but one consolidated government. From the extent of our country, its diversified interests, different pursuits, and different habits, it is too obvious for argument that a single consolidated government would be wholly inadequate to watch over and protect its interests; and every friend of our free institutions should be always prepared to maintain unimpaired and in full vigor the rights and sovereignty of the states and to confine the action of the general government strictly to the sphere of its appropriate duties. . . .

Plain as these principles appear to be, you will yet find there is a constant effort to induce the general government to go beyond the limits of its taxing power and to impose unnecessary burdens upon the people. Many powerful interests are continually at work to procure heavy duties on commerce and to swell the revenue beyond the real necessities of the public service, and the country has already felt the injurious effects of their combined influence. They succeeded in obtaining a tariff of duties bearing most oppressively on the agricultural and laboring classes of society and producing a revenue that could not be usefully employed within the range of the powers conferred upon Congress, and in order to fasten upon the people this unjust and unequal system of taxation extravagant schemes of internal improvement were got up in various quarters to squander the money and to purchase support. Thus one unconstitutional measure was intended to be upheld by another, and the abuse of the power of taxation was to be maintained by usurping the power of expending the money in internal improvements. You can not have forgotten the severe and doubtful struggle through which we passed when the executive department of the government by its veto[1] endeavored to arrest this prodigal scheme of injustice and to bring back the legislation of Congress to the boundaries prescribed by the Constitution. The good sense and practical judgment of the people when the subject was brought before them sustained the course of the Executive,[2] and this plan of unconstitutional expenditures for the purposes of corrupt influence is, I trust, finally overthrown.

The result of this decision has been felt in the rapid extinguishment of the public debt and the large accumulation of a surplus in the Treasury, notwithstanding the tariff was reduced and is now very far below the amount originally contemplated by its advocates. But, rely upon it, the design to collect an extravagant revenue and to burden you with taxes beyond the economical wants of the Government is not yet abandoned. The various interests which have combined together to impose a heavy tariff and to produce an overflowing Treasury are too strong and have too much at stake to surrender the contest. The corporations and wealthy individuals who are engaged in large manufacturing establishments desire a high tariff to increase their gains. Designing politicians will support it to conciliate their favor and to obtain the means of profuse expenditure for the purpose of purchasing influence in other quarters; and since the people have decided that the federal government can not be permitted to employ its income in internal improvements, efforts will be made to seduce and mislead the citizens of the several states by holding out to them the deceitful prospects of benefits to be derived from a surplus revenue collected by the general government and annually divided among the states; and if, encouraged by these fallacious hopes, the states should disregard the principles of economy which ought to characterize every republican government, and should indulge in lavish expenditures exceeding their resources, they will before long find themselves oppressed with debts which they are unable to pay, and the temptation will become irresistible to support a high tariff in order to obtain a surplus for distribution. Do not allow yourselves, my fellow-citizens, to be misled on this subject. The federal government can not collect a surplus for such purposes without violating the principles of the Constitution and assuming powers which have not been granted. It is, moreover, a system of injustice, and if persisted in will inevitably lead to corruption, and must end in ruin. The surplus revenue will be drawn from the pockets of the people—from the farmer, the mechanic, and the laboring classes of society; but who will receive it when distributed among the states, where it is to be disposed of by leading state politicians, who have friends to favor and political partisans to gratify? It will certainly not be returned to those who paid it and who have most need of it and are honestly

---

[1] The Maysville Road Bill veto, 1830.
[2] The election of 1832.

entitled to it. There is but one safe rule, and that is to confine the general government rigidly within the sphere of its appropriate duties. It has no power to raise a revenue or impose taxes except for the purposes enumerated in the Constitution, and if its income is found to exceed these wants it should be forthwith reduced and the burden of the people so far lightened. . . .

It was not easy for men engaged in the ordinary pursuits of business, whose attention had not been particularly drawn to the subject, to foresee all the consequences of a currency exclusively of paper, and we ought not on that account to be surprised at the facility with which laws were obtained to carry into effect the paper system. Honest and even enlightened men are sometimes misled by the specious and plausible statements of the designing. But experience has now proved the mischiefs and dangers of a paper currency, and it rests with you to determine whether the proper remedy shall be applied.

The paper system being founded on public confidence and having of itself no intrinsic value, it is liable to great and sudden fluctuations, thereby rendering property insecure and the wages of labor unsteady and uncertain. . . .

These ebbs and flows in the currency and these indiscreet extensions of credit naturally engender a spirit of speculation injurious to the habits and character of the people. We have already seen its effects in the wild spirit of speculation in the public lands and various kinds of stock which within the last year or two seized upon such a multitude of our citizens and threatened to pervade all classes of society and to withdraw their attention from the sober pursuits of honest industry. . . .

Some of the evils which arise from this system of paper press with peculiar hardship upon the class of society least able to bear it. A portion of this currency frequently becomes depreciated or worthless, and all of it is easily counterfeited in such a manner as to require peculiar skill and much experience to distinguish the counterfeit from the genuine note. These frauds are most generally perpetrated in the smaller notes, which are used in the daily transactions of ordinary business, and the losses occasioned by them are commonly thrown upon the laboring classes of society, whose situation and pursuits put it out of their power to guard themselves from these impositions, and whose daily wages are necessary for their subsistence. It is the duty of every government so to regulate its currency as to protect this numerous class, as far as practicable, from the impositions of avarice and fraud. . . .

Recent events have proved that the paper-money system of this country may be used as an engine to undermine your free institutions, and that those who desire to engross all power in the hands of the few and to govern by corruption or force are aware of its power and prepared to employ it. . . .

But when the charter for the Bank of the United States was obtained from Congress it perfected the schemes of the paper system and gave to its advocates the position they have struggled to obtain from the commencement of the federal government to the present hour. The immense capital and peculiar privileges bestowed upon it enabled it to exercise despotic sway over the other banks in every part of the country. From its superior strength it could seriously injure, if not destroy, the business of any one of them which might incur its resentment; and it openly claimed for itself the power of regulating the currency throughout the United States. In other words, it asserted (and it undoubtedly possessed) the power to make money plenty or scarce at its pleasure, at any time and in any quarter of the Union, by controlling the issues of other banks and permitting an expansion or compelling a general contraction of the circulating medium, according to its own will. The other banking institutions were sensible of its strength, and they soon generally became its obedient instruments, ready at all times to execute its mandates; and with the banks necessarily went also that numerous class of persons in our commercial cities who depend altogether on bank credits for their solvency and means of business, and who are therefore obliged, for their own safety, to propitiate the favor of the money power by distinguished zeal and devotion in its service. The result of the ill-advised legislation which established this great monopoly was to concentrate the whole moneyed power of the Union, with its boundless means of corruption and its numerous dependents, under the direction and command of one acknowledged head, thus organizing this particular interest as one body and securing to it unity and concert of action throughout the United States, and enabling it to bring forward upon any occasion its entire and undivided strength to support or defeat any measure of the government. In the hands of this formidable power, thus perfectly organized, was also placed unlimited dominion over the amount of the circulating medium, giving it the power to regulate the value of property and the fruits of labor in every quarter of the Union, and to bestow prosperity or bring ruin upon any city or section of the country as might best comport with its own interest or policy.

We are not left to conjecture how the moneyed power, thus organized and with such a weapon in its hands, would be likely to use it. The distress and alarm which pervaded and agitated the whole country when the Bank of the United States waged war upon the people in order to compel them to submit to its demands can not yet be forgotten. The ruthless and unsparing temper with which whole cities and communities were oppressed, individuals impoverished and ruined, and a scene of cheerful prosperity suddenly changed into one of gloom and despondency ought to be indelibly impressed on the memory of the people of the United States. If such was its power in a time of peace, what would it not have been in a season of war, with an enemy at your doors? No nation but the freemen of the United States could have come out victorious from such a contest; yet, if you had not conquered, the government would have passed from the hands of the many to the hands of the few, and this organized money power from its secret conclave would have dictated the choice of your highest officers and compelled you to make peace or war, as best suited their own wishes. The forms of your government might for a time have remained, but its living spirit would have departed from it.

. . .

Defeated in the general government, the same class of intriguers and politicians will now resort to the states and endeavor to obtain there the same organization which they failed to perpetuate in the Union; and with specious and deceitful plans of public advantages and state interests and state pride they will endeavor to establish in the different states one moneyed institution with overgrown capital and exclusive privileges sufficient to enable it to control the operations of the other banks. . . .

It is one of the serious evils of our present system of banking that it enables one class of society—and that by no means a numerous one—by its control over the currency, to act injuriously upon the interests of all the others and to exercise more than its just proportion of influence in political affairs. The agricultural, the mechanical, and the laboring classes have little or no share in the direction of the great moneyed corporations, and from their habits and the nature of their pursuits they are incapable of forming extensive combinations to act together with united force. . . .

The planter, the farmer, the mechanic, and the laborer all know that their success depends upon their own industry and economy, and that they must not expect to become suddenly rich by the fruits of their toil. Yet these classes of society form the great body of the people of the United States; they are the bone and sinew of the country—men who love liberty and desire nothing but equal rights and equal laws, and who, moreover, hold the great mass of our national wealth, although it is distributed in moderate amounts among the millions of freemen who possess it. But with overwhelming numbers and wealth on their side they are in constant danger of losing their fair influence in the government, and with difficulty maintain their just rights against the incessant efforts daily made to encroach upon them. The mischief springs from the power which the moneyed interest derives from a paper currency which they are able to control, from the multitude of corporations with exclusive privileges which they have succeeded in obtaining in the different states, and which are employed altogether for their benefit; and unless you become more watchful in your states and check this spirit of monopoly and thirst for exclusive privileges you will in the end find that the most important powers of government have been given or bartered away, and the control over your dearest interests has passed into the hands of these corporations.

The paper-money system and its natural associations—monopoly and exclusive privileges—have already struck their roots too deep in the soil, and it will require all your efforts to check its further growth and to eradicate the evil. The men who profit by the abuses and desire to perpetuate them will continue to besiege the halls of legislation in the general government as well as in the states, and will seek by every artifice to mislead and deceive the public servants. It is to yourselves that you must look for safety and the means of guarding and perpetuating your free institutions. In your hands is rightfully placed the sovereignty of the country, and to you everyone placed in authority is ultimately responsible. It is always in your power to see that the wishes of the people are carried into faithful execution, and their will, when once made known, must sooner or later be obeyed; and while the people remain, as I trust they ever will, uncorrupted and incorruptible, and continue watchful and jealous of their rights, the government is safe, and the cause of freedom will continue to triumph over all its enemies. . . .

While I am thus endeavoring to press upon your attention the principles which I deem of vital importance in the domestic concerns of the country, I ought not to pass over without notice the important considerations which should govern your policy toward foreign powers. It is unquestionably our true interest to cultivate the most friendly understanding with every nation and to avoid by every honorable means the calamities of war, and we shall best attain this object by frankness and sincerity in our foreign intercourse, by the prompt and faithful execution of treaties, and by justice and impartiality in our conduct to all. But no nation, however desirous of peace, can hope to escape occasional collisions with other powers, and the soundest dictates of policy require that we should place ourselves in a condition to assert our rights if a resort to force should ever become necessary. Our local situation, our long line of seacoast, indented by numerous bays, with deep rivers opening into the interior, as well as our extended and still increasing commerce, point to the navy as our natural means of defense. It will in the end be found to be the cheapest and most effectual, and now is the time, in a season of peace and with an overflowing revenue, that we can year after year add to its strength without increasing the burdens of the people. It is your true policy, for your navy will not only protect your rich and flourishing commerce in distant seas, but will enable you to reach and annoy the enemy and will give to defense its greatest efficiency by meeting danger at a distance from home. It is impossible by any line of fortifications to guard every point from attack against a hostile force advancing from the ocean and selecting its object, but they are indispensable to protect cities from bombardment, dockyards and naval arsenals from destruction, to give shelter to merchant vessels in time of war and to single ships or weaker squadrons when pressed by superior force. Fortifications of this description can not be too soon completed and armed and placed in a condition of the most perfect preparation. The abundant means we now possess can not be applied in any manner more useful to the country, and when this is done and our naval force sufficiently strengthened and our militia armed we need not fear that any nation will wantonly insult us or needlessly provoke hostilities. We shall more certainly preserve peace when it is well understood that we are prepared for war.

. . . The progress of the United States under our free and happy institutions has surpassed the most sanguine hopes of the founders of the Republic. Our growth has been rapid beyond all former example in numbers, in wealth, in knowledge, and all the useful arts which contribute to the comforts and convenience of man, and from the earliest ages of history to the present day there never have been thirteen millions of people associated in one political body who enjoyed so much freedom and happiness as the people of these

United States. You have no longer any cause to fear danger from abroad; your strength and power are well known throughout the civilized world, as well as the high and gallant bearing of your sons. It is from within, among your-selves—from cupidity, from corruption, from disappointed ambition and in-ordinate thirst for power—that factions will be formed and liberty endan-gered. It is against such designs, whatever disguise the actors may assume, that you have especially to guard yourselves. You have the highest of human trusts committed to your care. Providence has showered on this favored land blessings without number, and has chosen you as the guardians of freedom, to preserve it for the benefit of the human race. May He who holds in His hands the destinies of nations make you worthy of the favors He has be-stowed and enable you, with pure hearts and pure hands and sleepless vigi-lance, to guard and defend to the end of time the great charge He has com-mitted to your keeping.

C. Whig Ideology

• *Calvin Colton (1844)*

> The Whig party, a coalition of various anti-Jacksonian factions including National Republicans and Antimasons, never acquired a commanding na-tional leader like Jackson who could at once symbolize the party's diffuse aspirations and articulate its ideology. Here, the essential Whig principles and arguments are set forth by Calvin Colton (1789–1857), a journalist and what today would be called a "media specialist" for Henry Clay. Some-thing of the character of Whiggery is revealed by the fact that Colton be-gan his career as a clergyman and missionary, having graduated from Yale and Andover Theological Seminary. After spending four years in England as a correspondent for the *New York Observer*, he adopted the pen name "Junius" and wrote propaganda for the protective tariff and other Whig causes. Despite Colton's evangelical background, he became the official biographer and publicist for the notoriously ungodly Kentuckian, Henry Clay.
>
> It is noteworthy that Colton, after advancing the classic Whig doctrines that investment of capital creates jobs and that what is good for capitalists is good for the people, assumes the mantle of the *true* democrat, the *true* voice of the people, in assailing the ONE MAN POWER of Jackson and his "aristocratic" followers. The financial panic of 1837 and the subse-quent years of depression enabled Whigs to stigmatize Democrats as the party of demagoguery and arbitrary rule; having shattered the confidence of the business community and having created artificial divisions between rich and poor, so the theory went, the Democrats had threatened the very essence of America—a "country of self-made men."

Calvin Colton (1844)

The true and best interest of moneyed capital.

It is to give labor a fair reward, and to make it profitable. But as this can not be forced, as between the parties, trade being always a vountary transaction, the ability to do it can not be separated from the action of government. All workers, therefore, as well as moneyed capitalists—all laborers are deeply concerned in supporting a public policy, which will put labor in good demand, and thus enable it to command a good price. This depends entirely upon the proceeds of moneyed investments. While these are good, labor will be in demand, and the price of it, or its wages, will be proportionately high. Moneyed investments are sure to pay well, if it can be afforded; and the more they can afford, the better for them. But generally, this ability to give good wages, depends very much, sometimes entirely, on the policy of government, in the privileges it confers on such investments, and the chances it gives to them. If the government wars against them, instead of extending to them its fostering care, if it endeavors to cripple and break them down, instead of protecting and sustaining them, this hostility may and does injure the moneyed capitalist, by rendering his investments insecure and unproductive; but it injures the working classes of the community much more. The rich can hide themselves in a storm of government hostility, though they may be losers; but the poor perish, or are in great distress, for want of employment.

· · ·

A plain statement.

Nothing but an extraordinary infatuation could have shut the eyes of the people to the FACT, that moneyed capital employed in the country, is for the interests of labor; that its uses afford chances of improvement to those who have little, and give bread, clothing, and a home to the poor; that rich men seek to invest their funds where they can be employed by labor; that the modes of investment are naturally determined by the habits and wants of the commercial, agricultural, manufacturing, mechanical, and other laboring classes of the community; that what these want will be most productive to capitalists, because most beneficial to labor; that capital in large amounts . . . must necessarily be vested with corporate rights, to be secure for all concerned, and most effective for general good; that moneyed capitalists would never put their funds in other hands without such protection; that banks are necessary to furnish a circulating medium, convenient in form, and adequate for the trade and business of the country; that all these institutions had their origin in the wants and necessities of the people; that in putting

SOURCE: Calvin Colton, *The Junius Tracts*, No. VII: *Labor and Capital* (New York: Greeley and McElrath, 1844), pp. 8, 13–15.

down and destroying them, by legislation and government, the people only put down and destroy themselves; and that the greater the income of capital vested in these various forms, as a permanent state of things, so much greater the evidence of general prosperity.

But the revolution introduced in the financial policy of the government, and forced on the commercial habits of the people, from 1830 to 1840, broke up all these established relations of the different parts of the community toward each other, and left all in a mass of confusion and ruin, to be reorganized and set in order again, as best they could.

. . .

The chances of life in this country.

Ours is a country, where men start from an humble origin, and from small beginnings rise gradually in the world, as the reward of merit and industry, and where they can attain to the most elevated positions, or acquire a large amount of wealth, according to the pursuits they elect for themselves. No exclusive privileges of birth, no entailment of estates, no civil or political disqualifications, stand in their path; but one has as good a chance as another, according to his talents, prudence, and personal exertions. This is a country of *self-made men*, than which nothing better could be said of any state of society.

. . .

A retrospect.

Understanding, as we now do, if what we have said is correct, the relation between the labor of the country and its moneyed capital, we must look back with astonishment at the policy of the Federal Administration, from 1829 to 1841, when the cry rang through the land, and never ceased—DOWN WITH THE BANKS! DOWN WITH MANUFACTORIES! DOWN WITH CORPORATIONS! DOWN WITH CAPITALISTS! It is a history that one can hardly believe in! . . .

[F]or the period above named, we had a *re*-lapse and *col*-lapse in our national welfare, never to be forgotten; that an unlucky star rose in our hemisphere, ascended to its meridian, and marched to the western hills, leaving an OMINOUS TAIL BEHIND; that the people were persuaded for a time, that it was the TRUE SUN, and were hard to be convinced of its eccentric and ill boding character; that it brought famine, pestilence, and death; that demagogueism was the rage of its season, innoculating the poor with a mania against the rich, and the laborer with jealousy against the moneyed capitalist; that the love of ONE MAN POWER [Jackson], was the chief malady that afflicted the nation, and its ascendency the most remarkable occurrence of the time; that the long-established, simple, and democratic habits of the people, social and political, were superseded by the dictation of a Chief, and by the aristocratic assumptions of his menials; that new, unheard-of, and destructive doctrines were promulged for the government of the country; that a well-ordered system of currency was broken up and destroyed; that the useful relations between capitalists and the laboring classes, were violently assailed, and so far dissolved, as to bring great distress on the industrious and working population; that states and large corporations were first enticed to enlist in great enterprises, and then forced to suspend them, and to stop payment, by sudden changes in the policy and measures of the government; that our credit at home was prostrated, and abroad became the by-word and scorn of nations; that the shameless doctrine of the repudiation of debts, was for the first time avowed and sanctioned by legislative authority; that the superstructure and very foundations of society were shaken in the general convulsion; in short, that times, modes, customs, morals, and manners underwent a complete revolution, so that the republic that *was*, could hardly be recognised in the new state of things.

The Fear of Sectional Exclusion

A. Beginnings of Sectional Rivalry

• *Thomas Hart Benton (Recalling 1828)*

As we have suggested, the struggle to define rules governing the access to wealth and power divided along lines of class, occupation, ethnicity, and local interest, although no simple formula can explain the complexity of individual philosophies and commitments. The most dangerous line of division, the one which most American leaders sought to blur or in some way repress, was the division between South and North—between states dependent on slave labor and states which had once legitimized black slavery but now prided themselves on their commitment to free labor.

We cannot even begin to recount here the history of vacillating conflict and rivalry that finally led to the Civil War. The purpose of the two concluding selections of Unit Two is to suggest some of the connections between our preceding themes and the "irrepressible conflict" between North and South, a conflict which finally absorbed, compressed, and symbolized all the tensions between the anxious spirit of gain and the quest for moral order, self-improvement, and social righteousness.

Thomas Hart Benton (1782–1858) of Missouri, for thirty years a powerful voice in the Senate, describes in the selection following an ominous confrontation over the "Tariff of Abominations" of 1828, in which sectional jealousy temporarily became fused with economic interest. Benton's account cannot be read as a wholly accurate description of the conflict, but should rather be taken as the retrospective view of an ardent nationalist. Benton sees himself vainly struggling to reconcile the shifting interests of North and South, arguing that Henry Clay's "American System" of tariffs and internal improvements "should work alike in all parts of our America." When his efforts are defeated by backers of the American System, the worst fears of the Deep South seem confirmed. George McDuffie, a protégé of Calhoun's who had taken Calhoun's former seat in the House of Representatives, pictures the tariff as a tyrannical device for expropriating wealth from the South and redistributing it to the North. This early confrontation, in Benton's later view, had accentuated the South's fear of being excluded from equal access to national benefits. It should be added that Benton, a loyal supporter of Jackson and the Senate floor leader in the war against the Second Bank of the United States, was no friend of Southern extremism. In 1828 he was interested in promoting an alliance between the South and West in order to outflank the political alliance between the West's Henry Clay and New England's John Quincy Adams. But during the debates on the Compromise of 1850, he opposed further concessions to the South (Senator Foote of Mississippi drew a pistol on Benton) and hence lost the support of his Missouri constituents.

Thomas Hart Benton (Recalling 1828)

The question of a protective tariff had now not only become political, but sectional. In the early years of the federal government it was not so. . . .

In this early period the southern states were as ready as any part of the Union in extending the protection to home industry which resulted from the imposition of revenue duties on rival imported articles, and on articles necessary to ourselves in time of war; and some of her statesmen were among the foremost members of Congress in promoting that policy. . . .

After 1824 the New England states (always meaning the greatest portion when a section is spoken of) classed with the protective states [i.e., the New England states joined traditionally pro-tariff states like Pennsylvania]—leaving the South alone, as a section, against that policy. My personal position was that of a great many others in the three protective sections—opposed to the policy, but going with it, on account of the interest of the state in the protection of some of its productions. . . .

SOURCE: Thomas Hart Benton, *Thirty Years' View*, Vol. I (New York: D. Appleton and Co., 1854–1856), pp. 97, 100, 101.

I moved a duty upon indigo, a former staple of the South, but now declined to a slight production; and I proposed a rate of duty in harmony with the protective features of the bill. No southern member would move that duty, because he opposed the principle. I moved it, that the "American System," as it was called, should work alike in all parts of our America.

· · ·

The proposition for this duty on imported indigo did not prevail. In lieu of the amount proposed, and which was less than any protective duty in the bill, the friends of the "American System" (constituting a majority of the Senate) substituted a nominal duty of five cents on the pound. . . . A duty so contemptible, so out of proportion to the other provisions of the bill, and doled out in such miserable drops, was a mockery and insult; and so viewed by the southern members. It increased the odiousness of the bill, by showing that the southern section of the Union was only included in the "American System" for its burdens, and not for its benefits. Mr. McDuffie [George McDuffie, of South Carolina], in the House of Representatives, inveighed bitterly against it, and spoke the general feeling of the southern states when he said:

> Sir, if the union of these states shall ever be severed, and their liberties subverted, the historian who records these disasters will have to ascribe them to measures of this description. I do sincerely believe that neither this government nor any free government, can exist for a quarter of a century, under such a system of legislation. . . .
>
> Sir, when I consider that, by a single act like the present, from five to ten millions of dollars may be transferred annually from one part of the community to another; when I consider the disguise of disinterested patriotism under which the basest and most profligate ambition may perpetrate such an act of injustice and political prostitution, I cannot hesitate, for a moment, to pronounce this very system of indirect bounties, the most stupendous instrument of corruption ever placed in the hands of public functionaries.

B. "What Is It That Has Endangered the Union?"

• *John C. Calhoun* (1850)

John C. Calhoun (1782–1850), having begun his public career as a nationalistic Congressman and secretary of war, later emerged as the embittered theorist and ideologist of the extreme southern rights movement. An intellectual and in many ways a loner, Calhoun was mistrusted by both Democratic and Whig leaders who suspected that his overriding ambition to become President would always take precedence over party loyalty. Even in the Deep South, his political following was small, and his finely-spun logic was too abstract for most farmers, planters, and country lawyers. Calhoun made his chief contribution to sectional conflict during his brief and really accidental tenure as secretary of state (1844–1845), when he succeeded in linking the annexation of Texas with the defense of Negro slavery. By 1850, the year of his death, Calhoun had failed in his campaign to unite Southerners across party lines, but he had acquired great symbolic importance as a spokesman for southern principles, rectitude, and intransigence. Because he was too enfeebled to speak publicly in the great Senate debates on the Compromise of 1850, his grim speech opposing the admission of California as a free state was read by Senator J. M. Mason of Virginia. A masterful presentation and analysis of southern grievances, it was immediately recognized as a landmark in the history of sectional controversy.

In addressing the question, "what is it that has endangered the union?", Calhoun goes far beyond the immediate business of the Senate and shows with compelling logic, if one accepts his premises, how slavery and sectional divergence had become intermeshed with fundamental struggles over the access to wealth and power. In the selection below, we hear echoes of various questions presented earlier in Unit Two: the meaning of westward expansion for past conceptions of social order and national equilibrium; the significance of California in the years immediately following its annexation and gold rush; and the role of the government, ostensibly representing all regions, interests, and citizens, in apportioning public land and other benefits.

Calhoun's central grievance is not aimed at abolitionist extremists or indeed at any faction. Nor does he complain against nature or fate for allowing the North to outstrip the South in population, wealth, and productivity. Rather, he is convinced that the growing disparity in power between the two sections is the direct result of governmental policy, a policy which has benefited the entire North at the expense of the South. For this injustice he holds the people of the North responsible, much as Jefferson in his original draft of the Declaration of Independence held the people of Britain responsible for supporting a tyrannical government. Unlike most southern politicians at this time, Calhoun rejects the hope of relying on northern allies, on northern conservatism, or on the trade-offs of traditional bargaining. In one limited respect, his position resembles that of northern radicals (see Part 2, A, above) who demanded free and equal access to the public domain and who interpreted any exclusion or partiality as the first step toward "enslaving" the disadvantaged—the "true workingmen," in the eyes of the radicals; the South, in the eyes of Calhoun.

If this comparison seems ironic, there is a deeper irony in Calhoun's fear of southern enslavement to the North. First, he advances the thesis that unless the South is guaranteed equal rights and equal political power to protect those rights, there will be no barriers to inevitable northern encroachments and total southern dependency. Calhoun had no need to look to history or to other continents to find a model of such unlimited power and dependency. He was a slaveholder himself. But next we find Calhoun, speaking from a "slave-like" position of powerlessness and proclaiming that the South has no political means of resistance, delivering a virtual ultimatum to the North. It is up to the North, he says, which dominates a government "as absolute as that of the Autocrat [Czar] of Russia," to make permanent and guaranteed concessions of equal rights. In short, toward the end of his speech, Calhoun seems to be in the curious position of a "slave" demanding not only freedom and civil rights but one-half of his master's property! As Calhoun well knew, masters and autocrats were seldom so generous. But like a rebellious slave, Calhoun backs up his demand with the threat of escape—or secession—and of violence if the escape is resisted. The final irony is that in 1850 the South was probably strong enough, relative to the North, to have won its independence. Insofar as Calhoun's speech frightened northern moderates and contributed to compromise, it helped delay a showdown the North was certain to win if the North continued to gain in wealth, population, and power.

John C. Calhoun (1850)

To this question there can be but one answer: that the immediate cause is the almost universal discontent which pervades all the states composing the southern section of the Union. This widely-extended discontent is not of recent origin. It commenced with the agitation of the slavery question, and has been increasing ever since. The next question, going one step further back, is: what has caused this widely-diffused and almost universal discontent?

It is a great mistake to suppose, as is by some, that it originated with demagogues, who excited the discontent with the intention of aiding their personal advancement, or with the disappointed ambition of certain politicians, who resorted to it as a means of retrieving their fortunes. On the contrary, all the great political influences of the section were arrayed against excitement, and exerted to the utmost to keep the people quiet. The great mass of the people of the South were divided, as in the other section, into Whigs and Democrats. The leaders and the presses of both parties in the South were very solicitous to prevent excitement and to preserve quiet; because it was seen that the effects of the former would necessarily tend to weaken, if not destroy, the political ties which united them with their respective parties in the other section. Those who know the strength of the party ties will readily appreciate the immense force which this cause exerted against agitation, and in favor of preserving quiet. But, great as it was, it was not sufficient to prevent the wide-spread discontent which now pervades the section. No; some cause, far deeper and more powerful than the one supposed, must exist, to account for discontent so wide and deep. The question then

SOURCE: John C. Calhoun, "Speech on Henry Clay's Compromise Resolution on the Bill to Admit California, March 4, 1850," in Alexander Johnson, ed., *American Orations* (New York: G. P. Putnam's Sons, 1896), Vol. II, pp. 132, 134, 136–37, 139–41, 156–59.

recurs: what is the cause of this discontent? It will be found in the belief of the people of the southern states, as prevalent as the discontent itself, that they cannot remain, as things now are, consistently with honor and safety, in the Union. The next question to be considered is: what has caused this belief?

One of the causes is, undoubtedly, to be traced to the long-continued agitation of the slavery question on the part of the North, and the many aggressions which they have made on the rights of the South during the time. . . .

There is another lying back of it—with which this is intimately connected —that may be regarded as the great and primary cause. This is to be found in the fact, that the equilibrium between the two sections, in the government as it stood when the Constitution was ratified and the government put in action, has been destroyed. At that time there was nearly a perfect equilibrium between the two, which afforded ample means to each to protect itself against the aggression of the other; but, as it now stands, one section has the exclusive power of controlling the government, which leaves the other without any adequate means of protecting itself against its encroachment and oppression. To place this subject distinctly before you, I have, Senators, prepared a brief statistical statement, showing the relative weight of the two sections in the government under the first census of 1790, and the last census of 1840.

According to the former, the population of the United States, including Vermont, Kentucky, and Tennessee, which then were in their incipient condition of becoming states, but were not actually admitted, amounted to 3,929,827. Of this number the northern states had 1,997,899, and the southern 1,952,072, making a difference of only 45,827 in favor of the former states.

The number of states, including Vermont, Kentucky, and Tennessee, were sixteen; of which eight, including Vermont, belonged to the northern section, and eight, including Kentucky and Tennessee, to the southern,—making an equal division of the states between the two sections, under the first census. . . .

According to the last census the aggregate population of the United States amounted to 17,063,357, of which the northern section contained 9,728,920, and the southern 7,334,437, making a difference in round numbers, of 2,400,-000. The number of states had increased from sixteen to twenty-six, making an addition of ten states. In the meantime the position of Delaware had become doubtful as to which section she properly belonged. Considering her as neutral, the northern states will have thirteen and the southern states twelve, making a difference in the Senate of two Senators in favor of the former. According to the apportionment under the census of 1840, there were two hundred and twenty-three members of the House of Representatives, of which the northern states had one hundred and thirty-five, and the southern states (considering Delaware as neutral) eighty-seven, making a difference in favor of the former in the House of Representatives of forty-eight. The difference in the Senate of two members, added to this, gives to the North in the Electoral College, a majority of fifty. Since the census of

1840, four states have been added to the Union—Iowa, Wisconsin, Florida, and Texas. They leave the difference in the Senate as it was when the census was taken; but add two to the side of the North in the House, making the present majority in the House in its favor fifty, and in the Electoral College fifty-two.

The result of the whole is to give the northern section a predominance in every department of the government, and thereby concentrate in it the two elements which constitute the federal government,—majority of states, and a majority of their population, estimated in federal numbers. Whatever section concentrates the two in itself possesses the control of the entire government.

But we are just at the close of the sixth decade, and the commencement of the seventh. The census is to be taken this year, which must add greatly to the decided preponderance of the North in the House of Representatives and in the Electoral College. The prospect is, also, that a great increase will be added to its present preponderance in the Senate, during the period of the decade, by the addition of new states. Two territories, Oregon and Minnesota, are already in progress, and strenuous efforts are making to bring in three additional states from the territory recently conquered from Mexico; which, if successful, will add three other states in a short time to the northern section, making five states; and increasing the present number of its states from fifteen to twenty, and of its Senators from thirty to forty. On the contrary, there is not a single territory in progress in the southern section, and no certainty that any additional state will be added to it during the decade. The prospect then is, that the two sections in the Senate, should the effort now made to exclude the South from the newly acquired territories succeed, will stand before the end of the decade, twenty northern states to fourteen southern (considering Delaware as neutral), and forty northern Senators to twenty-eight southern. This great increase of Senators, added to the great increase of members of the House of Representatives and the Electoral College on the part of the North, which must take place under the next decade, will effectually and irretrievably destroy the equilibrium which existed when the government commenced.

Had this destruction been the operation of time, without the interference of government, the South would have had no reason to complain; but such was not the fact. It was caused by the legislation of this government, which was appointed as the common agent of all, and charged with the protection of the interests and security of all. The legislation by which it has been effected may be classed under three heads. The first is, that series of acts by which the South has been excluded from the common territory belonging to all the states as members of the Federal Union—which have had the effect of extending vastly the portion allotted to the northern section, and restricting within narrow limits the portion left the South. The next consists in adopting a system of revenue and disbursements, by which an undue proportion of the burden of taxation has been imposed upon the South, and an undue proportion of its proceeds appropriated to the North; and the last is a system of political measures, by which the original character of the government has been radically changed.

· · ·

To sum up the whole, the United States, since they declared their independence, have acquired 2,373,046 square miles of territory, from which the North will have excluded the South, if she should succeed in monopolizing the newly acquired terrtories, about three fourths of the whole, leaving to the South but about one fourth. . . .

. . . [I]f the South had retained all the capital which had been extracted from her by the fiscal action of the government; and, if it had not been excluded by the ordinance of 1787 and the Missouri Compromise, from the region lying between the Ohio and the Mississippi rivers, and between the Mississippi and the Rocky Mountains north of 36° 30′—it scarcely admits of a doubt, that it would have divided the emigration with the North, and by retaining her own people, would have at least equalled the North in population under the census of 1840, and probably under that about to be taken. She would also, if she had retained her equal rights in those territories, have maintained an equality in the number of states with the North, and have preserved the equilibrium between the two sections that existed at the commencement of the government. The loss, then, of the equilibrium is to be attributed to the action of this government.

· · ·

The result of the whole of those causes combined is, that the North has acquired a decided ascendency over every department of this government, and through it a control over all the powers of the system. A single section governed by the will of the numerical majority, has now, in fact, the control of the government and the entire powers of the system. What was once a constitutional federal republic is now converted, in reality, into one as absolute as that of the Autocrat of Russia, and as despotic in its tendency as any absolute government that ever existed.

As, then, the North has the absolute control over the government, it is manifest that on all questions between it and the South, where there is a diversity of interests, the interest of the latter will be sacrificed to the former, however oppressive the effects may be; as the South possesses no means by which it can resist, through the action of the government. But if there was no question of vital importance to the South, in reference to which there was a diversity of views between the two sections, this state of things might be endured without the hazard of destruction to the South. But such is not the fact. There is a question of vital importance to the southern section, in reference to which the views and feelings of the two sections are as opposite and hostile as they can possibly be.

I refer to the relation between the two races in the southern section, which constitutes a vital portion of her social organization. Every portion of the North entertains views and feelings more or less hostile to it. Those most opposed and hostile, regard it as a sin, and consider themselves under the most sacred obligation to use every effort to destroy it. Indeed, to the extent that they conceive that they have power, they regard themselves as implicated in the sin, and responsible for not suppressing it by the use of all and every means. Those less opposed and hostile, regarded it as a crime—an offense against humanity, as they call it; and, although not so fanatical, feel themselves bound to use all efforts to effect the same object; while those who are least opposed and hostile, regard it as a blot and a stain on the character of what they call the Nation, and feel themselves accordingly bound to give it no countenance or support. On the contrary, the southern section regards the relation as one which cannot be destroyed without subjecting the two races to the greatest calamity, and the section to poverty, desolation, and wretchedness; and accordingly they feel bound, by every consideration of interest and safety, to defend it.

This hostile feeling on the part of the North toward the social organization of the South long lay dormant, and it only required some cause to act on those who felt most intensely that they were responsible for its continuance, to call it into action. The increasing power of this government, and of the control of the northern section over all its departments, furnished the cause. It was this which made the impression on the minds of many, that there was little or no restraint to prevent the government from doing whatever it might choose to do. This was sufficient of itself to put the most fanatical portion of the North in action, for the purpose of destroying the existing relation between the two races in the South.

$$\bullet \quad \bullet \quad \bullet$$

Having now shown what cannot save the Union, I return to the question with which I commenced, how can the Union be saved? There is but one way by which it can with any certainty; and that is, by a full and final settlement, on the principle of justice, of all the questions at issue between the two sections. The South asks for justice, simple justice, and less she ought not to take. She has no compromise to offer, but the Constitution; and no concession or surrender to make. She has already surrendered so much that she has little left to surrender. . . .

But can this be done? Yes, easily; not by the weaker party, for it can, of itself do nothing,—not even protect itself—but by the stronger. The North has only to will it to accomplish it—to do justice by conceding to the South an equal right in the acquired territory, and to do her duty by causing the stipulations relative to fugitive slaves to be faithfully fulfilled, to cease the agitation of the slave question, and to provide for the insertion of a provision in the Constitution, by an amendment, which will restore to the South, in substance, the power she possessed of protecting herself, before the equilibrium between the sections was destroyed by the action of this government. There will be no difficulty in devising such a provision—one that will protect the South, and which, at the same time, will improve and strengthen the government, instead of impairing and weakening it. . . .

It is time, Senators, that there should be an open and manly avowal on all sides, as to what is intended to be done. If the question is not now settled, it is uncertain whether it ever can hereafter be; and we, as the representatives of the states of this Union, regarded as governments, should come to a distinct understanding as to our respective views, in order to ascertain whether the great questions at issue can be settled or not. If you, who represent the stronger portion, cannot agree to settle on the broad principle of justice and duty, say so; and let the states we both represent agree to separate and part in peace. If you are unwilling we should part in peace, tell us so, and we shall know what to do, when you reduce the question to submission or resistance. If you remain silent, you will compel us to infer by your acts what you intend. In that case, California will become the test question. If you admit her, under all the difficulties that oppose her admission, you compel us to infer that you intend to exclude us from the whole of the acquired territories, with the intention of destroying, irretrievably, the equilibrium between the two sections. We would be blind not to perceive in that case, that your real objects are power and aggrandizement; and infatuated, not to act accordingly.

Unit Three

The Plight of Outsiders in an "Open Society"

Introduction

By 1860, a growing number of southern leaders had been converted to views that had seemed extremist in 1850, when voiced by the dying Calhoun. The triumph of the sectional Republican party convinced such leaders that the North was determined to exclude the South from equal access to national resources and opportunities. The result, they believed, would be an irreversible drain of southern wealth, power, and moral influence leading to a condition of quasi-colonial dependence. The South, being no longer an equal partner in the federal compact, would then have no protection against northern economic and cultural imperialism.

These particular fears were complicated by the South's own exploitation of black slavery, an institution that made the region increasingly vulnerable to the moral censure of the Western world. But the southern example also highlights the more general issue of defining and responding to "deviance" in a supposedly open society. White Southerners were determined to avoid at all costs the consequences of being labeled un-American (the concept, if not the precise term, was very familiar). They were well aware of the fate of the powerless, of America's true outsiders. They had earlier placed their hopes on maintaining a kind of national pluralism based on mutual respect between free and slave societies; but as Calhoun warned, such mutual respect depended on preserving a balance of power.

This Unit is concerned with the limits and dimensions of cultural pluralism in antebellum America. The theme, like so many secular questions, has roots in religious history. In earlier centuries, Europeans had been far more attuned to religious differences than to ethnicity, or even race. Nations like England and France, while long tolerating a diversity of regional ethnic groups and subcultures, had tried to enforce religious uniformity. Until comparatively modern times, dissenters from an established church suffered persecution and often faced the ultimate alternatives of conversion or emigration. As examples, we need only recall the expulsion of Jews from Western Europe, the flight of Catholics and Puritan Separatists from Protestant England, and the migration of Huguenots from Catholic France. The modern idea of pluralism was a belated by-product of the slowly emerging religious toleration of the late seventeenth and eighteenth centuries. Although most of the American colonies originally sought religious uniformity within their borders, their movement toward religious freedom was more rapid and complete than that of Western Europe. Indeed, by the early nineteenth century even New England was completing the process of separating church from state. Protestants were discovering unexpected benefits from the principle of "voluntarism" and from interdenominational cooperation. Americans took increasing pride in their heritage as a refuge for the victims of European persecution.

There were definite limits, however, to this acceptance of religious diversity. The title of Part 1, "The Protestant Establishment," refers to a widely-held consensus, sanctioned by law and official pronouncements, that the United States was a Christian nation and that Protestant Christianity was a unifying force that endowed the nation with a high spiritual purpose. The selections in Part 1 indicate some of the outer limits of tolerance where deviation from vital communal norms was regarded as sufficient cause for persecution or exclusion. We begin with religious "deviants" for three reasons. First, it was religious freedom that distinguished America, especially in European eyes, as a genuinely open society. The definition of religious outsiders is thus of particular significance as an exception to a general rule. Second, as we shall later see, religion was a central element in debates over the possibility of assimilating Indians, blacks, and other "ethnic outsiders." Finally, the persecution of Mormons and Catholics illustrates patterns of thought that reappear in later selections. Here, it is sufficient to note the fear of church or corporate solidarity as an unfair and undemocratic advantage in political and economic rivalry; the belief that outsiders were being manipulated by America's Old World enemies or by a small group of unprincipled and self-serving leaders (the counterparts of "half-breed" Indian chieftains); and the demand for either assimilation or expulsion as a means of preserving America's "unity of character and custom."

In Part 2, we turn to "The Problem of Aborigines: Assimilation Versus Removal." Unlike other outsiders, the American Indians were the original *insiders* who still occupied millions of acres of valuable land, posing a barrier to the rapid exploitation of the nation's natural resources. The headnotes for this Part explain the evolution of America's contradictory Indian policies in some detail. The salient points can be briefly summarized here. The overriding consideration from the 1790s onward was the demand that Indians cede their lands to the federal government in order to open the vast territories west of the Appalachians to legal settlement. Initially, this motive was strongly reinforced by the strategic needs of national defense along British and Spanish-American frontiers.

After the War of 1812, the Indians' only allies were the missionary societies of the Northeast, a region where the native inhabitants had mostly been exterminated and which was several generations removed from the hatreds inspired by Indian raids and border warfare. Northeastern philanthropists promoted the ideal of Christianizing and civilizing Indians as an atonement for past wrongs and as a step toward future assimilation. Though the federal government endorsed this pious aim, it showed less enthusiasm for the missionaries' insistence that Indians be protected from the violence and fraud of frontiersmen, especially when the frontiersmen were supported by southern state legislatures. In fact, the goal of assimilation was based on the assumption that "civilized" Indians would need only small parcels of land for individual family farms and that their immense hunting preserves would thus be opened to white speculators and settlers. As the populous southern tribes discovered, progress in civilization offered no protection against the aggressive encroachments of the whites. The Cherokees, Creeks, Choctaws, and Chickasaws—the so-called civilized tribes—had by the 1820s moved far toward an agricultural economy supplemented by various artisan trades. But southern states, led by Georgia, made every effort to destroy tribal unity, customs, and leadership. Moreover, in practice it made little difference whether Indians had fought as America's allies or had been deprived of their lands, like many northwestern tribes, as punishment for siding with the British. By the 1830s, even many missionaries and humanitarians began to conclude that Indians would have to be removed west of the Mississippi for their own welfare and survival. Otherwise, subjected to harassment, demoralization, and internal division, they would be exterminated before they could be assimilated.

The goal of Indian removal had long been associated with westward expansion. The Louisiana Purchase of 1803 provided an unexpected and sparsely populated refuge where the eastern tribes would in theory be immune from white encroachments and corruption and would have sufficient time to prepare themselves for civilization. This general objective was favored by Jefferson and most of the leading statesmen of the next generation, but it was Andrew Jackson who provided the concrete implementation. As a military commander, Jackson had forced southern tribes to cede immense tracts of land, sometimes in exchange for land west of the Mississippi. But in 1830, during Jackson's first term as President, some 60,000 members of the "civilized tribes" still held millions of acres that included some of the richest soil in Georgia, Alabama, and Mississippi. Ten years later, the Indians had all been moved, with the exception of the rebellious Seminoles and a few remnants in tiny reservations, to relatively barren country in the West. Their former land constituted the heart of the Cotton Kingdom and thus of the southern slave system. Ostensibly, the eastern tribes had consented to this exchange and had received fair remuneration. In fact, various tribes including the Creeks, Cherokees, and ultimately the Seminoles were forced by the government to emigrate. As a gesture toward the ideal of assimilation, small plots of land were offered to the chieftains and heads of families of certain tribes. But between eighty and ninety percent of such "allotments" quickly passed into the hands of white speculators. Except for an extremely small minority of acculturated Indians, mainly of mixed blood, there was no room in America's open society for Indians—especially for Indians whose tribal and cultural integrity depended on land which white Americans were determined to buy or seize.

In Part 3, "The Discovery of Cultural Polarities," we can only sample other groups of outsiders who were sometimes likened to Indians and whose way of life challenged the ideal of middle-class Protestant homogeneity. Our focus is limited to points on the geographic periphery of American society. First, we consider the Hispanic border, where in the 1850s a United States Attorney for the recently annexed territory of New Mexico comments on the backwardness and moral depravity of the Mexican-Americans. Such attitudes help explain the defiant resistance, in the next selection, of the Texan rebel, Juan Cortina. We then move to the violent and booming Pacific port of San Francisco, where the gold rush had created a *de facto* cultural pluralism that greatly disturbed Anglo-Saxon proponents of law, order, and respectability. In response to the governor's call for Chinese exclusion, Norman Assing, a mafia-like godfather and the self-appointed spokesman for the Chinese community, skillfully defends Chinese immigration by appealing to Anglo-Saxon values. We then turn to the most notorious ghetto in New York City, which was the most heterogeneous Atlantic port, where reformers confronted an "anti-culture" of seemingly infinite moral depravity. As middle-class Americans gaped at the horrors of New York's Five Points, they sometimes expressed doubts whether its denizens could be rehabilitated and socialized before the moral contamination spread outward infecting the entire city and nation. But as with other outsiders, periodic efforts at assimilation were less successful than spatial segregation. In its own way, the ghetto became the urban counterpart of the Indian reservation.

In Part 4, "The Nonfreedom of 'Free Blacks,'" we discover that race in antebellum America was the preeminent symbol for excluding an entire category of people from any pluralistic compact. As explained in the selection by Martin Delany, the black abolitionist, oppression has always been easier and more severe when the oppressors have found groups with distinctive physical characteristics, "those who differed as much as possible, in some particulars, from themselves." In such situations, Delany argues, physical difference enables the oppressors to exploit popular prejudice against the oppressed, who are deprived of the normal protections of sympathetic identification. Delany's ingenious theory helps to account for the mental blocks which allowed most white Americans either to ignore "the Negro problem" or to treat it as an anomaly for which they bore no responsibility. In other words, it was an "except" or "but" which really failed to qualify the traditional American boasts of liberty, opportunity, and freedom from class struggle.

For the nation's future, it was an ominous sign that free blacks were coercively restricted to the status of an inferior caste, especially in the North. Since the gradual abolition of slavery in the northern states had brought blacks little genuine freedom or racial integration, the long-term prospects seemed even bleaker for the great mass of slaves in the South. To drive home the significance of this point, one must take note of the extraordinarily low proportion of blacks in the northern population. Though blacks constituted over fourteen percent of the nation's population in 1860, the proportion was less than one percent for the nonslaveholding states as a whole, ranging from 3.8 percent in New Jersey and 1.3 percent in New York to less than one percent in New England and the East North Central states. Yet even this tiny minority suffered from increasing legal, economic, and social discriminations.

Part 4 traces free black responses to this worsening condition. Beginning as early as 1817, most black leaders indignantly repudiated the solution proposed by the white American Colonization Society. Organized in 1816, the Colonization Society continued to promote the removal of free blacks to Africa, and was instrumental in founding the colony of Liberia as a kind of counterpart to the western Indian reservations. As the selections indicate, some blacks became so discouraged by the prospects of living in a racist society that they either cooperated with the white colonizationists or, like Martin Delany in the 1850s, organized colonization ventures of their own. Others, like David Walker, argued that the fate of free blacks was intimately linked with the fate of black slaves. From Walker's eloquent *Appeal* of 1829 to Henry Highland Garnet's militant *Address* of 1843, we sample a tradition of black abolitionism that turned the principles of the Declaration of Independence against the racism and hypocrisy of white America. It must be added that Garnet himself later turned to colonization. Frederick Douglass' strong appeals for black "industrial education" and economic opportunity bore little fruit, at least in the antebellum period. These selections poignantly indicate the racial limits of a self-proclaimed open society. They also formulate the goals of a truly democratic pluralism which we are still struggling to achieve.

In Part 5, we finally move to "The Polarized South: Outsiders Inside." Unlike other immigrants, blacks had originally been forcibly transported to America as slaves. Throughout the antebellum era, southern slavery remained the great generator of racial prejudice, a constant reminder that blacks were uniquely different from all other Americans—that their original and "normal" status was that of chattel property. This view was only partially undermined by the North's growing disapproval of slavery and desire to restrict its westward expansion. The blunt fact was that slave prices continued to rise, reflecting a growing demand and a confidence that the institution would continue to prosper and expand. In 1820, there were approximately 1,500,000 slaves in the United States; in 1860, nearly 4,000,000. Even more striking, in 1860 there were well over one-quarter million slaves in Florida and Texas, regions acquired after 1820 from Spain and Mexico. In 1860, the five "southwestern" states, Alabama, Mississippi, Louisiana, Arkansas, and Missouri, contained nearly 1,500,000 slaves; forty years earlier there had been only 155,600 slaves in the same states and territories.

As the basic system of production, Negro slavery dominated the economic and social structure of the entire South, profoundly affecting relations between whites as well as between whites and blacks. Yet in a peculiar way, slaves were truly "outsiders inside"—in white eyes, an alien and only half-understood people whose labor was essential for household maintenance as well as, for agriculture, trades, and industry. Though we have voluminous commentaries on the institution from white Southerners and travelers who mostly listened to white Southerners, no modern assessment can ignore the testimony of slaves themselves, who were in most respects the most expert witnesses. Thus Part 5 begins with slave voices, the first being the recorded testimony of Nat Turner, who in 1831 led a bloody and electrifying insurrection in Southampton County, Virginia. As in the more militant selections by free blacks, one is struck by the double-edged potentialities of religion, which could provide the inspiration and rationale for resistance as well as the faith and patience for endurance. These brief selections by blacks also give us glimpses of the complexities of cruelty and kindness, of struggle, accommodation, and anguish.

The South remained a polarized society for several reasons, as illustrated in the selections on "Managing Slaves and White Overseers." Because slaves were legally defined and treated as human personalities, responsible for crimes or meritorious service, they were subject to the techniques of moral influence and socialization described in Unit One. But because they were also legally defined and treated as chattel property, there were necessary limits to their socialization and assimilation. In response to their exploitation, the slaves themselves helped establish those limits. This fundamental contradiction pervaded not only the relations between slaves and masters but also the more complex interplay of power between slaves, overseers, and masters. The difficult situation of the white overseer, caught in the middle of this unstable system, leads us to the more generalized tensions and barriers between the slaveholding elite and poor whites. Despite the efforts of proslavery theorists to portray the South as a unified and harmonious society, race alone could be a dangerous and fragile basis for unity. As indicated by Hinton R. Helper in the last selection, racism could also be used in an attempt to rally the nonslaveholding whites against the planter elite and their black dependents. Finely-spun apologies for slavery could never altogether conceal the deep divisions and uncertainties in southern white society. And in a certain sense, the disparities and polarities of southern life were simply a microcosm of those of the nation at large, divided as it was between northern, southern, and western versions of the American dream.

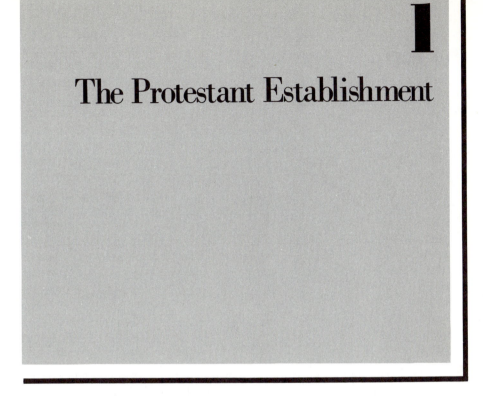

The Protestant Establishment

A. The Limits of Religious Dissent

- *Stephen Colwell* (*1854*)
- *Commonwealth* v. *Kneeland* (*1838*)

To understand both the definition and treatment of outsiders, one must begin with religion. For if American leaders boasted incessantly of the nation's religious freedom, they did not publicly question the prevailing dogma that America was a Christian nation, that Christianity, in Stephen Colwell's words, was "the very atmosphere in which our institutions exist . . . the cement by which they are bound together." This official view, upheld by courts of law and symbolically reaffirmed by the prayers and ceremonies of government, assumed that Christianity was a *unifying* force—the enduring source of cultural norms that enabled a highly diverse and freedom-loving people to live together in peace, sharing a common national identity and purpose. But if this generalized civil religion was supposedly nonsectarian and nonexclusive, what was to be done about non-Christians or about Americans who openly rejected the central doctrines of Christian faith? There were two alternatives to the long-range trend toward increasing toleration: exclusion, in one form or another; and renewed efforts at religious conversion as a step toward assimilation.

In the first selection, Stephen Colwell (1800–1871) presents a concise summary of the dominant view of civil religion. It should be emphasized that Colwell was not a minister but a lawyer, iron manufacturer, railroad promoter, and political economist who moved from his native Virginia first to Ohio and then to Pennsylvania. Like many entrepreneurs of his generation, Colwell somehow managed to spare some time and energy from managing industries and railroads and lobbying for protective tariffs, to take an active part in church affairs—helping to found, for example, a chair of Christian ethics at Princeton. The selection below provides clues to Colwell's sense of compelling and interrelated priorities. He heartily endorses the growing image of America as a land of refuge for the victims of persecution, a land where Christianity refuses aid from the state and confidently relies on its "moral" power. But this confident openness, Colwell stresses, should not be mistaken for an abdication from power, or for a free-for-all vacuum in which all religious claims are equally valid. For in Colwell's view, which was widely shared by American Protestants, the very survival of a refuge of religious toleration depends on Protestant principles and on the robust health of Protestant Christianity. When compared with the religious despotism of the rest of the world, Americans had shown astonishing "delicacy and forbearance" in the exercise of majoritarian power. On this point there was surely agreement even from the small minority of Jews, the only non-Christian immigrants from Europe, who in exchange for centuries of persecution could easily accommodate minor insults and disabilities or humor innocent if well-organized efforts at Christian conversion. More ominous, however, is Colwell's flat statement (not included here), that blasphemous publications, including an "irreverent rejection" of God and His holy religion, had always been indictable in America and punishable by common law. This warning qualifies Colwell's assurance that the power of Christianity is only "moral, not physical." And it adds bite to his final paragraph, appealing for a more vigorous application of political power, which is "safe only in the hands of those who are under Christian influences. . . ."

Some two decades earlier, the question of blasphemy had been legally tested in Massachusetts. The case of Abner Kneeland (1774–1844) was a sensation because "atheists," however defined, were a rarity in antebellum America; because it was therefore difficult to determine the limits of religious freedom granted by the "declaration of rights" embodied in state constitutions; and because Kneeland was a conscientious clergyman, of old New England and Revolutionary stock, who had become more revolutionary than his fellow Universalists—who were themselves regarded as far too revolutionary for orthodox New England tastes. By temperament a radical and a "seeker" of unknown religious truth, Kneeland had gradually abandoned belief in supernatural religion as he drifted around the Northeast preaching and publishing in Philadelphia and New York and, in the latter city, joining forces with the English free-thinkers, Robert Dale Owen and Frances Wright. Finally settling in Boston, he began in 1831 to edit a paper, the *Boston Investigator*, which defended a pantheistic faith that God was synonymous with nature and which daringly flaunted the kind of rational skepticism that had been commonplace two generations earlier among the *philosophes* of the European Enlightenment.

As the original 1833 indictment makes clear, it was Kneeland's provocative manner—his "bad intent" and determination to "give just offense"—that led to prosecution. The prosecutors faced a problem in the Massachusetts Declaration of Rights, which guaranteed both freedom of the press and freedom of religious belief. Defending Kneeland were such luminaries and reformers as William Ellery Channing, Ralph Waldo Emerson, Theodore Parker, and William Lloyd Garrison, joined by a triumvirate of orthodox Baptist ministers. But the Declaration of Rights also presented the opportunity—or necessity, as conservatives saw it—of setting limits to the open defiance of communal norms. Blasphemy, as defined by Chief Justice Lemuel Shaw, speaking for the majority of the court in Kneeland's final trial, "is a willful and malicious attempt to lessen men's reverence of God, by denying his existence, or his attributes as an intelligent creator, governor and judge of men, and to prevent their having confidence in him, as such." The state's attorney general further explained that legislators had understood the term "God" to mean "that Supreme, Intelligent Being who is alike revered by Christians, Jews and Mahometans, and not the material universe, which the defendant would substitute." After his conviction was thus upheld, Kneeland served sixty days in jail. If for liberals this made him a martyr for civil liberty, his case also marked in 1838 the outer limits of the Protestant establishment's tolerance. At least a symbolic exclusion or incarceration awaited the deviant who challenged the fundamental premises of what Colwell termed a "Christian civilization." It is worth noting that Kneeland, after being released from jail, moved on to the western territories, where he hoped to found a utopian community.

Stephen Colwell (1854)

It is apparent, then, from our statutory and our common law, from our constitutions and our social institutions, that Christianity is legally recognized as the popular [public] religion of this country. It is the very atmosphere in which our institutions exist; it is the cement by which they are bound together; it is the sanction of our penal laws; it is, in most cases, the security to which appeal is made by oath for official faithfulness; it is the guardian of judicial evidence; it is the basis of our morality, and the mould in which our civilization has been cast. The refuge we offer to men of all the world from intolerance, oppression and persecution, for opinion's sake, is offered under the influences of Christianity and according to its principles. We do

SOURCE: Stephen Colwell, *The Position of Christianity in the United States* (Philadelphia: Lippincott, Grambo & Co., 1854), pp. 67–69.

not strike the Christian flag when we thus open wide our doors to the world, announcing that here is liberty of worship for all—Christian toleration for all: we rather invite men to come beneath its folds and under its protection. We spread over all that Christian vesture which is without seam or line of division, the broad mantle of Christian charity. We ask only obedience to such laws as are necessary to the preservation of such institutions—institutions which can only subsist and thrive under the Christian flag and on the broad ground of Christian charity.

Christianity asks no aid, and will receive none, from the state, to enforce its precepts or its worship. Its only power is moral, not physical. It seeks to govern men by the intrinsic excellence of its precepts, and by presenting to them the moral and religious claims of the Creator upon all His creatures. It seeks the extension of Christian civilization and the amelioration of human condition, the amendment of legislation and the wholesome reformation of our social institutions, for the good of men as well as for the glory of God; but it expects to accomplish this good only by its moral and enlightening influence upon the minds and consciences of Christian men and those who lend themselves to Christian influences.

Christianity enjoys advantages here never before accorded to it by accident or by power. It wields no temporal power to make it feared; it wants no aid but that from its own friends. It enjoys for its generous toleration the heart-felt respect of all the intelligent and ardent friends of humanity. . . .

The Christians of the United States have received from their Fathers the most important trust ever committed to men. The political institutions of this country, springing from Christian liberality, Christian civilization and intelligence, designed solely to promote human well-being, are placed in their hands as implements to be employed for human welfare. They contain powers safe only in the hands of those who are under Christian influences—powers fraught in their proper or improper exercise, with more of good or evil for the human family, than were ever before entrusted to Christian hands. The Evangelical Christians of the United States can sway this power at their pleasure, for they have heretofore been and still are, largely in the majority. There has undoubtedly been undue delicacy and forbearance shown in the exercise of this power. Such has been this forbearance, indeed, that the question now is rather of the neglect than of the abuse of power.

Commonwealth *v.* Kneeland (1838)

> Under *St*[atute] 1782, *c.* 8, (Revised Stat. *c.* 130, § 15.) the denial of God, his creation, government, or final judging of the world, made wilfully, that is, with the intent and purpose to calumniate and disparage him and impair and destroy the reverence due to him, is blasphemy.

SOURCE: *Commonwealth v. Kneeland,* 20 Pick. 206 (1838), 206–7.

Under the same statute, cursing or contumeliously [insultingly] reproaching God, is blasphemy.

If the general averment in an indictment under this statute, alleges blasphemy in both of these modes, and if the language recited by way of specification and imputed to the defendant, amounts to such a denial, but without a contumelious reproaching, or amounts to a contumelious reproaching, but without a denial, the indictment is sufficient.

On an indictment for wilfully blaspheming the holy name of God, by denying God, his creation, etc. in the following words, viz. "The Universalists believe in a god which I do not; but believe that their god, with all his moral attributes (aside from nature itself,) is nothing more than a chimera of their own imagination," it was *held*, that after a conviction, if no evidence was erroneously admitted or rejected and no incorrect instructions to the jury in matter of law were given, it was to be taken as proved, that this language was used in the sense of a denial of God, and under the circumstances and with the intent and purpose laid in the indictment, so as to bring it within the statute.

The statute is not intended to prohibit the fullest inquiry and freest discussion for all honest and fair purposes, one of which is the discovery of truth; nor to prevent the simple and sincere avowal of disbelief in the existence and attributes of a supreme, intelligent being, upon suitable and proper occasions; nor to prevent or restrain the formation of any religious opinions or the profession of any religious sentiments whatever; but it is intended to punish a denial of God, made with a bad intent, and in a manner calculated to give just offense; and with this construction the statute is not repugnant to the 2d article of the Declaration of Rights, which declares that no subject shall be hurt, molested or restrained for his religious profession or sentiments, provided he does not disturb the public peace or obstruct others in their religious worship.

This statute (when applied to printed blasphemy) is not repugnant to the 16th article of the Declaration of Rights, which declares that the liberty of the press ought not to be restrained.

This article was intended to secure to the citizen the general liberty of publishing without the previous license of any officer of the government, but not to restrain the legislative power in relation to the punishment of injuries to individuals, or of the disturbance of the peace, by malicious falsehoods or obscene or profane publications or exhibitions.

THIS was an indictment, alleging that the defendant, on December 20, 1833, unlawfully and wickedly composed, printed and published in a newspaper called the Boston Investigator, of which he was the editor and publisher, a certain scandalous, impious, obscene, blasphemous and profane libel, in which he "did willfully blaspheme the holy name of God, by denying and contumeliously reproaching God, his creation, government, and final judging of the world, and by reproaching Jesus Christ and the Holy Ghost, and contumeliously reproaching the holy word of God." The indictment then sets forth an obscene article from the newspaper, concerning Jesus Christ, and extracts from another article turning into ridicule the subject of addressing prayers to God. It then alleges that the libel, in another part of it "contains the following scandalous, profane and blasphemous words, matters and things, of and concerning God, and of and concerning Jesus Christ, and of and concerning the final judging of the world by God, and of and concerning the holy scriptures, to wit:—

'1. Universalists believe in a god which I do not; but believe that their god, with all his moral attributes (aside from nature itself) is nothing more than a mere chimera of their own imagination.

'2. Universalists believe in Christ, which I do not; but believe that the whole story concerning him is as much a fable and a fiction as that of the god Prometheus, the tragedy of whose death is said to have been acted on the stage in the theatre at Athens, five hundred years before the Christian era.

'3. Universalists believe in miracles, which I do not; but believe that every pretension to them can be accounted for on natural principles, or else is to be attributed to mere trick and imposture.

'4. Universalists believe in the resurrection of the dead, in immortality and eternal life, which I do not; but believe that all life is mortal, that death is an eternal extinction of life to the individual who possesses it, and that no individual life is, ever was, or ever will be eternal:'

To the great scandal and contumelious reproach of God, and his holy name, his creation, government, and final judging of the world, of Jesus Christ, and the Holy Ghost, of the holy word of God, and of the Christian religion, against the peace," etc.

The indictment was found at the Municipal Court, January term 1834, and at the same term the defendant was tried, convicted, and sentenced to imprisonment for three months in the common gaol. From this judgment he appealed to the Supreme Judicial Court, and at November term 1835 he was tried before *Wilde* J[ustice] and convicted.

B. Excluding Mormons and Catholics

• *Anti-Mormonism in Illinois* (1845)
• *Thomas R. Whitney* (1856)

The early history of Mormonism illustrates the treatment accorded by a liberal, Protestant society to true deviants, in the literal sense of people who deviated from vital norms. Since the Mormons were not strange aliens from China or Ceylon, but rather farmers, tradesmen, and mechanics from generally rural parts of New England, New York, Pennsylvania, and the frontier Midwest, their experience of savage persecution helps us to identify what the non-Mormon majority interpreted as "vital norms," which could not be violated without forfeiting the basic rights and protections of a supposedly free society.

This history of conflict and persecution, which can only be touched upon here, also pulls together many thematic strands from our previous selections. When in 1830 Joseph Smith, Jr. founded the Mormon church (or Church of Jesus Christ of Latter-day Saints) in Upstate New York, basing his religious claims on divine revelation, he was threatened with an indictment for blasphemy. As the Mormons fled westward, they were unable to obtain a banking charter from the Ohio legislature and were nearly destroyed by the failure of Smith's venture in illegal banking. In frontier Missouri, where the Mormons purchased large tracts of public land, their farms and homes were confiscated after Governor L. W. Boggs proclaimed them enemies who "had to be exterminated, or driven from the state."

What aroused such popular rage was not the Mormons' practice of polygamy, which was not openly acknowledged until they had found a reasonably secure refuge in distant Utah (though it should be added that reports of polygamy in the early 1840s stoked the fires of anti-Mormonism in Illinois). For an individualistic society, the Mormons were enemies because of their corporate solidarity. Committed to establishing the Kingdom of God on earth, they did not regard religion as a weekend activity that could be divorced from political and economic life. And for anti-Mormons, this merging of religious and secular pursuits became most alarming when Mormon refugees from Missouri and Ohio, joined by thousands of converts from the East and eventually from England, built a virtually independent city-state, Nauvoo, in Hancock County, Illinois. By 1844, Mormons made up at least half the population of Hancock County, and Nauvoo was probably the largest city in Illinois, surpassing even Chicago. Because Mormons voted as a bloc in a state where Whigs and Democrats were closely matched, they had sufficient political power to exact extraordinary concessions from the legislature. For example, Smith presided as a Lieutenant General (the only one in the nation) over a Nauvoo Legion of some two thousand men. This private army, independent of the state militia, prevented an attempt to arrest Smith and extradite him to Missouri, where he had been charged with treason.

In Hancock County, an anti-Mormon party emerged under the leadership of Thomas C. Sharp, a young lawyer, Freemason, and editor of the *Warsaw Signal*, a paper published in one of Nauvoo's neighboring towns. Sharp and his followers claimed that the Mormons had been unscrupulous in their land transactions and other economic activities, which allegedly included wholesale theft, and had succeeded in living "above the law." When the law was thus reduced to "mere mockery," according to Sharp, the opinion of the "sensible men" of the community could justify a "summary execution." In 1844, Smith and his brother were in fact assassinated by a "mob" which was clearly well-organized and led by some of the county's most "respectable citizens." Much evidence indicates that Sharp was the key instigator of the plot, but in a highly dubious trial he and four other defendants were eventually acquitted of the charge of murder.

Our first selection is from an anti-Mormon letter written for Sharp's *Warsaw Signal*. It may well be a bogus letter written by Sharp himself, with intentional mistakes in grammar and spelling (Sharp was the son of a Methodist minister and had been educated at Dickinson College). The author makes a profession of personal tolerance, a device also common in anti-Catholic writing—that is, he is not opposed to Mormons as individuals and recognizes that there are "some good, law-abiding, peaceable citizens" within the church. Yet even such well-meaning dupes give added power to their dictatorial leaders, who threaten to subvert the basic principles of a free society. Purporting to speak for a grassroots, Jeffersonian America, in the untutored language of the common man, the writer views Mormons as members of a criminal conspiracy which has forfeited all claims of mutual trust and respect. It is significant that neither he nor most other anti-Mormons considered the option of conversion to a more traditional creed. While there were many Mormon apostates, conversion was an art at which the Mormons clearly excelled. It therefore appeared that the only remedy was expulsion, backed up by "summary execution" and other acts of mob violence.

Although there were many parallel themes in anti-Catholicism, they had a long history extending back to the Protestant Reformation. Unlike anti-Mormonism, anti-Catholicism absorbed large doses of ethnic prejudice since an increasing majority of Catholics were immigrants from Ireland or, to a lesser extent, from Germany and other Continental nations. Finally, Catholics were far too numerous and dispersed to be driven like the Mormons to a distant refuge. Even attempts to restrict their further immigration, in the 1850s, were immediately short-circuited by Constitutional scruples regarding the limits of federal authority. But it is worth noting that in 1834, when Missouri vigilantes drove Mormons from Jackson County, beginning a period of intermittent warfare that culminated four years later with the massacre at Haun's Mill of eighteen unarmed Mormon men and a boy, a Massachusetts mob attacked and burned the Catholic Ursuline Convent school at Charlestown. In 1844, within a few weeks of Joseph Smith's assassination, anti-Catholic mobs rampaged through the Irish districts of Philadelphia, burning churches and whole blocks of houses, exchanging lethal fire with Catholic defenders and with a militia that finally resorted to cannon and point-blank slaughter.

By 1830, the traditional Protestant slogan, "No Popery!", was revivified by evangelical revivalism and by an influx from England of propaganda opposing the 1829 Catholic Emancipation Bill, which had extended minimal political rights to English Catholics. But the major and growing source of anti-Catholicism was immigration, particularly by the 1840s when cheap transport and the promise of unskilled jobs attracted hundreds of thousands of Irish peasants who had been reduced to near starvation by the potato blight. Native workers feared displacement by immigrants who would work for the lowest wages. Alarmists pointed to the disproportionate number of Catholic immigrants who had become paupers, supported by public funds. On the other side, Catholic bishops, backed up by large electorates, served notice that they would no longer tolerate Protestant indoctrination in tax-supported schools. Indeed, by 1850 Archbishop John Hughes of New York, the leader of the Catholic counteroffensive, could echo the evangelical Protestants by affirming that "everybody should know that we have for our mission to convert the world—including the inhabitants of the United States— the people of the cities, and the people of the country, the officers of the navy and the marines, commanders of the army, the legislatures, the Senate, the Cabinet, the President, and all!"

The disastrous Philadelphia riots at least temporarily discredited violence. Urban capitalists were not only disturbed by the spectacle of mobs destroying private property but were suddenly impressed by the vulnerability of large cities to retaliation. In the tense aftermath of the Philadelphia bloodshed, Hughes had publicly warned that "if a single Catholic Church were burned in New York, the city would become a second Moscow [referring to the Russians' leveling of Moscow after its capture by Napoleon]." It is significant that Brigham Young, who succeeded Joseph Smith as the leader of the Mormons, made a similarly effective threat of burning Salt Lake City to the ground when faced in 1857 by an invasion of Utah by federal troops. Since anti-Catholic violence had proved to be a dangerous option, the only alternative was political action designed to weaken or annihilate Catholic power. A minor fuming in the late 1840s, this so-called Know-Nothing movement finally erupted in 1854 as a national volcano, smothering the Whig party, sweeping new leaders into power from Massachusetts to Louisiana, and transforming the structure of American politics.

For Know-Nothing leaders like Thomas R. Whitney (1807–1858), the Catholic church posed not simply the threat of corporate solidarity, like the Mormons, but the threat of corporate solidarity directed and manipulated by the despots of Europe. This international dimension was seemingly confirmed by the role of the Catholic church in helping to suppress republican movements in the European Revolutions of 1848. Whitney, a Know-Nothing Congressman from New York, was unable to foresee the eventual accommodation of the Catholic hierarchy to the forces of democratic pluralism. In the following selection, which strongly influenced an 1856 report of the House Committee on Foreign Affairs, he pictures Catholicism not as a religion but as a deceptive ideology allowing a small group of leaders to conspire for mastery of political and economic power.

Three points deserve further notice. First, Whitney plays on the familiar theme of speaking for the common people, upholding the noble inheritance of the Founding Fathers. His desire to arouse the apathetic leads to a second and rather surprising emphasis on the deceptiveness of the established parties, a subject seemingly unrelated to the Catholic church. But Whitney suggests that such artificial issues as the tariff, bank policy, and slavery have cheapened and degraded public life, allowing politicians like New York's Governor William Seward to become tools of Catholic manipulation. Third, the supposed betrayal of public trust for selfish political advantage points up the overriding need of preserving homogeneity, a "unity of character and custom" in the face of alien contamination. The nativist rhetoric is aimed at convincing Protestants of the necessity of harsher naturalization laws that would strip recent immigrants of equal political rights. It proved to be far easier, however, to deny the right of statehood to Mormon Utah than to deny the rights of citizenship to Catholic immigrants. Though Know-Nothings for a time held the balance of power in Congress, they were notably unsuccessful in supplementing social and religious discriminations with legally sanctioned inequalities.

Anti-Mormonism in Illinois (1845)

Mr. Editor.

On the all-absorbing question of Mormonism or Anti-Mormonism I as heretofore have remained silent, but after viewing dispassionately many Mormon outrages commited by the leaders of that fanatical sect in various parts of the country in defiance of all law, and after witnessing the many disgraceful exertions on the part of certain politicians to identify both political parties [Democratic and Whig] with "Mormonmobocracy" for the sole purpose of advancing the political interests of a few would-be office holders to the great detriment of the many (that the leaders of both parties of this Congressional district have done this during the last canvass cannot be denied.) It is truly humiliating to see talented and able men go and act the spanial to a set of base miserable rascals who are abusing the great privileges that was [sic] bought with the noblest blood that ever flowed, it is a low pitiable, contemptable kind of electioneering, that old Tom Jefferson would have been ashamed of—when a body of men acting under the garb of religion (as the Mormons themselves say they are) shall decide our elections and act together as a body politically, we may as well bid a final farewell to our liberties and the common rights of man.

Now Sir, under all these circumstances, it is high time that every individual in this community should come out and clearly define the position that he occupies. I too am an Anti-Mormon both in principle and in practice, although I have voted a consistent political ticket ever since I have arriven [sic] to the years of maturity, but sir if pure Jeffersonian principles cannot be

---

SOURCE: "Junius Secondus," manuscript letter sent to *The Warsaw Signal* [Warsaw, Illinois], from "Manuscript history of the Anti-Mormon disturbances in Illinois, 1845 . . . ," (New Haven: Beinecke Rare Book and Manuscript Library, Yale University).

sustained in this country without being strangled in the deadly coils of Mormon-mobocracy I would throw them to the four winds of Heaven and go for those principles best calculated to subserve the interest of the community, and the country in which I live. Mr. Editor when I speak harshly of the Mormons, I wish it to be perfectly understood I do not mean every individual that advocates the Mormon cause. By no means; that there are some good, law-abiding, peaceable citizens belonging to the Mormon profession I verily believe. I am not opposed to the Mormons either, simply because they are called Mormons or later day saints [sic]; but I am opposed to them because of the unprincipled manner in which the leaders of that fanatical sect, set at defiance the laws of the land, although they pretending declare themselves good law-abiding, peacable citizens and swear they will use every endeavor in their power to enforce the law in all cases, but sir such declamations are all a base cheatery, an idle delusion, for *their actions* certainly speak louder than words. . . .

Now, sir, we live to learn and we sometimes learn more sadly by experience than otherwise, call back to memory then for a moment the general course pursued by the heads of the Mormon church from its origin to the present day and it will be found to be one of rapine and plunder, first pretending to shelter themselves under the laws of the land from the halter or the dungeon, for commiting their ignominious deeds, and in the next place setting at defiance all law (as was the case in Missouri) claiming to be the chosen people of God; not subject to the laws of the state in any respect whatever, and receiving revelations direct from Heaven almost daily commanding them to take the property of the older citizens of the county and confiscate it to the use of the Mormon church. . . .

It was for the commission of such deeds together with deeds ten fold more dark and damning in their nature that finally led to their expulsion from that state, and one of the brightest pages in the history of Missouri is that, on which is written "Governor Boggs's exterminating order" directing that, that lawless rabble should be driven beyond the limits of the state, or exterminated at their own option—they choose the former,—a most unfortunate thing for the state of Illinois.

Strange to tell, yet such is the fact, they have commenced nearly the same operations here that they did in Missouri, setting at defiance the laws of the land, violating with impunity the highest moral and social obligations, they have attempted to subcidize [sic] the press, thereby attempting to corrupt the very fountains of public virtue,—they have went [sic] into the legislative halls and attempted to bribe the representatives of the people in thier seats and made them their tools.

They have in short, by a long series of high handed outrages, in violation of all law, against the rights, the peace and the liberties of the people, forfeited all claims (if any they ever had) to confidence and respect, and ought justly to receive the condemnation of every individual, not only in this community, but in this nation.

Thomas R. Whitney (1856)

If we analyze this subject closely, we may discover a peculiar force and point in the phraseology of the Constitution, as quoted in the preceding chapter. It will be perceived that the Constitution forbids Congress to pass any laws for the establishment of *religion*. This phrase covers the ground intended more completely than if it had used the words *a national Church*, instead of the simple and comprehensive word *religion*, because, whatever may be the association of ideas in this connection, the *Church* is one thing, and *religion* another. Religion sometimes, has but little to do with the Church, and it frequently occurs that the Church has less to do with religion. I mean the religion of Christ. What is the Church of Rome, for example, but a budget of mechanical and ostentatious forms and ceremonies, and a promoter of ignorance and low superstition? I find nothing of religion in the jugglery that first stifles intelligence, and then *compels* its illiterate dupes to believe that the figure of a woman painted on canvas, can and does exhibit signs of physical life, as the so-called "Winking Virgin," or that a dry thorn will emit drops of blood, on the anniversary of the crucifixion. These are a part of the machinery of the Roman Catholic *Church*, and they are but two instances in a catalogue of thousands of like absurdity. And what are they but *villainous* inventions, by which a few men hope to control the political interests, and temporal destinies of the whole earth? The intellect of man, when permitted to have full play, revolts at them, spurns them, despises them. When the mind is sufficiently enlightened to see through their web, it finds in them not only the vilest hypocrisy, but an absolute sacrilege, and an insult to the natural intelligence of the human race. . . .

This doctrine may have answered before the Reformation, and it may answer now in such of the Papal States as have not yet opened their eyes, or even in Brazil, Portugal, Spain, Mexico, or South America, where priestcraft still holds sway over reason, but it will not answer in the United States of North America.

• • •

As one of the people, I write for the people. I am one of the millions who have too long allowed a few men to do their political thinking for them. I have determined to think for myself, read for myself, and, as far as I can, to understand for myself, free from the dictation of any party or faction, and I believe it would be better for civil and religious liberty if all my countrymen would "go and do likewise." We have all been too long harnessed in the party traces of a few designing men, and we have allowed them to rule over us until our union and our free institutions have been brought to the very verge of annihilation—another step, and we plunge into the abyss of anarchy and national chaos! Too long we have worshipped "hickory poles" and "hard cider"—too long have the ambitious leaders of party thrown in our eyes the

SOURCE: Thomas R. Whitney, *A Defense of the American Policy* (New York: DeWitt and Davenport, 1856), pp. 64–65, 68–72.

dust of "tariff" and "free trade," "bank" or "no bank," "slavery" or "anti-slavery," till we have been blinded to the trust which our honest old grand-fathers left to us, and our dearest interests have been made the subjects of bargain and sale. The patriarchs of the nation left us the inheritance of temporal and spiritual freedom, with the Holy Bible and the Constitution for our guides. The one is now sacrilegiously desecrated, and the other is trampled under foot; the Bible is thrown from our schools at the dictation of Romish priests, and the Constitution is violated and ignored by the public enactment of fanatical legislation.

One of the surest guarantees of permanent nationality is the perfect homogeneousness of the people. It is, therefore, an important duty on the part of the statesman, to encourage all that pertains to unity of character and custom, and to discountenance every influence that tends to produce the opposite result. This duty is the more imperative in the United States, where the conflict of individual character and custom is kept so constantly active by an unceasing and multifarious [im]migration. The course recommended by Governor Seward, instead of lessening, would increase this heterogenous element by encouraging foreign languages and customs among the [im]migrants. Instead of forcing them into our body politic, and enforcing a unity of interest and feeling by instruction in the language and customs of America, Mr. Seward would encourage social antagonisms and multiplied nationalities within the American circle. A stronger evidence of his incapacity as a statesman could not exist.

Again, in the same paragraph of his message, he recommends that in schools supported at the public expense, the children of foreigners *should be taught by persons of the same religious faith.* This would be neither more nor less than the establishment of sectarian schools at the expense of the people. In this Mr. Seward distinctly violates two well understood principles of the American Republican system, thus again proving his unfitness for the responsible trusts reposed in him by his party. The first principle violated is, that the state shall not interpose in matters of religion among the people, or give encouragement to sectarians; and the second is, that no one religious sect shall be required to pay tribute to others—both of which would occur if Mr. Seward's recommendation was carried into effect.

· · ·

It is not the purpose of this volume to recapitulate the historical proofs of the political character of the Romish Church, nor to review in detail the evidences of its despotic nature. They are to be found in a thousand authentic works already within reach of every reader. It is sufficient for us to know:

I. That the Church is a political government, claiming temporal authority over every nation and people of the earth.

II. That it is now striving directly, to establish its temporal or political power in these United States, and

III. That its form of government is diametrically opposed to the genius of American Republicanism.

2

The Problem of
Aborigines: Assimilation
Versus Removal

A. The Hope of Christianization

- *American Board of Commissioners for Foreign Missions* (1824)
- *Henry Benjamin Whipple* (1860)

The outsiders posing a serious obstacle to American growth were not religious dissenters or alien immigrants but America's original inhabitants. Decimated by their vulnerability to Old World diseases, deprived after 1815 of the hope of European allies, Indians still occupied some of the richest land west of the Appalachians, especially in the future Cotton Kingdom. For white Americans, it was inconceivable that primitive tribal economies should long preempt such resources or prevent the government's sale of such "public" land for more productive use.

From the earliest colonial times, the relations of whites with Indians had been complex and inconsistent, since many tribes had proved to be indispensable as allies, suppliers, and customers while others had been treated as enemies or even slaves. In general, however, white perceptions split into polarized images of good Indians and bad Indians; noble savages and fiendish devils; Christianized pupils of civilization and degraded pagans who were only rendered more dangerous and treacherous by the white man's whiskey and guns.

These contrary images corresponded to the two objectives that began to govern public policy in the early nineteenth century. For the "good Indians," there was hope of acculturation and gradual assimilation, premised on religious conversion and on the breakdown of tribal units. For it was as select *individuals* that "good Indians" would meet the tests of civilization and become responsible citizens subject to the sovereignty of states. The irreclaimable majority, stupefied by the weight of custom and tribal loyalties, would then be removed for their protection to unoccupied lands west of the Mississippi. The truly "bad Indians" who violently resisted this supposedly benevolent social engineering would, for the most part, be exterminated.

Curiously, the Constitutional scruples that impeded federal control over immigration and even blocked federal regulation of interstate commerce in black slaves, had little effect on Indian policy. The Constitution itself says remarkably little about Indians, besides granting Congress the power "to regulate commerce with foreign nations, and among the several States, and with the Indian tribes." Yet the federal government essentially took over the former prerogatives and responsibilities of the British crown, requiring that any sale or transfer of Indian lands be validated by a prior federal treaty; that all commerce with Indians be subject to federal licensing and regulation (for example, even prohibiting the sale to Indians of alcohol).

Given the lack of funds and the pathetic weakness of federal bureaucracy in the antebellum era (both points of pride from a Jeffersonian and Jacksonian perspective), these pretensions of sovereignty were a bit absurd. Even a strongly centralized government would have had difficulty controlling or giving ample force to lonely agents and army officers scattered over thousands of miles of forest and mountain wilderness, harassed by local white traders, squatters, and state authorities. After the conclusion of the War of 1812, which unleashed a wild scramble for land west of the southern piedmont—especially in western North Carolina, northern Georgia, and parts of Tennessee, Alabama, and Mississippi—the federal government relied partly on the work of private missionaries, who received federal aid for continuing their efforts at educating and civilizing Indians. In line with the doctrines of environmentalism and socialization presented in Unit One, both missionaries and government officials assumed that influence could best be exerted by *example*. Once a few Cherokees, for example, had demonstrated the benefits of common schools, printing presses, workshops, family farms, and church attendance, the seeds of enlightenment would germinate with a multiplier effect, undermining tribal despotism and superstition, separating the self-improving Indians from the unregenerate. Everyone recognized that such an experiment in what today would be called "modernization" was a race against time, since federal authorities had no effective power to prevent encroachments on Indian land by white traders and settlers, tacitly or openly backed by state authorities. By the late 1820s, a Constitutional crisis finally exposed the underlying contradictions of federal policy. As a tribe like the Cherokees became increasingly "civilized," adopting not only schools and technology but a written constitution asserting sovereignty over their own domains, they posed an increasing challenge to the claims and expectations of an aggressive state like Georgia. In two important decisions, the Supreme Court denied Georgia's right to extend state laws to Cherokee lands, but limited Cherokee claims of sovereignty to those of a "domestic dependent nation," which was not authorized by the Constitution to bring suit in federal courts. As we shall see in subsequent selections, the federal government was committed to the policy of Indian removal, and President Jackson had no intention of even protecting the Cherokees from state harassment, as supposedly required by treaties (as interpreted by the Supreme Court).

Meanwhile, missionaries of various denominations argued over conflicting programs of "Christianization" and "civilization"—for example, over the way to deal with Cherokees who followed the white example of buying black slaves. The Cherokees were no less divided in deciding how to respond to white initiatives, what practices and institutions to emulate, and what tribal customs to preserve. Their success in maintaining a proud sense of tribal heritage and corporate identity, while learning new skills for survival, refuted the racist argument that Indians were incapable of adjusting to the demands of a modern age. In the first selection below, the Congregationalist Board of Commissioners for Foreign Missions specifically counters this racist ideology, knowing that it presents the central obstacle to publicly funded missionary work. In addressing Congress, the prestigious Board of Commissioners also attacks the supposed panacea of Indian removal, arguing that there is no longer any refuge large enough for a primitive hunting economy that would not soon be encroached upon by white civilization. The blunt alternatives are to "be *progressively civilized,* or *successively* perish."

The next selection moves ahead thirty-six years in time and over one thousand miles to the northwest, but the issues are much the same, the Indians' tribal destruction being simply farther advanced. In this text, Henry Benjamin Whipple (1822–1901), the first Episcopal Bishop of Minnesota, appeals directly to President Buchanan, describing the critical plight of the Sioux, Winnebago, and Chippewa tribes and proposing specific reforms in the government's Indian policy. In 1860, Whipple had served as Bishop of Minnesota for only a year, but had become increasingly discouraged by the degradation of the Indians and by the ineffectiveness of his appeals to Indian agents and government officials. He continued to beseech President Lincoln, Buchanan's successor, and his warnings were vindicated in 1862 when the Minnesota Sioux reached the breaking point and struck back, killing hundreds of white settlers and igniting an eventually self-destructive war. Even more than the American Board of Commissioners, Whipple advocates a protective paternalism linking church and government in a desperate, last-minute scheme of social engineering. His proposal for combining monetary payment with the issuance of "a medal on one side of which should be a pledge to abstain from intoxicating drinks for one year," is a perfect example of what later psychologists would call the science of "behavior modification."

American Board of Commissioners for Foreign Missions (1824)

In fulfillment of our commission, we beg leave, respectfully, to state to your honorable body, that a prominent object of the board we represent is, to extend the blessings of civilization and Christianity, in all their variety, to the Indian tribes within the limits of the United States. In carrying on this work of benevolence and charity, we are happy to acknowledge, with much gratitude, the aid received from the government, in making and supporting the several establishments made for accomplishing their purpose. The object of the government and of the Board is one, and, indeed, is common to the whole community. We trust, therefore, that the measure adopted by our board will not be deemed an improper interference with the concerns of the government, a thing at which our feelings would revolt; but, only as a proper act of co-operation of a portion of the citizens, in effecting a great and interesting *national* object.

The history of our intercourse with Indians, from the first settlement of this country, contains many facts honorable to the character of our ancestors, and of our nation—many, also, too many, which are blots on this character; and which, in reflecting on them, cannot fail to fill us with regret, and with concern, lest the Lord of nations, who holds in his hand the scales of equal and everlasting justice, should in his wrath say to us, "As ye have done unto these Indians, so will I requite you." We here allude to the neglect with which these aboriginal tribes have been treated in regard to their civil, moral, and religious improvement—to the manner in which we have, in many, if not most instances, come into possession of their lands, and of their peltry: also, to the provocations we have given, in so many instances, to those cruel, desolating, and exterminating wars, which have been successively waged against them; and to the corrupting vices, and fatal diseases, which have been introduced among them, by wicked and unprincipled white people. These acts can be viewed in no other light, than as national sins, aggravated by our knowledge, and their ignorance; our strength and skill in war, and their weakness—by our treacherous abuse of their unsuspicious simplicity, and, especially, by the light and privileges of Christianity, which we enjoy, and of which they are destitute. In these things we are, as a nation, verily guilty, and exposed to the judgments of that just Being, to whom it belongs to avenge the wrongs of the oppressed; under whose perfect government the guilty, who remain impenitent, can never escape just punishment. The only way, we humbly conceive, to avert these judgments, which now hang, with threatening aspect, over our country—to secure the forgiveness and favor of Him whom we have offended, and to elevate our national character, and render it exemplary in view of the world—is happily, that which has been

---

SOURCE: American Board of Commissioners for Foreign Missions, Memorial to the Senate and the House of Representatives, in American Society for Improving Indian Tribes, *First Annual Report*, 1824, pp. 66–68.

already successfully commenced, and which the government of our nation, and Christians of nearly all denominations, are pursuing with one consent, and with their combined influence and energies. The American Board of Commissioners for Foreign Missions view these facts as highly encouraging; and it is their earnest desire that the God of nations would speed the course so auspiciously commenced, and give direction, and his blessing, to our joint efforts; add numbers and strength to those already engaged in this good work; convince, and reconcile to the object, those who are now opposed to it; and, ultimately, crown our labors with the desired success.

The work in which we are engaged, we are sensible, is not only noble, and god-like, and worthy to command the best energies of our nature, but it is also a great, arduous, and difficult work, requiring patience, forbearance, perseverance, and unremitted and long continued efforts. Here is scope enough to employ the wisdom, the means, and the power of the nation; and the object is of sufficient magnitude and interest, to command the employment of them all.

We are aware of the great and only objection, deserving notice, that is made to our project, and which has been made by some men of distinction and influence in our country, whose opinion on other subjects is entitled to respect; and this is, that "it is *impracticable*; that Indians, like some species of birds and beasts, their fellow inhabitants of the forest, are *untameable*; and that no means, which we can employ, will prepare them to enjoy with us the blessings of civilization." In answer to this objection, we appeal to facts; facts not distant from us—not of a doubtful nature; but which exist, and are fast multiplying among us, under our own eyes and observation—to facts which cannot be doubted, and in such number and variety, as furnish indubitable evidence of the practicability of educating Indians in such manner, as to prepare them to enjoy all the blessings, and to fulfill all the duties, of civilized life. . . .

It being admitted, then, that the Indians within our jurisdiction *are* capable of receiving an education, which will prepare them to participate with us in all the blessings which we enjoy, these questions will naturally arise: Is it desirable that they should receive such an education? Are they willing to receive it? Have we the means of imparting it to them? These questions, your memorialists conceive, may, with confidence, be answered in the affirmative. It *is* desirable that our Indians should receive such an education as has been mentioned, we conceive, because the civilized is preferable to the savage state; because the Bible, and the religion therein revealed to us, with its ordinances, are blessings of infinite and everlasting value and which the Indians do not now enjoy. It is also desirable as an act of common humanity. The progress of the white population, in the territories which were lately the hunting grounds of the Indians, is rapid, and probably will continue and increase. Their game, on which they principally depend for subsistence, is diminishing, and is already gone from those tribes who remain among us. In the natural course of things, therefore, they will be compelled to obtain their support in the manner we do ours. They are, to a considerable extent, sensible of this already. But they cannot thus live, and obtain their support, till they receive the education for which we plead. There is no place on the earth to which they can migrate, and live in the savage and hunter state. The Indian tribes must, therefore, be *progressively* civilized, or *successively* perish.

Henry Benjamin Whipple (1860)

Having been called to the Episcopate of Minnesota, I find in my diocese several thousand Indians of the Sioux, Winnebago, and Chippewa tribes in whom I feel the deepest interest. They are American pagans whose degradation and helplessness must appeal to every Christian heart. From their past history they have peculiar claims upon the benevolence and protection of a Christian nation. The only hope for the Indians is in civilization and Christianization. They understand this, and I believe would welcome any plan which will save them from destruction.

The curse of the Indian country is the firewater which flows throughout its borders. Although every treaty pledges to them protection against its sale and use, and the government desires to fulfil this pledge, thus far all efforts have proved ineffectual.

The difficulties in the way are these: First, the policy of our government has been to treat the red man as an equal. Treaties are then made. The annuities are paid in gross sums annually; from the Indian's lack of providence and the influence of traders, a few weeks later every trace of the payment is gone. Second, the reservations are scattered and have a widely extended border of ceded lands. As the government has no control over the citizens of the state, traffic is carried on openly on the border. Third, the Indian agents have no police to enforce the laws of Congress, and cannot rely upon the officers elected by a border population to suppress a traffic in which friends are interested. Fourth, the army, being under the direction of a separate department, has no definite authority to act for the protection of the Indians. Fifth, if arrests are made, the cases must be tried before some local state officer, and often the guilty escape. Sixth, as there is no distinction made by the government between the chief of temperate habits and the one of intemperate, the tribe loses one of the most powerful influences for good, —that of pure official example.

With much hesitation I would suggest to those who have Indian affairs in charge and who, I trust, feel a deep solicitude for their welfare,—

First, whether, in future, treaties cannot be made so that the government shall occupy a paternal character, treating the Indians as their wards, and giving to them all supplies in kind as needed.

SOURCE: Henry Benjamin Whipple, *Lights and Shadows of a Long Episcopate* (New York: Macmillan, 1899), pp. 50–53.

Second, whether a United States Commissioner could not be located near all reservations with authority to try all violations of Indian laws.

Third, whether more definite instructions cannot be issued to all Indian agents to take prompt action to prevent the sale of ardent spirits to the Indians, and with full power to enforce the law.

Fourth, whether the department has power to strike from the roll of chiefs, the name of any man of intemperate habits, and thus make a pure, moral character the ground of government favor.

Fifth, whether the department has authority to issue a medal on one side of which should be a pledge to abstain from intoxicating drinks for one year, these medals to be given to all Indians at the time of payment, who will make this pledge.

Sixth, whether in the future the different bands of an Indian tribe may not be concentrated on one reservation.

Seventh, whether some plan cannot be devised to create in the Indians an interest in securing for themselves homes where they can live by the cultivation of the soil.

Eighth, whether practical Christian teachers cannot be secured to teach the Indians the peaceful pursuits of agriculture and the arts of civilization.

Be assured that I appreciate fully the perplexities which surround our relations to the Indians. My excuse for addressing you is my deep interest in this wronged people, whom the Providence of God has placed under my spiritual care. In my visits to them my heart has been pained to see the utter helplessness of these poor souls, fast passing away, caused in great part by the curse which our people have pressed to their lips.

B. The Rationale for Removal

- *James Monroe* (1817)
- *Andrew Jackson* (1830)

> For the great eastern tribes, the only realistic hope of survival, even by the mid-eighteenth century, lay in alliances with French, Spanish, or British efforts to check white American expansion. But such alliances only confirmed the white American view of Indians as treacherous enemies whose continuing presence would always endanger American security. Even for the "friendly" tribes who fought for the American cause, the defeat of pro-British Indians in the Revolution and especially in the War of 1812 meant disaster.
>
> For example, in 1814, during the War of 1812, General Andrew Jackson destroyed the heart of the Muskogee nation of the so-called Creeks, but with the aid of many Creek allies. At the Treaty of Fort Jackson he then imposed an indemnity upon allies and enemies alike, forcing the Muskogee nation to surrender some twenty million acres of land in Georgia and Alabama. After Jackson repelled a British invasion at the Battle of New

Orleans, which instantly made him a superhero and the most popular man in America, he delivered a succession of fatal blows to the southern tribes culminating with the first Seminole War of 1818 and with Jackson's unauthorized invasion of Spanish Florida. In a series of treaties between 1816 and 1820, the Chickasaws, Cherokees, and Choctaws ceded immense tracts of land east of the Mississippi in exchange for land west of the river. In addition to passing out thousands of dollars in bribes, Jackson reminded the chiefs of the fate of the rebellious Creeks. As the commanding general responsible for defending the South, his paramount concern was national security.

The rationale for removal went back in time at least to Jefferson, and in implementing this policy Jackson had the full support of President Monroe. In his first annual message, from which the first selection is taken, Monroe discussed America's strategic concerns in the face of the Latin American wars of independence from Spain, which posed a danger of European intervention while at the same time inviting American expansion, for self-defense, into Florida and Texas. As Monroe proceeds to point out, the nation's northern frontier with Canada—the scene of many military defeats during the recent War of 1812—had been rendered secure by the wholesale cession of Indian lands. As for the more vulnerable Gulf coast, Jackson had already cleared a broad swath through former Indian lands from Tennessee to Mobile. Within a few weeks, Monroe would order Jackson to pursue and punish the rebellious Seminoles, a vaguely worded order that Old Hickory would interpret to mean the conquest of Spanish Florida.

In a letter two months earlier, President Monroe had endorsed Jackson's views on Indian policy by concluding that "a compulsory process seems to be necessary, to break their habits, and to civilize them, and there is much cause to believe, that it must be resorted to, to preserve them." Without mentioning compulsion, Monroe's annual message of 1817 expands on the Americans' "duty" to preserve and improve "the native inhabitants" by putting their lands to better use. In other words, national security and prosperity happily coincided with what the government took to be the best interests of the Indians.

This theme is developed with much humanitarian rhetoric in the second selection, taken from Jackson's second annual message as President. By 1830, national security was no longer a central concern as in 1817, but Georgia's attempt to subject Cherokees and white missionaries to state law raised the spectre of dangerous internal conflict between state and federal jurisdictions. Though in some respects a nationalist, Jackson fervently believed in state autonomy and in scrupulous respect for jurisdictional boundaries. Above all, he was determined to prevent New England's recent outbreak of "philanthropic" sympathy for the Indians from shattering the fragile equilibrium between state and federal governments. Jackson's presentation is almost bitterly defensive. It should be read as the self-justification of a highly self-righteous leader, the chief architect of American Indian policy, whose overarching program had recently won Congressional approval. As a national leader, Jackson was especially indignant over moral censure by affluent and secure Northeasterners who had never seen a scalped child or a burned frontier settlement, who had never engaged Indians in combat or in prolonged treaty negotiations.

Two points in Jackson's speech deserve special attention: (1) the revelation of Jackson's underlying hostility toward tribal solidarity, echoing the themes of previous selections concerning the seemingly threatening *bond* uniting such groups as Freemasons, Catholics, Mormons, and monopolistic corporations. One must ask how such threatening collectivities differed from the supposedly natural bonds of family, community, and political state. (2) In a curiously literary flourish, Jackson builds on the familiar image of the Indians as a doomed race, drawing startling parallels between the succession of generations and the extinction of entire races. His paean to progress and perfectibility, conceived as an annihilation of all roots in the past, tells us more about the tensions within antebellum culture than one could learn from volumes of ordinary documents. One must remember that Jackson was by popular consent the archetypal American hero and philosopher of democracy; by 1830 every word he uttered was attuned to what he conceived to be the general will.

James Monroe (1817)

From several of the Indian tribes inhabiting the country bordering on Lake Erie purchases have been made of lands on conditions very favorable to the United States, and, as it is presumed, not less so to the tribes themselves.

By these purchases the Indian title, with moderate reservations, has been extinguished to the whole of the land within the limits of the State of Ohio, and to a part of that in the Michigan Territory and of the State of Indiana. From the Cherokee tribe a tract has been purchased in the State of Georgia and an arrangement made by which, in exchange for lands beyond the Mississippi, a great part, if not the whole, of the land belonging to that tribe eastward of that river in the States of North Carolina, Georgia, and Tennessee, and in the Alabama Territory will soon be acquired. . . .

A similar and equally advantageous effect will soon be produced to the south, through the whole extent of the states and territory which border on the waters emptying into the Mississippi and the Mobile. In this progress, which the rights of nature demand and nothing can prevent, marking a growth rapid and gigantic, it is our duty to make new efforts for the preser-

SOURCE: James Monroe, First Annual Message, December 2, 1817, in James D. Richardson, *A Compilation of the Messages and Papers of the Presidents*, Vol. 2 (New York: Bureau of National Literature, n.d.), pp. 585–86.

vation, improvement, and civilization of the native inhabitants. The hunter state can exist only in the vast uncultivated desert. It yields to the more dense and compact form and greater force of civilized population; and of right it ought to yield, for the earth was given to mankind to support the greatest number of which it is capable, and no tribe or people have a right to withhold from the wants of others more than is necessary for their own support and comfort. It is gratifying to know that the reservations of land made by the treaties with the tribes on Lake Erie were made with a view to individual ownership among them and to the cultivation of the soil by all, and that an annual stipend has been pledged to supply their other wants. It will merit the consideration of Congress whether other provision not stipulated by treaty ought to be made for these tribes and for the advancement of the liberal and humane policy of the United States toward all the tribes within our limits, and more particularly for their improvement in the arts of civilized life.

Among the advantages incident to these purchases, and to those which have preceded, the security which may thereby be afforded to our inland frontiers is peculiarly important. With a strong barrier, consisting of our own people, thus planted on the Lakes, the Mississippi, and the Mobile, with the protection to be derived from the regular [army] force, Indian hostilities, if they do not altogether cease, will henceforth lose their terror. Fortifications in those quarters to any extent will not be necessary, and the expense attending them may be saved.

Andrew Jackson (1830)

It gives me pleasure to announce to Congress that the benevolent policy of the government, steadily pursued for nearly thirty years, in relation to the removal of the Indians beyond the white settlements is approaching to a happy consummation. Two important tribes have accepted the provision made for their removal at the last session of Congress, and it is believed that their example will induce the remaining tribes also to seek the same obvious advantages.

The consequences of a speedy removal will be important to the United States, to individual States, and to the Indians themselves. The pecuniary advantages which it promises to the government are the least of its recommendations. It puts an end to all possible danger of collision between the authorities of the General and State governments on account of the Indians. It will place a dense and civilized population in large tracts of country now occupied by a few savage hunters. By opening the whole territory between

SOURCE: Andrew Jackson, Second Annual Message, December 6, 1830, in James D. Richardson, *A Compilation of the Messages and Papers of the Presidents*, Vol. 3 (New York: Bureau of National Literature, n.d.), pp. 1082–85.

Tennessee on the north and Louisiana on the south to the settlement of the whites it will incalculably strengthen the southwestern frontier and render the adjacent States strong enough to repel future invasions without remote aid. It will relieve the whole State of Mississippi and the western part of Alabama of Indian occupancy, and enable those States to advance rapidly in population, wealth, and power. It will separate the Indians from immediate contact with settlements of whites; free them from the power of the States; enable them to pursue happiness in their own way and under their own rude institutions; will retard the progress of decay, which is lessening their numbers, and perhaps cause them gradually, under the protection of the Government and through the influence of good counsels, to cast off their savage habits and become an interesting, civilized, and Christian community. These consequences, some of them so certain and the rest so probable, make the complete execution of the plan sanctioned by Congress at their last session an object of much solicitude.

Toward the aborigines of the country no one can indulge a more friendly feeling than myself, or would go further in attempting to reclaim them from their wandering habits and make them a happy, prosperous people. I have endeavored to impress upon them my own solemn convictions of the duties and powers of the General Government in relation to the State authorities. For the justice of the laws passed by the States within the scope of their reserved powers they are not responsible to this Government. As individuals we may entertain and express our opinions of their acts, but as a Government we have as little right to control them as we have to prescribe laws for other nations.

. . .

Humanity has often wept over the fate of the aborigines of this country, and Philanthropy has been long busily employed in devising means to avert it, but its progress has never for a moment been arrested, and one by one have many powerful tribes disappeared from the earth. To follow to the tomb the last of his race and to tread on the graves of extinct nations excite melancholy reflections. But true philanthropy reconciles the mind to these vicissitudes as it does to the extinction of one generation to make room for another. In the monuments and fortresses of an unknown people, spread over the extensive regions of the West, we behold the memorials of a once powerful race, which was exterminated or has disappeared to make room for the existing savage tribes. Nor is there anything in this which, upon a comprehensive view of the general interests of the human race, is to be regretted. Philanthropy could not wish to see this continent restored to the condition in which it was found by our forefathers. What good man would prefer a country covered with forests and ranged by a few thousand savages to our extensive Republic, studded with cities, towns, and prosperous farms, embellished with all the improvements which art can devise or industry execute, occupied by more than 12,000,000 happy people, and filled with all the blessings of liberty, civilization, and religion?

The present policy of the Government is but a continuation of the same progressive change by a milder process. The tribes which occupied the countries now constituting the Eastern States were annihilated or have melted away to make room for the whites. The waves of population and civilization are rolling to the westward, and we now propose to acquire the countries occupied by the red men of the South and West by a fair exchange, and, at the expense of the United States, to send them to a land where their existence may be prolonged and perhaps made perpetual. Doubtless it will be painful to leave the graves of their fathers; but what do they more than our ancestors did or than our children are now doing? To better their condition in an unknown land our forefathers left all that was dear in earthly objects. Our children by thousands yearly leave the land of their birth to seek new homes in distant regions. Does Humanity weep at these painful separations from everything, animate and inanimate, with which the young heart has become entwined? Far from it. It is rather a source of joy that our country affords scope where our young population may range unconstrained in body or in mind, developing the power and faculties of man in their highest perfection. These remove hundreds and almost thousands of miles at their own expense, purchase the lands they occupy, and support themselves at their new homes from the moment of their arrival. Can it be cruel in this Government when, by events which it can not control, the Indian is made discontented in his ancient home to purchase his lands, to give him a new and extensive territory, to pay the expense of his removal, and support him a year in his new abode? How many thousands of our own people would gladly embrace the opportunity of removing to the West on such conditions! If the offers made to the Indians were extended to them, they would be hailed with gratitude and joy.

And is it supposed that the wandering savage has a stronger attachment to his home than the settled, civilized Christian? Is it more afflicting to him to leave the graves of his fathers than it is to our brothers and children? Rightly considered, the policy of the General government toward the red man is not only liberal, but generous. He is unwilling to submit to the laws of the States and mingle with their population. To save him from this alternative, or perhaps utter annihilation, the General Government kindly offers him a new home, and proposes to pay the whole expense of his removal and settlement.

C. Indian Responses

- *Pushmataha* (1811)
- *Memorial and Protest of the Cherokee Nation* (1836)

Far from being a homogeneous people, the "Indians" were sharply divided by cultural traditions, tribal rivalries, and differing susceptibilities to the influences of white culture. Their response to white demands for assimilation or removal ranged from skillful warfare to stubborn negotiation and resigned acquiescence. Unfortunately for the historian, most of the expressions of Indian opinion were recorded by white listeners and are of at least questionable authenticity. Formal protests and petitions were often written by sympathetic whites or by "half-breed" leaders, much despised by Jackson and other Indian-fighters who in this regard contradicted their professed hopes for assimilation. Keeping these cautions in mind, numerous Indian documents are poignant, illuminating, and consistent with the known stand of various tribes.

Pushmataha (*c.* 1765–1824), represented in the first selection, was the Choctaw chieftain of the Six Town District. In 1811 he faced a momentous decision. War was about to erupt between America and Britain. With encouragement from British Canada, Tecumseh, the chief of the northwestern Shawnees, journeyed southward to recruit support from the more powerful southern tribes, promising a flow of weapons from the Gulf ports occupied by Spain, Britain's European ally against Napoleon. Indian militancy reached a peak in Tecumseh's appeal to the Creeks: "Let the white race perish! . . . They seize your land; they corrupt your women; they trample on the bones of your dead! Back whence they came, upon a trail of blood, they must be driven! Back—aye, back to the great water whose accursed waves brought them to our shores! Burn their dwellings—destroy their stock—slay their wives and children, that the very breed may perish. War now! War always! War on the living! War on the dead!"[1]

Pushmataha, in his 1811 speech to the Choctaws and Chickasaws, skillfully undercuts Tecumseh's seeming hysteria. Within the next months and years, Pushmataha's pro-American stance seemed to be vindicated by Tecumseh's disastrous defeat at the Battle of Tippecanoe (1811) and death at the Battle of the Thames (1813), and by Jackson's annihilation of the rebellious "Red Stick" Creeks at the Battle of Horseshoe Bend (1814). Pushmataha himself led loyal Choctaw forces to fight with Jackson against the Creeks, the British, and the Spanish. But by 1820 the Choctaw chieftain had futile second thoughts when his tribe received an ultimatum from Jackson at Doak's Stand, in Mississippi. In this fateful confrontation, Pushmataha openly accused his former ally of duplicity. In exchange for what Jackson termed a mere "slip" of five million acres of Choctaw land in Mississippi, Old Hickory offered a western "country of tall trees, many water courses, rich lands and high grass abounding in game of all kinds. . . ." Pushmataha knew better. He informed the Choctaws that the land was barren, the game scarce, and that the promised "preserve" was already occupied by white settlers. Jackson, in a characteristic explosion of anger, warned that a refusal to "consent" would mean the destruction of the Choctaw nation. By 1820 the Choctaws had no allies, and Pushmataha finally agreed to surrender the rich "Delta" lands of Mississippi, the heart of the

---

[1] J. F. H. Claiborne, *Mississippi as a Province, Territory and State* (Jackson Miss.: 1880), p. 317. As quoted in Robert V. Remini, *Andrew Jackson and the Course of American Empire, 1767–1821* (New York: Harper & Row, 1977), p. 188.

future Cotton Kingdom, in exchange for desolate tracts in Oklahoma and southwestern Arkansas.[1]

What made American Indian policy so morally deceptive was its appearance of fairness and legality. The government showed considerable patience in negotiating and renegotiating treaties that purported to show Indian consent; in providing for compensation in the form of provisions, transport, and western land; and in assuring chiefs and heads of families that they could remain on *individual* plots or allotments within the areas ceded to the United States. While the cessions of 1814–1820 opened up much of the South to white settlement, the so-called civilized tribes of Creeks, Choctaws, Chickasaws, and Cherokees retained vast holdings that were more than sufficient for agriculture, if not for an economy dependent on hunting. The final dispossession and relocation of entire tribes began only after the Indian Removal Act of 1830, which provided funds for acquiring all tribal lands and for transporting whole populations to the West.

The Choctaws were the first to sign a new treaty under the provisions of the Removal Act, and by 1831 were suffering the terrible hardships of an ill-planned and inadequately supplied migration. The Cherokees, encouraged by decisions of the Supreme Court and by the strength of humanitarian sentiment against removal, held firm. The overwhelming majority of Cherokees continued to resist removal even after a dissident group signed a treaty in 1835 accepting the government's terms. The second selection is from a memorial and protest submitted to Congress by John Ross, a mixed-blood chief, and other representatives of the Cherokee nation. Despite these substantiated claims of fraud, by 1838 the army began evicting Cherokees from their land and locking them in temporary stockades. There was no deliberate attempt at extermination, but thousands of Cherokees died as a result of individual white aggression, malnutrition, disease, and physical hardship as they were herded toward new settlements in the West.

Pushmataha (1811)

It was not my design in coming here to enter into a disputation with any one. But I appear before you, my warriors and my people, not to throw in my plea against the accusations of Tecumseh; but to prevent your forming rash and dangerous resolutions upon things of highest importance, through the instigations of others. I have myself learned by experience, and I also see many of you, O Choctaws and Chickasaws, who have the same experience of years

---

[1] Remini, *Andrew Jackson*, pp. 188, 394–95.

SOURCE: H. B. Cushman, *History of the Choctaw, Chickasaw and Natchez Indians* (Greenville, Texas: Headlight Printing House, 1899), pp. 315–18.

that I have, the injudicious steps of engaging in an enterprise because it is new. Nor do I stand up before you to-night to contradict the many facts alleged against the American people, or to raise my voice against them in useless accusations. The question before us now is not what wrongs they have inflicted upon our race, but what measures are best for us to adopt in regard to them; and though our race may have been unjustly treated and shamefully wronged by them, yet I shall not for that reason alone advise you to destroy them unless it was just and wise for you so to do; nor would I advise you to forgive them, though worthy of your commiseration, unless I believe it would be to the interest of our common good. We should consult more in regard to our future welfare than our present. What people, my friends and countrymen, were so unwise and inconsiderate as to engage in a war of their own accord, when their own strength, and even with the aid of others, was judged unequal to the task? I well know causes often arise which force men to confront extremities, but, my countrymen, those causes do not now exist. Reflect, therefore, I earnestly beseech you, before you act hastily in this great matter, and consider with yourselves how greatly you will err if you injudiciously approve of and inconsiderately act upon Tecumseh's advice. Remember the American people are now friendly disposed toward us. Surely you are convinced that the greatest good will result to us by the adoption of and adhering to those measures I have before recommended to you. . . .

My friends and fellow countrymen! you now have no just cause to declare war against the American people, or wreak your vengeance upon them as enemies, since they have ever manifested feelings of friendship towards you. It is besides inconsistent with your national glory and with your honor, as a people, to violate your solemn treaty; and a disgrace to the memory of your forefathers, to wage war against the American people merely to gratify the malice of the English.

The war, which you are now contemplating against the Americans, is a flagrant breach of justice; yea, a fearful blemish on your honor and also that of your fathers, and which you will find if you will examine it carefully and judiciously, forbodes nothing but destruction to our entire race. It is a war against a people whose territories are now far greater than our own, and who are far better provided with all the necessary implements of war, with men, guns, horses, wealth, far beyond that of all our race combined, and where is the necessity or wisdom to make war upon such a people? Where is the hope of success, if thus weak and unprepared we should declare it against them? Let us not be deluded with the foolish hope that this war, if begun, will soon be over, even if we destroy all the whites within our territories, and lay waste their homes and fields. Far from it. It will be put the beginning of the end that terminates in the total destruction of our race. And though we will not permit ourselves to be made slaves, or, like inexperienced warriors, shudder at the thought of war, yet I am not so insensible and inconsistent as to advise you to cowardly yield to the outrages of the whites, or willfully to connive at their unjust encroachments; but only not yet to have recourse to war, but to send ambassadors to our Great Father at Washington, and lay before him our grievances, without betraying too great eagerness for war, or manifesting any tokens of pusillanimity. Let us, therefore, my fellow countrymen, form our resolutions with great caution and prudence upon a subject of such vast importance, and in such fearful consequences may be involved. . . .

Be not, I pray you, guilty of rashness, which I never as yet have known you to be; therefore I implore you, while healing measures are in the election of us all, not to break the treaty, nor violate your pledge of honor, but to submit our grievances, whatever they may be, to the Congress of the United States, according to the articles of the treaty existing between us and the American people.

Memorial and Protest of the Cherokee Nation (1836)

The undersigned representatives of the Cherokee nation, east of the river Mississippi, impelled by duty, would respectfully submit, for the consideration of your honorable body, the following statement of facts: It will be seen, from the numerous subsisting treaties between the Cherokee nation and the United States, that from the earliest existence of this government, the United States, in Congress assembled, received the Cherokees and their nation into favor and protection; and that the chiefs and warriors, for themselves and all parts of the Cherokee nation, acknowledged themselves and the said Cherokee nation to be under the protection of the United States of America, and of no other sovereign whatsoever: they also stipulated, that the said Cherokee nation will not hold any treaty with any foreign power, individual State, or with individuals of any State: that for, and in consideration of, valuable concessions made by the Cherokee nation, the United States solemnly guaranteed to said nation all their lands not ceded, and pledged the faith of the government, that "all white people who have intruded, or may hereafter intrude, on the lands reserved for the Cherokees, shall be removed by the United States, and proceeded against, according to the provisions of the act, passed 30th March, 1802," entitled "An act to regulate trade and intercourse with the Indian tribes, and to preserve peace on the frontiers." It would be useless to recapitulate the numerous provisions for the security and protection of the rights of the Cherokees, to be found in the various treaties between their nation and the United States. The Cherokees were happy and prosperous under a scrupulous observance of treaty stipulations by the government of the United States, and from the fostering hand extended over them, they made rapid advances in civilization, morals, and in the arts and sciences. Little did they anticipate, that when taught to think and feel as the American citizen, and to have with him a common interest, they were to be

SOURCE: Memorial and Protest of the Cherokee Nation, June 22, 1836, *Exec. Doc.* No., 286, 24th Cong., 1st sess., pp. 1–2.

despoiled by their guardian, to become strangers and wanderers in the land of their fathers, forced to return to the savage life, and to seek a new home in the wilds of the far west, and that without their consent. An instrument purporting to be a treaty with the Cherokee people, has recently been made public by the President of the United States, that will have such an operation, if carried into effect. This instrument, the delegation aver before the civilized world, and in the presence of Almighty God, is fraudulent, false upon its face, made by unauthorized individuals, without the sanction, and against the wishes, of the great body of the Cherokee people. Upwards of fifteen thousand of those people have protested against it, solomnly declaring they will never acquiesce. . . .

D. The Indian as an Object of Sympathy and Hate

- *George Catlin* (1841)
- *Western Monthly Magazine* (1833)

Beginning in the 1820s, James Fenimore Cooper's *Leatherstocking Tales* established the red man as a popular subject for fictional romance. Cooper and his many imitators presented a gallery of Indian villains and noble savages, mostly pure figments of the literary imagination and all doomed, like Cooper's "Last Mohican," to extinction. George Catlin (1796–1872), the greatest early painter of Indians, was influenced by this romantic fascination with the idea of a perishing race. Having made the difficult transition from legal training to a successful career as a portrait painter, Catlin encountered in Philadelphia one day an imposing delegation of Indian braves from the Far West, and immediately vowed to use his art "in rescuing from oblivion the looks and customs of the vanishing races of native man in America." But instead of sitting in a Philadelphia studio and imagining what Indians were like, Catlin traveled extensively through the wilderness of the Far West, visiting some forty-eight tribes and, between 1829 and 1838, painting some six hundred portraits of Indian men and women.

As a child in Pennsylvania, Catlin had been nurtured on tales of Indian warfare—his own mother and grandmother had actually been captured by Indians. Yet he was one of the few Americans of his time who could accept Indian culture on its own terms, appreciating the value of radically different customs and institutions without expressing horror over "barbarism" and "superstition" or hope for the Indians' Christianization. In the following selection, Catlin is remarkably accurate and objective in his assessment of the consequences of Indian removal. In the East and in Europe, he at least aroused interest in Indian manners and customs by displaying his collection of paintings and artifacts. This popular road show helped to supplement his winter income as a portrait artist and to finance his western expeditions. But in the last analysis, Catlin like Cooper focused on a "lost world" and the seemingly inevitable costs of civilization. Realistically, Catlin knew that he was not simply painting the momentary features of *individuals* who were certain to age and die, but the exotic plumage of a human way of life which, like certain species of birds, could not survive the diseased touch of civilization. For his readers and viewers, this message could easily be sublimated into romantic and ultimately reassuring regret—life might be happier in a primitive Indian village, but since Indians belonged to the *past*, an enlightened civilization could at least view their remnants as a form of art and as a source of nostalgic inspiration. For living Indians, however, who looked to the future, the more immediate problem was "Indian hating."

In a magazine essay of 1829, James Hall had discussed the phenomenon of white hatred of Indians, citing the legend of one Colonel John Moredock who had dedicated his life to the vengeful slaying of Indians following the massacre of his family. Popular writers like Robert Montgomery Bird picked up the theme and, in effect, justified and glorified the extermination of red men. Herman Melville finally turned the tables in a blistering chapter on the "Metaphysics of Indian Hating," in *The Confidence Man,* in which he found an opposite meaning in the Moredock story. Much earlier, in 1833, *Western Monthly Magazine* had prefaced an account of Moredock's murderous obsession with a reasonably straightforward analysis of why frontiersmen hated Indians. Reprinted here as the second selection, this explanation of "Indian hating" raises as many questions as it answers.

George Catlin (1841)

The Indians of North America . . . are copper-colored, with long black hair, black eyes, tall, straight, and elastic forms—are less than two millions in number—were originally the undisputed owners of the soil, and got their title to their lands from the Great Spirit who created them on it,—were once a happy and flourishing people, enjoying all the comforts and luxuries of life which they knew of, and consequently cared for;—were sixteen millions in numbers, and sent that number of daily prayers to the Almighty, and thanks for His goodness and protection. Their country was entered by white men, but a few hundred years since; and thirty millions of these are now scuffling for the goods and luxuries of life, over the bones and ashes of twelve millions of red men; six millions of whom have fallen victims to the small-pox, and the remainder to the sword, the bayonet, and whiskey; all of which means of their death and destruction have been introduced and visited upon them by

---

SOURCE: George Catlin, *North American Indians; Being Letters and Notes on their Manners, Customs, and Conditions, Written During Eight Years' Travel Amongst the Wildest Tribes of Indians in North America, 1832–1839* (1st ed., New York: 1841; New York: Dover Publications, Inc., 1973), Vol. I, pp. 6–7; Vol. II, pp. 282–83.

acquisitive white men; and by white men, also, whose forefathers were welcomed and embraced in the land where the poor Indian met and fed them with "ears of green corn and with pemican." Of the two millions remaining alive at this time, about 1,400,000 are already the miserable living victims and dupes of white man's cupidity, degraded, discouraged, and lost in the bewildering maze that is produced by the use of whiskey and its concomitant vices; and the remaining number are yet unroused and unenticed from their wild haunts or their primitive modes, by the dread or love of white man and his allurements.

 · · ·

He who will sit and contemplate that vast Frontier, where, by the past policy of the government, one hundred and twenty thousand of these poor people (who had just got initiated into the mysteries and modes of civilized life, surrounded by examples of industry and agriculture which they were beginning to adopt), have been removed several hundred miles to the West, to meet a second siege of the whiskey-sellers and traders in the wilderness, to whose enormous exactions their semi-civilized habits and appetites have subjected them, will assuredly pity them. Where they have to quit their acquired luxuries, or pay ten times their accustomed prices for them—and to scuffle for a few years upon the plains, with the wild tribes, and with white men also, for the flesh and the skins of the last of the buffaloes; where their carnage, but not their *appetites*, must stop in a few years, and with the ghastliness of hunger and despair, they will find themselves gazing at each other upon the vacant waste, which will afford them nothing but the empty air, and the desperate resolve to flee to the woods and fastnesses of the Rocky Mountains; whilst more lucky white man will return to his comfortable home, with no misfortune, save that of *deep remorse* and a *guilty conscience*. Such a reader will find enough to claim his pity and engage his whole soul's indignation, at the wholesale and retail system of injustice, which has been, from the very first landing of our forefathers (and is equally at the present day, being), visited upon these poor, and naturally unoffending, untrespassing people.

In alluding to the cruel policy of removing the different tribes to their new country, west of the Mississippi, I would not do it without the highest respect to the motives of the government—and to the feelings and opinions of those worthy divines [ministers], whose advice and whose services were instrumental in bringing it about; and who, no doubt, were of opinion that they were effecting a plan that would redound to the Indian's benefit. Such was once my own opinion—but when I go, as I have done, through every one of those tribes removed, who had learned at home to use the ploughshare, and also contracted a passion, and a taste for civilized manufactures; and after that, removed twelve and fourteen hundred miles west, to a wild and lawless region, where their wants are to be supplied by the traders, at eight or ten times the prices they have been in the habit of paying; where whiskey can easily be sold to them in a boundless and lawless forest, without the restraints that can be successfully put upon the sellers of it in their civilized neighborhoods; and where also they are allured from the use of their ploughs, by the herds of buffaloes and other wild animals on the plains; I am compelled to state, as my irresistible conviction, that I believe the system one well calculated to benefit the interests of the vorcious land-speculators and Indian Traders; the first of whom are ready to grasp at their lands, as soon as they are vacated—and the others at the *annuities* of one hundred and twenty thousand extravagant customers. I believe the system is calculated to aid these, and perhaps to facilitate the growth and the wealth of the civilized border; but I believe, like everything else that tends to white man's aggrandizement, and the increase of his wealth, it will have as rapid a tendency to the poverty and destruction of the poor *red men*; who, unfortunately, *almost* seemed *doomed*, never in any way to be associated in interest with their pale-faced neighbors.

Western Monthly Magazine (1833)

The violent animosity which exists between the people of our frontier and the Indians, has long been a subject of remark. In the early periods of the history of our country, it was easily accounted for, on the ground of mutual aggression. The whites were continually encroaching upon the aborigines, and the latter avenging their wrongs by violent and sudden hostilities. The philanthropist is surprised, however, that such feelings should prevail now, when these atrocious wars have ceased, and when no immediate cause of enmity remains; at least upon our side. Yet the fact is, that the dweller upon the frontier continues to regard the Indian with a degree of terror and hatred, similar to that which he feels towards the rattlesnake or panther, and which can neither be removed by argument, nor appeased by any thing but the destruction of its object.

In order to understand the cause and the operation of these feelings, it is necessary to recollect that the backwoodsmen are a peculiar race. We allude to the pioneers, who, keeping continually in advance of civilization, precede the denser population of our country in its progress westward, and live always upon the frontier. They are the descendants of a people whose habits were identically the same as their own. Their fathers were pioneers. A passion for hunting, and a love for sylvan sports, have induced them to recede continually before the tide of emigration, and have kept them a separate people, whose habits, prejudices, and modes of life have been transmitted from father to son with little change. From generation to generation they have lived in contact with the Indians. The ancestor met the red men in battle upon the shores of the Atlantic, and his descendants have pursued the footsteps of the retreating tribes, from year to year, throughout a whole century,

SOURCE: "Indian Hating," *Western Monthly Magazine*, II (September, 1833), pp. 403–5.

and from the eastern limits of our great continent to the wide prairies of the west.

America was settled in an age when certain rights, called those of *discovery* and *conquest*, were universally acknowledged; and when the possession of a country was readily conceded to the strongest. When more accurate notions of moral right began, with the spread of knowledge, and the dissemination of religious truth, to prevail in public opinion, and regulate the public acts of our government, the pioneers were but slightly affected by the wholesome contagion of such opinions. Novel precepts in morals were not apt to reach men who mingled so little with society in its more refined state, and who shunned the restraints, while thew despised the luxuries of social life.

The pioneers, who thus dwelt ever upon the borders of the Indian hunting grounds, forming a barrier between savage and civilized men, have received but few accessions to their numbers by emigration. The great tide of emigration, as it rolls forward, beats upon them and rolls them onward, without either swallowing them up in its mass, or mingling its elements with theirs. They accumulate by natural increase; a few of them return occasionally to the bosom of society, but the great mass moves on.

It is not from a desire of conquest, or thirst of blood, or with any premeditated hostility against the savage, that the pioneer continues to follow him from forest to forest, ever disputing with him the right to the soil, and the privilege of hunting game. It is simply because he shuns a crowded population, delights to rove uncontrolled in the woods, and does not believe that an Indian, or any other man, has a right to monopolize the hunting grounds, which he considers free to all. When the Indian disputes the propriety of this invasion upon his ancient heritage, the white man feels himself injured, and stands, as the southern folks say, upon his reserved rights. . . .

Traditions of horses stolen, and cattle driven off, and cabins burned, are numberless; are told with great minuteness, and listened to with intense interest. With persons thus reared, hatred towards an Indian becomes a part of their nature, and revenge an instinctive principle. Nor does the evil end here. Although the backwoodsmen, properly so called, retire before that tide of emigration which forms the more stationary population, and eventually fills the country with inhabitants, they usually remain for a time in contact with the first of those who, eventually, succeed them, and impress their own sentiments upon the latter. In the formation of each of the western territories and states, the backwoodsmen have, for awhile, formed the majority of the population, and given the tone to public opinion.

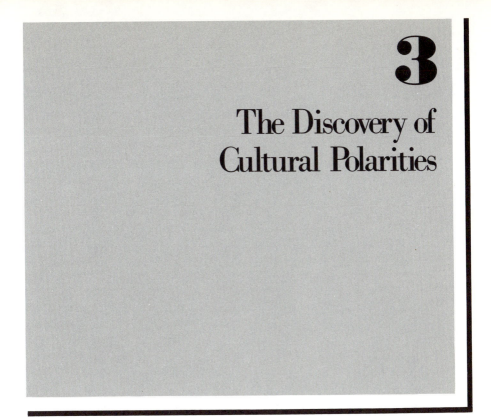

3

The Discovery of Cultural Polarities

A. Hispanic Americans

- *William W. H. Davis* (1857)
- *Juan Nepomuceno Cortina* (1859)

The acceptance of cultural and ethnic pluralism is a twentieth-century development. The alternatives presented to the Indians of assimilation, extinction, or removal presupposed a future of irresistible homogeneity. Yet spokesmen for the governing antebellum culture expressed continuing dismay over the discovery of pockets of seeming "anti-culture" in the hinterland—for example, in the more remote lumbering and mining districts and in the mountainous region later called Appalachia. Such settlements of squatters, hunters, and itinerant laborers had long been associated with criminality of one sort or another, and were thus subject to the punitive violence of self-appointed "regulators" and vigilantes who appeared periodically from colonial South Carolina to California in the days of the gold rush. Lawless settlements like Rogue's Harbor, in frontier Kentucky, were also traditionally vulnerable to religious revivalism. In popular legend, the roaring, irreverent Mike Finks, celebrated for their hard drinking and daring exploits, were doomed like the Indians to extinction (according to one story, Fink was finally knocked flat and properly chastised by Peter Cartwright, the frontier revivalist). By the 1840s, middle-class Americans could assume that following the removal of the Indians to the West, Christian civilization—in the form of schools, farms, and courthouses—would soon obliterate the pockets of "primitive," nonconforming whites who seemed to live like Indians.

But if the center of American society was thus secure, new challenges appeared around the periphery—in the Mexican (and French Canadian) border lands; in polyglot California; and in the slums of the great eastern port cities, especially New York. In the following two selections, we can only sample the complexity of cultural conflict along the Hispanic frontier, which had been greatly expanded as a result of the annexation of Texas (1845) and the acquisition of the territory extending from New Mexico to California (1848) in the Mexican War.

Though Anglo-Americans had treated Spanish and Mexican officials with the same respect accorded to any Europeans in peace or war in the past, the conflict over Texas encouraged a new and basically racist contempt for Hispanic-Americans. Increasingly, "North Americans" (a term used by Mexican-Americans) viewed Mexicans as a degenerate, three-breed race stigmatized by the worst traits of their Indian and African ancestors. The reasons for this shift in perspective were complicated and cannot be summarized without some distortion. It is sufficient to mention three points here: (1) the character of the North Americans who intruded upon and seized Mexican territory—men involved in wars against Indians and committed, for the most part, to the extension of Negro slavery; (2) the character of the Hispanic-Indian population along the Texan-New Mexican frontiers of Mexico—repeatedly described by officials from Mexico City, prior to United States conquest, as poor, ignorant, lethargic, fun-loving, and uninterested in "improvement" or "effective" government—the very traits attributed to North American backwoodsmen in the hills of Kentucky and Tennessee; (3) the growing popularity by the 1840s of racist modes of thought throughout the Anglo-American world, applied with little distinction to such technologically backward regions as Africa, India, China, and South America—regions which had little in common besides falling within the expanding world market dominated by the rising industrial powers.

Within this context, William W. H. Davis's description of the New Mexican people is significant because it probably represents the most balanced North American view recorded within the decade after New Mexico's conquest. Davis (1820–1910) was appointed United States Attorney for New Mexico in 1853. Though saturated with the ethnocentric prejudices of his time and culture, he was also a sensitive observer, alert to what he considered the positive characteristics of the Hispanic inhabitants of New Mexico. For example, Davis repeatedly stresses the affable, compliant, and temperate traits of Mexican-Americans. By contrast, Mexican officials in pre-annexation Texas described the Anglo-American settlers as pugnacious, vicious, and given to frequent drunkenness. Davis also takes pains (in passages not included here) to defend the physical bravery of Mexican males. Yet his overall assessment is negative. It should be read not as an objective portrayal but as a view distorted through the prism of official Anglo-American culture—a prism through which well-wishers also assessed the Chinese in California and the immigrant slumdwellers in New York City.

Davis, who later devoted his energies to Pennsylvania history, strikingly reflects the dominant values and prejudices of his time. Echoing the themes of Unit One, he perceives the Mexican-Americans as people who have never received moral training "in the American sense of the word." Horace Mann, Samuel Goodrich, and Lydia Child had all pointed to disturbing examples of *individuals* who had received deficient moral training. But according to Davis, the New Mexicans are an example of what happens when everyone is "allowed to grow up from infancy to manhood without being taught that it is wrong to indulge in vicious habits." Since Davis acknowledges that New Mexicans are not prone to riots or drunkenness, he is clearly thinking of sex. And throughout his account one senses the amazement and horror of the middle-class Protestant conscience confronting, for the first time, a sexually permissive society. One must quickly add that from a modern perspective this society was brutally exploitive. Davis is less concerned with sex, *per se*, than with the degradation of women and with the system of peonage and prostitution, which he likens to Negro slavery. Indeed, his response to human exploitation and brutalization resembles the response of contemporary reformers to both Negro slavery and urban prostitution. Like many reformers, he blends this humanitarian concern with conventional anti-Catholic and racist stereotypes, concluding, for example, that the New Mexican people have no present hope of "improving in color." This mixture of sympathy and contempt suggests the imperiousness of the culture to which tens of thousands of Hispanic Americans were unwillingly annexed.

While most of these people had no choice but to submit to North American hegemony, proudly preserving their own cultural heritage and adapting from the "gringos" whatever useful techniques and methods they could, a number of Mexican-Americans were pushed to violent resistance. Chicano historians have recently begun to rehabilitate the stereotyped "Mexican bandit," arguing that destitute Mexican-Americans did not see armed robbery as a crime but rather as a legitimate means of resisting oppression. Whatever the validity of this argument, Juan Cortina (1824–1892), though called a bandit, was not a Mexican variant on Jesse James and Butch Cassidy. The son of an established and wealthy family, Cortina fought for Mexico in the Mexican War and then became a respected landowning rancher in the disputed zone north of the Rio Grande, officially part of the United States after the Treaty of Guadalupe-Hidalgo (1848). Cortina deeply resented the arrogant bullying of his people, who under the cover of the law were continually being swindled of their land and livestock. Embroiled in some bitter personal conflicts in the Anglo-American outpost of Brownsville, Cortina led a raid on the border town on September 2, 1859, killing a number of enemies. Two days later, he issued a proclamation assuring "orderly people and honest citizens" that they had nothing to fear, but promising death to six or eight more "oppressors" who had persecuted, robbed, and spread terror among Mexican-American citizens.

The selection below is from a second proclamation, issued on November 23 after Cortina had defeated two punitive expeditions made up of American and Mexican troops. Calling for self-defense against the tyranny of Anglo-Americans and their repeated violation of rights guaranteed by the Treaty of Guadalupe-Hidalgo, Cortina vaguely refers to a secret society which will avenge Mexican wrongs. Yet as an American citizen, he also appeals to the governor-elect of Texas, Sam Houston. Reports that Cortina had seized Brownsville, massacred its Anglo-American inhabitants, and proclaimed a Republic of the Rio Grande, temporarily alarmed Washington and led to military mobilization. A detachment of American troops and Texas Rangers finally defeated Cortina, who retreated across the Rio Grande into Mexico. His exploits not only aggravated anti-Mexican sentiments in Texas but were used as an excuse for American military incursions into Mexican territory. Cortina, after serving as governor of the state of Tamaulipas, finally endured a long imprisonment at the hands of the dictatorial president Porfirio Díaz.

William W. H. Davis (1857)

The state of the mechanic arts among the New Mexicans is very low, and apparently without improvement since the earliest times. There are a few carpenters, blacksmiths, and jewelers among the natives, but, if ever so well skilled, it would be impossible for them to accomplish much with the rough tools they use. The gold and silver smiths excel all the other workmen, and some of their specimens, in point of ingenuity and skill, would do credit to the craft in any part of the world. Nearly all the lumber used for cabinet-making and building is sawed by hand, and carried to market on burros, two or three sticks or boards at a time, and sold by the piece. . . .

Before the Americans occupied the Territory, saw-mills were unknown, and their place was entirely supplied by hand-labor; but since that time two or three mills have been erected, which do a good business. A few flour-mills

SOURCE: W. W. H. Davis, *El Gringo: or, New Mexico and Her People* (New York: Harper and Brothers, 1857), pp. 211–23, 231–33.

have also been built, and the grain is better ground than formerly. In building they have no idea of architectural taste, but they construct their houses
in the same style as their ancestors—rather comfortable, but very homely
affairs.

. . .

When a Mexican travels he carries with him both bed and board, and
encamps on mountain or plain where night ovetakes him. He and all his
attendants go armed, which is a precaution highly necessary in whatever part
of the country you travel. In New Mexico there are no public houses by the
wayside in which the traveler can find rest and food for the night, and unless
he is able to reach some village where there are friends, he is obliged to en-
camp out. In some of the towns Americans have opened places of "enter-
tainment for man and beast," where a few can find tolerable accommodations at New York prices. Before the public house in Albuquerque hangs a
sign-board, on which is painted, in large letters, "Pacific and Atlantic Hotel,"
being considered the half-way house between the two oceans.

. . .

In some respects the New Mexicans are a peculiar and interesting people.
They are of Eastern origin, and in general possess all the vices of those whose
homes are washed by the blue waters of the Mediterranean Sea, whence a
branch of their ancestors originally came. When the Moors were expelled from
Spain, they left behind them, as a legacy to the people by whom they had
been conquered, many of their manners and customs, which, during their
residence in the country, had become firmly ingrafted into society. They had
intermarried with the Spaniards, and thus formed a mixed race, in whose
veins flowed the blood of both ancestors. Among the early adventurers who
came in quest of gold and fame into Mexico were many who had sprung
from this union of the Moor and Spaniard, and whose manners and customs
assimilated, to a considerable degree, with those of their Moslem ancestors.
. . . A thirst for further conquest, coupled with religious zeal, invited them
thither [to New Mexico], a distance of two thousand miles from the seat of
Spanish power in America. They streamed up the valley of the Del Norte
[the Rio Grande], and formed settlements upon the banks at the most favorable points that presented themselves, where they also established missions to
convert the native heathen, and military posts for defense, and became themselves permanent settlers. The Good Book as well as Nature taught them
that "it is not good for man to be alone," and so they considered the propriety of taking partners to share their exile and hardships. In this domestic
emergency there was but one alternative; their own fair countrywomen, "the
dark-eyed maids of Castile," were thousands of miles away, and could not
be obtained for wives, and they were therefore compelled, by force of circumstances, to look to the daughters of their Indian neighbors for help-meets.
This course was adopted, and all the settlers and gay cavaliers who were in
want of the gentler sex to smooth the pathway of life and keep their houses
in order, took to their bed and board Indian maidens. Here was a second

blending of blood and a new union of races; the Spaniard, Moor, and the aboriginal were united in one and made a new race, the Mexicans.

Among the present population there is found every shade of color, from the nut-brown, which exhibits a strong preponderance of the aboriginal blood, to the pure Castilian, who is as light and fair as the sons and daughters of the Anglo-Saxon race. Of the latter there are only a few families among the *ricos* who pride themselves upon not having Indian blood in their veins. The great mass of the population are very dark, and can not claim to be more than one fourth or one eighth part Spanish. The intermixture between the peasantry and the native tribes of Indians is yet carried on, and there is no present hope of the people improving in color.

• • •

While the Mexicans lack the courage and enterprise of our own people, they neither possess their turbulent and uneasy spirit. They are a peaceful and quiet race of people, and in their general disposition are rather mild and amiable. They are prone to order, and riots and kindred disturbances are almost unknown among them. They are temperate in their habits, and it is seldom that one becomes an habitual drunkard. When their passions are not aroused by anger they are universally kind, and in an intercourse of some years with them I have never received other than the most polite treatment from all classes. They bear a deadly hatred toward their enemy, and will manifest it whenever the opportunity offers. If they obtain an advantage over an enemy, they will oppress him beyond measure, and deem it a virtue; and, in return, they look for the same treatment when they are brought under in the wheel of fortune. They possess great talent for intrigue and chicanery, but lack stability and firmness of purpose. With all their faults, they are easily governed if they are treated with kindness and justice.

I regret that I am not able to speak more favorably of the morals of New Mexico, but in this particular the truth must be told. Probably there is no other country in the world, claiming to be civilized, where vice is more prevalent among all classes of the inhabitants. Their ancestors were governed in this matter by the standard of morality that prevailed in Southern Europe and along the shores of the Mediterranean, where morals were never deemed an essential to respectability and good standing in society. . . . The people of New Mexico have inherited all the vices of their ancestors, which they have continued to practice to this day. They have never received any moral training, in the American sense of the word, and have been allowed to grow up from infancy to manhood without being taught that it is wrong to indulge in vicious habits. The standard of female chastity is deplorably low, and the virtuous are far outnumbered by the vicious. Prostitution is carried to a fearful extent; and it is quite common for parents to sell their own daughters for money to gratify the lust of the purchaser, thus making a profit from their own and their children's shame. It is almost a universal practice for men and women to live together as husband and wife, and rear a family of children, without having been married. One thing which has greatly conduced to this condition of life in times gone by was the high price of the marriage fee. The peasantry could not afford to be married according to the rites of the Church, and as no other ceremony was legal, they were, in a measure, driven into this unlawful and sinful intercourse. This irregular mode of life is also encouraged by the matrimonial system practiced, which results in illy-advised matches, which, in a large number of instances, drives the parties to a separation, when one or both assume an illicit connection.

It is the custom for married men to support a wife and mistress at the same time, and but too frequently the wife also has her male friend. A gentleman of many years' residence in the country, and who has a thorough acquaintance with the people, assured me that such practices are indulged in by three-fourths of the married population. The marriage vow is held sacred by a very few, and the ceremony is more a matter of convenience than any thing else. The custom of keeping mistresses appears to be part of the social system, and the feelings of society are in no manner outraged by it, because the public opinion of the country sanctions it; and what seems to argue an exceedingly liberal code of morals is the fact that the standing of neither party is injured in the community in which they live, but they seem to maintain the same degree of respectability as though they did not thus violate the rules of propriety and decency. This mode of life is practiced openly and without shame. The parties keep up a regular domestic establishment, receive their friends, and appear together in public, as though their union was sanctioned by the holy rites of marriage, and blessed by the laws of God and man.

There are two or three causes for the almost universal looseness of morals among the native population, the principal of which is the entire absence of that necessary moral training which children receive in the States. In times gone by the Church conduced much to this state of things; a majority of the priests themselves lived in open prostitution, and the most abandoned characters retained their standing in the Church, if they were regular at the confessional, and paid the customary dues without fail. The organization of society is such that a large number are driven into this mode of life by sheer poverty. There are no employments to which indigent females can resort to make a respectable living, as in the States. All domestic labor is performed by Indian slaves, and women can find no occupation in housework for their own maintenance. Thus, when their parents die, and they are thrown upon their own resources for support, they have but the alternative of starving or adopting this degraded mode of life, which, not being considered in the least disreputable, neither driving them from society nor injuring their prospect of a subsequent marriage, is most generally embraced.

• • •

Another peculiar feature of New Mexico is the system of domestic servitude called peonism, that has existed, and still exists, in all the Spanish American colonies. It seems to have been an institution of the civil law, and in New Mexico is yet recognized by statute. The only practical difference between it and Negro slavery is, that the peones are not bought and sold in the market as chattels; but in other respects I believe the difference is in favor of the Negro. The average of intelligence among the peones is lower than that among the slaves of the southern States; they are not so well cared for, nor do they enjoy so many of the blessings and comforts of domestic life. In truth, peonism is but a more charming name for a species of slavery as abject and oppressive as any found upon the American continent.

The statutory law recognizing its existence in the Territory is dignified with the title of "Law regulating contracts between masters and servants." This is all well enough on paper, as far as it goes, but the statute is found to be all upon the side of the master. The wages paid is the nominal sum of about five dollars per month, out of which the peon has to support himself and family. The act provides, among other things, that if the servant does not wish to continue in the service of the master, he may leave him upon paying all that he owes him; this the poor peon is not able to do, and the consequence is that he and his family remain in servitude all their lives. Among the proprietors in the country, the master generally keeps a store, where the servant is obliged to purchase every article he wants, and thus it is an easy matter to keep him always in debt. The master is required to furnish the peon with goods at the market value, and may advance him two-thirds the amount of his monthly wages. But these provisions, made for the benefit of the peon, are in most instances disregarded, and he is obliged to pay an enormous price for every thing he buys, and is allowed to run in debt beyond the amount of his wages, in order to prevent him leaving his master. When parents are, as the statute terms it, "driven into a state of slavery," they have the right to bind their children out as peones, and with this beginning they become slaves for life. When a servant runs away from his master, the latter goes before a justice of the peace, or some other civil magistrate, and takes out a "warrant of the debt," which authorizes the arrest of the peon in any part of the Territory. One of the most objectionable features in the system is, that the master is not obliged to maintain the peon in sickness or old age. When he becomes too old to work any longer, like an old horse who is turned out to die, he can be cast adrift to provide for himself. These are the leading features of peonism, and, in spite of the new name it bears, the impartial reader will not be able to make any thing else out of it than slavery.

Juan Nepomuceno Cortina (1859)

Mexicans! When the State of Texas began to receive the new organization which its sovereignty required as an integrant part of the Union, flocks of vampires, in the guise of men, came and scattered themselves in the settlements, without any capital except the corrupt heart and the most perverse

---

SOURCE: *House Exec. Doc.*, No. 52, 36st Cong., 1st sess., 1860, pp. 80–82.

intentions. Some, brimful of laws, pledged to us their protection against the attacks of the rest; others assembled in shadowy councils, attempted and excited the robbery and burning of the houses of our relatives on the other side of the river Bravo; while others, to the abusing of our unlimited confidence, when we intrusted them with our titles [to land], which secured the future of our families, refused to return them under false and frivolous pretexts, all, in short, with a smile on their faces, giving the lie to that which their black entrails were meditating. Many of you have been robbed of your property, incarcerated, chased, murdered, and hunted like wild beasts, because your labor was fruitful, and because your industry excited the vile avarice which led them. A voice infernal said, from the bottom of their soul, "kill them; the greater will be our gain!" Ah! this does not finish the sketch of your situation. It would appear that justice had fled from this world, leaving you to the caprice of your oppressors, who become each day more furious towards you; that, through witnesses and false charges, although the grounds may be insufficient, you may be interred in the penitentiaries, if you are not previously deprived of life by some keeper who covers himself from responsibility by the pretence of your flight. There are to be found criminals covered with frightful crimes, but they appear to have impunity until opportunity furnish them a victim; to these monsters indulgence is shown, because they are not of our race, which is unworthy, as they say, to belong to the human species. But this race, which the Anglo-American, so ostentatious of its own qualities, tries so much to blacken, depreciate, and load with insults . . . does not fear . . . those subtle inquisitions which are so frequently made as to its manners, habits, and sentiments. . . .

· · ·

Mexicans! Is there no remedy for you? Inviolable laws, yet useless, serve, it is true, certain judges and hypocritical authorities, cemented in evil and injustice, to do whatever suits them, and to satisfy their vile avarice at the cost of your patience and suffering; rising in their frenzy, even to the taking of life, through the treacherous hands of their bailiffs. The wicked way in which many of you have been oftentimes involved in persecution, accompanied by circumstances making it the more bitter, is now well known, these crimes being hid from society under the shadow of a horrid night. . . .

Mexicans! My part is taken; the voice of revelation whispers to me that to me is entrusted the work of breaking the chains of your slavery, and that the Lord will enable me, with powerful arm, to fight against our enemies, in compliance with the requirements of that Sovereign Majesty [God], who, from this day forward, will hold us under His protection. On my part, I am ready to offer myself as a sacrifice for your happiness; and counting upon the means necessary for the discharge of my ministry, you may count upon my cooperation, should no cowardly attempt put an end to my days. This undertaking will be sustained on the following bases:

First. A society is organized in the State of Texas, which devotes itself sleeplessly until the work is crowned with success, to the improvement of the unhappy condition of those Mexicans resident therein; exterminating their tyrants, to which end those which compose it are ready to shed their blood and suffer the death of martyrs.

Second. As this society contains within itself the elements necessary to accomplish the great end of its labors, the veil of impenetrable secrecy covers "The Great Book" in which the articles of its constitution are written; while so delicate are the difficulties which must be overcome that no honorable man can have cause for alarm, if imperious exigencies require them to act without reserve.

Third. The Mexicans of Texas repose their lot under the good sentiments of the governor elect of the State, General Houston, and trust that upon his elevation to power he will begin with care to give us legal protection within the limits of his powers.

B. A Chinese-American Protest

• *Norman Assing* (1852)

The great gold rush of 1849 not only made San Francisco an "instant city" but also a city of striking ethnic diversity, rivalry, and violence. From a sleepy settlement of less than 3,000 inhabitants at the beginning of 1849, San Francisco had become by 1852 a wild, brawling port of some 35,000 souls, well over half of whom were foreign-born (see selection by Bayard Taylor, Unit Two, Part 1, B). The high incidence of crime and the ineffectiveness of law enforcement encouraged leading merchants to form a Vigilance Committee which attempted to rule by terror and by inflicting its own extralegal punishments. The Chinese merchants who dominated the various Chinese companies and associations also relied on extralegal justice in order to control the rank-and-file of indentured workers or "coolies." Though the Chinese still constituted only a tiny proportion of California's population, they aroused intense prejudice from Anglo-American and European settlers. In an attempt to exploit this racism for political gain, Governor John Bigler proposed in 1852 that the legislature restrict Chinese immigration.

The following selection is from Norman Assing's public letter to Governor Bigler protesting such a discriminatory and unconstitutional measure. Little is known about Assing. He refers to himself as a Christian and as a naturalized citizen of Charleston, South Carolina. He had arrived in San Francisco before 1850 and soon became a prominent merchant, the owner of the Macao and Woosung Restaurant, and an iron-fisted boss who, in Gunther Barth's words, ruled his community with "shrewdness, belligerency, and ruthlessness. . . ." On the occasion of "the first reported Chinese New Year celebration in the United States, on February 1, 1851, Assing 'gave a grand feast at his private home in San Francisco, with a number of policemen' and 'many ladies' among his guests."[1] He also led Chinese processions at public ceremonies commemorating the funeral of President Zachary Taylor and the admission of California as a state. Given the absence in California of Chinese gentry or mandarin officials, merchants like Assing appropriated all the traditional functions of leadership, combining, in Barth's words, "the prestige of mandarins, the wealth of gentry, the authority of family heads, the status of scholars, and the power of creditors. . . ."[2] But Assing met his match in the popular Miss Atoy, the empress of Chinese prostitutes, who went to court in order to block his extortionist attempts to rake off a percentage of her girls' earnings. And he apparently met his downfall when he extended his techniques of summary justice to non-Chinese offenders.

Assing's letter to Governor Bigler is a striking illustration of ethnic accommodation to the values and prejudices of American antebellum culture. As the self-appointed spokesman for Chinese California, Assing skillfully plays on the Americans' professed worship of industry, their prejudices against Indians and Negroes, and their habitual reference to the Declaration of Independence and the war with Great Britain. It was precisely this ability to address Anglo-Americans in the "language" of their culture that made men like Assing representatives of their own communities. For a time, their power over such communities could be virtually unlimited if they could pose, like Assing, as republicans and lovers of free institutions, and also resist the temptation of extending their power to the outside world. After the Civil War, as California lost the free-for-all fluidity of a frontier outpost, it became more apparent that the "Americanization" of Chinese leaders concealed a defensive, semi-autonomous structure of power and cultural solidarity—an "anti-culture" that seemed, like the Indian tribes, to defy fundamental standards of assimilation and individualism. By 1877, white hoodlums in San Francisco were setting fire to Chinese laundries, houses, and shops, and by 1882, Congress finally fulfilled Governor Bigler's wish of 1852 by suspending all Chinese immigration and even forbidding the naturalization of the Chinese already present in the country.

Norman Assing (1852)

To His Excellency Gov. Bigler

Sir:—I am a Chinaman, a republican, and a lover of free institutions; am much attached to the principles of the Government of the United States, and therefore take the liberty of addressing you as the chief of the government

---

[1] Gunther Barth, *Bitter Strength: A History of the Chinese in the United States, 1850–1870* (Cambridge, Mass.: Harvard University Press, 1964), p. 31.
[2] Barth, *Bitter Strength*, p. 31.
SOURCE: *Daily Alta California* (May 5, 1852).

of this state. Your official position gives you a great opportunity of good or evil. Your opinions through a message to a legislative body have weight, and perhaps none more so with the people, for the effect of your late message has been thus far to prejudice the public mind against my people, to enable those who wait the opportunity to hunt them down, and rob them of the rewards of their toil. You may not have meant that this should be the case, but you can see what will be the result of your propositions.

I am not much acquainted with your logic, that by excluding population from this state you enhance its wealth. I always have considered that population was wealth; particularly a population of producers, of men who by the labor of their hands or intellect, enrich the warehouses or the granaries of the country with the products of nature and art. You are deeply convinced you say "that to enhance the prosperity and to preserve the tranquility of this state, Asiatic immigration must be checked." This, your Excellency, is but one step towards a retrograde movement of the government, which, on reflection, you will discover; and which the citizens of this country ought never to tolerate. It was one of the principal causes of quarrel between you (when colonies) and England; when the latter pressed laws against emigration, you looked for immigration; it came, and immigration made *you what you are—* your nation what it is. It transferred you at once from childhood to manhood, and made you great and respectable throughout the nations of the earth. I am sure your Excellency cannot, if your would, prevent your being called, the descendant of an immigrant, for I am sure you do not boast of being a descendant of the red men. But your further logic is more reprehensible. You argue that this is a republic of a particular race—that the constitution of the United States admits of no asylum to any other than the pale face. This proposition is false in the extreme; and you know it. The declaration of your independence, and all the acts of your government, your people, and your history, are against you.

It is true, you have degraded the negro because of your holding him in involuntary servitude, and because for the sake of union in some of your states such was tolerated. And amongst this class you would endeavor to place us; and no doubt it would be pleasing to some would-be freemen to mark the brand of servitude upon us. But we would beg to remind you that when your nation was a wilderness, and the nation from whom you sprung *barbarous*, we exercised most of the arts and virtues of civilized life; that we are possessed of a language and literature, and that men skilled in science and the arts are numerous amongst us; that the productions of our manufactories, our sail and work-shops, form no small share of the commerce of the world; and that for centuries colleges, schools, charitable institutions, asylums and hospitals, have been as common as in your own land. That our people cannot be reproved for their idleness, and that your historians have given them due credit for the variety and richness of their works of art, and for their simplicity of manners, and particularly their industry. And we beg to remark, that so far as the history of our race in California goes, it stamps with the test of truth the fact that we are not the degraded race you would make us. We came amongst you as mechanics or traders, and following every honorable business of life. You do not find us pursuing occupations of a degrading character, except you consider labor degrading, which I am sure you do not; and if our countrymen save the proceeds of their industry from the tavern and the gambling house, to spend it in the purchase of farms or town lots or on their families, surely you will admit that even these are virtues. You say "you desire to see no change in the generous policy of this Government as far as regards Europeans." It is out of your power to say, however, in what way or to whom the doctrines of the Constitution shall apply. You have no more right to propose a measure for checking immigration, than you have to assume the right of sending a message to the Legislature on the subject. As far as regards the color and complexion of our race, we are perfectly aware that our population have been a little more tanned than yours.

Your Excellency will discover, however, that we are as much allied to the *African* race or the red man as you are yourself, and that as far as the aristocracy of *skin* is concerned, ours might compare with many of the European races; nor do we consider that your Excellency, as a Democrat, will make us believe that the framers of your declaration of rights ever suggested the propriety of establishing an aristocracy of *skin*.

C. The Five Points: The Response to Outsiders Inside

- *The Old Brewery* (1854)
- *McDowall's Journal* (1834)

Cultural polarities could be dramatized in the unequal confrontations between Indians and European immigrants, Asians and Westerners, or Hispanic and Anglo-Americans. They could also be compressed, even without ethnic or racial dimensions, within a few blocks of a major city like New York. The connecting link, in this instance, was poverty and deprivation.

On the surface, there was little in common between the Chicanos of the southwestern border, the Chinese of San Francisco, and the contemporary white denizens of New York's Five Points—a notorious ghetto centered at the intersection of five streets in lower Manhattan. But despite obvious differences, these Americans were all defined as outsiders. By the rules of the game, they were all barred from genuine access to the contests over wealth and power portrayed in Unit Two. They were also all perceived as deviating in threatening ways from the familial and sexual norms described in Unit One. The most shocking symbol of such deviation was prostitution —a vice repeatedly associated with the Mexicans and Chinese, and a word instantly evoked by the very mention of Five Points. For all three groups, sexual license also suggested miscegenation (at Five Points, the mixture of whites and blacks), and the exploitation and degradation of young women.

But above all, for middle-class whites these outsiders became exhibits of cultural antithesis—of what America should not be. The inhabitants of Five Points, like the Indians, Mexicans, Chinese, and even Utah Mormons, became the subject matter for sensational exposés which constituted a new genre of "travel literature." It was rare traveler, indeed, who failed to make the almost obligatory pilgrimage to Five Points and, once there, to gaze on a kind of Barnum museum of pimps, prostitutes, drunkards, and ragamuffins. Typically, the spectator's response moved through three stages: first, a voyeuristic shock and "thrill of horror," a phrase used by the prostitutes' self-appointed missionary, John R. McDowall; second, a compassionate desire to retrieve the fallen and downtrodden by setting up missions and houses of refuge for their rehabilitation; third, a fear that this concentration of sin, crime, and suffering could not be contained within a geographical "point" but would spread outward like a contagious disease. As McDowall warns in the second selection below, no one could be sure whether a trusted household maid carried on a secret, nighttime career in the vicinity of Five Points, or whether the "drawers and trunks" of one's children contained products from the same anti-culture, "books and pictures vile enough to make even licentiousness blush to look at them. One would think the devil had turned editor, and converted hell itself into a printing office."

We begin, in the first selection, with a concise description of the contrast between Five Points and the fashionable elegance of nearby Broadway. Less lurid than the lengthy descriptions in earlier popular literature, this account of 1854 was written by members of the Ladies Home Missionary Society of the Methodist Episcopal Church. By then, several religious and reform groups had established missions, day schools, homes for the friendless, and houses of industry in the Five Points area. Such reformers had come to realize that religious exhortation was of little use unless reinforced by education, vocational training, and jobs. But these carefully supervised asylums of Protestant morality and industry had little effect on the economic system which made the very subsistence of tens of thousands of New York women depend on intermittent work, mostly in the needletrades, for a small fraction of the wages paid for the lowliest male labor.

In the second selection, we backtrack to the first "discovery" of Five Points prostitution—or rather to its first sensational exposé—by John R. McDowall (b. 1801). A Princeton divinity student, McDowall was sent to Five Points in 1830 to distribute religious pamphlets for the American Tract Society. As he and his volunteer assistants began to uncover the sordid realities of prostitution, they formed a New York Magdalen Society and launched a monthly journal to publicize the sins of America's greatest metropolis. McDowall's first annual report, of 1834, infuriated the "respectable" citizens of New York. McDowall not only received obscene and threatening letters, but his journal was finally condemned by a grand jury as "an obscene and demoralizing publication." Despite these efforts at suppression, McDowall's campaign stimulated an antiprostitution crusade led by the New York Female Reform Society, which attracted massive support from the women of New England and Upstate New York.

The Old Brewery (1854)

A stranger, taking his position in Broadway, near the City Hospital, would find himself at one of the central points of the wealth, the fashion, and the commerce of the largest and most influential city of the Union. The Hospital, of massive stone, surrounded by fine trees and spacious grassplots, which present a beautiful oasis amid the desert of brick and sand that encompasses its outer railing, tells loudly that active benevolence has here its sphere, and Christian charity its appropriate work. Elegant stores, crowded with merchandise of the most costly description; carts bending beneath the pressure of valuable loads; handsome carriages, containing fair occupants, whose rich attire bespeaks an utter disregard of the value of money . . . everything betokens progress, wealth, and happiness. . . .

One minute's walk from that Broadway-point of wealth, commerce, and enjoyment, will place him in another world of vision, thought, and feeling. Passing down Anthony-street but two squares, a scene will be presented, forming so entire a contrast to that he has just left, that imagination would never have pictured, nor can language in its utmost strength successfully portray it. Standing at the lower end of Anthony-street, a large area, covering about an acre, will open before him. Into this, five streets, viz., Little-Water, Cross, Anthony, Orange, and Mulberry, enter, as rivers emptying themselves into a bay. In the center of this area is a small triangular space, known as "Paradise-square," surrounded by a wooden paling generally disfigured by old garments hung upon it to dry. Opposite this little park stands, or rather stood, the "Old Brewery," so famed in song and story. Miserable-looking buildings, liquor-stores innumerable, neglected children by scores, playing in rags and dirt, squalid-looking women, brutal men with black eyes and disfigured faces, proclaiming drunken brawls and fearful violence, complete the general picture. . . .

The "Five Points!" What does that name import? It is the synonym for ignorance the most entire, for misery the most abject, for crime of the darkest dye, for degradation so deep that human nature cannot sink below it. We hear it, and visions of sorrow—of irremediable misery—flit before our mental vision. Infancy and childhood, without a mother's care of a father's protection: born in sin, nurtured in crime; the young mind sullied in its first bloom, the young heart crushed before its tiny call for affection has met one answer-

SOURCE: *The Old Brewery, and the New Mission House at the Five Points* . . . By *Ladies of the Mission* (New York: Stringer and Townsend, 1854), pp. 31–35.

ing response. Girlhood is there; not ingenuous, blushing, confiding youth, but reckless, hardened, shameless effrontery, from which the spectator turns away to weep. Woman is there; but she has forgotten how to blush, and she creates oblivion of her innocent childhood's home, and of the home of riper years, with its associations of fond parental love and paternal sympathies, by the incessant use of ardent spirits. Men are there—whose only occupation is thieving, and sensuality in every form, of every grade, and who know of no restraint, except the fear of the strong police, who hover continually about these precincts. And boys are there by scores, so fearfully mature in all that is vicious and degrading, that soon, O how soon, they will be fit only for the prison and the gallows.

McDowall's Journal (1834)

The extent of prostitution in this city, as shown by facts already developed during our labors, and the alarming increase of the unhappy victims of seduction among us, of which we have attained the most demonstrative evidence, so far exceed all our own previous calculations, that we are prepared to anticipate skepticism and incredulity in others. Indeed, enough is in our possession to cause a thrill of horror to be felt by every virtuous man and woman in the community, such as was never produced by any exposé of vice which has ever met the public eye. Did not prudence and delicacy forbid the disgusting detail of what has been brought to our knowledge thus early in the history of this Society, every parent would tremble for the safety of his sons as well as his daughters. . . .

First, then, we would present the fact, that we have satisfactorily ascertained that the number of females in this city, who abandon themselves to prostitution, is not less than TEN THOUSAND!! The data on which this estimate is founded, are, first, the opinion of the Alderman, whose experience and observation for several years past, as Commissioner at Bellevue, enabled him to judge very accurately, and from whom we learned in the commencement of our labors, what we then thought improbable, that there were *"ten thousand harlots in this city."* But although we then judged that the number was overrated, we are driven to the painful admission, that his estimate was just, from our own observation in the partial census we have attempted.

We have the names, street, and number, of the houses of ill-fame in this city, notoriously inhabited by abandoned women; and also the houses of assignation where daily and nightly the pollution of girls and women of all ages and color, married and single, is habitually committed. Many of these sinks of iniquity are in respectable neighborhoods, disguised under the mask of boarding houses, dress makers, milliners, stores, and shops of various kinds.

SOURCE: *McDowall's Journal*, II (May, 1834), pp. 34, 37, 67, 70–71.

Some of them are large and elegant houses, provided with costly furniture, and have brass and silver plates on the doors, on which are engraved the real or fictitious names of the occupants.

These haunts of iniquity have been discovered partly by the aid of the police officers, partly by the girls and women who have been rescued from pollution by the Asylum, and partly by the vigilance of persons, male and female, employed by the Society. By these means we have arrived at very many of the secrets of these nests of abomination, the number of lewd women who reside or resort to each, the arts and intrigues by which the victims of seduction are procured, as well as the *names* of scores of the men and boys who are the seducers of the innocent, or the companions of the polluted. . . .

Besides these, we have the clearest evidence that there are hundreds of private harlots and kept misses, many of whom keep up a show of industry as domestics, seamstresses, nurses, etc., in the most respectable families, and throng the houses of assignation every night. Although we have no means of ascertaining the number of these, yet enough has been learned from the facts already developed to convince us that the aggregate of these is alarmingly great, perhaps little behind the proportion of the city of London, whose police reports assert on the authority of accurate researches, that the number of private prostitutes in that city, is fully equal to the number of public harlots.

. . .

We have ascertained from various sources, that each female of this class is visited, on the average, by *three* men or boys *daily*, and that each of these spend at least *fifty* cents for liquors, porter [ale], etc., besides the sum paid to the companions of their guilt, and the infamous myrmidons who procure and keep them. This will show that of the ten million times these women are visited, by men, for the purposes of prostitution in the course of a year, *five millions of dollars* are expended in addition to the items included in the above estimate.

From the reformed women in the several Asylums, it is ascertained that it is no uncommon thing for them to receive from ten to twenty dollars of a night, and frequently from Saturday night to Monday morning, they will receive fifteen to twenty-five men, and obtain, as their reward, from thirty to fifty dollars. These items will go far to sustain the justness of our former calculations, and are intended to afford some idea of the stupendous expense of this one single vice, the cause of so much pauperism and crime; filling our almshouses, hospitals, prisons, and penitentiaries, and destroying our race.

But what is all this waste of wealth compared with the ruin of the generation of young men, and the destruction of female purity? It is insignificant when compared to the overthrow of the peace of families, the premature dissolution of broken-hearted parents, the wretchedness and disgrace of community. But all this is as the dust in the balance, when weighed beside the loss of hundreds of thousands of immortal souls. All else is worse than worthless, when viewed in the light of the eternal world, for "her house is the way to death, and her path lays hold on hell."

In a former part of this report, we have hinted at the cruelty with which very many of these guilty and unfortunate girls are treated, by those in whose houses they are kept in a state worse than Algerine slavery. In many of the houses, some broken down rake is kept by the women who board the girls, in the double capacity of pimp and bully, or house dog. When any benevolent person visits the house for the purpose of persuading the females to leave their sinful courses, this vagabond interferes, and either compels the visiter to leave the house, or forcibly conveys the girls into another apartment. If a girl shows a desire to reform, drugs are given her in her drink, to stupify her senses, and she is often cruelly beaten by this monster in the form of a man. . . .

Another fact, as sustained by abundant proof in our possession, and one in which every class of the community is interested, is, that there are hundreds, if not thousands, of female domestics in this city, who serve in respectable families, who visit the houses of assignation at convient intervals, sometimes nightly, and by returning in tolerable season, escape detection by a lie in their mouths, and mingle with the daughters in the families where they live, passing for virtuous women. One of these, who has forsaken her evil ways, states, that she met one man every Tuesday night, and another every Friday night, for months together, without missing a single night, and without ever incurring suspicion.

• • •

Parents in the country, by sending their daughters to a city, to learn a trade, or to engage in domestic labor, expose their children to ten thousand snares, about which they, and the better part of the city population, know but little. Thousands of females, instead of being educated to make good housewives, are put out to learn trades, already overstocked with hands. Consequently, great numbers of these females are unable, by the avails of their industry, to support themselves. Hence, in an evil hour, they listen to the charmer's voice, yield to his embrace, and die in infamy.

• • •

It ought to be known that the community, especially our great cities, are inundated with a flood of books and pictures vile enough to make even licentiousness blush to look at them. One would think the devil had turned editor, and converted hell itself into a printing office. Those who have never seen them, can form no conception of their lust-exciting character.

But why mention and expose the fact? Because the venders of these books and pictures, of which there is an endless variety, are scattering them in every village and township throughout the country; and we feel bound in the sight of God, as faithful watchmen, to shout *danger!* . . .

In regard to these books and pictures, the ingenuity and art of man have been exhausted in devising the most lust-exciting representations and illustrations of pleasure that it is possible to invent; and pleasure too that it is impossible to purchase, except by the flagrant transgression of God's laws, and by the most direful consequences both to body and soul.

It is needless to add that these pictures and books are a mortal pestilence, from whose contaminating influence few sections of the country are free. We have evidence, facts, names, books, pictures, etc. To fathers and mothers we say, search the drawers and trunks of your children. Beware of the common pedlars who visit your abodes. Beware of dashing dandy-youth. Beware of print and fancy goods stores.

4

The Nonfreedom of "Free Blacks"

A. "Getting Rid of Them"

• *Thomas Jefferson* (1824)

For most white Americans, the prominent visibility of free blacks in non-servile roles reinforced the noxious reputation of New York's Five Points. Yet the blacks were not like white urbanites who had "fallen" into sin and degradation. Nor could they be likened to Asians who immigrated voluntarily and preserved an exotic culture within the self-contained recesses of a Chinatown. Free blacks were clearly not noble savages or crafty warriors who aroused terror by raiding frontier settlements. Among outsiders, their situation was unique and so disturbing that insiders tended to evade the topic in polite conversation. In contrast to the Indians, the Afro-Americans had been dispossessed and uprooted long ago from a distant continent. It was not their land but their labor, as slaves, that white Americans had coveted. By 1820, white Americans owned over 1.5 million black slaves. Since white Americans tended to think of slavery as the prescribed status for blacks, they looked upon the quarter-million free blacks, only ninety-nine thousand of whom lived in the North, as the unwanted debris of an unfortunate and undesirable institution. Far more assimilated and Christianized than the Indians, but treated with far more contempt, the free blacks epitomized more than any other group the fate of powerlessness in a republic that pretended to despise corporate power.

Racial prejudice was rampant throughout antebellum America, for the most part unashamed and thus devoid of modern hypocrisy. Blacks—or "niggers" to most white Americans—were publicly humiliated, ridiculed, and caricatured. Even before 1820, Congress had specifically limited naturalization to white resident aliens and had barred blacks from such public honors as militia duty and carrying the mail. Although no consistent rules governed citizenship and suffrage, blacks had a right to vote only in Massachusetts, Vermont, New Hampshire, Maine, and New York, and in the latter state only in accordance with discriminatory property-holding qualifications. Most states prohibited Negroes from marrying whites, from testifying against whites in court, and even from moving into the state in search of home or employment. In general, the historical processes of "democratization," immigration, and territorial expansion deepened the racism of the so-called free states. In states like Pennsylvania, the extension of the vote to all adult males specifically excluded black males. New states like Oregon prohibited blacks from owning real estate, from making legal contracts, and from instituting law suits. In California, in the 1850s, blacks were wholly vulnerable to assault or even murder since a black witness could not give admissible testimony in court.

Meanwhile, European immigrants quickly learned that Negro-baiting was the common denominator for communal acceptance and white American identity. Even by the 1850s, urban immigrants had succeeded in displacing blacks from the few skilled trades and services that blacks had traditionally occupied. The pioneering labor unions, struggling against heavy obstacles for sheer survival, viewed blacks as threatening enemies—since black workers were hardly in a position to turn down momentary employment as strike-breakers. During the antebellum era, most free Negroes in the North were shut out from any employment above the level of servants, seamen, and day laborers. Barred from hotels and restaurants, segregated in inferior schools, consigned like livestock to stinking pens on steamboats and trains, blacks were also crowded into "nigger pews" in white churches and "nigger districts" in white towns. The latter ghettos, or "little Africas" as they were often called, were repeatedly raided and burned to the ground by mobs of white vandals. As Alexis de Tocqueville concluded from his observations of 1831, well before the worst anti-black riots of that decade:

> If ever America undergoes great revolutions, they will be brought about by the presence of the black race on the soil of the United States; that is to say, they will owe their origin, not to the equality, but to the inequality of condition.
>
> • • •
>
> When the Negro dies, his bones are cast aside, and the distinction of conditions prevail even in the equality of death. Thus the Negro is free, but he can share neither the rights, nor the plea-

sures, nor the labor, nor the afflictions, nor the tomb of him whose equal he has been declared to be; and he cannot meet him upon fair terms in life or in death.[1]

This is the great "American Dilemma," a term given poignant meaning in 1944 by the Swedish social scientist Gunnar Myrdal, but a dilemma no less familiar to Thomas Jefferson, the apostle of American democracy. Jefferson's views on race and slavery have always been controversial; the issues are too complex to summarize here. It is sufficient to note that he was one of the largest slaveholders in his native Virginia and always depended for his livelihood on the labor of slaves; that he sincerely believed that slavery violated the fundamental principles of a republican society and should thus be abolished; and that he believed, with equal sincerity, that blacks were in some ways inferior to whites and that the two races could never coexist in the same society on a level of political and social equality.

In fact, Jefferson's vast correspondence and writings contain surprisingly few references to either blacks or black slavery. His *Notes on Virginia* (1784) vaguely suggests a plan for gradual emancipation and deportation, and also advances pseudo-scientific "suspicions" of Negro inferiority. But Jefferson waited until he was almost eighty-one, when he was revered as the Sage of Monticello and the patriarch of the Republic, to outline a detailed plan for "getting rid of them." In a letter of February 4, 1824, Jefferson carefully revealed his long-hidden thoughts to Jared Sparks, an influential New Englander and future president of Harvard, a southern-oriented religious liberal who had recently promoted the cause of "African colonization" in the *North American Review.* In 1816, a group of ministers and prominent political leaders had formed an American Colonization Society for the purpose of resettling America's free blacks in west Africa—as it turned out, in the colony of Liberia. They hoped at one stroke to rid America of an unwanted population while encouraging the Christianization and civilization of the "Dark Continent." It was this supposedly benevolent movement, supported by such figures as Madison, Monroe, Henry Clay, John Marshall, and William Crawford, to which Jefferson responded in his letter to Jared Sparks.

In our selection from this letter Jefferson first applauds the missionary aims of African colonization but then argues that it is wholly impracticable to think of such colonization as a means of removing the black race from America. In his own plan, Jefferson is not particularly concerned with the ultimate geographic destination of blacks (his mention of "St. Domingo" and "their Chief" refers to an offer that had recently been made by the president of Haiti, Jean Pierre Boyer). Nor is he troubled by the thought of separating black children from their parents and "putting them to indus-

---

[1] Alexis de Tocqueville, *Democracy in America*, Henry Reeve text, revised by Francis Bowen, corrected and edited by Phillips Bradley (New York: Vintage Books, 1955), Vol. I, p. 374; Vol. II, p. 270.

trious occupations, until a proper age for deportation." Jefferson *is* concerned with expense and with avoiding any "violation of private right" to property. He proposes selling land taken from the Indians and using the proceeds to pay the cost of transporting "the whole annual increase" of black chilren to some distant asylum or reservation, leaving "the old stock" to "die off in the ordinary course of nature." Behind these calculations and projections is the dream of an all-white America.

Thomas Jefferson (1824)

In the disposition of these unfortunate people, there are two rational objects to be distinctly kept in view. First. The establishment of a colony on the coast of Africa, which may introduce among the aborigines the arts of cultivated life, and the blessings of civilization and science. By doing this, we may make to them some retribution for the long course of injuries we have been committing on their population. . . .

The second object, and the most interesting to us, as coming home to our physical and moral characters, to our happiness and safety, is to provide an asylum to which we can, by degrees, send the whole of that population from among us, and establish them under our patronage and protection, as a separate, free and independent people, in some country and climate friendly to human life and happiness. That any place on the coast of Africa should answer the latter purpose, I have ever deemed entirely impossible. And without repeating the other arguments which have been urged by others, I will appeal to figures only, which admit no controversy. I shall speak in round numbers, not absolutely accurate, yet not so wide from truth as to vary the result materially. There are in the United States a million and a half of people of color in slavery. To send off the whole of these at once, nobody conceives to be practicable for us, or expedient for them. Let us take twenty-five years for its accomplishment within which time they will be doubled. Their estimated value as property, in the first place (for actual property has been lawfully vested in that form, and who can lawfully take it from the possessors?), at an average of two hundred dollars each, young and old, would amount to six hundred millions of dollars, which must be paid or lost by somebody. To this, add the cost of their transportation by land and sea to Mesurado [Liberia], a year's provision of food and clothing, implements of husbandry and of their trades, which will amount to three hundred millions more, making thirty-six millions of dollars a year for twenty-five years, with insurance of peace all that time, and it is impossible to look at the question a second time. I am aware that at the end of about sixteen years, a gradual detraction from

SOURCE: *The Writings of Thomas Jefferson* (Washington, D.C.: Thomas Jefferson Memorial Association, 1904), Vol. XVI, pp. 8–13.

this sum will commence, from the gradual diminution of breeders, and go on during the remaining nine years. Calculate this deduction, and it is still impossible to look at the enterprise a second time. I do not say this to induce an inference that the getting rid of them is forever impossible. For that is neither my opinion nor my hope. But only that it cannot be done in this way. There is, I think, a way in which it can be done; that is, by emancipating the afterborn, leaving them, on due compensation, with their mothers, until their services are worth their maintenance, and then putting them to industrious occupations, until a proper age for deportation. This was the result of my reflections on the subject five and forty years ago, and I have never yet been able to conceive any other practicable plan. It was sketched in the Notes on Viriginia [1784], under the fourteenth query. The estimated value of the new-born infants is so low (say twelve dollars and fifty cents), that it would probably be yielded by the owner gratis, and would thus reduce the six hundred millions of dollars, the first head of expense, to thirty-seven millions and a half; leaving only the expenses of nourishment while with the mother, and of transportation. And from what fund are these expenses to be furnished? Why not from that of the lands which have been ceded by the very states now needing this relief? And ceded on no consideration, for the most part, but that of the general good of the whole. These cessions already constitute one-fourth of the States of the Union. It may be said that these lands have been sold; are now the property of the citizens composing those states; and the money long ago received and expended. But an equivalent of lands in the territories since acquired [the Louisiana Purchase and Florida], may be appropriated to that object, or so much, at least, as may be sufficient; and the object, although more important to the slave states, is highly so to the others also, if they were serious in their arguments on the Missouri question. The slave states, too, if more interested, would also contribute more by their gratuitous liberation, thus taking on themselves alone the first and heaviest item of expense.

In the plan sketched in the Notes on Virginia, no particular place of asylum was specified; because it was thought possible, that in the revolutionary state of America, then commenced, events might open to us some within practicable distance. This has now happened. St. Domingo has become independent, and with a population of that color only; and if the public papers are to be credited, their Chief offers to pay their passage, to receive them as free citizens, and to provide them employment. This leaves, then, for the general confederacy, no expense but of nurture with the mother a few years, and would call, of course, for a very moderate appropriation of the vacant lands. Suppose the whole annual increase to be of sixty thousand effective births, fifty vessels, of four hundred tons burden each, constantly employed in that short run, would carry off the increase of every year, and the old stock would die off in the ordinary course of nature, lessening from the commencement until its final disapperance. In this way no violation of private right is proposed. Voluntary surrenders would probably come in as fast as the means to be provided for their care would be competent to it. Looking at my own State only, and I presume not to speak for the others, I verily believe that this surrender of property would not amount to more, annually, than half our present direct taxes, to be continued fully about twenty or twenty-five years, and then gradually diminishing for as many more until their final extinction; and even this half tax would not be paid in cash, but by the delivery of an object which they have never yet known or counted as part of their property; and those not possessing the object will be called on for nothing. I do not go into all the details of the burdens and benefits of this operation. And who could estimate its blessed effects? I leave this to those who will live to see their accomplishment, and to enjoy a beatitude forbidden to my age. But I leave it with this admonition, to rise and be doing. A million and a half are within their control; but six millions, (which a majority of those now living will see them attain,) and one million of these fighting men, will say, "we will not go."

I am aware that this subject involves some constitutional scruples. But a liberal construction, justified by the object, may go far, and an amendment of the Constitution, the whole length necessary. The separation of infants from their mothers, too, would produce some scruples of humanity. But this would be straining at a gnat, and swallowing a camel.

B. "We See, In Effect, Two Nations—One White and Another Black"

• *William Chambers (1854)*

If Jefferson at age eighty strikes us as shockingly brutal and insensitive, his concerns are at least put in a wider perspective by the brutal realities described by reasonably objective and fair-minded European travelers. No foreign observer summed up the plight of free blacks and the central issues of America's racial dilemma more succinctly than William Chambers (1800–1883), a gifted Scottish bookseller, publisher, and promoter of public knowledge and enlightenment. It was precisely thirty years after Jefferson's letter to Sparks that Chambers published his impressions of a visit, entitled *Things As They Are in America*; and with respect to race, Chambers' concerns were precisely those of Jefferson: the existential status of free blacks in the North; the geometric increase in the population of slaves, which had doubled every twenty-five years; and the bearing of these two facts on the fate of America's unprecedented experiment with democracy, an experiment which might well determine, in both Chambers' and Jefferson's views, the fate of the world.

Chambers, it should be stressed, did not share Jefferson's prejudice toward blacks. A truly self-made man, Chambers had accumulated his wealth by shrewdly catering to the growing British market for low-priced, high-quality "useful information," a project that culminated in the immensely popular ten-volume *Chambers's Encyclopaedia*. Anyone really familiar with Jefferson's biography is tempted to conclude that America's third President would have eagerly changed places with Chambers, whose career so closely matched Jefferson's inherent tastes, and who escaped the misfortune of having been born in a slaveholding society. Be that as it may, Chambers expresses a respect and fascination, typical of European liberals, for Jefferson's Declaration of Independence. It is that standard of idealism and mission against which he measures America's shortcomings.

William Chambers (1854)

A question constantly arises, in looking at the political fabric of the United States: "Will it last—does it not contain within itself the germs of dissolution?" In offering a few observations in reply, it will be necessary to touch upon what is admitted to be the most unpleasant social feature of this remarkable country.

When the American colonists renounced their allegiance to George III, and assumed an attitude of independence, it was confidently predicted that their nationality, unsupported by monarchical and aristocratic institutions, could not possibly endure beyond the first outburst of enthusiasm. The experience of eighty years has failed to realize these prognostications; and it may be said that the principle of self-reliance has never been so successfully tested as in the history of the United States. Left to themselves, and favored by breadth of territory, the progress of the American people has for many years been no ordinary phenomenon.

At the Declaration of Independence, the number of states was thirteen, with a population of about 3,000,000—a wonderfully small number, to have defied and beat off the British monarchy. In 1800, when several new states had been added to the confederacy, the population was little more than 6,000,000. During the next fifty years, there was a great advance. In 1850, when the number of states had increased to thirty-one, along with several territories not organized into states, the population had reached 23,191,918. At this point, it was 3,000,000 ahead of that of the island of Great Britain; and as at this ratio it doubles every twenty-five years, we might infer that towards the conclusion of the present century, the United States will possess a population of not far from 100,000,000.

Such are the prospects entertained by the Americans themselves, with perhaps too slight a regard for a seriously disturbing element in their calculations. The present population, as above stated, are not all white—exercising the

---

SOURCE: William Chambers, *Things As They Are in America* (London: William and Robert Chambers, 1857), pp. 354–63.

privileges and animated with the sentiments of freemen. In the number, are comprehended 3,204,345 slaves, and 433,643 persons of color nominally free, but occupying a socially degraded position. The presence of such an immense mass of population, alien in blood and aspect, in the midst of the commonwealth, is an awkward, and, I fear, a dangerous, feature in the condition of the United States, which cannot be passed over in any impartial estimate of the prospective growth and dignity of the country.

At the Revolution, there was, comparatively speaking, but a handful of negro slaves in the several states, introduced from Africa during the colonial administration; and it was probably expected by Washington and others, that in time the number would diminish, and that, finally, there would be none. The reverse, however, has been the result. In the New England States, New York, New Jersey, and Pennsylvania, slavery, wherever it existed, has been legally abolished, leaving generally a residuum of free negroes; but in the other older states, slavery is still in force, besides being ingrafted in various new states, which have been acquired by conquest or purchase; so that, as an institution with large vested interests, it is stronger and more lifelike than ever. According to the census of 1850, it existed in fifteen out of thirty-one states; in one of them, however—New Jersey—it was in the form of an expiring apprenticeship.

. . .

I repeat, it is difficult to understand what is the genuine public feeling on this entangled question; for with all the demonstrations in favor of freedom in the north, there does not appear in that quarter to be any practical relaxation of the usages which condemn persons of African descent to an inferior social status. There seems, in short, to be a fixed notion throughout the whole of the states, whether slave or free, that the colored is by nature a subordinate race; and that, in no circumstances, can it be considered equal to the white. Apart from commercial views, this opinion lies at the root of American slavery; and the question would need to be argued less on political and philanthropic than on physiological grounds. . . .

It may have been merely a coincidence, but it is remarkable, that all with whom I conversed in the States on the distinctions of race, tended to the opinion that the negro was in many respects an inferior being, and his existence in American an anomaly. The want of mental energy and forethought, the love of finery and of trifling amusements, distaste of persevering industry and bodily labor, as well as overpowering animal propensities, were urged as general characteristics of the colored population; and it was alleged, that when consigned to their own resources, they do not successfully compete with the white Anglo-Americans; the fact being added, that in slavery they increase at the same ratio as the whites, while in freedom, and affected with the vices of society, the ratio of increase falls short by one-third. From all that I have since heard of the free people of color, I believe these remarks to have been largely a result of prejudice. I had, indeed, reason to be surprised, when speaking a kind word for at least a very unfortunate, if not brilliant race, that the people of the northern states, though repudiating slavery, did not think more favorably of the negro character than those further south. Throughout the greater part of New England States, likewise in the states of New York, Pennsylvania, etc., there is a rigorous seperation of the white and black races. In every city, there are white and black schools, and white and black churches. No dark-skinned child is suffered to attend a school for white children. . . .

As an explanation of these distinctions, I was informed that white would not sit beside colored children; and further, that colored children, after a certain age, did not correspondingly advance in learning—their intellect being apparently incapable of being cultured beyond a particular point. From whatever cause, it was clear that a reluctance to associate with persons of negro descent was universally inculcated in infancy, and strengthened with age. The result is a singular social phenomenon. We see, in effect, two nations—one white and another black—growing up together within the same political circle, but never mingling on a principle of equality.

• • •

All the efforts, in my opinion, which may be made with a view to influencing the south in favor of emancipation, are valueless so long as there exists a determined resolution throughout northern society to consider the colored race, in all its varieties of shade, as beneath the dignity of human nature, and in no respect worthy to be associated with, countenanced, honored, or so much as spoken to on terms of equality. Excluded, by such inflexible and carefully nourished prejudices, from entertaining the slightest prospect of ever rising beyond the humblest position; condemned to infamy from birth; not tolerated in the railway-cars which are devoted to the use of the whites; turned away from any of the ordinary hotels, no matter what be the character, means, or style of dress of the applicants; in a word, treated from first to last as *Parias* —how can we expect that objects of so much contumely are to improve in their faculties or feelings, or to possess, in any degree, the virtue of self-respect? The wonder, indeed, is, that they conduct themselves so well as they do, or that they assume anything like the dress or manners of civilized persons.

Glad to have had an opportunity of calling attention to many cheering and commendable features in the social system of the Americans, I consider it not less my duty to say, that in their general conduct towards the colored race, a wrong is done which cannot be alluded to except in terms of sorrow and reproach. I cannot think without shame of the pious and polished New Englanders adding to their offenses on this score, the guilt of hypocrisy. Affecting to weep over the sufferings of imaginary dark-skinned heroes and heroines; denouncing in well-studied platform oratory the horrid sin of reducing human beings to the abject condition of chattels; bitterly scornful of southern planters for hard-hearted selfishness and depravity; fanatical on the subject of southern aggression; frantic at the spectacle of fugitive slaves seized and carried back to their owners—these very persons are daily surrounded by liberated slaves, or their educated descendants, yet shrink from them as if the touch were pollution, and look as if they would expire at the bare idea of inviting one of them to their house or table. Until this is materially changed, the people of the North place themselves in a false position, and do damage to the cause they espouse. If they think that negroes are MEN, let them give the world an evidence of their sincerity, by moving the reversal of all those social and political arrangements which now in the free states exclude persons of color, not only from the common courtesies of life, but from the privileges and honors of citizens. To speak plainly, why should not the free northern states take a first step toward consistency, by beginning to educate the colored along with white children in the ordinary public schools? And if to this movement, they were to add that of electing a colored person to Congress, the world would be satisfied that their principles are something more than a fanciful abstraction. As things remain, the owners of slaves are furnished with the excuse that emancipation, besides being attended with no practical benefit, would be an act of cruelty to their dependents; for that the education given to free persons of color only aggravates the severity of their condition—makes them feel a sense of degradation, from which, as slaves in a state of ignorance, they are happily exempted. Looking at the hapless position of the colored population in the northern states—nominally free, yet loathed and shunned as little better than the meanest of the lower animals—the great question, it appears to me, is, What is to be done with the slaves if they are set at liberty? Are they to grow up a powerful alien people within the commonwealth, dangerous in their numbers, but doubly dangerous in their consciousness of wrongs, and in the passions which may incite them to acts of vengeance?

Serious as is this question, there is one, perhaps, still more serious. Are the slaves to go on increasing in a geometrical ratio—6,000,000 in 1875, 12,000,000 in 1900; and so on through an infinitude of years? Sympathizing so far with the Americans in the dilemma in which circumstances have placed them, I cannot say they have acted with discretion in seeing this portentous evil widen in its sphere, and swell to such vast dimensions, as at length to go beyond the reach of all ordinary measures of correction. Nay, at this moment the canker is extending its ramifications over the boundless territories of the West; and it is to be feared that, in a few years hence, the northern and middle free states will be but a speck in comparison with the slave region. This is a thing which concerns not the Americans alone, but the whole civilized world. The highest intellects of Europe are looking with breathless wonder at the spread of the Anglo-Saxon race over the vast continent of America. They talk of the not distant time when there will be a nation counted by hundreds of millions, speaking the English tongue, and governed by the institutes of freemen. But always, in the midst of their glowing anticipations, there arises an odious spectre—human slavery—reminding them that it was this which blighted the old civilizations, Egypt, Greece, Rome—and why not America!

C. "Though We Are Not Slaves, We Are Not Free"

- *Protest from Black Philadelphia* (1817)
- *Abraham Camp* (1818)
- *A Black Memorial to the Citizens of Baltimore* (1826)

Proposals for Negro colonization went back to the Revolutionary era. They were sometimes supported by genuine abolitionists, such as Samuel Hopkins, and fiercely opposed by defenders of black slavery, such as William L. Smith. The pioneer who was the first, in 1815, to actually transport a group of free blacks to west Africa (Sierra Leone) was Paul Cuffe (1759–1817). A native of Massachusetts, Cuffe was the son of a former black slave and an Indian woman. A Quaker sea captain and shipowner, he contributed thousands of dollars of his own money to the experiment of African colonization and gave invaluable assistance and information to the founders of the American Colonization Society.

Despite the initial ambiguity of motives and purpose, there could be no doubt that the Colonization Society appealed mainly to white racist prejudices and assumptions. It directly challenged the long struggle of free blacks to prove, in the face of every legal, economic, and social obstacle, that they were responsible citizens and patriotic Americans. Hence, the leaders of Philadelphia's black community held a large protest meeting in January 1817, only a few weeks after the Colonization Society was officially formed. James Forten (1766–1842), a prosperous black sail-maker, had aided Paul Cuffe in the past and had praised the cause of African colonization. But Forten was suspicious of the pretended philanthropy of a white organization that included numerous slaveholders and powerful political leaders, and that used the white-imposed degradation of free blacks as justification for their mass "expatriation." Forten himself was a proud American. During the Revolution, he had served in the navy and had been captured by the British. In 1814 he, together with Absalom Jones and the Reverend Richard Allen, had mobilized 2,500 black volunteers to defend Philadelphia against a threatened British invasion. It was in this same spirit that Forten, Jones, and Allen mobilized black resistance to African colonization.

The first selection presents resolutions adopted by the January meeting in Allen's Bethel Church (Allen was the pastor, founder, and bishop of the African Methodist Episcopal Church). Though Colonization Society officials tried their best to win over Philadelphia's black leaders, Forten called another protest meeting in August that drew over three thousand black supporters. In New York and Boston, colonization was denounced not only by black men but by black women like Maria W. Stewart, who defied the taboo against women speaking in public.

Nevertheless, blacks were not unanimous in their rejection of African colonization. John B. Russworm, a graduate of Bowdoin College in 1826 (one of the first American blacks to receive a college degree) and the founder of *Freedom's Journal* (the first Negro newspaper in New York) emigrated to Liberia in 1829. The files of the American Colonization Society contain eloquent letters from far more obscure blacks who had become disillusioned by America's barriers to true freedom and opportunity. The second selection is from one of such letters, written in 1818 by Abraham Camp, who was then living in the Illinois Territory.

For free blacks who lived in a slave state like Maryland, the prospects seemed even grimmer. In the third selection, we turn to a memorial drafted in 1826 by some free blacks of Baltimore and addressed to the white community. While the memorial plays on the prejudices and rationalizations of whites—endorsing the conceit, for example, that the British bear the blame for slavery—it also contains an only thinly-veiled indictment of America's experiment in freedom. By accepting expatriation the memorial makes clear that the *true* Americans will be the blacks who brave the difficulties and dangers of founding a new nation in Africa where rights and privileges are not denied on the basis of race. This Baltimore memorial quickly provoked an angry remonstrance from the blacks of Philadelphia.

Protest from Black Philadelphia (1817)

At a numerous meeting of the people of color, convened at Bethel church, to take into consideration the propriety of remonstrating against the contemplated measure, that is to exile us from the land of our nativity; James Forten was called to the chair, and Russell Parrott appointed secretary. The intent of the meeting having been stated by the chairman, the following resolutions were adopted, without one dissenting voice.

Whereas our ancestors (not of choice) were the first successful cultivators of the wilds of America, we their descendants feel ourselves entitled to participate in the blessings of her luxuriant soil, which their blood and sweat manured; and that any measure or system of measures, having a tendency to banish us from her bosom, would not only be cruel, but in direct violation of those principles, which have been the boast of this republic.

Resolved, That we view with deep abhorrence the unmerited stigma attempted to be cast upon the reputation of the free people of color, by the promoters of this measure, "that they are a dangerous and useless part of the community," when in the state of disfranchisement in which they live, in the hour of danger they ceased to remember their wrongs, and rallied around the standard of their country.

Resolved, That we never will separate ourselves voluntarily from the slave population in this country; they are our brethren by the ties of consanguinity,

---

SOURCE: William Lloyd Garrison, *Thoughts on African Colonization*, Part II (Boston: Garrison and Knapp, 1832), p. 9.

of suffering, and of wrong; and we feel that there is more virtue in suffering privations with them, than fancied advantages for a season.

Resolved, That without arts, without science, without a proper knowledge of government, to cast into the savage wilds of Africa the free people of color, seems to us the circuitous route through which they must return to perpetual bondage.

Resolved, That having the strongest confidence in the justice of God, and philanthropy of the free states, we cheerfully submit our destinies to the guidance of Him who suffers not a sparrow to fall, without his special providence.

Abraham Camp (1818)

I am a free man of color, have a family and a large connection of free people of color residing on the Wabash, who are all willing to leave America whenever the way shall be opened. We love this country and its liberties, if we could share an equal right in them; but our freedom is partial, and we have no hope that it ever will be otherwise here; therefore we had rather be gone, though we should suffer hunger and nakedness for years. Your honor may be assured that nothing shall be lacking on our part in complying with whatever provision shall be made by the United States, whether it be to go to Africa or some other place; we shall hold ourselves in readiness, praying that God (who made man free in the beginning, and who by his kind providence has broken the yoke from every white American) would inspire the heart of every true son of liberty with zeal and pity, to open the door of freedom for us also.

A Black Memorial to the Citizens of Baltimore (1826)

We have hitherto beheld, in silence, but with the intensest interest, the efforts of the wise and philanthropic in our behalf. If it became us to be silent, it became us also to feel the liveliest anxiety and gratitude. The time has now arrived, as we believe, in which your work and our happiness may be promoted by the expression of our opinions. We have therefore assembled for that purpose, from every quarter of the city and every denomination, to offer you this respectful address, with all the weight and influence which our number, character and cause can lend it.

We reside among you, and yet are strangers; natives, and yet not citizens; surrounded by the freest people and most republican institutions in the world, and yet enjoying none of the immunities of freedom. This singularity in our

SOURCE: Carter Godwin Woodson, ed., *The Mind of the Negro as Reflected in Letters Written During the Crisis, 1800–1860* (New York: Russell & Russell, 1969), pp. 2–3.

SOURCE: "Memorial of the Free People of Colour to the Citizens of Baltimore," *The African Repository and Colonial Journal*, Vol. II (December, 1826), pp. 295–97.

condition has not failed to strike us as well as you: but we know it is irremediable here. Our difference of color, the servitude of many and most of our brethren, and the prejudices which those circumstances have naturally occasioned, will not allow us to hope, even if we could desire, to mingle with you one day, in the benefits of citizenship. As long as we remain among you, we must (and shall) be content to be a distinct caste, exposed to the indignities and dangers, physical and moral, to which our situation makes us liable. All that we may expect, is to merit by our peaceable and orderly behavior, your consideration and the protection of your laws.

It is not to be imputed to you that we are here. Your ancestors remonstrated against the introduction of the first of our race, who were brought amongst you; and it was the mother country that insisted on their admission, that her colonies and she might profit, as she thought, by their compulsory labor. But the gift was a curse to them, without being an advantage to herself. The colonies, grown to womanhood, burst from her dominion; and if they have an angry recollection of their union and rupture, it must be at the sight of the baneful institution which she has entailed upon them.

How much you regret its existence among you, is shown by the severe laws you have enacted against the slave-trade, and by your employment of a naval force for its suppression. You have gone still further. Not content with checking the increase of the already too growing evil, you have deliberated how you might best exterminate the evil itself. This delicate and important subject has produced a great variety of opinions: but we find, even in that diversity, a consolatory proof of the interest with which you regard the subject, and of your readiness to adopt that scheme which may appear to be the best. . . .

But if *you* have every reason to wish for our removal, how much greater are *our* inducements to remove! Though we are not slaves, we are not free. We do not, and never shall participate in the enviable privileges which we continually witness. Beyond a mere subsistence, and the impulse of religion, there is nothing to arouse us to the exercise of our faculties, or excite us to the attainment of eminence. Though under the shield of your laws we are partially protected, not totally oppressed; nevertheless, our situation will and must inevitably have the effect of crushing, not developing the capacities that God has given us. We are, besides, of opinion, that our absence will accelerate the liberation of such of our brethren as are in bondage, by the permission of Providence. When such of us as wish, and may be able, shall have gone before to open and lead the way, a channel will be left, through which may be poured such as hereafter receive their freedom from the kindness or interests of their masters, or by public opinion and legislative enactment, and who are willing to join those who have preceded them. As a white population comes in to fill our void, the situation of our brethren will be nearer to liberty; for their value must decrease and disappear before the superior advantages of free labor, with which their's can hold no competition.

Of the many schemes that have been proposed, we most approve of that of *African Colonization*. If we were able and at liberty to go whithesoever we would, the greater number, willing to leave this community, would prefer LIBERIA, on the coast of Africa. Others, no doubt, would turn them towards some other region: the world is wide.

. . .

We foresee that difficulties and dangers await those who emigrate, such as every infant establishment must encounter and endure; such as your fathers suffered when first they landed on this now happy shore. They will have to contend, we know, with the want of many things which they enjoyed here; and they leave a populous and polished society for a land where they must long continue to experience the solitude and ruggedness of an early settlement. But "Ethiopia shall lift her hands unto God." Africa is the only country to which they can go and enjoy those privileges for which they leave their firesides among you. The work has begun, and it is continuing. A foothold has been obtained, and the principal obstacles are overcome. The foundations of a nation have been laid, of which they are to be the fathers.

D. A Revolutionary Appeal

• *David Walker* (1829)

The most radical, brilliant, and uncompromising assessment of the condition of blacks in antebellum America has seldom received the respect it deserves. David Walker's *Appeal to the Colored Citizens of the World* is one of the classic documents in the history of American civilization. Like other such documents, it should ideally be read without abridgement, but selected extracts can at least draw attention to the pamphlet's central message.

We know far too little about David Walker (1785–1830). Born in North Carolina, he was legally free because his mother was a free black even though his father was a slave. There is no reason to doubt Walker's claim that he had traveled widely throughout the slave and free states. Self-educated, he clearly devoured every journal and newspaper he could lay his hands on, brooding over the recorded speeches of Henry Clay, John Randolph, and other luminaries whom he quotes at length, with biting commentary, in parts of the *Appeal* not included here. He also studied and pondered many volumes of history, searching for the crucial truth hidden between the lines of European and American self-congratulation. Walker's pamphlet is often studded with defensive displays of self-taught learning—with references to Sparta, Lycurgus, Tiberius, Mahomed II, Charles V, Las Casas, and black Haiti. In 1829, one must remember, no aspiring white politician could give a speech without referring to classical Greece and Rome, and to America's analogous perils and future grandeur.

In the mid-1820s, Walker settled down in Boston. On Brattle Street, near the bustling wharves, he opened a second-hand clothing shop geared to the maritime trade, which included black seamen. It is worth noting that Paul Cuffe, James Forten, and other black leaders were often connected in some way with maritime trades that provided blacks with unusual mobility and opportunities for interstate communication. In his *Appeal*, Walker pays lengthy tribute to Bishop Richard Allen of Philadelphia, whose abolitionist African Methodist Episcopal Church had inspired black resistance and solidarity throughout the country. These interstate networks are still obscure, but when South Carolina officials uncovered Denmark Vesey's slave conspiracy of 1822, which aimed at seizing Charleston and massacring the white population, they discovered among the plotters both black and white seamen as well as black Methodists who had been in touch with Bishop Allen's church. It seems probable that black merchant seamen transported the multiple copies of Walker's *Appeal* that suddenly turned up in such southern ports as Savannah and New Orleans. For Southerners, the probability was at least sufficient to bring new and stringent restrictions on even the temporary entry of foreign black seamen, as well as threatening remonstrances to the mayor of Boston.

Apart from these speculations, we know that Walker was a prominent member of the Massachusetts General Colored Association, which was dedicated to the abolition of slavery and to improving the condition of free blacks. He delivered lectures and served as the local agent for the New York Negro weeklies, *Freedom's Journal* and *Rights of All*. He subscribed to a fund to buy freedom for a young black poet in North Carolina, and from his own earnings paid the printing costs for three editions of his fervent *Appeal* to his brethren. Throughout this pamphlet, Walker refers to his enemies, white and black, and to the likelihood of his martyrdom. In 1830, he was found dead near the doorway of his shop. According to black tradition, Walker had been poisoned; there was no official verdict on the cause of his death.

Three themes of Walker's *Appeal* deserve particular attention. First, unlike most northern free blacks, he not only had first-hand knowledge of southern slavery but could place the institution within a coherent historical framework. Walker was well aware, for example, that whites had long enslaved fellow whites and that slavery based on racial distinctions was a relatively recent by-product of New World colonization. Instead of limiting his attention to the deplorable condition of free blacks in the North, Walker identified slavery as "the *source* from which most of our miseries proceed." It is this wider vision of racial oppression that gives force to Walker's scathing attack on the American Colonization Society (not included here), and that enables him to address his *Appeal* to the "colored citizens of the world."

The second point is that Walker's pamphlet is fueled with religious fervor and saturated with volatile Biblical imagery. In earlier selections, we have seen the Bible invoked to support the existing social order. Like other rebels in different ages, Walker finds a different message in God's revealed Word. He portrays Christ as an avenging "God of justice and of armies." He pictures white Americans as a heaven-defying people who, if they could, would "*dethrone* Jehovah and seat themselves upon his throne." And he warns whites that "your DESTRUCTION *is at hand,* and will be speedily consummated unless you REPENT."

Finally, Walker is almost obsessed with America's Revolutionary heritage and with its flawed symbol, Thomas Jefferson. He exhorts his black brethren to read and study Jefferson's *Notes on Virginia,* and especially spotlights the famous passage: "I advance it therefore as a suspicion only, that the blacks, whether originally a distinct race, or made distinct by time and circumstances, are inferior to the whites in the endowments both of body and mind." It is this passage that Walker satirizes when, after reviewing the history of whites as both pagans and Christians, he advances his own "suspicion of them, whether they are *as good by nature* as we are or not." But Walker's master stroke against Jefferson comes at the very end of his pamphlet when he quotes Jefferson's Declaration of Independence and then shouts out, "See your Declaration, Americans! ! ! Do you understand your own language?" After repeating the words about the right and duty of throwing off a despotic government, Walker candidly asks white Americans whether their sufferings under Britain were "one hundredth part as cruel and tyrannical as you have rendered ours under you?"

David Walker (1829)

My dearly beloved Brethren and Fellow Citizens:

Having traveled over a considerable portion of these United States, and having, in the course of my travels taken the most accurate observations of things as they exist—the result of my observations has warranted the full and unshakened conviction, that we, (colored people of these United States) are the most degraded, wretched, and abject set of beings that ever lived since the world began, and I pray God, that none like us ever may live again until time shall be no more.

• • •

I am fully aware, in making this appeal to my much afflicted and suffering brethren, that I shall not only be assailed by those whose greatest earthly desires are, to keep us in abject ignorance and wretchedness, and who are of the firm conviction that heaven has designed us and our children to be slaves and *beasts of burden* to them and their children.—I say, I do not only expect

SOURCE: David Walker, *Appeal, in Four Articles; Togther with a Preamble to the Colored Citizens of the World. . . .* (Boston: September 28, 1829; 3rd ed., Boston: D. Walker, 1830), pp. 11–12, 18–19, 24–29.

to be held up to the public as an ignorant, impudent and restless disturber of the public peace, by such avaricious creatures, as well as a mover of insubordination—and perhaps put in prison or to death, for giving a superficial exposition of our miseries, and exposing tyrants. But I am persuaded, that many of my brethren, particularly those who are ignorantly in league with slave-holders or tyrants, who acquire their daily bread by the blood and sweat of their more ignorant brethren—and not a few of those too, who are too ignorant to see an inch beyond their noses, will rise up and call me cursed.

. . .

Now I appeal to heaven and to earth, and particularly to the American people themselves who cease not to declare that our condition is not *hard*, and that we are comparatively satisfied to rest in wretchedness and misery, under them and their children. Not, indeed, to show me a colored President, a Governor, a Legislator, a Senator, a Mayor, or an Attorney at the Bar.— But to show me a man of color, who holds the low office of a Constable, or one who sits in a Juror Box, even on a case of one of his wretched brethren, throughout this great Republic ! !—But let us pass Joseph the son of Israel a little further in review, as he existed with that heathen nation.

" And Pharaoh called Joseph's name Zaphnath-paaneah; and he gave him " to wife Asenath the daughter of Potipherah priest of On. And Joseph " went out over all the land of Egypt."

Compare the above, with the American institutions. Do they not institute laws to prohibit us from marrying among the whites? I would wish, candidly, however, before the Lord, to be understood, that I would not give *a pinch of snuff* to be married to any white person I ever saw in all the days of my life. And I do say it, that the black man, or man of color, who will leave his own color (provided he can get one who is good for any thing) and marry a white woman, to be a double slave to her just because she is *white*, ought to be treated by her as he surely will be, viz; as a NIGGER ! ! ! It is not indeed what I care about intermarriages with the whites, which induced me to pass this subject in review; for the Lord knows, that there is a day coming when they will be glad enough to get into the company of the blacks, notwithstanding, we are, in this generation, leveled by them almost on a level with the brute creation; and some of us they treat even worse than they do the brutes that perish. I only made this extract to show how much lower we are held, and how much more cruel we are treated by the Americans, than were the children of Jacob, by the Egyptians.

. . .

I have been for years troubling the pages of historians to find out what our fathers have done to the *white Christians of America*, to merit such condign punishment as they have inflicted on them, and do continue to inflict on us their children. But I must aver, that my researches have hitherto been to no effect. I have therefore come to the immovable conclusion, that they (Americans) have, and do continue to punish us for nothing else, but for enriching them and their country. For I cannot conceive of any thing else. Nor will I ever believe otherwise until the Lord shall convince me.

The world knows, that slavery as it existed among the Romans, (which was the primary cause of their destruction) was, comparatively speaking, no more than a *cypher*, when compared with ours under the Americans. Indeed, I should not have noticed the Roman slaves, had not the very learned and penetrating Mr. Jefferson said, "When a master was murdered, all his slaves " in the same house or within hearing, were condemned to death."—Here let me ask Mr. Jefferson, (but he is gone to answer at the bar of God, for the deeds done in his body while living,) I therefore ask the whole American people, had I not rather die, or be put to death than to be a slave to any tyrant, who takes not only my own, but my wife and children's lives by the inches? Yea, would I meet death with avidity far! far!! in preference to such *servile submission* to the murderous hands of tyrants. Mr. Jefferson's very severe remarks on us have been so extensively argued upon by men whose attainments in literature, I shall never be able to reach, that I would not have meddled with it, were it not to solicit each of my brethren, who has the spirit of a man, to buy a copy of Mr. Jefferson's "Notes on Virginia," and put it in the hand of his son. For let no one of us suppose that the refutations which have been written by our white friends are enough—they are *whites*— we are *blacks*. We, and the world wish to see the charges of Mr. Jefferson refuted by the blacks *themselves*, according to their chance: for we must remember that what the whites have written respecting this subject, is other men's labors and did not emanate from the blacks. I know well, that there are some talents and learning among the colored people of this country, which we have not a chance to develop, in consequence of oppression; but our oppression ought not to hinder us from acquiring all we can.—For we will have a chance to develop them by and by. God will not suffer us, always to be oppressed. Our sufferings will come to an *end*, in spite of all the Americans this side of *eternity*. Then we will want all the learning and talents among ourselves, and perhaps more, to govern ourselves.—"Every dog must have its day," the American's is coming to an end.

But let us review Mr. Jefferson's remarks respecting us some further. Comparing our miserable fathers, with the learned philosophers of Greece, he says: "Yet notwithstanding these and other discouaging circumstances among " the Romans, their slaves were often their rarest artists. They excelled too " in science, insomuch as to be usually employed as tutors to their master's " children; Epictetus, Terence and Phaedrus, were slaves,—but they were of " the race of whites. It is not their *condition* then, but *nature*, which has produced the distinction." See this, my brethren! ! Do you believe that this assertion is swallowed by millions of the whites? Do you know that Mr. Jefferson was one of as great characters as ever lived among the whites? See his writings for the world, and public labors for the United States of America. Do you believe that the assertions of such a man, will pass away into oblivion unobserved by this people and the world? If you do you are much mistaken —See how the American people treat us—have we souls in our bodies? Are we men who have any spirits at all? I know that there are many *swell-bellied* fellows among us whose greatest object is to fill their stomachs. Such I do not mean—I am after those who know and feel, that we are Men as well as other people; to them, I say, that unless we try to refute Mr. Jefferson's arguments respecting us, we will only establish them.

But the slaves among the Romans. Every body who has read history, knows, that as soon as a slave among the Romans obtained his freedom, he could rise to the greatest eminence in the State, and there was no law instituted to hinder a slave from buying his freedom. Have not the Americans instituted laws to hinder us from obtaining our freedom? Do any deny this charge? Read the laws of Virginia, North Carolina, etc. Further: have not the Americans instituted laws to prohibit a man of color from obtaining and holding any office whatever, under the government of the United States of America? Now, Mr. Jefferson tells us that our condition is not so hard, as the slaves were under the Romans ! ! ! !

· · ·

The whites have always been an unjust, jealous unmerciful, avaricious and blood thirsty set of beings, always seeking after power and authority.—We view them all over the confederacy of Greece, where they were first known to be any thing, (in consequence of education) we see them there, cutting each other's throats—trying to subject each other to wretchedness and misery, to effect which they used all kinds of deceitful, unfair and unmerciful means. We view them next in Rome, where the spirit of tyranny and deceit raged still higher.—We view them in Gaul, Spain and in Britain—in fine, we view them all over Europe, together with what were scattered about in Asia and Africa, as heathens, and we see them acting more like devils than accountable men. But some may ask, did not the blacks of Africa, and the mulattoes of Asia, go on in the same ways as did the whites of Europe? I answer no—they never were half so avaricious, deceitful and unmerciful as the whites, according to their knowledge.

But we will leave the whites or Europeans as heathens and take a view of them as christians, in which capacity we see them as cruel, if not more so than ever. In fact, take them as a body, they are ten times more cruel, avaricious, and unmerciful than ever they were; for while they were heathens they were bad enough it is true, but it is positively a fact that there were not quite so audacious as to go and take vessel loads of men, women and children, and in cold blood and through devilishness, throw them into the sea, and murder them in all kind of ways. While they were heathens, they were too ignorant for such barbarity. But being christians, enlightened and sensible, they are completely prepared for such hellish cruelties. Now suppose God were to give them more sense, what would they do. If it were possible would they not *dethrone* Jehovah and seat themselves upon his throne? I therefore, in the name and fear of the Lord God of heaven and of earth, divested of prejudice either on the side of my color or that of the whites, advance my suspicion of them, whether they are *as good by nature* as we are or not. Their actions, since they were known as a people, have been the reverse, I do indeed suspect them, but this, as I before observed, is shut up with the Lord, we cannot exactly tell, it will be proved in succeeding generations.—The whites have had the essence of the gospel as it was preached by my master and his apostles —the Ethiopians have not, who are to have it in its meridian splendor—the Lord will give it to them to their satisfaction. I hope and pray my God, that they will make good use of it, that it may be well with them.

E. Organizing Free Blacks

• *First Annual Convention (1830)*

Three years before the organization (in Philadelphia) of the American Anti-Slavery Society, some forty black delegates from eight states assembled at Bishop Allen's Bethel Church. This was the first in a series of national Negro conventions that denounced slavery and the discriminatory "black laws" of northern states and considered various plans for "the speedy elevation of ourselves and brethren to the scale and standing of men." The following *Address* of the 1830 Convention takes off from the Declaration of Independence, respectfully disapproves of the American Colonization Society, but does endorse the idea of a refuge for American blacks in British Canada. In 1829, the city government of Cincinnati had decided to enforce Ohio's "black laws," informing the population of nearly three thousand free blacks that they would each have to post a $500 bond or leave the state. Encouraged by this official racism, a mob of several hundred whites attacked and pillaged Cincinnati's "Bucktown." Meanwhile, the Lieutenant-Governor of Upper Canada had given a favorable response to delegates from Cincinnati's black community, and the Canada Land Company had offered to sell the blacks four thousand acres. The resulting colony of Wilberforce never flourished. Weakened from the start by a lack of funds, the colony's prospects were also damaged when the mayor of Cincinnati, alarmed by the threat of a mass exodus of cheap labor, succeeded in delaying the enforcement of the expulsion law.

First Annual Convention (1830)

As much anxiety has prevailed on account of the enactment of laws in several states of the Union, especially that of Ohio, abridging the liberties and privileges of the Free People of Color, and subjecting them to a series of privations and sufferings, by denying them a right of residence, unless they comply with certain requisitions not exacted of the Whites, a course altogether incompatible with the principles of civil and religious liberty.

SOURCE: *Minutes and Proceedings of the First Annual Convention of the People of Colour* (Philadelphia: 1831), pp. 9–10.

In consideration of which, a delegation was appointed from the states of Connecticut, New York, Pennsylvania, Delaware, and Maryland, to meet in Convention in Philadelphia, to consider the propriety of forming a settlement in the province of Upper Canada, in order to afford a place of refuge to those who may be obliged to leave their homes, as well as to others inclined to emigrate with the view of improving their condition.

The said Convention accordingly met in Bethel Church, city of Philadelphia, on the 20th of September, 1830; and having fully considered the peculiar situation of many of their brethren, and the advantages to be derived from the proposed settlement, adopted the following

ADDRESS
TO THE FREE PEOPLE OF COLOR
OF THESE UNITED STATES

Brethren,

Impressed with a firm and settled conviction, and more especially being taught by that inestimable and invaluable instrument, namely, the Declaration of Independence, that all men are born free and equal, and consequently are endowed with unalienable rights, among which are the enjoyments of life, liberty, and the pursuits of happiness.

Viewing these as incontrovertable facts, we have been led to the following conclusions; that our forlorn and deplorable situation earnestly and loudly demand of us to devise and pursue all legal means for the speedy elevation of ourselves and brethren to the scale and standing of men.

And in pursuit of this great object, various ways and means have been resorted to; among others, the African [American] Colonization Society is the most prominent. Not doubting the sincerity of many friends who are engaged in that cause; yet we beg leave to say, that it does not meet with our approbation. However great the debt which these United States may owe to injured Africa, and however unjustly her sons have been made to bleed, and her daughters to drink of the cup of affliction, still we who have been born and nurtured on this soil, we, whose habits, manners, and customs are the same in common with other Americans, can never consent to take our lives in our hands, and be the bearers of the redress offered by that Society to that much afflicted country.

Tell it not to barbarians, lest they refuse to be civilized, and eject our christian missionaries from among them, that in the nineteenth century of the christian era, laws have been enacted in some of the states of this great republic, to compel an unprotected and harmless portion of our brethren, to leave their homes and seek an asylum in foreign climes: and in taking a view of the unhappy situation of many of these, whom the oppressive laws alluded to, continually crowd into the Atlantic cities, dependent for their support upon their daily labor, and who often suffer for want of employment, we have had to lament that no means have yet been devised for their relief.

These considerations have led us to the conclusion, that the formation of a settlement in the British province of Upper Canada, would be a great advantage to the people of color. In accordance with these views, we pledge ourselves to aid each other by all honorable means, to plant and support one in that country, and therefore we earnestly and most feelingly appeal to our colored brethren, and to all philanthropists here and elsewhere, to assist in this benevolent and important work.

F. The Coercion of a Black Priest

• *Peter Williams (1834)*

> In July 1834, the nation's mounting Negrophobia erupted in a savage anti-abolition riot in New York City. Spurred on by leaders of the Colonization Society, which had suffered disastrous losses of income following abolitionist attacks, a mob sacked the house of Lewis Tappan, a founder and benefactor of the American Anti-Slavery Society. Rioters also gutted a dozen Negro homes and burned the home and church of the Reverend Peter Williams (1780–1840), the first black priest in the American Episcopal Church. Troops began to restore order under martial law only when the property of wealthy whites appeared to be endangered.
>
> What most inflamed the mob were the charges that abolitionists were promoting racial "amalgamation," and that Williams had presided over an interracial marriage. In fact, the farthest the white abolitionists had gone toward "mixing" the races was in inviting a choir from Williams' church to sing at the May anniversary celebration of the American Anti-Slavery Society—and in Lewis Tappan's words, "the choirs sat separately on the orchestra, the whites on one side and the colored on the other!" But in immediate response to the riot, Benjamin T. Onderdonk, Bishop of the Protestant Episcopal Church in New York, dashed off a note to Peter Williams expressing sympathy "for you and your people" and advising him to resign at once "your connection, in every department, with the Anti-Slavery Society, and to make public your resignation." Williams was one of the six blacks on the Society's board of managers. In response, Williams addressed the following open letter to the citizens of New York.

Peter Williams (1834)

It has always been painful to me to appear before the public. It is especially painful to me to appear before them in the columns of a newspaper, at a time of great excitement like the present; but when I received Holy orders,

SOURCE: Carter Godwin Woodson, *The Mind of the Negro, op. cit.*, pp. 630–33.

I promised "reverently to obey my Bishop, to follow with a glad mind his godly admonitions, and to submit myself to his godly judgment."

My Bishop, without giving his opinions on the subject of Abolition, has now advised me, in order that the Church under my care "may be found on the Christian side of meekness, order, and self-sacrifice to the community," to resign connection with the Anti-Slavery Society, and to make public my resignation. There has been no instance hitherto, in which I have not sought his advice in matters of importance to the Church, and endeavored to follow it when given; and I have no wish that the present should be an exception.

But in doing this, I hope I shall not be considered as thrusting myself too much upon public attention, by adverting to some facts in relation to myself and the subject of the present excitement, in the hope that when they are calmly considered, a generous public will not censure me for the course I have pursued.

My father was born in Beekman street in this city, and was never, in all his life, further from it than Albany; nor have I ever been absent from it longer than three months, when I went to Haiti for the benefit of my brethren who had migrated there from this country. In the revolutionary war, my father was a decided advocate for American Independence, and his life was repeatedly jeopardized in its cause. Permit me to relate one instance, which shows that neither the British sword, nor British gold, could make him a traitor to his country. He was living in the state of Jersey, and Parson Chapman, a champion of American liberty, of great influence throughout that part of the country, was sought after by the British troops. My father immediately mounted a horse and rode round among his parishioners, to notify them of his danger, and to call them to help in removing him and his goods to a place of safety. He then carried him to a private place, and as he was returning a British officer rode up to him, and demanded in the most peremptory manner, "where is Parson Chapman?" "I cannot tell," was the reply. On that he drew his sword, and raising it over his head, said, "Tell me where he is, or I will instantly cut you down." Again he replied, "I cannot tell." Finding threats useless, the officer put up his sword and drew out a purse of gold, saying, "If you will tell me where he is, I will give you this." The reply still was, "I cannot tell." The officer cursed him and rode off.

This attachment to the country of his birth was strengthened and confirmed by the circumstances that the very day on which the British evacuated this city, was the day on which he obtained his freedom by purchase through the help of some republican friends of the Methodist Church, who loaned him money for that purpose, and to the last year of his life he always spoke of that day as one which gave double joy to his heart, by freeing him from domestic bondage and his native city from foreign enemies.

The hearing him talk of these and similar matters, when I was a child, filled my soul with an ardent love for the American government, and made me feel, as I said in my first public discourse, that it was my greatest glory to be an American.

A lively and growing interest for the prosperity of my country pervaded my whole soul and led to the belief, notwithstanding the peculiarly unhappy condition of my brethren in the United States, that by striving to become intelligent, useful and virtuous members of the community, the time would come when they would all have abundant reason to rejoice in the glorious Declaration of American Independence. . . .

These were among the feelings that led me into the ministry, and induced me to sacrifice all my worldly prospects, and live upon the scanty pittance which a colored minister must expect to receive for his labors, and to endure the numerous severe trials peculiar to his situation.

My friends who assisted me in entering into the ministry, know that if the Church with which I am connected as a Pastor, could have been established without my becoming its minister, I should have been this day enjoying the sweets of private life, and there has not been a day since I have entered upon the duties of my office, that I would not have cheerfully retired to earn my living in some humbler occupation, could I have done so consistently with my sense of duty.

By the transaction of last Friday evening, my church is now closed, and I have been compelled to leave my people. Whether I shall be permitted to return to them again, I cannot say, but whether or not, I have the satisfaction of feeling that I have labored earnestly and sincerely for their temporal and spiritual benefit, and the promotion of the public good.

In regard to my opposition to the Colonization Society it has extended no farther than that Society has held out the idea, that a colored man, however he may strive to make himself intelligent, virtuous and useful, can never enjoy the privileges of a citizen of the United States, but must ever remain a degraded and oppressed being. I could not, and do not believe that the principles of the Declaration of Independence, and of the Gospel of Christ, have not power sufficient to raise him, at some future day, to that rank. I believe that such doctrines tend very much to discourage the efforts which are making for his improvement at home. But whenever any man of color, after having carefully considered the subject, has thought it best to emigrate to Africa, I have not opposed to him, but have felt it my duty to aid him, in all my power, on his way, and I have the satisfaction of being able to prove that the most prominent and most useful men in the Colony have been helped there by me.

. . .

When I found that strong prejudices were forming against me, because of my disapprobation of some of the Society's measures, and that my usefulness was thereby affected, I ceased to speak on the subject, except in the private circle of my friends, or when my opinions were asked privately by others; and in my short address to the Phenix Society, last spring, I carefully avoided the subject; and the only sentiment I uttered, referring to it, was this: "Who that witnesses an assembly like this, composed of persons of all colors, can doubt that people of all colors can live in the same country, without doing each other harm?"

It was my anxiety to promote the object of the Phenix Society, which is the improvement of the people of color in this city, in morals, literature, and the mechanic arts, that brought me to an acquaintance with the members of the Anti-Slavery Society. For several years, I had given considerable attention to the education of our people, and was much interested about our public schools.

I was anxious that some of our youth should have the opportunity of acquiring a liberal education, and felt that it was my duty to strive to rear up some well qualified colored ministers. I selected two lads of great promise, and made every possible effort to get them a collegiate education. But the colleges were all closed against them. Anti-Slavery men generously offered to aid us in establishing a Manual Labor College, or High School, for ourselves, and to aid us in all the objects of the Phenix Society. I joined with them in this work heartily, and wished them all success, as I still do in their endeavors, by all means sanctioned by law, humanity and religion, to obtain freedom for my brethren, and to elevate them to the enjoyment of equal rights with the other citizens of the community; but I insisted that while they were laboring to restore us to our rights, it was exclusively our duty to labor to qualify our people for the enjoyment of those rights.

G. The "Killing Influence" of Prejudice

• *Theodore S. Wright* (1837)

Peter Williams came to the painful conclusion that he could do more for his people by working within the Episcopal Church than by retaining official ties with white abolitionism. Theodore Sedgewick Wright (1797–1847), so far as we know, never faced a similar ultimatum. Wright, a Presbyterian minister, was the first black to receive a degree from Princeton Theological Seminary. He continued to preside over a Negro Presbyterian church in New York City while actively participating in the bi-racial causes of abolitionism, temperance, public education, and moral self-improvement. In the face of prevailing taboos against social fraternization, Wright had sufficient stature among white abolitionists to be asked to lead a prayer, as one of the officiating clergymen, at the wedding of two great abolitionist leaders, Theodore Weld and Angelina Grimké. A leader of New York's black community during the most tumultuous years of early protest, Wright became an outspoken champion of the Liberty Party and an active defender of fugitive slaves. On September 20, 1837, the New York Anti-Slavery Society adopted a resolution condemning "the prejudice, peculiar to our country, which subjects our colored brethren to a degrading distinction in our worship, assemblies and schools, which withholds from them that kind and courteous treatment to which as well as other citizens, they have a right, at public houses, on board steamboats, in stages, and in places of public concourse. . . ." To this indictment, which could be extended in detail but applied with equal justice a century later, Wright responded with the following eloquent statement.

Theodore S. Wright (1837)

It is true that in these United States and in this state, there are men, like myself, colored with the skin like my own, who are not subjected to the lash, who are not liable to have their wives and their infants torn from them; from whose hand the Bible is not taken. It is true that we may walk abroad; we may enjoy our domestic comforts, our families; retire to the closet; visit the sanctuary, and may be permitted to urge on our children and our neighbors in well doing. But sir, still we are slaves—everywhere we feel the chain galling us. It is by that prejudice which the resolution condemns, the spirit of slavery, the law which has been enacted here, by a corrupt public sentiment, through the influence of slavery which treats moral agents different from the rule of God, which treats them irrespective of their morals or intellectual cultivation. This spirit is withering all our hopes, and ofttimes causes the colored parent as he looks upon his child, to wish he had never been born. Often is the heart of the colored mother, as she presses her child to her bosom, filled with sorrow to think that, by reason of this prejudice, it is cut off from all hopes of usefulness in this land. Sir, this prejudice is wicked.

If the nation and church understood this matter, I would not speak a word about that killing influence that destroys the colored man's reputation. This influence cuts us off from everything; it follows us up from childhood to manhood; it excludes us from all stations of profit, usefulness and honor; takes away from us all motive for pressing forward in enterprises, useful and important to the world and to ourselves.

In the first place, it cuts us off from the advantages of the mechanic arts almost entirely. A colored man can hardly learn a trade, and if he does it is difficult for him to find any one who will employ him to work at that trade, in any part of the state. In most of our large cities there are associations of mechanics who legislate out of their society colored men. And in many cases where our young men have learned trades, they have had to come to low employments for want of encouragement in those trades.

SOURCE: Carter Godwin Woodson, *Negro Orators and Their Orations* (Washington, D. C.: Associated Publishers, 1925), p. 93.

H. A Militant Appeal to Slaves

• *Henry Highland Garnet (1843)*

Theodore S. Wright was a close friend and mentor of Henry Highland Garnet (1815–1882), the grandson of an African Mandingo leader and one of the eminent black abolitionists. Unlike Wright, Garnet had been born into slavery in Maryland and as a youth had escaped to the North. After graduating from a white academy in New Hampshire, in the face of mob protest, and continuing his education at an abolitionist-sponsored institute in Upstate New York, Garnet had followed Wright into the ministry. A spell-binding orator, he had won increasing respect among white abolitionists until at age twenty-seven he delivered the following appeal to America's three million slaves at a convention of free blacks in Buffalo.

By 1843, northern black leaders had reached a critical crossroads. Their white abolitionist friends had continually cautioned them to keep a low profile, to prove their Christian worth by outdoing the whites in moderation, sobriety, and forgiveness. Yet southern slavery continued to expand, and it was clearly only a matter of time before the United States annexed the slaveholding Republic of Texas. Southern writers had already seized upon statistics from the 1840 census which seemingly showed that the emancipation of northern blacks had resulted in astonishingly high rates of insanity, deafness, blindness, and other abnormalities. It was of little avail that the flagrant errors of the 1840 census were exposed by white statisticians and by James McCune Smith, a distinguished black physician and abolitionist, a friend of Garnet's who had received his scientific training in Glasgow and Paris. In 1844, America's secretary of state, John C. Calhoun, exploited the false statistics on the deterioration of free blacks in angry communications with Britain over the annexation of Texas.

It was this larger context, aggravated by fatal divisions among white abolitionists, that Garnet faced in 1843. His impassioned speech at Buffalo conveys a new sense of the unending *hopelessness* of the blacks' condition in the United States—a condition that would be perpetuated, unless there was militant resistance, to their children's children. In this respect, Garnet's view of the future is precisely the opposite of that of hopeful whites. Like David Walker, he exposes the hypocrisy of white rhetoric and rationalization. But also like Walker, he draws on the powerful inspiration of the Declaration of Independence and the American faith in self-improvement. Garnet later exclaimed to a white woman abolitionist who was troubled by his suggestions of violence, that at least "there is one black American who dares to speak boldly on the subject of universal liberty." Yet Garnet really equivocates on the expediency of violence. He presents a curious scenario of slaves refusing to work until properly compensated and daring their masters to strike the first blow. Garnet is perhaps most American in his appeal to a native tradition of black resistance. He later reprinted an edition of his 1843 speech coupled with a biographical sketch of David Walker and the text of Walker's *Appeal*. By 1848, Garnet had shifted his hopes to Liberia and later founded his own African Colonization Society.

Henry Highland Garnet (1843)

Your brethren of the north, east, and west have been accustomed to meet together in National Conventions, to sympathize with each other, and to weep over your unhappy condition. In these meetings we have addressed all classes of the free, but we have never until this time, sent a word of consolation and advice to you. We have been contented in sitting still and mourning over your sorrows, earnestly hoping that before this day, your sacred liberties would have been restored. But, we have hoped in vain. Years have rolled on, and tens of thousands have been borne on streams of blood, and tears, to the shores of eternity. While you have been oppressed, we have also been partakers with you; nor can we be free while you are enslaved. We therefore write to you as being bound with you.

Many of you are bound to us, not only by the ties of a common humanity, but we are connected by the more tender relations of parents, wives, husbands, children, brothers, and sisters, and friends. As such we most affectionately address you. . . .

Two hundred and twenty-seven years ago, the first of our injured race were brought to the shores of America. They came not with glad spirits to select their homes, in the New World. They came not with their own consent, to find an unmolested enjoyment of the blessings of this fruitful soil. . . . Neither did they come flying upon the wings of Liberty, to a land of freedom. But, they came with broken hearts, from their beloved native land, and were doomed to unrequited toil, and deep degradation. Nor did the evil of their bondage end at their emancipation by death. Succeeding generations inherited their chains, and millions have come from eternity into time, and have returned again to the world of spirits, cursed, and ruined by American Slavery.

. . .

The colonists threw the blame upon England. They said that the mother country entailed the evil upon them, and that they would rid themselves of it if they could. The world thought they were sincere, and the philanthropic pitied them. But time soon tested their sincerity. In a few years, the colonists grew strong and severed themselves from the British Government. Their Independence was declared, and they took their station among the sovereign powers of the earth. The declaration was a glorious document. Sages

---

SOURCE: Henry Highland Garnet, *An Address to the Slaves of the United States of America* (New York: J. H. Tobitt, 1848), pp. 90–96.

admired it, and the patriotic of every nation reverenced the Godlike sentiments which it contained. When the power of Government returned to their hands, did they emancipate the slaves? No; they rather added new links to our chains. Were they ignorant of the principles of Liberty? Certainly they were not. The sentiments of their revolutionary orators fell in burning eloquence upon their hearts, and with one voice they cried, LIBERTY OR DEATH. O, what a sentence was that! It ran from soul to soul like electric fire, and nerved the arm of thousands to fight in the holy cause of Freedom. Among the diversity of opinions that are entertained in regard to physical resistance, there are but a few found to gainsay that stern declaration. We are among those who do not.

SLAVERY! How much misery is comprehended in that single word. What mind is there that does not shrink from its direful effects? Unless the image of God is obliterated from the soul, all men cherish the love of Liberty. . . . In every man's mind the good seeds of liberty are planted, and he who brings his fellow down so low, as to make him contented with a condition of slavery, commits the highest crime against God and man. Brethren, your oppressors aim to do this. They endeavor to make you as much like brutes as possible. When they have blinded the eyes of your mind—when they have embittered the sweet waters of life—when they have shut out the light which shines from the word of God—then, and not till then has American slavery done its perfect work.

TO SUCH DEGRADATION IT IS SINFUL IN THE EXTREME FOR YOU TO MAKE VOLUNTARY SUBMISSION. The divine commandments, you are in duty bound to reverence, and obey. If you do not obey them you will surely meet with the displeasure of the Almighty. He requires you to love him supremely, and your neighbor as yourself—to keep the Sabbath day holy—to search the Scriptures —and bring up your children with respect for his laws, and to worship no other God but him. But slavery sets all these at naught, and hurls defiance in the face of Jehovah. The forlorn condition in which you are placed does not destroy your moral obligation to God. . . .

Your condition does not absolve you from your moral obligation. The diabolical injustice by which your liberties are cloven down, NEITHER GOD, NOR ANGELS, OR JUST MEN, COMMAND YOU TO SUFFER FOR A SINGLE MOMENT. THEREFORE IT IS YOUR SOLEMN AND IMPERATIVE DUTY TO USE EVERY MEANS, BOTH MORAL, INTELLECTUAL, AND PHYSICAL, THAT PROMISE SUCCESS. If a band of heathen men should attempt to enslave a race of Christians, and to place their children under the influence of some false religion, surely, heaven would frown upon the men who would not resist such aggression, even to death. If, on the other hand, a band of Christians should attempt to enslave a race of heathen men and to entail slavery upon them, and to keep them in heathenism in the midst of Christianity, the God of heaven would smile upon every effort which the injured might make to disenthral themselves.

Brethren, it is as wrong for your lordly oppressors to keep you in slavery, as it was for the man thief to steal our ancestors from the coast of Africa.

You should therefore now use the same manner of resistance, as would have been just in our ancestors, when the bloody foot prints of the first remorseless soul thief was placed upon the shores of our fatherland. The humblest peasant is as free in the sight of God, as the proudest monarch that ever swayed a sceptre. Liberty is a spirit sent out from God, and like its great Author, is no respector of persons.

Brethren, the time has come when you must act for yourselves. It is an old and true saying, that "if hereditary bondmen would be free, they must themselves strike the blow." You can plead your own cause, and do the work of emancipation better than any others. . . .

Look around you, and behold the bosoms of your loving wives, heaving with untold agonies! Hear the cries of your poor children! Remember the stripes your father bore. Think of the torture and disgrace of your noble mothers. . . . Think how many tears you have poured out upon the soil which you have cultivated with unrequited toil, and enriched with your blood; and then go to your lordly enslavers, and tell them plainly, that YOU ARE DETERMINED TO BE FREE. Appeal to their sense of justice, and tell them that they have no more right to oppress you, than you have to enslave them. Entreat them to remove the grievous burdens which they have imposed upon you, and to remunerate you for your labor. Promise them renewed diligence in the cultivation of the soil, if they will render to you an equivalent for your services. . . .

Do this, and for ever after cease to toil for the heartless tyrants, who give you no other reward but stripes and abuse. If they then commence the work of death, they, and not you, will be responsible for the consequences. You had far better all die—*die immediately*, than live slaves, and entail your wretchedness upon your posterity. If your would be free in this generation, here is your only hope. However much you and all of us may desire it, there is not much hope of Redemption without the shedding of blood. If you must bleed, let it all come at once—rather, *die freemen, than live to be slaves*. It is impossible, like the children of Israel, to make a grand Exodus from the land of bondage.

• • •

Fellow-men! patient sufferers! behold your dearest rights crushed to the earth! See your sons murdered, and your wives, mothers, and sisters, doomed to prostitution! In the name of the merciful God! and by all that life is worth, let it no longer be a debateable question, whether it is better to choose LIBERTY or DEATH!

In 1822, Denmark Veazie [Vesey], of South Carolina, formed a plan for the liberation of his fellow men. In the whole history of human efforts to overthrow slavery, a more complicated and tremendous plan was never formed. He was betrayed by the treachery of his own people, and died a martyr to freedom. . . .

The patriotic Nathaniel Turner followed Denmark Veazie. He was goaded to desperation by wrong and injustice. By Despotism, his name has been recorded on the list of infamy, but future generations will number him among the noble and brave.

Next arose the immortal Joseph Cinque, the hero of the Amistad. He was a native African, and by the help of God he emancipated a whole ship-load of his fellow men on the high seas. And he now sings of liberty on the sunny hills of Africa, and beneath his native palm trees, where he hears the lion roar, and feels himself as free as that king of the forest. Next arose Madison Washington, that bright star of freedom, and took his station in the constellation of freedom. He was a slave on board the brig Creole, of Richmond, bound to New Orleans, that great slave mart, with a hundred and four others. Nineteen struck for liberty or death. But one life was taken, and the whole were emancipated, and the vessel was carried into Nassau, New Providence. Noble men! Those who have fallen in freedom's conflict, their memories will be cherished by the true-hearted, and the God-fearing, in all future generations; those who are living, their names are surrounded by a halo of glory.

We do not advise you to attempt a revolution with the sword, because it would be INEXPEDIENT. Your numbers are too small, and moreover the rising spirit of the age, and the spirit of the gospel, are opposed to war and bloodshed. But from this moment cease to labor for tyrants who will not remunerate you. Let every slave throughout the land do this, and the days of slavery are numbered. You cannot be more oppressed than you have been—you cannot suffer greater cruelties than you have already. RATHER DIE FREEMEN, THAN LIVE TO BE SLAVES. Remember that you are THREE MILLIONS. . . .

Let your motto be RESISTANCE! RESISTANCE! RESISTANCE!—No oppressed people have ever secured their liberty without resistance. What kind of resistance you had better make, you must decide by the circumstances that surround you, and according to the suggestion of expediency. Brethren, adieu. Trust in the living God. Labor for the peace of the human race, and remember that you are three millions.

I. An Appeal for Black Skilled Labor

• *Frederick Douglass (1853)*

Garnet's speech failed to win endorsement from the 1843 black convention and was even opposed by Frederick Douglass (1817?–1895), who was becoming the most famous black to have escaped from southern slavery and who would soon emerge as the most notable and respected black leader in America. Douglass had escaped to the North in 1838. For three years he worked as an unskilled laborer, but in 1841, after addressing an abolitionist meeting at Nantucket, he was hired by the Massachusetts Anti-Slavery Society as a full-time lecturer. In 1845, he published his classic *Narrative of the Life of Frederick Douglass, An American Slave*; within a few years some 30,000 copies had been printed in America and Britain. From 1845 to 1847, Douglass toured the British Isles delivering an immense number of lectures supporting antislavery, temperance, and other reforms. Upon his return to America, he settled in Rochester, New York, where he began publishing a reformist weekly, *The North Star*. He was the only male to take a prominent part in the 1848 women's rights convention at Seneca Falls (see Unit One, Part 5, B).

In 1853, Douglass was approached for advice by Harriet Beecher Stowe, a daughter of Lyman Beecher and a sister of Catharine and Henry Ward Beecher. In 1850, Harriet Beecher Stowe and her husband had been living in near poverty, and the next year she had been paid only $300 for the serial publication of her novel, *Uncle Tom's Cabin, or Life Among the Lowly*. But when published in book form in 1852, the antislavery novel sold 300,000 copies within a year. Though Stowe received no royalties on the million-and-a-half copies sold in Britain, she was suddenly wealthy and an international celebrity. Wanting to use some of her income to found a Negro school, she appealed to Douglass and others for suggestions.

In the following letter to Hariet Beecher Stowe, Douglass advances important arguments favoring the establishment of a black "industrial college." Though he ordinarily opposed all forms of racial segregation, Douglass apparently felt this was an opportunity that should not be missed. His most interesting points pertain to the liabilities of "overeducated" blacks in a racist society and the need for concentrating on industrial or mechanical skills—a line of argument later developed in a different historical context by Booker T. Washington. Above all, Douglass displays a striking concern for the collective welfare and advancement of the blacks as a people.

Because she received conflicting advice on the propriety of a separate black school and on the need for combatting slavery as the first priority, Stowe abandoned the idea of an industrial college.

Frederick Douglass (1853)

You kindly informed me, when at your house a fortnight ago, that you designed to do something which would permanently contribute to the improvement and elevation of the free colored people in the United States. You especially expressed interest in such of this class as had become free by their own exertions, and desired most of all to be of service to them. In what manner and by what means you can assist this class most successfully, is the subject upon which you have done me the honor to ask my opinion. . . . I assert then that *poverty, ignorance* and *degradation* are the combined evils; or in other words, these constitute the social disease of the free colored people of the United States.

SOURCE: Carter Godwin Woodson, *The Mind of the Negro, op. cit.*, pp. 654–57.

To deliver them from this triple malady, is to improve and elevate them, by which I mean, simply to put them on an equal footing with their white fellow countrymen in the sacred right to *"Life, Liberty,* and the pursuit of happiness." I am for no fancied or artificial elevation, but only ask fair play. How shall this be obtained? I answer, first, not by establishing for our use high schools and colleges. Such institutions are, in my judgment, beyond our immediate occasions and are not adapted to our present most pressing wants. High schools and colleges are excellent institutions, and will in due season be greatly subservient to our progress; but they are the result, as well as they are the demand of a point of progress, which we as a people have not yet attained. Accustomed as we have been, to the rougher and harder modes of living, and of gaining a livelihood, we cannot, and we ought not to hope that in a single leap from our low condition, we can reach that of *Ministers, Lawyers, Doctors, Editors, Merchants,* etc. These will doubtless be attained by us; but this will only be, when we have patiently and laboriously, and I may add, successfully, mastered and passed through the intermediate gradations of agriculture and the mechanical arts. Besides, there are—and perhaps this is a better reason for my views of this case—numerous institutions of learning in this country, already thrown open to colored youth. To my thinking, there are quite as many facilities now afforded to the colored people, as they can spare the time from the sterner duties of life, to avail themselves of. In their present condition of poverty, they cannot spare their sons and daughters two or three years at boarding-schools or colleges, to say nothing of finding the means to sustain them while at such institutions. . . .

We have two or three colored lawyers in this country; and I rejoice in the fact; for it affords very gratifying evidence of our progress. Yet it must be confessed, that in point of success, our lawyers are as great failures as our ministers. White people will not employ them to the obvious embarrassment of their causes, and the blacks, taking their *cue* from the whites, have not sufficient confidence in their abilities to employ them. Hence educated colored men, among the colored people, are at a very great discount.

It would seem that education and emigration go together with us, for as soon as a man rises amongst us, capable, by his genius and learning, to do us great service, just so soon he finds that he can serve himself better by going elsewhere. . . .

There is little reason to hope that any considerable number of the free colored people will ever be induced to leave this country; even if such a thing were desirable. This black man—*un*like the Indian—loves civilization. He does not make very great progress in civilization himself but he likes to be in the midst of it, and prefers to share its most galling evils, to encountering barbarism. Then the love of the country, the dread of isolation, the lack of adventurous spirit, and the thought of seeming to desert their "brethren in bonds," are a powerful check upon all schemes of colonization, which look to the removal of the colored people, without the slaves. The truth is, dear madam, we are *here,* and here we are likely to remain. Individuals emigrate

—nation never. We have grown up with this republic, and I see nothing in her character, or even in the character of the American people as yet, which compels the belief that we must leave the United States. If then, we are to remain here, the question for the wise and good is precisely that you have submitted to me—namely: What can be done to improve the condition of the free people of color in the United States?

The plan which I humbly submit in answer to this inquiry—and in the hope that it may find favor with you, and with the many friends of humanity who honor, love, and cooperate with you—is the establishment in Rochester, N. Y., or in some other part of the United States equally favorable to such an enterprise, of an INDUSTRIAL COLLEGE in which shall be taught several important branches of the mechanical arts. This college to be opened to colored youth. I will pass over the details of such an institution as I propose. . . . Never having had a day's schooling in all my life I may not be expected to map out the details of a plan so comprehensive as that involved in the idea of a college. I repeat, then, I leave the organization and administration to the superior wisdom of yourself and the friends who second your noble efforts.

The argument in favor of an Industrial College—a college to be conducted by the best men—and the best workmen which the mechanical arts can afford; a college where colored youth can be instructed to use their hands, as well as their heads; where they can be put into possession of the means of getting a living whether their lot in after life may be cast among civilized or uncivilized men; whether they choose to stay here, or prefer to return to the land of their fathers—is briefly this: Prejudice against the free colored people in the United States has shown itself nowhere so invincible as among mechanics. The farmer and the professional man cherish no feeling so bitter as that cherished by these. The latter would starve us out of the country entirely. At this moment I can more easily get my son into a lawyer's office to learn law than I can into a blacksmith's shop to blow the bellows and to wield the sledgehammer. Denied the means of learning useful trades we are pressed into the narrowest limits to obtain a livelihood. In times past we have been the hewers of wood and the drawers of water for American society, and we once enjoyed a monopoly in menial enjoyments [employments?—ed.] but this is so no longer. Even these enjoyments are rapidly passing away out of our hands. The fact is—every day begins with the lesson, and ends with the lesson—that colored men must learn trades; and must find new employment; new modes of usefulness to society, or that they must decay under the pressing wants to which their condition is rapidly bringing them.

We must become mechanics; we must build as well as live in houses; we must make as well as use furniture; we must construct bridges as well as pass over them, before we can properly live or be respected by our fellow men. We need mechanics as well as ministers. We need workers in iron, clay, and leather. We have orators, authors, and other professional men, but these reach only a certain class, and get respect for our race in certain select circles.

To live here as we ought we must fasten ourselves to our countrymen through their every day cardinal wants. We must not only be able to *black* boots, but to *make* them. At present we are unknown in the northern states as mechanics. We give no proof of genius or skill at the county, state, or national fairs. We are unknown at any of the great exhibitions of the industry of our fellow-citizens, and being unknown we are unconsidered.

J. Black Disillusionment

• *Martin Delany* (1852)

Harriet Beecher Stowe caught criticism from black and white abolitionists alike for having George Harris, the proud and talented fugitive slave in *Uncle Tom's Cabin*, write a long letter from France defending his decision to emigrate with his family to Liberia—"to *my country*,—my chosen, my glorious Africa!" But even by 1852, a number of black abolitionists like Martin Delany (1812–1885) were giving colonization a second look. From 1847 to 1849 Delany had worked with Frederick Douglass in publishing *The North Star*. He had then studied medicine at Harvard and worked as a doctor in Pittsburgh, the town to which his free black parents had migrated from western Virginia when he was a child. Like Douglass, Delany began to realize that the success of black professionals, editors, and lecturers had made no dent in the color wall. Unlike Douglass, Delany concluded that American blacks had only the two options of emigrating or suffering from continuing and hopeless degradation. This is the central message of *The Condition, Emigration, and Destiny of the Colored People of the United States*, which Delany published in 1852 and which reflected, like *Uncle Tom's Cabin*, the anger and disillusion evoked by the Fugitive Slave Law of 1850.

In our selection from this book, Delany first offers an intriguing theory of racial oppression, a theory borne out in many respects by recent historical research. Delany then reviews the history of the first Negro conventions and of the later black subservience to white abolitionists. It is the failure of white abolitionists to act on their professed convictions of equality that Delany finds most discouraging. In an appendix, not included here, he dreams of building a new and prosperous trading nation on the east coast of Africa. But when Delany later assembled a National Emigration Convention in 1854, he was eager to investigate possible sites in Haiti, Central America, and the Niger Valley of west Africa.

While most black leaders continued to reject colonization, events of the late 1850s brought a more open-minded reception to both emigration and appeals for slave revolution. Douglass, for example, said he would welcome news that the slaves had rebelled; he, Delany, and other black leaders were actively courted by John Brown, whose execution after the Harpers Ferry raid of 1859 made him a great hero and martyr among America's black population. By then, Delany had traveled to Africa, but his colonizing schemes were cut short by the Civil War. Back in America, he helped recruit Negro troops, received a commission of major in the Union army, and during Reconstruction served in the Freedmen's Bureau and as a trial justice in Charleston, South Carolina.

Martin Delany (1852)

The United States, untrue to her trust and unfaithful to her professed principles of republican equality, has also pursued a policy of political degradation to a large portion of her native born countrymen, and that class is the Colored People. Denied an equality not only of political, but of natural rights, in common with the rest of our fellow citizens, there is no species of degradation to which we are not subject.

Reduced to abject slavery is not enough, the very thought of which should awaken every sensibility of our common nature; but those of their descendants who are freemen even in the non-slaveholding states, occupy the very same position politically, religiously, civilly and socially (with but few exceptions) as the bondman occupies in the slave states.

In those states, the bondman is disfranchised, and for the most part so are we. He is denied all civil, religious, and social privileges, except such as he gets by mere sufferance, and so are we. They have no part nor lot in the government of the country, neither have we. They are ruled and governed without representation, existing as mere nonentities among the citizens, and excrescences on the body politic—a mere dreg in community, and so are we. . . .

Have we not now sufficient intelligence among us to understand our true position, to realize our actual condition, and determine for ourselves what is best to be done? If we have not now, we never shall have, and should at once cease prating about our equality, capacity, and all that.

Twenty years ago, when the writer was a youth, his young and yet uncultivated mind was aroused, and his tender heart made to leap with anxiety in anticipation of the promises then held out by the prime movers in the cause of our elevation.

In 1830 the most intelligent and leading spirits among the colored men in the United States . . . assembled in the city of Philadelphia, in the capacity of a National Convention, to "devise ways and means for the bettering of our condition." These Conventions determined to assemble annually, much talent, ability, and energy of character being displayed. . . .

SOURCE: Martin Delany, *The Condition, Emigration, and Destiny of the Colored People of the United States* (Philadelphia: M. Delany, 1852), pp. 14–30.

Among other great projects of interest brought before the convention at a previous sitting, was that of the expediency of a general emigration, as far as it was practicable, of the colored people to the British Provinces of North America. Another was that of raising sufficient means for the establishment and erection of a college for the proper education of the colored youth. These gentlemen long accustomed to observation and reflection on the condition of their people, saw at once, that there must necessarily be means used adequate to the end to be attained—that end being an unqualified equality with the ruling class of their fellow citizens. He saw that as a class, the colored people of the country were ignorant, degraded and oppressed, by far the greater portion of them being abject slaves in the South, the very condition of whom was almost enough, under the circumstances, to blast the remotest hope of success, and those who were freemen, whether in the South or North, occupied a subservient, servile, and menial position, considering it a favor to get into the service of the whites, and do their degrading offices. That the difference between the whites and themselves, consisted in the superior advantages of the one over the other, in point of attainments. That if a knowledge of the arts and sciences, the mechanical occupations, the industrial occupations, as farming, commerce, and all the various business enterprises, and learned professions were necessary for the superior position occupied by their rulers, it was also necessary for them. And very reasonably too, the first suggestion which occured to them was, the advantages of a location, then the necessity of a qualification. They reasoned with themselves, that all distinctive differences made among men on account of their origin, is wicked, unrighteous, and cruel, and never shall receive countenance in any shape from us, therefore, the first acts of the measures entered into by them, was to protest, solemnly protest, against every unjust measure and policy in the country, having for its object the proscription of the colored people, whether state, national, municipal, social, civil, or religious.

But being far-sighted, reflecting, discerning men, they took a political view of the subject, and determined for the good of their people to be governed in their policy according to the facts as they presented themselves. In taking a glance at Europe, they discovered there, however unjustly, as we have shown in another part of this pamphlet, that there are and have been numerous classes proscribed and oppressed, and it was not for them to cut short their wise deliberations, and arrest their proceedings in contention, as to the cause, whether on account of language, the color of eyes, hair, skin, or their origin of country—because all this is contrary to reason, a contradiction to common sense, at war with nature herself, and at variance with facts as they stare us every day in the face, among all nations, in every country—this being made the pretext as a matter of *policy* alone—a fact worthy of observation, that wherever the objects of oppression are the most easily distinguished by any peculiar or general characteristics, these people are the more easily oppressed, because the war of oppression is the more easily waged against them. This is the case with the modern Jews and many other people who have strongly-marked, peculiar, or distinguishing characteristics. This arises in this wise. The policy of all those who proscribe any people, induces them to select as the objects of proscription, those who differed as much as possible, in some particulars, from themselves. This is to ensure the greater success, because it engenders the greater prejudice, or in other words, elicits less interest on the part of the oppressing class, in their favor. This fact is well understood in national conflicts, as the soldier or civilian, who is distinguished by his dress, mustache, or any other peculiar appendage, would certainly prove himself a madman, if he did not take the precaution to change his dress, remove his mustache, and conceal as much as possible his peculiar characteristics, to give him access among the repelling party. This is mere policy, nature having nothing to do with it. Still, it is a fact, a great truth well worthy of remark, and as such we adduce it for the benefit of those of our readers, unaccustomed to an enquiry into the policy of nations.

In view of these truths, our fathers and leaders in our elevation, discovered that as a policy, we the colored people were selected as the subordinate class in this country, not on account of any actual or supposed inferiority on their part, but simply because, in view of all the circumstances of the case, they were the very best class that could be selected. They would have as readily had any other class as subordinates in the country, as the colored people, but the condition of society *at the time,* would not admit of it. In the struggle for American Independence, there were among those who performed the most distinguished parts, the most common-place peasantry of the provinces. English, Danish, Irish, Scotch, and others, were among those whose names blazoned forth as heroes in the American Revolution. But a single reflection will convince us, that no course of policy could have induced the proscription of the parentage and relatives of such men as Benjamin Franklin the printer, Roger Sherman the cobbler, the tinkers, and others of the signers of the Declaration of Independence. But as they were determined to have a subservient class, it will readily be conceived, that according to the state of society at the time, the better policy on their part was, to select some class, who from their political position—however much they may have contributed their aid as we certainly did, in the general struggle for liberty by force of arms—who had the least claims upon them, or who had the *least chance,* or was the *least potent* in urging their claims. This class of course was the colored people and Indians.

The Indians who in the early settlement of the continent, before an African captive had ever been introduced thereon, were reduced to the most abject slavery, toiling day and night in the mines, under the relentless hands of heartless Spanish taskmasters, but being a race of people raised to the sports of fishing, the chase, and of war, were wholly unaccustomed to labor, and therefore sunk under the insupportable weight, two millions and a half having fallen victims to the cruelty of oppression and toil suddenly placed upon their shoulders. And it was only this that prevented their farther enslavement as a class, after the provinces were absolved from the British Crown. It is true that their general enslavement took place on the islands and in the mining districts of South America, where indeed, the Europeans continued to enslave them, until a comparatively recent period; still, the design, the feeling, and inclination from policy, was the same to do so here, in this section of the continent.

Nor was it until their influence became too great, by the political position occupied by their brethren in the new republic, that the German and Irish peasantry ceased to be sold as slaves for a term of years fixed by law, for the repayment of their passage-money, the descendants of these classes of people for a long time being held as inferiors, in the estimation of the ruling class, and it was not until they assumed the rights and privileges guaranteed to them by the established policy of the country, among the leading spirits of whom were their relatives, that the policy towards them was discovered to be a bad one, and accordingly changed. Nor was it, as is frequently very erroneously asserted, by colored as well as white persons, that it was on account of hatred to the African, or in other words, on account of hatred to his color, that the African was selected as the subject of oppression in this country. This is sheer nonsense; being based on policy and nothing else, as shown in another place. The Indians, who being the most foreign to the sympathies of the Europeans on this continent, were selected in the first place, who, being unable to withstand the hardships, gave way before them.

But the African race had long been known to Europeans, in all ages of the world's history, as a long-lived, hardy race, subject to toil and labor of various kinds, subsisting mainly by traffic, trade, and industry, and consequently being as foreign to the sympathies of the invaders of the continent as the Indians, they were selected, captured, brought here as a laboring class, and as a matter of policy held as such. Nor was the absurd idea of natural inferiority of the African ever dreamed of, until recently adduced by the slaveholders and their abettors, in justification of their policy. This, with contemptuous indignation, we fling back into their face, as a scorpion to a vulture. And so did our patriots and leaders in the cause of regeneration know better, and never for a moment yielded to the base doctrine. But they had discovered the great fact, that a cruel policy was pursued towards our people, and that they possessed distinctive characteristics which made them the objects of proscription. These characteristics being strongly marked in the colored people, as in the Indians, by color, character of hair and so on, made them the more easily distinguished from other Americans, and the policies more effectually urged against us. For this reason they [the first black Conventions] introduced the subject of emigration to Canada, and a proper institution for the education of the youth.

At this important juncture of their proceedings, the afore-named white gentlemen [Garrison and other abolitionists] were introduced to the notice of the Convention, and after gaining permission to speak, expressed their gratification and surprise at the qualification and talent manifested by different members of the Convention, all expressing their determination to give the cause of the colored people more serious reflection.

•   •   •

At this important point in the history of our efforts, the colored men stopped suddenly, and with their hands thrust deep in their breeches-pockets, and their mouths gaping open, stood gazing with astonishment, wonder, and surprise, at the stupendous moral colossal statues of our Anti-Slavery friends and brethren, who in the heat and zeal of honest hearts, from a desire to make atonement for the many wrongs inflicted, promised a great deal more than they have ever been able half to fulfill, in thrice the period in which they expected it. And in this, we have no fault to find with our Anti-Slavery friends, and here wish it to be understood, that we are not laying any thing to their charge as blame, neither do we desire for a moment to reflect on them, because we heartily believe that all that they did at the time, they did with the purest and best of motives, and further believe that they now are, as they then were, the truest friends we have among the whites in this country. . . .

It should be borne in mind, that Anti-Slavery took its rise among *colored men*, just at the time they were introducing their greatest projects for their own elevation, and that our Anti-Slavery brethren were converts of the colored men, in behalf of their elevation. Of course, it would be expected that being baptized into the new doctrines, their faith would induce them to embrace the principles therein contained, with the strictest possible adherence.

The cause of dissatisfaction with our former condition, was, that we were proscribed, debarred, and shut out from every respectable position, occupying the places of inferiors and menials.

It was expected that Anti-Slavery, according to its professions, would extend to colored persons, as far as in the power of its adherents, those advantages nowhere else to be obtained among white men. That colored boys would get situations in their shops and stores, and every other advantage tending to elevate them as far as possible, would be extended to them. At least, it was expected, that in Anti-Slavery establishments, colored men would have the preference. Because, there was no other ostensible object in view, in the commencement of the Anti-Slavery enterprise, than the *elevation* of the *colored man*, by facilitating his efforts in attaining to equality with the white man. It was urged, and it was true, that the colored people were susceptible of all that the whites were, and all that was required was to give them a fair opportunity, and they would prove their capacity. That it was unjust, wicked, and cruel, the result of an unnatural prejudice, that debarred them from places of respectability, and that public opinion could and should be corrected upon this subject. That is was only necessary to make a sacrifice of feeling, and an innovation on the customs of society, to establish a different order of things. . . .

Thus, was the cause espoused, and thus did we expect much. But in all this, we were doomed to disappointment, sad, sad disappointment. Instead of realizing what we had hoped for, we find ourselves occupying the very same position in relation to our Anti-Slavery friends, as we do in relation to the pro-slavery part of the community—a mere secondary, underling position, in all our relations to them, and any thing more than this, is not a matter of course affair—it comes not by established anti-slavery custom or right, but like that which emanates from the proslavery portion of the community, by mere sufferance. . . .

And if it be urged that colored men are incapable as yet to fill these positions, all that we have to say is, that the cause has fallen far short; almost equivalent to a failure, of the tithe [one-tenth], of what it promised to do in half the period of its existence, to this time, if it have not as yet, now a period of twenty years, raised up colored men enough, to fill the offices within its patronage. We think it is not unkind to say, if it had been half as faithful to itself, as it should have been—its professed principles we mean; it could have reared and tutored from childhood, colored men enough by this time, for its own especial purpose. These we know could have been easily obtained, because colored people in general, are favorable to the anti-slavery cause . . . .

We are nevertheless, still occupying a miserable position in the community, wherever we live; and what we most desire is, to draw the attention of our people to this fact, and point out what, in our opinion, we conceive to be a proper remedy.

The Polarized South: Outsiders Inside

A. "So the Last Shall Be First, and the First Last" (Matthew, 20:16)

• *Nat Turner* (1831)

Negro slavery was founded on and sustained by violence. The entire structure of southern white paternalism was designed to soften and conceal this fact. But every slave child—and most southern whites—learned the lesson at an early age. The truth became clear every time a slave defied white authority, tried to escape, or was sold apart from spouse, parents, or children.

Because insurrections were far less frequent in the South than in the West Indies and Brazil, white Southerners were often able to convince themselves that slaves were "loyal" and content. Because blacks seemed to have internalized the more submissive precepts of Christianity, it was difficult to think of slavery as *"the state of War continued,"* in John Locke's definition, *"between a lawful Conqueror, and a Captive."*

But white complacency could never be quite the same after the events of August 22, 1831, in Southampton County, Virginia. In the early morning hours, Nat Turner (1800–1831) led a small group of fellow slaves into the home of Joseph Travis, Turner's nominal master and the stepfather of Turner's infant "owner," and killed the entire Travis family including the infant. Turner was a trusted Baptist preacher who later admitted he had

315

"no cause to complain" of Travis's treatment. Yet by August 23, Turner's vengeful force, increased to between sixty and eighty slaves and several free blacks, had massacred some sixty whites, more than half women and children. The local militia quickly defeated and dispersed Turner's rebels, and white troops and vigilantes proceeded to torture and kill large numbers of blacks in what a white general condemned as "inhuman butchery." Turner himself escaped capture until October 31. Before being tried and executed, he dictated long responses to questions from a white lawyer, Thomas R. Gray. Historians have generally accepted these so-called *Confessions*, from which this selection is taken, as authentic.

"Confession" is actually a rather misleading word. When Gray asks Turner whether he now considers himself mistaken in thinking that he was charged with the holy mission of fighting against the Serpent, or Devil, Turner snaps back, "Was not Christ crucified?" This exchange provides a key to Turner's apocalyptic vision—a vision based on the prohetic passages of the Bible that foretell the final unleashing of Satan, an epic struggle between the forces of good and evil, and the violent destruction of evil. Turner's mind soaked up Biblical passages like a sponge, and he was clearly aware of God's injunction in Ezekiel (10:5–6): "Go ye . . . and smite: let not your eye spare, neither have ye pity: Slay utterly old and young, both maids, and little children, and women: but come not near any man upon whom is the mark. . . ."

As a boy Turner had learned to read and write, and his slave parents had led him to believe he was "intended for some great purpose." Among the local slaves, he acquired considerable respect as a preacher. Slave religion, a mixture of Christian and African elements, was the crucial vehicle for sustaining a culture independent from the white world. In the interest of sheer survival, this religion usually aimed at patience, accommodation, and hope. But hope rested on a conviction that the time of suffering, like the Hebrews' bondage in Egypt, was limited. Turner had experienced religious visions early in life, and in 1828 had felt himself commissioned to lead the war against evil when the proper "signs" appeared. In 1831 an eclipse of the sun, followed in August by a greenish sunrise and an apparent black spot traversing the sun, signaled for Turner the Last Days. Even after the subsequent white panic began to subside, slaveholders could never again be certain whether Turner had been a lone fanatic, or whether there were other Nat Turners in their own households.

Nat Turner (1831)

And on the 12th of May, 1828, I heard a loud noise in the heavens, and the Spirit instantly appeared to me and said the Serpent was loosened, and

SOURCE: *The Confessions of Nat Turner, the Leader of the Late Insurrection in Southampton, Va.* (Baltimore: Published by Thomas R. Gray; Lucas & Deaver, printer; 1831).

Christ had laid down the yoke he had borne for the sins of men, and that I should take it on and fight against the Serpent, for the time was fast approaching when the first should be last and the last should be first. [Question] Do you not find yourself mistaken now? [Answer] Was not Christ crucified? And by signs in the heavens that it would be made known to me when I should commence the great work—and until the first sign appeared, I should conceal it from the knowledge of men—And on the appearance of the sign (the eclipse of the sun last February), I should arise and prepare myself, and slay my enemies with their own weapons. And immediately on the sign appearing in the heavens, the seal was removed from my lips, and I communicated the great work laid out before me to do, to four in whom I had the greatest confidence (Henry, Hark, Nelson, and Sam)—It was intended by us to have begun the work of death on the 4th of July last—Many were the plans formed and rejected by us, and it affected my mind to such a degree, that I fell sick, and the time passed without our coming to any determination how to commence—Still forming new schemes and rejecting them, when the sign appeared again, which determined me not to wait longer.

Since the commencement of 1830, I had been living with Mr. Joseph Travis, who was to me a kind master, and placed the greatest confidence in me: in fact, I had no cause to complain of his treatment of me. On Saturday evening, the 20th of August, it was agreed between Henry, Hark and myself, to prepare a dinner the next day for the men we expected, and then to concert a plan, as we had not yet determined on any. Hark, on the following morning, brought a pig, and Henry brandy, and being joined by Sam, Nelson, Will and Jack, they prepared in the woods a dinner, where, about three o'clock, I joined them. . . .

I saluted them on coming up, and asked Will how came he there, he answered, his life was worth no more than others, and his liberty as dear to him. I asked him if he thought to obtain it? He said he would, or lose his life. This was enough to put him in full confidence. Jack, I knew, was only a tool in the hands of Hark, it was quickly agreed we should commence at home (Mr. J. Travis') on that night, and until we had armed and equipped ourselves, and gathered sufficient force, neither age nor sex was to be spared (which was invariably adhered to). We remained at the feast, until about two hours in the night, when we went to the house and found Austin; they all went to the cider press and drank, except myself. On returning to the house Hark went to the door with an axe, for the purpose of breaking it open, as we knew we were strong enough to murder the family, if they were awakened by the noise; but reflecting that it might create an alarm in the neighborhood, we determined to enter the house secretly, and murder them whilst sleeping. Hark got a ladder and set it against the chimney, on which I ascended, and hoisting a window, entered and came down stairs, unbarred the door, and removed the guns from their places. It was then observed that I must spill the first blood. On which, armed with a hatchet, and accompanied by Will, I entered my master's chamber, it being dark, I could not give a death blow, the hatchet glanced from his head, he sprang from the bed and called his wife, it was his last word, Will laid him dead, with a blow of his axe, and Mrs. Travis shared the same fate, as she lay in bed. The murder of this family, five in number, was the work of a moment, not one of them awoke; there was a little infant sleeping in a cradle, that was forgotten, until we had left the house and gone some distance, when Henry and Will returned and killed it; we got here, four guns that would shoot, and several old muskets, with a pound or two of powder. We remained some time at the barn, where we paraded; I formed them in a line as soldiers, and . . . carrying them through all the manoeuvres I was master of. . . .

B. Slave Labor

• *Solomon Northup* (1855)

Slaves and former slaves left an astonishing amount of testimony concerning virtually every aspect of life under the South's "peculiar institution." This rich documentation can only be briefly sampled here, but is now fortunately accessible in well-edited, book-length anthologies.[1] While one must be cautious in judging the authenticity of some of the slave narratives published before the Civil War, Solomon Northup's story was corroborated in interviews and in judicial proceedings. Northup (1808– ?) was a free black, born in Upstate New York. In 1841 he and his family lived in Saratoga Springs, where he took on a hazardous job requiring travel to the South. Though Northup carried papers proving that he was a freeman and a citizen, slave dealers kidnapped him in Washington and shipped him off to New Orleans. Despite brutal beatings and threats of death, Northup managed to send off a letter appealing for help, but his friends had no way of tracing his destination. For nearly ten years, Northup worked as a slave on a cotton plantation leased by Edwin Eppes in Bayou Bœuf, Louisiana. Finally, in 1852, Northup's New York friends received another letter and were now able to enlist support from the governor of New York, the secretary of war, Supreme Court Justice Samuel Nelson, and other influential figures. Even in Louisiana, the authorities cooperated in securing Northup's freedom, though efforts to prosecute his enslavers were unavailing.

In writing a narrative of his experiences, *Twelve Years a Slave*, Northup received editorial assistance from David Wilson, a New York lawyer and state legislator who was not known for abolitionist sympathies. The account provides an authentic and chilling picture of slavery as experienced by a black who until the age of thirty-three had lived in relative freedom. As Northup

---

[1] See especially John W. Blassingame, ed., *Slave Testimony: Two Centuries of Letters, Speeches, Interviews, and Autobiographies* (Baton Rouge: Louisiana State University Press, 1977); and Willie Lee Rose, *A Documentary History of Slavery in North America* (New York: Oxford University Press, 1976).

makes clear, Edwin Eppes was an unusually harsh and at times sadistic master. Northup acknowledges that the character of masters could be as diverse as the range of human personalities. Yet the *system* of slavery subjected the individual slave to the worst traits and unrestrained outbursts of whomever he acquired as an owner. And the system was geared, as Northup also emphasizes, to the maximization of labor.

Solomon Northup (1855)

Edwin Epps [Eppes] . . . is a large, portly, heavy-bodied man with light hair, high cheek bones, and a Roman nose of extraordinary dimensions. He has blue eyes, a fair complexion, and is, as I should say, full six feet high. He has the sharp, inquisitive expression of a jockey. His manners are repulsive and coarse, and his language gives speedy and unequivocal evidence that he has never enjoyed the advantages of an education. He has the faculty of saying most provoking things. . . . At the time I came into his possession, Edwin Epps was fond of the bottle, his "sprees" sometimes extending over the space of two whole weeks. Latterly, however, he had reformed his habits, and when I left him, was as strict a specimen of temperance as could be found on Bayou Bœuf. When "in his cups," Master Epps was a roystering, blustering, noisy fellow, whose chief delight was in dancing with his "niggers," or lashing them about the yard with his long whip, just for the pleasure of hearing them screech and scream, as the great welts were planted on their backs. When sober, he was silent, reserved and cunning, not beating us indiscriminately, as in his drunken moments, but sending the end of his rawhide to some tender spot of a lagging slave, with a sly dexterity peculiar to himself.

He had been a driver and overseer in his younger years, but at this time was in possession of a plantation on Bayou Huff Power, two and a half miles from Holmesville, eighteen from Marksville, and twelve from Cheneyville. It belonged to Joseph B. Roberts, his wife's uncle, and was leased by Epps. His principal business was raising cotton, and inasmuch as some may read this book who have never seen a cotton field, a description of the manner of its culture may not be out of place.

The ground is prepared by throwing up beds or ridges, with the plough—back-furrowing, it is called. Oxen and mules, the latter almost exclusively, are used in ploughing. The women as frequently as the men perform this labor, feeding, currying, and taking care of their teams, and in all respects doing the field and stable work, precisely as do the ploughboys of the North.

The beds, or ridges, are six feet wide, that is, from water furrow to water

---

SOURCE: Solomon Northup, *Twelve Years a Slave* (New York: Miller, Orton and Mulligan, 1855), pp. 162–68, 206–7.

furrow. A plough drawn by one mule is then run along the top of the ridge or center of the bed, making the drill, into which a girl usually drops the seed, which she carries in a bag hung round her neck. Behind her comes a mule and harrow, covering up the seed, so that two mules, three slaves, a plough and harrow, are employed in planting a row of cotton. This is done in the months of March and April. Corn is planted in February. When there are no cold rains, the cotton usually makes its appearance in a week. In the course of eight or ten days afterwards the first hoeing is commenced. This is performed in part, also, by the aid of the plough and mule. The plough passes as near as possible to the cotton on both sides, throwing the furrow from it. Slaves follow with their hoes, cutting up the grass and cotton, leaving hills two feet and a half apart. This is called scraping cotton. In two weeks more commences the second hoeing. This time the furrow is thrown towards the cotton. Only one stalk, the largest, is now left standing in each hill. In another fortnight it is hoed the third time, throwing the furrow towards the cotton in the same manner as before, and killing all the grass between the rows. About the first of July, when it is a foot high or thereabouts, it is hoed the fourth and last time. Now the whole space between the rows is ploughed, leaving a deep water furrow in the center. During all these hoeings the overseer or driver follows the slaves on horseback with a whip, such as has been described. The fastest hoer takes the lead row. He is usually about a rod in advance of his companions. If one of them passes him, he is whipped. If one falls behind or is a moment idle, he is whipped. In fact, the lash is flying from morning until night, the whole day long. The hoeing season thus continues from April until July, a field having no sooner been finished once, than it is commenced again.

In the latter part of August begins the cotton picking season. At this time each slave is presented with a sack. A strap is fastened to it, which goes over the neck, holding the mouth of the sack breast high, while the bottom reaches nearly to the ground. Each one is also presented with a large basket that will hold about two barrels. This is to put the cotton in when the sack is filled. The baskets are carried to the field and placed at the beginning of the rows.

When a new hand, one unaccustomed to the business, is sent for the first time into the field, he is whipped up smartly, and made for that day to pick as fast as he can possibly. At night it is weighed, so that his capability in cotton picking is known. He must bring in the same weight each night following. If it falls short, it is considered evidence that he has been laggard, and a greater or less number of lashes is the penalty.

. . .

There are few sights more pleasant to the eye, than a wide cotton field when it is in the bloom. It presents an appearance of purity, like an immaculate expanse of light, new-fallen snow. . . .

The hands are required to be in the cotton field as soon as it is light in the morning, and, with the exception of ten or fifteen minutes, which is given them at noon to swallow their allowance of cold bacon, they are not permitted to be a moment idle until it is too dark to see, and when the moon is full, they often times labor till the middle of the night. They do not dare to stop even at dinner time, nor return to the quarters, however late it be, until the order to halt is given by the driver.

The day's work over in the field, the baskets are "toted," or in other words, carried to the gin-house, where the cotton is weighed. No matter how fatigued and weary he may be—no matter how much he longs for sleep and rest—a slave never approaches the gin-house with his basket of cotton but with fear. If it falls short in weight—if he has not performed the full task appointed him, he knows that he must suffer. And if he has exceeded it by ten or twenty pounds, in all probability his master will measure the next day's accordingly. So, whether he has too little or too much, his approach to the gin-house is always with fear and trembling. Most frequently they have too little, and therefore it is they are not anxious to leave the field. After weighing, follow the whippings; and then the baskets are carried to the cotton house, and their contents stored away like hay, all hands being sent in to tramp it down. If the cotton is not dry, instead of taking it to the gin-house at once, it is laid upon platforms, two feet high, and some three times as wide, covered with boards or plank, with narrow walks running between them.

This done, the labor of the day is not yet ended, by any means. Each one must then attend to his respective chores. One feeds the mules, another the swine—another cuts the wood, and so forth; besides, the packing is all done by candle light. Finally, at a late hour, they reach the quarters, sleepy and overcome with the long day's toil. Then a fire must be kindled in the cabin, the corn ground in the small hand-mill, and supper, and dinner for the next day in the field, prepared. All that is allowed them is corn and bacon, which is given out at the corncrib and smoke-house every Sunday morning.

. . .

There may be humane masters, as there certainly are inhuman ones—there may be slaves well-clothed, well-fed, and happy, as there surely are those half-clad, half-starved and miserable; nevertheless, the institution that tolerates such wrong and inhumanity as I have witnessed, is a cruel, unjust, and barbarous one. Men may write fictions portraying lowly life as it is, or as it is not—may expatiate with owlish gravity upon the bliss of ignorance—discourse flippantly from arm chairs of the pleasures of slave life; but let them toil with him in the field—sleep with him in the cabin—feed with him on husks; let them behold him scourged, hunted, trampled on, and they will come back with another story in their mouths. Let them know the *heart* of the poor slave—learn his secret thoughts—thoughts he dare not utter in the hearing of the white man; let them sit by him in the silent watches of the night—converse with him in trustful confidence, of "life, liberty, and the pursuit of happiness," and they will find that ninety-nine out of every hundred are intelligent enough to understand their situation, and to cherish in their bosoms the love of freedom, as passionately as themselves.

C. Slave Voices

- *George Skipwith* (1847)
- *Lucy Skipwith* (1863)
- *Maria Perkins* (1852)

In contrast to Edwin Eppes, John Hartwell Cocke was an enlightened Virginia planter. Though one of the largest slaveholders in the state, he once termed slavery "the great cause of all the great evils of our land," and continued to serve as senior vice-president of the American Colonization Society. He was also a leader in the national temperance, Bible, Sunday-school, and missionary societies. In contrast to Solomon Northup, George Skipwith belonged to the trusted slave elite and wrote dutiful reports to his absent master, John Hartwell Cocke. The first selection is from one of George Skipwith's letters to Cocke. While revealing an unusual relationship between master and slave, the letter also echoes one of Northup's key themes—disputes over the amount of labor performed and a resulting infliction of brutal punishment.

The second selection moves on in time to the critical year of the Civil War, when Lucy Skipwith reports to Cocke that "there is no white person here at present." Like George Skipwith, Lucy is trying to please her master and is telling him what she thinks he wants to hear. But she also serves her own interests and conveys a complex picture of the relationship between white and black power.

The third selection is an eloquent and moving cry of distress from Maria Perkins to her husband, who is owned by a different master. Apart from her anguish over the separation of their family, it is notable that she is concerned over the fate of personal possessions that are scattered as far west from Charlottesville as Staunton, on the other side of Virginia's Blue Ridge Mountains.

George Skipwith (1847)

Sir   hopewell July the 8 1847

on the forth day of July i reseved your letter dated may the 25. i wrote to you the 15 of June the second time gieving you a true statement of the crops, horses, hogs, and chickens. but i am sorry that I shall have to [write] you princeable about other matters. I hav a good crop on hand

SOURCE: Cocke Family Letters, University of Virginia Library, Charlottesville. John Blassingame, ed., *Slave Testimony: Two Centuries of Letters, Speeches, Interviews, and Autobiographies* (Baton Rouge: Louisiana State University Press, 1977), pp. 66–68.

for you, borth of cotton and corn. this you know could not be don without hard work. i have worked the people but not out of reason. and i have whiped none without a caus   the persons whome i have correct i will tell you thir name and thir faults. Suky who I put to plant som corn and after she had been there long anuf to have been done i went there and she had hardly began it   i gave her some four or five licks over her clothes   i gave isham too licks over his clothes for coveering up cotten with the plow. I put frank, isham, Evally, Dinah, Jinny evealine and Charlott to sweeping cotten going twice in a roe. and at a Reasonable days worke they ought to hav plowed seven accers a peice. and they had been at it a half of a day. and they had not done more than one accer and a half and i gave them ten licks a peace upon their skins   i gave Evlyann eight or ten licks for misplacing her hoe. that was all the whiping I hav done from the time that I pitched the crop untell we commenced cutting oats. . . . when i come to them at twelve o clocke, they had cut some nineteen roes. and it would not take them more than ten minutes to cut one roe. Shadrack was the ruler among them, i spoke these words to him, you do not intend to cut these oats untill i whip every one of you. Shadrack did not say any thing to me. but Robert spoke these words saying that he knoed when he worked. i told him to shut his lips and if he spoke a nother worde i would whip him right of[f]   but he spoke again the second time saying that he was not afraid of being whiped by no man. i then gave him a cut with the whip. he then flong down his cradle and made a oath and said that he had as live die as to live and he said that he did not intend to stay here. he then tried to take the whip out of my hand, but i caught him fast by the collar and holed him. i then told the other boys to strip him and they don so   i then whiped untell i thought that he was pretty could   but i was deseived for as soon as i leave him and went to the hoe hands, he come up to the house to our preacher and his family becaus he knoed that they would protect him in his Rascality for he had herd that they had said that they were worked to death and that they were lowed no more chance for liveing than they were dogs or hogs. tho the preacher did not say any thing to me about whiping Robert neither to mas John but went down to the Shop and holed about an hours chat with the negroes   i do not knoe what his chat was to them but i ask Dr. Weeb. what was good for a negro that w[as] whipt albut to death and he had much to say about it. Dr. Weeb saw that his chat was calculated to incurage the people to rebel against me, and he went and told mas John about what he had herd and mas John took him and come up here to see if he was punished in the way he had herd. but as soon as the Dr put his hand upon him he told mas John that there was nothing the matter with him. mas John then ordered him to his worke and told him that he did not have what his crime was deserving him, and at some lesure time he intend to give him a good wallening and then he would knoe how to behave him self. he rode over the land and saw what they had done, and instead of finding fault of me he said i ought to have given the other three the same.

Lucy Skipwith (1863)

Hopewell Aug 15th 1863

Dear master

I received your last letter & have carefully considered its contents. & I hope to write more sattisfactory than I have done heretofore. the white people who have stayed on the plantation are always opposed to my writing to you. & always want to see my letters and that has been the reason why my letters has been Short but there is no white person here at present. mr Handy is gone home to return no more. I do not know who mr. Powell will get to take his place. The health of the people is not very good at present. we have four laid up at this time but they are getting better. Cain has been pulling fodder for more than a week. & it will take him a week more to finish it.

The cotton is opening very fast & it will soon be open enough to commence picking it out. The weather at present is quite rainy & has been for the last two or three days which makes it hard on the fodder. There is three mulberry trees that has fruit besides the old tree. The Scuppernong grapes have proper frames to run upon & they are full of fruit. . . .

We have our morning prayers regularly. I have not kept up the Sabbath School regularly. Some white people in the neighborhood has said that they would punish me if they caught me at it and I have been afraid to carry it on unless some grown white man was living here. but I will commence Teaching again as soon as this talk dies out.

Maria Perkins (1852)

Charlottesville, Oct. 8th, 1852.

Dear Husband   I write you a letter to let you know my distress   my master has sold albert to a trader on Monday court day and myself and other child is for sale also and I want you to let [me] hear from you very soon before next cort if you can I don't know when   I don't want you to wait till Christmas I want you to tell dr Hamelton and your master if either will buy me they can attend to it know and then I can go afterwards. I don't want a trader to get me   they asked me if I had got any person to buy me and I told them no   they took me to the court houste too   they never put me up a man buy the name of brady bought albert and is gone I don't know where

SOURCE: John Blassingame, ed., *Slave Testimony: Two Centuries of Letters, Speeches, Interviews, and Autobiographies,* p. 79.

SOURCE: Ulrich B. Phillips, *Life and Labor in the Old South* (Boston: Little, Brown and Co., 1929), p. 212. Reprinted by permission of the publisher.

they say he lives in Scottesville   my things is in several places some is in staunton and if I should be sold I don't know what will become of them   I don't expect to meet with the luck to get that way till I am quite heartsick nothing more   I am and ever will be your kind wife   Maria Perkins.

D. Managing Slaves and White Overseers

- *De Bow's Review* (1855)
- *Farmers' Register* (1837)
- *Stancil Barwick* (1855)

Of the various "outsiders" considered in Unit Three, only the slaves were harnessed to a system of production which made their labor indispensable to the society in which they lived. A few white Southerners might dream of Negro colonization as a kind of extension of Indian removal, but most planters knew removal could never be a viable option as long as slave labor remained the source of their wealth and power, constituting the very basis of the social system.

Historically, the other option for dealing with outsiders was acculturation and assimilation, by instilling in them the norms and aspirations of middle-class American Protestants. But to "civilize" slaves in this way would soon undermine their utility as human "beasts of burden" performing the heavy labor so essential for the very civilization to which they would be assimilated!

The slaveholding elite tried to solve this problem by compromise. Within narrow limits, they tried to assimilate Negro slavery to the ideology of moral uplift and perfectibility presented in Unit One. The author of the second selection below, "Remarks on Overseers, and the Proper Treatment of Slaves," uses the very imagery of northern educators when he writes: "The character of the negro is much underrated. It is like the plastic clay, which, may be molded into agreeable or disagreeable figures, according to the skill of the molder." But if black slaves were frequently likened to children, it was essential to make their childlike status *perpetual*, since unlike real children they could not be allowed to grow toward the self-reliance and responsibilities of adulthood. This need to categorize blacks as perpetual children was partly met by racist theories that branded Africans as a "primitive" people still living at the "childhood" stage of human development. But despite this comforting rationalization, the values of republicanism and progressive Christianity, which the South shared with the rest of the nation, were in constant conflict with the imperatives of a labor system based on coercion. One must grasp this fundamental contradiction in order to understand the otherwise bizarre character of southern writings on slavery—the familiar American rhetoric of religious and moral improvement coupled with language that seems to refer to the care and management of livestock.

This duality of thought is especially striking when white Southerners were addressing *themselves* instead of the outside world. The first selection below is from an essay on the "Management of Negroes." It belongs to the genre of practical, how-to-do-it literature and presents the norms of order, efficiency, and humanity to which enlightened planters aspired. In paragraphs omitted here, the author sets forth detailed standards regarding proper food, sleep, clothing, and housing. The anxieties aroused by having to deal with "outsiders inside"—outsiders who can never be wholly subjected to the modes of acculturation described in Unit One—are suggested by the author's warning that white children are often irreparably corrupted by their early fraternization with black slaves.

The second selection is a sample of similar "advice literature" but deals with the hired white managers, or overseers, who could stand as intermediaries between an owner and his slaves. While overseers could spare owners from some of the burdens of authority, they also complicated the meaning and transmission of power. This point is illustrated by the third selection, a defensive and revealing letter from an overseer, Stancil Barwick, to his employer, Colonel J. B. Lamar, of Macon, Georgia. Like many overseers, Barwick complains that slaves have undermined his authority by appealing directly to their master.

De Bow's Review (1855)

The negroes should be required to keep their houses and yards clean; and in case of neglect should receive such punishment as will be likely to insure more cleanly habits in future.

In no case should two families be allowed to occupy the same house. The crowding a number into one house is unhealthy. It breeds contention; is destructive of delicacy of feeling, and it promotes immorality between the sexes. . . .

The master should never establish any regulation among his slaves until he is fully convinced of its propriety and equity. Being thus convinced, and having issued his orders, implicit obedience should be required and rigidly enforced. Firmness of manner, and promptness to enforce obedience, will save much trouble, and be the means of avoiding the necessity for much whipping. The negro should feel that his master is his lawgiver and judge; and yet is his protector and friend, but so far above him, as never to be approached save in the most respectful manner. That where he has just cause, he may, with due deference, approach his master and lay before him

---

SOURCE: *De Bow's Review*, XIX (September, 1855), pp. 360–63.

his troubles and complaints; but not on false pretexts or trivial occasions. If the master be a tyrant, his negroes may be so much embarrassed by his presence as to be incapable of doing their work properly when he is near.

It is expected that servants should rise early enough to be at work by the time it is light. In sections of country that are sickly, it will be found conductive to health in the fall to make the hands eat their breakfast before going into the dew. In winter, as the days are short and nights long, it will be no encroachment upon their necessary rest to make them eat breakfast before daylight. One properly taken care of, and supplied with good tools, is certainly able to do more work than under other circumstances. While at work they should be brisk. If one is called to you, or sent from you, and he does not move briskly, chastise him at once. If this does not answer, repeat the dose and double the quantity. When at work I have no objection to their whistling or singing some lively tune, but no *drawling* tunes are allowed in the field, for their motions are almost certain to keep time with the music.

. . .

In the intercouse of negroes among themselves, no quarrelling nor opprobrious epithets, no swearing nor obscene language, should ever be allowed. Children should be required to be respectful to those who are grown, more especially to the old, and the strong should never be allowed to impose on the weak. Men should be taught that it is disgraceful to abuse or impose on the weaker sex, and if a man should so far forget and disgrace himself as to strike a woman, the women should be made to give him the hickory and ride him on a rail. The wife, however, should never be required to strike her husband, for fear of its unhappy influences over their future respect for and kindness to each other.

The negroes should not be allowed to run about over the neighborhood; they should be encouraged to attend church, when it is within convenient distance. Where there are pious negroes on a plantation who are so disposed, they should be allowed and encouraged to hold prayer meetings among themselves; and when the number is too great to be accommodated in one of the negro houses, they should have a separate building for the purpose of worship. Where it can be done, the services of a minister should be procured for their special business. By having the appointments for preaching at noon, during summer, and at night during winter, the preacher could consult his own convenience as to the day of the week, without, in the least, interfering with the duties of the farm.

A word to those who think and care but little about their own soul or the soul of the negro, and yet desire a good reputation for their children. Children are fond of the company of negroes, not only because the deference shown them makes them feel perfectly at ease, but the subjects of conversation are on a level with their capacity; while the simple tales, and the witch and ghost stories so common among negroes, excite the young imagination and enlist the feelings. If in this assococation the child becomes familiar with indelicate, vulgar, and lascivious manners and conversation, an impression is made upon the mind and heart which lasts for years—perhaps for life. Could we, in all cases, trace effects to their real causes, I doubt not but many young men and women of respectable parentage and bright prospects, who have made shipwreck of all their earthly hopes, have been led to the fatal step by the seeds of corruption which, in the days of childhood and youth, were sown in their hearts by the indelicate and lascivious manners and conversation of their father's negroes.

Farmers' Register (1837)

When negroes are accustomed to an overseer, and you dispense with the services of one, they *must* be exposed to a great deal of temptation, far more than they can resist. And education has not taught them the difference between right and wrong; at any rate, their ideas on the subject must be confused. What they learn of the moral code, is gathered from observation, and the example of others, their superiors. How can any person, who, has no overseer, be all at hours with his negroes, when he is delivering his grain for example? Let him turn his back, and a cunning fellow will help himself to a bushel of corn or wheat, and he will never be informed upon by his fellow laborers, though ever so honest; for an informer, in their eyes, is held in greater detestation than the most notorious thief.

I admit that many overseers are vain, weak tyrants, "dressed in a little brief authority," but probably a larger proportion of farmers of Virginia are indifferent cultivators of the soil. I regard an overseer as an indispensable agent, whose first qualities should be honesty and firmness, united with forbearance and good temper. Sobriety is a *sine qua non*. A written agreement should be drawn up between the employer and the employed, to be signed by both, setting forth the terms, and mentioning the most important requisitions, which will occur to every one. An overseer's wages should always be paid in money; for if you give him a part of the crops, your land will be worked to death, and never have a dozen loads of manure spread upon it. In addition to this, your views and his will frequently come into collision.

Your overseer should be treated with marked respect; for if you treat him contemptuously or familiarly, your authority and his are injured. He should not be allowed to strike a negro with his fist or a stick, nor ever to punish with severity; for it is not the severity, but certainty of punishment, that wins implicit obedience.

The subject before me turns my thoughts to the food, houses, and clothing of the negro. The master should ever bear in mind, that he is the guardian and protector of his slaves, who if well treated and used, are the happiest laboring class in the world.

· · ·

SOURCE: *Farmers' Register*, V (September, 1837), pp. 301–2.

Liberally and plentifully fed, warmly clad and housed, your negroes work harder and more willingly, will be more healthy, and their moral character be improved, for they will not be urged, by a hungry longing for meat, to steal their masters' hogs, sheep, and poultry, or to make predatory excursions upon his neighbors. Your negroes will breed much faster when well clothed, fed and housed; which fact, offers an inducement to those slave owners, whose hearts do not overflow with feelings of humanity.

The character of the negro is much underrated. It is like the plastic clay, which, may be molded into agreeable or disagreeable figures, according to the skill of the molder. The man who storms at, and curses his negroes, and who tells them they are a parcel of infernal rascals, not to be trusted, will surely make them just what he calls them; and so far from loving such a master, they will hate him. Now, if you be not suspicious, and induce them to think, by slight trusts, that they are not unworthy of some confidence, you will make them honest, useful, and affectionate creatures.

Stancil Barwick (1855)

Dear Sir:　I received your letter on yesterday ev'ng was vary sorry to hear that you had heard that I was treating your Negroes so cruely. Now sir I do say to you in truth that the report is false thear is no truth in it. No man nor set of men has ever seen me mistreat one of the Negroes on the Place. Now as regards the wimin loosing children, Treaty [a slave] lost one it is true. I never heard of her being in that way until she lost it. She was at the house all the time, I never made her do any work at all. She said to me in the last month that she did not know she was in that way her self untill she lost the child. As regards Louisine she was in the field it is true but she was workt as she please. I never said a word to her in any way at all untill she com to me in the field and said she was sick. I told her to go home. She started an on the way she miscarried. She was about five months gone. This is the true statement of case. Now sir a pon my word an honnor I have tride to carry out your wishes as near as I possibly could doo. Ever since I have been on the place I have not been to three neighbours houses since I have been hear I com hear to attend to my Businiss　I have done it faithfully the reports that have been sent must have been carried from this Place by Negroes the fact is I have made the Negro men work an made them go strait that is what is the matter an is the reason why that my Place is talk of the settlement. I have found among the Negro men two or three hard cases an I have had to deal rite Ruff but not cruly at all. Among them Abram has been as triflin as any man on the place. Now sir what I have wrote you is truth an it cant be disputed by no man on earth.

source:　From Ulrich B. Phillips, ed., *Plantation and Frontier* (Cleveland: A. H. Clark; 1909), pp. 312–13.

E. "A Distinct and Rather Dispicable Class"

• *Frederick Law Olmsted* (1856)

The son of a wealthy Connecticut merchant, Frederick Law Olmsted (1822–1903) dabbled at scientific agriculture, journalism, and world travel before becoming America's foremost landscape architect—the creator of New York City's Central Park and numerous other parks from Boston to San Francisco. In 1852, Olmsted accepted an assignment from the *New York Times* to travel through the southern slave states in search of objective and dispassionate truth. His extensive journeys resulted in three books which were accepted by northern contemporaries and by later historians as the most accurate accounts ever written of the slaveholding South.

Olsted did approach his subject with certain strong preconceptions. He was convinced, for example, that free labor is always cheaper and more productive than slave labor. In discussing the free white workers of the South, he therefore needed to explain why supposedly superior free labor was not displacing the costly and inefficient labor of slaves. As we can see below, Olsted suggests two answers: (1) Negro slavery stifles the incentives of whites by degrading the image of labor; (2) The "poor whites" are "said to be extremely ignorant and immoral, as well as indolent and unambitious." Olsted frequently relied on the opinion of slaveholding informants, though he was also an acute observer.

We still have much to learn about the social and economic status of non-slaveholding whites. Far from conforming to the stereotyped picture of indolent "poor whites," most of the nonslaveholders owned land and operated family farms. Their great handicap, when competing with slaveholders, was their inability to hire nonfamily labor to take advantage of the profits possible from expanded production. Free labor was in short supply precisely because land was plentiful, and most white Southerners preferred family farming to working for wages. There can also be no doubt that many whites disdained certain kinds of work that had long been associated with slaves. When Olmsted refers to the "high wages" commanded by Negroes working on railroads and in tobacco factories, he means "wages" paid to owners who have "hired out" their slaves. For slaves provided a highly mobile form of labor that could be applied to the fluctuating demands of the market. Nonslaveholders, engaged for the most part in self-sufficient agriculture, lived on the periphery of this expanding market economy. Deprived of the immense capital gains which rising slave prices gave to the owners of "human capital," the nonslaveholders lived in a world of constricted horizons—a world that could best be escaped by joining the slaveholding class.

Frederick Law Olmsted (1856)

I learned that there were no white laboring men here who hired themselves out by the month. The poor white people that had to labor for their living, never would work steadily at any employment. "They mostly followed boat-ing"—hiring as hands on the bateaus that navigate the small streams and canals, but never for a longer term at once than a single trip of a boat, whether that might be long or short. At the end of the trip they were paid by the day. Their wages were from fifty cents to a dollar, varying with the demand and individual capacities. They hardly ever worked on farms except in harvest, when they usually received a dollar a day, sometimes more. In harvest-time, most of the rural mechanics closed their shops and hired out to the farmers at a dollar a day, which would indicate that their ordinary earn-ings are considerably less than this. At other than harvest-time, the poor white people, who had no trade, would sometimes work for the farmers by the job; not often at any regular agricultural labor, but at getting rails or shingles, or clearing land.

He [Mr. Newman, Olmsted's informant] did not know that they were particular about working with negroes, but no white man would ever do cer-tain kinds of work (such as taking care of cattle, or getting water or wood to be used in the house), and if you should ask a white man you had hired, to do such things, he would get mad and tell you he wasn't a nigger. Poor white girls never hired out to do servants' work, but they would come and help another white woman about her sewing or quilting, and take wages for it. But these girls were not very respectable generally, and it was not agreeable to have them in your house, though there were some very respectable ladies that would go out to sew. Farmers depended almost entirely upon their negroes; it was only when they were hard pushed by their crops, that they got white hands to help them any.

Negroes had commanded such high wages lately, to work on railroads and in tobacco-factories, that farmers were tempted to hire out too many of their people [i.e., their slaves], and to undertake to do too much work with those they retained, and thus they were often driven to employ white men, and to give them very high wages by the day, when they found themselves getting much behindhand with their crops. He had been driven very hard in this way this last season; he had been so unfortunate as to lose one of his best women, who died in child-bed just before harvest. The loss of the woman and her child, for the child had died also, just at that time, came very hard upon him. He would not have taken a thousand dollars of any man's money for them. He had had to hire white men to help him, but they were poor sticks and would be half the time drunk, and you never know what to depend

SOURCE: Frederick Law Olmsted, *A Journey in the Seaboard Slave States* (New York: Dix and Edwards, 1856), pp. 82–85.

upon with them. One fellow that he had hired, who had agreed to work for him all though harvest, got him to pay him some wages in advance (he said it was to buy him some clothes with, so he could go to meeting, Sunday, at the Court-House), and went off the next day, right in the middle of harvest, and he never had seen him since. He had heard of him—he was on a boat —but he didn't reckon he should ever get his money again.

Of course, he did not see how white laborers were ever going to come into competition with negroes here, at all. You never could depend on white men, and you couldn't *drive* them any; they wouldn't stand it. Slaves were the only reliable laborers—you could command them and *make* them do what was right.

From the manner in which he always talked of the white laboring people, it was evident that, although he placed them in some sort on an equality with himself, and that in his intercourse with them he wouldn't think of asserting for himself any superior dignity, or even feel himself to be patronizing them in not doing so, yet he, all the time, recognized them as a distinct and a rather despicable class, and wanted to have as little to do with them as he conveniently could.

I have been once or twice told that the poor white people, meaning those, I suppose, who bring nothing to market to exchange for money but their labor, although they may own a cabin and a little furniture, and cultivate land enough to supply themselves with (maize) bread, are worse off in almost all respects than the slaves. They are said to be extremely ignorant and im-moral, as well as indolent and unambitious. That their condition is not as unfortunate by any means as that of negroes, however, is most obvious, since from among them, men *sometimes* elevate themselves to positions and habits of usefulness, and respectability. They are said to "corrupt" the negroes, and to encourage them to steal, or to work for them at night and on Sundays, and to pay them with liquor, and also to constantly associate licentiously with them. They seem, nevertheless, more than any other portion of the community, to hate and despise the negroes.

F. The Proslavery Argument

- *Thomas R. Dew* (1832)
- *William Harper* (1837)

Like the North, the antebellum South had a small class that today would be termed "intellectuals." These were the ministers, lawyers, professors, journalists, and novelists who felt at home with abstract ideas and reasoned argument; who were familiar with the Western heritage of social philosophy; and who felt it a social duty to place immediate problems within an organized and ostensibly objective system of meaning.

Like their northern counterparts, the southern intellectuals were rather remote from the family farmers, artisans, and shopkeepers who made up most of the population. They contributed to an ideology which tended to justify and give a higher social purpose to the governing class—in the South, the large slaveholders. At the same time, the southern intellectuals held up standards of selfless duty and moral stewardship that could be used to measure the shortcomings of the rich and powerful. In many respects, their social theory was simply a variation, played in a more conservative key, on the common American themes of moral influence, responsible self-government, "cheerful obedience," "separate spheres," and national mission (see Unit One). Like many northern writers and preachers, they were primarily concerned with the disintegrative effects of popular sovereignty, individualism, and economic expansion. They sought to find American substitutes for the authoritarian institutions that had supposedly ensured stability, social unity, and historical continuity in the past. What distinguished the southern intellectuals was their need to assimilate Negro slavery to this larger vision of moral improvement and ordered historical progress.

In actuality, the proslavery ideology owed much to transplanted northern ministers and to Southerners who had been educated at northern colleges like Princeton and Yale. The second generation of major southern apologists also drew heavily on the contemporary social theorists of Europe, particularly those reacting against the alienating and dehumanizing effects of laissez-faire capitalism. Here we shall limit our attention to two of the relatively early but highly influential attempts to rationalize the polarities of southern life.

Thomas R. Dew (1802–1846), the author of the first selection, was a respected professor of history, metaphysics, and political economy at William and Mary (in 1836 he became president of the college). In this *Review of the Debates in the Virginia Legislature*, Dew is responding to an unprecedented and, to him, alarming legislative debate that had rocked the entire South during the winter of 1831–1832. Following the Nat Turner insurrection, several legislators, especially from the nonslaveholding western counties, had demanded that steps be taken for the gradual emancipation and deportation of all slaves. The legislature had refused to even authorize a committee to study the feasibility of emancipation. But for the first and last time in history, a southern legislature had heard speeches denouncing slavery as a social evil. Tidewater planters, who had always monopolized the state's political power, had faced the spectre of nonslaveholders contending that a form of property which endangered public security could no longer be tolerated.

Dew's arguments are designed to silence such heretical outbursts. Unlike most later apologists, he does not deny that slavery, abstractly considered, is wrong. But as a utilitarian, he insists that institutions and policies must be judged by their consequences, and that the options of deportation or of attempted assimilation would lead to far worse evils than slavery. Above all, Dew rests his case on the inviolability of private property as the very basis of civilization. He also holds that a given system of labor influences "our moral and religious character" and determines "the social and political state of man" (a thesis to be advanced by Karl Marx years later). Hence Negro slavery, far from being a superficial excrescence, lay at the center of the southern social order. For Dew, as for an increasing number of southern intellectuals, Americans were fortunate in being able to rely for productive labor on a supposedly inferior race.

This theme is more aggressively developed by Chancellor William Harper (1790–1847) of South Carolina. The son of a Methodist missionary, Harper was born in the British slave colony of Antigua. After studing law in South Carolina, he served as Chancellor of Missouri Territory, as a United States Senator from South Carolina, and as a judge and Chancellor of the same state. An ardent defender of states rights, Harper became one of the most outspoken critics of the egalitarian philosophy embodied in the Declaration of Independence: "Is it not palpably nearer the truth to say that no man was ever born free, and that no two men were ever born equal? Man is born in a state of the most helpless dependence on others." Starting from this tough-minded "realism" regarding human power, Harper tries to expose the hypocrisy of so-called "free societies" which simply disguise the compulsions that make men work. In the 1850s, this proslavery critique of the North was more brilliantly elaborated in George Fitzhugh's *Sociology for the South, or the Failure of Free Society*, and *Cannibals All! or Slaves Without Masters*.

Thomas R. Dew (1832)

. . . A race of people, differing from us in color and in habits, and vastly inferior in the scale of civilization, have been increasing and spreading, "growing with our growth, and strengthening with our strength," until they have become interwined and intertwisted with every fibre of society. Go through our southern country, and every where you see the negro slave by the side of the white man; you find him alike in the mansion of the rich, the cabin of the poor, the workshops of the mechanics, and the field of the planter. Upon the contemplation of a population framed like this, a curious and interesting question readily suggests itself to the inquiring mind:—Can these two distinct races of people, now living together as master and servant, be ever separated? Can the black be sent back to his African home, or will the day ever arrive when he can be liberated from his thraldom, and mount upwards in the scale of civilization and rights, to an equaiity with the white? This is a question of truly momentous character. . . .

SOURCE: From *The Pro-Slavery Argument* (Philadelphia: Lippincott, Grambo and Co., 1853), pp. 287–90, 384, 386–87, 420–23, 451–52.

Revolutionary France, actuated by the most intemperate and phrenetic zeal for liberty and equality, attempted to legislate the free people of color, in the Island of St. Domingo, into all the rights and privileges of the whites; and, but a season afterwards, convinced of her madness, she attempted to retrace her steps. But it was too late. The deed had been done. The bloodiest and most shocking insurrection [of slaves] ever recorded in the annals of history had broken out, and the whole island was involved in frightful carnage and anarchy, and France, in the end, has been stript "of the brightest jewel in her crown," the fairest and most valuable of all her colonial possessions. Since the revolution, France, Spain and Portugal, large owners of colonial possessions, have not only not abolished slavery in their colonies, but have not even abolished the slave trade in practice.

In our southern slaveholding country, the question of emancipation has never been seriously discussed in any of our legislatures, until the whole subject, under the most exciting circumstances, was, during the last winter [1831–1832] brought up for discussion in the Virginia Legislature, and plans of partial or total abolition were earnestly pressed upon the attention of that body. It is well known that, during the last summer, in the county of Southampton, in Virginia, a few slaves, led on by Nat Turner, rose in the night, and murdered, in the most inhuman and shocking manner, between sixty and seventy of the unsuspecting whites of that county. The news, of course, was rapidly diffused, and, with it, consternation and dismay were spread throughout the state, destroying, for a time, all feeling of security and confidence; and, even when subsequent development had proved that the conspiracy had been originated by a fanatical negro preacher (whose confessions prove, beyond a doubt, mental aberration), and that this conspiracy embraced but few slaves, all of whom had paid the penalty of their crimes, still the excitement remained, still the repose of the commonwealth was disturbed, for the ghastly horrors of the Southampton tragedy could not immediately be banished from the mind—and *rumor*, too, with her thousand tongues, was busily engaged in spreading tales of disaffection, plots, insurrections, and even massacres, which frightened the timid, and harassed and mortified the whole of the slaveholding poulation. During this period of excitement, when reason was almost banished from the mind . . . we are not to wonder that, even in the lower part of Virginia, many should have seriously inquired if this supposed monstrous evil could not be removed from our bosom? Some looked to the removal of the free people of color, by the efforts of the Colonization Society, as an antidote to all our ills. Some were disposed to strike at the root of the evil: to call on the General Government for aid, and, by the labors of *Hercules*, to extirpate the curse of slavery from the land.

. . .

There is slave property of the value of $100,000,000 in the State of Virginia, etc., and it matters but little how you destroy it, whether by the slow process of the cautious practitioners, or with the frightful despatch of the self-confident *quack*; when it is gone, no matter how, the deed will be done, and Virginia will be a desert.

We shall now proceed to examine briefly, the most dangerous of all the wild doctrines advanced by the abolitionists in the Virginia Legislature, and the one which, no doubt, will be finally acted upon, if ever this business of emancipation shall be seriously commenced. *It was contended that property is the creature of civil society, and is subject to action, even to destruction.* . . .

"My views are briefly these," said Mr. [Charles James] Faulkner; "they go to the foundation upon which the social edifice rests—property is the creature of civil society. So long as that property is not dangerous to the good order of society, it may and will be tolerated. But, sir, so soon as it is ascertained to jeopardize the peace, the happiness, the good order, nay the very existence of society, from that moment the right by which they hold their property is gone, society ceases to give its consent, the condition upon which they are permitted to hold it is violated, their right ceases."

• • •

The doctrine of these gentlemen, so far from being true in its application, is not true in theory. The great object of government is the protection of property;—from the days of the patriarchs down to the present time, the great desideratum has been to find out the most efficient mode of protecting property. There is not a government at this moment in Christendom, whose peculiar practical character is not the result of the state of property.

• • •

We have thus examined fully this scheme of emancipation and deportation, and trust we have satisfactorily shown, that the whole plan is utterly impracticable, requiring an expense and sacrifice of property far beyond the entire resources of the state and federal governments. We shall now proceed to inquire, whether we can emancipate our slaves with permission that they remain among us.

Emancipation without Deportation.—We candidly confess, that we look upon this last mentioned scheme as much more practicable, and likely to be forced upon us, than the former. We consider it, at the same time, so fraught with danger and mischief both to the whites and blacks—so utterly subversive of the welfare of the slaveholding country, in both an economical and moral point of view, that we cannot, upon any principle of right or expediency, give it our sanction. Almost all the speakers in the Virginia Legislature seemed to think there ought to be no emancipation without deportation. . . .

Even the northern philanthropists themselves admit, generally, that there should be no emancipation without removal. Perhaps, then, under these circumstances, we might have been justified in closing our review with a consideration of the colonization scheme; but as we are anxious to survey this subject fully in all its aspects, and to demonstrate upon every ground the complete justification of the whole southern country in a further continuance of that system of slavery which has been originated by no fault of theirs, and continued and increased contrary to their most earnest desires and petitions, we have determined briefly to examine this scheme likewise. . . .

The ground upon which we shall rest our arguments on this subject is, *that the slaves, in both an economical and moral point of view, are entirely unfit for a state of freedom among the whites*; and we shall produce such proofs and illustrations of our position, as seem to us perfectly conclusive. That condition of our species from which the most important consequences flow, says Mr. [James] Mill, the Utilitarian, is the necessity of labor for the supply of the fund of our necessaries and conveniences. It is this which influences, perhaps more than any other, even our moral and religious character, and determines more than everything else besides, the social and political state of man. . . .

We shall, therefore, proceed at once to inquire what effect would be produced upon the slaves of the South in an economical point of view, by emancipation with permission to remain—whether the voluntary labor of the freedman would be as great as the involuntary labor of the slave? Fortunately for us, this question has been so frequently and fairly subjected to the test of experience, that we are no longer left to vain and fruitless conjecture. Much was said in the legislature of Virginia about superiority of free labor over slave, and perhaps, under certain circumstances, this might be true; but, in the present instance, the question is between *the relative amounts of labor which may be obtained from slaves before and after their emancipation*. Let us, then, first commence with our country, where, it is well known to everybody, that slave labor is vastly more efficient and productive than the labor of free blacks.

Taken as a whole class, the latter must be considered the most worthless and indolent of the citizens of the United States. It is well known that throughout the whole extent of our Union, they are looked upon as the very *drones* and *pests* of society. Nor does this character arise from the disabilities and disfranchisement by which the law attempts to guard against them. In the non-slaveholding States, where they have been more elevated by law, this kind of population is in a worse condition, and much more troublesome to society, than in the slaveholding, and especially in the planting States.

· · ·

It is said slavery is wrong, in the *abstract* at least, and contrary to the spirit of Christianity. To this we answer as before, that any question must be determined by its circumstances, and if, as really is the case, we cannot get rid of slavery without producing a greater injury to both the masters and slaves, there is no rule of conscience or revealed law of God which *can* condemn us. . . .

With regard to the assertion that slavery is against the spirit of Christianity, we are ready to admit the general assertion, but deny most positively, that there is anything in the Old or New Testament, which would go to show that slavery, when once introduced, ought at all events to be abrogated, or that the master commits any offence in holding slaves. The children of Israel themselves were slaveholders, and were not condemned for it. All the patriarchs themselves were slaveholders; Abraham had more than three hundred. . . .

When we turn to the New Testament, we find not one single passage at all calculated to disturb the conscience of an honest slaveholder. No one can read it without seeing and admiring that the meek and humble Saviour of the world in no instance meddled with the established institutions of mankind; he came to save a fallen world, and not to excite the black passions of men, and array them in deadly hostility against each other.

William Harper (1837)

President [Thomas R.] Dew has shown that the institution of slavery is a principal cause of civilization. Perhaps nothing can be more evident than it is the sole cause. If anything can be predicated as universally true of uncultivated man, it is that he will not labor what is absolutely necessary to maintain his existence. Labor is pain to those who are unaccustomed to it, and the nature of man is averse to pain. Even with the training, the helps and motives of civilization, we find that this aversion cannot be overcome in many individuals of the most cultivated societies. The coercion of slavery alone is adequate to form man to habits of labor. Without it, there can be no accumulation of property, no providence for the future, no tastes for comfort or elegancies, which are the characteristics and essentials of civilization. He who has obtained the command of another's labor, first begins to accumulate and provide for the future, and the foundations of civilization are laid.

• • •

What is the essential character of *slavery*, and in what does it differ from the *servitude* of other countries? If I should venture on a definition, I should say that where a man is compelled to labor at the will of another, and to give him much the greater portion of the product of his labor, there *slavery* exists; and it is immaterial by what sort of compulsion the will of the laborer is subdued. It is what no human being would do without some sort of compulsion. He cannot be compelled to labor by blows. No—but what difference does it make, if you can inflict any other sort of torture which will be equally effectual in subduing the will? if you can starve him, or alarm him for the subsistence of himself or his family? And is it not under this compulsion that the *freeman* labors? I do not mean in every particular case, but in the general. Will any one be hardy enough to say that he is at his own disposal, or has the government of himself? True, he may change his employer if he is dissatisfied with his conduct towards him; but this is a privilege he would in the majority of cases gladly abandon, and render the connection between them indissoluble.

SOURCE: From *The Pro-Slavery Argument* (Philadelphia: Lippincott, Grambo and Co., 1853), pp. 3–4, 52–58.

There is far less of the interest and attachment in his relation to his employer, which so often exists between the master and the slave, and mitigates the condition of the latter. An intelligent English traveler has characterized as the most miserable and degraded of all beings, "a masterless slave." And is not the condition of the laboring poor of other countries too often that of masterless slaves? Take the following description of a *free* laborer, no doubt highly colored, quoted by the author to whom I have before referred.

"What is that defective being, with calfless legs and stooping shoulders, weak in body and mind, inert, pusillanimous and stupid, whose premature wrinkles and furtive glance, tell of misery and degradation? That is an English peasant or pauper, for the words are synonymous. His sire was a pauper, and his mother's milk wanted nourishment. From infancy his food has been bad, as well as insufficient; and he now feels the pains of unsatisfied hunger nearly whenever he is awake. But half clothed, and never supplied with more warmth than suffices to cook his scanty meals, cold and wet come to him, and stay by him with the weather. . . .

"His [marriage] partner and his little ones being like himself, often hungry, seldom warm, sometimes sick without aid, and always sorrowful without hope, are greedy, selfish, and vexing; so, to use his own expression, he hates the sight of them, and resorts to his hovel, only becaue a hedge affords less shelter from the wind and rain. . . ."

$$\bullet \quad \bullet \quad \bullet$$

That they are called free, undoubtedly aggravates the sufferings of the slaves of other regions. They see the enormous inequality which exists, and feel their own misery, and can hardly conceive otherwise, than that there is some injustice in the institutions of society to occasion these. They regard the apparently more fortunate class as oppressors, and it adds bitterness that they should be of the same name and race. They feel indignity more acutely, and more of discontent and evil passion is excited; they feel that it is mockery that calls them free. Men do not so much hate and envy those who are separated from them by a wide distance, and some apparently impassable barrier, as those who approach nearer to their own condition, and with whom they habitually bring themselves into comparison. The slave with us is not tantalized with the name of freedom, to which his whole condition gives the lie, and would do so [even] if he were emancipated tomorrow. The African slave sees that nature herself has marked him as a separate—and if left to himself, I have no doubt he would feel it to be an inferior—race, and interposed a barrier almost insuperable to his becoming a member of the same society, standing on the same footing of right and privilege with his master.

That the African negro is an inferior variety of the human race, is, I think, now generally admitted, and his distinguishing characteristics are such as peculiarly mark him out for the situation which he occupies among us. . . .

Let me ask if this people do not furnish the very material out of which slaves ought to be made, and whether it be not an improving of their condition to make them the slaves of civilized masters?

G. Polarized South, Polarized Nation

• *Hinton R. Helper* (*1857*)

The proslavery ideology failed to convince all white Southerners. But the challengers of a dominant ideology, especially one that is militantly enforced and that conceals explosive potentialities for violence, are often rather wild eccentrics. This generalization at least holds true for Hinton R. Helper (1829–1909).

Helper was the son of a small farmer in western North Carolina. Though he claimed that his father at one time owned a few slaves, Helper himself worked in the fields and then in a store from which he embezzled several hundred dollars in cash, later promising to pay back his employer. Enticed by the gold rush, he traveled in 1850 to New York and sailed off to California via Cape Horn. Helper's three years in California produced little gold but did yield an embittered book, *The Land of Gold*, which presented hostile caricatures of the Chinese, Jews, Indians, and Irish. Throughout his long life, Helper was an inveterate racist. His contempt for blacks exceeded that of the proslavery theorists. But after returning to North Carolina, he began to brood over the plight of nonslaveholding whites and concluded that they, far more than the blacks, were the victims of slavery. Helper found confirmation for this view in the statistics of the 1850 Census, which showed in spectacular contrasts that the North was forging ahead of the South by every positive measurement.

Helper prudently moved north to New York in order to complete his sensational book on "the impending crisis of the South." Viewed from one perspective, the resulting exposé is instantly discredited by Helper's racial prejudice, by his naive reading of statistics, and by his exaggerated view of a backward, subservient South, blighted by the twin curses of blacks and black slavery. Viewed from another perspective, only a "kook" like Helper —whose ancestors' original German name had literally meant "helper" or "abettor"—was capable of striking the planter oligarchy at its vulnerable Achilles heel. Southern leaders had shown not only anger but confidence and resourcefulness in dealing with outside critics, including the most recent and threatening critic, Harriet Beecher Stowe. But in 1857, when Horace Greeley's *New York Tribune* began promoting Helper's "inside story" as if it were an exposé by a fugitive Catholic nun or the revelation from one of Brigham Young's emancipated Mormon wives, the South exploded in frenzy.

What deepened the outrage was Helper's unseemly alliance with the new Republican party. It was bad enough that a Southerner, a self-appointed spokesman for the "poor whites," should make invidious comparisons between the progress of North and South. Far more intolerable was Helper's revolutionary appeal to nonslaveholders, suggesting a violent overthrow of planter domination.

But for astute southern leaders, it was Helper's racism that posed the lethal threat. These leaders knew that in any final showdown, their power would depend on the grassroots Negrophobia of white farmers and villagers, not on finely-spun theories justifying the political economy of slavery. By combining racism with a populist attack on the planter oligarchy—"the lords of the lash"—Helper drove a wedge through the heart of proslavery ideology. In so doing, he threatened not only to mobilize the nonslaveholding whites of the South but to forge an alliance with northern farmers and workingmen who, because of racial prejudice, had usually spurned the appeals of abolitionists. It was for these reasons that southern officials publicly burned copies of Helper's book and persecuted anyone indiscreet enough to display it. For similar reasons, the Republican party adopted a "compendium" of the book as a semi-official text.

For all its defects, *The Impending Crisis of the South* occupies a unique place in American political history. No other work has rivaled it as a symbol of subversion in the eyes of some Americans and of freedom of expression in the eyes of others. In the critical presidential campaign of 1860, Republicans distributed over one hundred thousand copies while Southerners burned and denounced the book. Meanwhile, Congress stormed over Helper's text. Though John B. Sherman of Ohio was slated to be Speaker of the House of Representatives, his casual endorsement of Helper deprived him of this honored post. Such a volatile reaction to a "mere book," unparalleled in American history, dramatized the deepening polarities of American society—and the uncertainties over the fate of outsiders when no one could be wholly certain of remaining inside.

Hinton R. Helper (1857)

It is a fact well known to every intelligent Southerner, that we are compelled to go to the North for almost every article of utility and adornment, from matches, shoepegs and paintings, up to cotton-mills, steamships and statuary; that we have no foreign trade, no princely merchants, nor respectable artists; that, in comparison with the Free States, we contribute nothing to the literature, polite arts and inventions of the age; that, for want of profitable employment at home, large numbers of our native population find themselves necessitated to emigrate to the West, while the Free States retain not only the larger proportion of those born within their own limits, but induce, annually, hundreds of thousands of foreigners to settle and remain amongst them; that almost everything produced at the North meets with ready sale, while, at the same time, there is no demand, even among our own citizens, for the productions of Southern industry; that, owing to the absence of a proper system of business among us, the North becomes, in one way or anoth-

SOURCE: Hinton R. Helper, *The Impending Crisis of the South* (New York: A. B. Burdick, 1859), pp. 25–26, 28–29, 40, 42–43.

er, the proprietor and dispenser of all our floating wealth, and that we are dependent on Northern capitalists for the means necessary to build our railroads, canals and other public improvements; that if we want to visit a foreign country, even though it may lie directly south of us, we find no convenient way of getting there except by taking passage through a Northern port; and that nearly all the profits arising from the exchange of commodities, from insurance and shipping offices, and from the thousand and one industrial pursuits of the country, accrue to the North, and are there invested in the erection of those magnificent cities and stupendous works of art which dazzle the eyes of the South, and attest the superiority of free institutions!

· · ·

And now that we have come to the very heart and soul of our subject, we feel no disposition to mince matters, but mean to speak plainly and to the point, without any equivocation, mental reservation, or secret evasion whatever. The son of a venerated parent, who, while he lived, was a considerate and merciful slaveholder, a native of the South, born and bred in North Carolina, of a family whose home has been in the valley of the Yadkin for nearly a century and a half, a Southerner by instinct and by all the influences of thought, habits and kindred, and with the desire and fixed purpose to reside permanently within the limits of the South, and with the expectation of dying there also—we feel that we have the right to express our opinion, however humble or unimportant it may be, on any and every question that affects the public good. . . .

And now to the point. In our opinion, an opinion which has been formed from data obtained by assiduous researches and comparisons, from laborious investigation, logical reasoning, and earnest reflection, the causes which have impeded the progress and prosperity of the South, which have dwindled our commerce and other similar pursuits, into the most contemptible insignificance; sunk a large majority of our people in galling poverty and ignorance, rendered a small minority conceited and tyrannical, and driven the rest away from their homes; entailed upon us a humiliating dependence on the Free States; disgraced us in the recesses of our own souls, and brought us under reproach in the eyes of all civilized and enlightened nations—may all be traced to one common source, and there find solution in the most hateful and horrible word, that was ever incorporated into the vocabulary of human economy —*Slavery*.

· · ·

In making up these [statistical] tables we have two objects in view; the first is to open the eyes of the non-slaveholders of the South to the system of deception that has been so long practiced upon them, and the second is to show slaveholders themselves—we have reference only to those who are not too perverse, or ignorant, to perceive naked truths—that free labor is far more respectable, profitable, and productive, than slave labor. In the South, unfortunately, no kind of labor is either free or respectable. Every white man who is under the necessity of earning his bread, by the sweat of his brow, or by manual labor, in any capacity, no matter how unassuming in deportment, or exemplary in morals, is treated as if he were a loathsome beast, and shunned with disdain. His soul may be the very seat of honor and integrity, yet without slaves—himself a slave—he is accounted as nobody, and would be deemed intolerably presumptuous, if he dared to open his lips, even so wide as to give faint utterance to a three-lettered monosyllable, like yea or nay, in the presence of an august knight of the whip and the lash.

. . .

The lords of the lash are not only absolute masters of the blacks, who are bought and sold, and driven about like so many cattle, but they are also the oracles and arbiters of all the non-slaveholding whites, whose freedom is merely nominal, and whose unparalleled illiteracy and degradation is purposely and fiendishly perpetuated. How little the "poor white trash," the great majority of the Southern people, know of the real condition of the country, is, indeed, sadly astonishing. The truth is, they know nothing of public measures, and little of private affairs, except what their imperious masters, the slave-drivers, condescend to tell, and that is but precious little, and even that little, always garbled and one-sided, is never told except in public harangues; for the haughty cavaliers of shackles and handcuffs will not degrade themselves by holding private converse with those who have neither dimes nor hereditary rights in human flesh.

Whenever it pleases, and to the extent it pleases, a slaveholder to become communicative, poor whites may hear with fear and trembling, but not speak. They must be as mum as dumb brutes, and stand in awe of their august superiors, or be crushed with stern rebukes, cruel oppressions, or downright violence. If they dare to think for themselves, their thoughts must be forever concealed. The expression of any sentiment at all conflicting with the gospel of slavery, dooms them at once in the community in which they live, and then, whether willing or unwilling, they are obliged to become heroes, martyrs, or exiles. . . .

Non-slaveholders are not only kept in ignorance of what is transpiring at the North, but they are continually misinformed of what is going on even in the South. Never were the poorer classes of a people, and those classes so largely in the majority, and all inhabiting the same country, so basely duped, so adroitly swindled, or so unpardonably outraged.

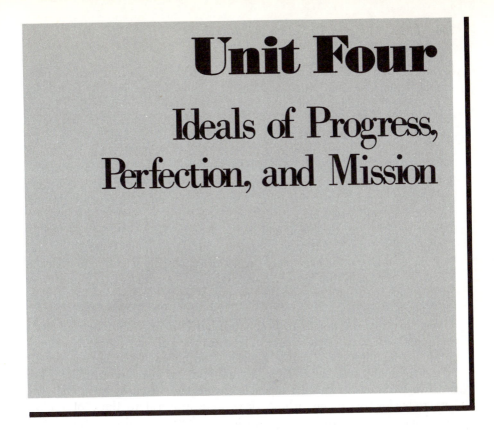

Unit Four

Ideals of Progress, Perfection, and Mission

Introduction

From the competitive pursuit of wealth and power, we moved in Unit Three to the poor and the powerless, to the jagged edges of American culture where theories of moral influence, consent, and contract could neither prevent nor disguise brute violence. The sharp polarities of American life—the lack of gradations, for example, between the assimilation and removal of Indians or between the slavery of blacks and the freedom of whites—now lead us on to the unifying realm of ideals. It can be argued, of course, that ideals had little effect on the actual disparities and inequalities of American society, and may even have fostered illusions and deepened convictions of national self-righteousness. But except for saying that such arguments are oversimplified, this is not the place for such a debate. The fact remains that American culture has been permeated with ideals of progress, perfection, and mission. The United States was unique among nineteenth-century nations in being formally "dedicated," as Lincoln put it, to a "proposition" or ideal—according to Lincoln, the ideal of equality. In each of the preceding Units, we have encountered ideals of progress, perfection, and mission in various contexts. We are now prepared to examine these ideals more systematically.

Although visions of a better life had traditionally been religious in origin, often focusing on a worldly millennium of universal peace and happiness, we begin Part 1 with discussions of science and technology. The reason, quite simply, is that the rapid progress in scientific knowledge, especially knowledge of fundamental principles of cause and effect, brought "otherworldly" dreams within the mundane realm of historical possibility. Instead of having to await some revolutionary expression of God's will, it appeared that science itself might be a divine revelation that would gradually link human desires with human will and ability. It was this faith that long preserved an uneasy but buoyant marriage between science and religion. During the antebellum era, religion remained the dominant partner in this union, providing the matrix for academic instruction in the natural sciences as well as the rules for judging heresy or for threatening ultimate divorce. Yet as we shall see in Part 2, religion drew much of its new optimism from the divine "wonders" revealed by science and from the exemplary success of supposedly scientific methods of reasoning—especially the inductive or "Baconian" method of reasoning from discrete facts which might contradict otherwise irrefutable logic based on false but plausible premises.

We can leave the details to headnotes, but it is important here to stress that prior to the Civil War science in America was still very much an amateur enterprise, an adjunct to "natural theology," in no way separate conceptually or institutionally from what later became know as the "humanities." The first two selections in Part 1 happen to have been written by men who were lawyers by profession, but whose views were identical to those of leading experimental scientists who happened to have been trained in theology. For example, given more space, we might well have included parallel selections from major scientists like Edward Hitchcock. Hitchcock, the founder of the first state geologic survey and chairman of the pioneering Association of Geologists and Naturalists (which in 1847 became the American Association for the Advancement of Science), was also a trained theologian, who succeeded Heman Humphrey (Unit One, Part 1, A) as president of Amherst College, and whose most famous work was entitled *The Religion of Geology and Its Connected Sciences*. Antebellum America was by no means deficient in impressive scientific achievements, but they were never far removed from religion and moral philosophy on one side, or from technology and social use on the other.

In part 2, we devote considerably more space to the broad subject of "Revivals, Holiness, and the American Conversion of the World." For if one had to identify the most significant development in antebellum culture, compelling arguments would point to evangelical revivalism—a force that dramatically increased church membership, that exerted a profound influence on political loyalties and social reform, that affected southern slaves as well as their masters, and that supplied the rhetoric and symbolism that ultimately persuaded both North and South that they stood at Armageddon, battling for the Lord. By the 1840s, European visitors agreed that the United States had become the most "religious" nation in the world—in the sense of churchgoing, of voluntary contributions, and of public appeals to religious values. It is of crucial importance that this widespread evangelizing of America occurred just before the mass immigration of European Catholics and the beginnings of genuine industrialization.

Viewed from one perspective, the features of a modern, urban, pluralistic society were engrafted into a culture already seething with the anxieties and millennial expectations of evangelical Protestantism. But this view would miss the complex and dynamic interplay between religion and material growth. If religious revivals were hailed as the only hope for counteracting the greed and selfishness generated by "universal liberty and boundless prosperity," they were also engines of enterprise, inspiring visions of practical achievement that linked material progress with the Christianization of the world.

The selections in Part 2, while sampling varieties of both revivalist and nonrevivalist religious experience, point to the central tension of antebellum Protestantism. On the one hand, there is the yearning to become "twice-born," to rise above the stunting and demeaning pursuit of individual gain, and to subordinate American life on all levels to the transcendent law of the Gospel. On the other hand, there is growing agreement that Christianity can be *effective* in the nineteenth century only by making the fullest use of nineteenth-century methods of science and social organization. Hence, we shall see Christians exulting over America's material growth and power, confident that advances in technology and world trade assure the imminent conversion of Muslims, heathen, and "uncivilized" peoples of all kinds. Simultaneously, we can glimpse deeper fears that religious purity will become engulfed in the very tide of progress which is supposed to carry it to the far shores of the globe. The great question for evangelical leaders was how the ideal of perfect holiness could be given practical effect without becoming so engaged in the whirl of modern life as to become indistinguishable from every other competing demand. Their answer, as we have already suggested, lay in a new faith in human ability, an ability limited only by the strength of will.

The secular testing ground for this new sense of ability and strength of will was social reform. In Part 3, we turn to the so-called Temperance Reformation, in many ways the catalyst of social reform and the movement most closely intermeshed with evangelical religion. During the first two decades of the nineteenth century, temperance societies were local in character and allied with more general movements to suppress vice and public disorder. Beginning in the mid-1820s, the temperance cause gained rapid momentum as the nation's leading moral reform. To understand the growing demand for total abstinence from all alcoholic beverages, one must take account of the extraordinary amount of liquor that Americans drank—a level of *per capita* consumption far exceeding that of today. But the goal of national sobriety also reflected changing attitudes toward individual responsibility, standards of public behavior, the allocation of family and national resources, and what today would be termed "lifestyles." Above all, the goal of total abstinence provided a secular and "patriotic" test for the religious emphasis on ability, decision, and new birth. However temperance reformers might differ on theological doctrines of sin, they could agree that the drinker who persisted in drinking was destroying man's noblest gift, the capacity for rational self-control. And by destroying God's gift of perfectibility, the alcoholic was also a traitor and enemy to America's world mission.

Though temperance was predominately a middle-class reform, the cause won increasing support from groups of urban artisans and journeymen who had little use for middle-class organizations but who identified drinking as an obstacle to economic advancement and self-respect. In the early 1840s, the movement entered a new populist phase as groups of reformed drunkards formed "Washingtonian" societies, arousing new hope and compassion for men who previously had been regarded as irreclaimable.

But as we have seen in Unit Three, alcohol had long been a crucial symbol in the treatment and perception of various "out-groups," particularly Indians and working-class immigrants. Against Indians, whites had intentionally used liquor as a kind of chemical warfare agent to undermine resistance and soften targets of conquest. The effectiveness of this agent, despite the efforts of missionaries and other well-wishers, was then used as confirmation of the Indians' supposed depravity. Heavy drinking also became a symbol of the supposed depravity of immigrants, especially the Irish. While it is often said that alcohol was one of the few solaces for victims of exploitation, it should be added that Irish laborers and slumdwellers were probably no less temperate than most American farmers and artisans of the pre-1830s. What had changed, largely as a result of Protestant revivalism, was the growth of enclaves of sobriety which viewed tipsy behavior not as relaxed merriment or a blowing off of steam but as an intolerable flaunting of sin. Mass immigration added growing momentum to this collision between drinking and nondrinking subcultures. It also collapsed evangelical faith in "moral suasion," which had taken for granted relatively homogenous communities susceptible to Protestant exhortation. Part 3 concludes with the shift toward coercion, or state prohibition laws in the 1850s. While this shift in reform strategy reflected a new mood of realism and a growing reliance on political action, the temperance reformation was no less concerned with morally purifying the state—that is, with ending any state complicity, through licensing or taxation, with the liquor trade.

Abolitionism, the subject of Part 4, eventually moved toward a similar strategy of regenerating American government. From the early 1830s, the development of abolitionism was very complex and therefore cannot be summarized here. In Part 4, we begin with retrospective writings after the movement had reached maturity and had achieved a degree of respectability, when reformers were able to look backward and begin to reconstruct their own history and place in human history. In these first selections, two themes deserve special notice. The first is the sense of a new moral era or "dispensation," based on the historical promise of the Declaration of Independence but translating political revolution into moral and spiritual demands, much as the New Testament had supposedly built on and superseded the Old Testament. The second theme, emerging out of the factional divisions and rivalries of the abolition movement, is a redefinition of democratic ideals, a sense of widening *secular* possibilities—of challenging various forms of inequality that had long been accepted as inevitable by both church and state. The subsequent selections backtrack several decades to examine some of the more revealing conflicts over abolitionist commitments and priorities, particularly the competing claims of religious revivalism and of protests against "wages slavery." Like Part 3, Part 4 concludes with the shift toward coercion and righteous power, in this case Lysander Spooner's attempt to interpret the Constitution as an antislavery document empowering both courts and lawmakers to restore to slaves their natural and inalienable liberty.

The sense of widening secular possibilities animated a multitude of movements in quest of new social harmonies, the theme of Part 5. There was such a profusion of proposals and experiments that we must be content with covering only a few examples of social perfectionism. Instead of focusing on the history of such communitarian settlements as New Harmony, Brook Farm, and Oneida, the selections are intended to illuminate the underlying spirit of discontent and hope. The alert reader will hear echoes of the environmentalism and yearning for self-improvement documented in Unit One; the concern over "the anxious spirit of gain" and the monopolization of power presented in Unit Two; the profound and half-repressed misgivings of a society officially committed to equality but unified only at the price of excluding and exploiting the groups represented in Unit Three; and finally, the faith, rooted in both the sciences and revivalism discussed in this Unit, in finding simple formulas for achieving unlimited perfection. While the selections in Part 5 reveal a remarkable openness to experiment, and a willingness to question any custom, institution, or dogma, they also suggest an erratic vacillation between two poles: the "come-outer" movement of withdrawal from all complicity with social violence and sin; and the temporary "gathering" of saints or would-be perfectionists in an alternative community—a cellular anti-America or regenerated America which in time, it was hoped, would purge the national organism of sin.

The utopian communities failed to renovate the social order, but the pervasive visions of utopia, combined with revivalism, Transcendentalism, and various reform movements, gave a new thrust to the traditional belief in America's uniqueness as a "New Israel," bearing, in the words of Herman Melville, "the ark of the liberties of the world." Except for the most disillusioned critics, it was only a short jump from condemning America's shortcomings to applauding Abraham Lincoln's resolve that "this nation, under God, shall have a new birth of freedom," so "that government of the people, by the people, for the people, shall not perish from the earth." What made the jump easier, of course, was the conviction that slavery was the only serious obstacle to America's "new birth," and that slavery was being destroyed in the agonizing self-purgation of civil war.

Part 6, "Transcending Human History," traces the steps toward this critical leap of faith. We are not concerned with the perennial debate over the "causes" of the Civil War, but rather with explaining how dissenting ideals of nonviolence and social harmony could become absorbed within the nationalistic tradition of America as a "Redeemer Nation." First, it is necessary to highlight the appeal of this tradition, not by quoting aggressive jingoists and champions of Manifest Destiny, but by conveying the spirit of hope and excitement that America's physical expansion stimulated among sensitive poets, novelists, and immigrant scientists. Minds that were acutely aware of the nation's imperfections were also steeped in the Enlightenment's faith in the future. And by the mid-nineteenth century, few liberal minds could doubt that most of the world was still trapped in the tyrannies, deceptions, and endless chains of injustice spawned by Old World history. After making every allowance for disturbing shortcomings, it still appeared that America alone had escaped from the contagions of the past. No other nation had been "conceived in liberty" or consciously "brought forth" as the fulfillment of universal and timeless ideals. It followed that America's dramatic growth in population, wealth, and settled area could only be interpreted as a positive confirmation of the revolutionary "experiment" and as a hopeful sign for the future of all humankind.

What made this faith convincing was the conviction that the present was a mere preface to a glorious future that belonged to America. Hence, material progress, even if temporarily based on "the anxious spirit of gain," would ultimately dissolve all contradictions, disparities, and disharmonies. It was precisely because America was free from the burdens of history, from the weight of a feudal and barbaric past, that most evils could be dismissed as transient, accidental, and peripheral. For a time, most Northerners and many Southerners regarded Negro slavery in this very light—as an anomaly that was destined to disappear in time. But by the time of America's conquest of Mexico, in 1847, it was becoming clear that national and material progress, far from eroding the frontier outposts of slavery, had become inextricably linked to the "progress" of a southern "Slave Power." In the eyes of many Northerners, including nonabolitionists, this was an ominous and intolerable development. Increasingly, all the imperfections of democracy, all the forces of coercion, exploitation, and disharmony that could no longer be rationalized or cloaked by various fictions, became concentrated in the supreme symbol of the southern "Slave Power"—an evil force alien to America's mission, a counterpart to the historic despotisms of the Old World, a serpent loose in the world's last Eden.

Yet most Southerners were no less dedicated to moral progress or to America's mission of redeeming the world. They had simply assimilated Negro slavery into the religious and scientific faith in perfectibility. In the words of William Henry Holcombe, the enslavement of supposedly inferior races was "an integral link in the grand progressive evolution of human society as an indissoluble whole." The selection from Holcombe expresses the dominant southern view that America could have been a harmonious nation pursuing a common mission, since there were no intrinsic conflicts of interest between North and South. The fatal anomaly was not slavery but the success in the North of fanatical and misguided agitation against slavery. As Calhoun had warned in 1850 (Unit Two, Part 6, B), this moral polarization would enable the North to exploit its growing superiority in wealth, population, and productivity. Unless checked by guarantees of equal power and mutual respect, ideological division over slavery would pose a direct threat to southern security.

The supreme irony is that the fears of southern slaveholders were grounded in the realities of American experience documented in Unit Three—that is, in the fate of various outcast groups, including blacks, who had been excluded from the "American dream." Of course southern leaders, picturing themselves in the vanguard of progress, enlightenment, and Christian morality, could not think of sharing a common cause with Indians, blacks, and Irish immigrants. They knew, however, that once stripped of power and stigmatized as morally inferior and backward, they would face two options: physical "removal" or secession; or being subjected to swarms of missionaries armed with an arsenal of political and economic weapons, intent on moral conversion and on establishing perpetual moral dependency.

Beginning with the sectional crisis over the Kansas-Nebraska Bill in 1854, these opposing fears and commitments solidified into two irreconcilable views of America's revolutionary heritage and future mission. For the South, the defense of Negro slavery was an intrinsic part of this heritage and mission. For northern reformers and even for a pragmatic politician like Lincoln, there could be no hope of fulfilling the vision of the Founding Fathers until the public was assured that slavery was "in the course of ultimate extinction."

Oddly enough, both sides shared the belief (with a few individual exceptions) that the national family would be harmonious if everyone perceived Negro slavery in its true light. In other words, except for the misperceptions of the other side, there were no basic flaws or inherent contradictions in American culture. This assumption meant that both sides could optimistically reaffirm their commitment to America's mission even when accepting the necessity of a single and ultimate act of fraternal warfare, a sacrificial act of purgation or vindication that would give a second birth to the principles of the Revolution. Indeed, in many ways both North and South prepared to reenact the War of Independence, which had also been a civil war, to prove that they alone were the true heirs and custodians of the national mission.

1

Science, Machines, and Human Progress

A. The Influence of Baconian Philosophy

• *Samuel Tyler* (1843)

Most antellum readers would have been puzzled and disturbed by the title and subsequent fame of a work published in 1896, Andrew Dickson White's ponderous *History of the Warfare of Science with Theology*. In the pre-Darwinian era (which by chance coincided with the era before the Civil War), there was widespread confidence that science confirmed divine revelation and could thus be taught as a branch of applied theology. Of course, educated Americans were familiar with the persecution of great scientists like Galileo, but since most educated American were Protestants, they could blame that on Catholic bigotry and superstition. Somewhat more embarrassing was the fact that a few extreme conservatives continued to associate science with the wild strain of philosophic radicalism and atheism that had supposedly brought on the French Revolution. This historic ploy was sufficiently troubling to require scornful rebuttals from hundreds of Anglo-American writers, including Samuel Tyler, who dismissed the French "Enlightment" as a perversion of both science and political philosophy. In Britain and America, even the most orthodox Protestants embraced science as a reinforcement to "common sense" and moral progress. Above all, they embraced science as an invincible ally against a new enemy that threatened both revealed religion and common-sense pragmatism—the mystical "transcendental philosophy" spawned by post-Napoleonic Germany.

Science, when defined as historically anti-materialist and anti-mystical, became an inexhaustible wellspring for American ideals of perfection, progress, and mission. What made the scientific method so compellingly attractive was its promise of continuous material and intellectual improvement without infringement on the fundamental boundaries of belief, authority, and social organization. In a tribute typical of the mid-nineteenth century, Samuel Tyler hails science as the great unifying and integrating force that links the wonders of nature with the discoveries of man. The unearthly achievements of a Newton, who weighs and measures "planet after planet," and holds "worlds in the hollow of his hands," culminate in the practical applications of steam power. The steam engine, according to Tyler, is "revolutionizing the world" without violence or political turmoil, "annihilating time and space by its speed, and bringing the most remote parts of the earth together." For Tyler and his contemporaries there was no distinction between pure and applied science. Science was at once "sublime" and utilitarian, imbued with the romance of discovery and disciplined by human needs.

Tyler (1809–1877) was a distinguished Maryland lawyer, the son of a tobacco planter, and a supporter of the Confederacy during the Civil War. In his spare time, he wrote articles on logic and metaphysics that attracted the attention of a celebrated British philosopher, Sir William Hamilton. Like many lawyers, clergyman, and scientists of his time Tyler looks upon Francis Bacon (1561–1626) as the patron saint of modern science, the originator of an inductive method which is accessible to all men, which has demolished the fanciful metaphysics of antiquity, and which has unified all branches of knowledge. No doubt Tyler exaggerates the importance of Bacon and of English contributions to science. But what matters is the symbolic significance attached to "Baconian philosophy" as an assured source of progress coupled with stability.

The Baconian philosophy, in this prevailing view, was more than a method for uncovering the secrets of the universe. It gave assurance that human science and technology were sanctioned by the fundamental design of the universe—by the laws and principles of nature which were lying in wait, so to speak, for human discovery and use. When Tyler repeats Bacon's familiar maxim that "knowledge is power," he means not only that the progress of knowledge transforms human life, but that such effective knowledge is in *moral* conformity with the laws governing the expansion of gas and the movement of planets, laws designed for the comfort and benefit of mankind. For minds like Tyler's, there was no suspicion of conflict between nature and human "improvement." And in most respects Tyler expresses the dominant mentality of the future, as evidenced by his enthusiasm for a speed that annihilates time and space, and by his extravagant rhetoric on scientific agriculture—rhetoric that would better describe developments of the twentieth century. Perhaps most surprising, given Tyler's commitment to the South, is his enthusiasm for Britain's imperialistic crusade to civilize the world. He knew that slavery could have no place in a civilization defined by British standards. But he also knew that progress, when guided by Baconian philosophy, was always accompanied by stability and by the need "to walk in the plain and sober paths of common sense."

Samuel Tyler (1843)

. . . Bacon wished to make every power of nature work for man, the winds, the waters, gravity, heat and all the mighty energies, which lie like the fabled giants of old under the mountains. These he wished to unloose from their fetters, and bring as servants under the dominion of man. Such are the grand conceptions which Bacon proclaimed to the world. . . .

Not long after the death of Lord Bacon, in 1626, the Royal Society was established for the promotion of the sciences, and all England resounded with his praise. The philosophers [meaning also, scientists] of England almost adored his genius. They felt that he had a true English mind. That he was the father of English philosophy [science]. That the English mind had at last given to it a method of philosophizing suited to its practical and common sense turn. And, behold the results written upon the glorious records of English philosophy!

In every department of physical science, England has made the leading discoveries; and other nations, though their scientific labors have been so brilliant, have done little more than extend her researches and verify her theories.

* * *

What more delightful employment can the speculative philosopher have than the grand contemplation of the discoveries which we have been considering! To one who loves truth for its own sake, and feels delight in the mere contemplation of harmonious and mutually dependent truths, the knowledge of such great truths are of sufficient value to repay him for the labor of discovery, even if they did not admit of any practical application. To know what it is that paints the beautiful colors of the rainbow, and covers the hills and valleys in green, and gives the delicate tints to the flowers which illuminate the fields; to know that the scathing lightnings which rush with such tremendous fury from the vast magazines of the heavens, is the same with the spark rubbed from the cat's back; to know that the water which we drink and which appears so simple, is composed of two gases, one of which

SOURCE: [Samuel Tyler], "Influence of the Baconian Philosophy," *Biblical Repertory and Princeton Review*, XV (1843), pp. 484–85, 489–94, 505–6.

is more combustible than gunpowder, and produces instant death when inhaled, and the other is the supporter of combustion, though the two united is the chief agent by which we extinguish fire; to know that the planets of such vast magnitude, and moving with such velocity through such boundless space are held in their orbits by the same force which causes an apple to fall to the ground; to know the times of eclipses and the returns of comets dashing with a velocity quicker than thought over millions of miles of space and returning with unerring certainty to the goal whence they set out: and all the other wonders which natural philosophy reveals, must forever, as mere matters of intellectual contemplation, be considered as inestimable treasures. And the mere process of investigation according to the Baconian method, is one of the noblest and most delightful employments. The philosopher at almost every stage of his progress, is meeting with hints of greater things still undiscovered, which cheers the mind amidst its toil, with the hope of making still further progress; and new fields of discovery are continually opening in prospect and the light of his present discoveries throwing enough of their rays across the darkness before him, to reveal as much of other new truths as will stimulate him to continued exertion for their discovery; thus curiosity is ever kept alive, and exhausted energies renovated in the laborious pursuit of knowledge.

How utterly insignificant as mere matters of intellectual contemplation, is all the physical philosophy of the ancients in comparison with these magnificent discoveries in the different sciences! And what can form a more striking contrast than the sublime argumentation of Newton and the petty sophistry of the philosophers of the middle age[s]! What are the eloquent reveries of Plato and the ingenious reasoning of Aristotle in comparison with the mighty mensuration by which Newton beginning with the dust on the balance measures the earth, and rising in the sublime argument measures planet after planet and weighing them, balances one against the other, and not content with holding as it were, worlds in the hollow of his hands, he measures and weighs systems of worlds. . . .

We see then, that as a mere matter of intellectual contemplation to satisfy the speculative mind, the Baconian philosophy is preëminently sublime. We will now show that it is also eminently practical; and in this particular, it differs from all the philosophy of the ancients, who thought that the only use of philosophy, was in its influence upon the mind in elevating it above the concerns of life, and thus purifying and preparing it for the philosophical beatitude of their heaven, into which none but philosophers were to enter; and that the practical affairs of life belonged to those of common endowments who are fated by destiny to be mere "hewers of stone and drawers of water" [that is, slaves]. But far different is the spirit of the Baconian philosophy. Humbling itself before Christianity, it acknowledges it to be a revelation from heaven, pointing out the same way to future bliss, for the peasant and the philosopher. . . .

It is then the great excellence of the Baconian philosophy, that even those of its discoveries which have contributed most to the satisfaction of the speculative intellect and are apparently the most remote from everything like practical application to the comforts of man, have frequently been applied to the most useful purposes of life. The discovery of the nature of light by Newton, at once led him to attempt a practical application of it; and though nothing of importance resulted from his labors, yet Hall and afterwards Dolland constructed achromatic telescopes, which could never have been done, if the fact of the different refrangibility of the different rays of light had not been known; and this discovery was thus applied to the arts in accordance with the utilitarian spirit of the Baconian philosophy. Scarcely had Franklin discovered the nature of lightning, before he constructed an apparatus to protect our buildings on land and our ships on the sea from the ravages of the electric fluid [lightning]. And thus by a discovery apparently so remote from all practical utility he disarmed the spirit of the storm of his thunders, and thereby showed to the world that knowledge is power. But the most fruitful practical applications have been made of chemistry. It has been applied to agriculture, to medicine, and to the mechanical arts. By analyzing the nature of soils, and applying the principles thereby ascertained, to the improvements of agriculture, it has made the most sterile waste so fertile, as to yield all the various fruits of the earth in the richest abundance. Where not a blade of grass grew, now the most abundant harvests gladden the sight, as they spread out in ocean waves over the fields where chemistry has shed its fertilizing dews. And by its magic power, chemistry has released the various medical agents which lie embedded in the innumerable vegetable and mineral products of nature, and handed them over to the healing art, to aid the vital powers in throwing off from the body the many diseases which prey upon man. And its application to the mechanic arts, has bestowed the richest blessings upon man. Sir H. Davy applied its principles in the construction of the safety lamp; by which man is enabled to walk with comparative safety in the bottoms of dark mines, with a light, amidst a gas more explosive than gunpowder, where, without this lamp, the miner is frequently exposed to as much danger as though he were walking in a magazine of powder with a lighted torch; and thus thousands of lives and millions of money are saved by this one application of science to art. But the crowning invention of all, the one which constitutes the chief glory of science in its application to art, is the steam-engine. A profound chemical knowledge applied by the most exquisite mechanical skill, enabled James Watt to bring the steam-engine, which had been invented by Savery and Newcomen, to a degree of perfection which renders it the most valuable of all inventions of art. It brings under the control of man an agent more potent than a hundred giants, swifter than the Arabian horse, and capable of assuming more forms in mechanism, than a Proteus, so as to apply itself to all kinds of work. It can pull a hundred wagons as easily as one—perform one kind of labor as easily as another. It is on the ocean, it is on the rivers, it is on the mountains, it is in the valleys, it is at the bottom of mines, it is in shops, it is everywhere at work. It propels the ship, it rows the boat, it cuts, it pumps, it hammers, it cards, it spins, it weaves, it washes, it cooks, it prints, and releases man of nearly all bodily toil. This mighty agent is revolutionizing the world—annihilating time and space by its speed, and bringing the most remote parts of the earth together. And all this mighty power is gained by a scientific knowledge of the nature of the atmosphere which we breathe, and the water which we drink and applying this knowledge to mechanism, so as to make these so familiar objects work for man.

Here let us pause, and reflect upon the benefits conferred on England by the Baconian philosophy. It has made her the greatest nation in the world. It has done more to develop her wealth than all the legislation of all the statesmen who have adorned her history by their financial skill. It has given her hundreds of bushels of wheat, thousands of yards of cloth, and bestowed innumerable comforts, where without its instrumentality, there would have been but one. It has enabled her to extend her commerce over the whole earth, and bring into her treasury countless millions of wealth. And this commerce is the source of her great power, both in war and peace, and is the means by which she is controling the destinies of the world. And though her whole policy is to extend her commerce by cultivating the arts of peace, yet it is true, that she sometimes (and we abhor the wickedness of it) pushes her commerce by the thunders of her cannon into regions where ignorance forbids its entrance; but the people who are thus treated, will in time learn, that is is equally for their benefit, with that of England, that her trade is extended to their shores, and they will feel that peace is the true policy of the world, and that all men are mutually interested in each other's welfare and should live like members of one family. The commercial spirit of England is also the power which pioneers the way for the other great influences which she is exerting upon the civilization of the world. Her sciences, her arts and her literature are carried on the wings of her commerce over the whole earth. And the Christian religion is soon found smoothing the thorny pillow of the dying man, and pouring the balm of consolation over his drooping spirit, in every clime where British commerce has placed her foot.

But the Baconian philosophy is not confined to physical nature, as has been often asserted. It embraces all knowledge. Bacon expressly says that his method of investigation is intended to be applied to all the sciences. "Some may raise this question (says he) rather than objection, whether we talk of perfecting natural philosophy alone according to our method, or the other sciences also, such as logic, ethics, politics. We certainly intend to comprehend them all. And as common logic, which regulates matters by syllogisms, is applied not only to natural, but also to every other science, so our inductive method likewise comprehends them all." And in his advancement of learning, where he defines the boundaries of the different sciences, he has devoted as much attention to the intellectual and moral sciences as to the physical.

· · ·

We now feel ourselves free to declare, that Bacon has done more to advance the progress of the human mind than any uninspired man[1] known to history. There are no writings in the whole of literature, which take so profound a view of human nature, and point out so exalted a destiny for man, as his. With a philosophical forecast unparalleled in the world, he has given anticipations of some of the greatest discoveries of modern science. . . .

The nations which have been most under its influence have risen superior to all the rest of the human family, and have advanced progressively, and their speed is daily accelerated, to a degree of intellectual development, moral superiority, and political power, which seem to indicate that it is destined to form the type of the civilization of a greater part, if not of all of the human race. And that this progress is likely to be perpetual, is also indicated by the fact that England, the nation which has most assiduously cultivated this philosophy stands at the head of modern civilization, and is not only the great progressive and regenerative nation of modern times, but is also eminently conservative, possessing in happy combination the elements of both progress and stability. She never loses sight of ancient landmarks in her progressive movements. How often, for example, has she thrown her conservative influence over the troubled waters of European politics, even when the commotion received its first impulse from the influence of her own principles of government! . . .

We have, therefore, strong reason to hope, that the Baconian philosophy sanctified by the spirit of Christianity, will pour its sanative floods over all the earth, and bring back all nations from the delirious wanderings of the transcendental philosophy, to walk in the plain and sober paths of common sense.

B. A Defense of "Mechanism" and Technology

• *Timothy Walker* (*1831*)

Like Samuel Tyler, Timothy Walker (1802–1856) was a lawyer by profession. Although he had grown up with little schooling on a Massachusetts farm, Walker had prepared himself for Harvard, and after teaching mathematics at George Bancroft's Round Hill School, had moved on to Ohio where he edited the *Western Law Journal* and sought to educate the public on the "moral sublimity" of the law.

In the following essay, Walker is responding to an anonymous writer in the *Edinburgh Review* who had attacked the "midnight hag," Mechanism, warning that "men are grown mechanical in head and in heart, as well as in hand"; and who had advanced the heretical suspicion that, far from progressing morally, "in true dignity of soul and character, we are, perhaps, inferior to most civilized ages." This was to challenge the fundamental

---

[1] Any man not supernaturally inspired by God, like the Biblical prophets and apostles.

premises, hopes, and dogmas of the dominant American culture. The issues raised were momentous and would arouse increasing debate over the next century-and-a-half. Indeed, it is remarkable that as early as 1831 Walker could bring such a "modern" perspective to the questions of work, leisure, and technological unemployment.

While purporting to defend "Mechanism" and the "Mechanical Philosophy," Walker is not entirely clear on the meaning of the terms. He devotes much space to the wonders and promise of technology, which he considers an unmitigated blessing to humanity. On this point there was virtually no dissent in America, which unlike England never experienced a "Luddite" movement of artisans smashing machines that threatened their livelihood. But by "Mechanism" Walker means something more than the material advantages of technology. He tries to refute the charge that machines are mechanizing human character and relationships. Walker's answer, which would become part of the official ideology of the future, is that machines increase leisure, and that leisure is the necessary and sufficient condition for an improved and more democratically accessible "culture." In other words, only the painful necessity of labor prevents ordinary people from becoming philosophers, poets, and painters.

Timothy Walker (1831)

. . . In plain words, we deny the evil tendencies of Mechanism, and we doubt the good influences of his [the writer in the *Edinburgh Review*] Mysticism. We cannot perceive that Mechanism, as such, has yet been the occasion of any injury to man. Some liberties, it is true, have been taken with Nature by this same presumptuous intermeddler. Where she denied us rivers, Mechanism has supplied them. Where she left our planet uncomfortably rough, Mechanism has applied the roller. Where her mountains have been found in the way, Mechanism has boldly levelled or cut through them. Even the ocean, by which she thought to have parted her quarrelsome children, Mechanism has encouraged them to step across. As if her earth were not good enough for wheels, Mechanism travels it upon iron pathways. . . .

Still further encroachments are threatened. The terms uphill and downhill are to become obsolete. The horse is to be unharnessed, because he is too slow; and the ox is to be unyoked, because he is too weak. Machines are to perform all the drudgery of man, while he is to look on in self-complacent ease.

But where is the harm and danger of this? Why is every lover of the human race called on to plant himself in the path, and oppose these giant strides of

---

SOURCE: [Timothy Walker], "Defence of Mechanical Philosophy," *North American Review*, XXXIII (1831), pp. 123–25.

Mechanism? Does this writer fear, that Nature will be dethroned, and Art set up in her place? Not exactly this. But he fears, if we rightly apprehend his meaning, that mind will become subjected to the laws of matter; that physical science will be built up on the ruins of our spiritual nature; that in our rage for machinery, we shall ourselves become machines. . . .

And, on the face of the matter, is it likely that mechanical ingenuity is suicidal in its efforts? Is it probable that the achievements of mind are fettering and enthralling mind? Must the proud creator of Mechanism stoop to its laws? By covering our earth with unnumbered comforts, accommodations, and delights, are we, in the words of this writer, descending from our "true dignity of soul and character?" Setting existing facts aside, and reasoning in the abstract, what is the fair conclusion? To our view, directly the contrary. We maintain, that the more work we can compel inert matter to do for us, the better will it be for our minds, because the more time shall we have to attend to them. So long as our souls are doomed to inhabit bodies, these bodies, however gross and unworthy they may be deemed, must be taken care of. Men have animal wants, which must and will be gratified at all events; and their demands upon time are imperious and peremptory. A certain portion of labor, then, must be performed, expressly for the support of our bodies. But at the same time, as we have a higher and nobler nature, which must also be cared for, the necessary labor spent upon our bodies should be as much abridged as possible, in order to give us leisure for the concerns of this better nature. The smaller the number of human beings, and the less the time it requires to supply the physical wants of the whole, the larger will be the number and the more the time left free for nobler things. Accordingly, in the absolute perfection of machinery, were that attainable, we might realize the absolute perfection of mind. In other words, if machines could be so improved and multiplied, that all our corporeal necessities could be entirely gratified, without the intervention of human labor, there would be nothing to hinder all mankind from becoming philosophers, poets, and votaries of art. The whole time and thought of the whole human race could be given to inward culture, to spiritual advancement. But let us not be understood as intimating a belief, that such a state of things will ever exist. This we do not believe, nor is it necessary to our argument. It is enough, if there be an approach thereto. And this we do believe is constantly making. Every sober view of the past confirms us in this belief.

In the first ages of the world, when Mechanism was not yet known, and human hands were the only instruments, the mind scarcely exhibited even the feeblest manifestations of its power. And the reason is obvious. As physical wants could only be supplied by the slow and tedious processes of hand-work, every one's attention was thereby completely absorbed. By degrees, however, the first rudiments of Mechanism made their appearance, and effected some simple abbreviations. A portion of leisure was the necessary result. One could now supply the wants of two, or each could supply his own in half the time previously required. And now it was, that mind began to develop its energies, and assert its empire over all other things. Leisure gave rise to thought, reflection, investigation; and these, in turn, produced new inventions and facilities. Mechanism grew by exercise. Machines became more numerous and more complete. . . .

But unhappily the progress has not been gradual. Of late, Mechanism has advanced [by leaps], and the world has felt a temporary inconvenience from large numbers being thrown suddenly out of employment, while unprepared to embark in any thing else. But this evil must be from its nature temporary, while the advantage resulting from a release of so large a proportion of mankind from the thraldom of physical labor, will be as lasting as the mind. And hence it is, that we look with unmixed delight at the triumphant march of Mechanism. So far from enslaving, it has emancipated the mind, in the most glorious sense. From a ministering servant to matter, mind has become the powerful lord of matter. Having put myriads of wheels in motion by laws of its own discovering, it rests, like the Omnipotent Mind, of which it is the image, from its work of creation, and pronounces it good.

C. The Motors of Perpetual Progress

• *Thomas Ewbank* (1849)

In the last selection, Timothy Walker suggested that science and technology would ultimately elevate the human mind to godlike omnipotence. Thomas Ewbank, writing eighteen years later, extends the religious parallel so far as to equate sin with "deviations from the principles of science" and to assert that only when mechanical science "is fully expored and universally applied can man attain his destiny, and evil be swept from the earth." Ewbank might be dismissed as an eccentric if his faith had not been so closely in tune with that of the future, and if his anticipation of computers, automation, and unlimited sources of energy had not been so uncannily on target.

Born in England, Thomas Ewbank (1792–1870) worked up the ladder of industrial apprenticeship as a coppersmith, tinsmith, and brass founder, learning as a lowly shopworker the recent innovations in the science of metallurgy. At age twenty-seven, he emigrated to the United States, where he did well as a manufacturer of metal tubing and where, as an inventor, his patents for such devices as improved steam safety valves soon won official approval—at a time when patented inventions were becoming accepted as the clearest index of historical progress. By 1842, Ewbank had devoted considerable study to the principles of technology, and had published a widely used work on the history and science of "hydraulic and other machines for raising water." In 1849, President Taylor appointed Ewbank United States commissioner of patents, and it is from one of his Patent Office reports that the following selection is taken.

As one might expect, Ewbank pictures inventors as the priests of the future, waging war on the unscientific sins of waste and inefficiency, leading humanity toward an earthly millennium of universal prosperity, democracy, and peace. In this respect, his outlook is surprisingly similar to that of Thorstein Veblen and other technocratic theorists of the early twentieth century. But Ewbank's principle concern is energy—or in his vocabulary, "motors," meaning not merely engines but any agents imparting "motion" and energy. In his view, motors are the key to progress, the "chief levers of civilization." We lack space to include his historical account of the progression from "animal forces" to hydraulic and steam power, or his speculations about the possible future use of "electric motors" and "explosive forces." It is sufficient to say that Thomas Ewbank was one of the few antebellum Americans who was intellectually prepared, if suddenly transported by a time machine, for the technological achievements of our own era. Like Francis Bacon, he believed that the goal of science was "the effecting of all things possible." And even by 1849, the understanding of scientific principles had advanced far enough to make almost anything seem possible, if only a nation had sufficient resources and determination. The California gold rush gives Ewbank the perfect occasion, in his eloquent conclusion, for linking national priorities with resources and determination. In a voice that is often echoed today, he calls for the discovery of new sources of energy instead of a wasteful search for glittering but unproductive grains of gold.

Thomas Ewbank (1849)

Newly acquired truths in physics are keys, each of which unlocks a world of wonders. Every new art gives birth to a thousand. The range of discovery is undoubtedly illimitable—a truth that has only dawned recently with full conviction even upon savants. A century ago few minds were prepared to receive it, and fewer to act on it. . . .

The study of nature's mechanisms, of God's own applications of the same principles and materials He has given inventors to work with, is only beginning. The UNIVERSE is before inventors, and all its elements and energies invite their attention. There is, therefore, no danger in expecting or attempting too much, provided they aspire not beyond where Nature herself has gone, and even then illusions vanish with experiment.

· · ·

Inventors, then, are revealers and expounders of the practical doctrines of civilization, and more than any other class have they shown us how to lessen life's evils and multiply its good. The connection of morals with expanding science and art, and the necessity of their union to the elevation of the species, are beginning to elicit attention. It is now perceived that deviations from

SOURCE: [Thomas Ewbank], *Report of the Commissioner of Patents*, 1849, *House Doc.*, 31st Cong., 1st sess., Pt. 1, no. 20, pp. 487–90, 496–98, 510–11.

principles of science—either in agriculture, arts, manufactures, in processes or pursuits of any kind—are errors, and all errors, in an extended sense, are SINS—are violations of Divine laws. And though sins of ignorance they carry, and will for ever carry, their punishment with them, viz: in imperfect results and the infliction of unnecessary inconveniences, expenses, and toil, in spending strength for naught.

Not till mechanical as well as ethical science is fully explored and universally applied can man attain his destiny, and evil be swept from the earth. . . .

Nothing is clearer than that mechanical inventions are ordained to animate, clothe, and adorn, a naked and torpescent world—to infuse into the species the elements of increasing vigor and felicity. Even as arts multiply and flourish, the chief labor of working out the great problems of existence continues to devolve upon inventors. Without them the prospects and hopes of the present had neither been seen nor felt. It is they who, by discovering new physical truths, are establishing the grandest of moral ones—*Perpetual Progress*—illimitable advancement in social, civil, and intellectual enjoyments.

. . .

If machinery doesn't *think*, it does that which nothing but severe and prolonged thinking can do, and it does it incomparably better. In the composition of astronomical and nautical tables, accuracy is everything. . . .

Now, automata have been made to work out arithmetical problems with positive certainty and admirable expedition; relieving mathematicians and others of an incalculable amount of mental drudgery—drudgery that has worn out the strongest constitutions. Moreover, they carry the use of numbers further than the clearest intellects dare follow—to an extent that language lacks terms to express. In human computations, minute errors creep in and corrupt the whole, often requiring months of the closest ratiocination to find out; but calculating machines detect their own mistakes at once, correct them, and then shutting out the interference of human fingers as well as heads, and with them the chance of marring the work, they print their tables as well as compose them—thus producing works to which entire confidence can safely be given.

. . .

To proclaim perfect, that is, absolute liberty to the sciences and arts, is to establish the sanctity of human rights on their surest, because of their natural foundations. Had rulers never been permitted to meddle with them—to cripple under the pretence of protecting them—to smother genius while affecting to foster it—our current marvels had been developed ages ago, and devices and discoveries yet in the womb of the future had been in universal use now.

Leave the arts free, and the world can never become a desert again. There can be no decay of nations without a decline in them; but when they are no longer fostered, or when such only are cherished as tend to aggrandize the great, empires *must* become extinct and their proudest monuments crumble away. Ancient legislators did not understand this, and the present disordered condition of a great part of the earth is the result of their ignorance. They preferred the exaltation of a class to that of the masses, mistook magnificence for power, and military force and idle display for prosperity. What are the accounts of their contests, and what the relics of their palaces and pyramids but monuments of their folly—sad reminiscences of populous cities, now desolate wastes—of people once mighty, now no longer known. Had they perceived that nothing can be lasting that is not beneficial to society at large, and had they under that conviction devoted the treasures they squandered to the general diffusion of science and art, the earth had not now been sprinkled with the tombstones of nations.

. . .

Inventions for modifying and conveying motion from one machine to another, or for distributing it to various parts of the same machine, frequently evince striking ingenuity; but the disclosure of useful forces indicates a higher order of research, and is fraught with vastly more important results. Improvements in mechanism are to a certain extent limited and local, but the advent of a new motive agent would be felt throughout the circle of the sciences—as exemplified in the case of steam. It would open new channels of industry and wealth, and give rise to devices and applications novel and innumerable.

Man rises with the motors. His growth begins with them, and only as he extends their applications or adds to their number, can he increase in real stature. Nothing can compensate for their absence, for nothing valuable can he acquire but through them. Steps of a ladder resting upon earth and reaching to heaven, he is without them an earth-worm, with them almost a God. His destinies are and ever must be wound up in them.

The chronology or human condition is comprehended in the cycles of the motors, and in them will that condition be best studied and understood. We are not to suppose that the annals of nations are for ever to be meted out in petty dynasties, or those of the species by mere circles of years; on the contrary, the probability increases that eras will be determined by revolutions in science, and the condition of generations measured by their chief motive-agents.

. . .

To conclude:—Notwithstanding those of bygone and the more successful inquiries of recent days, but exceedingly few of her secrets have yet been drawn out of Nature. Environed by her, it is but little that is comprehended of what she is doing above, beneath, about us; yea, with us and within us—little of the grand scheme of creation and of the principles and processes at work on it. Our wisest men are but pupils in normal schools—freshmen in their rudiments. True, we know much compared with the deplorable ignorance of the past, yet what we have acquired is only the A B C of either science or art. Those who fondly imagine the arts at their culmination, and steam the last of inorganic motors, would shrink with awe, could they contemplate the grandeur of human destiny, in an epoch of which our day is but the dawning.

And, certainly, whoever confers this splendid gift of a new motor on the world, will be ranked with the noblest of earth's sons. The goal is a tempting one, and the more so since the keenest spirits in two hemispheres are striving to reach it. We are ignorant who will receive the crown, but we know who will not, viz., those who pay divine honors to pelf [money], and whose aspirations never soar above the common objects of vulgar ambition. Generally, the rich revelations of science are made to those who love them for themselves, not for what they can be sold for. They come down to those who seek them, who, by industrial study and research, struggle to find them out, and who prize them when found, as expressions of Divine thoughts for the good of the species.

For months past, crowds have been hastening across every latitude, on their way to the newly-discovered realms of gold. An epidemic rages to gather and hoard that, which, except as a symbol, has little more value than its weight of inert sandstone or granite. A people's treasure is in useful labor; there is no wealth, and can be none but what it creates. Every good, great or small, is purchased by it. Savages with boundless territories and fertile lands, are indigent and often destitute because they work not. A single day's labor of a peasant or a mechanic, tends to relieve human wants and increases human comforts. It produces that which is not to be had without it, and to which tons of glittering ore can contribute nothing. In fine, there is no wealth but labor—no enjoyments but what are derived from it.

But, to those who are ambitious of ennobling themselves and really enriching their country, *placers* inexpressibly more precious than any to be found on the Sacramento, are invitingly open. Let them dig in THE MINES OF THE MOTORS, and they will bring to light, active, fruitful, and everlasting sources of true opulence.

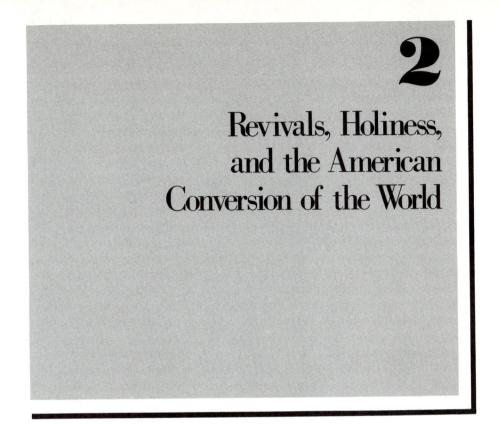

2

Revivals, Holiness, and the American Conversion of the World

A. True Progress Depends on Christianity

• *New Englander* (*1847*)

As we have seen, the Americans who made a new religion out of science were not avowedly antireligious or anticlerical. In this respect, they differed markedly from the French *philosophes* of the eighteenth century and from later generations of Continental and Latin American radicals who looked upon science as a secular weapon against religious authority. To understand antebellum American ideals of perfectibility and mission, one must remember that for the most part the American clergy had not only supported the Revolution of 1776 but had assimilated much of the world view associated with the philosophy of natural rights. This made it easier for their nineteenth-century successors to associate the progress of secular liberty and equality with the progress of scientific knowledge, and to explain both of these interrelated blessings as the historical product of "true" Christianity—or in other words, as history's manifestation of God's will.

For the writer of the following essay on Christianity and progress, whose assumptions were widely shared in all parts of the country, technological achievement gives scientific verification not only to Christianity but to the more purified and truer strains of Christianity, such as those in the United

States: "We have only to point to the indisputable fact, that the world over, the line which divides the progressive from the stationary and the retrograde, is the same which divides Christianity from Mohammedanism and heathenism; and that in Christendom, those nations stand highest, into which true Christianity has most thoroughly penetrated." In effect, this is to say that the best and truest religion is that which flourishes in the most advanced and productive nations. But such chauvinism, which would reduce spirituality to a mere appendage of national power, is softened by two important qualifications. First, our writer makes it clear that America is the fortunate beneficiary of a thousand-year struggle for liberty, which must be passed on as a trust to posterity. Second, like most moralists of his time, he tries in the end to keep religious truth distinct from national prowess, warning that there is no inevitability to the connection between spiritual purity and worldly power. The American people, he is confident, "will go onwards with accumulating power. But there is a fearful uncertainty whether their progress will be beneficent or destructive." In trying at once to harness religious ideals to the expansive energies of American life while striving to preserve such ideals as objctive reference points for national self-evaluation, this anonymous writer expresses a central dilemma of American religion.

New Englander (1847)

Archimedes had graved on his tombstone the cylinder and sphere, mementoes of his demonstrations in pure mathematics, leaving to forgetfulness his mechanical inventions, because he deemed science degraded by being made to aid in labor. But in these days use is the incitement to invention, and science deems it her proudest trophy to facilitate labor and to make common as the stones comforts which once wealth alone could enjoy. Once books were ponderous folios; now they are penny-magazines and facts for the million. Once learning was walled up in cloisters and universities; now we have academies, and common schools, and colleges, almost as common. . . .

• • •

This movement commenced, not with the American Revolution, not with the sailing of the Mayflower, not with the rise of English Puritanism, not with the Protestant Reformation. Already must the people have arisen from the lowest depths, before any of these movements could have been possible. Far back in the dark ages, when the people were serfs, bought and sold sometimes with the soil to which they were attached . . . when the barons in their castles exercised the power of life and death, of war and peace, and Euro-

SOURCE: "The Dependence of Popular Progress Upon Christianity," *New Englander*, V (July, 1847), pp. 433–35, 437–38, 442.

pean society was a chaos, originated the long conflict for popular rights. . . .

Thus have the people been rising, gathering strength with the progress of ages; sometimes crushed for long ages; again bursting barriers strong as the ribs of earth, and heaving off burdens heavy as the Andes. Thus have the people been rising, like a huge continent lifting its black mass from the ocean's bottom, at first, it may be, with upheaved, broken strata, and yawning fissures, and sweeping currents, but preparing for coming life and fruitfulness and beauty. Such is the movement in the midst of which we live, and which is heaving with it, us and all our institutions.

· · ·

Having thus glanced at what popular progress has been and what it still needs to be, we propose to show its dependence on Christianity.

It needs only a glance at history to see that the progress of man has been directly proportioned to the influences of Christianity. We have only to contrast oriental stagnation of mind with western activity—oriental despotism with western constitutions. We have only to ask, why has Mohammendanism, with the mighty vigor of its youth, developed a civilization so miserable and retrogressive; while around Christianity, although [originally] weakened by corruption and plunged in the midst of barbarians, has been wrought a civilization so elastic, vigorous, and progressive? We have only to point to the indisputable fact, that the world over, the line which divides the progressive from the stationary and the retrograde, is the same which divides Christianity from Mohammendanism and heathenism; and that in Christendom, those nations stand highest, into which true Christianity has most thoroughly penetrated. Were there nought else to declare it, Christianity would show its path among the nations by its effects. . . . Nor is the history of ancient Greece and Rome an exception. Theirs was a civilization in which vice rotted under the gauze of refinement, and corruption steamed beneath the silks of luxury. Theirs were forms of liberty under which the populace were ignorant, turbulent, and factious, and, with the exception of limited municipal privileges in a few cities, oppressed beneath a tyrannical aristocracy.

· · ·

We proceed to show that the connection between Christianity and popular progress must be maintained and made more intimate and complete. The people will go onwards with accumulating power. But there is a fearful uncertainty whether their progress will be beneficent or destructive. Here, then, we see the necessity of Christian influence. There is no safety if progress be not guided by the principles and imbued with the spirit of Christ's religion. . . .

The influence of Christianity is essential to prevent popular progress from being purely selfish, and consequently cruel and tyrannical.

B. The Science of Revivalism

- *Charles Grandison Finney* (1835)
- *Frances Trollope* (1832)
- *Lyman Beecher* (1831)

The last selection posed a momentous but still highly abstract dilemma: how could Christian "influence," when much of its authority and legitimacy depended on material progress, redeem and morally purify material progress? Antebellum Americans were above all a practical people who tended to seek in improved organization the solution of all problems. Their answer to the above dilemma was the religious revival, a dynamic method of organizing which promised to reconcile and periodically readjust the claims of worldly ambition and spiritual duty. Charles Grandison Finney (1792–1875), the acknowledged king of antebellum revivalists, was quite explicit in viewing revivalism as a form of natural science.

The son of Connecticut migrants, Finney grew up in Upstate New York where he studied law and was admitted to the bar. He then experienced a shattering religious conversion that led him to study theology much as he had studied law, that is mostly on his own with the guidance and encouragement of a professional mentor. Though he scorned formal seminary training, Finney was finally licensed and ordained by the local presbytery of the Presbyterian church, and in 1824 he began igniting religious fervor in the small towns of western New York. Finney's "new measures" of preaching were no doubt enhanced by his imposing height, his athletic build, and his outflow of vibrant energy. But Finney's informal style and reliance on direct, heart-to-heart talk were also in tune with the values of Upstate New York—a region where the Erie Canal was revolutionizing social and economic life and where a marketing center like Rochester, the fastest growing town in America, was seething with hope, turmoil, and anxiety. A figure like Finney had little appeal for the thousands of young migrant laborers who moved in and out of the canal towns, crowding the cheap taverns and boarding houses and alarming the custodians of law and order. But as his revivals spread from Utica and Troy to his final stunning triumphs at Rochester in 1830, Finney became a virtual savior in the eyes of merchants, bankers, tradesmen, and aspiring artisans. For middle-class women, he had an even more charismatic appeal.

Having won national fame, Finney was summoned in 1832 to New York City by the wealthy merchants and philanthropists, Arthur and Lewis Tappan. There he presided over the Tappans' Chatham Street Chapel, intended to be a beachhead of evangelism and reform in the midst of New York's slums. In 1835, Finney accepted a Tappan-supported professorship in theology at Oberlin College, in Ohio. The Tappans had subsidized Oberlin as a liberal alternative to Lane Theological Seminary in Cincinnati, whose trustees had recently suppressed all student discussion of slavery.

Finney's following remarks were published in the year he left New York for Oberlin, at the height of his career as a revivalist and at a time when many of his converts and disciples had abandoned revivalism to assume leadership in the abolitionist crusade. Here Finney advances the ingenious argument that it is precisely because material progress stimulates so many worldly excitements and distractions that the spread of Christianity requires a science of conversion—or in today's terms, a psychology of behavior modification. In recognizing the importance of human emotion and "excitability," Finney is reacting against what he considered an overly intellectual approach to religion. He also wants to remove religious conversion from the realm of supernatural mystery or passive mysticism, subjecting the phenomenon to rules of cause and effect that are open to human study and control. Far from secularizing something holy, Finney argues that such psychological manipulation is in line with God's intention that we use all our self-improving powers, that we apply the techniques of engineering to revivals as well as to building canals. Indeed, in a nation so distracted by canal-building and by idealistic reforms like abolitionism, true religion can survive only by becoming more effective and more powerful in its appeal. It is true that Finney does express ambivalence toward the need of combatting "declension" and keeping up with the frantic rush of American life. He soothes himself with the thought that the revivalist's tension, competition, and overwork will lessen as the millennium approaches. When religion became so immersed in "the anxious spirit of gain," faith in divine ideals may have necessitated faith in a coming Golden Age that would soon vindicate all struggles and temporary compromises with sin.

In the second selection, Frances Trollope (1780–1863) presents an unflattering description of an Indiana camp meeting, a frontier form of revivalism that had originated in Kentucky at the turn of the century. Mrs. Trollope, the mother of the great English novelist Anthony Trollope and ultimately a well-known novelist herself, resided in America from 1827 to 1830 during which time her husband failed miserably in a speculative venture at Cincinnati. Desperate for money after returning to England, Mrs. Trollope wrote a popular account of American society which instantly won her fame in Europe and indignant resentment in the United States. The following account is biased by Mrs. Trollope's general distaste for "democratic manners" and by her Anglican prejudices against religious emotionalism and Methodist preaching. But such distortion is more than counterbalanced by her British gift for understatement and satirical wit. Thanks to Mrs. Trollope's sharp eye for detail, we also get an invaluable glimpse of what camp meetings meant for tens of thousands of Americans who lived in rural isolation and who trekked by foot or wagon to these great religious festivals. Especially noteworthy is the presence of black participants who, though apparently segregated in a separate tent, are very must part of the collective performance. In religious revivalism, the flow of influence between blacks and whites always moved in two directions.

There was also a two-way flow of influence between New England and the more unruly and uninhibited "West," including Finney's "burned-over district"—so named because it was so thoroughly swept by the fires of revivalism. New England money and missionary work had helped encourage the religous excitement in western New York and Ohio. But by 1827 New England leaders like Asahel Nettleton and Lyman Beecher were becoming alarmed by Finney's "new measures," such as urging women to pray in public and conducting protracted meetings of several days' duration. In a famous nine-day confrontation at New Lebanon, New York, on the Massachusetts border, Nettleton and Beecher advised Finney to cool his preaching and avoid social improprieties. Beecher said, "Finney, I know your plan . . . you mean to come into Connecticut and carry a streak of fire to Boston. But if you attempt it, as the Lord liveth, I'll meet you at the state line, and call out all the artillerymen, and fight every inch of the way to Boston, and then I'll fight you there."[1] But four years later Beecher invited Finney to Boston and, in effect, capitulated to Western revivalism.

In our third selection, published at the time of this reconciliation, Beecher defends revivals as the only hope for preserving virtue in the midst of "universal liberty and boundless prosperity." There is no clearer summary of the self-assigned mission of evangelical Protestantism in the Age of Jackson, or of the dangers perceived in a frantic scramble for wealth that threatened to snap the fundamental bonds of social cohesion. Lyman Beecher (1775–1863) was the father of Catharine and Henry Ward Beecher (Unit One, Parts 1 and 4), and of Harriet Beecher Stowe. Though himself the son of a Connecticut blacksmith, he studied for the ministry at Yale. In 1826, having achieved some fame as an eloquent preacher and temperance reformer, he established himself in Boston where he waged war on Unitarians and Roman Catholics. In 1832, appointed president of the new Lane Theological Seminary, he moved west to Cincinnati.

Charles Grandison Finney (1835)

A "Revival of Religion" presupposes a declension. Almost all the religion in the world has been produced by revivals. God has found it necessary to take advantage of the excitability there is in mankind, to produce powerful excitements among them, before he can lead them to obey. Men are so spiritually sluggish, there are so many things to lead their minds off from religion, and to oppose the influence of the Gospel, that it is necessary to raise an excite-

---

[1] *The Autobiography of Lyman Beecher*, Barbara M. Cross, ed., 2 vols. (Cambridge, Mass.: The Belknap Press of Harvard University Press, 1961), vol. II, p. 75.

SOURCE: Charles G. Finney, *Lectures on Revivals of Religion* (New York: Fleming H. Revell Co., n.d.), pp. 9–15.

ment among them, till the tide rises so high as to sweep away the opposing obstacles. They must be so excited that they will break over these counteracting influences, before they will obey God. Not that excited feeling is religion, for it is not; but it is excited desire, appetite and feeling that prevents religion. The will is, in a sense, enslaved by the carnal and worldly desires. Hence it is necessary to awaken men to a sense of guilt and danger, and thus produce an excitement of counter feeling and desire which will break the power of carnal and worldly desire and leave the will free to obey God. . . .

There is so little *principle* in the church, so little firmness and stability of purpose, that unless the religious feelings are awakened and kept excited, counter worldly feeling and excitement will prevail, and men will not obey God. They have so little knowledge, and their principles are so weak, that unless they are excited, they will go back from the path of duty, and do nothing to promote the glory of God. The state of the world is still such, and probably will be till the millennium is fully come, that religion must be mainly promoted by means of revivals. How long and how often has the experiment been tried, to bring the church to act steadily for God, without these periodical excitements. Many good men have supposed, and still suppose, that the best way to promote religion, is to go along *uniformly*, and gather in the ungodly gradually, and without excitement. But however sound such reasoning may appear in the abstract, *facts* demonstrate its futility. If the church were far enough advanced in knowledge, and had stability of principle enough to *keep awake*, such a course would do; but the church is so little enlightened, and there are so many counteracting causes, that she will not go steadily to work without a special interest being awakened. As the millennium advances, it is probable that these periodical excitements will be unknown. Then the church will be enlightened, and the counteracting causes removed, and the entire church will be in a state of habitual and steady obedience to God. The entire church will stand and take the infant mind, and cultivate it for God. Children will be trained up in the way they should go, and there will be no such torrents of worldliness, and fashion, and covetousness, to bear away the piety of the church, as soon as the excitement of a revival is withdrawn.

It is very desirable it should be so. It is very desirable that the church should go on steadily in a course of obedience without these excitements. Such excitements are liable to injure the health. Our nervous system is so strung that any powerful excitement, if long continued, injures our health and unfits us for duty. If religion is ever to have a pervading influence in the world, it cannot be so; this spasmodic religion must be done away. Then it will be uncalled for. . . . Then there will be no need that ministers should wear themselves out, and kill themselves, by their efforts to roll back the flood of worldly influence that sets in upon the church. But as yet the state of the Christian world is such, that to expect to promote religion without excitements is unphilosophical and absurd. The great political, and other worldly excitements that agitate Christendom, are all unfriendly to religion, and divert the mind from the interests of the soul. Now these excitements can only be counteracted by *religious* excitements. And until there is religious principle in the world to put down irreligious excitements, it is vain to try to promote religion, except by counteracting excitements. This is true in philosophy, and it is a historical fact.

• • •

I. A revival of religion is not a miracle

1. A miracle has been generally defined to be, a Divine interference, setting aside or suspending the laws of nature. [A revival] is not a miracle in this sense. All the laws of matter and mind remain in force. They are neither suspended nor set aside in a revival.

2. It is not a miracle according to another definition of the term miracle —*something above the powers of nature*. There is nothing in religion beyond the ordinary powers of nature. It consists entirely in the *right exercise* of the powers of nature. It is just that, and nothing else. When mankind become religious, they are not *enabled* to put forth exertions which they were unable before to put forth. They only exert the powers they had before in a different way, and use them for the glory of God.

3. It is not a miracle, or dependent on a miracle, in any sense. It is a purely philosophical [scientific] result of the right use of the constituted means—as much so as any other effect produced by the application of means. There may be a miracle among its antecedent causes, or there may not. The apostles employed miracles, simply as means by which they arrested attention to their message, and established its divine authority. But the miracle was not the revival. The miracle was one thing; the revival that followed it was quite another thing. The revivals in the apostles' days were connected with miracles, but they were not miracles. . . .

I wish this idea to be impressed on all your minds, for there has long been an idea prevalent that promoting religion has something very peculiar in it, not to be judged of by the ordinary rules of cause and effect; in short, that there is no connection of the means with the result, and no tendency in the means to produce the effect. No doctrine is more dangerous than this to the prosperity of the church, and nothing more absurd.

Suppose a man were to go and preach this doctrine among farmers, about their sowing grain. Let him tell them that God is a sovereign, and will give them a crop only when it pleases him, and that for them to plow and plant and labor as if they expected to raise a crop is very wrong, and taking the work out of the hands of God, that it interferes with his sovereignty, and is going on in their own strength; and that there is no connection between the means and the results on which they can depend. And now, suppose the farmers should believe such doctrine. Why, they would starve the world to death.

Just such results will follow from the church's being persuaded that promoting religion is somehow so mysteriously a subject of Divine sovereignty, that there is no natural connection between the means and the end. What *are* the results? Why, generation after generation has gone down to hell. No doubt more than five thousand million have gone down to hell, while the church has been dreaming, and waiting for God to save them without the use of means. It has been the devil's most successful means of destroying souls. The connection is as clear in religion as it is when the farmer sows his grain. . . .

II. I am to show what a revival is

It is the renewal of the first love of Christians, resulting in the awakening and conversion of sinners to God. In the popular sense, a revival of religion in a community is the arousing, quickening, and reclaiming of the more or less backslidden church and the more or less general awakening of all classes, and insuring attention to the claims of God.

It presupposes that the church is sunk down in a backslidden state, and a revival consists in the return of a church from her backslidings, and in the conversion of sinners.

Frances Trollope (1832)

The prospect of passing a night in the back-woods of Indiana was by no means agreeable, but I screwed my courage to the proper pitch, and set forth determined to see with my own eyes, and hear with my own ears, what a camp-meeting really was. I had heard it said that being at a camp-meeting was like standing at the gate of heaven, and seeing it opening before you; I had heard it said, that being at a camp-meeting was like finding yourself within the gates of hell; in either case there must be something to gratify curiosity, and compensate one for the fatigue of a long rumbling ride and a sleepless night.

We reached the ground about an hour before midnight, and the approach to it was highly picturesque. The spot chosen was the verge of an unbroken forest, where a space of about twenty acres appeared to have been partially cleared for the purpose. Tents of different sizes were pitched very near together in a circle round the cleared space; behind them were ranged an exterior circle of carriages of every description, and at the back of each were fastened the horses which had drawn them thither. Through this triple circle of defense we distinguished numerous fires burning brightly within it; and still more numerous lights flickering from the trees that were left in the enclosure. . . .

Four high frames, constructed in the form of altars, were placed at the four corners of the inclosure; on these were supported layers of earth and sod, on which burned immense fires of blazing pine-wood. On one side a rude

---

SOURCE: Frances Trollope, *Domestic Manners of the Americans* (London: Whittaker, Treacher and Co., 1832), pp. 139–43.

platform was erected to accommodate the preachers, fifteen of whom attended this meeting, and with very short intervals for necessary refreshment and private devotion, preached in rotation, day and night, from Tuesday to Saturday.

When we arrived, the preachers were silent; but we heard issuing from nearly every tent mingled sounds of praying, preaching, singing, and lamentation. The curtains in front of each tent were dropped, and the faint light that gleamed through the white drapery, backed as it was by the dark forest, had a beautiful and mysterious effect, that set the imagination at work; and had the sounds which vibrated around us been less discordant, harsh, and unnatural, I should have enjoyed it; but listening at the corner of a tent, which poured forth more than its proportion of clamor, in a few moments chased every feeling derived from imagination, and furnished realities that could neither be mistaken nor forgotten. . . .

Great numbers of persons were walking about the ground, who appeared like ourselves to be present only as spectators; some of these very unceremoniously contrived to raise the drapery of this tent at one corner, so as to afford us a perfect view of the interior.

The floor was covered with straw, which round the sides was heaped in masses, that might serve as seats, but which at that moment were used to support the heads and the arms of the close-packed circle of men and women who kneeled on the floor.

Out of about thirty persons thus placed, perhaps half a dozen were men. One of these, a handsome-looking youth of eighteen or twenty, kneeled just below the opening through which I looked. His arm was encircling the neck of a young girl who knelt beside him, with her hair hanging dishevelled upon her shoulders, and her features working with the most violent agitation; soon after they both fell forward on the straw, as if unable to endure in any other attitude the burning eloquence of a tall grim figure in black, who, standing erect in the center, was uttering with incredible vehemence an oration that seemed to hover between praying and preaching; his arms hung stiff and immoveable by his side, and he looked like an ill-constructed machine, set in action by a movement so violent as to threaten its own destruction, so jerkingly, painfully, yet rapidly, did his words tumble out; the kneeling circle ceasing not to call, in every variety of tone, on the name of Jesus; accompanied with sobs, groans, and a sort of low howling inexpressibly painful to listen to. . . .

One tent was occupied exclusively by Negroes. They were all full-dressed, and looked exactly as if they were performing a scene on the stage. One woman wore a dress of pink gauze trimmed with silver lace; another was dressed in pale yellow silk; one or two had splendid turbans; and all wore a profusion of ornaments. The men were in snow white panataloons, with gay colored linen jackets. One of these, a youth of coal-black comeliness, was preaching with the most violent gesticulations, frequently springing high from the ground, and clapping his hands over his head. Could our missionary societies have heard the trash he uttered, by way of an address to the Deity, they might perhaps have doubted whether his conversion had much enlightened his mind.

At midnight, a horn sounded through the camp, which, we were told, was to call the people from private to public worship; and we presently saw them flocking from all sides to the front of the preacher's stand. . . . There were about two thousand persons assembled.

One of the preachers began in a low nasal tone, and, like all other Methodist preachers, assured us of the enormous depravity of man as he comes from the hands of his Maker, and of his perfect sanctification after he had wrestled sufficiently with the Lord to get hold of him, *et cetera*. The admiration of the crowd was evinced by almost constant cries of "Amen! Amen!" "Jesus Jesus!" "Glory! Glory!" and the like.

•   •   •

The exhortation nearly resembled that which I had heard at "the revival," but the results was very different; for, instead of the few hysterical women who had distinguished themselves on that occasion, above a hundred persons, nearly all females, came forward, uttering howlings and groans so terrible that I shall never cease to shudder when I recall them. They appeared to drag each other forward, and on the word being given, "let us pray," they fell on their knees; but this posture was soon changed for others that permitted greater scope for the convulsive movements of their limbs; and they were soon all lying on the ground in an indescribable confusion of heads and legs. They threw their limbs with such incessant and violent motion, that I was every instant expecting some serious accident to occur.

Lyman Beecher (1831)

The dangers which threaten these United States, and the free institutions here established, are numerous and appalling. They arise, in part, from our vast extent of territory, our numerous and increasing population, from diversity of local interests, the power of selfishness, and the fury of sectional jealousy and hate. All these are powerful causes of strife, and never were they in more powerful or terrific action.

These causes, alone sufficient to set on fire the course of nature, have, during several of the last years, been wielded, concentrated, and blown into fury, by a mad ambition. The thirst of power and dominion has fallen upon some of our leading politicians, to whom the ordinary elements of strife seem tame and lazy in the work of ruin; and they—regardless of consequences, and with a view to subserve their own political ends—have heated the furnace of anger seven-fold, and raised to a seven-fold height the winds and waves of political commotion.

SOURCE: "The Necessity of Revivals of Religion to the Perpetuity of Our Civil and Religious Institutions," *The Spirit of the Pilgrims* (1831), pp. 467–69, 471.

To these must be added the corrupting influence of a pre-eminent national prosperity, productive of voluptuousness, extravagance, and rash speculation, and leading, in many instances, to reckless poverty and misery.

The increase of intellectual power too, without a corresponding increase of moral restraint, and this connected with the universality of suffrage, presents an ocean of unstable mind to the ruthless power of mad ambition.

Nor are these our only sources of danger. There is the atheistic, anti-social conspiracy which, amid the war of elements, would blot out the sun, suspend moral attraction, dissolve society, and turn out the whole family of human animals into one common field of unbridled appetite and lust. And there is religious party spirit, destroying the confidence of the great Christian denominations in one another, inflaming them with jealousy and hatred, and paralyzing their energy of action against a common foe, and for the cause of their common Lord. . . .

Another danger not to be overlooked, arises from the intrigues of Catholic Europe, through the medium of our own Catholic population, to give a predominance to their religion with all its antirepublican tendencies, and thus to divide us, and destroy our institutions. . . .

Let me then call the attention of my readers to *our only remaining source of hope—GOD—and the interpositions of his Holy Spirit, in great and general Revivals of Religion, to reform the hearts of this people, and make the nation good and happy.*

There is for us assuredly but one remedy, and that is, such a state of the affections towards God and our neighbor, as the Law and the Gospel require: —Not the ascendency of Christians over the world, but the world, in the day of God's power, becoming Christian. . . .

It is not to be supposed a thing beyond the power of God, to effect such a change of human character as will reconcile universal liberty and boundless prosperity, with their permanence and purity. Neither reason nor philosophy requires us to suppose, that God has created a race whom he cannot, if it seems good to him, reclaim and govern, in accordance with the highest degree of temporal prosperity.

The benevolence and mercy of God would lead us to infer, from what he has done in providing redemption, that he will do much more than he has yet done in its application. Everything shows that his purposes are tending to intellectual, and civil, and social results, much beyond what has ever before existed. And this analogy, coupled with his mercy, would lead us to anticipate a more than corresponding moral and religious amelioration. In this too we are confirmed by the considerations, that every other cause has been tried and has completely failed.

• • •

The government of God is the only government which will hold society against depravity within and temptation without; and this it must do by the force of its own law written upon the heart. This is that unity of the Spirit and that bond of peace which alone can perpetuate national purity and tranquillity—that law of universal and impartial love by which alone nations can be kept back from ruin. There is no safety for republics but in self-government, under the influence of a holy heart, swayed by the government of God.

C. The Promise of American Protestantism

- *William Ellery Channing* (*c. 1831*)
- *Philip Schaff* (*1855*)

Visions of Christian perfectibility and mission were by no means limited to revivalists. We have already examined William Ellery Channing's thoughts on self-culture (Unit One, Part 4). As the symbolic leader of American Unitarianism and for forty years pastor at the Federal Street Church in Boston, Channing also preached a humane, rational, and hopeful view of human destiny that inspired a host of younger men and women to work for improving the condition of the blind, the deaf, the insane, the imprisoned, and the enslaved. For Channing, "the essence of the Christian religion," the title of the discourse from which the following selection is taken, is the moral perfection of man.

As Channing conceives it, this principle of perfectibility is universal and rationally accessible. There is no suggestion of supernatural mystery, sin, divine passion, or the ecstasy of redemption—although Channing's great emphasis on "mind" does contain hints of latent, indwelling powers similar to those celebrated by his Transcendentalist followers. But moral progress for Channing is primarily a function of intellectual progress. He is cheered by the recent European revolutions of 1830 because "men are now moved, not merely by physical wants and sufferings, but by ideas, by principles, by the conception of a better state of society, under which the rights of human nature will be recognized, and greater justice be done to the mind in all classes of the community." Note that Channing agrees with more orthodox Protestants, like Lyman Beecher, on the dangers of universal liberty and prosperity when unaccompanied by internalized self-restraints. It is his faith in the irreversible triumph of reason, exemplified in the United States, that allows him to applaud revolutions against despotism as historic signposts toward "a state of society more fit to perfect human beings." And here he expresses the very essence of American liberalism.

In assessing the promise of American Protestantism, Philip Schaff (1819–1893) is no less haunted by the spectre of despotic and revolutionary Europe. Nearly forty years younger than Channing, Schaff arrived in America in 1844, two years after Channing's death. Born in Switzerland, Schaff had received the world's most advanced theological and philosophical training in German universities, and would, in all probability, have become a professor of theology at the University of Berlin had he not accepted an unexpected appointment at the new and remote German Reformed (Calvinist)

Seminary at Mercersburg, Pennsylvania. By the early 1840s, Mercersburg Seminary had already become a frontier outpost for the latest conservative currents of German scholarship, a potent counterforce to the revivalistic "new measures" which, borrowed by some German-Americans from Finney, had begun to undermine the dicipline and unity of the German Reformed Church.

What particularly distinguished Schaff from the American revivalists was his respect for the sacramental, institutional, and historical character of the Christian church. Instead of viewing the Protestant Reformation as a revolutionary emancipation from Roman superstition and corruption, Schaff and his Mercersburg colleagues saw Protestantism as simply a logical and historical development of the more progressive tendencies within Catholicism. Indeed, even in the brief selection here, one catches glimpses of an ecumenical vision—of a Christian church reunited in essential goals and purpose if not in formal organization. This spirit of toleration subjected Schaff to severe censure in an era of mounting nativism and anti-Catholic prejudice. But ironically, Schaff expresses a deeper faith in American institutions than did the nativists. After acknowledging the liabilities of America's "voluntary system"—for example, the painful readjustment of immigrant churches which were used to state support and now faced the competitive and distracting pressures described by Finney—Schaff ultimately finds in voluntarism the great strength and historical mission of American Protestantism. In America, where all churches are deprived of state support and where even Catholicism is reduced to the status of one among many denominations, Christianity has only "moral means of influencing the world" (an observation that echoes some of the themes of Unit One). For Schaff this means a hopeful energizing of religion, the promise of translating into practical experience the historical and theological truths uncovered by German scholarship —especially the truth of a single, universal church.

William Ellery Channing (*c.* 1831)

I believe that Christianity has one great principle, which is *central*, around which all its truths gather, and which constitutes it the glorious gospel of the blessed God. I believe that no truth is so worthy of acceptation and so quickening as this. In proportion as we penetrate into it, and are penetrated by it, we comprehend our religion, and attain to a living faith. This great principle can be briefly expressed. It is the doctrine that "God purposes, in his unbounded fatherly love, to perfect the human soul; to purify it from all sin; to create it after his own image; to fill it with his own spirit; to unfold it for ever; to raise it to life and immortality in heaven,—that is, to communicate to

---

SOURCE: W. E. Channing, "The Perfect Life: The Essence of the Christian Religion," *Channing's Works* (Boston: American Unitarian Association, 1895), pp. 1001, 1003–5.

it from himself a life of celestial power, virtue, and joy." The elevation of men above the imperfections, temptations, sins, sufferings, of the present state, to a diviner being,—this is the great purpose of God, revealed and accomplished by Jesus Christ; this it is that constitutes the religion of Jesus Christ,—glad tidings to all people: for it is a religion suited to fulfill the wants of every human being.

In the New Testament I learn that God regards the human soul with unutterable interest and love; that in an important sense it bears the impress of his own infinity, its powers being germs, which may expand without limit or end; that he loves it, even when fallen, and desires its restoration; that he has sent his Son to redeem and cleanse it from all iniquity; that he for ever seeks to communicate to it a divine virtue which shall spring up, by perennial bloom and fruitfulness, into everlasting life. In the New Testament I learn that what God wills is our perfection; by which I understand the freest exercise and perpetual development of our highest powers,—strength and brightness of intellect, unconquerable energy of moral principle, pure and fervent desire for truth, unbounded love of goodness and greatness, benevolence free from every selfish taint, the perpetual consciousness of God and of his immediate presence, co-operation and friendship with all enlightened and disinterested spirits, and radiant glory of divine will and beneficent influence, of which we have an emblem—a faint emblem only—in the sun that illuminates and warms so many worlds. Christianity reveals to me this moral perfection of man, as the great purpose of God.

When I look into man's nature, I see that moral perfection is his only true and enduring good; and consequently the promise of this must be the highest truth which any religion can contain. The loftiest endowment of our nature is the moral power,—the power of perceiving and practising virtue, of discerning and seeking goodness.

. . .

Mind is the great object to be enjoyed; and this is true to a greater extent than we imagine. Even outward, material Nature derives its chief power of contributing to our happiness, by being a manifestation of mental or spiritual excellence. No one truly enjoys the creation, but he who sees it everywhere as radiant with *mind*, and as for ever showing forth the perfection of its author. We think, perhaps, that Nature has a beauty of its own, in which we can delight, without reference to any reality above it. But natural beauty is an image or emblem of harmonious qualities of the mind. It is a type of spiritual beauty. And he, to whom the last is not known by consciousness, by the dawning of beauty in his own soul, can know and feel but little of the former. Thus the perfection of our own minds makes us the heirs of all good, whether in the outward or the spiritual worlds. Let us, then, look to no other happiness. . . .

At this period, we see a mighty movement of the civilized world. Thrones are tottering, and the firmest establishments of former ages seem about to be swept away by the torrent of revolution. In this movement I rejoice, though not without trembling joy. But I rejoice, only because I look at it in the light of the great truth which I have this day aimed to enforce; because I see, as

I think, in the revolutionary spirit of our times, the promise of a freer and higher action of the human mind,—the pledge of a state of society more fit to perfect human beings. I regard the present state of the world in this moral light altogether. The despotisms, which are to be prostrated, seem to be evils, chiefly as they have enslaved men's faculties, as they have bowed and weighed down the soul. The liberty, after which men aspire, is to prove a good only so far as it shall give force and enlargement to the mind; only so far as it shall conspire with Christianity in advancing human nature. Men will gain little by escaping outward despotism, if the soul continues enthralled. Men must be subjected to some law; and unless the law in their own breast, the law of God, of duty, of perfection, be adopted by their free choice as the supreme rule, they will fall under the tyranny of selfish passion, which will bow their necks for an outward yoke.

I have hope in the present struggle of the world, because it seems to me more spiritual, more moral, in its origin and tendencies, than any which have preceded it. It differs much from the revolts of former times, when an oppressed populace or peasantry broke forth into frantic opposition to government, under the goading pressure of famine and misery. Men are now moved, not merely by physical wants and sufferings, but by ideas, by principles, by the conception of a better state of society, under which the rights of human nature will be recognized, and greater justice be done to the mind in all classes of the community. There is then an element—spiritual, moral, and tending towards perfection—in the present movement; and this is my great hope. When I see, however, the tremendous strength of unsubdued passions, which mix with and often overpower this conception of a better order of society; when I consider the success with which the selfish, crafty, and ambitious have turned to their own purposes the generous enthusiasm of the people; when I consider the darkness which hangs over the nations, the rashness with which they have rushed into infidelity and irreligion, as the only refuge from priestcraft and superstition; and when I consider how hard it is for men, in seasons of tumult and feverish excitement, to listen to the mild voice of wisdom teaching that moral perfection alone constitutes glory and happiness,—I fear. I fear not for the final results; not for the *ultimate* triumphs of truth, right, virtue, piety; not for the gradual melioration of men's lot: but for those nearer results, those immediate effects, which the men of this generation are to witness and to feel.

Philip Schaff (1855)

. . . While in Europe ecclesiastical institutions appear in historical connection with Catholicism, and even in evangelical [Protestant] countries, most of the city and village churches, the universities, and religious foundations, point to

SOURCE: Philip Schaff, *America: A Sketch of Its Political, Social and Religious Character,* Perry Miller, ed. (Cambridge, Mass.: The Belknap Press of Harvard University Press, 1961), pp. 72–74, 78–79, 96–99, 102–03. Reprinted by permission of the publishers.

a mediaeval origin; in North America, on the contrary, every thing had a Protestant beginning, and the Catholic church has come in afterwards as one sect among the others, and has always remained subordinate. In Europe, Protestanism has, so to speak, fallen heir to Catholicism; in America, Catholicism under the wing of Protestant toleration and freedom of conscience, has found an adopted home, and is everywhere surrounded by purely Protestant institutions. . . .

The Roman church has attained social and political importance in the eastern and western states only within the last twenty years, chiefly in consequence of the vast Irish emigration; but it will never be able to control the doctrines of the New World, though it should increase a hundred fold.

Another peculiarity in the ecclesiatical condition of North America, connected with the Protestant origin and character of the country, is the separation of church and state. The infidel reproach, that had it not been for the power of the state, Christianity would have long ago died out; and the argument of Roman controversialists, that Protestantism could not stand without the support of princes and civil governments, both are practically refuted and utterly annihilated in the United States. The president and governors, the congress at Washington, and the state legislatures, have, as such, nothing to do with the church, and are by the Constitution expressly forbidden to interfere in its affairs. State officers have no other rights in the church, than their personal rights as members of particular denominations, The church, indeed, everywhere enjoys the protection of the laws for its property, and the exercise of its functions; but it manages its own affairs independently, and has also to depend for its resources entirely on voluntary contributions. As the state commits itself to no particular form of Christianity, there is of course also no civil requisition of baptism, confirmation, and communion. Religion is left to the free will of each individual, and the church has none but moral means of influencing the world.

・　・　・

. . . It is truly wonderful, what a multitude of churches, ministers, colleges, theological seminaries, and benevolent institutions are there founded and maintained entirely by free-will offerings. In Berlin there are hardly forty churches for a population of four hundred and fifty thousand, of whom, in spite of all the union of church and state, only some thirty thousand attend public worship. In New York, to a population of six hundred thousand, there are over two hundred and fifty well-attended churches, some of them quite costly and splendid. . . . In the city of Brooklyn, across the East River, the number of churches is still larger in proportion to the population, and in the country towns and villages, especially in New England, the houses of worship average one to every thousand, or frequently even five hundred, souls. . . .

The voluntary system unquestionably has its great blemishes. It is connected with all sorts of petty drudgery, vexations, and troubles, unknown in well endowed established churches. Ministers and teachers, especially among the recent German emigrants in America, who have been accustomed to state provision for religion and education, have very much to suffer from the free system. They very often have to make begging tours for the erection of a church, and submit to innumerable other inconveniences for the good cause, till a congregation is brought into a proper course, and its members become practised in free giving.

But, on the other hand, the voluntary system calls forth a mass of individual activity and interest among the laity in ecclesiastical affairs, in the founding of new churches and congregations, colleges and seminaries, in home and foreign missions, and in the promotion of all forms of Christian philanthropy.

. . . .

. . . America is the classic land of sects, where in perfect freedom from civil disqualification, they can develop themselves without restraint. . . . But in the term *sect-system* we refer at the same time to the whole ecclesiastical condition of the country. For there the distinction of church and sect properly disappears; at least the distinction of established church and dissenting bodies, as it is commonly understood in England and Germany. In America, there is, in fact, no national or established church; therefore no dissenter. There all religious associations, which do not outrage the general Christian sentiment and the public morality (as the Mormons, who, for their conduct, were driven from Ohio and Illinois), enjoy the same protection and the same rights. . . .

Favored by the general freedom of conscience, the representatives of all the forms of Christianity in the Old World, except the Greek [Orthodox]—for we here leave out of view the isolated Russian colony in the Northwest of America—have gradually planted themselves in the vast field of the United States by emigration from all European countries, and are receiving reinforcements every year. There is the Roman with his Tridentinum and pompous mass; the Episcopal Anglican with his Thirty-nine Articles and Book of Common Prayer; the Scotch Presbyterian with his Westminster Confession, and his presbyteries and synods; the Congregationalist, or Puritan in the stricter sense, also with the Westminster Confession, but with his congregational independence; the Baptist, with his immersion and anti-paedobaptism [baptism of infants]; the Quaker, with his inward light; the Methodist, with his call to repentance and conversion, and his artificial machinery; the Lutheran, now with all his symbols . . . ; the German Reformed and Reformed Dutch, with the Heidelberg Cathechism and the Presbyterian Synodal polity; the Unionist, either with the consensus of both confessions, or indifferently rejecting all symbols; the Moravian community, with its silent educational and missionary operations; and a multitude of smaller sects besides, mostly of European origin, but some of American. . . .

This confusion of demoninations and sects makes very different impressions on the observer from different theological and religious points of view. If he makes all of individual Christianity, and regards the conversion of men as the whole work of the church, he will readily receive a very favorable impression of the religious state of things in America. It is not to be denied, that by the great number of churches and sects this work is promoted; since they multiply the agencies, spur each other on, vie with each other, striving to outdo one another in zeal and success. . . . There are in America probably more awakened souls, and more individual effort and self-sacrifice for religious purposes, proportionally, than in any other country in the world, Scotland alone perhaps excepted. . . .

But on closer inspection the sect system is seen to have also its weaknesses and it shady side. It brings all sorts of impure motives into play, and encourages the use of unfair, or at least questionable means for the promotion of its ends. It nourishes party spirit and passion, envy, selfishness, and bigotry. It changes the peaceful kingdom of God into a battle-field, where brother fights brother, not, of course, with sword and bayonet, yet with loveless harshness and all manner of detraction, and too often subordinates the interests of the church universal to those of his own party.

• • •

We believe . . . that the present divided condition of Protestantism, is only a temporary transition state, but that it will produce something far more grand and glorious, than Catholicism ever presented in its best days. Protestantism after all still contains the most vigorous energies and the greatest activity of the church. It represents the progressive principle of history. It is Christianity in motion. Hence more may be expected from it than from the comparative stagnation of the Roman or Greek Catholicism. . . . But this requires the previous fulfillment of the mission of Protestantism, the transforming of each individual man into a temple of God. Out of the most confused chaos God will bring the most beautiful order; out of the deepest discords, the noblest harmony; out of the most thoroughly developed Protestantism, the most harmonious and at the same time the freest Catholicism. What wild controversy has already raged, what violent passion has been kindled among theologians, about the doctrine of the Eucharist! And yet this sacrament is the feast of the holiest and deepest love, the symbol of the closest fellowship of Christ and the church. The one, holy, universal, apostolic church is an article not only of faith, but also of hope, to be fully accomplished only with the glorious return of Christ.

D. Holiness Through Submission

- *Phoebe Palmer* (1851)
- *Quarterly Christian Spectator* (1853)

In nineteenth-century America, the great majority of church members were women, and by mid-century, women like Phoebe Palmer (1807–1874) were taking an active leadership in religious revivals, publications, and organizations. Born in New York City, Phoebe Palmer was the daughter of English Methodist immigrants and the wife of a Methodist homeopathic physician. Together with her husband, Mrs. Palmer converted thousands of Americans and Canadians in camp meetings and "holiness revivals," reaping especially rich "harvests" during the great wave of urban revivalism of 1857–1858. Mrs. Palmer's informal "Tuesday meetings," held at her home in New York City, attracted a galaxy of Methodist leaders including bishops and college professors. A gifted organizer and pioneer in urban philanthropy, she led the Methodist home mission movement, seeking to aid and redeem the destitute and even the inmates of New York's Tombs prison. In the 1850s, Mrs. Palmer received much of the credit for establishing the Methodist Five Points' Mission on the site of the demolished Old Brewery, the city's most noxious slum (see Unit Three, Part 3, C).

There were subtle differences between Phobe Palmer's conception of perfectionism and inspiration to philanthropy and that of such figures as Finney and Channing. For Mrs. Palmer, the core of all religion is to be sought in "the way of holiness," the title of her book from which this selection is taken. Her book was so popular that it went through thirty-six editions in the decade before the Civil War. Though some modern readers may find Mrs. Palmer's prose saccharine and simple-minded, it was precisely tuned to the central concern of tens of thousands of Americans who yearned but did not feel worthy to be "twice-born Christians." Mrs. Palmer's great message is that holiness is not beyond anyone's reach. It is not necessary to wait for some soul-shattering influx of spirit; no extraordinary powers are required. All that is needed, in this "shorter" and only way, is total submission to the will of God. For the mark of true holiness is having nothing more to give.

The author of the second selection is also concerned with finding "a shorter way" to religious conversion, not of individual Americans but of the entire world. Much as Mrs. Palmer argues against individual procrastination and feelings of inability, this anonymous essayist seeks to counter the pessimism and "practical unbelief" that dwells on obstacles, postponing the global triumph of Christianity "to a great, indefinite distance in the future." Expressing the militant Protestant and Anglo-American chauvinism ascendant in the 1850s, he applauds the advance of British imperialism and the impending collapse of the Turkish empire. In the expansion of Western trade and technology he finds a progressive force that is compelling "the uncivilized to acknowledge their inferiority" and humbly accept the religion of civilization. Since most of the world's population is in some way "subject to" nominally Christian governments, our essayist asserts that the time has arrived for "the speedy conversion of the world." Essentially he offers material encouragement for the immensely popular vision embodied in Reginald Heber's great missionary hymn,

> From Greenland's icy mountains,
> From India's coral strand,
> Where Afric's sunny fountains
> Roll down their golden sand.

> . . . . In vain with lavish kindness
> The gifts of God are strown;
> The heathen in his blindness
> Bows down to wood and stone.

One should compare Mrs. Palmer's "feminine" ideal of individual submission with the second author's imperialist ideal of civilization compelling pagan and infidel nations to submit to Protestant Christianity. Both selections stress the discovery of a new *ability*, associated with knowledge, and the critical importance of *decision*. In both cases ability and decision lead to the assertion of a supposedly saving and emancipating power—for Mrs. Palmer the power is directed against the intemperance, ignorance, and depravity of New York's Five Points; for the promoter of world conversion, the power is aimed at the poverty and benighted customs of what eventually would be called the Third World.

Phoebe Palmer (1851)

"I HAVE thought," said one of the children of Zion to the other, as in love they journeyed onward in the way cast up for the ransomed of the Lord to walk in; "I have thought," said he, "whether there is not a *shorter way* of getting into this way of holiness than some of our   *   *   *   brethren apprehend?"

"Yes," said the sister addressed, who was a member of the denomination alluded to; "Yes, brother, THERE IS A SHORTER WAY! O! I am sure this long waiting and struggling with the powers of darkness is not necessary. There is a shorter way." And then, with a solemn feeling of responsibility, and with a realizing conviction of the truth uttered, she added, "But, brother, there is but one way."

Days and even weeks elapsed, and yet the question, with solemn bearing, rested upon the mind of that sister. . . .

How many, whom Infinite Love would long since have brought into this state, instead of seeking to be brought into the possession of the blessing at once, are seeking a preparation for the reception of it! They feel that their *convictions* are not deep enough to warrant an approach to the throne of grace, with the confident expectation of receiving the blessing *now*. Just at this point some may have been lingering months and years. Thus did the sister, who so confidently affirmed "there is a shorter way." And here, dear child of Jesus, permit the writer to tell you just how that sister found the "shorter way."

SOURCE: Phoebe Palmer, *The Way of Holiness* (New York: 1851), pp. 17–21, 32.

On looking at the requirements of the word of God, she beheld the command, "Be ye holy." She then began to say in her heart, "Whatever my former deficiencies may have been, God requires that I should *now* be holy. Whether *convicted* [of sin], or otherwise, *duty is plain.* God requires *present* holiness." On coming to this point, she at once apprehended a simple truth before unthought of, i.e., *Knowledge is conviction.* She well knew that, for a long time, she had been assured that God required holiness. But she had never deemed this knowledge a sufficient plea to take to God—and because of present need, to ask a present bestowment of the gift.

Convinced that in this respect she had mistaken the path, she now, with renewed energy, began to make use of the knowledge already received, and to discern a "shorter way."

Another difficulty by which her course had been delayed she found to be here. She had been accustomed to look at the blessing of holiness as such a high attainment, that her general habit of soul inclined her to think it almost beyond her reach. This erroneous impression rather influenced her to rest the matter thus:—"I will let every high state of grace, in name, alone, and seek only to be *fully conformed to the will of God, as recorded in his written word.* My chief endeavors shall be centered in the aim to be an humble *Bible Christian.* By the grace of God, all my energies shall be directed to this one point. With this single aim, I will journey onward, even though my faith may be tried to the uttermost by those manifestations being withheld, which have previously been regarded as essential for the establishment of faith."

On arriving at this point, she was enabled to gain yet clearer insight into the simplicity of the way. And it was by this process. After having taken the Bible as the rule of life, instead of the opinions and experience of professors [i.e., those who professed to be saved], she found, on taking the blessed word more closely to the companionship of her heart, that no one declaration spoke more appealingly to her understanding than this: "Ye are not your own, ye are bought with a price [i.e., saved by Christ's sacrifice], therefore glorify God in your body and spirit which are his."

By this she perceived the duty of *entire consecration* in a stronger light, and as more sacredly binding, than ever before. Here she saw God as her Redeemer, claiming, by virtue of the great price paid for the redemption of body, soul, and spirit, the *present and entire service* of all these redeemed powers.

. . .

But she did not at the moment regard the state into which she had been brought as the "way of holiness," neither had the word holiness been the most prominent topic during this solemn transaction. *Conformity to the will of God in all things* was the absorbing desire of her heart. Yet after having passed through these exercises she began to give expression to her full soul thus: "I am wholly thine!—Thou dost reign unrivaled in my heart! There is not a tie that binds me to earth; every tie has been severed, and now I am wholly, wholly thine!" While lingering on the last words, the Holy Spirit appealingly repeated the confident expressions to her heart, thus: What! wholly the Lord's? Is not this the holiness that God requires? What have you more to render? Does God require more than all? Hath he issued the command, "Be ye holy," and not given the ability, with the command, for the performance of it? Is he a hard master, unreasonable in his requirements? She now saw, in a convincing light, her error in regarding holiness as an attainment beyond her reach. . . .

Quarterly Christian Spectator (1853)

. . . Come,—come the golden age of peace, and light, and love,—the age when idolatry, with its foul and bloody orgies, and superstition, with its maddening incantations and its besotting follies, and despotism, with its rod of iron and its chains, and priestly domination, with its heavier fetters for the soul, shall have been swept away before the march of truth; and the earth, renewed in more than pristine beauty, decked with all the ornaments of human industry and art, and crowded with an enlightened, peaceful, happy population, shall reflect the smiles and resound with the praises of its Maker. . . .

Our wish is to show, that the *field of the world* is white to the harvest,— that the facilities to effort, and the encouragements to great effort, for the speedy conversion of all nations, which are peculiar to these times, are such as ought to call forth the utmost energy of every disciple of Christ, in the great work of spreading the knowledge of the Savior through the world. The question is, are efforts for the *speedy* conversion of the world, chimerical? Is it practicable, within any limited period of time, to send the knowledge of the gospel to all the habitations of mankind? Ought we, individually and unitedly, and with all our strength, to address ourselves to the work of subduing the world for Christ, and in the expectation of a speedy success? . . .

The majority of the human race is at present either nominally Christian, or subject to the governments of nominally Christian nations. Fifty years ago, it was far otherwise; but now, of the seven hundred and thirty-seven millions, which, according to the best estimates, make up the population of the globe, about three hundred and eighty-eight millions are either nominally, Christian, or subject to nominally Christian governments.

The Mohammedan and popish powers, which once constituted the greatest external obstacle to the progress of the religion of the Bible, are declining. The great Mohammedan empire in India has become entirely extinct; and a British governor-general in Calcutta, sways the scepter of the Great Mogul. The great and dreaded empire of the Turks, whose cresent has hung so long with baleful aspect over the fairest regions of the world, blighting the scenes of all that is

---

SOURCE: "Encouragements to Effort, for the Speedy Conversion of the World," *Quarterly Christian Spectator*, VII (March, 1853), pp. 1–2, 4–5, 10–11.

sacred in history, is already dismembered, impoverished, half-revolutionized, and, like some wounded monster, exhausted and faint, is staggering to its fall. . . .

Look next at *the great extension of commerce.* The whole world is continually explored and agitated by the spirit of commercial enterprise. The productions of every clime and region find their way to every other. The policy of governments is changing in this respect. Formerly, trade was almost every where restricted, lest it should impoverish; each government sought to make its subjects buy and sell of one another. Now, trade, the fair interchange of commodities among different nations, is almost every where encouraged, for it is found to enrich all the parties engaged in it. . . .

Commerce diffuses civilization, and excites every where the spirit of improvement. It diffuses civilization, by giving to savage tribes whom it visits, new ideas of comfort, and by thus forming them to habits of industry. It diffuses civilization, by diffusing knowledge, and by imparting the improvements of the more intelligent and favored nations to those who are less so. It promotes the spirit of improvement, not only in these ways, but by bringing different nations into contact with each other, and compelling the ignorant to see their ignorance, and the uncivilized to acknowledge their inferiority. In this way, the Turk already feels, that the Christian dogs of Europe, as in his barbarian pride he once called them, know more, and are better off, than himself. In this way, the Chinese must, ere long, become ashamed of his national vanity. In this way, all the Mohammedan and pagan nations on the globe, are either prepared, or are fast preparing, to listen with deference to the teachers of the religion, the *only* religion, of civilization. . . .

Wherever you choose to commence a missionary work, thither you can send missionaries, at a comparatively trifling expense, by the ordinary conveyances of commerce; and you can hear from them frequently, of their successes and their wants, after they reach there; and thither you can send them, at your pleasure or their need, supplies and helpers, and all that is required for the successful prosecution of their labors. Your missionaries too, can no where feel themselves beyond the reach of the sympathy and aid of the churches. Every impulse that is given to the cause at home, is felt by the remotest laborer abroad.

• • •

Missionaries have already gone to all sorts of men; and every where they have had success enough, at least, to show, that they are engaged in no impracticable enterprise. Do you ask, whether China can be penetrated, and whether the Chinese can be taught the lessons of the gospel? While you ask, China is penetrated; Chinese Christians are at this moment spreading abroad among their countrymen, the knowledge of the gospel. . . .

The indolent, voluptuous, cruel savage of the Pacific,—he too has felt the power of the gospel; and O, what wonders has the gospel wrought among those isles that gem the bosom of the southern deep! What more desperate experiment can there be? Go to frozen Labrador,—go where, under the rigor of a polar sky, the dwarfish Greenlander maintains a precarious existence amid the everlasting conflict of the elements,—there the experiment has been tried; and there the wretched native, sitting in his snow-built cabin, through the long, dark watches of his sunless winter, has rejoiced in the splendor of the sun of righteousness. And, to add one more particular to this recital, the African, about whom philosophers have sometimes doubted, whether he is human,—the African, both as we find him far away from the appropriate seat of his race and kindred, crushed under a horrid slavery, and as we find him in his native wilds,—has been sought out by the officiousness of Christian love; and he too is a witness, that the world can be evangelized. . . .

We would ask our readers now, do we not hear, as it were, in these exhibitions of success, the voice of our Savior, the voice of our God, coming from the heavens, and from all the regions of the earth,—coming from the four winds, and from every mountain, and plain, and sea, and island, and telling us of the approach of that blessed consummation for which his elect have so long been waiting? Lift up your eyes, and look upon the field, which is the world, —it is white already to the harvest. Oh, the deafness of that man, who will not hear!—the blindness of that man, who will not discern the signs of the times! God bids us look upon the aspect of the earth hastening to a crisis, such as earth never yet has known. God calls us as with a voice from heaven, Put in the sickle and reap, for the harvest of the earth is ripe.

3

The Temperance Reformation

A. Moral Influence: The Diffusion of Knowledge

- *Lyman Beecher* (1826)
- *Thomas S. Grimké* (1833)

Temperance was the first of the mass movements for social reform. It served as a model and training ground for future abolitionists, feminists, prison reformers, and communitarians. It far outdid all other antebellum movements by recruiting over one million followers and by winning support in the South and West as well as in the Northeast. Even by the 1820s, "temperance" meant not moderate drinking but total abstinence from distilled liquor (most temperance reformers also excluded beer and wine, though the sacramental use of wine continued to arouse sharp debate).

Temperance reformers, though sometimes portrayed as religious cranks and killjoys, were responding to a genuine social problem. Beginning in the eighteenth century, improvements in distillation, transportation, and distribution had made spiritous liquor cheap and universally accessible (by the 1820s, the price of whiskey had fallen to 25¢ a gallon). By the 1820s, *per capita* consumption had risen to an all time record. In parts of Massachusetts (and England) for which statistics are available, *per capita* consumption of hard liquor was well over twice that of today, and most of the consuming was done by males. It was no accident that alcohol became popularly identified as the major source of domestic discord, or that women played such a prominent part in the temperance movement (see Unit One). And while some of the moral concern can be attributed to new desires to reduce public rowdiness and disorder, to increase the efficiency and productivity of labor, and to lower the costs of public welfare, there is also evidence that alcoholism was becoming a rampant American disease.[1] If the temperance reformers failed to emancipate the nation from the "demon rum," they at least contributed to a marked decline in *per capita* consumption—a decline that accentuated the division between drinkers and nondrinkers, or in a larger sense between drinking and nondrinking subcultures.

In the first selection, we turn again to Lyman Beecher because he was a great propagandist whose classic *Six Sermons* on intemperance left an enduring imprint on the movement. No other writer appealed so brilliantly to the anxieties of moderate drinkers or succeeded so well in dramatizing the social and psychological allures that had led many of his friends and fellow ministers to the habitual consumption of alcohol. Note how Beecher builds upon the religious themes of ability, decision, and new birth that we examined in Part 2, except that sin is now secularized and naturalized as a self-deceiving "state of internal sensation"; conversion and holiness are translated into the mental and bodily regeneration following the decision not to drink. Beecher also echoes writings on the Baconian method (Part 1) when he finds the remedy for intemperance in the "correct application of general principles" and predicts that the "moral influence" of enlightened public opinion will be as certain and irresistible in effect as the law of gravitation. Though exuberant over the prospect of a millennium of sobriety, Beecher holds out no hope for the tipplers who have crossed the threshhold of reclamation. Like the "nonelect," the condemned sinners in the Calvinist theology which Beecher was beginning to modify, there is an entire "generation of drunkards" doomed to "hasten out of time." And here, one should consider the implications of social class. Beecher's arguments are aimed at the Christian middle class. He warns against censuring the middle-class distillers and distributors of liquor, who are merely responding to consumer demand. Beecher leaves little doubt that the "generation of drunkards" is a class of self-destroying workers joined by a few black sheep who have disgraced the most respectable families.

In the second selection, Thomas S. Grimké also appeals to arguments based on facts "as in the inductive philosophy," but hails the "Temperance Reformation" as both a modern counterpart to the Protestant Reformation and an expression of loyalty to country and republican principles. A South Carolinian, Grimké (1786–1834) was the son of a Revolutionary patriot who also happened to be a wealthy slaveholder. Hence, Thomas Grimké, a

---

[1] See W. J. Rorabaugh, *The Alcoholic Republic: An American Tradition* (New York: Oxford University Press, 1979).

prominent South Carolina lawyer and state senator, speaks from an entirely different world from that of Beecher (though both men had graduated from Yale). It should be added, however, that Grimké was not a typical South Carolina slaveholder. His sisters, Sarah and Angelina, both migrated to the North and became converts to abolitionism and feminism (see Unit One, Part 5). Grimké himself supported such causes as Bible and tract societies, manual training schools, the peace movement, higher education for women, and foreign missions. Like many northern and western reformers, he considered temperance the keystone in this grand arch of scientific enlightenment and moral improvement.

Lyman Beecher (1826)

No sin has fewer apologies than intemperance. The suffrage of the world is against it; and yet there is no sin so naked in its character, and whose commencement and progress is indicated by so many signs, concerning which there is among mankind such profound ignorance. All reprobate drunkenness; and yet, not one of the thousands who fall into it, dreams of danger when he enters the way that leads to it.

The soldier, approaching the deadly breach, and seeing rank after rank of those who preceded him swept away, hesitates sometimes and recoils from certain death. But men behold the effects upon others . . . they see them begin, advance, and end, in confirmed intemperance, and unappalled rush heedlessly upon the same ruin.

A part of this heedlessness arises from the undefined nature of the crime in its early stages, and the ignorance of men, concerning what may be termed the experimental [empirical] indications of its approach. Theft and falsehood are definite actions. But intemperance is a state of internal sensation, and the indications may exist long, and multiply, and the subject of them not be aware that they are the signs of intemperance. It is not unfrequent, that men become irreclaimable in their habits, without suspicion of danger. . . .

Intemperance is the sin of our land, and, with our boundless prosperity, is coming in upon us like a flood; and if anything shall defeat the hopes of the world, which hang upon our experiment of civil liberty, it is that river of fire, which is rolling through the land, destroying the vital air, and extending around an atmosphere of death.

. . .

It is a matter of undoubted certainty, that habitual tippling is worse than periodical drunkenness. The poor Indian, who, once a month, drinks himself

SOURCE: Lyman Beecher, *Six Sermons on the Nature, Occasions, Signs, Evils and Remedy of Intemperance*, 8th ed. (Boston: T. R. Marvin, 1829), pp. 6–7, 9, 17, 26–27, 43–45, 54–56, 64–66, 86–87.

dead all but simple breathing, will out-live for years the man who drinks little and often, and is not, perhaps, suspected of intemperance. The use of ardent spirits daily, as ministering to cheerfulness, or bodily vigor, ought to be regarded as intemperance. No person, probably, ever did or ever will receive ardent spirits into his system once a day, and fortify his constitution against its deleterious effects, or exercise such discretion and self government as that the quantity will not be increased, and bodily infirmities and mental imbecility be the result, and, in more than half the instances, inebriation. Nature may hold out long against this sapping and mining of the constitution, which daily tippling is carrying on; but, first or last, this foe of life will bring to the assault enemies of its own formation. . . .

· · ·

Ardent spirits, given as a matter of hospitality, is not unfrequently the occasion of intemperance. In this case the tempation is a stated inmate of the family. The utensils are present, and the occasions for their use are not unfrequent. And when there is no guest, the sight of the liquor, the state of the health, or even lassitude of spirits, may indicate the propriety of the "prudent use," until the prudent use becomes, by repetition, habitual use—and habitual use becomes irreclaimable intemperance. In this manner, doubtless, has many a father, and mother, and son, and daughter, been ruined forever.

· · ·

In the commencement of this evil habit, there are many who drink to excess only on particular days, such as days for military exhibition, the anniversary of our independence, the birth-day of Washington, Christmas, New Year's day, election, and others of the like nature. When any of these holidays arrive, and they come as often almost as saints' days in the calendar, they bring with them, to many, the insatiable desire of drinking, as well as a dispensation from the sin, as efficacious and quieting to the conscience, as papal indulgences. . . .

There are others who feel the desire of drinking stirred up within them by the associations of place. They could go from end to end of a day's journey without ardent spirits, were there no taverns on the road. But the very sight of these receptacles of pilgrims awakens the desire "just to step in and take something." And so powerful does this association become, that many will no more pass the tavern than they would pass a fortified place with all the engines of death directed against them. There are in every city, town, and village, places of resort, which in like manner, as soon as the eye falls upon them, create the thirst of drinking. . . .

· · ·

There is no remedy for intemperance but the cessation of it. Nature must be released from the unnatural war which is made upon her, and be allowed to rest, and then nutrition, and sleep, and exercise, will perform the work of restoration. Gradually the spring of life will recover tone, appetite will return, digestion become efficient, sleep sweet, and the muscular system vigorous, until the elastic heart with every beat shall send health through the system, and joy through the soul. . . .

Are there then set times, days, and places, when you calculate always to indulge yourselves in drinking ardent spirits? Do you stop often to take something at the tavern when you travel, and always when you come to the village, town, or city? This frequency of drinking will plant in your system, before you are aware of it, the seeds of the most terrific disease which afflicts humanity. Have you any friends or companions whose presence, when you meet them, awakens the thought and the desire of drinking? Both of you have entered on a course in which there is neither safety nor hope but from instant retreat.

Do any of you love to avail yourselves of every little catch and circumstance among your companions, to bring out "a treat?" "Alas, my lord, there is death in the pot."

Do you find the desire of strong drink returning daily, and at stated hours? Unless you intend to travel all the length of the highway of intemperance, it is time to stop. Unless you intend soon to resign your liberty forever, and come under a despotism of the most cruel and inexorable character, you must abandon the morning bitters, the noontide stimulant, and the evening bowl.

Do any of you drink in secret, because you are unwilling your friends or the world should know how much you drink? You might as well cut loose in a frail boat before a hurricane, and expect safety: you are gone, gone irretrievably, if you do not stop.

• • •

In every city and town the poor-tax, created chiefly by intemperance, is augmenting. . . . [T]he frequency of going upon the town [relying on public welfare] has taken away the reluctance of pride, and destroyed the motives to providence which the fear of poverty and suffering once supplied. The prospect of a destitute old age, or of a suffering family, no longer troubles the vicious portion of our community. They drink up their daily earnings, and bless God for the poor-house, and begin to look upon it as, of right, the drunkard's home, and contrive to arrive thither as early as idleness and excess will give them a passport to this sinecure of vice. Thus is the insatiable destroyer of industry marching through the land, rearing poor-houses, and augmenting taxation: night and day, with sleepless activity, squandering property, cutting the sinews of industry, undermining vigor, engendering disease. . . .

Add the loss sustained by the subtraction of labor, and the shortened date of life, to the expense of sustaining the poor, created by intemperance; and the nation is now taxed annually more than the expense which would be requisite for the maintenance of government, and for the support of all our schools and colleges, and all the religious instruction of the nation. Already a portion of the entire capital of the nation is mortgaged for the support of drunkards. . . .

Every intemperate and idle man, whom you behold tottering about the streets and steeping himself at the stores, regards your houses and lands as pledged to take care of him,—puts his hands deep, annually, into your pockets, and eats his bread in the sweat of your brows, instead of his own; and with marvellous good nature you bear it. If a robber should break loose on the highway, to levy taxation, an armed force would be raised to hunt him from society. But the tippler may do it fearlessly, in open day, and not a voice is raised, not a finger is lifted.

• • •

Intemperance in our land is not accidental; it is rolling in upon us by the violation of some great laws of human nature. In our views, and in our practice as a nation, there is something fundamentally wrong; and the remedy, like the evil, must be found in the correct application of general principles. It must be a universal and national remedy.

What then is this universal, natural, and national remedy for intemperance? IT IS THE BANISHMENT OF ARDENT SPIRITS FROM THE LIST OF LAWFUL ARTICLES OF COMMERCE, BY A CORRECT AND EFFICIENT PUBLIC SENTIMENT; SUCH AS HAS TURNED SLAVERY OUT OF HALF OUR LAND, AND WILL YET EXPEL IT FROM THE WORLD. . . .

We are not therefore to come down in wrath upon the distillers, and importers, and venders of ardent spirits. None of us are enough without sin to cast the first stone. For who would have imported, or distilled, or vended, if all the nominally temperate in the land had refused to drink? It is the buyers who have created the demand for ardent spirits, and made distillation and importation a gainful traffic. And it is the custom of the temperate too, which inundates the land with the occasion of so much and such unmanageable temptation. Let the temperate cease to buy—and the demand for ardent spirits will fall in the market three fourths, and ultimately will fail wholly, as the generation of drunkards shall hasten out of time.

To insist that men, whose capital is embarked in the production, or vending of ardent spirits, shall manifest the entire magnanimity and self-denial, which is needful to save the land, though the example would be glorious to them, is more than we have a right to expect or demand. Let the consumer do his duty, and the capitalist, finding his employment unproductive, will quickly discover other channels of useful enterprise. . . .

This however cannot be done effectually so long as the traffic in ardent spirits is regarded as lawful, and is patronized by men of reputation and moral worth in every part of the land. Like slavery, it must be regarded as sinful, impolitic, and dishonorable. That no measures will avail short of rendering ardent spirits a contraband of trade, is nearly self-evident.

• • •

No great melioration of the human condition was ever achieved without the concurrent effort of numbers, and no extended, well-directed application of moral influence, was ever made in vain. Let the temperate part of the nation awake, and reform, and concentrate their influence in a course of systematic action, and success is not merely probable, but absolutely certain. And cannot this be accomplished?—cannot the public attention be aroused, and set in array against the traffic in ardent spirits, and against their use? With just as much certainty can the public sentiment be formed and put in motion, as the waves can be moved by the breath of heaven—or the massy rock, balanced on the precipice, can be pushed from its centre of motion;—and when the public sentiment once begins to move, its march will be as resistless as the same rock thundering down the precipice. Let no man then look upon our condition as hopeless, or feel, or think, or say, that nothing can be done. The language of Heaven to our happy nation is, "be it unto thee even as thou wilt," and there is no despondency more fatal, or more wicked, than that which refuses to hope, and to act, from the apprehension that nothing can be done.

Thomas S. Grimké (1833)

The Temperance Reformation is peculiarly Christian, American. The great characteristics of Christianism, and of the political institutions of our country, are stamped upon its face. It appeals to the sense of duty and the spirit of usefulness. Its arguments, as in the inductive philosophy, are gathered from facts. Observation and experience are its tests; while health, order, industry and happiness, in a word, the good of the people, are the object of its labors, and the reward of its victory. Assailed at once by prejudice and interest, by self-confidence, inveterate habits, and even hospitality, by the lovers of plea-sure and the victims of vice, it has met these antagonists calmly, openly, fear-lessly. It has met, and conquered them, in the name and for the sake of humanity and liberty, of religion, morals and social order. . . .

I shall not speak of such patriotism and such patriots [as statemen, warriors, and martyrs]. They are the stars, and the planets, and the comets, which adorn the firmament of public life; and pour out their flood of glory on distant lands and remote ages. I speak of a patriotism, which is *the very sunlight of society*, cheerful, diffusive, invigorative: and of a patriot, who like the sun-beam, is benevolent and useful, tho' scarcely ever noticed. . . . I shall speak then, of the patriotism of the people in private life, not of the patriotism of their rulers in public. I speak of the patriot, as found in the humblest citizen of our country, at the fireside and the social circle. . . .

To provide for the *health* of the community, is one of the duties of patriot-ism. And is not the Temperance Reformation one of the most simple yet powerful agents in the establishment and preservation of health? . . .

In a word, the vice of intemperance is the prolific parent of disease in every age and condition of life, and in every state of society, whether civilized or barbarous. And is not the Temperance Reformation the cause of GENUINE PATRIOTISM; since its object is to deliver every community from so vast an amount of loathsome, excruciating and obstinate disease, and to transmit to children, and to children's children, a sound constitution?

The preservation of *property* and *life* is among the most important duties of a good government. Almost all the civil and political institutions of society embrace these, directly or indirectly, as primary objects. They are inseparable from the chief ends of society; because, without security to them, society can-

SOURCE: Thomas S. Grimké, *Address on the Patriot Character of the Temperance Refor-mation* (Charleston: Observor Office Press, 1833), pp. 5, 7–11.

not exist. We shall hereafter speak of the great value of temperance in promoting the spirit of industry and frugality, in relation to the individual and his family: and we cannot doubt its vast importance, when we consider to what an extent we ourselves and our property are either in the power, or are actually entrusted to the care of others. . . .

How often life has been endangered or lost, or property either ruined or impaired in value, from the intemperance of others, needs neither argument to convince us, nor facts to illustrate and corroborate the position. The records of our criminal courts, are of themselves the highest evidence of the melancholy truth. . . . Assuredly, that is an enlightened and merciful patriotism which provides the means of safety for so many lives and so much property. *And what but the* PATRIOTISM *of the* TEMPERANCE REFORM *has ever had the wisdom to devise, and the courage to execute so benevolent a plan?*

It is equally the duty of patriotism to cultivate among the people the spirit of *industry and economy.* But what can be a more formidable enemy to them than the immoderate use of spirituous liquors? Experience has set beyond all controversy this truth, as a rule, little less than universal, that intemperance is the mother of irregular habits in business of every description; whether in the field or in the city, on the land or the ocean. The absence of frugality follows inevitably. How many of the young have traced the ruin of their prospects to the sin of intemperance! How many of the middle aged have beheld in this, the loss of property and credit! How many of the old have looked back from the pallet of straw and the hovel of wretchedness, to the comforts of competency or the enjoyments of wealth, and have found the cause of their misery in the inebriating cup! What multitudes have been crowded into our pauper establishments, and hospitals, and lunatic asylums, from their indulgence in this vice; and instead of an honored tomb, among relatives and friends, have been laid unnoticed and unmourned in the burial ground of the stranger and outcast! And is it not the office of enlightened patriotism, to relieve the individual and society from the countless variety of evils that flow from intemperance, thro' idleness and prodigality? . . . What, then, shall we say of the patriotism, which saves not merely one man, but thousands and tens of thousands, from the public receptacles of the sick, the maniac and the pauper? Which purifies the atmosphere of public and private business, and establishes on sure foundations, the habits of industry and economy? Shall we not say, that, such patriotism is full of benevolence and wisdom? *And what is the* TEMPERANCE *cause but such* PATRIOTISM?

B. Compassion for the Fallen

- *John Bartholomew Gough* (1869, *recalling the early 1840s*)
- *Abraham Lincoln* (1842)

In 1840, the temperance movement took a new direction when a group of reformed drunkards organized a Washingtonian Temperance Society in Baltimore, capitalizing on the theme of patriotism and aiming at essentially the same goals as the modern Alcoholics Anonymous. As we have seen, Lyman Beecher considered drunkards irreclaimable. Old guard temperance leaders had little taste for fraternizing with reformed alcoholics, who often seemed like seedy characters of disreputable background. But the spectacular growth of the Washingtonian movement, which imitated the parades and public theatrics of election campaigns, soon brought limited concessions and cooperation from the established temperance societies.

Washingtonians had a clear advantage in converting the intemperate. By speaking from personal experience, dramatizing the horrors of self-deception, remorse, and loss of self-control, they could persuade hundreds of thousands of men to "sign the pledge" of total abstinence. Like fugitive slaves from the South, they were living proof that escape was possible. Yet the reformed drunkards could not altogether escape the stigma of having once been enslaved to alcohol, particularly since their effectiveness as public speakers depended on dramatizing their former degradation. Moreover, some of the most popular platform speakers, such as John Bartholomew Gough, were forced to admit occasional and sensational lapses—as when Gough was found in a New York house of prostitution after a week's binge. In fact, Gough was not a Washingtonian; and the success of the Washingtonians in providing one another with mutual and fraternal support was somewhat obscured by their association with men like Gough in spectacular campaigns to collect public pledges. Like the contemporary campaigns to collect votes or religious conversions, these quantitative triumphs were often temporary and therefore disillusioning.

Gough (1817–1886) came from a poor English family who had shipped him off to America when he was twelve. After working on a farm for two years, he drifted to New York City where he learned the book-binding trade, dabbled at acting (he had a remarkable voice), and took to drink. In 1842, when seemingly a hopeless alcoholic, he stunned a temperance meeting with a vivid account of his sufferings. Within a decade, Gough had won international fame as a platform orator. Forgiven by his church and by the general public for his last lapse from temperance (the details of which were discreetly whitewashed), he went on to deliver thousands of lectures for increasingly high fees and to claim credit for hundreds of thousands of signed pledges. The following selection is a sample of his written style, but one must try to imagine his performance on the stage, reenacting the violence of delirium tremens.

One seldom associates Abraham Lincoln (1809–1865) with the temperance cause, but one of his early public speeches was an address, on Washington's birthday, to the Washingtonians of Springfield, Illinois. At this time, Lincoln had just turned thirty-three. He was a successful, ambitious lawyer with years of experience in the Illinois legislature. The next year, 1843, he would be sent to Congress. Growing up in a hard-drinking, violent society, Lincoln had resolved early in life to abstain from alcohol. No aspiring Yankee was more committed to the ethic of self-control and self-improvement. Yet few aspiring Yankees could express Lincoln's charitable view that "such of us as have never fallen victims have been spared more by the absence of appetite than from any mental or moral superiority over those who have." Lincoln's speech may be unique in temperance literature for its humor (a quality not conspicuous in any reform), its compassion, and its suspension of moral judgment. No less important is Lincoln's sense of national mission.

John Bartholomew Gough (1869)

Will it be believed that I again sought refuge in rum? Yet so it was. Scarcely had I recovered from the fright, than I sent out, procured a pint of rum, and drank it all in less than an hour. And now came upon me many terrible sensations. Cramps attacked me in my limbs, which racked me with agony; and my temples throbbed as if they would burst. So ill was I, that I became seriously alarmed, and begged the people of the house to send for a physician. They did so; but I immediately repented having summoned him, and endeavored, but ineffectually, to get out of his way when he arrived. He saw at a glance what was the matter with me, ordered the persons about me to watch me carefully, and on no account to let me have any spiritous liquors. Everything stimulating was rigorously denied me; and then came on the drunkard's remorseless torturer—delirium tremens, in all its terrors, attacked me. For three days, I endured more agony than pen could describe, even were it guided by the mind of Dante. Who can tell the horrors of that malady, aggravated as it is by the almost ever-abiding consciousness that it is self-sought? Hideous faces appeared on the walls, and on the ceiling, and on the floors; foul things crept along the bedclothes, and glaring eyes peered into mine. I was at one time surrounded by millions of monstrous spiders, that crawled slowly over every limb, whilst the beaded drops of perspiration would start to my brow, and my limbs would shiver until the bed rattled again. Strange lights would dance before my eyes, and then suddenly the very blackness of darkness would appall me by its dense gloom. All at once, whilst gazing at a frightful creation of my distempered mind, I seemed struck with sudden blindness. I knew a candle was burning in the room, but I could not see it—all was so pitchy dark. I lost the sense of feeling, too, for I endeavored to grasp my arm in one hand, but consciousness was gone. I put my hand to my side, my head, but felt nothing, and still I knew my limbs and frame *were* there. And then the scene would change: I was falling—falling swiftly as an arrow—far down into some terrible abyss. . . .

By the mercy of God, I survived this awful seizure; and when I rose, a weak, broken-down man, and surveyed my ghastly features in a glass, I thought of my mother, and asked myself how I had obeyed the instructions I had

---

SOURCE: *Autobiography and Personal Reminiscences of John B. Gough* (Springfield, Mass.: Bill, Nichols and Co., 1869), pp. 103–5.

received from her lips, and to what advantage I had turned the lessons she taught me. I remembered her countless prayers and tears,—thought of what I had been but a few short months before, and contrasted my situation with what it then was. Oh! how keen were my own rebukes; and, in the excitement of the moment, I resolved to lead a better life, and abstain from the accursed cup.

For about a month, terrified by what I had suffered, I adhered to my resolution; then my wife came home, and, in my joy at her return, I flung my good resolutions to the wind, and, foolishly fancying that I could now restrain my appetite, which had for a whole month remained in subjection, I took a glass of brandy. That glass aroused the slumbering demon, who would not be satisfied by so tiny a libation. Another and another succeeded, until I was again far advanced in the career of intemperance. The night of my wife's return, I went to bed intoxicated.

Abraham Lincoln (1842)

Although the temperance cause has been in progress for near twenty years, it is apparent to all that it is just now being crowned with a degree of success hitherto unparalleled.

The list of its friends is daily swelled by the additions of fifties, of hundreds, and of thousands. The cause itself seems suddenly transformed from a cold abstract theory to a living, breathing, active, and powerful chieftain. . . .

The warfare heretofore waged against the demon intemperance has somehow or other been erroneous. Either the champions engaged or the tactics they adopted have not been the most proper. These champions for the most part have been preachers, lawyers, and hired agents. Between these and the mass of mankind there is a want of approachability, if the term be admissible, partially, at least, fatal to their success. They are supposed to have no sympathy of feeling or interest with those very persons whom it is their object to convince and persuade.

And again, it is so common and so easy to ascribe motives to men of these classes other than those they profess to act upon. The preacher, it is said, advocates temperance because he is a fanatic, and desires a union of the church and state; the lawyer from his pride and vanity of hearing himself speak; and the hired agent for his salary. But when one who has long been known as a victim of intemperance bursts the fetters that have bound him, and appears before his neighbors "clothed and in his right mind," a redeemed specimen of long-lost humanity, and stands up, with tears of joy trembling in his eyes, to tell of the miseries once endured, now to be endured no more

SOURCE: Abraham Lincoln, "Address Before the Springfield Washingtonian Temperance Society, February 22, 1842," *Complete Works*, Vol. I, J. G. Nicolay and J. Hay, eds. (n.p., Lincoln Memorial University: 1894), pp. 193–200, 202–3, 205–9.

forever; of his once naked and starving children, now clad and fed comfortably; of a wife long weighed down with woe, weeping, and a broken heart, now restored to health, happiness, and a renewed affection; and how easily it is all done, once it is resolved to be done; how simple his language!—there is a logic and an eloquence in it that few with human feelings can resist. They cannot say that he desires a union of church and state, for he is not a church member; they cannot say he is vain of hearing himself speak, for his whole demeanor shows he would gladly avoid speaking at all; they cannot say he speaks for pay, for he receives none, and asks for none. Nor can his sincerity in any way be doubted, or his sympathy for those he would persuade to imitate his example be denied.

In my judgment, it is to the battles of this new class of champions that our late success is greatly, perhaps chiefly, owing. But, had the old-school champions themselves been of the most wise selecting, was their system of tactics the most judicious? It seems to me it was not. Too much denunciation against dram-sellers and dram-drinkers was indulged in. This I think was both impolitic and unjust. . . . When the dram-seller and drinker were incessantly told—not in accents of entreaty and persuasion, diffidently addressed by erring man to an erring brother, but in the thundering tones of anathema and denunciation with which the lordly judge often groups together all the crimes of the felon's life, and thrusts them in his face just ere he passes sentence of death upon him—that they were the authors of all the vice and misery and crime in the land; that they were the manufacturers and material of all the thieves and robbers and murderers that infest the earth; that their houses were the workshops of the devil; and that their persons should be shunned by all the good and virtuous, as moral pestilences—I say, when they were told all this, and in this way, it is not wonderful that they were slow, very slow, to acknowledge the truth of such denunciations, and to join the ranks of their denouncers in a hue and cry against themselves.

To have expected them to do otherwise than they did—to have expected them not to meet denunciation with denunciation, crimination with crimination, and anathema with anathema—was to expect a reversal of human nature, which is God's decree and can never be reversed.

When the conduct of men is designed to be influenced, persuasion, kind, unassuming persuasion, should ever be adopted. It is an old and a true maxim "that a drop of honey catches more flies than a gallon of gall." So with men. If you would win a man to your cause, first convince him that you are his sincere friend. . . . On the contrary, assume to dictate to his judgment, or to command his action, or to mark him as one to be shunned and despised, and he will retreat within himself, close all the avenues to his head and his heart; and though your cause be naked truth itself, transformed to the heaviest lance, harder than steel, and sharper than steel can be made, and though you throw it with more than herculean force and precision, you shall be no more able to pierce him than to penetrate the hard shell of a tortoise with a rye straw. Such is man, and so must he be understood by those who would lead him, even to his own best interests.

On this point the Washingtonians greatly excel the temperance advocates of former times. Those whom they desire to convince and persuade are their old friends and companions. They know they are not demons, nor even the worst of men; they know that generally they are kind, generous, and charitable, even beyond the example of their more staid and sober neighbors. . . .

But I have said that denunciations against dram-sellers and dram-drinkers are unjust, as well as impolitic. Let us see. . . .

When all such of us as have now reached the years of maturity first opened our eyes upon the stage of existence, we found intoxicating liquor recognized by everybody, used by everybody, repudiated by nobody. It commonly entered into the first draught of the infant and the last draught of the dying man. From the sideboard of the parson down to the ragged pocket of the houseless loafer, it was constantly found. Physicians precribed it in this, that, and the other disease; government provided it for soldiers and sailors; and to have a rolling or raising, a husking or "hoedown," anywhere about without it was positively insufferable. So, too, it was everywhere a respectable article of manufacture and merchandise. The making of it was regarded as an honorable livelihood, and he who could make most was the most enterprising and respectable. Large and small manufactories of it were everywhere erected, in which all the earthly goods of their owners were invested. Wagons drew it from town to town; boats bore it from clime to clime, and the winds wafted it from nation to nation; and merchants bought and sold it, by wholesale and retail, with precisely the same feelings on the part of the seller, buyer, and bystander as are felt at the selling and buying of plows, beef, bacon, or any other of the real necessaries of life. Universal public opinion not only tolerated but recognized and adopted its use.

It is true that even then it was known and acknowledged that many were greatly injured by it; but none seemed to think the injury arose from the use of a bad thing, but from the abuse of a very good thing. The victims of it were to be pitied and compassionated, just as are the heirs of consumption and other hereditary diseases. Their failing was treated as a misfortune, and not as a crime, or even as a disgrace. If, then, what I have been saying is true, is it wonderful that some should think and act now as all thought and acted twenty years ago? and is it just to assail, condemn, or despise them for doing so? The universal sense of mankind on any subject is an argument, or at least an influence, not easily overcome. The success of the argument in favor of the existence of an overruling Providence mainly depends upon that sense; and men ought not in justice to be denounced for yielding to it in any case, or giving it up slowly, especially when they are backed by interest, fixed habits, or burning appetites.

. . .

By the Washingtonians this system of consigning the habitual drunkard to hopeless ruin is repudiated. They adopt a more enlarged philanthropy; they go for present as well as future good. They labor for all now living, as well as hereafter to live. They teach hope to all—despair to none. As applying to their cause, they deny the doctrine of unpardonable sin; as in Christianity it is taught, so in this they teach—"While the lamp holds out to burn, The vilest sinner may return." And, what is a matter of more profound congratulation, they, by experiment upon experiment and example upon example, prove the maxim to be no less true in the one case than in the other. On every hand we behold those who but yesterday were the chief of sinners, now the chief apostles of the cause.

• • •

But it is said by some that men will think and act for themselves; that none will disuse spirits or anything else because his neighbors do; and that moral influence is not that powerful engine contended for. Let us examine this. Let me ask the man who could maintain this position most stiffly, what compensation he will accept to go to church some Sunday and sit during the sermon with his wife's bonnet upon his head? Not a trifle, I'll venture. And why not? There would be nothing irreligious in it, nothing immoral, nothing uncomfortable—then why not? Is it not because there would be something egregiously unfashionable in it? Then it is the influence of fashion; and what is the influence of fashion but the influence that other people's actions have on our actions—the strong inclination each of us feels to do as we see all our neighbors do? Nor is the influence of fashion confined to any particular thing or class of things; it is just as strong on one subject as another. Let us make it as unfashionable to withhold our names from the temperance cause as for husbands to wear their wives' bonnets to church, and instances will be just as rare in the one case as the other.

"But," say some, "we are no drunkards, and we shall not acknowledge ourselves such by joining a reformed drunkards' society, whatever our influence might be." Surely no Christian will adhere to this objection. If they believe as they profess, that Omnipotence condescended to take on himself the form of sinful man, and as such to die an ignominious death for their sakes, surely they will not refuse submission to the infinitely lesser condescension, for the temporal, and perhaps eternal, salvation of a large, erring, and unfortunate class of their fellow-creatures. Nor is the condescension very great. In my judgment such of us as have never fallen victims have been spared more by the absence of appetite than from any mental or moral superiority over those who have. Indeed, I believe if we take habitual drunkards as a class, their heads and their hearts will bear an advantageous comparison with those of any other class. There seems ever to have been a proneness in the brilliant and warm-blooded to fall into this vice—the demon of intemperance ever seems to have delighted in sucking the blood of genius and of generosity. What one of us but can call to mind some relative, more promising in youth than all his fellows, who has fallen a sacrifice to his [the demon's] rapacity? . . .

If the relative grandeur of revolutions shall be estimated by the great amount of human misery they alleviate, and the small amount they inflict, then indeed will this be the grandest the world shall ever have seen.

Of our political revolution of '76 we are all justly proud. It has given us a degree of political freedom far exceeding that of any other nation of the earth.

In it the world has found a solution of the long-mooted problem as to the capability of man to govern himself. In it was the germ which has vegetated, and still is to grow and expand into the universal liberty of mankind. But, with all these glorious results, past, present, and to come, it had its evils too. It breathed forth famine, swam in blood, and rode in fire; and long, long after, the orphan's cry and the widow's wail continued to break the sad silence that ensued. These were the price, the inevitable price, paid for the blessings it bought.

Turn now to the temperance revolution. In it we shall find a stronger bondage broken, a viler slavery manumitted, a greater tyrant deposed; in it, more of want supplied, more disease healed, more sorrow assuaged. By it no orphans starving, no widows weeping. By it, none wounded in feeling, none injured in interest; even the dram-maker and dram-seller will have glided into other occupations so gradually as never to have felt the change, and will stand ready to join all others in the universal song of gladness. . . .

Happy day when—all appetites controlled, all poisons subdued, all matter subjected—mind, all conquering mind, shall live and move, the monarch of the world. Glorious consummation! Hail, fall of fury! Reign of reason, all hail!

And when the victory shall be complete—when there shall be neither a slave nor a drunkard on the earth—how proud the title of that land which may truly claim to be the birthplace and the cradle of both those revolutions that shall have ended in that victory. How nobly distinguished that people who shall have planted and nurtured to maturity both the political and moral freedom of their species.

C. Coercion Replaces Moral Suasion

• *American Temperance Magazine* (1852)

In 1851, Maine became the first state to outlaw the manufacture and sale of alcoholic beverages. The result of aggressive political manipulation, this celebrated "Maine law" reflected a new hostility toward liquor dealers as well as a growing disillusion over the effectiveness of moral suasion. The following defense of legal prohibition typifies the new mood of hard realism that was beginning to pervade various reforms. In part, this emphasis on utility and tangible results reflects a new respect for scientific thinking (see Part 1): hence, the writer below tells us that speculative reason and mere "words" must give way to the proven laws of cause and effect. The appeal to public safety as an excuse for coercion also reflects the alarm of middle-class Protestants whose homogeneous communities were being drastically transformed by waves of Irish-Catholic immigration. Though other states followed Maine's example, most of the laws were soon repealed after immigrant and other anti-reform groups discovered the political rewards of an antitemperance coalition.

In view of our previous discussions of moral influence and perfectibility (including those in Unit One), it is important to note that the test of self-improvement was an individual act of will overcoming some genuine temptation (see, for example, Wally Barclay's mastery of temptation in the Catharine Sedgwick selection, Unit One, Part 1, B). But this risky self-discipline presupposed the social pressures of a homogeneous community sharing a Protestant scheme of values. As we have seen in Unit Three, American society was never really homogeneous, and this fact was especially dramatized by the Catholic immigration of the late 1840s. For proponents of the Maine law and similar measures of the early 1850s, it was no longer safe to rely on the individual's mastery of temptation. The crucial act of will was now to be performed by the *state*, removing temptation beyond the walls of a less confident society.

American Temperance Magazine (1852)

This is a utilitarian age. The speculative has in all things yielded to the practical. Words are mere noise unless they are things. . . .

In this sense, moral suasion is moral balderdash. "Words, my lord, words" —worse than words, they are a delusion. How long have they been sounded in the public ear and sounded in vain? The drunkard's mental and physical condition pronounces them an absurdity. He is ever in one or other extreme —under the excitement of drink, or in a state of morbid collapse. Will it be said that words of suasion will commend themselves to a drunken man? Will he hear or heed them, or if he hear will there not be a prompting devil within, jeering at their blessedness? Reason with a man when all reason has fled, and it is doubtful whether he or you is the greater fool. But take him while in the other mood. Does he then need your counsel? Who can impart a bitterer poignancy to his memory? Who can picture to him remorse deeper than his own? Who impart to the past revel a character of darker horror better than his own racked brain? Self-reproach is his one unchanging feeling; reformation his single purpose. He is to himself a subject of abhorrence. He shudders to remember the actual debasement to which he reduced himself. His whole frame is in revulsion. . . .

Still he is sure to fall, and fall he does. Why? Temptation meets him. He hesitates. He is lost. He concludes that one glass, or it may be less, would restore the tone of his nerves. But beyond that he would not go. He drinks, and feels an agreeable heat pervade him. Surely another would heighten the sensation of delight this one had given rise to. His hesitation this time is short—he drinks again, and the old appetite is once more awakened. There is no longer any hesitation; another and another follow, and the feeling of the

SOURCE: "The Maine Law vs. Moral Suasion," *American Temperance Magazine*, III (1852), pp. 137–39.

morning becomes a subject of mockery to him. He scoffs at his own want of heart. He laughs to scorn all the counsels of prudence. He rises into the maniac. Moral suasion! Bah!

Place this man we have been describing out of the reach of temptation. He will have time to ponder. His mind and frame recover their native vigor. The public-house does not beset his path. Another and another day dawn upon him and find him clear and collected, confirming his purpose, and imparting joy as well as firmness to his resolution. This is the true suasion. Thus, and thus only, will reformation and temperance be secured. And how is this accomplished? Never except through the instrumentality of the law. If it were possible to reason the drunkard into soberiety, it would not be possible to make the rumseller forego his filthy gains. Try your moral suasion on him, and he will point to his wife or children. . . . The only logic he will comprehend, is some such ordinance as this, coming to him in the shape and with the voice of law—you shall not sell. The object of law and government is the public safety . . . and you shall not accumulate wealth by driving a trade resulting inevitably in the ruin, mentally and physically, of hundreds; and the equally inevitable ruin of thousands in point of comfort, respectability, and worldly station.

Abolitionism and Moral Progress

A. The Lessons and Imperatives of History

• *William Goodell* (1853)

Like the temperance crusade, abolitionism drew on religious ideals of moral perfection and social mission. But for temperance reformers, the enemy lay close at hand in each community, and the conflict involved the rights and values of diverging subcultures for which the freedom to drink or the "enslavement" to drink was a crucial symbolic issue. Although black slavery had once been a national institution, by the 1830s it had been wholly repudiated by the laws of the northern states. Hence abolitionists were somewhat in the position of temperance reformers speaking out from prohibitionist states. While they aroused violent opposition within the free states, the fundamental conflict was sectional and involved the rights and powers of state and national governments within the federal system.

As the following selections make clear, abolitionism also differed from temperance in attacking not simply a habitual mode of behavior and economic consumption but an exploitive system of production which dominated the society and politics of an entire region.

It is true that in the early 1830s abolitionists relied on techniques of moral suasion, exhorting southern Christians to free their slaves, much as temper-

411

ance reformers exhorted moderate drinkers to sign the pledge. But the militant southern reaction to such efforts soon forced abolitionists to re-examine basic questions of civil rights and political responsibility. As abolitionism broadened into a more popular, egalitarian movement, it defied containment by national leaders, platforms, or organizations. Protest against the oppression of black slaves radiated outward into protest against the oppression of free blacks, women, and white workers. Historians have tended to dwell on the divisiveness of this process—on the schisms and warring factions, the disputes over the rival claims of segregated blacks, disfranchised women, and "wage slaves." Yet in a larger view, the significant point is a new sense of *secular* possibility marked by highly diverse attempts to redefine democratic ideology. What gave unity and *esprit* to the abolitionist movement was the insistence on dissolving polarities and inequities long accepted as inevitable.

Any reformation requires a particular version of "historical truth"—a shared understanding of how corruptions became entrenched and how, at a particular moment in time, enlightenment emerged. Usually a movement is well advanced before such a "history" is made explicit and coherent. The following selection is taken from William Goodell's *Slavery and Antislavery*, originally published in 1852. No American abolitionist wrote a more masterful analysis of the movement's origins, its relations to evangelical religion, and its expanding ties with the forces of democratic progress.

Goodell (1792–1878) was born in a frontier settlement in Upstate New York but spent much of his youth in New England. After viewing Asia and Europe as a merchant seaman and then suffering financial losses as a merchant, he began writing and lecturing for various reform causes, especially temperance. He was one of the organizers of the American Anti-Slavery Society, and for a time edited the Society's official paper, *The Emancipator*. Goodell was active in founding the Liberty party and in pushing one wing of the abolitionist movement toward a broader assault on various forms of inequality. The following selection indicates how Goodell, while orthodox in his religious beliefs, could find religious justification for extending antislavery into a radical critique of racial prejudice and the "aristocracy of wealth." Goodell's rendition of antislavery history is obviously not impartial, but it is both more accurate and more penetrating than the accounts of many later historians.

William Goodell (1853)

The study of history is like a journey, or an exploring tour, in the course of which, cheering prospects are sometimes unexpectedly succeeded by scenes less promising, but necessary to be traversed, or the proposed end is not

SOURCE: William Goodell, *Slavery and Anti-Slavery* (New York: William Goodell, 1853), pp. 118–20, 122–23, 125–26, 128–30, 132–33, 139–40, 387–90.

reached. If we would faithfully explore a country, we must not confine our attention to the pleasant portions of it. If we would improve it, we must acquaint ourselves with the unseemly features and untoward influences to be removed or remedied. . . .

The marked decline of the spirit of liberty in this country for half a century after the Revolution, is a fact too palpable to escape notice. . . .

The details to be presented will appear credible enough when we shall have become conversant with the moral causes at work beforehand. . . . To the reader who never stops to inquire after moral causes, or who reads on, without keeping them steadily in mind, the perusal of history can be of little value. It can supply him with no guide to the future, no element of congruity for the past. Such causes constitute, in reality, the most essential ingredient of true history. They are facts, at wholesale, fountains of facts, from whence all minor facts flow. . . .

We may not be able, always, to distinguish causes from effects, nor to designate the precise point, in the history, where the defection began, nor decide positively what portion of the body politic was first corrupted, or first became corrupting. But we can note down a few general facts.

We shall first venture to suggest, that the regard for human liberty and the opposition to the slave trade and slavery, that were manifested during the revolutionary period, may have failed to prove permanent and abiding because, in respect to great numbers of the people, including some prominent citizens, those sentiments were not as deep seated and as disinterested as they should have been, and therefore a change in the aspect of public affairs would naturally bring with it a change in the manifestation of such sentiments. To suppose otherwise would be to suppose an unprecedented purity of purpose, of which no other nation has yet furnished a parallel. This suggestion does not discredit the fact of an actual declension. It only indicates one of the causes of it. Without any previous tendency to declension, other causes would have had little power.

It is easy to see that, in many ways, the revolutionary period presented peculiar inducements to the abolition of the slave trade and slavery. To fight for their own liberties while enslaving others, was an incongruity too glaring to consist with national reputation, or with intelligent self-respect. Like all other men, in times of pressing danger and sore calamity, our fathers might make solemn promises of amendment, which would be liable to be forgotten and disregarded, on the return of security and peace. The fear of an insurrection of the slaves, or of their desertion to the enemy in time of war, might present an argument in favor of their emancipation that would influence many minds, until the danger had passed away. Such, indeed, was the fact.

· · ·

The experiment of putting a stop to the slave trade during the existence of slavery—and the policy of attempting to abolish either the one or the other, or both of them, by the mere force of moral suasion, without corresponding and adequate political action, was fully tried by the philanthropists and patriots of the revolutionary period, and with a result that should prove a caution to all their successors who may be engaged in the cause of human freedom. To maintain penal laws against any other forms of crime, and permit this crime of crimes to go "unwhipt of justice," is a solecism in legislation, in jurisprudence, and in civil polity, without a parallel for inconsistency and folly. This capital error we put down as one of the leading causes or outstanding signs of the lamentable defection of this nation from the principles of civil government they had marked out for themselves, in their declaration of human rights, and their definition of the objects and characteristics of a legitimate and just civil government.

"The ruse of gradualism"—the strategy of delay—the contamination of temporary compromise, was another kindred error, (if it may be called another) and the same with which the friends of liberty have been frequently beset, and sometimes foiled, in their more recent as well as more early endeavors.

. . .

When the private and the public purse were replenished, when prosperity had succeeded to poverty, when wealth, at the opening of the present century, rolled in upon the nation, the former habits of disinterested or even of patriotic devotion to public affairs and the interests of human freedom did not return. The pursuit of wealth had begotten the inordinate love of it. Inattention to the demands of liberty and justice had resulted in the disregard of them. Inequality of possession, continually increasing and in striking contrast to earlier times, had undermined the spirit of equality, and introduced aristocratic tastes. Humanity and human rights were less valued than wealth. The concentration of capital created a new element of political power, and diverted it from its former channels. The possession of wealth, or of talents prostituted to the support of its claims, instead of a disinterested advocacy of human liberty and equal justice, supplied passports to seats in the state and national councils, to places of authority and power. Here was another cause, and another step in the downward tendencies of the nation; the beginnings of that powerful aristocracy of wealth that afterwards openly opposed the discussion of the slave question.

The want of a thorough, consistent, and Christian democracy, therefore, is distinctly visible in the origin and continuation of the pro-slavery policy of the national government, and to this fact, as to a comprehensive cause, the present ascendency of the slave power may be traced. Had the "Federalists" been more democratic in their theory of civil government—had the "Democrats" (or "Republicans," as they were then called) reduced their own theory to practice, the system of American slavery would have been abolished at an early period of our history.

In close connection with the preceding facts, it should be noticed that the excesses of the first French Revolution, commencing soon after our Federal Government went into operation, must have contributed largely, as we know it did, to bring democratic principles into disrepute, to increase and fortify the jealousies and fears of conservatists [conservatives], and confirm the impression of insecurity to life, to property, and to civil order, if large masses of men should at once be released from absolute control. If millions of educated and polished Frenchmen could not be transferred at once from a state of mere political servility to a state of civil and political freedom, without becoming fired with the frenzy of demons, abjuring all the restraints of religion, subverting the state, proscribing the church, engulfing society and property in the wildest chaos or disorder; drenching the land with blood, and exterminating each other by the rapid succession and violent proscription of rival factions, how could it be thought safe or prudent to release suddenly from a state of still deeper degradation a more ignorant population of slaves? . . .

The horrors of the French Revolution, like the perverted story of "the horrors of St. Domingo," some time afterwards, have ever since been on the lips of the conservators of slavery. So late as the beginnings of the present anti-slavery agitation, in 1833, the "reign of terror" in France, and "the horrors of St. Domingo," were successfully adverted to by opposers; and the doctrines of immediate and unconditional emancipation, as taught by [Jonathan] Edwards [Jr.], were systematically confounded with the "Jacobinism of the first French Revolution"—a misrepresentation less excusable now, than during the dimness and confusion near the close of the last century. . . .

A Christianity crippled by an alliance with even the most pure and elevated description of aristocracy, is incompetent to the task of securing human freedom. A democracy, or a philanthropy, however ardent and radical, that is not based upon the Christianity of the Bible, is equally impotent, for the same sublime mission.

Among the influences tending strongly to bribe the public sentiment, and change the political tendencies of the country, especially at the South, on the slave question, have been justly reckoned the increased and unforeseen profitableness of slave labor, in consequence of the invention of the cotton-gin, by Mr. Whitney. . . . This economical view of the subject must have become the more prominent as the moral influences and the generous enthusiasm of the revolutionary period gave place to plans of individual thrift and accumulation. Then it was that the blighting influences of slavery must have begun to be felt; but a wonderful change was at hand, the almost magical result of a labor-saving machine, in the hands, not of the laborer himself, but of the capitalist who controlled him, and appropriated the avails of his labor. And thus, at the very moment when the more worthy and noble considerations in favor of liberty had almost ceased to occupy the slaveholder's attention, the most powerful temptations were presented to his cupidity and avarice. Under this temptation, he fell. And the policy of the national government was, in consequence, changed.

There is still another and a most potent element and evidence of deterioration, on this subject, that we know not how to treat of, as its magnitude and its meanness demand. Whenever we attempt to speak or write upon it, we feel our cheeks burning with indignation and shame. We know not how or in what terms to describe it, to what origin to trace it, or by what considerations to attempt to dislodge it from the minds of sane men. From its flat contradiction of the Bible, we should characterize it as decidedly of infidel parentage, yet we find it nestling in the bosom of the Church. . . . Were it less murderous and less blasphemous, we might laugh at it; were it less ludicrous, we might reason against it; were it less mean, we could enter the lists against it, as an object of honorable warfare. We should attribute it to sheer vulgarity and ignorance (where we find it signally at home) but that we meet with it also in circles claiming refinement and learning. We allude to the infatuation that virtually predicates humanity upon the hue of the skin, that disbelieves that "God had made of one blood all nations of men," that arrogates to less than one-sixth part of the human race the exclusive monopoly of our common humanity, that thus falsifies the self-evident truths of our Declaration of Independence, and sets up, in the temples of Jehovah, the monuments of heathen caste. . . .

In countries not familiarized with a population of colored slaves (as in Russia and Poland, where the serfs are all whites), the prejudice against colored people is unknown, and its existence among us is there discredited, or considered an inexplicable phenomenon. In France, in England, in Germany, and throughout all Europe, though the *Jews* are a degraded caste, the educated *negro* has free access, and on terms of unquestioned equality, to the very highest circles of society. It is reserved to a nation pluming itself upon being the world's teacher of the doctrine of human equality, to deny the common courtesies of life, along with the essential rights of humanity, to a large part of the human species (to the very race first proficient in literature and civilization), on account of their color! Thus do we invite and merit a world's scorn!

Were it not for this stupid prejudice against color, the sceptre of the slaveholding oligarchy would drop powerless at once, and the nation would be disenthralled.

. . .

There were moral, religious, and social influences at work, preparatory to an unprecedented agitation of the slave question. The missionary enterprise, in its youthful vigor, was an effort for "evangelizing the world." It was deliberately proposed as a *work to be done.* It was based on a belief that the promises and predictions of the Scriptures afforded a divine guaranty for its accomplishment. Bible, Tract, and Education Societies were commended and patronized as auxiliaries to this magnificent undertaking. The anniversaries [annual meetings] of these were enlivened with glowing descriptions of the approaching millennium, when all should know the Lord, from the least to the greatest, and sit under *their own* vines and fig-trees, secure in their rights. . . . The time was set for furnishing every family on the earth with Bibles. The chronology of the prophetic periods was computed, and the close of the present century, it was believed, was to witness the completed work of the "conversion of the world." To be "up and doing" was the watchword, and our American love of liberty, equality, and "free institutions," was gratified with the assurance that all the despotisms of the earth were to crumble at the Prince Emanuel's [Christ's] approach!

Was all this to be accomplished without Bibles, and education, and marriage, and family sanctities, and liberation for American slaves? Who could believe it? Whatever our missionary and evangelizing orators intended, whatever *they* were thinking of, they were God's instruments for putting into the minds of others "thoughts that burned," for the emancipation of the enslaved. The writer and many others well remember that the tone of our May anniversaries of religious societies, from 1825 to 1832, was such as has been described. And the suddenness with which this tone was changed, when Bibles, education, and family sanctities were demanded for slaves, did not escape notice. But the fires kindled could not be extinguished.

The same period was distinguished by "revivals of religion," in which prominence was given to the old doctrine of [Samuel] Hopkins and [Jonathan] Edwards, demanding "immediate and unconditional repentance" of all sin, as the only condition of forgiveness and salvation. This was urged in direct opposition to the vague idea of a gradual amendment, admitting "a more convenient season"—a prospective, dilatory, indefinite breaking off from transgression—an idea that had been settling upon the churches for thirty or forty years previous—an incubus upon every righteous cause, and every holy endeavor. It is easy to see the bearing of such religious awakenings upon the mode of treating the practice of slaveholding, unless it were believed to be righteous. A more perfect antagonism to the ethics and operations of the Colonization Society could not well be imagined. A collision was inevitable, whenever the subject should be introduced, and the Society itself could scarcely avoid introducing it.

Simultaneously with all this, and more or less connected with it, there came over the religious community an increasing spirit of inquiry in respect to Christian ethics, and the bearing of the religious principle upon the social relations and political duties of man. Peace Societies had been formed. Temperance Societies were in progress. The Institution of Free Masonry had been arraigned. The influence of theatres, of lotteries, and the morality of lottery grants by legislatures, were brought under rigorous review. The treatment of the aborigines of our country, especially of the Cherokees, by Georgia and the Federal Government, and the imprisonment of the missionaries among the Cherokees, became subjects of earnest attention. Christians began to be reminded that they were citizens, and that Christianity had its claims upon them in their civil relations. . . .

In short, it was a period of unwonted if not unprecedented moral and political inquiry. Was it possible that the slave question should escape the scrutiny of such an age? Assuredly it *did* not, and for the obvious reason that there was in progress a new and strong development of the human mind in the direction of such investigations. How short-sighted are those who think that the agitation originated only with a few "fanatics," and that all would be quiet if they could be silenced or crushed!

Along with the new spirit of moral enterprise and inquiry, there came likewise the new and appropriate methods of their manifestation and culture among the masses of the people. Newspapers were no longer confined to party politics and commerce, nor the reading of them to the select few. Religious newspapers were among the novelties of the times. These were followed by papers designed to promote the reforms and discuss the moral questions of the day. Voluntary lectures and agents of societies were abroad. Promiscuous [open to both sexes] conventions as well as protracted religious meetings were held, and laymen found they had tongues. To write for the public was no longer the monopoly of professional authors and quarterly and monthly reviewers. Whoever pleased might become an editor of a newspaper, and whoever chose to subscribe for it, at a trifling expense, was introduced into the "republic of letters." Not only did the great masses become readers of public journals, but to a great and growing extent, contributors, likewise. The custom of writing anonymously, encouraged the timid: the most dependent could stand here on a level with the most powerful, and sometimes smile to see their productions arrest the public attention. Farmers and mechanics, journeymen and apprentices, merchants and clerks—females as well as males —participated in the privilege. From the counting-house, from the anvil, from the loom, from the farm-yard, from the parlor, perhaps from the kitchen, there came paragraphs for the perusal (perhaps for the reproval and instruction) of Senators and Doctors of the Law. History, that often busies itself with petty details pertaining to those who have been falsely called great, need not count it undignified to notice revolutions in human condition like these —revolutions more sublime than those that transfer from one dynasty to another, princely crowns. No one can comprehend, in their causes and distinctive characteristics, the existing agitations in America, who does not take into account the new power and the changed direction of the public press, constituting a new era in human history.

Was it strange, at such a period, when *laborers* of almost all classes were giving free utterance to their thoughts, that the morality of unpaid and forced labor began to be questioned—that the chivalry of whipped women, and the civilization of selling babes at auction by the pound—began to be scrutinized? The rail-car, in 1838, the electric telegraph ten years afterwards, were scarcely greater innovations or greater curiosities than were voluntary lecturers, free public conventions, and moral and religious weekly journals, with their free correspondence, from 1825 to 1830. Was nothing, then, to have been expected —is nothing now to be attributed to this new moral and educating power?

B. The Burden of All Reformers

• *William Lloyd Garrison* (1860)

The secession crisis of 1860 accentuated the abolitionists' need for historical retrospection. Here William Lloyd Garrison (1805–1879), who in popular imagination continued to symbolize a movement that had never really accepted his leadership, places antislavery within the widest context of global history and human progress. Events of the 1850s had enormously enhanced Garrison's prestige and public influence, but a generation earlier he had been one of the most hated men in America. No one could speak more eloquently on the reformer's burden of unpopularity—of being charged with betraying a common fidelity to church, country, and white supremacy.

Born in Massachusetts, Garrison was the son of a drunken sailor who deserted his family before William was three. In his native Newburyport, Garrison learned the printing trade, then moved on to Boston where he worked as a compositor and began writing anonymous letters and essays attacking, among other things, intemperance, Sabbath-breaking, and war. Garrison gained his first notoriety when his gift for vituperative rhetoric, directed against a Newburyport merchant who was shipping slaves from Maryland to Louisiana, resulted in a libel suit that landed Garrison in a Baltimore jail. After being bailed out by Arthur Tappan, Garrison went on in 1831 to found the famous *Liberator*, which was supported for some years by the subscriptions of free blacks. Garrison's prestige at the founding meeting of the American Anti-Slavery Society depended less on this pioneer publication than on his recent trip to England, at the successful culmination of the British struggle for West Indian emancipation, where he had received the blessings of highly revered British abolitionists. From 1833 on, he remained the most controversial figure in various American reforms, his acrimonious pen continually defying the rules of tact, propriety, moderation, and common sense, yet winning new converts while alienating old friends. As we can see from his following view of history, Garrison's remarkable self-confidence rested on an identification with reformers, agitators, and revolutionaries from the time of the Old Testament prophets. If most other abolitionists were less extreme and less self-confident, they had all suffered from persecution and from the charge of religious "infidelity"; by 1860, we can assume, virtually all would have cheered Garrison's righteous response.

William Lloyd Garrison (1860)

Every great reformatory movement, in every age, has been subjected alike to popular violence and to religious opprobrium. The history of one is essentially that of every other. Its origin is ever in obscurity; its earliest supporters are destitute of resources, uninfluential in position, without reputation; it is denounced as fanatical, insane, destructive, treasonable, infidel. The tactics resorted to for its suppression are ever the same, whether it be inaugurated by the prophets, by Jesus and his apostles, by Wickliffe, Luther, Calvin, Fox, or any of their successors. Its opponents have scornfully asked, as touching its pedigree, "is not this the carpenter's son?" They have patriotically pronounced it a seditious attempt to play into the hands of the Romans, to the subversion of the state and nation. They have piously exclaimed against it

SOURCE: William Lloyd Garrison, *The "Infidelity" of Abolition* (New York: American Anti-Slavery Society, 1860), pp. 3–10.

as open blasphemy. They have branded it as incomparably more to be feared and abhorred than robbery and murder.

No other result has been possible, under the circumstances. The wrong assailed has grown to a colossal size: its existence not only implies, but demonstrates, universal corruption. It has become organic—a part of the habits and customs of the times. It is incorporated into the state; it is nourished by the church. Its support is the test of loyalty, patriotism, piety. It holds the reins of government with absolute mastery. . . .

Now, to attack such a wrong, without fear or compromise—to strip off the mask, and exhibit it in all its naked deformity—to demand its immediate suppression, at whatever cost to reputation or worldly interest—must, of necessity, put the reformer seemingly in antagonism to public quietude and good order, and make the whole social, political and religious structure tremble to its foundations. He cannot be a good citizen; for he refuses to be law-abiding, and treads public opinion, legislative enactment, and governmental edict, alike under his feet. He cannot be sane; for he arraigns, tries and condemns, as the greatest sinners and the worst criminals, the most reputable, elevated, revered, and powerful members of the body politic. He cannot love his country; for he declares it to be "laden with iniquity," and liable to the retributive judgments of Heaven. He cannot possess humility; for he pays no regard to usage, precedent, authority, or public sentiment, but defies them all. . . .

Every nation has its "peculiar institution," its vested interest, its organized despotism, its overmastering sin, distinct from every other nation. The conflict of reform is ever geographical as an issue, because the evil assailed is never world-wide: it may be universal in its tendencies, but it is local in its immediate results. It is easy to denounce Monarchy in America, Slavery in Europe, Protestantism in Italy, Democracy in Russia, Judaism in Turkey; because it is to take the popular side in every such case. An iniquitous system, which, if vigorously assailed in one country, may excite a bloody persecution, and cause the whole land to tremble with consternation and fury, in another country may be denounced not only with impunity, but to general acceptance; for the special abomination thus opposed not existing therein, it is seen in its true character. . . .

The one great, distinctive, all-conquering sin in America is its system of chattel slavery—co-existent with the settlement of the country—for a considerable time universally diffused—at first, tolerated as a necessary evil—subsequently, deplored as a calamity—now, defended in every slave state as a most beneficent institution, upheld by natural and revealed religion—in its feebleness, able to dictate terms in the formation of the Constitution—in its strength, controlling parties and sects, courts and legislative assemblies, the army and navy, Congress, the National Executive, the Supreme Court—and having at its disposal all the offices, honors and revenues of the government, wherewith to defy all opposition, and to extend its dominion indefinitely. Gradually abolished in six of the thirteen states which formed the Union, it has concentrated itself in the southern and southwestern portion of the

Republic, covering more than one-half of the national territory, and aiming at universal empire.

The victims of this terrible system being of African extraction, it has engendered and established a complexional caste, unknown to European civilization; pervading all parts of the United States like a malaria-tainted atmosphere; in its development, more malignant at the North than at the South; poisoning the life-blood of the most refined and the most depraved alike; and making the remotest connection with the colored race a leprous taint. Its spirit is as brutal as it is unnatural; as mean as it is wicked; as relentless as it is monstrous. It is capable of committing any outrage upon the person, mind or estate of the negro, whether bond or free. . . . No religious creed, no form of worship, no evangelical discipline, no heretical liberality, either mitigates or restrains it. Christian and Infidel, Calvinist and Universalist, Trinitarian and Unitarian, Episcopalian and Methodist, Baptist and Swendenborgian, Old School and New School Presbyterian, Orthodox and Hicksite Quaker, all are infected by it, and equally ready to make an innocent natural distinction the badge of eternal infamy, and a warrant for the most cruel proscription. As a nation sows, so shall it also reap. The retributive justice of God was never more strikingly manifested than in this all-pervading negrophobia, the dreadful consequence of chattel slavery. . . .

Such, then, was the system—so buttressed and defended—to be assailed and conquered by the Abolitionists. And who were they? In point of numbers, as drops to the ocean without station or influence; equally obscure and destitute of resources. Originally, they were generally members of the various religious bodies, tenacious of their theological views, full of veneration for the organized church and ministry, but ignorant of the position in which these stood to "the sum of all villanies." What would ultimately be required of them, by a faithful adherence to the cause of the slave, in their church relations, their political connections, their social ties, their worldly interest and reputation, they knew not. Instead of seeking a controversy with the pulpit and the church, they confidently looked to both for efficient aid to their cause. Instead of suddenly withdrawing from the pro-slavery religious and political organizations with which they were connected, they lingered long and labored hard to bring them to repentance. . . . They sought to liberate the slave, by every righteous instrumentality—and nothing more. But to their grief and amazement, they were gradually led to perceive, by the terrible revelations of the hour, that the religious forces on which they had relied were all arrayed on the side of the oppressor; that the North was as hostile to emancipation as the South; that the spirit of slavery was omnipresent, invading every sanctuary, infesting every pulpit, controlling every press, corrupting every household, and blinding every vision; that no other alternative was presented to them, except to wage war with "principalities, and powers, and spiritual wickedness in high places," and to separate themselves from every slaveholding alliance, or else to . . . substitute compromise for principle, and thus betray the rights and liberties of the millions in thraldom, at a fearful cost to their own souls. If some of them faltered, and perished by the way; if others deserted the cause, and became its bitterest enemies; if others still withdrew from the ranks . . . the main body proved fearless and incorruptible, and, through the American Anti-Slavery Society and its auxiliaries, have remained steadfast to the present hour.

Religion is, in every land, precisely and only what is popularly recognized as such. To pronounce it corrupt, spurious, oppressive, and especially to demonstrate it to be so, is ever a proof of "infidelity"—whether among Pagans or Mahommedans, Jews or Christians, Catholics or Portestants. In the United States, it is the bulwark of slavery—the untiring enemy of Abolitionism. How, then, has it been possible for the Abolitionists to establish a religious character, or to avoid the imputation of infidelity, while in necessary and direct conflict with such a religion? To say that they ought not to assail it, is to denounce them for refusing to go with the multitude to do evil, for being governed by the standard of eternal justice, for adhering to the Golden Rule.

To what, or to whom, have they been infidel? If 'to the cause of the enslaved, let it be shown. But this is not pretended; and yet this is the only test by which they are to be tried. They have but one bond of agreement— the inherent sinfulness of slavery, and, consequently, the duty of immediate emancipation. As *individuals*, they are of all theological and political opinions; having an undeniable right to advocate those opinions, and to make as many converts to them as possible. An an *organization*, they meet for a common object in which they are agreed, to endorse nothing but the right of the slave to himself as paramount to every other claim, and to apply no other principle as a rule whereby to measure sects, parties, institutions and men.

. . .

If, therefore, it be an infidel Society, it is so only in the sense in which Jesus was a blasphemer, and the Apostles were "pestilent and seditious fellows, seeking to turn the world upside down." It is infidel to Satan, the enslaver; it is loyal to Christ, the redeemer. It is infidel to a Gospel which makes man the property of man; it is bound up with the Gospel which requires us to love our neighbors as ourselves, and to call no man master. It is infidel to a Church which receives to its communion the "traffickers in slaves and the souls of men"; it is loyal to the Church which is not stained with blood, nor polluted by oppression. . . . It is infidel to all blood-stained compromises, sinful concessions, unholy compacts, respecting the system of slavery; it is devotedly attached to whatever is honest, straightforward, invincible for the right.

C. Explaining "Immediate Emancipation"

- *The New-England Anti-Slavery Society* (1833)
- *Declaration of the National Anti-Slavery Convention* (1833)
- *Instructions to Theodore Dwight Weld* (1833)

By 1830, British abolitionists were demanding the "immediate emancipation" of West Indian slaves by act of Parliament. Americans quickly adopted the slogan and made it the central principle and article of faith of the rejuvenated antislavery movement. Yet reformers in the two countries faced entirely different situations. America did not have a central government that was unlimited in power and committed to the goal of emancipation. Unlike the West Indies, American slave states were not dependent colonies which had long been pressured to improve the condition of their slaves and which ultimately had few options besides delay and holding out for maximum monetary compensation. In America, therefore, there was much confusion over the meaning of "immediate emancipation."

Garrison's New-England Anti-Slavery Society, founded in 1832, was the first organization to transform the phrase into official doctrine, although the phrase itself had appeared in earlier antislavery writings and had even been endorsed, with qualifications, by earlier organizations. In the first selection, the New England Garrisonians try to head off objections by exposing the absurdity of gradual emancipation and by spelling out the expected consequences of immediatism. Three points deserve special notice. First, echoing the themes of Unit One, there is much emphasis on the autonomous family, noncoercive discipline, individual self-possession, and self-improvement. Second, it is assumed that emancipated slaves will continue to work for their former owners. Third, it is unclear whether "just wages" will be determined by the market forces of supply and demand or by the paternalistic benevolence of planters who will regard their former enemies as "grateful friends and servants."

The principle of immediatism was also adopted by the self-styled "Convention" that met in Philadelphia in December 1833 to organize the American Anti-Slavery Society. The second selection is taken from the Convention's "Declaration of Sentiments," written by Garrison and consciously modeled on the Declaration of Independence. We have already examined the style of an earlier antimasonic "Declaration of Independence" (Unit Two, Part 5, A) and a later feminist "Declaration of Sentiments" (Unit One, Part 5, B); there is no need to comment further on the parallel lists of grievances or "assemblage of horrors." What is easily missed by the modern reader—though unmistakable to any thoughtful Christian of 1833—is the symbolic allusion to Mosaic and Christian "dispensations" or moral orders. In effect, the Founding Fathers and the original Declaration of Independence are identified with the Old Testament law of retribution, of "eye for eye, tooth for tooth." Like the New Testament, the abolitionists' Declaration claims to supersede the achievements of a bloody and warlike age, completing in a moral and spiritual realm the promises that the Revolution had left unfulfilled. In this sense, the abolitionists' Declaration is both a subtle rebuke to the Revolutionary generation for evading the question of slavery while shedding blood for its own liberty, and a pledge to the nation—and to slaveholders—that the cause of immediate emancipation is the cause of peace.

But how could the public be persuaded that immediate emancipation provided the only assurance of peace? From the outset it was clear that the power of the written word had to be reinforced by personal appeals and face-to-face confrontation. For this gigantic task religious revivals—and such offspring as societies for distributing Bibles and tracts—furnished the obvious precedents. It was no accident that Arthur Tappan, chairman of the excutive committee of the new American Anti-Slavery Society, selected Theodore Dwight Weld as the Society's first traveling agent in the West. Weld (1803–1895) had been one of Finney's converts, a member of Finney's "holy band" of revivalists, and had traveled extensively in both North and South promoting temperance, antislavery, and the integration of manual labor with "literary" education. Weld could not participate in the organization of the American Anti-Slavery Society because he was then in Cincinnati studing theology at Lane Seminary, which he had recently helped to found. Though he declined the Society's appointment and did not assume the duties of an agent until later in 1834, his official instructions—given here in the third selection—tell much about the abolitionists' early tactics, expectations, and assumptions concerning communal influence. The shrewd advice on avoiding argument over specific plans also suggests that an insistence on simple moral principle was not so naive as it might appear.

The New-England Anti-Slavery Society (1833)

The New-England Anti-Slavery Society maintains that the slaves ought instantly to be emancipated from their fetters. It acknowledges no claims upon their persons by their masters. It regards the holders of slaves as guilty of a heinous sin. . . . It says to every individual—"Let the principle be clearly and firmly established in your mind that there is, and can be, no such thing as *property in man*, and you cannot, as a patriot, a philanthropist, or a disciple of Christ, oppose the immediate liberation of the slaves—you cannot but demand that liberation—you cannot be satisfied with any thing short of an immediate liberation." It is not for men of Christian integrity to calculate how far it is expedient to do wrong. . . .

A very singular kind of logic prevails at the present day. "I concede," says one, "that slavery in the *abstract* is very wicked; but I am opposed to immediate abolition." Slavery in the *abstract*? What does the objector mean? *Abstract* slavery never did, and never can exist. He means, perhaps—his language implies nothing else—that it is most atrocious to *think* of enslaving human beings; but, in fact, to buy, or sell, or hold them in fetters, is by no means sinful! That is to say—if a man should merely *meditate* the destruction of the houses of his fellow-citizens by fire, without any doubt he ought to be hung;—but if he should actually set them on fire, and run from street to street with the burning brand in his hand, to destroy others, why then he

---

SOURCE: "Annual Report of the New-England Anti-Slavery Society," *The Abolitionist*, I (January, 1833), pp. 20–21.

would not be guilty. It would only be necessary for him to cry aloud to the firemen—"I am as much opposed to arson, in the *abstract*, as you are; but see! the houses are on fire!—My abstract theory has assumed a practical shape, and therefore I am exonerated from blame. I am opposed to an immediate extinguishment of the fire. Put it out very gradually. . . ."

The Board of Managers are satisfied that the doctrine of immediate abolition is opposed by many, not because they really mean to justify crime, but simply through ignorance or a misapprehension of its nature. It is associated in their minds with something undefinable, yet dreadful—they see, in imagination, cities and villages in flames, and blood flowing in torrents, and hear the roll of drums, the shouts of blood-thirsty savages, and the shrieks of the dying—and thus bringing upon themselves a strong delusion, they naturally stand aghast at the proposition. All this ruffling of mind is indeed ridiculous; but as it originates unwittingly in error, it merits a charitable allowance rather than satire.

What, then, is meant by IMMEDIATE ABOLITION?

It means, in the first place, that all title of property in the slaves shall instantly cease, because their Creator has never relinquished his claim of ownership, and because none have a right to sell their own bodies or buy those of their own species as cattle. Is there any thing terrific in this arrangement?

It means, secondly, that every husband shall have his own wife, and every wife her own husband, both being united in wedlock according to its proper forms, and placed under the protection of law. Is this unreasonable?

It means, thirdly, that parents shall have the control and government of their own children, and that the children shall belong to their parents. What is there sanguinary in this concession?

It means, fourthly, that all trade in human beings shall be regarded as felony, and entitled to the highest punishment. Can this be productive of evil?

It means, fifthly, that the tremendous power which is now vested in every slaveholder to punish his slaves without trial, and to a savage extent, shall be at once taken away. Is this undesirable?

It means, sixthly, that all those laws which now probit the instruction of the slaves, shall instantly be repealed, and others enacted, providing schools and instruction for their intellectual illumination. Would this prove a calamity?

It means, seventhly, that the planters shall employ their slaves as free laborers, and pay them just wages. Would this recompense infuriate them?

It means, eighthly, that the slaves, instead of being forced to labor for the exclusive benefit of others by cruel drivers, and the application of the lash upon their bodies, shall be encouraged to toil for the mutual profit of themselves and their employers, by the infusion of new motives into their hearts, growing out of their recognition and reward as men. Is this diabolical?

It means, finally, that right shall take the supremacy over wrong, principle over brute force, humanity over cruelty, honesty over theft, purity over lust, honor over baseness, love over hatred, and religion over heathenism. Is this wrong?

This is our meaning of Immediate Abolition.

Having thus briefly defined the extent of immediate abolition, it may be useful to state some of its probable, nay, certain benefits.

It will remove the cause of bloodshed and insurrection. No patrols at night, no standing army, will be longer needed to keep the slaves in awe. The planters may dismiss their fears, and sleep soundly; for, by one act, they will have transformed their enemies into grateful friends and servants.

Declaration of the National Anti-Slavery Convention (1833)

More than fifty-seven years have elapsed since a band of patriots convened in this place to devise measures for the deliverance of this country from a foreign yoke. The cornerstone upon which they founded the TEMPLE OF FREEDOM was broadly this—"that all men are created equal; that they are endowed by their Creator with certain inalienable rights; that among these are life, LIBERTY, and the pursuit of happiness." At the sound of their trumpet-call, three millions of people rose up as from the sleep of death, and rushed to the strife of blood; deeming it more glorious to die instantly as freemen, than desirable to live one hour as slaves. . . .

We have met together for the achievement of an enterprise, without which, that of our fathers is incomplete, and which, for its magnitude, solemnity, and probable results upon the destiny of the world, as far transcends theirs, as moral truth does physical force.

In purity of motive, in earnestness of zeal, in decision of purpose, in intrepidity of action, in steadfastness of faith, in sincerity of spirit, we would not be inferior to them.

Their principles led them to wage war against their oppressors, and to spill human blood like water, in order to be free. *Ours* forbid the doing of evil that good may come, and lead us to reject, and to entreat the oppressed to reject, the use of all carnal weapons for deliverance from bondage—relying solely upon those which are spiritual, and mighty through God to the pulling down of strong holds.

Their measures were physical resistance—the marshalling in arms—the hostile array—the mortal encounter. *Ours* shall be such only as the opposition of moral purity to moral corruption—the destruction of error by the potency of truth—the overthrow of prejudice by the power of love—and the abolition of slavery by the spirit of repentance.

Their grievances, great as they were, were trifling in comparison with the

---

SOURCE: "Declaration of the National Anti-Slavery Convention," *The Abolitionist,* I (December, 1833), p. 178.

wrongs and sufferings of those for whom we plead. Our fathers were never slaves—never bought and sold like cattle—never shut out from the light of knowledge and religion—never subjected to the lash of brutal taskmasters.

But those, for whose emancipation we are striving,—constituting at the present time at least one-sixth part of our countrymen—are recognized by the laws, and treated by their fellow beings, as marketable commodities—as good[s] and chattels—as brute beasts;—are plundered daily of the fruits of their toil without redress;—really enjoy no constitutional nor legal protection from licentious and murderous outrages upon their persons;—are ruthlessly torn asunder —the tender babe from the arms of its frantic mother—the heart-broken wife from her weeping husband—at the caprice or pleasure of irresponsible tyrants; —and, for the crime of having a dark complexion, suffer the pangs of hunger, the infliction of stripes, and the ignominy of brutal servitude. They are kept in heathenish darkness by laws expressly enacted to make their instruction a criminal offence.

Instructions to Theodore Dwight Weld (1833)

You are hereby appointed and commissioned, by the Executive Committee of the American Anti-Slavery Society, instituted at Philadelphia in 1833, as their Agent, for the space of one year commencing with the first day of January, 1834, in the State of Ohio and elsewhere as the Committee may direct.

The Society was formed for the purpose of awakening the attention of our whole community to the character of American slavery, and presenting the claims and urging the rights of the colored people of the United States; so as to promote, in the most efficient manner, the immediate abolition of slavery, and the restoration of our colored brethren to their equal rights as citizens. . . .

The Committee welcome you as a fellow-laborer in this blessed and responsible work; the success of which will depend, in no small degree, under God, on the results of your efforts. Their ardent desires for your success will continually attend you; you will have their sympathy in trials; and nothing, they trust, will be wanting, on their part, for your encouragement and aid.

They commend you to the kindness and co-operation of all who love Zion; praying that the presence of God may be with you, cheering your heart, sustaining you in your arduous labors, and making them a means of a speedy liberation of all the oppressed.

The people of color ought at once to be emancipated and recognized as citizens, and their rights secured as such, equal in all respects to others, according to the cardinal principle laid down in the American Declaration of Inde-

SOURCE: *Letters of Theodore Dwight Weld, Angelina Grimké Weld and Sarah Grimké, 1822–1844*, Gilbert H. Barnes and Dwight L. Dumond, eds. (New York: Appleton-Century-Crofts, 1934, Vol. I, pp. 124–27; reprint ed., New York: DaCapo Press, 1970). Reprinted by permission of Elizabeth B. Pumphrey.

pendence. Of course we have nothing to do with any *equal* laws which the states may make, to prevent or punish vagrancy, idleness, and crime, either in whites or blacks.

Do not allow yourself to be drawn away from the main object, to exhibit a detailed PLAN of abolition; for men's consciences will be greatly relieved from the feeling of present duty, by any objections or difficulties which they can find or fancy in your plan. Let the *principle* be decided on, of immediate abolition, and the plans will easily present themselves. What ought to be done can be done. If the *great* question were decided, and if half the ingenuity now employed to defend slavery were employed to abolish it, it would impeach the wisdom of American statemen to say they could not, with the Divine blessing, steer the ship through.

You will make yourself familiar with FACTS, for they chiefly influence reflecting minds. Be careful to use only facts that are well authenticated, and alway state them with the precision of a witness under oath. You cannot do our cause a greater injury than by overstating facts. . . .

In traversing your field, you will generally find it wise to visit first several prominent places in it, particularly those where it is known our cause has friends. In going to a place, you will naturally call upon those who are friendly to our objects, and take advice from them. Also call on ministers of the gospel and other leading characters, and labor specially to enlighten them and secure their favor and influence. Ministers are the hinges of community, and ought to be moved, if possible. If they can be gained, much is gained. But if not, you will not be discouraged; and if not plainly inexpedient, attempt to obtain a house of worship; or if none can be had, some other convenient place—and hold a public meeting, where you can present our cause, its facts, arguments and appeals, to as many people as you can collect, by notices in pulpits and newspapers, and other proper means.

Form auxiliary societies, both male and female, in every place where it is practicable. Even if such societies are very small at the outset, they may do much good as centers of light, and means of future access to the people. Encourage them to raise funds and apply them in purchasing and circulating anti-slavery publications gratuitously; particularly the Anti-Slavery Reporter, of which you will keep specimens with you, and which can always be had of the Society at $2.00 per 100. You are at liberty, with due discretion, to recommend other publications, *so far* as they advocate our views of immediate abolition. We hold ourselves responsible only for our own.

D. Conflicts of Conscience and Priority

- *Theodore Weld to Lewis Tappan* (1835)
- *Charles Grandison Finney to Theodore Weld* (1836)

The decision to launch a national antislavery crusade in 1834 soon led to painful tensions over commitments and priorities. Much of the difficulty arose from the fact that the wealthy Tappan brothers, having already begun to fund an incredibly ambitious campaign to Christianize New York City and the transAppalachian West, were now insistent on making abolitionism part of the project. It was Tappan money that sent Garrison to England and supported Weld at Cincinnati, that brought Finney to New York City, that paid Lyman Beecher's salary as president of Lane Seminary, and that financed most of the activities and publications of the American Anti-Slavery Society. Yet Beecher regarded Garrison as a dangerous fanatic, and both he and Finney feared that immediatism was not necessarily the cause of peace—that unless subordinated to religious control, it threatened to stifle the works of revivals and breed a spirit of civil war.

Early in 1834 these internal strains erupted into heated conflict. At Lane Seminary, Weld led an eighteen-day "protracted meeting" on slavery, making abolitionism a test of religious commitment. The institution's trustees were especially outraged by what they termed "niggerism," meaning the students' fraternization and fellowship with Cincinnati's free blacks. An attempt to expel Weld and other leaders led to the mass exodus of most of Lane's students. The Tappans, as Lane's major benefactors, never forgave Lyman Beecher for not publicly opposing the conservative trustees. As an alternative, the Tappans helped to establish Oberlin College and sent Finney there to take charge of theological training. Many of the "Lane rebels" ended up at Oberlin under Finney's tutelage; others joined Weld's band of abolitionist agents, adapting Finney's "new measures" to the purposes of secular reform.

But as the following two letters reveal, tensions persisted even among trusted friends. In the first selection, Weld tries to allay Lewis Tappan's suspicions that Finney, like Beecher, is weak in antislavery zeal and fearful of losing public favor. In this case, the bond between Weld and Tappan was the knowledge of mutual persecution—Weld having repeatedly faced hostile, missile-throwing crowds; Tappan having watched a mob gut his New York house. Though Finney had suffered no martyrdom for abolition, Weld defends his courage and his right to choose priorities. In the second letter, Finney questions Weld's own priorities.

Theodore Weld to Lewis Tappan, November 17, 1835

I am quite at a loss what to say in reply to that part of your last letter which treats of brother Finney. That Finney is a coward I cannot believe and for this simple reason: I have seen in him more frequent and more striking exhibi-

SOURCE: *Letters of Theodore Dwight Weld, Angelina Grimké Weld and Sarah Grimké, 1822–1844*, Vol. I, pp. 242–43, 318–20.

tions of courage physical and moral than in any other man living. That brother Finney has been (as you say you fear) "sinning against conviction" I cannot believe. An acquaintance with him of the most *intimate* character for *nine years* forbids me to harbor the suspicion for a moment. Everything in his character and history—all that I have seen of him—(and nobody has seen more of him) goes utterly against it.

Nobody on earth could convince me that *you* were deliberately "sinning against conviction." And if you were to do *just the things* which you allege against brother F. I could account for it on a supposition far more charitable than to suppose that you were sinning against conviction. I have looked over all the facts and details in your letter on this subject and have talked the whole over and over with brother Finney, and I find my mind exactly in this state. 1—I do not believe he has been *"afraid"* of anything except of *doing wrong.* 2—I believe he is an abolitionist in full. 3—That he has given the subject as much prominence in his preaching, and at Communions, etc., *as he conscientiously believed was his duty.* 4—I have no doubt but he has thought, felt, said and done less on the subject than he should have done. I have no doubt but he ought to have given it more prominence in his public prayers and preaching. He could have encouraged the monthly concert for the abolition of slavery more heartily. This I have told him in full.

The truth is Finney has always been in revivals of religion. It is his great business, aim and *absorbing passion* to promote them. He has never had hardly anything to do with Bible, tract, missionary, education, temperance, moral reform and antislavery societies. The three last he has joined and has decidedly committed himself before the public in favor of their principles, and taken a bold and high stand with reference to them at the Communion table. Finney feels about rivivals of religion and the promotion of the church and ministry in doctrines and measures, just as you and I do about antislavery. Now I feel as tho Finney could take hold of you and me and upbraid us, because we feel so little and pray with so little faith and fervor, and labor with so little of the tireless activity of [Saint] Paul, in summoning men night and day with tears to repent; and that, too, as far at least as I am concerned with far more reason for the upbraiding than you have for upbraiding him with his coldness and unfaithfulness in the cause of anti-slavery. God has called some *prophets,* some *apostles,* some *teachers.* All the members of the body of Christ have not the same office. Let [Edward] Delavan drive temperance, [John R.] McDowell moral reform, Finney revivals, Tappan antislavery, etc. Each of these is bound to make his own *peculiar* department his *main* business, and to promote *collaterally* as much as he can the other objects. I have no doubt but Finney has erred in not giving as much *collateral* attention to anti-slavery as the present emergent crisis demands. And I am equally certain that I have not done as much collaterally to promote temperance and revivals while I have been lecturing on slavery as I ought, and I havent a particle of doubt but you can say the same. . . .

Charles Grandison Finney to Theodore Weld, July 21, 1836

My particular object in writing to you at the present time is to talk with you a little about the present state of the church, our country, abolition, etc. Br[other] Weld is it not true, at least do you not fear it is, that we are in our present course going fast into a civil war? Will not our present movements in abolition result in that? Shall we not ere long be obliged to take refuge in a military despotism? Have you no fear of this? If not, why have you not? Nothing is more manifest to me than the present movements will result in this, unless your mode of abolitionizing the country be greatly modified. To suggest to some minds what I have here said would be evidence either of a pro-slavery spirit, or of cowardice. But D[ea]r Weld you *think,* and certainly you can not but discern the signs of the times. Now what is to be done? How can we save our country and affect the speedy abolition of slavery? This is my answer. What say you to it? The subject is now before the public mind. It is upon the conscience of every man, so that now every new convert will be an abolitionist of course. Now if abolition can be made an append[a]ge of a general revival of religion all is well. I fear no other form of carrying this question will save our country or the liberty or soul of the slave. One most alarming fact is that the absorbing abolitionism has drunk up the spirit of some of the most efficient moral men and is fast doing so [to] the rest, and many of our abolition brethren seem satisfied with nothing less than this. This I have been trying to resi[s]t from the beginning as I have all along foreseen that should that take place, the church and world, ecclesiastical and state leaders, will become embroiled in one common infernal squabble that will roll a wave of blood over the land. The causes now operating are in my view as certain to lead to this result as a cause is to produce its effect, unless the public mind can be engrossed with the subject of salvation and make abolition an appendage, just as we made temperance an appendage of the revival in Rochester. Nor w'd this in my judgment retard the work at all. I was then almost alone in the field as an Evangelist. Then 100,000 were converted in one year, every one of which was a temperance man. The same w'd now be the case in abolition. We can now, with you and my theological class, bring enough laborers into the field to, under God, move the whole land in 2 years. . . .

I believe we are united in the opinion here that abolition can be carried with more dispatch and with infinitely more safety in this indirect than in any other way. . . . The fact is, D[ea]r W[eld], our leading abolitionists are good men, but there are few of them *wise* men. Some of them are reckless. Others are so denunciatory as to kill all prayer about it. There is very little confidence and concert among many of our abolitionists. It is high time that we understood each other. . . .

But enough of this. Suffice it to say that unless we can come to a better understanding among ourselves, act more harmoniously and wisely and piously, I fear that all the evils and horrors of civil war will be the consequence.

E. Chattel Slavery versus "Wages Slavery"

• *William West* (1847)

Religious leaders like Finney were not alone in questioning abolitionist priorities. From quite a different direction, spokesmen for the rights of the working class had long accused the abolistionists, especially in Britain, of ignoring forms of oppression that were worse than plantation slavery and closer to home. The same arguments were gleefully endorsed and expanded upon by proslavery apologists, a fact which tempted abolitionists to lump all critics together by the dangerous device of guilt by association. But like Finney, most of the labor radicals abhorred black slavery and feared only that a selective assault on one evil would divert attention from even larger and more basic problems—for Finney, the conquest of sin; for National Reformers like George Henry Evans, the abolition of special privilege and dependency based on the monopolization of land (see Unit Two, Part 2).

Logically, there was no necessary conflict between opposing both black slavery and the oppression of white workers. In actuality, there is evidence that growing numbers of artisans supported the abolition movement, and by 1847 a few abolitionist leaders like William Goodell were calling for a broad political attack on all forms of special privilege including land monopoly, protective tariffs, military establishments, and the British oppression of Ireland. The fact remains that the leading spokesmen for American abolitionism, whatever their differences on other matters, agreed that black slavery was unique in its sinfulness, its degradation of victims, and its danger to America's mission. To blur the distinction between chattel slavery and lesser forms of injustice, they believed, could only encourage the moral lethargy that had long found excuses for defining as pieces of property human beings who happened to have black skins.

A debate over this question of priorities reached a heated climax in 1847, in the pages of Garrison's *Liberator*. Following the lead of Evans, William West, a National Reformer, crossed swords with Garrison in a series of letters and editorial rebuttals. Like Evans, West believed that the "usurpation" of land deprived the mass of workers of independence and of any meaningful freedom of employment. In comparing "wages slavery" with chattel slavery, West was on the firmest ground in a letter of March 20, which dramatized the suffering and starvation of Irish cottagers. But in a sequel of April 23, from which the following selection is taken, he focuses on the disintegration of northern workers' families and the sexual exploitation of working women, appropriating a favorite theme of abolitionist literature. West's motive may have been to exhort abolitionists to join a grand alliance with National Reformers and northern workingmen. But the more critics like West repeated the very arguments Southerners were making in defense of slavery, the more abolitionists felt compelled to defend the essential justice of a free market society in which *"wages-slaves,"* as Edmund

Quincy pointed out in the *Liberator*, instead of clamoring for owners, were demanding reforms, " 'voting themselves farms,' and altering the laws of the land by their ballots!" A final point that should not be overlooked is that Garrison's *Liberator* gave full space to critics like Evans and West.

William West (1847)

Slavery has been called the "sum of all villanies." This description of it does not apply to chattel slavery. That is, at least, free from hypocrisy. It does not disguise itself. It appears to be precisely what it is. The whips and the chains, the cruelties of the internal traffic, and the "horrors of the middle passage," all of the crimes and enormities peculiar to that system, are seen and known of all men. Give even the devil his due. He does *not* here assume the form of divinity. *Wages* slavery only is that system of it, to which the above description is justly applicable. Is not that so *deceptive* in its character, that even many lovers of liberty (yourself among the number) have mistaken it for freedom? Do but consider this question fairly. Ask yourself sincerely, wherein is that difference between wages and chattel slavery, which should entitle the former to the name of liberty? Is there *one* evil produced by the chattel system, which is not also produced by the wages? "Chattel slaves are sold at auction." Yes; but so are wages' slaves—with this difference only, that while the former need give themselves no trouble about finding purchasers (to *sell* them being the business of their owners, who must feed, and *well feed*, too, even FATTEN their property for the market), while the latter must do their utmost to sell themselves (a business, in which, *if they fail*, they cannot live, except by beggary, theft, prostitution, or some other equally disreputable means). Society denies *the right of life* to the wages slave, able to work, who cannot find it to do, while it secures that right (for a time, at least) to him whom old age, disease or disinclination has rendered unable or unwilling to labor. The honest worker must die because he is young and strong, and enjoys good health. The pauper or the criminal may live (a miserable life, and sometimes not a little of it in the alms-house or the prison), because he is a pauper or a criminal. "But husbands are torn from their wives, and wives from their husbands, parents from their children, and children from their parents." True; but husbands are torn from their wives, and wives from their husbands, parents from their children, and children from parents, even more frequently under the *wages* than under the *chattel* system of slavery. Millions of foreigners have come to this country, within the last twenty years—too many of them crowded into the steerage of vessels, covered with vermin, and suffering from the most loathsome diseases that flesh is heir to, as negroes

---

SOURCE: *The Liberator* (April 23, 1847).

have been packed into the holds of slavers on the "middle passage." Of these, thousands are children who have forsaken their parents and hundreds are husbands who have deserted their wives . . . but leaving one's father and mother, and abandoning one's wife, is none the less heart-rending, because it is done voluntarily. And here, two out of every three of the children of native-born citizens are forced to leave the homes of their parents (in a pecuniary sense) because their parents cannot *support* them at home; and three out of every five marriages prove to be a source of so much unhappiness, from domestic quarrels originating in pecuniary difficulties, that if the married parties do not separate, it is by no means because they would not be glad to do so, if they could without applying to the courts, and thereby save their reputations; or if the law did not require them to commit adultery, assault and battery, or some other equally heinous offence, in order to obtain a decree of divorce. "But the persons of female chattel slaves may be violated by their owners." Granted; but for every female chattel slave who is violated, at least half a dozen females wages slaves are *seduced*. Wherever wages slavery is substituted for chattel slavery, universal prostitution, both legal and illegal, must ultimately take the place of partial concubinage. Which of these forms of licentiousness is most repulsive and degrading, the reader must decide for himself.

F. Reinterpreting the Constitution

• *Lysander Spooner* (1845)

For a movement that sought to fulfill American ideals and restore equal rights and protections to all people, abolitionism was burdened with a perplexing liability. Until the 1840s, at least, virtually all its supporters accepted what William M. Wiecek has called the "federal consensus" regarding the Constitution: "(1) only the states could abolish or in any way regulate slavery within their jurisdictions; (2) the federal government had no power over slavery in the states."[1] The Garrisonians eventually denounced the Constitution as " a covenant with death, and an agreement with hell," and preached "disunion from slaveholders." Political abolitionists called for maximum action within the limits of the federal consensus, such as prohibiting slavery in the territories, barring interstate slave trade, and emancipating slaves in the District of Columbia. But in a nation whose mission was governed by a written charter, there seemed no way of overcoming the protections the charter purportedly gave to slaveholders.

In the 1840s, however, a number of theorists began to challenge the legal positivism which presupposed that law can be nothing more than the expressed will of lawmakers. Lysander Spooner, for example, insisted that law

---

[1] *The Sources of Antislavery Constitutionalism in America, 1760–1848* (Ithaca, N.Y.: Cornell University Press, 1977), p. 16.

is not an arbitrary rule "that can be established by mere will, numbers or power" but rather "an intelligible principle of right, necessarily resulting from the nature of man. . . .". Although Spooner (1808–1887) lacked formal education, having worked until age twenty-five on his father's Massachusetts farm, he began a law practice after a brief period of "reading" law in a private firm. Spooner's powers of logic were such that they commanded the respect of abolitionists who disagreed with his extreme position that slavery was unconstitutional and hence illegal even in the existing southern states. His prestige among reformers is all the more remarkable when one learns that Spooner was a deist who publicly attacked the premises of revealed religion.

The key to Spooner's thought is his reverence for the order of nature and the supremacy of natural law. Since he believed that slavery was absolutely contrary to natural law, one might conclude that the Constitution and other man-made laws were in a certain sense irrelevant. Yet Spooner identified natural law with ancient British rules such as the writ of *habeas corpus*, a protection against illegal imprisonment which a British court had used in 1772 to free a black slave. In the eyes of Spooner and a few other legal theorists, this celebrated *Somerset* decision had outlawed slavery in the colonies as well as in England by proscribing the institution as contrary to common law. Moreover, as Spooner goes on to argue in the following selection, the Constitution embodies natural-law and common-law principles and empowers the federal government to protect the rights of all people against tyrannical infringements by the states. In some respects, Spooner anticipates the principles of the Fourteenth Amendment which prevent any state from abridging the "privileges or immunities of citizens," depriving any person of "life, liberty, or property without due process of law," and denying "to any person within its jurisdiction the equal protection of the laws." But Spooner increasingly put his main hope in somehow convincing judges that there was an obligation to free individual slaves as if they were captives illegally held by bandits or kidnappers. In the late 1850s, Spooner became implicated in the violent plots of John Brown and devised his own wild plan for organizing revolutionary southern governments composed of blacks and nonslaveholding whites.

Lysander Spooner (1845)

It is a common assertion that the general government has no power over slavery in the states. If by this be meant that the states may reduce to slavery the citizens of the United States within their limits, and the general govern-

SOURCE: Lysander Spooner, *The Unconstitutionality of Slavery* (Boston: B. Marsh, 1853; 1st ed., 1845), pp. 270–76.

ment cannot liberate them, the doctrine is nullification, and goes to the destruction of the United States government within the limits of each state, whenever such state shall choose to destroy it.

The pith of the doctrine of nullification is this, viz., that a state has a right to interpose between her people and the United States government, deprive them of its benefits, protection, and laws, and annul their allegiance to it.

If a state have this power, she can of course abolish the government of the United States at pleasure, so far as its operation within her own territory is concerned; for the government of the United States is nothing, any further than it operates upon the persons, property, and rights of the people. If the states can arbitrarily intercept this operation, can interpose between the people and the government and laws of the United States, they can of course abolish that government. And the United States Constitution, and the laws made in pursuance thereof, instead of being "the supreme law of the land," "anything in the Constitution or laws of any state to the contrary notwithstanding," are dependent entirely upon the will of the state governments for permission to be laws at all.

A state law reducing a man to slavery, would, if valid, interpose between him and the Constitution and laws of the United States, annul their operation (so far as he is concerned), and deprive him of their benefits. It would annul his allegiance to the United States; for a slave can owe no allegiance to a government that either will not, or cannot protect him.

If a state can do this in the case of one man, she can do it in the case of any number of men, and thus completely abolish the general government within her limits.

But perhaps it will be said that a state has no right to reduce to slavery the people *generally* within her limits, but only to hold in slavery those who were slaves at the adoption of the Constitution, and their posterity.

One answer to this argument is, that at the adoption of the Constitution of the United States, there was no legal or constitutional slavery in the states. Not a single state constitution then in existence, recognized, authorized, or sanctioned slavery. All the slaveholding then practiced was merely a private crime committed by one person against another, like theft, robbery, or murder. All the statutes which the slaveholders, through their wealth and influence, procured to be passed, were unconstitutional and void, for the want of any constitutional authority in the legislatures to enact them.

But perhaps it will be said, as is often said of them now, that the state governments *had all power that was not forbidden to them.* But this is only one of those bald and glaring falsehoods, under cover of which, even to this day, corrupt and tyrannical legislators enact, and the servile and corrupt courts, who are made dependent upon them, sustain, a vast mass of unconstitutional legislation, destructive of men's natural rights. Probably half the state legislation under which we live is of this character, and has no other authority than the pretence that the government has all power except what is prohibited to it. The falsehood of the doctrine is apparent the moment it is considered that our governments derive all their authority from the grants of the people. Of necessity, therefore, instead of their having all authority except what is forbidden, they can have none except what is granted.

Everybody admits that this is the true doctrine in regard to the United States government; and it is equally true of the state governments, and for the same reason. The United States Constitution (amendment 10) does indeed specially provide that the U. S. government shall have no powers except what are delegated to it. But this amendment was inserted only as a special guard against usurpation. The government would have had no additional powers if this amendment had been omitted. The simple fact that all a government's powers are delegated to it by the people, proves that it can have no powers except what are delegated. And this principle is as true of the state governments, as it is of the national one; although it is one that is almost wholly disregarded in practice. . . .

But suppose, for the sake of the argument, that slavery had been authorized by the state constitutions at the time the United States Constitution was adopted, the Constitution of the United States would nevertheless have made it illegal; because the United States Constitution was made "the supreme law of the land," "anything in the constitution or laws of any state to the contrary notwithstanding." It therefore annulled everything inconsistent with it, *then existing* in the state constitutions, as well as everything that should ever after be added to them, inconsistent with it. It of course abolished slavery as a legal institution (supposing slavery to have had any legal existence to be abolished), if slavery were inconsistent with anything expressed, or legally implied, in the Constitution.

Slavery is inconsistent with nearly everything that is either expressed or legally implied in the Constitution. All its express provisions are general, making no exception whatever for slavery. All its legal *implications* are that the Constitution and laws of the United States are for the benefit of the *whole* "people of the United States," and their posterity.

The preamble expressly declares that "We the people of the United States" establish the Constitution for the purpose of securing justice, tranquillity, defense, welfare, and liberty, to "ourselves and our posterity." This language certainly implies that all "the people" who are parties to the Constitution, or join in establishing it, are to have the benefit of it, and of the laws made in pursuance of it. The only question, then, is, who were "the people of the United States?"

We cannot go out of the Constitution to find who are the parties to it. And there is nothing in the Constitution that can limit this word "people," so as to make it include a part, only, of "the people of the United States." The word, like all others, must be taken in the sense most beneficial for liberty and justice. Besides, if it did not include *all* the then "people of the United States," we have no *legal* evidence whatever of a single individual whom it did include. There is no legal evidence whatever in the Constitution, by which it can be proved that any one man was one of "the people," which will not also equally prove that the slaves were a part of the people. There is nothing in the Constitution that can prove the slaveholders to have been a part of "the people," which will not equally prove the slaves to have been also a part of them. And there is as much authority in the Constitution for excluding slaveholders from the description, "the people of the United States," as there is for excluding the slaves. The term "the people of the United States" must therefore be held to have included *all* "the people of the United States," or it can legally be held to have included none. . . .

The United States government, then, being in theory formed by, and for the benefit of, the whole "people of the United States," the question arises, whether it have the power of securing to "the people" the benefits it intended for them? Or whether it is dependent on the state governments *for permission* to confer these benefits on "the people?" This is the whole question. And if it shall prove that the general government has no power of securing to the people its intended benefits, it is, in no legal or reasonable sense, a government.

But *how* is it to secure its benefits to the people? That is the question.

The first step, and an indispensable step, towards doing it, is to secure to the people their personal liberty. Without personal liberty, none of the other benefits intended by the Constitution can be secured to an individual, because, without liberty, no one can prosecute his other rights in the tribunals appointed to secure them to him. If, therefore, the Constitution had failed to secure the personal liberty of individuals, all the rest of its provisions might have been defeated at the pleasure of the subordinate governments. But liberty being secured, all the other benefits of the Constitution are secured, because the individual can then carry the question of his rights into the courts of the United States, in all cases where the laws or Constitution of the United States are involved.

This right of personal liberty, this *sine qua non* to the enjoyment of all other rights, is secured by the writ of *habeas corpus*. This writ, as has before been shown, necessarily denies the right of property in man, and therefore liberates all who are restrained of their liberty on that pretence, as it does all others that are restrained on grounds inconsistent with the intended operation of the Constitution and laws of the United States. . . .

As the government is bound to dispense its benefits impartially to all, it is bound, first of all, after securing "the public safety, in cases of rebellion and invasion," to secure liberty to all. And the whole power of the government is bound to be exerted for this purpose, *to the postponement, if need be,* of everything else save "the public safety, in cases of rebellion and invasion." And it is the constitutional duty of the government to establish as many courts as may be necessary (no matter how great the number), and to adopt all other measures necessary and proper, for bringing the means of liberation within the reach of every person who is restrained of his liberty in violation of the principles of the Constitution.

We have thus far . . . placed this question upon the ground that those held in slavery are constitutionally a part of "the people of the United States," and parties to the Constitution. But, although this ground cannot be shaken, it is not necessary to be maintained, in order to maintain the duty of Congress to provide courts, and all other means necessary, for their liberation.

The Constitution, by providing for the writ of *habeas corpus*, without making any discrimination as to the persons entitled to it, has virtually declared, and thus established it as a constitutional principle, that, in this country, there can be no property in man; for the writ of *habeas corpus*, as has before been shown, necessarily involves a denial of the right of property in man. By declaring that the privilege of this writ "shall not be suspended, unless when, in cases of rebellion or invasion the public safety may require it," the Constitution has imposed upon Congress the duty of providing courts, and if need be, other aids, for the issuing of this writ in behalf of all human beings within the United States, who may be restrained on claim of being property. Congress are bound by the Constitution to aid, if need be, a foreigner, an alien, an enemy even, who may be restrained as property. And if the people of any of the civilized nations were now to be seized as slaves, on their arrival in this country, we can all imagine what an abundance of constitutional power would be found, and put forth, too, for their liberation.

Without this power, the nation could not sustain its position as one of the family of civilized nations; it could not fulfil the law of nations, and would therefore be liable to be outlawed in consequence of the conduct of the states. For example. If the states can make slaves of anybody, they can certainly make slaves of foreigners. And if they can make slaves of foreigners, they can violate the law of nations; because to make slaves of foreigners, is to violate the law of nations. Now the general government is the only government known to other nations; and if the states can make slaves of foreigners, and there were no power in the general government to liberate them, any one of the states could involve the whole nation in the responsibility of having violated the law of nations, and the nation would have no means of relieving itself from that responsibility by liberating the persons enslaved; but would have to meet, and conquer or die in, a war brought upon it by the criminality of the state.

The Quest for New Social Harmonies

A. Man the Reformer

• *Ralph Waldo Emerson* (*1841*)

Emerson (1803–1882) was not a reformer but a "man-of-letters"—in some respects America's central and most influential literary figure of the nineteenth century. He knew reformers of all kinds, attended their meetings, inspired them with ringing phrases, but remained aloof from all causes except his own. This he variously summed up as the cause of the nonconformist who seeks "to enjoy an original relation to the universe" and "to guide men by showing them facts amidst appearances." Though Emerson could applaud the critical, nonconformist *spirit* of reform, he feared the inevitable conformity of association and basically believed that social evils could be ameliorated only by individual self-regeneration.

Nevertheless, for a number of reasons, Emerson helps to illuminate the logical transition between reforms like temperance and abolition, which attacked a particular social evil, and more generalized quests to renovate the entire social order. First, as suggested in the following selection, Emerson senses that once an era of reform is underway, no traditional practice or institution is immune from criticism. Second, Emerson understands that this critical spirit is rooted historically in religious judgments of worldly

441

selfishness and compromise and is the end result of a succession of reforma-
tions and protests which, like a rising flood, have broken through all formal
restraints of church, creed, and theology. Here Emerson speaks from personal experience, since he had been brought up and educated by leaders of
the Unitarian rebellion against Calvinism (itself a rebellion against Catholicism), and had then rebelled himself against the remnants of revealed religion, such as the belief in New Testament miracles, within his father's
liberal creed.

Finally, unlike abolitionists and temperance reformers, Emerson has little
faith that society can be *fundamentally* improved by militant struggles
against some positive objectification of evil. For in Emerson's eyes, society
is shot through with imperfections. As he wrote in another essay, three
years later: "The wave of evil washes all our institutions alike. Do you
complain of our marriage? Our marriage is no worse than our education,
our diet, our trade, our social customs." But paradoxically, this very ubiq-
uity of evil opens the way for a relatively simple solution, since Emerson
considers evil to be merely the privation of good—not a force or presence
but an absence of harmony, of wholeness. In this respect, his outlook is
similar to that of the perfectionists and utopian socialists to whom we shall
soon turn, expect that Emerson always mistrusted communal quests for
new harmonies and relied instead on discovering a new communion between
the "infinitude of the private man" and what he termed the "Oversoul."

Ralph Waldo Emerson (1841)

In the history of the world the doctrine of Reform had never such scope as
at the present hour. Lutherans, Herrnhutters, Jesuits, Monks, Quakers, Knox,
Wesley, Swedenborg, Bentham, in their accusations of society, all respected
something—church or state, literature or history, domestic usages, the market
town, the dinner table, coined money. But now all these and all things else
hear the trumpet, and must rush to judgment—Christianity, the laws, commerce, schools, the farm, the laboratory, and not a kingdom, town, statute,
rite, calling, man, or woman, but is threatened by the new spirit.

What if some of the objection whereby our institutions are assailed are
extreme and speculative, and the reformers tend to idealism? That only
shows the extravagance of the abuses which have driven the mind into the
opposite extreme.

· · ·

. . . I content myself with the fact that the general system of our trade
(apart from the blacker traits, which, I hope, are exceptions denounced and

SOURCE: Ralph Waldo Emerson, "Man the Reformer," *Complete Works* (Boston:
Houghton Mifflin Co., 1903–1904), Vol. I, pp. 228–29, 232–35, 247–48.

unshared by all reputable men) is a system of selfishness; is not dictated by the high sentiments of human nature; is not measured by the exact law of reciprocity, much less by the sentiments of love and heroism, but is a system of distrust, of concealment, of superior keenness, not of giving but of taking advantage. . . . I do not charge the merchant or the manufacturer. The sins of our trade belong to no class, to no individual. One plucks, one distributes, one eats. Every body partakes, every body confesses—with cap and knee volunteers his confession, yet none feels himself accountable. He did not create the abuse; he cannot alter it. What is he? an obscure private person who must get his bread. That is the vice—that no one feels himself called to act for man, but only as a fraction of man. . . .

But by coming out of trade you have not cleared yourself. The trail of the serpent reaches into all the lucrative professions and practices of man. Each has its own wrongs. Each finds a tender and very intelligent conscience a disqualification for success. Each requires of the practitioner a certain shutting of the eyes, a certain dapperness and compliance, an acceptance of customs, a sequestration from the sentiments of generosity and love, a compromise of private opinion and lofty integrity. Nay, the evil custom reaches into the whole institution of property, until our laws which establish and protect it seem not to be the issue of love and reason, but of selfishness. Suppose a man is so unhappy as to be born a saint, with keen perceptions but with the conscience and love of an angel, and he is to get his living in the world; he finds himself excluded from all lucrative works; he has no farm, and he cannot get one; for to earn money enough to buy one requires a sort of concentration toward money, which is the selling himself for a number of years, and to him the present hour is as sacred and inviolable as any future hour. Of course, whilst another man has no land, my title to mine, your title to yours, is at once vitiated. Inextricable seem to be the twinings and tendrils of this evil, and we all involve ourselves in it the deeper by forming connections by wives and children, by benefits and debts.

Considerations of this kind have turned the attention of many philanthropic and intelligent persons to the claims of maual labor, as a part of the education of every young man. If the accumulated wealth of the past generation is thus tainted—no matter how much of it is offered to us—we must begin to consider if it were not the nobler part to renounce it, and to put ourselves into primary relations with the soil and nature, and abstaining from whatever is dishonest and unclean, to take each of us bravely his part, with his own hands, in the manual labor of the world.

But it is said, "What! will you give up the immense advantages reaped from the division of labor, and set every man to make his own shoes, bureau, knife, wagons, sails, and needle? This would be to put men back into barbarism by their own act." I see no instant prospect of a virtuous revolution; yet I confess I should not be pained at a change which threatened a loss of some of the luxuries or conveniences of society, if it proceeded from a preference of the agricultural life out of the belief that our primary duties as men could be better discharged in that calling. Who could regret to see a high con-science and a purer taste exercising a sensible effect on young men in their choice of occupation, and thinning the ranks of competition in the labors of commerce, of law, and of state?

. . .

I do not wish to be absurd and pedantic in reform. I do not wish to push my criticism on the state of things around me to that extravagant mark that shall compel me to suicide, or to an absolute isolation from the advantages of civil society. If we suddenly plant our foot and say—I will neither eat nor drink nor wear nor touch any food or fabric which I do not know to be inno-cent, or deal with any person whose whole manner of life is not clear and rational, we shall stand still. Whose is so? Not mine; not thine; not his. . . .

But the idea which now begins to agitate society has a wider scope than our daily employments, our households, and the institutions of property. We are to revise the whole of our social structure, the state, the school, religion, marriage, trade, science, and explore their foundations in our own nature; we are to see that the world not only fitted the former men, but fits us, and to clear ourselves of every usage which has not its roots in our own mind. What is a man born for but to be a Reformer, a Remaker of what man has made; a renouncer of lies; a restorer of truth and good, imitating that great Nature which embosoms us all, and which sleeps no moment on an old past, but every hour repairs herself, yielding us every morning a new day, and with every pulsation a new life?

B. A Manifesto Against Individualism

• *Robert Owen (1825)*

> Robert Owen (1771–1858) was a pioneer socialist and inspirer of com-munitarian experiments in Britain and the United States. Born in Wales, he achieved spectacular success early in life as a cotton textile manufacturer in Manchester, England. Unlike most entrepreneurs of his generation, Owen became deeply disturbed by the social evils spawned by industrialization and sought to find ways of ensuring that machines would benefit workers instead of displacing them. At his New Lanark mill, in Scotland, he built a paternalistic community distinguished by such enlightened innovations as model housing, sickness and old-age insurance, and schools instead of labor for small children. Disappointed by the failure of his schemes for national factory regulation, Owen embarked on several ambitious plans for creating egalitarian communities that would integrate agriculture with industry. The most famous of these experiments was at New Harmony, Indiana, a site Owen purchased from some German religious communitarians known as Rappites.
>
> In 1825, upon his arrival in America, Owen presented the principles of his "New System of Society" in a formal address to the Senate and House

of Representatives. The government's tolerance and curiosity are worthy of note, since one can hardly imagine Karl Marx being invited to address Congress in 1870. Owen was no Marx, but he had renounced religion and was a thoroughgoing materialist who insisted that human character, behavior, and values are entirely the product of environmental influence. As we have seen in Unit One, Americans were beginning to suggest that almost any results could be obtained by manipulating the environment of children. Owen extended this promise of infinite perfectibility to adults. But the goals he aimed at were hardly in tune with Peter Parley or the "Rollo Code." In his "Declaration of Mental Independence," promulgated on July 4, 1826, Owen called for the abolition of a "trinity" of evils: private property; absurd and irrational systems of religion; and a form of marriage founded on both private property and irrational religion.

The following selection is from Owen's initial address to the settlers at New Harmony, who had been carefully selected and who included some eminent European scientists. Note that his enmity toward individualism, as the cardinal defect of modern society, echoes some of the concern over "the anxious spirit of gain" which we encountered in Unit Two. Note also the parallels between faith in applying new scientific principles and the theme of scientific progress in Part 1 of this Unit. Yet it is significant that Owen, a representative both of the Old World and of the British industrialization that was beginning to revolutionize the world, seems somehow more innocent than the supposedly innocent Americans. In his single-minded pursuit of a simple and easier way to harmony, he is more "American" than the Americans—more oblivious to the experience of history, more committed to a dream. New Harmony had a short and tumultuous history—from 1825 to 1828. The final irony is that it failed, not because the enterprise was inherently impossible—witness the longevity of many religious communities —but largely because of Owen's own practical shortcomings as a manager, the very role in which he had excelled as a capitalist entrepreneur.

Robert Owen (1825)

I am come to this country, to introduce an entire new state of society; to change it from the ignorant, selfish system, to an enlightened, social system, which shall gradually unite all interests into one, and remove all cause for contest between individuals.

The individual system has heretofore universally prevailed; and while it continues, the great mass of mankind must remain, as they comparatively are at present, ignorant, poor, oppressed, and, consequently, vicious, and mis-

SOURCE: "Address Delivered by Robert Owen, April 27, 1825," *The New-Harmony Gazette*, I (October 1, 1825), pp. 1–2.

erable; and though it should last for numberless ages, virtue and happiness cannot be attained, nor can man, strictly speaking, become a rational being.

Until the individual system shall be entirely abandoned, it will be useless to expect any substantial, permanent improvement in the condition of the human race; for this system ever has been, and must remain, directly opposed to universal charity, benevolence and kindness; and until the means were discovered, and can be brought into practice, by which universal charity, benevolence and kindness, can be made to pervade the heart and mind of every human being, a state of society in which "peace on earth and good will to man" shall exist, must remain unknown and unenjoyed by mankind.

These invaluable blessings can be obtained only under a social system; a system derived from an accurate knowledge of human nature, and of the circumstances by which it is, or may be, governed.

This knowledge has been, until now, hidden from man; he therefore knew not how to put the social system into practice; for without this knowledge, the social system is utterly impracticable. . . .

The knowledge of our nature, and of the circumstances which govern the character and conduct of man, are to be acquired only by attending to the facts which exist around us, and to the past history of the human species.

These facts and this history demonstrate, that all men are formed by a creative power, and by the circumstances which are permitted to surround them from birth; and that no man has ever had any will, or power, or control, in creating himself, nor in forming the circumstances which exist around him at birth, in his childhood, in youth, or in manhood. He is a being, then, whose general nature, whose individual, or personal nature, and whose artificial acquirements, or character, have been formed for him. He cannot, therefore, become a proper subject for praise or blame, nor for artificial reward or punishment, or artificial accountability; but he becomes a being capable of being formed into the extremes of good or bad, and to experience the extremes of happiness or misery, by, and through the circumstances which shall exist around him at birth, in childhood, in youth, and in manhood. . . .

These fundamental principles being understood, and the real nature of man being thus laid open to us, the proceedings requisite to produce good instead of evil, and happiness instead of misery, become obvious and easy of practice.

I have bought this property [New Harmony, Indiana], and have now come here to introduce this practice, and to render it familiar to all the inhabitants of this country.

But to change from the individual to the social system; from single families with separate interests, to communities of many families with one interest, cannot be accomplished at once; the change would be too great for the present habits of society; nor can it be effected in practice, except by those who have been long acquainted with each other, and whose habits, condition and sentiments, are similar; it becomes necessary, therefore, that some intermediate measures should be adopted, to enable all parties, with the least inconvenience, to change their individual, selfish habits, and to acquire the superior habits requisite to a social state; to proceed, if I may so express myself, to a halfway house on this new journey from poverty to wealth; from ignorance to intelligence; from anxiety to satisfaction of mind. . . .

C. The Completion of Perfection

• *John Humphrey Noyes* (1837)
• Declaration of Sentiments, *Boston Peace Convention* (1838)
• *Albert Brisbane* (1843)

Despite the example of Owen, the more radical American quests for perfection tended to be religious in inspiration. One should be cautious, however, in drawing rigid distinctions in this period between religious and secular motivation. If Owen was regarded as an infidel because he repudiated institutional religion, his goals were the traditional Christian goals of "universal charity, benevolence, and kindness." Hundreds of Americans dissatisfied with the competitive struggle for success moved easily back and forth from religious to secular, or from secular to religious communities.

John Humphery Noyes (1811–1886) was the most radical and, in many ways, the most successful of all American communitarians. Noyes was also obsessed by a messianic vision—the conviction that Christ had returned to earth in 70 A.D., that the long-awaited millennium was well underway, and that this discovery had opened the way for him and his followers to achieve a state of sinless perfection. Noyes had been brought up by a strong-minded father, a Dartmouth graduate and Vermont Congressman, who had rejected religious belief. After following in his father's footsteps, graduating from Dartmouth with high honors and then studying law, Noyes experienced a religious conversion that led him to Andover Theological Seminary and then to Yale. But his quest for perfect holiness soon resulted in his dismissal as a heretical fanatic. In March, 1837, Noyes drifted into Garrison's antislavery office in Boston, where he found a receptive audience for his doctrines of perfectionism and withdrawal from all complicity with sinful government. Our first selection is from a remarkable follow-up letter that Noyes addressed to Garrison on March 22, 1837, spelling out the paradox of Christian unity—"the birth of a ransomed world" through extreme renunciation. Garrison did not follow Noyes to the next step of a separate perfectionist community, soon moved by Noyes from Putney, Vermont to Oneida, New York. But the Garrisonian reformers were deeply influenced by Noyes' repudiation of all governments founded and dependent on physical force.

The second selection, from another "Declaration of Sentiments," owes much to Noyes as well as to other radical "non-resistants" who carried to an extreme conclusion the American belief in voluntarism combined with the Biblical injunction in Matthew: "Whosoever shall smite thee on thy right cheek, turn to him the other also." Not all pacifists condemned defensive wars, let alone law suits, but this Declaration emanated from a "Peace Convention" of Garrisonians who wanted nothing to do with any form of coercion—except the moral and psychological coercion of rhetoric. Unlike Noyes, these non-resistants invested less hope in new social practice than in the power of words and in the evangelizing techniques of the temperance and abolition movements. It should be added, however, that within a few years other non-resistants and pacificists like William Ladd were calling not only for disengagement from military force but for new international institutions that would arbitrate or judicially resolve disputes between nations.

From the rich seedbed of the 1840s and early 1850s, one could easily multiply examples and varieties of perfectionism. Here, in the third selection, a final sample must suffice, illustrating the surprisingly popular phase of communitarianism inspired, in theory, by Charles Fourier, an eccentric French utopian who died in 1837. It is perhaps unfortunate that Albert Brisbane (1809–1890), the American author of our selection, is usually identified as merely a disciple and popularizer of Fourier. A native of Batavia, New York, in the "burned-over district," Brisbane was well-read in social philosophy even at the age of eighteen, when he sailed off to Europe to learn what he could about "the social destiny of man," a phrase he later chose for the title of his most famous book. In Paris, Brisbane studied with such leading philosophers and historians of the Sorbonne as Victor Cousin and François Guizot, both soon destined to become ruling figures in the French government. As a student in Berlin, he was dissatisfied with the lectures of Hegel, Europe's greatest but aging philosopher, whose method had not yet been discovered by a schoolboy named Karl Marx. In Turkey and eastern Europe, Brisbane pondered the meaning of massive destitution. In short, Brisbane was hardly an innocent and gullible American tourist when he became entranced by Fourier's formula for eliminating poverty and dignifying manual labor by the device of cooperative communities, or phalanxes. Even after two years of personal tutelage under Fourier, Brisbane was quite prepared to modify his master's theories to fit American conditions.

Brisbane was not directly responsible for the scores of utopian communities, even those roughly modeled on the Fourier phalanx, that mushroomed throughout the Northeast and Old Northwest in the 1840s. No doubt the yearning for communal solidarity, especially in the prolonged aftershock of economic depression, outweighed the speculative appeal of social theories imported from France. Still, thanks to his influence on Horace Greeley, Brisbane had access for a time to the unprecedented national readership of the New York *Tribune*. Later, he propagated the doctrines of Associationism in such publications as the *Plebeian*, the *Phalanx*, and the *Dial* (edited by Margaret Fuller and originally the organ of the Transcendentalists).

The selection here from the *Phalanx* owes less to Fourier's complicated scheme for harmonizing innate "passions" than to a growing American desire, documented in previous selections, to escape from the pressures and isolation of a competitive society; to move beyond political democracy to a new sense of social fraternity; and, as also seen in the writings of Noyes and the pacifists, to replace physical coercion by somehow putting "science in the hands of citizens."

John Humphrey Noyes (1837)

I am willing that all men should know that I have subscribed my name to an instrument similar to the Declaration of '76, renouncing all allegiance to the government of the United States, and asserting the title of Jesus Christ to the throne of the world. . . .

When I wish to form a conception of the government of the United States (using a personified representation), I picture to myself a bloated, swaggering libertine, trampling on the Bible—its own Constitution—its treaties with the Indians—the petitions of its citizens: with one hand whipping a negro tied to a liberty-pole, and with the other dashing an emaciated Indian to the ground. On one side stand the despots of Europe, laughing and mocking at the boasted liberty of their neighbor; on the other stands the Devil. . . . In view of such a representation, the question urges itself upon me—"What have I, as a Christian, to do with such a villain?" I live on the territory which he claims—under the protection, to some extent, of the laws which he promulgates. Must I therefore profess to be his friend? God forbid! I will rather flee my country. But every other country is under the same reprobate authority. I must, then, either go out of the world, or find some way to live where I am, without being a hypocrite or a partaker in the sins of the nation. . . . Every person who is, in the usual sense of the expression, a citizen of the United States, i.e., a voter, politician, etc., is at once a slave and a slaveholder —in other words, a subject and a ruler in a slaveholding government.

• • •

My hope of the millennium begins where Dr. [Lyman] Beecher's expires— viz., AT THE OVERTHROW OF THIS NATION.

The signs of the times clearly indicate the purpose of God to do his strange work speedily. The country is ripe for a convulsion like that of France; rather, I should say, for the French Revolution reversed. Infidelity roused the whirlwind in France. The Bible, by anti-slavery and other similar movements, is doing the same work in this country. So, in the end, Jesus Christ, instead of a bloodthirsty Napoleon, will ascend the throne of the world. The convulsion which is coming will be, not the struggle of death, but the travail of childbirth—the birth of a ransomed world.

SOURCE: *William Lloyd Garrison, 1805–1879, The Story of His Life* (New York: Century Co., 1885), pp. 145–47.

Declaration of Sentiments, Boston Peace Convention (1838)

We register our testimony, not only against all wars, whether offensive or defensive, but all preparations for war; against every naval ship, every arsenal, every fortification; against the militia system and a standing army; against all military chieftains and soldiers; against all monuments commemorative of victory over a fallen foe, all trophies won in battle, all celebrations in honor of military or naval exploits; against all appropriations for the defense of a nation by force and arms, on the part of any legislative body; against every edict of government requiring of its subjects military service. Hence, we deem it unlawful to bear arms, or to hold a military office.

As every human government is upheld by physical strength, and its laws are enforced virtually at the point of the bayonet, we cannot hold any office which imposes upon its incumbent the obligation to compel men to do right, on pain of imprisonment or death. We therefore voluntarily exclude ourselves from every legislative and judicial body, and repudiate all human politics, worldly honors, and stations of authority. If *we* cannot occupy a seat in the legislature or on the bench, neither can we elect *others* to act as our substitutes in any such capacity.

It follows, that we cannot sue any man at law, to compel him by force to restore anything which he may have wrongfully taken from us or others; but if he has seized our coat, we shall surrender up our cloak, rather than subject him to punishment.

. . .

The triumphant progress of the cause of TEMPERANCE and of ABOLITION in our land, through the instrumentality of benevolent and voluntary associations, encourages us to combine our own means and efforts for the promotion of a still greater cause. Hence, we shall employ lecturers, circulate tracts and publications, form societies, and petition our state and national governments, in relation to the subject of UNIVERSAL PEACE. It will be our leading object to devise ways and means for effecting a radical change in the views, feelings, and practices of society, respecting the sinfulness of war and the treatment of enemies.

Albert Brisbane (1843)

A social reform is the continuation, the completion of our great political movement of 1776. By our revolution, we effected a great Political Reform, or a reform in the old, time-honored and firmly established *Political System*,

SOURCE: "Declaration of Sentiments Adopted by the Peace Convention," *William Lloyd Garrison, 1805–1879, The Story of His Life* (New York: Century Co., 1885), pp. 231–33.

SOURCE: Albert Brisbane, "Exposition of Views and Principles," *The Phalanx*, I (October 5, 1843), pp. 4–5.

which we had received from Europe, but there reform has ceased; we have retained and preserved the *Social System*, which we received from the same source, unaltered and untouched. It rests with the People and the leaders of the People of this generation to continue and consummate the great work of Reform commenced by their noble ancestors. The invaluable principles of liberty and equality which they established in the political system of our country, must be extended by the men of the present day to its social system. They effected a Political reform and secured to us the blessings of *political* liberty and equality, we must effect a Social reform and bequeath to our posterity the far more precious boon of *social* liberty and equality! Their combat was to reform unjust and oppressive political Institutions; ours must be to reform unjust and more oppressive social Institutions. They contended against the outrageous usurpations of tyrannical power; we must contend against the blighting influences of unnatural social arrangements; but whilst theirs was the triumph of the Sword, ours must be the triumph of Reason . . . ours must be a victory which will *unite* our fellow-men—our brothers; for the Sword in the hands of warriors, there must be Science in the hands of citizens; for hostile blows between adverse parties, there must be friendly conference between amicable interests; for violence and blood, there must be conciliation and peace. . . .

Instead of an amelioration of social evils and an immensely improved condition of the people, the same oppressive evils which exist under monarchical forms of government, exist also in this land of political liberty, modified only by circumstances of a temporary character. The Working Classes, who form the great majority of the population, are subjected to the same harassing cares and anxieties of life; they are equally the drudges of ill-requited and exhausting toil; they are as dependent upon capital as the laboring masses of Europe, and like them, are Hirelings, bound in the thraldom of menial Servitude. Political freedom, and the equality of civil rights, which they possess, afford them no protection against the tyranny of *industrial bondage* to which they are subjected under a false system of Industry; and no security against reductive and depressing competition, unjust monopoly, or a coalition of capital opposed to the interests of labor, and the power of machinery in the hands of a few, which works *against* instead of *for* the mass. . . .

Why have not political freedom and democratic institutions been able to eradicate these various complicated evils, and secure happiness to all classes in society?

The reason is easily explained. We have destroyed the false *Political System* of Europe and replaced it by a true one, but we have left standing and unmolested the *Social Organization* in all its branches of injustice, falseness and iniquity. We have engrafted good and sound political institutions upon a false foundation—upon defective and corrupt social institutions, which have engendered the same evils and miseries in this as in the old world.

We have the same repugnant, degrading and ill-requited system of Industry as Europe; the same system of Free Competition, or false rivalry and envious strife and anarchy in the field of commerce and industry; the same menial and slavish system of Hired Labor or Labor for Wages; the same wasteful, intricate and grasping system of Trade; the same exclusive ownership of machinery by capital, or machinery monopolized by a few, which competes with the laborer and drives him from the field of Industry; the same complicated system of Law; and at the root of all social falseness, the same system of isolated or separate Households.

* * *

Under our system of isolated and separate households, with separate interests and separate pursuits, instead of association and combination among families, there is the most deplorable waste, which is one of the primary sources of the general poverty that exists; and discord, antagonism, selfishness, and an anti-social spirit are engendered. Woman is subjected to unremitting and slavish domestic duties: political liberty enfranchises Woman as little as it does the Laborer. The wives of the poor are complete domestic drudges, whose whole time is absorbed in complicated household cares and occupations, and the women of the more favored classes who escape the burthen of toil of the isolated household, do so only at the expense of a class of their fellow-creatures who are reduced to the most menial Servitude, to a degrading bondage and dependence directly at war with the spirit of political and christian equality which we profess to revere so sacredly in theory. The present servile system of domestic Servitude which makes a degraded class of one portion of the population, is a dead rebuke to all pretensions to Democracy, and if a new Social Order cannot be established, based upon "Associated households" (by which nine-tenths of domestic labors will be economized), and upon dignified and attractive Industry, so that this and all other species of servitude, will be abolished, not a hope remains for the future Social Elevation of the race.

Transcending Human History: Americans as "Pioneers of the World"

A. "We Have Monopolized the Best of Time and Space"

- *Gulian C. Verplanck (1836)*
- *Bronson Alcott (1834)*
- *Walt Whitman (1846)*

We have taken note of two common ingredients in the American reformers' sense of mission. First, they attached extraordinary importance to the Declaration of Independence, not only as a symbolic bench mark dividing ages of monarchic despotism from a new era of political liberty, but also as a model for future acts of self-emancipation. Second, believing that they, at least, had escaped from the ignorance, deceptions, and constraints of the past, reformers sought to apply transcendent standards of love and justice to the here and now, rejecting traditional excuses for violence, cruelty, and human degradation.

In some respects, these patterns of thought were part of a wider cultural concern with America's uniqueness and world mission. There were many aggressive nationalists, for example, who detested reformers but who were no less devout in revering the "Spirit of '76" and in contemplating visions of America's future perfection. Even the most bitter opponents of abolitionism, temperance, pacifism, and feminism, generally shared the conviction that the United States had escaped from the limits of past civilizations; like a space probe, to use a modern metaphor, America had seemingly burst free from the gravitational field of past history. Reformers and anti-reformers were similarly amazed and inspired by the nation's growth in population, technology, settled territory, wealth, and productivity. The difference was that reformers dwelled on the costs and perils of success (including some of the flagrant social crimes and national hypocrisies we have glimpsed in Unit Three). Many other Americans who were not necessarily inferior to reformers in human decency, good will, or common sense, remained confident that most social costs and perils could be met by growth and expansion—that domestic imperfections, conflicts, and polarities would ultimately be dissolved by the combined radiance of prosperity and republican institutions. This latter faith usually presupposed the "manifest destiny" of an American "empire for liberty," unimpeded by monarchic enemies and their unwitting American dupes (such as abolitionists, who were often accused of being the tools of a British plot to divide the nation).

This abbreviated background is essential for understanding the concluding themes of Unit Four as we move first from specific reforms to more generalized visions of America's mission and "futurity," as Walt Whitman called it; and then finally turn to the collision between such cosmic visions of harmony and perfection and the divisive issue of slavery.

The initial and, in many ways, central question, as the following three selections suggest, is the way the past was perceived, repudiated, used, and invoked. Antebellum Americans were remarkably attuned to history. Over one-fourth of all best-selling books of the period were histories or historical in subject matter. Periodicals and even newspapers devoted a large proportion of space to history of one kind or another. Yet paradoxically, much of this fascination centered either on the heroic epic of winning independence or on accounts of Old World vices, intrigues, and oppressions which Americans had escaped. While the reading of such history could reinforce the sense of America's mission as the "hope of mankind," the culmination of millennia of human yearning and struggle, it could also feed a spirit of self-congratulation that either minimized or denied the injustices that troubled reformers. History, when conceived as a morass of Old World evil and conflict that Americans could view as if from a separate planet, became a substitute for reform. It identified transcendent ideals with *existing* American trends and institutions, not with goals requiring future struggle.

Our first sample of nationalistic rhetoric is by Gulian C. Verplanck (described in Unit Two, Part 3, C). Neither Verplanck nor the other authors we have chosen were aggressive jingoists eager for America to fight the world. One of the points we wish to illustrate is the appeal of optimistic nationalism to some of the most sensitive and original American minds. Thus the second selection is from a diary entry of April 22, 1834 by Amos Bronson Alcott (1799–1888). A Transcendentalist and genuine innovator in child-centered teaching, Alcott personified the image of the starry-eyed reformer. In this brief passage, he also epitomizes a view of America's relation to the past and to "nature" that was at least as conducive to expansive nationalism as to reform.

The final selection is from an editorial by Walt Whitman (1819–1892) who in 1846 is already marveling at the prospect of America's Centennial thirty years hence. Whitman eventually would become the greatest and most original American poet of the nineteenth century, but in the mid-1840s he was an intensely excitable dreamer and idealist who gloried in America's expansion and Manifest Destiny. At the outset of the Mexican War, he predicted that the Yucatán peninsula would "add a bright star to the 'Spangled Banner.' "[1] In his early twenties Whitman was a wandering teacher, typesetter, journalist, and local cheerleader for the Democratic party. In 1846, he began editing the *Brooklyn Eagle*, from which our selection is taken. Already a poet of American boundlessness, Whitman spins off a striking image of the nation as a vast refuge for "the degrading, starving and ignorant ones of the Old World . . . transplanted thither. . . ." Seemingly buoyant with unlimited confidence, in the end he protests too much his disbelief in the "horror" of America's possible failure. Such mixed anticipations do much to enrich our understanding of the symbolic meaning that Whitman—and Lincoln—later attached to the Civil War.

Gulian C. Verplanck (1836)

The actual state and the probable future prospects of our country, resemble those of no other land, and are without a parallel in past history. Our immense extent of fertile territory opening an inexhaustible field for successful enterprise, thus assuring to industry a certain reward for its labors, and preserving the land, for centuries to come, from the manifold evils of an overcrowded, and consequently degraded population—our magnificent system of federated republics, carrying out and applying the principles of representative democracy to an extent never hoped or imagined in the boldest theories of the old speculative republican philosophers. . . .

[T]he unconstrained range of freedom of opinion, of speech, and of the press, and the habitual and daring exercise of that liberty upon the highest subjects—the absence of all serious inequality of fortune and rank in the condition of our citizens—our divisions into innumerable religious sects, and the consequent co-existence, never before regarded as possible, of intense religious zeal, with a great degree of toleration in feeling and perfect equality of rights

---

1 Frederick Merk, *Manifest Destiny and Mission in American History: A Reinterpretation* (New York: Alfred A. Knopf, 1963), p. 202.

SOURCE: Gulian C. Verplanck, *The Advantages and Dangers of the American Scholar* (New York: Wiley and Long, 1836), pp. 5–6.

—our intimate connection with that elder world beyond the Atlantic, communicating to us, through the press and emigration, much of good and much of evil not our own, high science, refined art, and the best knowledge of old experience, as well as prejudices and luxuries, vices and crimes, such as could not have expected to spring up in our soil for ages—all these . . . have given to our society, through all its relations, a character exclusively its own, peculiar and unexampled.

Bronson Alcott (1834)

To us the past *is* of value. Not, however, in the way of example; for the parallel is wanting, the analogy is dim. Circumstances are widely different. Man is operating on vastly different external relations. We are spread over a wider space; we have freer air; Nature spreads itself around us on a wider scale; our situation is wholly new. Nor are *men* the same. Physical differences have molded us in accordance with their spirit. Our physical and intellectual make are national; and, despite the foreign associations of our ancestral education, Nature has assumed her rightful influence and has shaped us in her molds. Living on the accumulated treasures of the past in a new theatre of action, we have monopolized the best of time and space, and stand on a vantage ground to which no people have ever ascended before.

Walt Whitman (1846)

Thirty years from this date, America will be confessed the *first nation* on the earth. We of course mean that her power, wealth, and the happiness and virtue of her citizens will then obtain a pitch which other nations cannot favorably compare with. Her immense territory is filling up with a rapidity which few eyes among us have realized. And back of what can possibly be filled up in fifty years, lay enormous untravelled plains and forests, fat of their own riches, and capable of sustaining nations like the greatest in Europe. The mind is lost in contemplating such incalculable acres—and the lover of his race, whose fellowship is not bound by an open or dividing line, yearns that the degrading, starving and ignorant ones of the Old World, whatever and whoever they are, should be transplanted thither, where their cramped natures may expand, and they do honor to the great humanity they so long have been a blot upon. . . . Yet it is well, as it is. For the time will surely

source: *Journals of Bronson Alcott*, Odell Shepard, ed. (Boston: Little, Brown and Co., 1938), pp. 40–41.

source: [Walt Whitman], *Brooklyn Daily Eagle*, Nov. 24, 1846. In Cleveland Rogers and John Black, eds. *Gathering of the Forces* (New York: G. P. Putnam's Sons, 1920), Vol. I, pp. 27–28.

come—that holy millennium of liberty—when the "Victory of endurance born" shall lift the masses of the down-trodden of Europe, and make them achieve something of that destiny which we may suppose God intends eligible for mankind. And this problem is to be worked out through the people, territory, and government of the United States. If it should fail! O, dark were the hour and dreary beyond description the horror of such a failure—which we anticipate not at all!

B. "The Past Is Dead, and Has No Resurrection"

• *Herman Melville* (1850)

Born the same year as Whitman, Herman Melville (1819–1891) was the greatest novelist of his time. Given the above quotation from Melville about the death of the past, there is an irony in the fact that the consensual judgment of his greatness emerged many decades after his death, and that he is probably the most *resurrected* literary figure of the entire nineteenth century. The irony is all the more striking when one considers that Melville devastated through satire the prevailing dogmas concerning civilization as a force of resurrection. Since he was anything but a conformist, it is unconventional to include him as a chanter of hymns to America's divine destiny.

The profusion of Melville biographies and literary criticism cannot be summarized here. Suffice it to say that his heritage mixed illustrious but distant strains of Scottish, New England, and Dutch-New York ancestry with immediate childhood poverty; that as a teenager he experimented with odd jobs as a clerk and schoolteacher and then shipped out as a cabin-boy on a voyage to Liverpool; and that at age twenty he embarked on a momentous whaling voyage to the South Pacific where he finally deserted ship, lived an idyllic life with cannibals in the Marquesas Islands, and eventually enlisted as a seaman on a frigate of the United States navy, which in 1844 finally discharged him in Boston. These romantic adventures provided Melville with the material for two exotic and popular novels, *Typee* and *Omoo*, which outraged supporters of Christian missionaries by idealizing the primitive life of South Sea islanders, but which also provided Melville with sufficient security by 1847 for him to marry the daughter of Lemuel Shaw, the Chief Justice of Massachusetts.

Melville's concentrated productivity during the next few years staggers belief. Of the five novels then published, *Moby-Dick* (1851) justly claims attention as the masterpiece of the so-called American Renaissance. The following selection is from a less ambitious work, *White Jacket* (1850), which deals with the life Melville witnessed on an American frigate or "man-of-war."

The immediate context of our selection is a sincere and impassioned attack, relatively conventional in reformist rhetoric, on the barbarity of flogging seamen in the navy. It is worth noting that abolitionists had long focused attention on the whip as a symbol of slavery, and that apologists for slavery had long pointed to the nearly universal acceptance of whipping as a normal punishment in the armed services. Melville, speaking not as a scholarly theorist but with the authority of experience, first dramatizes the indefensible cruelty of corporal punishment. But then, seizing upon the justification of flogging by British example and historical precedent, he launches into a remarkable discourse on America's moral mission, a discourse ringing with Biblical parallels.

Writing in the immediate aftermath of America's triumph in the Mexican War, when the Pacific Northwest and Southwest were both secure possessions, Melville is confident that "we Americans are the peculiar, chosen people—the Israel of our time," a people bearing "the ark of the liberties of the world." The image of American Israelites, escaping Old World bondage and taking on the global burdens of a new "dispensation," was as old as the New England Puritans. But for Melville's generation, the stakes of America's experiment are not even limited to "our first birthright—embracing one continent of earth. . . ." The stakes involve all mankind, and the outcome of a sacred event, to which Melville refers with uncharacteristic clumsiness: "Seventy years ago we escaped from thrall." Since we have come to accept the inevitability of Lincoln's phrasing in the Gettysburg Address, one wonders whether Melville would seem more "natural" if he had said, "three score and ten years ago we escaped from . . ."?

Herman Melville (1850)

The world has arrived at a period which renders it the part of Wisdom to pay homage to the prospective precedents of the Future in preference to those of the Past. The Past is dead, and has no resurrection; but the Future is endowed with such a life, that it lives to us even in anticipation. The Past is, in many things, the foe of mankind; the Future is, in all things, our friend. In the Past is no hope; the Future is both hope and fruition. The Past is the text-book of tyrants; the Future the Bible of the Free. Those who are solely governed by the Past stand like Lot's wife, crystallised in the act of looking backward, and forever incapable of looking before.

Let us leave the Past, then, to dictate laws to immovable China. . . . But for us, we will have another captain to rule over us—that captain who ever marches at the head of his troop, and beckons them forward, not lingering in the rear, and impeding their march with lumbering baggage-wagons of old precedents. *This* is the Past.

SOURCE: Herman Melville, *White Jacket* (London: Constable and Co., 1922, standard ed.), pp. 188–89.

But in many things we Americans are driven to a rejection of the maxims of the Past, seeing that, ere long, the van of the nations must, of right, belong to ourselves. There are occasions when it is for America to make precedents, and not to obey them. We should, if possible, prove a teacher to posterity, instead of being the pupil of bygone generations. More shall come after us than have gone before; the world is not yet middle-aged.

Escaped from the house of bondage, Israel of old did not follow after the ways of the Egyptians. To her was given an express dispensation; to her were given new things under the sun. And we Americans are the peculiar, chosen people—the Israel of our time; we bear the ark of the liberties of the world. Seventy years ago we escaped from thrall; and besides our first birthright—embracing one continent of earth—God has given to us, for a future inheritance, the broad domains of the political pagans, that shall yet come and lie down under the shade of our ark, without bloody hands being lifted. God has predestinated, mankind expects, great things from our race; and great things we feel in our souls. The rest of the nations must soon be in our rear. We are the pioneers of the world; the advance-guard, sent on through the wilderness of untried things, to break a new path in the New World that is ours. In our youth is our strength; in our inexperience, our wisdom. At a period when other nations have but lisped, our deep voice is heard afar. Long enough have we been skeptics with regard to ourselves, and doubted whether, indeed, the political Messiah had come. But he has come in *us*, if we would but give utterance to his promptings. And let us always remember that with ourselves, almost for the first time in the history of earth, national selfishness is unbounded philanthropy; for we cannot do a good to America, but we give alms to the world.

C. America as the Modern Rome

• *Arnold Guyot* (1849)

Even recent immigrants contributed to the ideology of America's divine mission. Born in Switzerland and educated in Germany, Arnold Guyot (1807–1884) was a noted geographer and geologist who received his doctorate at the University of Berlin and who, along with Jean Louis Agassiz, made pioneering studies of glaciers and glaciation. In 1848, Guyot followed Agassiz to America and the following year he delivered the Lowell Institute Lectures at Boston. Although Guyot's subject was the relation between the earth and its human inhabitants, he here presents a vision of world progress guided by the "persuasion," not brute force, of an American empire. In 1854, Guyot received a professorship in physical geography and geology at Princeton.

Arnold Guyot (1849)

And what continent is better adapted than the American, to respond to the wants of humanity in this phase of its history?

The nations of Europe might easily be drawn out and arrayed within its vast confines. Its fertile soil secures prosperity to all, in exchange for their labor. Its forests, its treasures of coal laid up in quantities surpassing everything of the kind to be found in any part of the globe, prepare an inexhaustible support, and allow a future extension of industry to a degree and in proportions unknown elsewhere. . . .

Thus we may, perhaps, foresee that the American Union, already the most numerous association of men that has ever existed voluntarily united under the same law, will be able hereafter to become, even within the limits of its present confines, a true social world, transcending in grandeur and unity the most impressive spectacles of human greatness the history of past ages holds up to our view.

Finally, the oceanic position of the American continent secures its commercial prosperity, and creates, at the same time, the means of influence upon the world. It commands the Atlantic by its ports, while Oregon and California open the route of the Pacific Ocean and the East. America, also, is so placed as to take an active part in the great work of the civilization of the world, so admirably begun by Europe.

As Greece, then, gave the ancient world instruction and culture, so Europe instructs and refines the modern world, and all mankind; and as Rome wrought out the social work of antiquity, America seems called to do the same service for modern times, and to build up in the New World the social state of which the Old World dreamed.

But while Rome accomplished her task by brute force, made a mere outside work, and brought about only an imperfect fusion of the nations, America is doing hers by persuasion. Drawing to her the free will of the sons of all the races, she binds them by one faith, and is thus preparing a true brotherhood of man. The one had only gross material arms; the other has spiritual arms. Between the two lies the whole distance that separates the heathen from the Christian world, and the progress made during two thousand years.

• • •

You see, gentlemen, this picture transports us into the future. *There* stands the goal, and we are only now at the starting point. But this lofty goal may serve as a guiding star for the present, to preserve it from losing its way. In what measure and through what perils it shall be given to mankind, and to America in particular, to attain it, is known to God alone, and future ages will teach the issue to the world; but what we do know is, that it will be in proportion as man shall be faithful to the law of his moral nature, which is the divine law itself.

SOURCE: Arnold Guyot, *The Earth and Man* (Boston: Gould and Lincoln, 1857; 1st ed., 1849), pp. 324–27.

Asia, Europe, and North America, are the three grand stages of humanity in its march through the ages. Asia is the cradle where man passed his infancy, under the authority of law, and where he learned his dependence upon a sovereign master. Europe is the school where his youth was trained, where he waxed in strength and knowledge, grew to manhood, and learned at once his liberty and his moral responsibility. America is the theatre of his activity during the period of manhood; the land where he applies and practices all he has learned, brings into action all the forces he has acquired, and where he is still to learn that the entire development of his being and his own happiness are possible only by willing obedience to the laws of his Maker.

D. Slavery as the Barrier to Fulfillment

- *Theodore Parker* (1855)
- *Abraham Lincoln* (1858)

The Kansas-Nebraska Act of 1854 suddenly dramatized the fears and divisions underlying American dreams of world mission. Senator Stephen Douglas, the architect of the bill, was an ardent nationalist determined that the vast territory west of Missouri and Iowa be opened for settlement and for a transcontinental railroad. He was so determined, in fact, that in exchange for southern support he was willing to make what he considered a merely symbolic concession—repeal of the Missouri Compromise which had prohibited slavery north of 36° 30′ latitude. But for Easterners like Theodore Parker (1810–1860) and Westerners like Abraham Lincoln, the concession threatened the future meaning of America and the very survival of free institutions.

The first selection is a brief excerpt from Parker's long and famous speech on "the Nebraska Question." The passage simply shows how belief in the imminent extinction of slavery was becoming the fulcrum for grandiose visions of America's progress and leadership. Although Parker is confident that slavery is doomed by the unfolding of God's will in human history, he is all the more outraged by temporary betrayals of America's Revolutionary heritage and glorious destiny. A dissident Unitarian minister, Parker was immensely proud of being the grandson of the Lexington Minute Man who on April 19, 1775 allegedly said, "If they mean to have a war, let it begin here." In addition to delivering radical sermons and lectures calling for a wide range of social reforms, Parker incited crowds to rescue captured fugitive slaves and joined the secret committee that backed John Brown's raid.

The second selection is from Lincoln's great "House Divided" speech of 1858, accepting the nomination by Illinois Republicans to run against Stephen Douglas for the Senate. In Unit One, we discussed the "house divided" theme as applied to family government. It was commonplace to extend family metaphors to the nation, especially when referring as Parker does to "what our fathers have done," and when appealing for fraternal unity in furthering America's mission. By condensing such associations in a few unforgettable phrases, Lincoln ingeniously amplifies their emotional impact. He also raises immeasurably the stakes of a political contest. One branch of the family, the Democrats, have conspired to build a "piece of machinery" that includes the Kansas-Nebraska Act and the Dred Scott decision and that is designed to make slavery "lawful in all the states, old as well as new, North as well as South." This subversion of America's ideals and mission, Lincoln suggests, can be prevented only by the political victory of the new Republican party, which will ensure that slavery is put "in the course of ultimate extinction."

Theodore Parker (1855)

Half a million immigrants annually find a shelter on our shores. "Westward the course of empire takes its way." Aye, it will come eastward—and Asia already begins to send us her children. What a noble destination is before us if we are but faithful. Shall politicians come between the people and the eternal Right—between America and her history! When you remember what our fathers have done; what we have done—substituted a new industrial for a military state, the self-rule of this day for the vicarious government of the middle ages; when you remember what a momentum the human race has got during its long run—it is plain that slavery is on the way to end.

As soon as the North awakes to its ideas, and uses its vast strength of money, its vast strength of numbers, and its still more gigantic strength of educated intellect, we shall tread this monster underneath our feet. See how Spain has fallen—how poor and miserable is Spanish America. She stands there a perpetual warning to us. One day the North will rise in her majesty, and put slavery under our feet, and then we shall extend the area of freedom. The blessing of Almighty God will come down upon the noblest people the world ever saw—who have triumphed over Theocracy, Monarchy, Aristocracy, Despotocracy, and have got a Democracy—a government of all, for all, and by all—a Church without a Bishop, a State without a King, a Community without a Lord, and a Family without a Slave.

Abraham Lincoln (1858)

If we could first know where we are, and whither we are tending, we could better judge what to do, and how to do it. We are now far into the fifth year since a policy was initiated [Kansas-Nebraska Act] with the avowed

---

SOURCE: Theodore Parker, "The Nebraska Question," *Additional Speeches, Addresses, and Occasional Sermons*, Vol. I (Boston: Little, Brown and Co., 1855), pp. 379–80.

SOURCE: Abraham Lincoln, "Speech Delivered at Springfield, Illinois, June 16, 1858," *Complete Works*, Vol. IV, J. G. Nicolay and J. Hay, eds. (n.p.: Lincoln Memorial University, 1894), pp. 1–3, 14–15.

object and confident promise of putting an end to slavery agitation. Under the operation of that policy, that agitation has not only not ceased but has constantly augmented. In my opinion, it will not cease until a crisis shall have been reached and passed. "A house divided against itself cannot stand." I believe this government cannot endure permanently half slave and half free. I do not expect the Union to be dissolved—I do not expect the house to fall —but I do expect it will cease to be divided. It will become all one thing, or all the other. Either the opponents of slavery will arrest the further spread of it, and place it where the public mind shall rest in the belief that it is in the course of ultimate extinction; or its advocates will push it forward till it shall become alike lawful in all the states, old as well as new, North as well as South.

Have we no tendency to the latter condition?

Let any one who doubts carefully contemplate that now almost complete legal combination—piece of machinery, so to speak—compounded of the Nebraska doctrine and the Dred Scott decision. Let him consider not only what work the machinery is adpated to do, and how well adapted; but also let him study the history of the construction, and trace, if he can, or rather fail, if he can, to trace the evidences of design and concert of action among its chief architects, from the beginning.

. . .

Our cause, then, must be intrusted to, and conducted by, its own undoubted friends—those whose hands are free, whose hearts are in the work, who do care for the result. Two years ago the Republicans of the nation mustered over thirteen hundred thousand strong. We did this under the single impulse of resistance to a common danger, with every external circumstance against us. Of strange, discordant, and even hostile elements, we gathered from the four winds, and formed and fought the battle through, under the constant hot fire of a disciplined, proud, and pampered enemy. Did we brave all then to falter now?—now, when that same enemy is wavering, dissevered, and belligerent? The result is not doubtful. We shall not fail—if we stand firm, we shall not fail. Wise counsels may accelerate or mistakes delay it, but, sooner or later, the victory is sure to come.

E. "Submission or Secession"

• *William Henry Holcombe* (1860)

While the South was virtually unanimous in opposing Lincoln's election as President, there was much division over the strategy and tactics of response. William Henry Holcombe's defiant pamphlet, *The Alternative*, attempts to disguise this internal conflict but expresses the doctrines that finally prevailed in various secession conventions.

Holcombe (1825–1893) was hardly a typical southern leader. When he was a youth, his Virginian parents emancipated their slaves and moved to Indiana. Holcombe himself studied medicine at the University of Pennsylvania, and in Cincinnati he began winning a national reputation for his success in the homeopathic treatment of cholera. It was not until 1852 that he moved to Mississippi and fully identified himself with the cause of the Deep South.

What is most remarkable about the following defense of secession and southern nationhood is the way it mirrors themes we have been examining throughout Unit Four. Holcombe claims that proslavery principles are based on inductive science. Far from being a "retrograde movement," Negro slavery for Holcombe is "an integral link in the grand progressive evolution of human society as an indissoluble whole." The institution is an instrument given by Providence to the white race for subduing the tropics and civilizing supposedly inferior races. Holcombe's overriding theme is the inherent harmony of progress—the harmony between southern duty and interest, between the true interests of inferior and superior races, between slave-labor and free-labor systems. In this denial of essential or necessary conflicts, Holcombe is at one with northern writers on America's civilizing mission. For such northern writers, Negro slavery was an aberration or excrescence which had somehow blinded Southerners to their own true interests. For Holcombe, it is antislavery fanaticism that has not only deluded the northern mind but has literally driven it mad "in its hostility to our institutions." Finally, in vowing to resist tyranny, Southerners shared national illusions of America's omnipotence—in Holcombe's case, the fatal illusion that because the industrial world depends on southern cotton, the South "holds the peace of the world in its hands."

William Henry Holcombe (1860)

A sectional party [the Republicans], inimical to our institutions, and odious to our people, is about taking possession of the federal government. The seed sown by the early abolitionists has yielded a luxuriant harvest. When Lincoln is in place, Garrison will be in power. The Constitution, either openly violated or emasculated of its true meaning and spirit by the subtleties of New England logic, is powerless for protection. We are no longer partners to a federal compact, but the victims of a consolidated despotism. Opposition to slavery, to its existence, its extension and its perpetuation, is the sole cohesive element of the triumphant faction. It did not receive the countenance of a single vote in any one of the ten great cotton states of the South! The question is at length plainly presented: submission or secession. The only alternative left us is this: *a separate nationality or the Africanization of the South.*

SOURCE: W. H. Holcombe, *The Alternative: A Separate Nationality, or the Africanization of the South* (New Orleans: Delta Mamoth Job Office, 1860), pp. 1–2, 4, 6–8.

He has not analyzed this subject aright nor probed it to the bottom, who supposes that the real quarrel between the North and the South is about the territories, or the decision of the Supreme Court, or even the Constitution itself; and that, consequently, the issues may be stayed and the dangers arrested by the drawing of new lines and the signing of new compacts. The division is broader and deeper and more incurable than this. The antagonism is fundamental and ineradicable. The true secret of it lies in the total reversion of public opinion which has occured in both sections of the country in the last quarter of a century on the subject of slavery.

It has not been more than twenty-five years since Garrison was dragged through the streets of Boston with a rope around his neck, for uttering abolition sentiments; and not thirty years since, the abolition of slavery was seriously debated in the legislature of Virginia. Now, on the contrary, the radical opinions of Sumner, Emerson and Parker, and the assassination schemes of John Brown, are applauded in Faneuil Hall [in Boston], and the whole southern mind with an unparalleled unanimity, regards the institution of slavery as righteous and just, ordained of God, and to be perpetuated by man. We do not propose to analyze the causes of this remarkable revolution, which will constitute one of the strangest chapters of history. The fact is unquestionable.

· · ·

This pro-slavery party includes, with insignificant exceptions, nine millions of people of Anglo-Saxon blood. It is diffused over territory sufficient for a mighty empire. It contends that its principles are based upon large and safe inductions, made from an immense accumulation of facts in natural science, political economy and social ethics. It holds the most prominent material interests, and thereby the peace of the world in its hands; a wise provision of Providence for its protection, since those who cannot be controlled by reason, may be withheld by fear.

· · ·

Certain physical and spiritual peculiarities of the Negro necessitate his subjection to the white man. It is for his own good that he is subjected. As long as this was doubtful or not clearly seen, the South itself was opposed to slavery. It remonstrated with England for imposing the institution upon it, and with Massachusetts for insisting upon a continuance of the slave-trade for twenty years after the adoption of the federal compact. The South is now fully convinced of the benefits and blessings it is conferring upon the Negro race. It is beginning to catch a glimpse of the true nature and extent of its mission in relation to this vast and growing institution. The government of the South is to protect it; the Church of the South is to christianize it; the people of the South are to love it, and improve it and perfect it. God has lightened our task and secured its execution by making our interests happily coincide with our duty.

We anticipate no terminus to the institution of slavery. It is the means whereby the white man is to subdue the tropics all around the globe to order and beauty, and to the wants and interests of an ever-expanding civilization. What may happen afar off in the periods of a millennial Christianity we cannot foresee. No doubt the Almighty in his wisdom and mercy has blessings in store for the poor Negro, so that he will no longer envy the earlier and more imposing development and fortunes of his brethren. Some shining Utopia will beckon him also with beautiful illusion into the shadowy future. But with those remote possibilities we need not trouble ourselves. His present duty is evidently "to labor and to wait."

The southern view of the matter, destined to revolutionize opinion throughout the civilized world, is briefly this: African slavery is no retrograde movement, no discord in the harmony of nature, no violation of elemental justice, no infraction of immutable laws, human or divine—but an integral link in the grand progressive evolution of human society as an indissoluble whole.

The doctrine that there exists an "irrepressible conflict" between free labor and slave labor is as false as it is mischievous. Their true relation is one of beautiful interchange and eternal harmony. When each is restricted to the sphere for which God and nature designed it, they both contribute their full quotas to the physical happiness, material interests, and social and spiritual progress of the race. They will prove to be not antagonistic but complementary to each other in the great work of human civilization. From this time forth, the subjugation of tropical nature to man; the elevation and christianization of the dark races, the feeding and clothing of the world, the diminution of toil and the amelioration of all the asperities of life, the industrial prosperity and the peace of nations, and the further glorious evolutions of Art, Science, Literature and Religion, will depend upon the amicable adjustment, the co-ordination, the indissoluble compact between these two social systems, now apparently rearing their hostile fronts in the northern and southern sections of this country.

The only "irrepressible conflict" is between pro-slavery and anti-slavery opinion. Here indeed collision may be inconceivably disastrous, and fanaticism may thrust her sickle into the harvest of death. The pro-slavery sentiment is unconquerable. It will be more and more suspicious of encroachment and jealous of its rights. It will submit to no restriction, and scouts the possibility of any "ultimate extinction." Nothing will satisfy us but a radical change of opinion, or at least of political action on the subject of slavery throughout the northern states. The relation of master and slave must be recognized as right and just, as national and perpetual. The Constitution must be construed in the spirit of its founders, as an instrument to protect the minority from the domination of an insolent majority. The slavery question must be eliminated forever from the political issues of the day. No party which contemplates the restriction of our system and its ultimate extinction can be tolerated for a moment. In assuming this bold attitude we simply assert our obvious rights and discharge our inevitable duty.

Now the northern mind is equally determined and defiant. It has literally gone mad in its hostility to our institutions. The most conservative of the

Republican party look forward complacently to the restriction and ultimate extinction of slavery, in other words, to the Africanization of the South and our national destruction. We will see to it that they precipitate no such calamity upon *us*, and we warn them to look carefully to their own fate.

F. "A New Birth of Freedom"

• *Abraham Lincoln (1863)*

The great hope of the Confederacy was European intervention, which would have assured southern independence. Though a majority of the British cabinet favored recognizing the South, the danger of a joint Anglo-French intervention had begun to subside by the end of 1862. Still, everyone knew that a major southern victory on northern soil would create almost irresistible pressures for European mediation. On July 4, 1863 this southern hope evaporated as Robert E. Lee prepared to withdraw his decimated army from the Battle of Gettysburg and Ulysses S. Grant accepted the surrender of 30,000 Confederate troops at Vicksburg. On July 7, in response to a serenade and a cheering crowd, President Lincoln thanked Almighty God and then said: "How long ago is it?—eighty odd years—since on the Fourth of July for the first time in the history of the world a nation by its representatives, assembled and declared as a self-evident truth that 'all men are created equal.' " Lincoln then went on to note the remarkable coincidence of the two great victories on the "Fourth of July just passed, when we have a gigantic Rebellion, at the bottom of which is an effort to overthrow the principle that all men were created equal. . . ." It was "a glorious theme," he added, "and the occasion for a speech, but I am not prepared to make one worthy of the occasion."

By November 19 Lincoln was prepared, when commemorating the military cemetery at Gettysburg. His words are so well known that we seldom consider their meaning. It is hoped that the preceding selections in this book will add resonance to Lincoln's themes of birth, bloody sacrifice, rebirth, and immortal mission.

Abraham Lincoln (1863)

Four score and seven years ago our fathers brought forth on this continent, a new nation, conceived in Liberty, and dedicated to the proposition that all men are created equal.

SOURCE: Abraham Lincoln, final text of the Gettysburg Address, from the *Collected Works of Abraham Lincoln*, Vol. VII, edited by Roy P. Basler (New Brunswick, N.J.: Rutgers University Press, 1953), p. 23. Copyright 1953 by the Abraham Lincoln Association. Reprinted by permission of Rutgers University Press.

Now we are engaged in a great civil war, testing whether that nation, or any nation so conceived and so dedicated, can long endure. We are met on a great battle-field of that war. We have come to dedicate a portion of that field, as a final resting place for those who here gave their lives that that nation might live. It is altogether fitting and proper that we should do this.

But, in a larger sense, we can not dedicate—we can not consecrate—we can not hallow—this ground. The brave men, living and dead, who struggled here, have consecrated it, far above our poor power to add or detract. The world will little note, nor long remember what we say here, but it can never forget what they did here. It is for us the living, rather, to be dedicated here to the unfinished work which they who fought here have thus far so nobly advanced. It is rather for us to be here dedicated to the great task remaining before us —that from these honored dead we take increased devotion to that cause for which they gave the last full measure of devotion—that we here highly resolve that these dead shall not have died in vain—that this nation, under God, shall have a new birth of freedom—and that government of the people, by the people, for the people, shall not perish from the earth.

Chronology, 1820-1860

1820
Missouri Compromise
Reelection of James Monroe without opposition symbolizes "Era of good Feelings."

1822
Denmark Vesey's conspiracy to lead massive slave uprising in South Carolina exposed.

1823
President issues the Monroe Doctrine.

1824
Congress enacts higher protective tariff.
Supreme Court, in *Gibbons* v. *Ogden*, extends power of Congress to regulate commerce.
John Quincy Adams elected President by House of Representatives after failure of any candidate to win electoral majority.

1825
Monroe calls for voluntary removal of Eastern Indians to lands west of the Mississippi.
Completion of Erie Canal.
Beginning of Charles Grandison Finney's religious revivals in New York State.
Founding of New Harmony community in Indiana.

1826
Disappearance and probable murder of William Morgan ignites anti-Masonic movement in New York State.
Founding of American Society for the Promotion of Temperance.

1827
Extension of 1818 United States–British agreement on joint occupation of the Oregon country.

1828
John C. Calhoun's anonymous *South Carolina Exposition and Protest*.
Congress passes "Tariff of Abominations."
Appearance of workingmen's parties in Eastern cities.
Election of Andrew Jackson as President brings triumphant victory to new Democratic party.

1829
David Walker's *Appeal to the Colored Citizens of the World*.

1830
Jackson vetoes Maysville Road Bill.
Congress passes bill authorizing Indian removal.
Webster-Hayne debate on land policy and nature of the Union.
Anti-Masonic party holds first national party convention.
Joseph Smith, Jr. publishes The Book of Mormon.
William Ellery Channing's *Remarks on National Literature*.

1831
Nat Turner's slave insurrection in Virginia.
William Lloyd Garrison begins *The Liberator*.
Finney's religious revival reaches its climax in Rochester, New York.
McCormick invents reaper.
Jackson purges Calhoun faction from his administration after Peggy Eaton affair.
Mormons migrate from New York State to Ohio; establish outpost near Independence, Missouri.

1832
Beginning of Jackson's war against Bank of the United States.

Special convention in South Carolina nullifies new protective tariff.
Virginia legislative debates over allowing a committee to report on future abolition of slavery.
Jackson reelected President.

1833
Congress provides for a gradual lowering of tariffs, but passes Force Bill authorizing Jackson to enforce federal law in South Carolina.
Formation of American Anti-Slavery Society.
Publication of New York *Sun*, first "penny press."
Emergence of Whig party, formed by Jackson's opponents.

1834
Students quit Lane Theological Seminary, in Cincinnati, after stormy debates over slavery.
Abolitionist agitation intensifies.

1835
Jackson calls for suppression of abolitionist propaganda.
Garrison nearly lynched by Boston mob.
Long war against Seminole Indians and runaway slaves begins in Florida.
Roger B. Taney succeeds Marshall as chief justice.

1836
Jackson's Specie Circular.
Congress adopts the Gag Rule, automatically tabling antislavery petitions.
Abolitionists begin to deluge Congress with petitions.
Texas proclaims independence from Mexico.
Martin Van Buren elected President.

1837
Financial panic brings many bank failures and suspension of specie payment.
The American steamer, *Caroline*, burned in Niagara River after carrying supplies to Canadian rebels.
American support for Canadian insurrection worsens U.S.-British relations.
Supreme Court, in *Charles River Bridge* v. *Warren Bridge*, places community rights above special privileges guaranteed by contract.
Elijah P. Lovejoy is first abolitionist martyr.
Presbyterian Church divides as Old School expels much of New School faction.
Massachusetts creates first state board of education; appoints Horace Mann secretary.
Emerson's address on "the American Scholar."

1838
John Quincy Adams's filibuster defeats move to annex Texas by joint resolution.
Rift in American Peace Society leads to formation of radical New England Non-Resistance Society.
Emerson delivers "Divinity School Address," a Transcendentalist manifesto.

1839
A major depression begins, leading to widespread bankruptcies and default of several states.
Mormons establish city-state of Nauvoo, Illinois.

1840
Congress passes Van Buren's Independent Treasury Act.
Bitter conflict between Catholics and Protestants over religious instruction in New York State public schools.
Division in abolitionist ranks as conservatives withdraw from American Anti-Slavery Society.
Washingtonian temperance movement launched.
James G. Birney runs for President as Liberty party candidate.
William H. Harrison elected; Whigs in power.

1841
Harrison's death makes John Tyler President.
Frederick Douglass, escaped from slavery in 1838, begins lecturing for Massachusetts Anti-Slavery Society.
Slaves mutiny on the ship *Creole*, bound from Virginia to New Orleans; are freed when they take ship to British colony of Nassau.
Congress passes general preemption law allowing squatters to purchase 160 acres of public land at minimum of $1.25 per acre.
Dorothea Dix begins crusade in behalf of insane.
Brook Farm founded.

1842
Webster-Ashburton Treaty settles disputed U.S.-Canadian boundary; provides for extradition of fugitives.
Tyler agrees to higher tariff after Whigs abandon demands for a distribution to the states of surplus federal revenue.
Dorr Rebellion in Rhode Island.

1843
Economic recovery begins.
"Oregon Fever"; first overland caravans to Oregon.

Duff Green, Calhoun, and others begin planning imperial expansion to thwart British plots to undermine American slavery. Growing radicalism among blacks evidenced in a Convention of the Free People of Color, at Buffalo, New York.

1844
Senate rejects Calhoun's Texas annexation treaty.
Calhoun, as secretary of state, incorporates defense of slavery as part of America's foreign policy.
Congress repeals Gag Rule.
Joseph Smith, Jr., assassinated at Carthage, Illinois.
Slavery issue splits Methodist Episcopal Church into Northern and Southern camps.
James K. Polk elected President.

1845
Before Tyler retires, Texas annexed by joint resolution of Congress.
Polk gives an aggressive reformulation to the Monroe Doctrine.
John Slidell's unsuccessful mission to Mexico to negotiate purchase of New Mexico and California.
Polk risks war with England by asserting America's right to "All Oregon" and terminating joint-occupation agreement.
Failure of Ireland's potato crop marks beginning of mass emigration to United States.
Sectional division of the Baptists.
Henry David Thoreau retreats to Walden Pond.

1846
Beginning of Mexican War. General Zachary Taylor invades Mexico from the north. The "Mormon Battalion" marches with S. W. Kearney's army to southern California.
U.S.-British dispute over Oregon settled.
Wilmot Proviso fuses question of slavery's expansion with consequences of Mexican War.
Walker tariff, adopted for revenue only, eliminates principle of protection.
Elias Howe patents sewing machine.

1847
General Winfield Scott captures Vera Cruz and Mexico City.
Mormons arrive in Great Salt Lake Valley.
Publicity campaign for annexation of Cuba.
Calhoun's resolutions in Senate, affirming right to take slaves into any United States territory.

1848
Treaty of Guadalupe Hidalgo ends Mexican War.
Secret attempts to purchase Cuba from Spain.
Gold discovered on American River in California.
Women's Rights Convention held in Seneca Falls, New York.
Van Buren, running for President on Free-Soil ticket, receives 10 percent of popular vote.
Zachary Taylor elected President.

1850
In Congress, violent sectional debate culminates in Compromise of 1850.
Taylor's death makes Millard Fillmore President.
Nashville convention considers the South's stake in the Union.
Clayton-Bulwer Treaty.
Nathaniel Hawthorne's *The Scarlet Letter*.

1851
Indian Appropriations Act, designed to begin consolidating Western tribes on reservations.
Herman Melville's *Moby Dick*.

1852
Massachusetts adopts first state compulsory education law.
Harriet Beecher Stowe's *Uncle Tom's Cabin*.
Franklin Pierce elected President.

1853
Upsurge of political nativism, the Know-Nothings.
Gadsden Purchase from Mexico, for $10 million, of 45 thousand square miles below Gila River, needed for a railroad route from the South to the Pacific.

1854
Spectacular Know-Nothing election victories signify critical shift in voter loyalties.
Kansas-Nebraska Bill rekindles sectional controversy over slavery.
Republican party emerges.
Railroads link New York City with the Mississippi.
Commodore Perry opens Japan to American trade.
Treaty to annex Hawaii negotiated but dropped for lack of public support.
Ostend Manifesto regarding Cuba.
Thoreau's *Walden*.
George Fitzhugh's *Sociology for the South*.
As result of election frauds, proslavery settlers in Kansas victorious.

1855
Beginning of "Bleeding Kansas."
Massachusetts desegrates the public schools.
Walt Whitman's *Leaves of Grass*.

1856
John Brown's murderous raid at
Pottawatomie.
Preston Brooks's attack on Senator
Charles Sumner.
James Buchanan elected President.
Democratic platform calls for annexing
Cuba.
Republican platform indicts slavery and
polygamy as "twin relics of barbarism."

1857
Financial panic and depression.
Dred Scott decision.
Tariff lowered to 20 percent.
Buchanan sends army to Utah to suppress
Mormons.
In Kansas, Lecompton constitution ratified
as free-state men refuse to vote.
Beginning of great urban religious revival.
Hinton Helper's *Impending Crisis of the
South*.

1858
In Kansas referendum, Lecompton
constitution overwhelmingly rejected.
Stephen Douglas joins Republicans in
opposing acceptance of Lecompton
constitution.
Lincoln-Douglas debates.

1859
A Southern commercial convention at
Vicksburg calls for reopening African slave
trade.
Kansas voters ratify a constitution
prohibiting slavery.
John Brown's raid on Harper's Ferry.
Discovery of Comstock lode.

1860
Democratic party deadlocked at Charleston
convention finally divides along sectional
lines at Baltimore. Constitutional Union
party nominates John Bell. Republicans
nominate Abraham Lincoln, who wins.
Senator John J. Crittenden unsuccessfully
offers series of constitutional amendments
to settle the sectional controversy.
South Carolina secedes from the Union.

1 2 3 4 5 6 7 8 9 0

DATE DUE